# EPISTEMOLOGY

*Philosophical Issues, 14, 2004*

# EPISTEMOLOGY

*Philosophical Issues Volume 14*

Edited by Ernest Sosa and Enrique Villanueva

**Blackwell Publishing** | Boston MA & Oxford UK

Blackwell Publishing, Inc.
350 Main Street
Malden, MA 02148 USA

Blackwell Publishing, Ltd.
9600 Garsington Road
Oxford OX4 2DQ
United Kingdom

Library of Congress Cataloging-in-Publication Data has been applied for.

ISBN 1-4051-1972-1
ISSN 1533-6077

# Contents

**Book Symposium**

*Philosophical Issues, 14, Epistemology, 2004*

# Editorial Preface

This volume includes main papers delivered at the 15th SOFIA conference, held in Porto Alegre, Brazil, in May of 2004, as well as papers invited specifically for the volume. We express our gratitude to the following institutions and persons for supporting the conference: the Pontifícia Universidade Católica do Rio Grande do Sul – PUCRS, and its Philosophy Department. Special thanks to Claudio de Almeida, of that Department, who led the organization of the conference in Porto Alegre. We express our gratitude to the Instituto de Investigaciones Juridicas de la Universidad Nacional Autónoma de México and its head Dr. Diego Valadés Rios for continuous support in SOFIA activities.

*Ernest Sosa* and *Enrique Villanueva*
Co-Editors

# A NATURALIZED APPROACH TO THE *A PRIORI*[1]

Louise Antony
The Ohio State University

A familiar complaint against naturalized epistemology is that it leaves no room for *norms*—that it abandons the traditional normative goals of theories of knowledge in favor of merely descriptive goals (Kim 1994). In the minds of many critics, this complaint is closely connected with a second, viz., that naturalization leaves no room for the a priori (Haack 1993). In earlier work, I've tried to meet both these challenges head on (Antony 2000). I've tried to show that naturalized epistemology has room for both normativity *and* the a priori—that indeed, a naturalist can provide a needed explanation of a priori access to epistemic norms.

But when I looked around for allies in this noble mission, I discovered that many prominent naturalists agreed with the critics on at least this point: that a naturalized approach to knowledge requires repudiation of the a priori (Devitt forthcoming, Kitcher 2000, Maddy 2000).[2] Michael Devitt goes so far as to *define* "naturalism" in a way that rules out the possibility of a priori knowledge:

> It is overwhelmingly plausible that *some* knowledge is empirical, justified by experience. The attractive thesis of naturalism is that *all* knowledge is; there is only one way of knowing. (Devitt forthcoming)

I certainly do not understand epistemological naturalism in this way. Devitt's definition conflates naturalism with *empiricism*, but this is both wrongheaded and ironic. It's wrongheaded for a naturalist to be an empiricist, because our best scientific theories of cognition have it that empiricism is false. Naturalistic methodology in the study of knowledge (human and non-human) has produced ample support for the existence of *a priori* elements in cognition, and indeed, for their necessity in even the most mundane cognitive achievements. It's ironic, because a naturalized approach to the study of knowledge can actually provide a quite satisfying account of the *a priori*. Why waste it?

This paper, then, is directed mainly to my fellow naturalists, but I hope my message will reach anti-naturalists as well. If naturalism can accommodate the *a priori*, then we'll be that much closer to an account of how naturalism can make a place for epistemic norms, and intuitions about those norms.

Let me start by recovering the route by which philosophers have come to hold that naturalism must reject the *a priori*, and see where things have gone wrong. Then I'll set out the positive account of the *a priori* that I think naturalism has to offer. Not to be mysterious: the account says, in essence, that the *a priori* is innateness plus reliability. Innateness explains our *access* to the *a priori*; reliability—as it does generally—explains our *justification*. I'll concede that this account will not provide a perfect reconstruction of the traditional notion, but it should be pretty satisfying.

Why do naturalists reject the *a priori*? Central to a naturalized approach to knowledge is commitment to confirmational holism and the Quine-Duhem Thesis: no statement is immune from revision in light of experience. This suggests the following argument against the possibility of knowing any statement *a priori*. A statement knowable *a priori* is one whose justification is independent of experience. To say that the justification for belief in such a statement is independent of experience is to say that there could be no experience in light of which one ought to revise belief in such a statement. Therefore, if there were statements knowable *a priori*, then there would be statements immune from revision in light of experience, and the Q-D Thesis would be false. But it's true, so there are no statements knowable *a priori*.

This way of reasoning, clearly, puts the Q-D Thesis directly at odds with the thesis that there are *a priori* knowable truths. One can, in this connection, cite the authority of Quine, who says, infamously, that not even the laws of logic are immune from revision—that *in extremis*, it might be rational to give up one of these, provided that doing so would gain us enough elsewhere.

> Any statement can be held true come what may, if we make drastic enough revisions elsewhere in the system. Even a statement very close to the periphery can be held true in the face of recalcitrant experience by pleading hallucination or by amending certain statements of the kind called logical laws. Revision even of the logical law of the excluded middle has been proposed as a means of simplifying quantum mechanics; and what difference is there in principle between such a shift and the shift whereby Kepler superseded Ptolemy, or Einstein Newton, or Darwin Aristotle? (Quine 1953)

Putnam, a decade or so later, fleshed out the "proposal" to emend logic in light of quantum mechanical phenomena, although it was the laws of distribution, rather than the law of the excluded middle, that Putnam wanted to drop from his "quantum logic." Putnam considered that quantum mechanics provided an empirical falsification of classical propositional logic, in exactly the same way that general relativity theory falsified Euclidean geometry, and thought that the whole matter showed "that logic is, in a certain sense, a natural science." (Putnam 1968)

Now I do want to accept confirmational holism, so I am going to have to address this argument. But for the moment, I want to counterpoise it with another. Apart from the emphasis on the empirical interconnectedness of all belief, naturalized epistemology sounds a second theme. The positive part of naturalized epistemology is its advocacy of an empirical approach to the study of knowledge. This approach involves, centrally, the project of treating epistemic achievements as constituting a natural kind, susceptible to scientific investigation. This approach grows out of Quine's construal and subsequent critique of Carnap's programme of rational reconstruction.

Quine saw positivism as failing by its own lights in the project of vindicating scientific practice. Carnap (at least on Quine's reading of him) offered rational reconstruction as a solution to a problem in *normative epistemology*, one that arises on an empiricistic view of knowledge. The problem is this: if it is experience and experience alone that justifies belief, how can we justify acceptance of a science that contains *a priori* elements? Carnap's solution was to segregate the *a priori* elements of theories from the empirical elements, and then explain the *a priori* elements as "conventional." The empirical elements could then be arranged in a hierarchy of dependency on sensory data, where the structure of the hierarchy is determined by the conventions that generated the *a priori* elements.

Quine, of course, objected to every feature of this proposal. But the overall thrust of the critique was global: Carnap's characterization of the structure of scientific confirmation was *false*, and a false story can vindicate nothing. If what we want to understand is how empirical knowledge is possible, we gain nothing by telling just-so stories about how theories *would* have been justified *had* they been derived in a certain way from the evidence.

> But why all this creative reconstruction, all this make-believe? *The stimulation of his sensory receptors is all the evidence anybody has to go on, ultimately, in arriving at his picture of the world.* Why not just see how this construction proceeds? Why not settle for psychology? (Quine 1971, 63) [My emphasis]

Quine's complaint, I believe, is that the kind of idealization inherent in rational reconstruction strips away exactly the features of actual inquiry that make the matter of vindication pressing in the first place—better to confront squarely the fact that we seem, somehow, by routes that do not match those that we judge intuitively to be necessary for epistemic reliability, to obtain substantive bodies of knowledge about the external world.

Quine is clearly urging the abandonment of pretheoretic—and hence, aprioristic—assumptions about knowledge, and to this extent, eschewing the *a priori*. But Quine did not take his own advice in regard to the abandonment of "first philosophies." Note the italicized sentence in the quotation above: significantly, it records what was in fact an aprioristic presumption on Quine's part, and one that would be refuted as soon as researchers began taking his advice to "settle for psychology" to heart. As it turns out, we have a great deal more "to go on" than the stimulation of our sensory receptors—we have a richly structured mind well suited to producing knowledge in environments of the sort in which we find ourselves. Taken at face value—and applied seriously—Quine's injunctions to naturalize the study of knowledge point directly toward the two elements of the account of the *a priori* I intend to defend.

The existence of knowledge is the starting point, the explanandum, of a scientific approach to epistemology. The question of *warrant* becomes the question of what processes and procedures do, as a matter of empirical fact, enable us to gather and process information about ourselves, each other, and our external environment. If a process works, it works—there is only the question of understanding *how* it works. In this way, a naturalized approach leads to a general account of warrant in terms of *reliability*. At the same time, a realistic investigation into our epistemic practices, whether these are the individualistic, largely unconscious solutions to everyday epistemic challenges—how far away is that car? Who is that approaching me? What language do my parents speak?—or, alternatively, large-scale, explicit and socially mediated theory construction, yields massive support for the existence of native elements in epistemic achievement. Sensory data vastly underdetermines theory, and yet theory arises, and is tested, and continues to survive. If this is so, it must be that something is being contributed by the subject, and that the contribution is salutary.

The starting point of such a naturalized, reliabilist epistemology, then, must be what we know, or can come to discover about the knowing subject herself. Although Quine's commitment to behavioristic psychology, motivated, remember, by *philosophical* arguments against the legitimacy of mentalistic posits, prevented him from embracing cognitivist psychology, it would appear that Chomsky's work on language acquisition constitutes the parade case for the naturalized approach. The story is surely familiar by now. Begin with a mundane epistemic achievement: human children's acquisition, within the first few years of life, before they have mastered much of anything that requires explicit instruction, of an intricate symbolic system that can be used for the expression and communication of messages unbounded in both their variety and their complexity. Observe the *actual* conditions under which this achievement occurs (as opposed to the *hypothetical* conditions under which "radical translation" takes place): exposure to a body of data that is both flawed and fragmentary, at least relative to the demands of theories of general learning. (These defects remain whether we construe "learning" mentalistic-ally, in terms of the operation of a general-purpose inductive logic, or behavioristically, in terms of patterns of conditioned responses to environ-mental stimuli. Things look considerably worse on the latter picture, when we deprive the child of the ability to make conjectures about the rules governing the phenomena she is exposed to.) Conclusion: human children are receiving unauthorized help—God is telling them the answers.

The rehabilitation of mentalistic psychology, and, more importantly for present purposes, of *nativism*, ought therefore to be regarded as a natural consequence of putting into practice Quine's injunctions to eschew armchair philosophizing about the nature of knowledge. But once we recognize that there is an independent variable in the construction of knowledge—one that lives *inside the subject's head*, we have a new basis upon which the tradi-tional distinction between the *a priori* and the *a posteriori* can be—partially, but satisfactorily—reconstructed. What I am recommending is that we now treat the distinction primarily as an etiological distinction. The *a priori* elements of knowledge are those elements that reflect or derive solely from features of our native[3] cognitive machinery; knowledge that additionally involves information supplied by the senses is *a posteriori*.

Consider, for example, the fact that I am inclined to infer

(3) It's Belgium

from

(1) It's Friday

and

(2) If it's Friday, then this is Belgium.

That (3) follows from (1) and (2) is something that anyone (who believes in the *a priori* at all) would say I know *a priori*. On my account, that's just to say that the inclination to perform the inference reflects the structure of a reliable cognitive machine: the hypothesized syntactic engine inside my head.

The qualification "reliable" is crucial to the account, for it forestalls the standard objection to analyzing the *a priori* in terms of innateness. The objection is that innateness in itself can *only* explain the etiology of belief, never its justification. That much surely is right: explaining what causes me to infer (3) from (1) and (2) is one thing, and explaining how I am *warranted* in so inferring is quite another. It hardly follows from the mere fact that I am built to reason in a certain way (or, for that matter, that I am built to believe certain propositions) that I have good epistemic reasons to so reason.

It is worth noting that this normative question can still arise in the context of a naturalistic programme. This is, in itself, an answer to those critics of naturalism who charge that naturalization means abandoning the traditional goals of epistemology. Speaking descriptively, we can note the ubiquity of a certain epistemic habit; nothing then prevents us from going on to ask, prescriptively, whether we ought to indulge it. (Although if I am right about the origins of this inferential practice, there may be no serious prospect for reform—but that possibility arises in any case.) Once the question is asked, though, the reliabilism of the account tells us exactly where to look for an answer: to the processes that produce the belief, to the mechanisms that subserve the inference. Are they, or are they not, reliable? If they are, then I have all the warrant I can ever need (or expect to get). If I have reliable cognitive machinery, then my reasoning will tend to track the truth. *A priori* warrant turns out to be simply an instance of epistemic warrant generally—no separate account, and certainly no "occult faculty" is needed.

What, exactly, is known *a priori* on this account? The refocusing of epistemology on the prerequisites of everyday knowledge yields two kinds of arguments for the existence of *a priori* elements in the development of human knowledge, corresponding to two types of *a priori* elements in human knowledge.

1) Direct empirical arguments: these support, by familiar empirical methods, the *de facto* involvement of innate information in extant cognitive achievements. This category includes native knowledge of the universal features of humanly natural language, just discussed, but also a variety of other native endowments central to our ability to recognize human faces, to infer shape from motion, to understand the psychological states of our conspecifics, and much else. Note that these are all achievements that *could* have been accomplished, at least in principle, without native short-cuts.[4] That we are not *in fact* able to manage without them is treated not as accidental to epistemic life, but as part of the conditions that constitute the phenomena of human knowledge.

I speak of innate *information*. I do not mean to say that such information must be explicitly represented. This information could be "present" in the form of native constraints on hypothesis formation, or as native biases for some forms of inference over others. In the case of innate linguistic knowledge, for example, the body of information constituting "universal grammar" *might* be present in the form of explicit rules, represented and stored from birth (or close thereto), and explicitly involved in the computational process of formulating, projecting, and confirming hypotheses about the child's target language. More plausibly, though, the information that constitutes UG is embodied in structural constraints on the formulation of hypotheses (on the rules-and-representations approach) or in the set of parameters the setting of which constitutes the child's idiolectual grammar, or I-language (on the principles-and-parameters approach).

2) Transcendental Arguments: these point out the necessary presence of *a priori* elements as preconditions of empirical learning, which therefore cannot, even in principle, be accounted for empirically. This type of argument is still empirical because of the crucial premise that learning of the relevant sort actually occurs. Empiricists have long recognized the existence of the *a priori* in this sense. Hume had to grant the aprioricity of the principle of induction, and Quine acknowledged the need for an innate "similarity space" in order for the process of operant conditioning—much less scientific experimentation—to get off the ground. To these we may add concepts like identity, "all," and "some," barring some as-yet-unimagined empiricistic account of concept learning that can proceed without assuming the existence of mental mechanisms the presence of which would suffice for crediting the organism with possession of these concepts.

More controversially, we may also add what Tyler Burge has called "*a priori* defeasible warrants." The idea here, due to Burge, is that the practices of treating certain kinds of experiences as warrants for beliefs is a precondition of treating anything as warrant for any belief. (Burge 1993) The following are all examples: believing that p on the basis of seeing that p, on the basis of remembering that p, on the basis of being told that p, and even on the basis of its seeming to one that p.[5] Clearly such warrants must be counted defeasible—I can learn that my eyes are not to be trusted in certain circumstances, or even that they are not to be trusted if they tell me certain things. In such instances, our *a priori* warrant is overridden. But there can be no empirical justification *in general* for trusting one's perceptions, since empirical justification depends, constitutively, on trusting one's senses.

In sum: naturalists ought, by their own principles, to acknowledge that innate elements play an ineliminable role in the generation of human knowledge. Moreover, because of the role these elements play, our epistemic dependence upon them must be deemed *a priori*. If such dependence can be shown to be warranted by the lights of a reliabilist account of warrant, then we have the basis of a naturalistic explanation of the *a priori*. I might add that if such dependence *cannot* be shown to be warranted, then it's hard to see how we could ever have any knowledge at all.

I'm now ready to lay out two distinctions that will help me defend my account. First I'll explain the distinctions; then I'll deploy them.

(I) We must distinguish between (a) accepting as valid a certain inference, or a certain pattern of inference, and (b) believing a proposition that expresses a rule characterizing that pattern of inference. So, for example, we need to distinguish the accepting of instances of

p

p $\rightarrow$ q

⎯⎯⎯⎯⎯

q

as valid, from believing

$$(p \ \& \ (p \rightarrow q)) \rightarrow q$$

to be a generally or necessarily true proposition. To put it another way: accepting inferences as valid, and believing propositions are *not fungible*.[6]

(II) We need also to distinguish between *possessing warrant* (i.e., being warranted) from *explaining warrant* (i.e., explaining how or why one is warranted). This is a distinction that epistemologists in general are inclined to accept. In the case of a reliabilist epistemology, the distinction amounts to the distinction between possessing and employing a reliable epistemic method or mechanism, and explaining how or why the mechanism is reliable.

The first distinction will help me straighten out a muddle, due, I believe, to Quine, about a cluster of issues about involving revisability and logic. The second distinction will enable me to respond to the residual doubts anti-naturalists will probably have about my account of warrant. So, to begin.

The idea that naturalism requires rejection of the a priori undoubtedly involves Quine's arguments, in "Two Dogmas of Empiricism" (Quine 1953) and elsewhere, for the holism of confirmation. In "Two Dogmas," Quine writes:

> Any statement can be held true come what may, if we make drastic enough adjustments elsewhere in the system. Even a statement very close to the periphery can be held true in the face of recalcitrant experience by pleading hallucination or by amending certain statements of the kind called logical laws. Conversely, by the same token, no statement is immune to revision. Revision even of the logical law of the excluded middle has been proposed as a means of simplifying quantum mechanics; and what difference is there in principle between such a shift and the shift whereby Kepler superseded Ptolemy, or Einstein Newton, or Darwin Aristotle? (Quine 1953, 43)

This passage recalls the following quick argument against the possibility of a priori knowledge sketched above:

1) No statement is immune from revision in light of experience. (The Quine-Duhem Thesis)
2) For a statement to be known a priori, it must be knowable independently of experience.
3) For a statement to be knowable independently of experience, it must be immune from revision in light of experience.

---

4) No statement can be known a priori.

Now there are two lines of objection to this argument that I do not want to pursue in any detail. The first has to do with the question whether it is statements or propositions that should be regarded as the objects of knowledge. It appears, as Descartes famously observed, that I can know that I exist without recourse to any sensory experience, and that (more to the point), there is no sensory experience that can cause me to doubt this. But what, exactly, is the content of my epistemic state in this case? If it is the *statement*, "I am here now," then premise (1), the Quine-Duhem Thesis, is simply false. On the other hand, the defender of the Q-D Thesis might insist that the content of an epistemic state should be regarded as a proposition, and that the proposition expressed by an utterance or thought-tokening of "I am here now" is perfectly empirical, and susceptible to revision in light of experience. Such a reply would then require reformulation of the Q-D Thesis, and of the argument; and something would need to be said about the Cartesian argument. Proper discussion of these issues would take us too far afield.

There is a second objection that I endorse, but that I don't want to make the whole of my case. The argument as I've formulated it fails to allow for the possibility of *defeasible* a priori warrants. Warrant, on my view, is reliability, across the board. And reliability does not have to be *perfect* reliability. If then, there are *defeasible* a priori warrants, the third premise is simply false: there just is no conflict between my first possessing positive non-empirical warrant for a given proposition, and then subsequently acquiring empirical grounds for rejecting that same proposition. But such a reply would not go to the heart of the naturalist's dissatisfaction. My reliabilist view of justification serves to expand the notion of the a priori so as to make possible a priori knowledge of what would otherwise have been classified as empirical statements; but the naturalist is interested in the status of the statements traditionally taken to be knowable a priori, statements like those that express the laws of logic and of mathematics. As a naturalist, it will be urged, I ought to allow that such statements as *those* are susceptible to revision in light of experience, and if that's so, do I want to allow that my warrant for these beliefs is also defeasible?

What seems dizzying about the suggestion that it might, at least in principle, be rational to give up a law of logic is the self-undermining character of the proposal. The word "revision" in the Q-D Thesis has to mean "*real* revision," and it has to mean "*rational* revision." That is, the Q-D Thesis has got to be talking about our actually altering our beliefs, as opposed to superficially mouthing some new sentence, and the alteration must be one that is rationally obligatory, given our experience. But how can these two conditions be jointly satisfied? If I feel under rational obligation to do anything, it is surely because of my commitment to logic; if I truly give up that commitment, how could I any longer feel rationally obliged to do anything?

It would seem that giving up (for example) the Law of Non-Contradiction, would be tantamount to giving oneself license to believe anything at all. And yet Quine himself, in his own discussions of confirmation holism, writes as if logical constraint must somehow survive even the most radical changes in belief: "Any statement can be held true come what may, *if we make drastic enough adjustments elsewhere in the system.*" (Quine 1953, 43, my emphasis.) So suppose we wish to hold true some logical contradiction—fine, says Quine, *provided* we're prepared to accept the consequences of doing so, and have the stomach for it. But this is puzzling—why the proviso? If giving up a law of logic—or, correlatively, embracing a contradiction—just *is* changing one's logic, why, once we give them up, are the old rules still in force? Consider, in this connection, the following puzzling passage:

> A conflict with experience at the periphery occasions readjustments in the interior of the field. Truth values have to be redistributed over some of our statements. Re-evaluation of some statements entails re-evaluation of others, because of their logical interconnections—the logical laws being in turn simply certain further statements of the system, certain further elements of the field. Having re-evaluated one statement we must re-evaluate some others, whether they be statements logically connected with the first or whether they be the statements of logical connections themselves. (Quine 1953, 42)

On the one hand, logical laws are "simply certain further statements of the system, certain elements of the field." But on the other hand, they seem to possess some kind of transcendent, normative force: "Having re-evaluated one statement we *must* re-evaluate some others." The existence of "logical interconnections" among statements means that we are not free to pick and choose which statements to re-evaluate: "re-evaluation of some statements *entails* [my emphasis] re-evaluation of others."[7]

Here is where the distinction between a priori warrant, and a priori knowledge of a proposition can be put to work: the distinction allows us to drive a wedge between giving up the *belief* that a law of logic is true, and *altering our logic*. On the classical computationalist view, the mind is, *inter alia*, a syntactic engine.[8] The logic that we *use* is that system of rules that characterizes the rules governing the manipulations of representations by the mental machinery. Beliefs, on the other hand, involve stored representations, so that giving up a belief is a matter of data management—shifting a representation out of one's "belief box." But data management itself, like all cognitive operations, is constrained by the general system of rules. These rules may be such as to ensure that the addition or elimination of certain beliefs will have far-reaching consequences both for the rest of one's belief set, and for one's behavior, hence the likelihood of "drastic adjustments elsewhere." But at the same time, there is no reason to suppose, and every reason to deny, that the addition or elimination of a belief will alter the overall architecture of one's cognitive machinery. To alter that, one presumably would need surgery.

Whether or not one possesses a priori warrant, on my account, depends on the reliability of one's cognitive machinery. Idealizing to the design of such machinery, to the competence embodied in the machine, we have reason to think that at least part of our logical apparatus is a mechanism of valid deductive inference, and hence that we do have a priori warrant for (at least some) of our intuitive judgments of validity (leaving room for interaction effects and other sources of performance error). But possession of such warrants does not entail possession of any particular belief; in particular, it does not entail that one possess a belief in any particular logical law, not even if the law is the one that captures the pattern of inference one is a priori warranted in accepting as valid. That being so, "giving up" belief in such a law, for whatever reason, is not tantamount to changing one's logic.

If all this is so, we can, as naturalists, accept the Quine-Duhem Thesis alongside the existence of a priori warrants. The Q-D Thesis concerns the relation among various elements of our belief sets, and states that none of them is evidentially insulated from any of the others. Specifically, it concerns the fate of statements that serve as *premises* in arguments the conclusions of which are predictions about sensory experience. Conceivably, one could include an explicit statement of some putative logical law among the premises of a piece of empirical reasoning, and then, by the Q-D Thesis, that statement would be a candidate for revision along with all the others. But the laws that govern both the original inferences and any subsequent revisions prompted by experience—these are not themselves premises in those inferences. It is thus possible to concede the revisability of logical *beliefs* without turning the nature of logical *warrant* into something empirical.

One final note on the Q-D Thesis and its relevance to questions of the a priori. Quine took it for granted that any proffered account of the a priori would appeal, at some point or other, to the notion of analyticity. Insofar as a naturalist accepts this assumption, it will appear that any argument against analyticity is equally an argument against the a priori. But my account makes no appeal to analyticity. In particular, I am not relying on the possibility of there being what Georges Rey calls "M-rules," rules that give the identity conditions for concepts, and that give the extension of the concept in all possible circumstances. (Rey 1998, 37 ff.) Rey points to the empirical possibility that psychological theory might be able to effect a principled distinction between M-rules for a concept (say, BACHELOR → UNMARRIED) and mere beliefs involving that concept ("Bachelors drive sports cars"). M-rules, for example, might turn out to be elements in an encapsulated parsing mechanism; if we possessed such a mechanism, we would find ourselves psychologically incapable of even entertaining the possibility of a married bachelor. Rey is agnostic about the existence of such rules, and says only that *were* there to be rules of this sort, "they could afford a basis for analytic *a priori* knowledge in a way that need pose no threat to a naturalized epistemology." (Rey 1998, 37) I am pretty skeptical that such a picture can be made to work. In particular, I suspect that the familiar Quinean considerations against analyticity can still be brought to bear against it,[9] and so it is no part of my burden here to defend the possibility of this "analytic a priori."

I turn now to the second distinction, between *possessing* and *explaining* warrant. I want to use this distinction to defend against the charge, sure to be made by anti-naturalists, that I have conflated warrant and mere causation. The worry is that what I've given is simply a causal explanation of one's propensity to accept certain inferences as valid, and to reject others as invalid. What reason is there, it will be asked, to think that the mechanisms that underlie and explain such dispositions provide epistemic warrant? My answer will be anticipated: the mechanisms provide warrant if and only if they are reliable. So much follows from my general reliabilism.

But the question may be pressed: how do I *know* my cognitive machinery is reliable? As a reliabilist, I am within my rights to refuse to answer this question. I am warranted in performing and accepting the inferences I perform and accept just in case the subserving mechanisms are reliable, and it need not be the case in order for them to *be* reliable that I *know* them to be reliable. To insist otherwise would be to urge upon me the principle, roundly rejected by epistemologists of almost every stripe, that in order to know that p, I must know that I know that p. (Or more conservatively, to promote the principle that to be warranted in accepting p, I must be warranted in believing that I am warranted in accepting p.)[10]

Still, as a good naturalist, I can provide a more satisfying response. The question of my warrant for claiming that my cognitive machinery is reliable ought properly to be treated as a demand for an *explanation* of the warrant—a theory of the mechanism that makes its reliability evident. This is a thoroughly empirical project, and involves at least two steps.

The first step is simply to investigate the cognitive machinery itself. Such an investigation might yield surprising results. Although I can perform inferences a priori, I cannot necessarily discover, by introspection alone, the character of the cognitive processes that underlie those inferences by introspection alone. I may, perhaps, feel that I have direct intuitions as to the content of the true logical laws, but if I'm right to insist on a distinction between possessing a logic, and possessing a belief about logic, there should be room for divergence. Certainly it must be possible, on anyone's view, for us to have an intuition—or for it to seem to us that we are having an intuition—that some proposition is true, when it's actually false. Frege, let us not forget, thought that the Axiom of Comprehension was self-evident.

Here's a plausible picture that accommodates these considerations: our beliefs about what the logical laws are based on introspective surveys of the inferences we accept (and, as may be, are a priori warranted in accepting). Since the survey is introspective, and need involve no sense experience, it falls on the "inside" side of the etiological divide in terms of which I propose to reconstruct the a priori/a posteriori distinction. Hence, the deliverances of introspection so conceived could count as yielding a priori knowledge just when and to the extent that the relevant form of introspection provides reliable access to the (reliable) processes introspected.

Still, introspection, if it has this character, must be counted as defeasible. It is an empirical question, for us to answer through scientific investigation, what exactly goes on when we are seized by "intuitions" about the nature of mind, the requirements for knowledge, or the myriad other subjects we philosophers discourse about. It may be that we are especially authoritative on such subjects, or on some, but not on others. The data of introspection may well turn out to carry weight—but like other data, they may, on occasion, be overriden.

Note, in this connection, the fact that the data of introspection are not unequivocal, and they certainly are not interpersonally robust. Intuitionists do not accept as valid the same class of inferences as classicists, and it is of course a matter of great controversy whether this shows that the connective "not" means something different for intuitionists from what it means for classicists. (It is a further empirical question whether intuitionists and classicists actually operate with different logics, or whether the differences are more superficial.)

Moreover, insofar as our beliefs about the logical laws depend on introspective *surveys*, they are warranted *inductively*. And so we run a risk of hasty generalization. We may fail to conjure up in imagination the counterexamples that would have altered our conclusions about what the laws of logic are. Vann McGee has argued, by displaying such alleged counterexamples, that *modus ponens* (my paradigm case!) is not a universally valid rule of inference for the conditional. (McGee 1985) He concludes:

> The methodological moral to be drawn from this is that, when we formulate general laws of logic [read: when we attempt to characterize the overall structure of our cognitive machinery], we ought to exercise the same sort of caution we exercise when we make inductive generalizations in the empirical sciences. We must take care that the instances we look at in evaluating a proposed generalization are diverse as well as numerous. (McGee 1985, 468)

McGee goes on to say that there is nothing here to trouble those who maintain that logic is "an *a priori* science." It could well be, he says, that we are able to recognize the validity of an instance of a valid rule by means of an a priori intuition, without our also being able to recognize by similar means *which* rule it is in accordance with which we are reasoning.[11]

Once we have characterized the cognitive mechanism, we are in a position to assess its reliability. This is a matter of assessing the epistemic practices that engage that equipment. Overall epistemic success—whether it is the everyday success of inferring shape from motion or the world-historical success of constructing a scientific theory of motion—vindicates whatever a priori elements figure crucially in the epistemic strategies that produce the success. Let me emphasize once more that this is *not* to say that warrant for one's ground-level a priori judgments awaits the outcome of empirical investigation into the reliability of the mechanisms that produce them. I am warranted in drawing my a priori inferences just in case the mechanisms by which I draw them are reliable ones.[12] But what my account does allow for is something that might bother defenders of the traditional a priori: it allows for the empirical justification of epistemic practices the cogency of which we nonetheless appreciate a priori. I am not sure that this should be any more paradoxical than the fact that we can empirically confirm the predictions of arithmetic.

Let me close by raising one final issue. I will not be able to provide an adequate treatment here, but I can sketch the shape I think such a treatment ought to take. The issue is an apparent disconnect between the *de facto* externalist reliability of certain inferences and our intuitive requirements for justification. Paul Boghossian, for example, writes that "[l]arge numbers of inferences that we are in no intuitive way justified in performing are necessarily truth-preserving," and thus perfectly reliable. In such cases, the subject "comes to hold a belief as the result of a reliable process, but his doing so is clearly epistemically irresponsible." (Boghossian 2001, 2–4) There are two promising lines of reply to this objection. In the first place, it is not at all clear that just because an inference from one statement to another is truth-preserving, that there is a reliable process of belief-fixation corresponding to it. But of course I have offered no account of mental processes that would enable me to make this response even remotely satisfying, and I think, anyway, that there's a deeper, and, if you will, more *reliable* reply to the objection.

Epistemic responsibility, I want to say, has no place in an account of knowledge, *per se*, that is, in an account of epistemic achievement. Its proper home, rather, is in an account of the norms of *knowledge-claims*. Suppose, counterfactually, that I have a gift of mathematical intuition that allows me to simply "see" that theorems of number theory are true. A naturalistic account of such a gift would have to explain how such an epistemic feat was possible, but it would not require that *I* be able to articulate any such account. On the other hand, if I now ask you to *take my word for it* that a certain proposition is a theorem of number theory, *it would be epistemically irresponsible for me not to provide a proof*. It is, as it were, bad epistemic manners for me to fail to offer you reasons to accept my claims beyond the bare assertion of my authority, given that the ability I am tacitly claiming for myself is so highly unusual. We don't, in general, think people epistemically irresponsible when they unreflectingly trust their senses, particularly if they're doing so in conditions we recognize (from our own experience) to be propitious, but we do want some minimal evidence of reliability in cases that are more arcane—when I report something you find surprising, for example, or something you generally believe I am not in a good position to know. The suggestion, in short, is to go Austinian (Austin 1946/1970) about justification, and keep to pure reliabilism about knowledge.

In sum, my account allows us to reconstruct, within a naturalized framework, everything that we could reasonably want in the way of a theory of a priori knowledge. A priori access is explained by the special etiology of a priori beliefs; a priori warrant is conferred on beliefs arrived at a priori when and only when the interior processes that give rise to the beliefs are reliable—in accord with the general account of warrant offered by reliabilism. If we want more than that—if we want to be warranted in believing that our a priori beliefs are warranted—then empirical investigation is necessary.

### Notes

1. Versions of this paper have been delivered at Ohio State University, The University of Canterbury, and at the 2003 Dubrovnik Conference on Metaphysics and Epistemology at the Inter-University Center in Dubrovnik, Croatia. It descends from a paper delivered at the Rutgers Epistemology Conference in 2002. I'd like to thank my audiences at all these venues for provocative and useful discussion of the ideas contained herein, especially Alex Byrne, Albert Casullo, Julian Cole, David Henderson, Terry Horgan, Nenad Miscevic, Matthias Steup, William Taschek, and Ralph Wedgwood. I'd also like to thank Joe Levine, George Pappas, Georges Rey, and Stewart Shapiro for many hours of discussion, and Christopher Peacocke and Paul Boghossian for helpful correspondence.
2. A notable exception is Georges Rey. The account of the a priori I develop here is very similar to the account he gives (in Rey 1993 and Rey 1998), and owes much to it, although there are differences in emphasis and in detail between our two views.
3. Actually, the requirement that it be *native* cognitive machinery is too strong. Cognitive machinery produced by surgery would, on my account, be equally capable of generating *a priori* warrants. The only kind of modification of the cognitive machine that should be ruled out is one that occurs through empirical learning, if such a modification is even possible. I'll have more to say about "changing one's logic" below.
4. One theory of autism has it that the disorder consists primarily in an absence of an innate "theory of mind." See Frith 1989, and Baron-Cohen 1996. It's consistent with this theory, and it does sometimes happen, that affected individuals puzzle out for themselves a rudimentary set of psychological generalizations that help them interpret the facial expressions and vocal tones of the non-autistic people around them. The inadequacy of these learned "theories" in providing genuine social competence to those autistic individuals who manage to develop

them shows the case to be the exception that proves the rule. See Williams 1994 for an autistic person's own account of her difficulties in trying to make sense of the verbal and gestural displays of her acquaintances.

5. I must admit, however, that it is unclear how, on my view, one can make sense of this last kind of warrant. Whereas perception, memory, and testimony can be plausibly regarded as reliable processes of belief-fixation (in perhaps descending order of strength), I don't see that the same can be said for the process of "seeming." Perhaps it could be shown that, more often than not, things that seem to me to be the case are the case, but I wouldn't bet money.

6. I take this to be the point of Lewis Carroll's fable, "What the Tortoise Said to Achilles:"

> "Let's make that quite clear. I accept $A$ and $B$ and $C$ and $D$. Suppose I *still* refused to accept $Z$?"
> "Then Logic would *force* you to do it!" Achilles triumphantly replied. "Logic would tell you 'You can't help yourself. Now that you've accepted $A$ and $B$ and $C$ and $D$, you *must* accept $Z$!' So you've no choice, you see."
> "Whatever Logic is good enough to tell me is worth *writing down*," said the Tortoise. "So enter it in your book, please. We will call it
> ($E$) If $A$ and $B$ and $C$ and $D$ are true, $Z$ must be true. Until I've granted *that*, of course I needn't grant $Z$. So it's quite a *necessary* step, you see?"
> "I see," said Achilles; and there was a touch of sadness in his tone.

(Carroll, 1895)

7. See Shapiro 2000 for discussion of the idea of a transcendent logic.
8. The distinction I am proposing does not depend upon the computational model; one can frame the distinction in terms of any of a variety of naturalistic conceptions of mind. However, exposition is easiest in terms of classical computationalism.
9. See Levine 1993 for discussion.
10. Cf. Rey 1998 on the "KK" Principle.
11. For critical discussion of McGee's argument, see Sinnott-Armstrong, et al., 1986. William Lycan has argued, independently, for the invalidity of *modus ponens* (Lycan 1993).
12. I was less clear about this than I should have been in an earlier discussion of this issue (Antony 2000). Thanks to Richmond Campbell and Joe Levine for raising questions about the account of the a priori given there.

## Works Cited

Antony, Louise. 2000. Naturalized epistemology, morality, and the real world. *Canadian Journal of Philosophy*, Supplementary Volume 26, ed. Richmond Campbell and Bruce Hunter. 103–137.

Austin, J. L. 1946/1976. Other minds. Reprinted in *Philosophical Papers*, J. L. Austin. Oxford: Oxford University Press. 2nd Edition, 76–116.

Baron-Cohen, Simon. 1996. *Mindblindness: An Essay on Autism and Theory of Mind.* Cambridge, MA: MIT Press.

Burge, Tyler. 1993. Content preservation. *The Philosophical Review*. 102 (4) (October): 457–488.

Carroll, Lewis. 1895. What the tortoise said to achilles. *Mind* 4, No. 14 (April): 278–280.

Devitt, Michael. Forthcoming. There Is No A Priori. In *Contemporary Debates in Epistemology*. Ed. Ernest Sosa and Matthias Steup. Oxford: Blackwell Publishers.

Frith, Uta. 1989. *Autism: Explaining the Enigma*. Oxford: Blackwell Publishers.

Haack, Susan. 1993. *Evidence and Inquiry*. Oxford: Blackwell Publishers.

Kim, Jaegwon. 1994. What is naturalized epistemology? In *Naturalized Epistemology*, 2nd edition, Ed. Hilary Kornblith, 1–14. Cambridge, MA: MIT Press.

Kitcher, Philip. 2000. A priori knowledge revisited. In *New Essays on the A Priori*. Ed. Paul Boghossian and Christopher Peacocke. Oxford: Oxford University Press.

Levine, Joseph. 1993. Intentional Chemistry. *Grazer Philosophische Studien* 46: 103–134.

Lycan, William G. 1993. MPP, RIP. In *Philosophical Perspectives*, 7. Ed. James Tomberlin. Atascadero, CA: Ridgeview Publishing Company.

Maddy, Penelope. 2000. Naturalism and the a priori. In *New Essays on the A Priori*. Ed. Paul Boghossian and Christopher Peacocke. Oxford: Oxford University Press.

McGee, Vann. 1985. A counterexample to Modus Ponens. *The Journal of Philosophy* 85: 82, 462–471.

Putnam, Hilary. 1968. The logic of quantum mechanics. Reprinted in *Mathematics, Matter and Method: Philosophical Papers, Vol. 1*. Cambridge, England: Cambridge University Press, 1975.

Quine, W. V. O. 1953. Two Dogmas of Empiricism. *From a Logical Point of View*. Cambridge, MA: Harvard University Press.

——— 1971. Epistemology Naturalized. Reprinted in *Empirical Knowledge: Readings from Contemporary Sources*, ed. Roderick Chisholm and Robert Swartz. Englewood Cliffs, N. J.: Prentice Hall, 1973.

Rey, Georges. 1993. The unavailability of what we mean: a reply to Quine and Fodor and LePore. In *Grazer Philosophische Studien* 46: 61–101.

——— 1998. A naturalistic a priori. *Philosophical Studies* 92: 25–43.

Shapiro, Stewart. 2000. The status of logic. In *New Essays on the A Priori*. Ed. Paul Boghossian and Christopher Peacocke. Oxford: Oxford University Press.

Sinnott-Armstrong, Walter, James Moor, and Robert Fogelin. 1986. A defense of modus ponens. *The Journal of Philosophy* 86: 83, 296–300.

Williams, Donna. 1994. *Somebody, Somewhere: Breaking Free From the World of Autism*. London: Jessica Kingsley.

*Philosophical Issues, 14, Epistemology, 2004*

# THE A PRIORI AUTHORITY OF TESTIMONY

Robert Audi
University of Notre Dame

The growing literature on testimony contains much discussion of the extent to which testimony is similar to other sources of knowledge and justification, particularly perception introspection, reason, and memory. One enduring question is whether it is basic in the way those sources apparently are. Another major question is whether testimony has a certain kind of a priori justificatory authority, i.e., whether it is an a priori truth (if a truth at all) that, at least with certain qualifications, beliefs based on testimony are prima facie justified. It is the second question that mainly concerns me here. One might think that if testimony is not basic in the relevant sense, then it cannot have a priori epistemic authority of any kind. I have argued elsewhere[1] that testimony is not a basic source of justification or knowledge—at least not in the way the four just mentioned are—but a negative answer to the question of basic epistemic status does not (as I shall show) require a negative answer to the question of a priori justificatory authority.

I want to begin by pursuing a related question that I believe has not so far been adequately explored: the possibility of a *limited* kind of basic justificatory power on the part of testimony. I will then proceed to the other main business of the paper, concerning the possibility that, whether or not testimony has basic justificatory power, it has an a priori role in justification.

## I. Two Types of Epistemic Source

It is natural to consider an epistemic source to be unqualifiedly basic only if it can supply what it is a source of—say, justified beliefs—without depending on the operation of another epistemic source. Perception is, for justification, basic in this sense if any source of justification is, whereas (to take an important example) inference can generate justified beliefs only if some other epistemic source plays an essential role in the justificatory grounding of its premise(s).[2] Inferring a proposition from premises that we are *not* justified in believing does not (by itself) justify our believing it.

To say, however, that a source, such as testimony, is not basic for justification leaves open something of much importance for the epistemology of testimony: whether it may be a *conditionally basic source* of justification.[3] By this I mean a source that is basic with respect to some degree of justification for believing a proposition *given* an appropriate degree independently possessed by the subject. The (epistemically) prior justification may be taken to derive, directly or indirectly, from one or more basic sources of justification. Unlike, say, sensory experience, a conditionally basic source cannot produce justification for a belief where the belief has none to begin with; but it can raise the level of justification that a belief (or other element) has on the basis of one or more other sources.

A ladder might provide a useful analogy. In isolation, it does not facilitate climbing. It must be grounded if it is to enable one to climb; but, once properly grounded, it may allow climbing to a great height. No particular limiting height need be indicated, however. To be sure, an ordinary ladder can support no heavier a climber than its grounding can sustain; but we can imagine a kind of ladder whose rungs have a certain amount of independent sustaining capacity, yet not enough to bear the full weight of a climber on their own. Suppose, then, that we think of a high level of justification, say one high enough to imply that a *true* belief having that degree of justification constitutes knowledge (provided the belief does not suffer from a fourth condition problem of the kind that shows why justified true belief *need* not constitute knowledge). We might then say that a conditionally basic source might or might not be one that can take us over that threshold.

A conditionally basic source might also be called a *secondary* source, but it is still a basic one because the resulting justification, the justification it distinctively contributes, is (one might argue) not grounded in—though it *depends* on—the originative, unqualifiedly basic source(s) in question. (The base of the ladder, but not its rungs, rests on the ground.) If testimony has this power, we might call it a generative source with respect to *some* degree of justification. But owing to the epistemic precondition of some degree of justification from another source of it, testimony would be only conditionally basic. If it is even conditionally basic, however, this would be some reason to expect it to have a priori epistemic authority—at least, it would be some reason if, as rationalists tend to, one took the standard basic sources to have a high degree of such authority.

To see how testimony might be conditionally basic for justification, suppose that, from experience over time, a child has some degree of justification for generally trusting its parents and hence, normally, some degree of inductive justification for believing a given thing they say. (They have usually been right about food, clothing, shelter, and much else, and we might suppose that even a quite young child can—in an unselfconscious way—inductively generalize on the basis of the retained beliefs formed from noticing such regularity.) Given this background, a parent's *saying* that *p*, for instance that it will rain tomorrow, might in itself provide justification that goes beyond the justification the child would have for this on the basis of (for instance) a sibling's *report* that the parent said this. The parentally given, testimony-based justification might add to the child's antecedent inductive justification for accepting parental attestations in general; the latter is itself ultimately grounded at least largely in (for instance) perceptual, memorial, and intuitive sources.

If testimony is a conditionally basic source of justification, this might also bear on its capacity to contribute to *knowledge* on the part of the recipient. Suppose the recipient's inductive justification for believing *p* is not strong; then perhaps (as suggested earlier) additional justification generated by testimony that *p* could be strong enough to take the recipient's belief over the threshold to being justified in some full-blooded way, for instance in a way that enables it to constitute knowledge if *p* is true *and* there are no defeaters of the kind that can prevent justified true belief from being knowledge. In this latter case, we might consider testimony a conditionally basic source of knowledge as well as of justification. For knowledge, however, there are conditions here that go beyond those needed for justification. Let me explain.

I assume that it is possible (as in the case of children just learning to speak) to acquire testimony-based knowledge without becoming justified in believing the proposition in question.[4] Thus, one condition here would be that the attester not know that *p*; otherwise, the recipient could (on my view) acquire knowledge that *p* even apart from the justification provided by the testimony (this might indeed hold on any plausible externalist account of knowledge).[5]

A further condition might be that to achieve knowledge that *p* by virtue of the added justification gained from testimony in the indicated (derivative) way, the recipient must have some initial *knowledge* of a certain kind, say, of the attester's being generally credible and of the content of the testimony, at least knowledge to the effect that it is *p* (as opposed to something else) that the attester said. But I leave this open. In any case, knowledge that *p* which arises from a combination of testimony-based justification and independent justification would not be testimony-based in the full-blooded sense. The justificatory or epistemic grounding of the recipient's belief would derive only in part from that source and, without non-testimony-based knowledge on the part of the recipient, would not be sufficient to enable the belief to constitute knowledge.

If there are conditionally basic sources of justification, a great deal must be said to determine what level of *initial* justification is needed in order for a such a source to generate justification. Another question is how much greater the *resultant* level of a belief's justification can be owing to one or another kind of testimony. These matters may be left open here. My point is that particularly if one takes it (as Thomas Reid may have) that the recipient of testimony is (characteristically) responding to the attester's *belief*—or at least a presumption thereof—and not just to a linguistic or other symbolic act, one may find it plausible to argue that testimony is a conditionally basic source of justification and perhaps of knowledge as well.[6] I do not claim that it is normally (or ever) such a source. I simply want to leave that possibility open and take account of some of its implications.

In leaving the possibility open, we need not assume that only a coherence theory of justification can explain it. Granted, it may be true that someone's attesting that *p* is coherence-making relative to a recipient of the testimony's believing *p*. But this need not be because the two intrinsically "cohere." (I take it that believing that *p* seems to cohere in some intuitive way with someone's telling one that *p*.) The coherence-making relation in question may be at least partly grounded in the explanatory connection between one person's attesting to a proposition and another's believing it *on that basis* (hence *because* of the testimony). Explanation, however, is not only a coherence-making relation but also the kind of relation foundationalist theories often appeal to in accounting for justification. On a foundationalist theory that gives testimony a conditionally basic role in grounding justification, my justification in believing *p* might be in part due to this belief's being explained by someone's telling me that *p*; and this explanatory relation might connect the belief either with a purportedly a priori ground— the testimony itself—or with some empirical ground, say the attester's presumed experiential basis for believing *p*.

A contrasting account of testimony-based justification might be offered from a broadly Humean point of view. On an inductivist account of such justification (which might be coherentist or, more likely, foundationalist), my justification for a testimony-based belief that *p* might be grounded in my background justification for thinking that the truth of *p* is at least part of what best explains why the attester is saying that *p*. The account of testimony-based justification sketched above, in allowing testimony to be a conditionally basic source and in not ascribing its justificatory power to inductively supporting elements, is consistent with its having a priori authority; the Humean inductivist account is not, since justification for drawing an empirically justified inductive inference is both needed for, and can be a sufficient ground for, the justification of a testimony-based belief.[7] The testimony contributes to that justification as a datum supporting the inductive basis for holding the belief; but it has no independent justificatory role. The former non-reductivist account, then, is the one to be explored in assessing the prospects for the a priori authority of testimony.

## II. A Case for the A Priori Justificatory Authority of Testimony

It may seem that if testimony is not at least a conditionally basic source of justification, then its justificatory authority must be entirely derivative and that one must have broadly inductive justification for believing it if one derives justification from testimony at all. But it has been plausibly argued that "We are a priori prima facie entitled to accept something that is prima facie intelligible and presented as true."[8] This is a strong claim. It affirms a kind of epistemological rationalism that is not entailed even by taking testimony to be a conditionally basic source of justification. (An empiricist could regard a source of testimony as a basic justificatory source, but not take it to have a priori authority.) Let me suggest a possible rationalization of the basic idea, in four stages.

*The natural grounds of belief.* We might plausibly argue that

(1) it is a priori (an a priori truth) that at least in those who have the conceptual sophistication which goes with learning a natural language as rich as English, perception, introspective consciousness, and conceptual reflection tend to produce beliefs and to do so in a *way* that yields prima facie justification for holding them.

This is not to say that *every* perception, or every introspective or reflectional experience, produces belief; but (in people having the indicated degree of sophistication) they all may be plausibly taken to *tend* to produce one or more beliefs, and, as epistemically basic sources of beliefs, to do so in a way that yields justification of the beliefs that are produced by them in normal ways. If, for instance, seeing print is the basis of our believing there is print before us, we tend to be justified in so believing. The idea that our experiences (of the kind in question) tend to produce belief does not imply that beliefs can have no other source (such as wishful thinking). But, although this is not entailed by the non-statistical, propensity notion of a tendency that is in question, there is some plausibility in holding that most of our beliefs are experientially produced.

*Testimony as a natural expression of belief.* We might also argue that

(2) it is a priori that *believing* a proposition carries a tendency to attest to it in the kinds of situations in which testimony is natural, as where a person one knows asks for information.

There are two points here. First, as Reid put it in speaking of God as implanting in us "principles that tally with each other," "The first of these principles is, a propensity to speak truth...Truth is always uppermost, and is the natural issue of the mind..."[9] Doubtless he was thinking of the normal case of speaking truth in which we believe what we affirm and do not merely utter a true proposition. One might go further (and this is my second point): a tendency to avow what one believes seems partly constitutive of the very concept of believing.[10]

Whether this second point holds or not, the natural expression view is most plausible when restricted, as it should be, to *undefeated testimony*, the kind that occurs in the absence of such factors as confused formulation, internal inconsistency in what is affirmed, the appearance of deception, and conflict with apparent facts evident in the situation in which the testimony is given, as where a man who is howling and limping says he is fine. The situations of normal testimony, by contrast, are the typical kinds in which we say things to our children and friends, answer questions by acquaintances, and express our needs or desires. Call the kind of attestation characteristic of such cases (which is usually undefeated) *normal testimony*.

A further restriction seems desirable here. The normal testimony in question should be what we might call *primary*. This is the basic kind of testimony given in saying that *p* (at least in the broad sense in which a conventional gesture, such as nodding, can be conceived as saying). Testimony in publications and reported by others may be called *secondary*. There are at least two interconnected reasons for calling it secondary. I take these in turn.

The first reason is conceptual. If secondary testimony could not be seen as both in a certain way distant from, and also appropriately continuous with, primary testimony (the everyday "direct" kind), it would not have the role it does in relation to the notion of justification. If, for instance, someone's saying that *p* is merely caused by primary testimony, and not a *conveyance* of the content carried by the originative speaking, writing, or other symbolic act, it is not secondary testimony at all. Suppose I mishear Jen's attestation that it is unusually hot, instead taking her to say 'humid', but I am aware that I did not hear her very clearly. A bit later, I might be caused to think about the weather by someone asking how she is taking the heat; I might then look at her fanning herself, and, reconstructing what she said for the inquirer, say to that third party, 'She said it's unusually hot'. This might be called *attempted* secondary testimony, but it is not genuine secondary testimony despite the coincidence of content and the causal line to the original testimony. It reproduces, but does not convey, her testimony.

The second consideration is this. To receive secondary testimony *as* such, we must take it that the attester has affirmed *p*, if only mentally, and (other things equal) would have attested to it in person on the originative occasion if on that occasion it was not attested to but only written in a letter. Still, in receiving secondary testimony we do not have the contextual element of getting testimony in person, an element that is arguably of considerable epistemic significance.[11] This point does not imply that testimony cannot be *written*. If I cannot speak, I can still give you testimony by writing before your eyes. The crucial distinction is in part a matter of the difference between a kind of direct presentation as opposed to one that is in a certain way indirect. In speaking of normal testimony for purposes of arguing for its a priori authority, I shall intend primary testimony.[12]

*The preservative role of memory.* Now suppose, in addition, that

> (3) it is a priori that the sorts of beliefs that undefeated normal testimony expresses (or at least appears to express) are among the kinds that memory preserves and that arise from perception, introspective consciousness, conceptual reflection, and inference from propositions believed on the basis of these sources.[13]

What supports taking (3) to be a priori is the thought that it is all but incoherent to suppose people are in general making up what they tell us in undefeated normal testimony. Given this, and given a plausible theory of human life in which testimony has a central place, it is arguably a priori that there is reason to believe that much of what people say, far from being fabricated, is *retained* in their memories. If this is a priori, one might go on to argue that there is a priori reason to think the retained beliefs tend to be traceable to some kind of experience (including reflection)—the kind that is a basic source of justification.

*Testimony as a prima facie representation of facts.* If (1)–(3) are true, then belief tends to reflect the world—inner or outer—that produces it, memory tends to preserve belief, and testimony tends to express belief. It might be claimed to follow from (1)–(3) that

> (4) it is a priori that (and we can thus have a priori justification for believing) undefeated normal testimony is prima facie credible.

Call this the *thesis of the a priori epistemic authority of testimony.* The underlying intuitive idea is roughly that we can see a priori that undefeated normal testimony tends to express beliefs which are ultimately grounded in the standard basic sources: either directly produced by those sources or inferentially grounded in their cognitive products, and (apart from beliefs formed or re-formed at the time) retained by memory.[14] If we are realists, we might say that such testimony reflects a natural progression in which information goes from the world, to the mind, to the mouth.

It is, to be sure, one thing to say we are a priori justified in *believing that* a *kind* of testimony is credible and another thing to say that it is a priori that we are justified in (non-inferentially) *believing that kind of testimony.* I am assuming, however, that if (4) is true, then beliefs *based on* undefeated normal testimony are prima facie justified. This is not asserted by (4); but it may be plausibly claimed to follow from a source's being (a priori) prima facie credible (hence prima facie worthy of belief) that there is justification for believing its outputs and that a belief *based* on that source is prima facie justified.[15]

To assess the epistemic authority thesis (i.e., 4), we must remember that one can be justified *in* believing something without actually believing it. Certainly many people would not form a belief of this thesis without an occasion for appropriate reflection on it. Defending the thesis does not require denying this evident psychological fact.

It would be at best difficult to establish the premises of the suggested argument. (I take it as obvious that it is not formally valid and, apart from regimenting its premises, it is best taken as a plausibility argument.) None of the premises is even close to something uncontroversially a priori. The weakest is perhaps (3), which affirms the reliability of memory at least in *preserving* our beliefs, so that by and large, if we seem to remember that *p* (and believe it on that basis), then we have at least retained the belief that *p* (whether or not we actually *remember that p*—which would entail its truth—by contrast with believing it out of wishful thinking, a possibility (3) does not adequately take into account). This is *internal reliability*, as opposed to what we might call the *external reliability* of memory, i.e., its reliability as measured by the proportion of memorially retained (or apparently memorially retained) beliefs (or non-doxastic representations such as mental pictures of people or events) that are *veridical*.

I cannot see that we are a priori justified in holding (3), though I *do* believe a good case can be made that memory beliefs are a priori *prima facie* justified.[16] If so, then even if it is not a priori that they ultimately derive from other basic sources of justification, such as perception, they may be taken by recipients of testimony to be prima facie justified. You tell me something you are justified in believing; I believe it on the basis of your testimony; do I not then have a justifying basis for it?

Suppose, for the sake of argument, that undefeated normal testimony does tend to express beliefs justified for the attester. It is far from clear that our knowing, even a priori, that the kinds of beliefs that tend to be expressed in undefeated normal testimony are *justified*, memorially or in any other likely way, for the *attester* will sustain the claim that it is a priori that *we*, who believe propositions on the basis of normal, undefeated testimony, are thereby (prima facie) justified in believing those propositions.[17]

There are many issues here. For one thing, even assuming that it is a priori that undefeated normal testimony tends to express beliefs justified for the attester, that such beliefs tend to be *true* is not self-evidently a priori; and internalists (usually in part because of how they interpret Cartesian demon worlds) tend to deny that it is a priori. (If an externalist notion of justification is in question, it is likely to be considered at best an empirical truth that the attester's beliefs—or any others—tend to be justified.) In reply, it might be noted that it is *also* not self-evidently a priori that beliefs justified by sensory experience tend to be true, and that this does not seem to prevent our being (normally) justified in believing propositions that we justifiedly believe others to believe on the basis of their sense-experience. This is an important point I want to leave open here, but it can support the a priori authority thesis (4) only if certain contrasts between testimony and the standard basic sources can be undermined.[18]

One may still ask, however, why it isn't a priori that believing p on the basis of someone else's justifiedly believing it is sufficient for justifiedly believing it oneself. Might we not argue as follows: since (a) the attester tends to be justified in what is attested to and (b) the content of a testimony-based belief is supported by whatever justification the attester has, (c) the latter beliefs tend to be true? Let me make two related points here.

First, even leaving aside whether these premises can be plausibly considered a priori, it is important to see that there *being* a justification for the attester's belief that p does not imply that the recipient's belief that p *has* that justification (or any other). This holds even if the original justification is perceptual and even if the attester's grounds for p render it objectively probable. Second, and more important here, even if the recipient is justified on some ground or other in thinking the attester is justified in believing p, the latter's justification could still be grounded on such inadequate bases as plausible but unsound reasoning, or on hallucination, or on false but credible testimony. This is obvious in a way that prevents the recipient's being automatically justified in believing that p, *simply* by virtue of taking the attester to be justified in believing that p.

Another factor weighing against this *secondary justification thesis*, as we might call it, is this. There are plainly enough cases of unjustified attestations to raise the question whether any *tendency* to be justified that testimony-based beliefs have is strong enough to ground justification for believing testimony in general, as opposed to, say, plausible testimony.

Suppose that despite the problems I have noted, (1)–(3) or some similar principles can be seen, a priori, to provide us with justification for *believing* the attester is justified in believing that p. Might this second-order justified belief not devolve justification on the recipient's testimony-based belief of the proposition attested to? This is doubtful. For one thing, justifiedly believing that someone is justified in believing something does not imply that one justifiedly believes it oneself. There are still other obstacles in the way of showing that testimony has a priori epistemic authority. Recall the premise we started with: that it is a priori that normal undefeated testimony *tends* to express justified beliefs. I am not going to try to show that this premise is false, or even only an empirical truth, or too weak to sustain the a priori authority of testimony. But unjustified testimony, as well as justified testimony that is false, is common; and clearly much work must be done to construct an account of normal, undefeated testimony that does not beg questions in favor of the a priori authority view. These are large issues, and here I simply record doubt that it can be shown (at least along lines closely akin to those pursued here) that we have prima facie a priori justification to take normal testimony to express justified belief.

Let us assume, then, that nothing so far said adequately supports the thesis of the a priori justificatory sufficiency of testimony. There is a closely related argument that might support that thesis and thereby the apparently entailed broad conclusion that testimony-based *beliefs* are (a priori) prima facie justified. Suppose (controversially) that we do not know a priori that justified beliefs tend to be true. It might still be a priori that

> (5) if our only good explanation for a proposition we are amply justified in believing entails the likely truth of a further proposition, we are prima facie justified in believing the latter proposition.

What good explanation do we have for someone's giving undefeated normal testimony that *p* which does not entail the likely truth of that proposition (i.e., its being more probable than its negation)? A case can be made that there is none.

Does holding that (5) is a priori, however, depend on theses (1)–(3) or any similar principles claiming a priori status for principles pertinent to testimony? This is not obvious. Perhaps the principles connecting the standard basic sources of belief with the natural cases of undefeated testimony (which seem to include most normal testimony)—the principles underlying such propositions as (1)–(3)—need only be empirical to help us understand how (5) is to be applied so as to support the a priori authority thesis. Perhaps it can be shown that the substantive contents of (1)–(3)—their contents with 'it is a priori that' deleted—need not themselves be a priori in order for it to be a priori that they are essential to our best explanation of undefeated normal testimony.

This line of thinking does not imply that testimony-based beliefs are inferential after all. Its thrust concerns the epistemic, not the psychological, status of those beliefs. That there *is* a justificatory argument for the (prima facie) credibility of normal testimony does not imply that justified beliefs based on such testimony must also be based on that argument or any constituent in it, such as (5). Still, the *justification* of testimony-based beliefs would (on this approach) be grounded in *justification* for employing some such argument. This point does not seem paralleled for the standard basic sources. They do not appear to need the kind of inductive underpinning just outlined.

Is the suggested inductivist line "Humean?" If the Humean approach forswears all substantive a priori justification (the "non-analytic" kind in question), it is not. Nor is it Humean in implying that our justification for a testimony-based belief is wholly inductive. The suggestion is rather that the justification of testimony-based beliefs rests on both an essential inductive element and an essential a priori element. The main inductive element is our justification for taking the attester's saying that $p$ to support its truth (perhaps owing to causal or empirical probability connections that enable us to view the testimony as best explained by propositions entailing its truth). The main a priori element is (5) itself or something close to it. Whether, given these assumptions, the justifiedness of testimony-based beliefs should be taken to *reduce* to inductive justification is in part a question of whether such justification can depend on an a priori epistemic principle and is left open.[19]

Although a case can be made for the apriority of something like (5), even its truth is not uncontroversial. Still, supposing one could show that (5) is a priori, it is controversial whether it is a priori that our only good explanation of undefeated normal testimony entails its truth or probable truth. What counts as our only good explanation of an empirical phenomenon is arguably in part a pragmatic or even subjective matter. Perhaps this is not so in the case of testimony. If it is not, that might be argued to be only because something close to (1)–(3) is a priori after all. That, however, is at best difficult to show.

### III. Testimony-based Acceptance

If the main points in the previous section are sound, the kind of case I have explored for the a priori authority thesis does not succeed. Rather than pursue other dimensions of what might be called the epistemological case for this view, however, I propose to move in a different direction that may take us further.

Let me start with an important distinction. It may not have escaped notice that I have spoken of the case for the a priori authority of testimony in relation to belief, not *acceptance*. These are not always distinguished, but they differ significantly. In my view, 'accept' does not even seem natural for most of the normal, as opposed to, say, courtroom, cases of testimony. The model so natural for philosophers, of accepting what is said only after careful consideration, should not be allowed to intrude here: it is misleading to say that I *accept* the ordinary things my family and friends say to me. Typically, I simply believe my family and friends, i.e., believe what they tell me. In the contexts where 'accept' is natural (for propositions), it contrasts with 'reject' and 'withhold'; and in that probably central use, acceptance does not entail belief. We can accept something while withholding—or simply not forming—belief.

Now I think that there *is* an a priori principle to the effect that if one needs to act and cannot do that without certain information (for instance, directions to a place one must find on pain of death), then in the absence of reasons to doubt testimony that one can see provides such information, one should *accept* that testimony and is justified in so doing. For instance, the agent should act on it in appropriate ways, tentatively use it as a basis for inference, abstain from rejecting it if, merely from a general skeptical disposition, the agent is tempted to do so, and so forth. Skepticism at the theoretical level is one thing; but in practice we would not be fully rational if, when there is no positive reason to doubt testimony (or that it provides information we need), we did not take it as worthy of acceptance, however tentative, as a basis for action. Indeed, an even wider principle may be a priori: that in everyday life we should accept testimony as prima facie credible unless we have reason to do otherwise.

These principles may be special applications of a comprehensive principle to the effect that we have prima facie reason to take what we consider to be our only means (or only realistically possible means) to an end that we see we must realize. But such principles are *practical*, not epistemic. They are nonetheless very important for seeking knowledge and justified belief. They are also good candidates to explain many of the major points that apply to the epistemological significance of testimony, including, I think, some denied by Hume. The most salient of these is that one needs no inductive justification for accepting undefeated normal testimony. Another point relevant here is that one need not draw an inference to the effect that testimony *is* acceptable (or true) as a basis for rationally accepting it.

It may seem that even the kinds of practical principles in question presuppose that testimony is taken to have some *epistemic* authority. If one did not consider it to have *some* credibility—some *believability* as opposed to just *acceptability*, we might say—why waste energy taking it into account? Here it must be borne in mind that I am assuming the agent must act and has no preferable alternative source of information regarding how to achieve the end that (from the agent's point of view) must be realized. Granted that the testimony should be rejected if it has only a zero probability of satisfying the informational need, it can have a higher probability than that if merely undefeated (I am taking grounds for ascribing a zero probability as prima facie defeating), whereas the probability of achieving the end if, from lack of significantly probable instrumental information, one does not act at all, *is* zero. This is *not* to deny that practical rationality depends on theoretical ("epistemic") rationality in some ways.[20] If *S* is to act *rationally* in using merely undefeated testimonial information, *S* must have some justification for believing the instrumental principle in question (or something similar). But this point does not entail that testimony itself has a priori epistemic authority.

Talk of acceptance of testimony may bring to mind other plausible practical principles in this range—*principles of epistemic regulation*, we might call them, by contrast with epistemic and justificational principles proper. The former are among the principles important in "the ethics of belief."[21] One is that if someone tells us, with apparent sincerity, that *p*, then unless we have reason to do otherwise, we should be prepared to take *p* as a basis for inference and as potential evidence. The idea is roughly that undefeated normal testimony is a defeasible a priori ground for acceptance. What we accept, even if we do not believe it, may lead to our forming justified beliefs or acquiring knowledge. These may be of the proposition itself, since we may acquire adequate grounds for it; but what we accept may also be like a rope we cast aside once we climb it to get to firm ground. The inferences one tentatively draws from what one merely accepts may lead to reconsidering the matter at hand and to discovering important truths that disconfirm the proposition initially accepted.

Another regulation principle is that if, with apparent sincerity, someone attests to a proposition obviously incompatible with a proposition one believes, then one should (prima facie) reconsider that proposition (say, by seeking further evidence). The idea here is roughly that undefeated normal attestation to a proposition obviously incompatible with one's beliefs is a defeasible a priori ground for something like accepting it for the sake of argument: perhaps only for a brief moment, but in some cases until one can determine a ground favoring one proposition or the other. These principles are not perfectly parallel: other things equal, testimony must have greater plausibility to justify reconsideration of a proposition we already believe than to justify acceptance of one we neither believe nor disbelieve.

Epistemic regulation principles bear, for instance, on what we should take as a premise, even if only suppositionally, on what we should use to guide a search for evidence, and on what propositions we should use as grounds for action or, on the other hand, withhold pending further information. It is essential to see that the soundness of such principles would not imply that testimony has the *kind* of a priori justificatory authority that has been claimed for it as a ground for belief. We should ask, then, how much of the data supporting the justificatory autonomy of testimony can be accounted for by such practical principles. Suppose that the kind of case I have sketched in support of the a priori justificatory sufficiency of testimony does not succeed, as I shall assume it does not. I would stress how much of what needs to be said about the role of testimony can be accommodated by practical epistemic regulation principles. They are also important in their own right, and they are essential for a comprehensive theory of justification, even if not for epistemology narrowly conceived.

To be sure, perhaps some other case for the a priori justificatory authority of testimony would succeed. Assume this for the sake of argument. Does it follow that the contrasts I have drawn between the standard basic sources and testimony are unsound? I believe not. Nor do I take it to follow simply from a source's being epistemically basic that its epistemic authority is a priori. The question whether testimony is an epistemically basic source must be distinguished from the question whether it has a priori justificatory authority.

One might think that if testimony has such authority—as anti-reductionists generally claim—then it *is* a basic source of justification. But that does not follow. What we have seen is that testimony could be so connected with the basic sources that its justificatory power and a priori authority derive from theirs. This would not imply either that its authority is ultimately inductive or that testimony is basic in the way the standard sources are, and it can be argued with or without the purportedly a priori principle that we are justified in believing what best explains something we justifiedly believe. A clearly successful case using either strategy, however, has (so far as I know) yet to be made.

\*\*\*

It should be plain that the contrasts I have drawn between testimony and the standard basic sources of justification and knowledge do not imply that testimony is inessential in a normal human life or that its authority in cognitive matters is only contingent and empirical. One reason for this is that not all cognitive matters are *doxastic*—matters of belief. But even apart from that point, it should be clear that testimony is both globally and focally essential in our lives: we depend on it in an overall way for an adequate view of the world, and we rely on specific attestations for knowledge or justification regarding specific propositions. Testimony is indeed of virtually unlimited breadth in its epistemic power: nearly anything that can be known firsthand can also be known on the basis of testimony. Testimony is a source of basic knowledge; it is normally the starting point of everyone's conceptual learning; it may perhaps be a conditionally basic source of justification and perhaps of knowledge as well; it may even have a measure of a priori justificatory authority, as it surely does of practical authority; and it is, as Reid saw, as natural a source of knowledge and justification as any of the others.[22]

## Notes

1. In "The Place of Testimony in the Fabric of Knowledge and Justification," *American Philosophical Quarterly* 34, 4 (1997) and "Testimony, Credulity, and Veracity," forthcoming in a collection edited by Jennifer Lackey and Ernest Sosa.

2. Taking perception to be a basic source in this sense does not require viewing it as generating indefeasible justification, nor does it commit one to a naïve, atomistic theory of concept acquisition. Although it does not permit one to hold epistemological coherentism, it does allow endorsing *conceptual coherentism*, the view (in part) that concepts are acquired, and operate, in families. These points are developed in my *Epistemology* (London and New York: Routledge, 2003), esp. ch. 7.

3. For further discussion of what constitutes a conditionally basic source, see my "The Foundationalism-Coherentism Controversy." There the main question pursued is whether coherence is a conditionally basic source of justification.

4. This is argued in my "The Place of Testimony in the Fabric of Knowledge and Justification," *American Philosophical Quarterly* (1997).

5. Would the imagined case falsify the plausible view that, at least normally, testimony-based belief constitutes testimony-based *knowledge* only if the attester knows that *p*? This view is controversial. That testimony can yield knowledge that *p* in the recipient without the attester's knowing that *p* has been plausibly argued by both Jennifer Lackey and Peter Graham. See, e.g., her "Testimonial Knowledge and Transmission," *Philosophical Quarterly* 49 (1999); and his "Conveying Information," *Synthese* 123 (2000), "The Reliability of Testimony," *Philosophy and Phenomenological Research* 61 (2000), and "Transferring Knowledge," *Nous* 34 (2000). I have briefly defended the knowledge requirement against both authors in "Testimony, Credulity, and Veracity," cited above. Here it is enough to note that since the belief in question would qualify as knowledge only on the basis of some degree of justification coming from a non-testimonial source (or at least a different testimonial source that itself confers some degree of justification on the belief in question only in virtue of some justification from a non-testimonial source), this belief would be only in part based on the testimony. If it counts as knowledge in part on the basis of justification from another source, it must be in part based on that source (a point that would likely be accepted even apart from a causal notion of the basis relation in question).

6. Consider, e.g., Reid's "first principle" *That certain features of the countenance, sounds of the voice, and gestures of the body, indicate certain thoughts and dispositions of the mind* (*Essays on the Intellectual Powers*, reprinted in part in Ronald Beanblossom and Keith Lehrer, eds., *Thomas Reid's Inquiry and Essays* [Indianapolis: Hackett, 1983], 279). For him these features, sounds, gestures, and presumably other expressive aspects of human behavior are "natural signs": "It seems to me incredible, that the notions men have of the expression of features, voice, and gesture, are entirely the fruit of experience" (p. 280). Now it may be that Reid took testimony to be characteristically accompanied by natural signs of believing what is attested to; he might have thought of testimony as naturally *indicating*, not as just *reporting*, or linguistically expressing, *belief*. In that case, it is easy to see how he could regard as so natural the kind of credulity that enables one to form testimony-based beliefs non-inferentially and without either screening for insincerity or seeking some premise to support what is attested to.

7. On one kind of Humean account, testimony-based beliefs would be in some sense inferential, an implication that seems false to their nature as directly resting on the testimony. My suggested Humean account does not have this

disadvantage, since it requires only *justification for drawing* the relevant inference, which does not imply either that *S* draws it or that the belief in question is based on the premises of the relevant argument. A case for the non-inferential character of testimony-based beliefs is made in my "The Place of Testimony," cited above.

8. See Tyler Burge, "Content Preservation," *Philosophical Review* 102 (1993), p. 472. His case for his view is lengthy and complex, and in rationalizing the view I suggest a different, though prima facie compatible, line of argument. My focus is justification rather than entitlement, which he distinguishes from justification; but the difference (which is probably not great given my concept of justification) does not affect the a priori status problem as pursued in this paper.

9. See Thomas Reid, *An Inquiry into the Human Mind on the Principle of Common Sense*, Chapter VI, Sec. 24.

10. I have defended a highly qualified form of this view in "The Concept of Believing," *The Personalist* 53, 1 (1972).

11. The epistemic significance of this element of receiving primary testimony in a context is perhaps *in part* a matter of the intervention of agency, by the attester or, more commonly, someone else such as a printer or oral reporter, in the causal chain tracing to the original attestation. The significance of agency in such cases and of other differences between testimony and the standard basic sources is examined in my "Testimony, Credulity, and Veracity."

12. There are further distinctions to be made here. For instance, if written testimony is in longhand, this may affect its epistemic status at least for some recipients. I may know another's handwriting as well as the person's voice and may be as sensitive to telltale signs in its appearance as I am to elements of intonation. But even if, in some cases, it can be more plausible than the comparable spoken testimony, the handwritten testimony is still secondary.

13. Three qualifications. First, given what I say about the issue, 'normal testimony' may be left vague without begging questions. Second, I am assuming that usually (sincere) testimony expresses beliefs retained in memory, but there are of course cases in which what one attests to others is based on present experience or reflection. In any event, cases in which the attester relies on memory are crucial for the epistemology of testimony. Third, I ignore the point that memory preserves some kinds of things much better than others, tends to decay over time, and so forth.

14. I do not find this thesis expressed in Burge, op. cit., but he says something akin to it and—for reasons I indicate shortly—different from his main a priori acceptability thesis: "It is not just the rationality of a source that marks an a priori prima facie connection to truth. The very content of an intelligible message does so as well. For content is constitutively dependent, in the first instance, on patterned connections to a subject matter, connections that insure in normal circumstances a baseline of true thought presentations" (p. 471). The argument I have sketched is intended to yield a similar connection between testimony and truth, but without depending on Burge's externalist theory of content. (It is, however, consistent with that theory.) For treatments of that theory as specially pertinent to testimony, see Richard Foley, *Intellectual Trust in Oneself and Others* (Cambridge: Cambridge University Press, 2001), esp. ch 4;

and Jonathan E. Adler, *Belief's Own Ethics* (Cambridge, MA: MIT Press, 2002), esp. ch 5.

15. The belief should be assumed to be "wholly" based on the testimony, but this is not to imply that there are no non-testimonial necessary conditions for its justification. This is not to deny that a belief can be based on both testimonial and inductive grounds; but that is not unqualifiedly a testimony-based belief, which is the kind in question.

16. In critically appraising C. A. J. Coady's view that testimony is necessarily reliable, Peter J. Graham helpfully explains how the reliability of memory is crucial for that of testimony. See his "The Reliability of Testimony," cited above.

17. Cf. Richard Foley's thesis that "[I]nsofar as it is rational for me to believe that someone else believes P, I automatically have at least a weak reason to believe P myself. I do not need to know anything special about the person . . . All else being equal, it is incoherent for me not to trust the other person, given that I trust myself" (op. cit., p. 105). This second-order-belief thesis, as we might call it, seems weaker than the claim in question in the text; but Foley's defense of it, including his defense of the incoherence thesis, suggests some of the reasons why the case I have outlined for the epistemic a priori authority of testimony might be found plausible.

18. I have in mind especially the contrasts between testimony and the standard basic sources described in "Testimony, Credulity, and Veracity"

19. The prospects for a Humean reductionist view are discussed by C. A. J. Coady in *Testimony* (Oxford: The Clarendon Press, 1992); by Elizabeth Fricker in a number of papers, including "Trusting Others in the Sciences: A Priori or Empirical Warrant," *Studies in History and Philosophy of Science* 33 (2002) and by Peter J. Graham in "Reductionism and Anti-Reductionism about Testimony" (forthcoming), as well as in my "Place of Testimony in the Fabric of Justification and Knowledge." Note that I again ignore the point that if one's justification in believing *p* is based on certain elements, one's belief is also based on it, hence would presumably be in some sense inferential in this case.

20. The kind of dependence that practical reason has on theoretical reason is discussed in some detail in my *Architecture of Reason* (Oxford and New York: Oxford University Press, 2001), esp. ch. 5.

21. For related discussion of the ethics of belief, see my "Doxastic Voluntarism and the Ethics of Belief," *Facta Philosophica* I, 1 (1999); and, for an extensive historically informed treatment of many of its aspects, Nicholas Wolterstorff, *John Locke and the Ethics of Belief* (Cambridge: Cambridge University Press, 1996).

22. For helpful comments on earlier versions of this paper I particularly want to thank Thomas Kelly, Jennifer Lackey, Ted. A. Warfield, and, especially, Peter J. Graham.

*Philosophical Issues, 14, Epistemology, 2004*

# EXTERNALIST JUSTIFICATION WITHOUT RELIABILITY

Michael Bergmann
Purdue University

Externalist analyses of epistemic properties typically include some sort of reliability requirement. Such analyses applied to *justification* fall prey to a simple yet persuasive counterexample: the beliefs of a victim of a deceptive demon can be justified despite their being formed in completely unreliable ways.[1] In this paper I will propose a way of analyzing justification that enables us to hang on to the externalism without the reliability requirement. As an added bonus, the proposed analysis of justification yields an account of the elusive connection between justification and truth.[2]

I begin with the assumption, congenial to many internalists, that the following *evidentialist* proposal is prima facie plausible and at least *close* to being a correct account of at least *one* important sort of epistemic justification:

$E_F$: S's belief B is justified iff B is a *fitting* doxastic response to S's evidence.[3]

In the first part of the paper I argue that the notion of fittingness employed in $E_F$ is best understood in terms of the notion of proper function. This conclusion lends support to the nonreliabilist externalist analysis of justification I propose and defend in the second part of the paper. For since that analysis is a refinement of $E_F$ understood in terms of proper function, I expect it to share to a large extent in $E_F$'s prima facie plausibility. The final section deals with objections.

## I. Fittingness and Proper Function

My path to defending a nonreliabilist externalism about justification begins with the evidentialist thesis, $E_F$, and makes its way first to the conclusion of section I: that $E_F$ is best understood in terms of proper function. Let's begin, then, by trying to understand evidentialism.

## A. Evidentialism

What exactly is a subject's evidence? I take it that it is limited to what the subject is aware of.[4] Thus, in order for a belief to be a fitting doxastic response to a subject's evidence, it must be a fitting doxastic response to what that subject is aware of (or to some relevant part thereof). I will assume that we have some grasp of what it is for a belief to *fit* one's evidence and that, with respect to certain clear cases, we have some fairly firm intuitions concerning whether the belief in question does or doesn't fit the subject's evidence. The very ease with which we make sense of the examples used by evidentialists to illustrate their position testifies to the plausibility of these last two assumptions. When, for example, Feldman and Conee say that the belief that *there is something green before one* fits the evidence that a normal person has in ordinary circumstances when looking at a plush green lawn in broad daylight or that the belief that *sugar is sour* does not fit our gustatory experience, we have no trouble understanding or accepting such claims.[5]

A standard line taken by evidentialists is endorsement of the following three claims:[6]

> *Nonreliability*: the fittingness of doxastic response B to evidence E is not contingent upon E's being a reliable indicator of B's truth.

> *Objectivity*: the fittingness of doxastic response B to evidence E is objective fittingness (in the sense that fittingness from the subject's perspective isn't sufficient for it).

> *Necessity*: the fittingness of doxastic response B to evidence E is an essential property of that response to that evidence.[7]

Nonreliability is extremely plausible. Just as it seems possible for a demon victim to have justified beliefs, so also it seems possible for her beliefs to fit her evidence. Her only problem is that her evidence isn't rightly connected to the world. So I join the evidentialist in accepting Nonreliability. I also accept Objectivity (which will be explained in some detail below). Consequently I follow the evidentialist in denying that objective fittingness depends on reliability. But then what *does* it depend on? The evidentialist's answer to this question is given by Necessity: the objective fittingness of doxastic response B to some evidence E is an *essential* property of that response to that evidence; it isn't a contingent property that depends on some other condition being satisfied. Here is where the evidentialist and I part company.

Notice first that the fact that the fittingness of doxastic response B to evidence E isn't contingent upon E's being a reliable indicator of B's truth doesn't prove that it isn't contingent upon anything. So Nonreliability doesn't entail Necessity. Thus, we aren't *forced* to give the Necessity-inspired evidentialist answer mentioned above to the question: "If objective fittingness doesn't depend on reliability, what does it depend on?" My answer to that question is that, contrary to what Necessity suggests, objective fittingness depends on proper function. In section I.D I will draw upon some suggestions of Thomas Reid's in order to develop an objection to Necessity[8]—an objection that points to proper function as that on which objective fittingness depends. Before getting to that objection, however, I'll need to say a little more, in the next two subsections, about Objectivity. For unless we first get clear on certain implications of Objectivity, I won't be able to explain the counterexample to Necessity that I have in mind.

## B. Objectivity

According to Objectivity, the fittingness *from the subject's perspective* of doxastic response B to her evidence isn't sufficient for B's *actually* fitting her evidence. In order to explain this claim, it will be helpful to distinguish between the main evidence for a belief, on the one hand, and connectors and disconnectors on the other.

Consider a person, Jane, who has managed somehow to become an adult without any exposure (directly or via testimony) to the phenomenon of a straight object looking bent when immersed in water. And suppose that Jane for the first time comes upon a straight stick immersed in water and, upon seeing it, forms the false belief that it is bent. The natural thing to say is that Jane's evidence for this belief is her visual experience (which, we may assume, is like the visual experience you and I have when we see such a thing). Consider next Tim, a logically perceptive man who learns from an informer who delights in obfuscation that

(1) If John goes to the party then {if Judy goes to the party then {if Jan goes to the party then the party will be a lot of fun}}.

Upon learning this, Tim immediately forms the belief that

(2) If John and Judy and Jan go to the party, then the party will be a lot of fun.

In this case, the natural thing to say is that Tim's evidence for his belief that (2) is his belief that (1). I'll refer to evidence of this sort—the sort we are naturally inclined to point to when identifying a person's evidence—as 'the main evidence' for a belief.

Now, some people think that the main evidence for our beliefs doesn't always constitute our total relevant evidence for them. For example, in the

Jane case, there may be, in addition to the visual experience on which she bases her belief that the stick is bent, the strong *felt* inclination to take her visual sensations as indicative of the truth of the belief in question.[9] Those of us who are completely familiar with the phenomenon of water distorting the appearance of a straight stick lack this felt inclination (at least it isn't as strong in us). As a result, some think our total evidence is somewhat different from Jane's. We can call Jane's strong felt inclination a 'connector' between her main evidence and her belief based on that evidence. It's a connector we lack. Another (related) difference is that we are inclined to think that the main evidence on which Jane relies is *not* indicative of the truth of the belief she bases on it. This provides us with a *disconnector* between the main evidence and the belief in question—a disconnector Jane lacks.[10] So if we think of these connectors and disconnectors as parts of one's total evidence, then *our* total evidence when we view a stick looking bent in water is different from *Jane's* when she considers such a sight (even if the main evidence—the way it visually appears—is the same).

In the Tim case there could be a connector too. Let us suppose it is the strong felt inclination to take the truth of (1) to entail the truth of (2). It is easy to imagine those less logically perceptive than Tim failing to see this sort of connection. We could describe this difference by saying that although these others have the same main evidence Tim has, they don't have the same total relevant evidence since they lack a connector he possesses.[11]

With this terminology at our disposal, we can return to our discussion of Objectivity. The view with which proponents of Objectivity disagree is the subjectivist view according to which a belief fits the subject's evidence if (though perhaps not only if) the subject's evidence consists of both her main evidence and a connector that connects her main evidence to her belief. In opposition to this suggestion, the supporter of Objectivity claims that if the subject's belief fails to fit the subject's main evidence, it won't help merely to add to her evidence a connector connecting that main evidence with the belief. Consider, for example, the following belief and pieces of evidence:

| Belief | Main Evidence | Connector |
| --- | --- | --- |
| B1. The first person belief: "There is small-ish hard round object in my hand". | ME1. Tactile sensations of the type you experience when you grab a billiard ball. | C1. The strong felt inclination to take ME1 to be indicative of the truth of B1. |
| | ME2. Olfactory sensations of the type you experience when you smell a meadow full of flowers.[12] | C2. The strong felt inclination to take ME2 to be indicative of the truth of B1. |

The subjectivist opponent of Objectivity might acknowledge that B1 fits ME1 and that it doesn't fit ME2. But she will add that B1 *does* fit the combined evidence of ME2 together with C2 because by adding C2 to ME2 (and adding no disconnectors[13]) we get subjective fittingness. The proponent of Objectivity rejects this suggestion. She says that since B1 doesn't fit ME2, it won't help merely to add C2 even if we stipulate that no disconnectors are present. The objective failure of B1 to fit the subject's evidence (ME2) isn't altered by adding C2 to the subject's evidence base; if B1 fails to fit ME2, it also fails to fit ME2 + C2 (the combination of sensation ME2 and connector C2).

Paradigm evidentialist Richard Feldman appears to be endorsing Objectivity so construed when he points out that one can't get justification for one's beliefs merely by thinking one has good reasons for them.[14] Other evidentialists such as Bruce Russell, Paul Moser and Richard Fumerton also seem to agree with Objectivity. For although they say that reliability isn't sufficient for E's being good evidence for B, they pay the same compliment to *thinking that E is good evidence for B*.[15] In each case, the idea seems to be that if a belief doesn't fit one's main evidence, then merely adding a connector joining that belief with that main evidence won't help.

## C. Learned and Unlearned Doxastic Responses

A possible concern about Objectivity arises in connection with its suggestion that if a belief doesn't fit the subject's main evidence then merely adding a connector won't help. Consider B1 and ME2. Why couldn't a person learn, in the way one learns to associate certain smells with gasoline or paint (i.e., by experiencing their constant conjunction), to associate olfactory experience ME2 with the truth of B1? Then one would have learned to have C2 whenever one has ME2, in which case B1 could be a fitting response to ME2 + C2 after all.

That concern about Objectivity strikes me as a sensible one. To handle it, we need to distinguish learned from unlearned doxastic responses. The distinction isn't easy to draw, but it is something like this. *Learned* doxastic responses, such as an experienced birdwatcher's immediate bird identifications after a quick look (or listen), are ones a person comes to have only after first finding out independently (i.e., without relying in any essential way on other instances of that same type of doxastic response) that there is a correlation between the truth of such beliefs and the experiences to which they eventually become immediate responses. By contrast, an *unlearned* doxastic response to experience is a hardwired or automatic response that occurs (perhaps only after a certain level of cognitive development) without the subject first independently finding out that there is a correlation between the truth of the belief in question and the experience to which it is a response.[16]

We can also distinguish learned from unlearned *connectors*. Suppose C is a connector that connects main evidence ME with a belief B. If C is acquired by first independently finding out that there is a correlation between the truth of B and the occurrence of ME, then C is a *learned* connector. However, if C isn't acquired by first learning independently of a correlation between the truth of B and the occurrence of ME—if, instead, a person simply has C without learning independently that there is such a correlation—then C is an *unlearned* connector. With these distinctions in mind, we can state the claim of Objectivity more carefully as follows: some unlearned doxastic responses to one's evidence are unfitting and merely adding an *unlearned* connector to one's evidence won't change that.

## D. Necessity

So far I'm in agreement with the evidentialist. I accept Objectivity. And, as I noted earlier, because I also accept Nonreliability, I follow the evidentialist in denying that objective fittingness depends on reliability. This brings us to the all-important question: "What *does* it depend on?" You will recall that the evidentialist's Necessity-inspired answer was that the objective fittingness of doxastic response B to some evidence E is an *essential* property of that response to that evidence, not a contingent property that depends on some other condition being satisfied. In this subsection, I will be arguing that Necessity is false.

To do this, I will need to employ some assumptions implicit in Objectivity. In particular, I will be assuming that there can be unlearned doxastic responses that are objectively fitting as well as ones that are objectively *un*fitting (in the ways described in the previous two subsections).[17] What follows is a description of a possible case in which the billiard ball belief B1[18] is a fitting unlearned doxastic response to ME2 and an unfitting unlearned doxastic response to ME1. Such a case is a counterexample to Necessity because in the actual world, B1 is a fitting unlearned doxastic response to ME1[19] and an unfitting unlearned doxastic response to ME2.

Thomas Reid emphasized that there doesn't seem to be any logical connection between our sense experiences and the content of the beliefs based on them. For example, the tactile sensations we experience when touching a hard surface seem to have no logical relation to (nor do they resemble) the content of the hardness beliefs they prompt. In light of this he said that "no man can give a reason why the sensations of smell, or taste, or sound, might not have indicated hardness".[20] Considering the matter in the abstract, tactile sensations do not seem to be any more suited than olfactory sensations to being indicators of hardness. Thus, it seems there could have been cognizers like us in outward appearance who experience, upon grabbing a billiard ball, a sensation that is qualitatively of the same type as one of our actual world sensations of smell.[21] And it seems possible that the natural *unlearned* doxastic response of such a cognizer to that "olfactory"[22] sensation is the first-person belief "There is a smallish hard round object in my hand" (i.e., B1). There is nothing about the process of *grabbing a billiard ball then experiencing ME2 then holding B1* that makes it intrinsically less suitable (as a natural unlearned process for a cognizer to undergo) than the process of *grabbing a billiard ball then experiencing ME1 then holding B1*. In each case, there is a causal chain from an external stimulus to an experience to a belief. And in each case, the experience has the same functional role of connecting that stimulus with B1. The only difference is that in the one case, the experience playing this functional role is ME1 whereas in the other it is ME2.[23]

This Reidian example suggests *two* things: first, that it is possible for billiard ball belief B1 to be an *unlearned* doxastic response to "olfactory" sensation ME2; second, that it is possible for such an unlearned response to be natural for a cognizer, even an entire species of cognizers. The first claim seems relatively uncontroversial—the possibility of a certain kind of cognitive malfunction in humans entails it. But the second seems plausible too.[24] It is no less plausible than the possibility of a species of cognizers whose experienced color spectrum is inverted with respect to ours.

It might be helpful here to say something in support of a crucial feature of this objection to Necessity, namely, its suggestion that brain-damaged humans could have the *same* evidence base for B1 (i.e., ME2) as do the possible cognizers in the Reidian example. Consider first normal humans. It seems that, for them, B1 is an unlearned doxastic response to ME1—something that occurs without their first learning *independently* that hardness is correlated with such tactile experiences.[25] Similar remarks apply to the possible cognizers in the Reidian example: B1 is, for them, an unlearned doxastic response to ME2. And the same thing can be said of the brain-damaged humans: due to some sort of injury, B1 is, for them, an *unlearned* doxastic response to ME2. You might think that normal humans also have, as a part of their evidence base for B1, an unlearned connector C1 (where what this amounts to is that they have a sense that B1 is the appropriate belief to hold given the circumstances, i.e., their experiencing ME1). But we could simply stipulate that the possible cognizers in the Reidian example have in their evidence base for B1 a similar sort of *unlearned* connector (only it is C2 rather than C1). And we could add that, due to the same injury that causes them to form B1 in response to ME2, the brain-damaged humans also have an *unlearned* connector C2—a sense that B1 is an entirely appropriate belief to hold in their circumstances, i.e., their experiencing ME2. Furthermore, we could stipulate that in neither the Reidian case nor the brain-damaged human case is there anything else in the subjects' evidence base that is relevant to their holding B1.[26]

What should we say of a species of cognizers for whom the natural unlearned response to grabbing a billiard ball is to experience ME2 and then form B1? It seems we should say that for such cognizers, B1 is a fitting unlearned response to ME2 and an unfitting unlearned response to ME1. This shows that the fittingness of an unlearned doxastic response is a contingent feature of it, a feature that depends in some cases on the species of the cognizer who has the response. Necessity is, therefore, false.[27]

## E. Proper Function

Having rejected Necessity, we must return to the question that prompted our discussion of it, namely: "If objective fittingness doesn't depend on reliability, what does it depend on?" The counterexample to Necessity considered in section I.D suggests that the fittingness of a doxastic response depends, in some cases at least, on the species of the cognizer who has it. What is it about the species of a cognizer that determines such fittingness in those cases? An answer that immediately suggests itself is that what makes a belief a fitting unlearned doxastic response to an experience has to do with the way the cognitive faculties of the cognizer in question are *supposed to* function. For clearly that is something that can vary from species to species. *Our* cognitive faculties are supposed to function so that when we experience tactile sensation ME1, our unlearned doxastic response is B1. Not so the cognizers described in the previous subsection. *Their* faculties are supposed to function so that when those cognizers experience "olfactory" sensation ME2, their unlearned doxastic response is B1. The sense in which our faculties and theirs are *supposed to* function in the ways just specified is the same as the sense in which our hearts are supposed to function so that they beat less than 200 times a minute when we are at rest. And the 'supposed to' of heart function is clearly connected with the notion of proper function. This suggests that the fittingness of a doxastic response to evidence is contingent upon the *proper function* of the cognitive faculties of the person in question. And this, in turn, suggests that the evidentialist claim $E_F$ is equivalent to something like the following (where a *PF-induced* response is one resulting from the proper functioning of the subject's cognitive faculties):

$E_{PF}$: S's belief B is justified iff B is a *PF-induced* doxastic response to S's evidence.

## II. Justification and Proper Function

### A. Refining $E_{PF}$

$E_{PF}$ isn't intended as a careful analysis. It is meant to be a rough statement (in need of refinement) of the position suggested by combining evidentialism with my objections to Necessity. The first refinement I want to recommend is that we expand our focus from evidence (thought of as something the subject is *aware* of) to something more general:

$I_{PF}$: S's belief B is justified iff B is a PF-induced doxastic response to the *input* to S's belief-forming systems.

What besides evidence counts as input to one's belief-forming systems? My proposal is that anything that is what John Pollock calls an 'internal state' of a believer counts as such input.[28] According to Pollock, a state or circumstance-type is internal if it is accessible (in a *nonepistemic* sense) to our "automatic processing systems", to the "cognitive mechanisms that direct our epistemic cognition"; it needn't be accessible to *us*.[29] The sense in which our cognition has this sort of access—the sense in which it "notes" that we are in these states—is "metaphorical. It is the same as the sense in which a computer program accessing a database might be described as noting that some particular item is contained in it."[30] Since the access to these internal states is neither *epistemic* nor access by *us*, we can require input in the form of such states without committing ourselves to internalism.

The reason I prefer $I_{PF}$ to $E_{PF}$ is that $E_{PF}$ suggests that a necessary condition of justification is having evidence. And if having evidence is thought of as involving the subject's being aware of something, then $E_{PF}$ seems to be imposing an awareness requirement on justification. Since I think there are severe problems associated with imposing awareness requirements on justification, I'd like to avoid any suggestion that I'm imposing one.[31] Furthermore, since evidence is perhaps the most prominent sort of input to *our* belief-forming systems, there will be a wide range of standard cases in which the different implications of $I_{PF}$ and $E_{PF}$ are not noticeable. The result is that the prima facie plausibility of $E_{PF}$ (which arises from a consideration of these standard cases together with the section I argument for the rough equivalence of $E_F$ and $E_{PF}$) will carry over in large part to $I_{PF}$.

In the remainder of the paper I will propose and defend an analysis of justification that can be viewed as a more careful statement of the idea behind $I_{PF}$.

## B. An Analysis of Justification

Plantinga has proposed the following analysis of *warrant* (i.e., that which makes the difference between knowledge and mere true belief):

$W_{PF}$: S's belief B is warranted iff each of the following conditions is satisfied:
  (i)   the cognitive faculties producing B are *functioning properly*
  (ii)  the cognitive environment in which B is produced is sufficiently similar to the one for which S's faculties were "designed"[32]

(iii) the modules of the "design" plan governing the production of B are directly aimed at the production of *true* beliefs

(iv) there is a high objective probability that a belief formed in accord with those modules in that sort of cognitive environment is true.[33]

He adds condition (iv) because he recognizes that the first three conditions don't entail reliability, and he thinks warrant should entail reliability.

A similar line of reasoning leads me to think he should add a fifth condition we can call a 'no-defeater condition':

(v) S does not take B to be defeated.

For warrant should entail a no-defeater condition, but Plantinga's four conditions don't.[34] There could be cognizers designed by a literal creator not only to form beliefs in a reliable way but also to take each of their reliably formed beliefs to be defeated. Furthermore, they could have been designed so that although they took their beliefs to be defeated, they ignored this fact and continued to hold them. Such beliefs would *not* be warranted even if they satisfied Plantinga's four conditions.[35]

My proposed account of justification is just my modified version of Plantinga's account of warrant (i.e., his account together with the fifth condition I just mentioned) *without* Plantinga's condition (ii)—the environmental condition. Once that condition is dropped, his account ceases to be reliability-entailing. Thus, to a first approximation, we may say that:

$J_{PF}$: S's belief B is justified iff (i) S does not take B to be defeated[36] and (ii) B is produced by cognitive faculties that are (a) functioning properly, (b) truth-aimed and (c) reliable in the environments for which they were "designed".

To see how this analysis is a refinement of $I_{PF}$, it's important to notice that clause (ii) is to be understood so that it entails that S's doxastic response to the input to her belief-forming systems is due to the proper functioning of S's faculties. As Plantinga points out, when we say cognitive faculties are functioning properly, the basic idea is that their functioning results in the appropriate doxastic response to the circumstances in which they are operating (which will include, rather prominently, the input to the subject's belief-forming systems).[37]

## C. Motivating the Last Two Sub-Clauses of $J_{PF}$

Why does $J_{PF}$ require that the belief be produced by *truth-aimed* cognitive faculties that are *reliable* in the environments for which they were "designed"? Why not require, in addition to the no-defeater clause, merely that they be produced by *properly functioning* cognitive faculties? The answer here is very much like the explanation Plantinga gives for including clauses like (ii)(b) and (ii)(c) in his account of *warrant*.[38] The main difference is that when Plantinga adds such clauses to his account of warrant, they entail that the belief is produced by a cognitive faculty that produces mostly true beliefs, whereas they do not have that consequence when added to my account of justification. The reason that the addition of such clauses doesn't make my account reliability-entailing is that I've dropped the "right environment" clause included in Plantinga's account. $J_{PF}$, therefore, is not a *reliabilist* account of justification despite the fact that it includes a clause having to do with reliability. It is because it isn't a reliabilist account that it is able to avoid the standard evil demon objection to reliabilist accounts of justification mentioned in the opening paragraph of this paper.

To return, then, to the question at hand, let me explain why I've added clauses (ii)(b) and (ii)(c) having to do with the cognitive faculty in question being truth-aimed and reliable in the right environment. My inclusion of clause (ii)(b), requiring that the faculty be truth-aimed, is due to the following sort of counterexample to the suggestion that clauses (i) and (ii)(a) are sufficient for justification. Suppose that the cognitive faculties of the cognizer in question were created by some benevolent being interested in the well-being of the cognizer. However, suppose also that the particular faculty producing the belief we are considering is intended by its creator not to produce *true* beliefs but, rather, to produce beliefs that will minimize psychological trauma (even if that involves regularly producing false beliefs). Then it seems that beliefs being produced by such a cognitive faculty won't be *epistemically* fitting responses to the input to the subject's belief forming system though they may be appropriate in some other sense. This would be a case of a belief that isn't justified (since it isn't an epistemically fitting doxastic response) even though it is produced by a properly functioning cognitive faculty.

Or suppose some evil demon intentionally designs creatures to form mostly false beliefs. For example, suppose that this malevolent creator decides to make Vic in such a way that his natural unlearned doxastic response to ME2 (the "olfactory" experience) is to form the billiard ball belief B1. Vic's cognitive faculties are, therefore, designed to function in much the same way as are the faculties of the possible cognizers described in my Reidian counterexample to Necessity in section I.D. The difference is that the beliefs of those cognizers are mostly true if their cognitive faculties are functioning properly in the environment for which they were "designed" whereas Vic's beliefs (including B1) are not. Now we noted earlier that the beliefs of those possible cognizers mentioned in I.D—beliefs like B1—are (epistemically) fitting responses to their evidence. But consider Vic who has been designed (by the demon who is intent on having Vic form mostly false beliefs) to form the false billiard ball belief B1 in response to the "olfactory" experience ME2. Is Vic's belief B1 an *epistemically* fitting response to ME2? It seems not. It's true that we can't blame Vic for holding the belief; so his epistemic blamelessness might give his belief a *subjective* sort of epistemic justification. But that won't be enough to make his belief *objectively* epistemically fitting. Nor will the fact that he was created by a designer who *intended* that he respond in this non-truth-conducive way to his experiences.

For the same reason, if the evil demon wanted a creature to have mostly false beliefs but decided to achieve this, in part, by having that creature believe B1 in response to the "tactile" experience ME1 (in a context where experiencing ME1 rarely occurs when B1 is true), we should conclude that *that* creature's belief B1 is not an epistemically fitting response to ME1. Hence, that creature's belief B1 isn't objectively justified (since it isn't an epistemically fitting response to his evidence) despite the fact that it is produced by cognitive faculties functioning properly in the sense that they are functioning so as to achieve their intended purpose. To avoid these sorts of counterexamples (ones like those given in this paragraph as well as ones like those mentioned in the previous two paragraphs), it is important to add clause (ii)(b) to $J_{PF}$ requiring that the belief be formed by a properly functioning faculty that is *aimed at truth*.

To see the importance of clause (ii)(c), consider a creature designed by one of Hume's infant deities. And suppose that, although this incompetent creator was trying to make a believer with reliable faculties, it instead created one whose faculties produce mostly false beliefs when placed in the environment in which it was intended by its creator to produce true beliefs. For example, suppose this infant deity intentionally created Ric in such a way that, like Vic described above, his natural unlearned doxastic response to ME2 is to form B1. But, contrary to what this bumbling creator hoped, this belief (like most of the other beliefs Ric forms) is false when produced in the intended environment by faculties functioning as they were designed to function. Is Ric's belief B1 an epistemically fitting response to ME2? It seems not. And the same would be true if the infant deity had designed a creature to form B1 in response to ME1 (rather than ME2), intending (but utterly failing to bring it about) that such a belief is true when formed in that way in the intended environment. Given the failed design attempt, the belief in question may be, in some sense, the output of properly functioning cognitive faculties (since those faculties are, in some sense, operating in the way they were designed to operate). But it doesn't seem to be an epistemically fitting response to the subject's evidence.

What the considerations in the previous paragraph suggest is that beliefs produced by properly functioning truth-aimed cognitive faculties do not result in epistemically fitting doxastic responses to one's evidence *if* the faculties in question aren't *successfully* aimed at truth—i.e., if they aren't likely to produce true beliefs when operating in the environment for which they were "designed". Hence, clause (ii)(c) of $J_{PF}$.

I should comment on the fact that what I've been saying in this subsection about demon cases might seem to conflict with my suggestion, in the first paragraph of the paper, that the evil demon counterexamples to reliabilism are plausible. According to those counterexamples, a belief can be justified, even objectively justified, in cases where the belief isn't reliably formed but is instead the result of misleading experiences produced by a deceptive demon. Yet in this subsection I point out the implausibility of the suggestion that the beliefs of a creature created by an evil demon to have unreliable beliefs are objectively justified. The explanation for this apparent conflict is that although I agree that in *some* evil demon cases (in which the subject's beliefs aren't reliably formed) the subject's beliefs *are* objectively justified, I don't think this is true in *all* such cases. What is true in most demon cases is that the subject's beliefs are subjectively justified, in the sense that the subject is epistemically blameless in holding them (since it is beyond her control to do otherwise). Furthermore, it is also true that we are sometimes quite sure that the demon victim is *supposed to* hold a certain perceptual belief in response to some sensory experience (as, for example, when an ordinary *human* comes, part way through her life, under the influence of a deceptive demon). If we *are* sure about such "supposed to" claims, then, with respect to cases in which such a demon victim holds the belief we think she is supposed to hold (given the experiences she is having), we may conclude that that belief is objectively justified, despite the fact that the experiences in question are illusory ones produced by the demon. However, when the demon victim is designed and created by the demon to hold unreliably formed beliefs, things are different.

Now that we have $J_{PF}$ before us and understand some of the motivation for it, let's consider two of its virtues.

## D. *Virtue One of $J_{PF}$: Handling of Cases*

One virtue of $J_{PF}$ is that it handles certain examples better than reliabilism or Necessity-endorsing internalism handles them. Some of these examples involve the reliable cognizers described in section I.D, whose natural unlearned response to ME2 is B1 and whose natural reaction to grabbing a billiard ball is to experience ME2. I'll call the complete description of the natural way of functioning for those cognizers 'design plan B'. And I'll call the complete description of our natural way of functioning 'the human design plan'.[39]

Here are the six cases (in each case, the doxastic response is unlearned):

*Case I*: A human forms B1 in response to the tactile sensation ME1. B1 is a normal reliably formed belief.

*Case II*:  A human forms B1 in response to ME1. However, ME1 is produced by a deceptive demon, not by actual contact with a billiard ball (nothing like such contact occurs on the occasion in question). The result is that B1 is not reliably formed.

*Case III*:  Due to cognitive malfunction caused by a radiation overdose, a human forms B1 in response to ME2. The same overdose also prevents her from noticing anything wrong with forming this belief in this way. Since ME2 isn't a reliable indicator of the truth of B1, the result is that B1 is not reliably formed.

*Case IV*:  A nonhuman cognizer with "design" plan B forms B1 in response to "olfactory" sensation ME2. This belief is a normal reliably formed belief of such a cognizer.

*Case V*:  A nonhuman cognizer with "design" plan B forms B1 in response to ME2. This belief is a normal unlearned doxastic response for such a creature to ME2. However, ME2 is produced by a deceptive demon, not by actual contact with a billiard ball (nothing like such contact occurs on the occasion in question). The result is that B1 is not reliably formed.

*Case VI*:  Due to cognitive malfunction caused by a radiation overdose, a nonhuman cognizer with "design" plan B forms B1 in response to "tactile" sensation ME1. The same overdose also prevents her from noticing anything wrong with forming this belief in this way. Since ME1 isn't (in this situation) a reliable indicator of the truth of B1, the result is that B1 is not reliably formed.

In both case IV and case V, B1 seems to be justified. For in those cases, just as in cases I and II, B1 is a natural and fitting unlearned response to the main evidence despite the fact that, in case V, the belief is formed in an unreliable way. And since case VI is like case III in that B1 is a malfunctioning and *unfitting* unlearned response to the subject's main evidence, B1 seems to be unjustified in case VI.

We can summarize all six cases as follows:[40]

| Case | Which "Design" Plan? | Functioning Properly? | Which Environment? | Which Move From Ground to Belief? | Reliably Formed? | Justified? |
|------|------|------|------|------|------|------|
| I | human | yes | appropriate | ME1 → B1 | yes | yes |
| II | human | yes | demon | ME1 → B1 | no | yes |
| III | human | no | appropriate | ME2 → B1 | no | no |
| IV | plan B | yes | appropriate | ME2 → B1 | yes | yes |
| V | plan B | yes | demon | ME2 → B1 | no | yes |
| VI | plan B | no | appropriate | ME1 → B1 | no | no |

Reliabilist accounts get cases II and V wrong. Internalist accounts endorsing Necessity get cases IV, V and VI wrong. For the belief ground in cases IV and V is the same as the belief ground in case III and yet, contrary to what such internalist accounts entail, B1 is *not* unjustified in cases IV and V even though it *is* unjustified in case III. Likewise, despite the fact that the belief ground in case VI is the same as the belief ground in cases I and II, B1 is justified in cases I and II but not in case VI. By contrast, $J_{PF}$ gets all six cases right.

## E. Virtue Two of $J_{PF}$: Justification and Truth

Another virtue of $J_{PF}$ is that it provides an account of the justification-truth connection that doesn't lead to the usual troubles. Stewart Cohen has argued that although there seems to be a nontrivial connection between justification and truth, there seems to be no good account of that connection.[41] He considers and, for reasons I find persuasive, rejects two types of accounts: (i) reliabilist accounts, according to which there is an objective connection between justification and truth, and (ii) subjectivist accounts that say that what matters is that there is a justification-truth connection *from the subject's perspective*.[42]

But there are two other accounts he doesn't consider—understandably since they hadn't been proposed at the time. One is $J_{PF}$. According to it, the connection between justification and truth comes through the notion of an appropriate environment: there is a high objective probability that a justified belief will be a true belief *if* the properly functioning faculties that produce it are operating in the environment *for which they were "designed"*. This explains the connection between justification and truth while avoiding the evil demon counterexamples to reliabilism. The other account is Sosa's virtue reliabilism. According to it, "justification is relative to environment".[43] Thus, the demon victim's beliefs are justified relative to *our* environment because the virtuous dispositions producing her belief are reliable in our environment; but those same beliefs aren't justified relative to the victim's environment because the dispositions in question aren't reliable in the victim's environment.[44]

The advantage of $J_{PF}$ over Sosa's virtue reliabilism is that the proponent of $J_{PF}$ can recognize a nonrelativized concept of justification whereas Sosa can't. But it seems that we do have the notion of justification *simpliciter*. This is important because although it is natural to think that the beliefs of demon victims aren't reliably formed in their environments, it isn't very natural at all to think of their beliefs as *unjustified relative to their environments*. That relativized concept of justification doesn't seem to be one we have in our pretheoretical repertoire of concepts. What we think of the demon victims is just that their beliefs exemplify justification *simpliciter*.[45] The problem is that Sosa needs, but doesn't seem to have, some principled way of selecting *the* environment in which reliability matters for nonrelativized justification. $J_{PF}$ *has* a principled way of doing that: the environment that matters is the one for which the cognizer's faculties were "designed".


## III. Objections

### A. Objection One: Proper Function and Naturalism[46]

$J_{PF}$ employs several notions in a way that might seem uncongenial to a naturalistic frame of mind. The three "offensive" notions are the *proper function* of a cognitive faculty, its *aim* and the environment for which it was *designed*. The proper function of a thing is the way it is supposed to function. The aim of a thing is the goal to which it is supposed to contribute. The environment for which a thing was "designed" is the environment in which its functioning the way it is supposed to function *is supposed to* result in that thing's contributing to the goal to which it is supposed to contribute. What makes $J_{PF}$'s employment of these notions potentially unacceptable to the naturalist is that, although they may not be problematic when applied to artifacts, they do seem problematic when applied to living organisms or their parts, which, according to naturalists, aren't artifacts. Some people express this sort of worry by saying that proper function analyses commit their proponents to theism or some other view according to which humans have an intelligent designer.

There is a large and growing literature on functions and goals.[47] Many naturalists are quite confident that the notion of a goal and of a function can be understood naturalistically and applied to living organisms (or their parts) even if these organisms are not the product of intelligent design. But when it comes to the idea of a function a thing is *supposed to* have or a goal to which it is *supposed to* contribute, some naturalists are more skeptical. Let's examine some of the possible views one could hold concerning the normativity implied by the "supposed to" talk.

First, consider the following three claims: the human heart is supposed to function so that it beats less than 200 times a minute when the person is at rest; the human heart is supposed to contribute to the goal of circulating blood and, ultimately, to the survival of the human in question; the type of environment in which a heart's functioning that way is supposed to result in the survival of the human of which it is a part is an environment relevantly similar to the one in which we find ourselves. These "supposed to" claims seem very sensible and natural. But can they survive as more than just ordinary ways of speaking? Is it literally true that there is a function a human heart is *supposed to* have, that there is goal to which it is *supposed to* contribute and that there is such a thing as the type of environment in which its functioning in this way is *supposed to* contribute to that goal? And are such claims, taken literally and seriously, compatible with naturalism?

There are (at least) three positions one could take in response to these questions. Let's say that "supposed to" talk is *reducible* to naturalistically acceptable talk just in case it is possible to give truth conditions for "supposed to" claims (applied to parts of living organisms) using only naturalistically acceptable concepts. The *reductivist* position is that "supposed to" talk is reducible to naturalistically acceptable talk. According to this view, the serious "supposed to" claims mentioned in the previous paragraph are true and compatible with naturalism.[48] The other two positions—nonreductive realism and eliminativism—are nonreductivist views insofar as they agree that "supposed to" talk is not reducible to naturalistically acceptable talk. According to *nonreductive realism*, serious "supposed to" claims are true and incompatible with naturalism (so naturalism is false).[49] According to *eliminativism*, serious "supposed to" claims are neither true nor compatible with naturalism.[50] The eliminativist with respect to the serious "supposed to" claims says that, strictly speaking, there is no such thing as the *proper* function of organisms (or their parts) or the *right* environment for them; these normative notions need to be eliminated from our careful conversation which will instead employ notions that are more friendly to naturalism—notions such as *statistically normal* or *evolutionarily selected* functions or environments (or even functions *valued by us*).

Each of these three positions has its proponents; each has a legitimate claim to be taken seriously even by those who reject it. Which position is the correct one? Obviously, I can't resolve this issue here. But I will say this. In sections I.D and I.E I have defended the view that the notion of fittingness is conceptually tied to the idea of there being a *right* way for a cognizer's cognitive faculties to function—a way its faculties are *supposed to* function. If I'm right about *that*, then whatever position one takes with respect to the normativity of "supposed to" claims about an organism's (or its parts') functions and goals—whether reductivism, nonreductive realism or eliminativism—one ought to take that same position with respect to fittingness. But Objectivity is opposed to eliminativism with respect to fittingness. And Nonreliability is opposed to at least one strand of reductivism with respect to fittingness. So those who find Objectivity and Nonreliability plausible are forced to be nonreductive realists with respect to fittingness or to come up with some nonreliabilist way of being a reductivist about fittingness. Such people should, therefore, be either nonreductive realists or a certain kind of reductivist about the commonsense "supposed to" claims concerning functions and goals; eliminativism is not an option for them.

In sum, my response to those naturalists who find the notion of proper function naturalistically unacceptable (i.e., my response to eliminativists about this sort of "supposed to" talk) is twofold. First, my claim that the notion of fittingness is conceptually tied to the notion of proper function is compatible with eliminativism about the normativity of proper function. So at least that part of my argument avoids this naturalistic challenge. Second, upon accepting the conclusion that there is that conceptual tie between fittingness and proper function (and, therefore, between justification and proper function), one can take the plausibility of Objectivity and Nonreliability to provide us with a reason for rejecting eliminativism and certain versions of reductivism about proper function.

## B. Objection Two: The Supervenience Thesis

The supervenience thesis (as it is sometimes called[51]) says that normative properties supervene on nonnormative ones. Applied to epistemology, and, in particular, to justification, it says that justification supervenes on nonnormative properties—that there couldn't be a difference in justification without a difference in nonnormative properties. The plausibility of the supervenience thesis might give rise to the following complaint about proper function accounts of epistemic justification: "The goal in understanding epistemic concepts such as justification is to give analyses of them in terms of nonnormative properties; but since *proper function* is a normative concept, analyses in terms of it are unsatisfying or uninteresting or in some other way unacceptable."

Although this objection seems to be taken seriously by some people,[52] I fail to see what the trouble is. The proponent of a proper function account of epistemic justification is like the Chisholmian who thinks epistemic concepts are reducible to ethical concepts.[53] Each thinks that epistemic evaluation is reducible (at least in part) to another sort of evaluation. But that in no way commits them to a rejection of the supervenience thesis. If epistemic properties are reducible to proper function (or ethical) properties and proper function (or ethical) properties are reducible to nonnormative properties, then the supervenience thesis holds. So I see no reason to think the supervenience thesis conflicts in any way with the analysis of justification given in this paper. It's true that it would be nice to conjoin my proper function analysis of justification with an analysis of proper function in terms of nonnormative properties and that I haven't done that here.[54] But that doesn't make it uninteresting to explain one normative notion in terms of another in the way Chisholm does—not unless the *only* sort of analysis of interest in epistemology is an analysis of epistemic properties in terms of nonnormative (rather than merely nonepistemic) ones.

## C. Objection Three: Swampman

Against proper function analyses of epistemic properties, Ernest Sosa (1993) uses Donald Davidson's example of Swampman who comes into existence by accident as a result of a lightning strike. Swampman is supposed to be a molecule for molecule replica of Donald Davidson, complete with Davidson's beliefs, memories, experiences and dispositions. Given his origin, it seems that Swampman has no design plan, not even in the sense in which faculties "designed" by evolution have a design plan. Thus, according to this objection, we can't say that his beliefs satisfy the proper function requirement. But since Davidson's beliefs are justified why not say the same of Swampman's?

By way of response, consider what we'd say of Swampman's heart and lungs. Assuming Davidson's heart and lungs were in fine shape at the time of the accidental duplication, the thing to say about Swampman's heart and lungs is that they are healthy. Furthermore, it seems plausible to say that Swampman is a human (molecular replication implies DNA replication after all). We might feel *some* hesitation about saying Swampman's heart is healthy and that he's a human. But saying so is far *more* plausible than saying that Swampman's heart and lungs are not healthy (either because they are unhealthy or because the concept of health doesn't apply) or that Swampman has Davidson's DNA but is not a human.

Now, if we find it plausible to say that Swampman's heart and lungs are healthy, it is reasonable also to conclude that his heart and lungs are functioning the way they are *supposed to function.* And if we can say that about his heart and lungs, we can say the same about his cognitive faculties. It's true there is no literal designer and no evolutionary origin. But because of the physical similarities (down to the DNA level), we are inclined to think of Swampman as being human. And that leads us to think that Swampman is supposed to function in the way humans are supposed to function.[55]

In this paper I've argued that $J_{PF}$ is superior to both reliabilist and Necessity-endorsing internalist accounts of justification. In doing so, I've defended the following two claims in a way that recognizes a nonrelativized concept of justification: (i) there is a satisfying externalist account of the justification-truth connection; (ii) there is a plausible externalist account of justification that avoids the evil demon counterexamples to reliabilism. The truth of these claims shows that epistemologists need to be careful *not* to take the failures of reliabilism to be failures of externalism.[56]

## Notes

1. This objection to reliabilism is proposed by Cohen (1984, 280–82), Foley (1985, section I), Lehrer (1990, 166) and Moser (1985, 240–241).
2. The larger project here is that of defending externalism and objecting to internalism. By presenting a nonreliabilist but still externalist account of justification, I take the sting out of the now standard evil demon objection (just mentioned in the text) to externalism about justification. See my 2000a, my 2000b and my forthcoming paper "A Dilemma for Internalism" for other contributions to this

larger project, which includes both attacks on internalism as well as defenses of externalism against other objections.

3. The more standard way of stating the evidentialist's thesis is to have the right-hand side of the 'iff' say something like "B fits S's evidence" (see Feldman and Conee 1985). I'm assuming that doxastic response B is a fitting response to S's evidence only if (i) B fits S's evidence and (ii) B is formed in response to S's evidence. Clause (ii) is a way of adding a sort of basing requirement. Since justification, as I'll be thinking of it in this paper, is *doxastic* justification rather than merely *propositional* justification, the addition of such a requirement is quite unremarkable. Doxastic justification is justification a person's *belief* has only if that belief is properly based. Propositional justification is justification enjoyed by a *proposition* for a person if that person's evidence is such that a belief in that proposition would be doxastically justified if she were to hold it on the basis of that evidence. (See Firth 1978, 218 for more on this distinction.) The notion of doxastic justification corresponds (roughly) to Feldman and Conee's notion of well-foundedness (see their 1985, 24). And the notion of propositional justification seems to correspond to what Feldman and Conee think of as justification *simpliciter*.

4. See Feldman 1988a.

5. Feldman and Conee 1985, 15.

6. Of these three claims—Nonreliability, Objectivity and Necessity—the first is the one most obviously endorsed by evidentialists. I'll explain later (in section I.B) why I think Feldman and other evidentialists hold Objectivity. As for Necessity, I'll just point out that Chisholm seems to hold it when he asserts (1986, 53) that epistemic properties supervene on the psychological properties that constitute our evidence base. And Feldman and Conee seem to hold it when they combine their claim (1985, 16) that "the epistemic justification of an attitude depends only on evidence" with their claim (1985, 15) that an attitude is epistemically justified if and only if that attitude *fits* the evidence. Who counts as an evidentialist? Perhaps the clearest examples are Feldman and Conee (1985). But evidentialist sympathies can also be discerned in the writings of Chisholm (1977), Moser (1985, 1989), Fumerton (1995), Haack (1993, 1997), and Russell (2001).

7. The idea is that if B is a fitting response to E, then, even if B could be an unfitting response to evidence that includes E *and more besides*, it couldn't be an unfitting response to E by itself.

8. Notice that in rejecting Necessity I am not saying that the relation of supervenience holding between justification and its supervenience base is contingent. For even if it were true that belief B's *justification* supervened (of necessity) on the fittingness of doxastic response B to the subject's evidence (which happened to be E), that wouldn't entail that the *fittingness* of doxastic response B to evidence E was an essential property of it.

9. A felt inclination to do X is an experience of feeling inclined to do X. It isn't merely a disposition.

10. Thus, disconnectors will be a sort of undercutting defeater (see Plantinga 2000, 359 and Pollock 1986, 39 for a discussion of undercutting defeaters). Notice that *lacking a connector* between a belief and one's main evidence isn't by itself sufficient for *having a disconnector*.

11. I am *not* suggesting that justification *requires* a connector between one's beliefs and one's main evidence. That smells of regress problems. I'm just explaining what connectors are and noting that they may be present in some cases.

12. Since a meadow full of flowers usually has a number of different kinds of flower (as well as a variety of nonflowering plants) each of which has a distinctive odor, the type of olfactory experience one has upon smelling a meadow full of flowers has many components. In this way it resembles the tactile experience one has upon grabbing a billiard ball, an experience that also has many components.

13. How could a person's total relevant evidence for B1 consist of only ME2 and C2 without any disconnectors? Wouldn't she glance at her hand or attempt to use the hand in which she thinks there is a small hard ball? Wouldn't others inform her that it is crazy for her to think, on the basis of ME2, that she is holding a small hard ball? These are certainly possibilities, likely ones even. But all we need is a possible example where no such disconnectors are present.

14. See his 1988b, 411. See also sections II and III of Feldman and Conee 1985 where they say that if B fails to fit one's evidence, it won't help to add subjective factors such as *trying one's best to hold only beliefs that fit one's evidence* or *being blameless in holding B*. They insist that even with those factors present, B still fails to fit the subject's evidence.

15. See Russell's 2001, 37–38, especially his comments on the believers raised in the benighted religious community whom he thinks of as subjectively justified but not objectively justified. See also Moser's 1989 (38–42, 47–52 and 202–3) and Fumerton's 1995 (8–20, 113–16 and chapter 7), where they emphasize that merely believing that one's evidence E is good evidence for B isn't sufficient for B's justification since E might not *in fact* make B objectively probable.

16. This distinction is similar to and inspired by Reid's distinction between original and acquired perception. See Reid 1969, 300–305 and Reid 1970, 210–11 (parts of the latter are in Reid 1983, 87–88). It is basically the same as Goldman's distinction between beliefs produced by native processes and beliefs produced by acquired methods (see his 1986, 93–95).

17. It is because my objection to Necessity relies on a counterexample employing these assumptions that I had to discuss Objectivity and explain its implications *before* giving the objection.

18. I call B1 a 'billiard ball belief' for convenience even though the concept of a billiard ball is not included in its content.

19. Objection: Is B1 really an *unlearned* doxastic response to ME1 for normal humans? Perhaps psychological research will show (or has shown) that it is *learned*.

    Reply: Maybe so. But suppose psychological research had shown that B1 is (as Reid believed) an *unlearned* doxastic response to ME1. Would that have given us a reason to take such beliefs to be unjustified? No. So it seems possible for there to be creatures for whom B1 is justified in virtue of being believed on the basis of ME1 even though B1 is (for them) an *unlearned* doxastic response to ME1. The possibility of such creatures is all I need to make my case.

20. Reid 1970, 63–64/Reid 1983, 39–40.

21. Perhaps sensations supervene on brain states. Then we have to imagine, first, that sensations of the same qualitative type as our olfactory sensations could supervene on physical states (call them X-states) other than those on which ours

supervene (cf. the Martians in section I of Lewis 1980). Second, we imagine a creature who is like us in outward appearance and who, upon grabbing a billiard ball in its hand, causes itself to go into an X-state.

22. I use quotation marks to indicate that although the sensation in question is qualitatively of the same type as *our* olfactory sensations, it may not, in the circumstances in question, be properly thought of as an olfactory sensation in the ordinary sense (since that sense may have functional role implications).

23. I should note that the cognizers in this Reidian example are such that *all* of the experiences produced in them by the sorts of activities that produce tactile experiences in us are what we would call 'olfactory experiences'. So it isn't just *B1's* ground that is different in this way.

24. Cf. Greco 1999, 277 and 2000, 173–74.

25. See note 19.

26. See note 13.

27. Plantinga's argument (1993a, 54–63) that the *warrant*-conferring power of a belief ground is a contingent feature of it is similar to my objection to Necessity. The main difference (aside from the fact that he focuses on warrant and I focus on justification) is that his examples are less convincing than the Reidian one I employed in this subsection. One problem with Plantinga's examples is that many of them involve *learned* doxastic responses. This leads to the concern discussed in section I.C—a concern that the Reidian example, which focuses on *unlearned* doxastic responses, sidesteps. Another problem is that one of Plantinga's examples (1993a, 62–63) is met with understandable resistance by Bruce Russell (see Russell's 2001, 45–46) who seems to think that Plantinga's example involves treating a doxastic response that must be *learned* as if it can be an appropriate *unlearned* doxastic response. I think Plantinga's example can survive Russell's criticisms. But the Reidian example is better because it involves a belief that clearly *can* be an appropriate unlearned doxastic response.

28. See Pollock 1986, 133–34. I should note that I *reject* the view that the term 'internal', as Pollock uses it, is helpful in making sense of the internalism-externalism debate in epistemology. See Plantinga 1993a, 180–81 for more on this.

29. See Pollock 1986, 133 and Pollock and Cruz 1999, 133 & 136.

30. Pollock and Cruz 1999, 136.

31. For a discussion of these problems as well as a defense of the view that imposing such requirements is at the heart of internalism, see my forthcoming paper "A Dilemma for Internalism".

32. The quotation marks are to indicate that the design in question needn't involve a literal designer. For discussion of how to make sense of design talk without postulating a literal designer, see section III.A below.

33. This is *not* a direct quotation (for his exact wording, see chapters 1 and 2 of Plantinga 1993b, especially p. 19 and pp. 46–47). Plantinga insists that this is still only a first approximation. For further details, qualifications and emendations see his 1993b as well as his 1996, his 1997 and his 2000 (156–61).

34. It is widely believed, even by externalists, that a belief isn't warranted if the person holding it takes it to be defeated (see for example Goldman 1986, 62–63 & 112–12 and Nozick 1981, 196). The same, I assume, is true of objective justification. See my 1997 for a discussion of this condition and its connection with internalism and externalism.

35. Plantinga says that warrant depends on the proper functioning of our defeater systems (1993b, 41). So he is aware of the concern I'm raising. However, what he doesn't acknowledge is that conditions (i)-(iv) don't entail the satisfaction of condition (v).

36. This clause requires that the subject not *take* her belief to be defeated. But shouldn't there also be a clause requiring that the belief not *in fact* be defeated, whether the subject takes it to be or not? Or, if there is such a requirement on justification (i.e., that the belief not in fact be defeated) but its satisfaction is guaranteed by the satisfaction of the proper function requirement, then why not think the satisfaction of the "no believed defeater" requirement is also guaranteed by the satisfaction of the proper function requirement? (My thanks to an anonymous referee for drawing these questions to my attention.)

There is much to be said here. But the short response is this. Yes, there is a requirement that the belief (we'll call it 'B') not *in fact* be defeated. What this amounts to is the requirement that the subject have no belief or experience that, when added to her previous beliefs and experiences, has the result that B becomes an epistemically inappropriate response to the input to her belief-forming systems. (For more on this way of thinking about defeaters, see Plantinga 2000, 359–66 and my forthcoming paper "Defeaters and Higher-Level Requirements".) Does the fact that the subject's cognitive faculties are functioning properly guarantee that this "no actual defeater" requirement will be satisfied? No. For the faculties might not be truth-aimed; and they might not be reliable in the environment for which they were "designed". (See section II.C for further discussion of these possibilities.) Would the satisfaction of the proper function requirement, together with the satisfaction of clauses (ii)(b) and (ii)(c) from $J_{PF}$, guarantee that the "no actual defeater" requirement is satisfied? No. For it may be that those conditions are satisfied and yet the subject takes her belief B to be defeated (see the example just given in the text to motivate the addition of clause (v) to Plantinga's account). That would be enough to make B an epistemically inappropriate response to the input to her belief-forming systems. In short, the "no actual defeater" requirement is satisfied only if the "no believed defeater" requirement is satisfied. Furthermore, if each of the conditions mentioned in $J_{PF}$ is satisfied, the "no actual defeater" requirement is satisfied too.

37. 1993b, 22–24.

38. See Plantinga's 1993b, 11–20 and 26–28.

39. As Plantinga points out (1993b, 22–24), we can think of "design" plans as sets of circumstance-response pairs (or circumstance-response-goal triples).

40. The six cases can also be described so that the belief ground in each case includes an *unlearned* connector. Just replace all appearances of 'ME1' (in the above descriptions of the six cases as well as in the table below) with 'ME1 + C1'; likewise, replace all appearances of 'ME2' with 'ME2 + C2'. In the demon and malfunction cases, this connector in question is caused by the demon or by the radiation overdose.

41. See Cohen 1984.

42. In section II of his 1984, Cohen objects to reliabilist accounts of justification on the grounds that they fail to attribute justification to demon victims. And in

section III he objects to subjectivist accounts on the grounds that they implausibly require for justification what we rarely have, namely, further beliefs about the reliability of our beliefs.

43. Sosa 1991,144.
44. This view is developed in Sosa 1991,140–44 and 284–90.
45. For a similar concern about views like Sosa's, see Goldman 1993, 101–3.
46. For other ways to handle a variety of objections to talk about proper function, see Plantinga's 1993b, 1993c, 1995 and 1996.
47. See Nissen 1997, Boorse (unpublished manuscript) and the introduction to Allen, Bekoff and Lauder 1998 for summaries of the relevant literature.
48. Karen Neander (1991a and 1991b) holds this view as do Fred Dretske (1994 and 2000) and Robert Koons (2000).
49. This view is endorsed by Alvin Plantinga (1993b) and perhaps also by Bedau (1993).
50. This view seems to be endorsed by John Searle (1992, 238) and by Christopher Boorse (unpublished manuscript).
51. Steup 1996, 30–36.
52. For example, by one of the referees for this paper.
53. See Chisholm 1986 and 1991. For objections to Chisholm's position, see Firth 1978.
54. But see the references in notes 48 and 49 for attempts at and discussions of such analyses.
55. Compare with Plantinga's response to the Swampman objection in his 1993c, 76–78.
56. Thanks to John Greco, Kevin Meeker, Trenton Merricks, Alvin Plantinga, three anonymous referees and especially Michael Rea and Matthias Steup for reading and providing insightful comments on earlier drafts. Thanks also to Christopher Boorse and Richard Feldman for helpful discussions of some of the ideas presented here. Finally, I would like to acknowledge the support of the Pew Evangelical Scholars Program while I worked on this paper.

# References

Allen, Colin, Mark Bekoff and George Lauder (eds.). 1998. *Nature's Purposes: Analyses of Function and Design in Biology*. Cambridge, MA: MIT Press.
Bedau, Mark. 1993. "Naturalism and Teleology." In Steven Wagner and Richard Warner (eds.), *Naturalism: A Critical Appraisal*, pp. 23–5. Notre Dame: University of Notre Dame Press.
Bergmann, Michael. 1997. "Internalism, Externalism and the No-Defeater Condition." *Synthese* 110: 399–417.
———. 2000a. "Deontology and Defeat." *Philosophy and Phenomenological Research* 60: 113–28.
———. 2000b. "Externalism and Skepticism." *The Philosophical Review* 109: 159–94.
———. Forthcoming. "A Dilemma for Internalism." In Thomas Crisp, Matthew Davidson and David Vander Laan (eds.), *Knowledge and Reality: Essays in Honor of Alvin Plantinga*. Dordrecht: Kluwer Academic Publishers.
———. Forthcoming. "Defeaters and Higher-Level Requirements." *The Philosophical Quarterly*.
Boorse, Christopher. Unpublished. "Functions: A Current Scorecard."

Chisholm, Roderick. 1977. *Theory of Knowledge* (2nd Edition). Englewood Cliffs, NJ: Prentice Hall.

———. 1986. "Self-Profile." In Radu Bogdan (ed.), *Roderick M. Chisholm*, pp. 3–77. Dordrecht: D. Reidel.

———. 1991. "Firth and the Ethics of Belief." *Philosophy and Phenomenological Research* 51: 119–28.

Cohen, Stewart. 1984. "Justification and Truth." *Philosophical Studies* 46: 279–95.

Dretske, Fred. 1994. "If You Can't Make One, You Don't Know How it Works." In Peter French, Theodore Uehling and Howard Wettstein (eds.), *Midwest Studies in Philosophy, 19, Philosophical Naturalism*, pp. 468–82. Notre Dame: University of Notre Dame Press.

———. 2000. "Norms, History, and the Constitution of the Mental." In *Perception, Knowledge and Belief: Selected Essays*, pp. 242–58. New York: Cambridge University Press.

Feldman, Richard. 1988a. "Having Evidence." In D.F. Austin (ed.), *Philosophical Analysis*, pp. 83–104. Dordrecht: Kluwer Academic Publishers.

———. 1988b. "Subjective and Objective Justification in Ethics and Epistemology." *The Monist* 71: 405 19.

Feldman, Richard and Earl Conee. 1985. "Evidentialism." *Philosophical Studies* 48: 15–34.

Firth, Roderick. 1978. "Are Epistemic Concepts Reducible to Ethical Concepts?" In A.I. Goldman and J. Kim (eds.), *Values and Morals*, pp. 215–29. Dordrecht, Holland: D. Reidel.

Foley, Richard. 1985. "What's Wrong With Reliabilism?" *The Monist* 68: 188–202.

Fumerton, Richard. 1995. *Metaepistemology and Skepticism*. Lanham: Rowman and Littlefield.

Goldman, Alvin. 1986. *Epistemology and Cognition*. Cambridge: Harvard University Press.

———. 1993. "Epistemic Folkways and Scientific Epistemology." In Alvin Goldman (ed.), *Readings in Philosophy and Cognitive Science*, pp. 95–116. Cambridge, MA: MIT Press.

Greco, John. 1999. "Agent Reliabilism." In James Tomberlin (ed.), *Philosophical Perspectives, 13, Epistemology (A Supplement to Noûs)*, pp. 273–96. Cambridge, MA: Blackwell Publishers.

———. 2000. *Putting Skeptics In Their Place*. New York: Cambridge University Press.

Haack, Susan. 1993. *Evidence and Inquiry: Towards Reconstruction in Epistemology*. Oxford: Blackwell Publishers.

———. 1997. "A Foundherentist Theory of Empirical Justification." In Louis Pojman (ed.), *The Theory of Knowledge: Classical and Contemporary Readings*, Second Edition, pp. 283–93. Belmont, CA: Wadsworth.

Koons, Robert. 2000. *Realism Regained: An Exact Theory of Causation, Teleology and the Mind*. New York: Oxford University Press.

Lehrer, Keith. 1990. *Theory of Knowledge*. Boulder: Westview Press

Lewis, David. 1980. "Mad Pain and Martian Pain." In Ned Block (ed.), *Readings in Philosophy of Psychology, Volume 1*, pp. 216–22. Cambridge, MA: Harvard University Press.

Moser, Paul. 1985. *Empirical Justification*. Boston: D. Reidel.

———. 1989. *Knowledge and Evidence*. New York: Cambridge University Press.

Neander, Karen. 1991a. "Functions as Selected Effects: The Conceptual Analyst's Defense." *The Philosophy of Science* 58: 168–84.

———. 1991b. "The Teleological Notion of Function." *Australasian Journal of Philosophy* 69: 454–68.

Nissen, Lowell. 1997. *Teleological Language in the Life Sciences*. Lanham: Rowman and Littlefield.

Nozick, Robert. 1981. *Philosophical Explanations*. Cambridge: Belknap of Harvard University Press.

Plantinga, Alvin. 1993a. *Warrant: The Current Debate*. New York: Oxford University Press.

———. 1993b. *Warrant and Proper Function*. New York: Oxford University Press.

———. 1993c. "Why We Need Proper Function." *Noûs* 27: 66–82.

———. 1995. "Reliabilism, Analyses and Defeaters." *Philosophy and Phenomenological Research* 55: 427–64.

———. 1996. "*Respondeo*." In Jonathan Kvanvig (ed.), *Warrant in Contemporary Epistemology: Essays in Honor of Plantinga's Theory of Knowledge*, pp. 307–78. New York: Rowman and Littlefield.

———. 1997. "Warrant and Accidentally True Belief." *Analysis* 57:140–45.

———. 2000. *Warranted Christian Belief*. New York: Oxford University Press.

Pollock, John. 1986. *Contemporary Theories of Knowledge*. Savage, MD: Rowman and Littlefield.

Pollock, John and Joseph Cruz. 1999. *Contemporary Theories of Knowledge* (2nd Edition). Lanham, MD: Rowman and Littlefield.

Reid, Thomas. 1969. *Essays on the Intellectual Powers*. Cambridge, MA: MIT Press.

———. 1970. *An Inquiry into the Human Mind*, (ed.) Timothy Duggan. Chicago: University of Chicago Press.

———. 1983. *Inquiries and Essays*, (eds.) Ronald Beanblossom and Keith Lehrer. Indianapolis: Hackett Publishing.

Russell, Bruce. 2001. "Epistemic and Moral Duty." In Matthias Steup (ed.), *Knowledge, Truth and Duty: Essays on Epistemic Justification, Responsibility, and Virtue*, pp. 34–48. New York: Oxford University Press.

Searle, John. 1992. *The Rediscovery of the Mind*. Cambridge, MA: MIT Press.

Sosa, Ernest. 1991. *Knowledge in Perspective: Selected Essays in Epistemology*. New York: Cambridge University Press.

———. 1993. "Proper Function and Virtue Epistemology." *Noûs* 27:51–65.

Steup, Matthias. 1996. *An Introduction to Contemporary Epistemology*. Upper Saddle River, NJ: Prentice Hall.

*Philosophical Issues, 14, Epistemology, 2004*

# REALISM AND THE NATURE OF PERCEPTUAL EXPERIENCE

Bill Brewer
University of Warwick

*Realism* concerning a given domain of things is the view that the things in that domain exist, and are as they are, quite independently of anyone's thought or experience of them. The realism that I am concerned with here is *empirical realism*, that is, realism concerning *empirical things*, which are the ordinary persisting things presented to us in our perception of the world around us. Empirical realism is thus the doctrine that the tables, tress, people and other animals, which we see, feel, hear, and so on, exist, and are as they are, quite independently of anyone's thought or experience of them. My question is which account of the nature of perceptual experience is most conducive to this commonsense realist world-view.

I start, in section I, by partitioning the possible accounts of the nature of perceptual experience into two groups, and clarifying in some detail precisely what this distinction between them consists in. In section II, I argue that accounts of one of these two fundamental kinds are either inconsistent with empirical realism or entail that our knowledge of empirical things is irremediably severely limited in a way that is sufficiently counterintuitive to constitute a *reductio*. In section III, I further divide the alternative accounts of the nature of perceptual experience into two, and offer some provisional grounds at least for exploring the merits of those in the more ambitious, and less familiar, of these sub-groups.[1] Section IV presents a new approach to how such accounts should treat various kinds of perceptual illusion, which I argue is extremely promising. I conclude, in section V, with a summary of my results.

I

Perceptual experience in some way presents us with the world of empirical things around us: the *empirical world*. A fundamental distinction can be drawn between accounts of the nature of such experience as follows.

(1) Perceptual experience itself is to be construed as awareness of mind-dependent entities.

(2) Perceptual experience is to be construed as mind-dependent awareness of potentially mind-independent things.

Although the distinction is commonplace and pre-theoretically accessible, it is seldom, if ever, made absolutely explicit. On my understanding, it concerns the relative priority of the individuation, on the one hand, of subjective experiences themselves, and, on the other hand, of the empirical things of which those experiences may constitute a presentation. The underlying thought here is that perceiving involves a way of being conscious, *perceptual experience*, and that the most fundamental question is therefore how to characterize the ways of being conscious that perceiving involves. I take the opposition between (1) and (2) to consist in a difference of opinion over how this question is to be answered. Proponents of (1) characterize the ways of being conscious that are involved in perceiving without any reference whatsoever to the ways mind-independent empirical things might be, whereas proponents of (2) insist that these ways of being conscious can only be characterized in terms of the ways such things might be or actually are in the empirical world perceived. Thus, according to (1), the experiences involved in perceiving are to be characterized prior to, and independently of, any characterization of the empirical things that are in some way to be presented by them. In contrast, the force of (2) is to insist that perceptual experiences themselves can only be characterized by appeal to a prior and independent characterization of the empirical things that they may present.

These two possibilities correspond, respectively, to the standard way of thinking of the relation between secondary qualities and experiences of those qualities, on the one hand, and primary qualities and experiences of those qualities, on the other. Thus, the orthodoxy has it that the most basic distinctions concerning the secondary qualities are between, say, red-type and green-type *experiences*, and the rest, conceived quite independently of the question of what their worldly correlates, if any, may be. The characterization of such experiences is prior to, and independent of, any characterization of the worldly qualities that are in some way presented by them. Having given such a characterization, of red-type experiences, say, we may then define a property—redness—which applies to mind-independent objects, as that of being disposed to produce those kinds of experiences—red-type ones—or, alternatively, as the property of having whatever underlying physical constitution happens in the actual world to ground that disposition. Conversely, on the standard view, the most basic distinctions concerning the primary qualities are those between, say, squareness and circularity, and the rest, *as properties of mind-independent things*. Having first identified which property squareness is, we can then identify square-type experiences as those that present something as having *that property*—squareness. So, the relevant experiences are to be characterized only by appeal to a prior, and independent, characterization of the worldly qualities that they may present.[2]

Thus, (1) is to be explicated by what I call the *secondary quality model*.

(S) Perceptual experiences are to be characterized prior to, and independently of, any characterization of the empirical things that are in some way presented by them.

Similarly, (2) is to be explicated by the corresponding *primary quality model*.

(P) Perceptual experiences can only be characterized by appeal to a prior, and independent, characterization of the empirical things that they may present.

This clarification of the initial partition of accounts of the nature of perceptual experience by (1) and (2), and especially its explication by appeal to a standard view of the distinction between primary and secondary qualities, brings out the possibility of various mixed positions, on which some features of experience are to be characterized according to (S), whilst others are to be characterized according to (P). Accordingly, I intend by (S) to identify only those accounts on which *every* feature of perceptual experience is to be characterized prior to, and independently of, any characterization of the empirical things that are in some way presented. (P) applies to any account on which at least *some* features of perceptual experience can only be characterized by appeal to a prior, and independent, characterization of the empirical things that may be presented.

## II

I contend that (S) is either inconsistent with empirical realism, or entails a highly counterintuitive, and utterly irremediable, ignorance concerning empirical things, which I argue should be treated as a *reductio ad absurdum*. This is not, or at least not just, the familiar point that proponents of (1) are unavoidably prone to scepticism, because there are perceptually identical scenarios in which the relevant mind-dependent entities remain the same whilst the external world varies dramatically. There are well known epistemic externalist responses to that point, of the kind inspired by Dretske and Nozick,[3] and, regardless of the ultimate merits of these views, the debate is at the least a delicate one.[4] The worry is rather that the realist proponent of (S) is bound to deny a person a certain kind of basic knowledge, or even understanding, of *what kinds of entities* the various kinds of empirical things might be. To put it crudely, it is not that we have a perfectly good understanding of the basic natures of empirical things, but must admit that our beliefs about them have dubious epistemic credentials. Rather, we must face the fact that we are constitutionally incapable of grasping the basic natures of empirical things at all.

The question to press against the proponent of (S), in order to launch this line of objection, is what conception can she possibly make available to a person of the empirical things supposedly presented to him in perception?[5]

A first suggestion is that a person should conceive of empirical things as composed out of the entities of which he is directly aware in such perception as their parts. On this view, a conception of empirical things is constructed on the basis of perception by regarding empirical things themselves as constructions out of the entities of which perceptual experiences are a person's direct awareness. The whole point of the current account of the nature of perceptual experience, though, is that these are *mind-dependent* entities. The result is precisely Berkeley's position.[6] Although there is some latitude in the details of its development, it is, as he is fully aware, bound to lead to a form of empirical idealism. For, if empirical things are conceived as a construct of some kind out of mind-dependent entities, then they cannot themselves be genuinely mind-independent. It may be possible to accommodate, within this way of thinking, a degree of incompleteness and inaccuracy in a given person's view of the empirical world; but the world itself is absolutely explicitly *mind-dependent* in nature.

The obvious alternative, which is of course the standard realist view, given this account of the nature of perceptual experience, is that a person should think of empirical things as the *explanatory causes* of such experience. Empirical things, on this view, are effectively theoretical postulates, involved in explanation of the order and nature of perceptual experience. Now, such experience *may* have mind-independent causes. For all the subject knows, though, it may equally well not have. In any case, this recipe provides him with no inkling whatsoever of what such things, in themselves, might actually be. For, according to (S), perceptual experiences are to be characterized prior to, and independently of, any characterization of the empirical things that are in some way presented by them. That is to say, no reference whatsoever may be made to empirical things in the characterization of such experiences themselves. So nothing can possibly be discovered about the natures of such things from a person's having those experiences. In Michael Ayers' (1991) terms, perceptual experiences are simply *blank effects*. What on earth the empirical things that cause them might be like is quite obscure so far as a person's possession of these experiences themselves is concerned. Hence perceptual experience fails to provide any proper conception of the nature of such things at all. Put the other way around, whatever it may be that a person comes to think of in this way as the explanatory causes of his experience, it is not the constituents of the *empirical* world: *this* world, the world we all know and love, of tables, trees, people and other animals. So, even if the relevant causes of experience did turn out, fortuitously, as it were, to be mind-independent, this would be no help at all to the *empirical* realist. For his concern is with the mind-independence of the very things that *are* presented to us in perception in this way.

Proponents of (S) are therefore quite incapable of providing a person with any satisfactory conception of mind-independent empirical things at all. Either they provide a perfectly intelligible conception of something that is bound to be mind-dependent, or they gesture in the direction of something that *may* be mind-independent, yet of which they provide no illuminating conception whatsoever, and which is therefore not a constituent of the *empirical world* that is presented in perception· whatever else it may be, it certainly isn't one of *these*—a table, tree, person or other animal.[7]

There may appear to be a way for the advocate of (S) to avoid my objection to the second approach outlined above, of identifying empirical things as the *explanatory causes* of perceptual experience. She may attempt to characterize them simply as *powers* actually to produce our actual experience, and counterfactually to produce suitably related alternative experience in suitably related circumstances, rather as the mysterious noumenal grounds of such powers. This is really just a form of phenomenalism, though, and does not constitute a vindication of empirical realism at all. It is in fact quite closely related to the explicit idealism of the first approach that I considered above to the question of how proponents of (S) might account for a person's conception of the natures of the empirical things presented to him in perception. According to the current suggestion, empirical things are not to be constructed directly out of mind-dependent entities as their parts, as on that earlier view. Rather, true sentences 'about' physical objects are held to be true *purely in virtue of* the basic facts about the actual and counterfactual order of appropriate perceptual experiences.[8] Still, there *are*, on both accounts, strictly speaking, no mind-independent tables, trees, people or other animals. Although sentences such as 'the table remains as it is in my office when I leave' are indeed true, on the present view, they are true solely in virtue of the fact that I and others would have perceptual experiences of various kinds if we remained in, or (re-) entered, my office—whatever exactly that is held to involve—and not in virtue of the existence in reality of a mind-independent thing that *is* my table, whose existence and nature is the categorical ground of such experiential counterfactuals. Thus, we may clarify what we always had in mind as *empirical realism* as follows. There is in reality a domain of entities, which are presented to us in perception, to which we refer with our ordinary terms for empirical things—table, tree, person, and the like—and whose mind-independent natures determine the truth or falsity of our beliefs expressed using these terms. The current phenomenalist account does not secure empirical realism for the proponent of (S).

There is, perhaps, a more significant worry at this point, though. Proponents of (S) who wish to identify empirical things as the *explanatory causes* of perceptual experience face the following choice. Either tables, trees, people, and so on, are construed simply as powers to produce such experience in us, or they are construed as the categorical grounds of those powers. My objection to the former is that it entails a version of phenomenalism, which is incompatible with empirical *realism*; and to the latter I object that it fails to provide any genuine conception of the constituents of the *empirical* world at all, and so equally fails to vindicate *empirical* realism. The difficulty, in the latter case, is that we are consigned to complete ignorance of the basic natures of the proposed empirical things, which therefore cannot actually *be*, as they are supposed to be, the constituents of the world that is presented to us in perception. Friends of (S) may well reply that my inference, from the fact that their view leaves us quite ignorant in this way about the basic natures of empirical things to the conclusion that they therefore fail to provide an adequate construal of the constituents of the empirical world that is presented to us in perception, is invalid. For such ignorance is precisely, and necessarily, a person's epistemic position with respect to the things presented to her in perception.[9]

So the crucial question now is whether the thesis that we are irremediably ignorant of the basic natures, that is to say, the intrinsic, categorical properties, of empirical things, which, following Langton (1998), I call the *Humility Thesis* (HT), is a *reductio ad absurdum* of (S), or a substantive philosophical truth, derivable from (S) rather than in any tension with it.

First, it must be stressed just how strongly counterintuitive (HT) is. It is not just the mild, and no doubt true, claim that there are some categorical properties of empirical things that we happen not to know, or even the idea that we will very likely never know all of them. It is rather the far more radical claim that we are necessarily, irremediably, utterly ignorant of every single one of them. For, recall that (S) requires that perceptual experiences are to be characterized prior to, and independently of, any characterization of the empirical things that are in some way presented by them. Hence the characterization of experience cannot make any reference *at all* to the nature of empirical things themselves. So nothing about the categorical natures of such things in the world can possibly be known simply in virtue of being the subject of perceptual experience.

Second, it is equally important, as I mentioned earlier, properly to distinguish (HT) from any standard sceptical challenge to our knowledge of the external world. It is not that we have a clear conception of a way the empirical world might be, which is nevertheless of questionable epistemic standing. Rather, any purported such conception is bound to be entirely lacking in determinacy as to the basic natures of its constituent ingredients:

the empirical things themselves, whose condition it purports to characterize. That is to say, proponents of (S) endorsing (HT) in this way face a serious threat to the very idea that the mind-independent things that they postulate in causal explanation of perceptual experience really *are* empirical things at all. For empirical things are by definition those things that are presented to us in perception—tables, trees, people and other animals, etc. In being so presented to him, a person seems at the very least to have some conception of what the basic natures of such things would be, were there actually to be any in mind-independent reality. So (S)'s proposed 'empirical things', of whose basic natures we are constitutionally ignorant, cannot be genuine empirical things at all. Thus (S) fails, as I contend, to provide a genuine vindication of *empirical* realism.

Third, there is implicit in the discussion of the previous paragraph the following direct argument against (HT). Empirical things are those things, such as tables, trees, people and other animals, which are presented to us in perception. We are aware of the basic natures of the things that are presented to us in perception. Therefore, we are not constitutionally ignorant of the basic natures of empirical things.

Of course, the supporter of (HT) will deny the premise that we are aware of the basic natures of the things that are presented to us in perception. Indeed, Langton's (1998) Kantian argument explicitly moves from the perceptual presentation of empirical things to our ignorance of their basic natures via premises concerning the causal nature of perception and the irreducibility of relational to intrinsic properties. The idea is that perception essentially involves a person's being experientially affected by empirical things; and, since the nature of such effects, as with the relation between cause and effect quite generally, is logically independent of the basic natures of their empirical causes, with no a priori connections discernible between them, perception can furnish no knowledge of the basic natures of empirical things.

The general principle concerning causation is mistaken, though. For there are many cases of a priori, necessarily connected causally related phenomena. For example, the rolling behaviour of round wheels, of appropriate rigidity and so on, is an a priori necessary consequence of their shape, on which it nevertheless causally depends. This is the great insight of Locke's mechanism: the smith appreciates, *without trial or experiment*, as he says, that "the turning of one Key will open a Lock, and not the turning of another" (1975, IV.iii.25). Furthermore, the causal dependence of experiences of primary qualities on the primary qualities of their objects is a paradigm case of this phenomenon, as explicitly articulated by (P). For the intrinsic nature of experiences of squareness, say, is on that account to be characterized precisely in terms of that very property of mind-independent things that they present, that is, squareness, and upon which they nevertheless normally causally depend. Thus, Langton's Kant is right that

(S) leads to (HT), but wrong in assuming that this is obligatory, however unacceptable it may be. For, (S) is not the only account of the nature of perceptual experience: (P) is an explicit alternative, which does not entail (HT). So I propose that we should treat the derivation of (HT), as I recommend above, as a *reductio* of (S), and an invitation at least to explore the credentials of (P).

I therefore assume in what follows that perceptual experience is to be construed as mind-dependent awareness of potentially mind-independent things. That is to say, perceptual experiences can only be characterized by appeal to a prior, and independent, characterization of the empirical things that they may present.

# III

The standard way in which the characterization of perceptual experiences may be thought to be dependent upon a prior characterization of empirical things is the *Content View* (CV), which holds that sentences describing ways empirical things may be in the mind-independent world in one way or another characterize experiences by giving their *representational content*: the way they represent such things as being out there. When an experience with such a content is appropriately caused by things' being roughly as described, then it presents those things as being just that way.

Here I simply raise two difficulties for (CV), before turning my attention to what I regard as a more promising approach. The first is really just a challenge, both to identify the vehicles of perceptual representation, and to give an account of how those vehicles attain their representational content. The difficulty is just that, although this approach is definitely the orthodoxy, no agreed satisfactory response has so far been given on either score. The second problem can be put in the form of a dilemma. Are the representational contents of perceptual experiences also possible contents of non-experiential thought or belief? If so, then what is added, in perception, to yield its characteristically conscious, *experiential*, nature; and how is this experiential additive to be accommodated in a satisfactorily naturalistic world-view? If not, then how are we to identify the essentially experiential representational contents, and explain their status as such? Again, the dilemma simply presents a challenge to proponents of (CV); but still, it is one that has resolutely resisted any convincing treatment that I am aware of.[10]

I have so far traced a portion of the following natural route towards (CV). (1) is motivated jointly by (a) a commonsense phenomenological conviction, that perception acquaints us with a domain of entities whose basic natures themselves constitute the subjective character of perceptual experience, and (b) the conclusion of a traditional philosophical argument from illusion, that these direct objects of acquaintance cannot be tables, trees people and other animals themselves, for in cases of illusion their properties differ; hence mind-independent empirical things are presented only indirectly in perception. This is (S); and I argued above that it cannot sustain any satisfying empirical realism. Proponents of (CV) move on by rejecting (a) the phenomenological conviction in favour of (b) the philosophical conclusion. Perceiving is not to be thought of, in the first instance, as being acquainted with any kind of entity whose basic nature constitutes its subjective character. Instead, it is to be construed as somehow entertaining a representation of a way the mind-independent world might be, whose degree of accuracy or inaccuracy in connection with how things actually are out there determines the extent to which the relevant perception is veridical or illusory.

Given the two difficulties raised above, I suggest that we at least take seriously the idea of reversing the preferences definitive of (CV), by jettisoning (b) the philosophical conclusion of the argument from illusion in favour of (a) the commonsense phenomenological conviction that perception involves acquaintance with entities whose basic natures constitute its subjective character. On such a view, the phenomenon of illusion does not force us to distinguish any such entities from mind-independent things. Thus, perception is an openness to, or acquaintance with, mind-independent empirical things themselves, whose basic natures and perceptible qualities constitute what it is like to be presented with them in this way. What it is like for a person, perceiving the world as she is, is to be characterized by citing the perceptible features of the specific mind-independent empirical things that are accessible to her in perception, given her point of view on the world and the relevant perceptual conditions. In contrast with (CV), I call this the *Object View* (OV).

A certain amount of work in cognitive psychology, and especially psychophysics, gives the initial impression of sympathy towards (S), and therefore an inclination towards some form of idealism. This comes out in the apparent assumption that perceptual experiences are 'located' in some way 'downstream' of neural perceptual processing, and are therefore quite independent of their worldly causes, if any, or whatever these may turn out to be. At the same time, I think that there is a perfectly natural way of taking the guiding questions in this area as deeply sympathetic to (P) in its current (OV) form. A major goal of this work is to uncover the role of various neural processing systems in subserving perceptual consciousness of various specific kinds; and the approach is to investigate which of the actual perceptible features of the empirical things around a person, or other animal, are made accessible to him by the operation of which such systems. That is to say, the background picture is precisely that the nature of the perceptual consciousness that is the target of investigation is to be understood in terms of the perceptible features of the mind-independent empirical things that are made accessible to the subject in question by the functioning of the neural processing systems under study as these enable his various differential responses to them.

The obvious challenge to (OV), of course, is to give a proper account of perceptual illusion. How, if perceptual experiences are to be characterized by the perceptible features of the actual mind-independent empirical things that are made accessible to the subject in them, are such illusions ever possible? It is this issue to which I now turn.


## IV

The key idea is Berkeley's (1975a, 1975b), that the locus of error in cases of illusion is the subject's judgements, or expectations, about the world, rather than any aspect of perceptual experience itself. On the current proposal, this simply acquaints him with various mind-independent things, whose actual perceptible features constitute the subjective quality of his experience. There are two slightly different types of illusion along these lines, of which the Müller-Lyer and the stick part-submerged in water are paradigm examples respectively. I shall explain in some detail how each is to be accommodated, according to (OV), and develop some further speculations concerning related cases of each type.[11]

1. *The Müller-Lyer*. The standard description of this case is that the two lines, which are really identical in length, nevertheless look different in length. I claim that, in normal conditions, good lighting, orthogonal viewing, and so on, perceptual experience itself presents the very lines out there, distributed in space as they actually are. In particular, their identity in length is a perceptible feature of the lines, which is made experientially accessible to the normal subject. Nevertheless, *judgement* is understandably led astray by the hashes in arriving at the conclusion that the lines are different in length. On a popular view, this is due to the fact that one wrongly equates the length of each line with the distance between the centroids of the trianges two-thirds constituted by the relevant hashes, to which attention is quite naturally drawn. Even when a person knows that the lines are equal in length, and so does not *actually* judge that they are different in length, still, he feels an inclination to make that judgement of difference, for the reason just given, and this is what the persistence of the 'illusion' consists in, even for those of us in the know. I would make two points in favour of my claim of experienced identity in length. First, if asked to point to the ends of the two lines, normal subjects point accurately, that is to say, they experience the endpoint of each line to be where it actually is. These pairs of points are of course equidistant. That is to say, the extents of space that the two lines are perceptually presented as occupying are identical. Their identity in length is a perceptible feature in part constitutive of

normal subjects' experience of them. Second, the characteristic experience of gradual removal of the misleading hashes is not one of the lines changing in apparent length, but rather a realization that a previous judgement, or inclination to judgement, of difference in length was mistaken. That is to say, the constancy of the lines' actual distribution in space as the hashes are removed is evident; that this is an identity in extent between the two lines becomes gradually more obvious, and therefore the previous judgement of difference becomes evidently in error.

It might be objected that this account fails to do justice to the robust sense in which the lines still *look* unequal in length, however familiar one may be with the illusion. Indeed, they still look unequal in length to a person so familiar with the illusion that she has no residual inclination whatsoever to judge that they are unequal. My reply is that even in this case, the subjective character of her experience evidently makes the mistaken judgement of inequality in length natural and explicable. This is what it means to say that they look unequal in length: the actual distribution of the lines and hashes in space, which constitute the subjective character of her experience, make manifest to her the naturalness and explicability of a judgement of inequality however disinclined she may be herself actually to make it. Consider a parallel case of inferential illusion. There are some invalid mathematical inferences, in which a carefully concealed division by zero is made, for example, which remain evidently misleading even to a decently skilled mathematician who is utterly disinclined to believe their conclusion. For he can easily 'see' how others might be taken in by them: they retain that 'look' of validity. Other invalid inferences are poorly constructed, and so clearly would not fool anyone. The Müller-Lyer is in my view analogous to the former. The lines look unequal in length, in this sense, even to somebody who knows full well that they are not. Taking her experience at face value, and disregarding extraneous information about how the illusion works, this makes a mistaken judgement of inequality in length evidently natural and explicable.

I would interpret Bruce Bridgeman's (1997) fascinating experiments on frame-shifting illusions along similar lines; and this has significant implications for various theories about the bifurcation of visual processing pathways between a primarily action-guiding system and one more concerned with the identification and categorization of perceptually presented items. The basic frame-shifting illusion consists of the brief successive presentation, firstly, of a target object centrally placed in a rectangular frame, followed, second, by a display identical except for the translation of the frame a little to the left, say. Subjects robustly judge that the target object has moved to the right. Bridgeman modifies the conditions by moving the central target object half the distance to the left that the frame is moved in that same direction, in the second presentation. Subjects are divided into two groups and asked what they see in two different ways: first, simply to say what they think happened; second, to point to the target object in both presentations. Those in the first group mistakenly think that the target object moved to the right. Those in the second group correctly point to the target object in both presentations: that is, they track its actual movement to the left.

One interpretation of these results is that conscious perceptual experience is itself ambiguous, or inconsistent, on the issue of the direction of the movement of the target object. We have to recognize two separate, anatomically distinguishable, visual processing systems, which subserve action-guidance and judgement respectively. In Bridgemen's conditions, these simultaneously yield contradictory experiences. The subjective qualities of perceptual experiences can be variously interrogated, and the product of such interrogation may depend upon the variety of interrogation adopted. The idea of a single fact about how things are in experience is therefore to be rejected (see, e.g., Milner & Goodale, 1995). I disagree with this interpretation. The subjective qualities of experience, in both original and modified conditions, are constituted by the actual spatial distribution of the various displays as these are accessible to the subject. This is what explains reliable tracking of the actual movement of the target object to the left in subjects' pointing in the Bridgeman case. Mistaken judgements, on the other hand, reflect a perfectly natural, and no doubt evolutionarily well-grounded, standing assumption, implicit in the move from perceptual presentation to beliefs about how things are in the world presented, that movements in the frame are far less likely than movements in the target, and hence that changes in relative positions should be assigned to the latter rather than to the former. Generalizing the point, interrogation of perceptual processing in connection with action-guidance yields information concerning the neural enabling of conscious perceptual experience, whereas interrogation in connection with anatomically distinct systems involved in the identification and categorization of perceptually presented items brings out the various assumptions implicit in the transition between direct perceptual openness to mind-independent empirical things, on the one hand, and our judgements, beliefs and expectations concerning them, on the other.

A diametrically opposed interpretation of Bridgeman's results is also available, on which experience itself illusorily, and unambiguously, presents the target as moving to the right, which explains subjects' mistaken judgements; correct tracking of its actual movement to the left in pointing being explained by the fact that parameters for visually-guided action are set by *non-conscious* visual representations. I do not mean to deny the coherence of this interpretation, or to deny that blindsight patients' success in certain action-tasks directed at targets in their blind field cry out for the postulation of non-conscious visual representations in the control and guidance of basic action in some cases. Nor do I wish to claim that subjects' actions quite generally offer an infallible guide to the subjective character of their experience however much this may conflict with other evidence, from their judge-ments, both about the world and about their experience, and from other sources. My point is far more limited. It is simply that the illusion that Bridgeman creates does not on its own constitute a counterexample to (OV). As things stand, the interpretation that I offer above is at the very least on a par with its various alternatives.

Other illusions involve blurring of some kind. For example, writing seen from a distance 'looks blurred'; but no mind-independent empirical thing is blurred. My description of this phenomenon is that the perceptible features accessible in such experiences are relatively indeterminate, perhaps that there is such and such a rough distribution of dark shapes on a light back-ground, or whatever: genuine features of the distant word itself, but insuffi-ciently specific to uniquely determine which word it is, or even that it is a word as opposed to an abstract pattern. The blurredness consists in the subject's perfectly understandable incapacity to determine in judgement which word is seen, or even that what he sees is a word at all.

Relatedly, if an object is moved rapidly from side to side in front of a person's eyes, her visual experience of it begins to blur. Yet the object itself is not blurred in any way. In this case my account appeals to indeterminacy due to limitations of spatio-temporal, rather than purely spatial, acuity. Over a given short time-frame, the object is correctly visually placed *some-where* in the range of its rapid movement, but cannot at any point be more precisely placed. This is its actual feature that constitutes the subjective character of the subject's perceptual experience.

2. *The stick part-submerged in water.* Here, the standard description is that a straight stick part-submerged in water nevertheless illusorily looks bent, or broken. I claim that the mind-independent things whose actual features and distribution in space constitute the subjective nature of this experience are the upper, unsubmerged, part of the stick, and the image from the subject's point of view of the lower half of the stick, refracted, as it is, through the water. Perfectly respectable optics ray diagrams allow the entirely mind-independent construction of the relevant refracted image. The 'illusion' consists in the error in judgement of taking that image to be identical to the lower half of the stick itself. Compare the case of shadows. Macroscopic material objects cast visible shadows in sunlight. When we look at these shadows, the subjective qualities of our experiences are par-tially constituted by their perceptible features, such as their size and shape. Shadows are perfectly objective optical phenomena, and so are refracted images. The difference is just that the former are not inclined to mislead us in our judgements about how things are in the world we perceive, whereas the latter are. This is all that illusions of the current kind consist in. The stick *looks bent* in the sense that its submerged part produces a refracted image that is naturally and perfectly explicably apt to be identified with that part of the stick itself in the mistaken judgement that the stick *is* bent.

Consider, finally, the classic case of Stratton's (1896) inverting spectacles. Initially, the subjective qualities of the subject's perceptual experience are constituted by the perceptible features of the images of persisting things produced by the spectacles. Again, these are a perfectly mind-independent product of the distribution of such things in the world around him and the optical properties of the inverting lenses. Then, as he gets used to the spectacles, and in particular as he re-establishes working active engagement in the world, direct perceptual access to those persisting things themselves is re-enabled too. Thus, it becomes the case, once more, that the subjective qualities of his perceptual experience, and especially its spatial orientation, are constituted by the relevant features of those very things out there in the world beyond his inverting spectacles.

'Illusions', then, are absolutely not cases in which there is some kind of misrepresentation of reality by perceptual experience. For the subjective qualities of perceptual experiences are constituted by the various features of mind-independent things that are accessible to the subject, given the relevant conditions of perception, including possibly intervening devices, in those experiences. Rather, they are cases in which the way that the subject is most naturally inclined to judge the world to be, given which features of mind-independent reality are accessible to him in experience in this way, is systematically out of line with the way things actually are out there. Notice, therefore, that illusions constitute a direct counterexample, on my view, to Evans' (1982) influential *outer judgement model* of introspection, according to which knowledge of the subjective qualities of perceptual experience is to be attained by subjects' prefixing the judgements that they are naturally inclined to make, ignoring any extraneous information that they may have, about the way things are in the world around them, with the operator 'it seems to me that . . .'. This is especially clear in the case of the Müller-Lyer. For, in this case, the judgement that subjects are naturally inclined to make about the lines they see is that they are unequal in length. So, Evans' formula yields the following experiential self-ascription: 'it seems to me that the lines are unequal in length'. Yet I claim that the subjective qualities of subjects' experience are constituted by the actual spatial qualities of the presented lines, which are in fact equal in length.

Not every case of a perceptual experience prompting a mistaken judgement constitutes an illusion. For example, if someone suddenly, and falsely, comes to believe that the world is about end on seeing a particular arrangement of furniture in a room, then this is clearly not a case of visual illusion of any kind. I do not have a fully satisfactory characterization here; but what we count as perceptual illusions are just those cases of perceptual experience *naturally* and *explicably* leading to mistaken judgements about the world, along the various lines sketched above.

I should also say here, both that there are clearly many more cases to consider, and also that the details of the specific accounts that I have so far given may well need to be amended in various ways. I do contend, though, that (OV) has ample scope to provide a satisfactory account of all illusions along some such lines. Indeed, (OV) is in my view demonstrably no worse off in this respect than any version of (CV). According to (CV), illusions are cases in which the world's being a certain way naturally and explicably gives rise to a perceptual representation of its being some systematically distorted way. Whatever account is given here, of the relevant distortion, is equally available on (OV), as an explanation of the way in which perceptual experience whose subjective character is constituted by the world's being precisely that way in the relevant respects naturally and explicably results in correspondingly mistaken judgements.

Of course, an entirely different account has to be given of pure hallucination, although I would begin by stressing the comparative rarity of genuine such cases, in which there is absolutely no perceptual access to anything at all in the mind-independent empirical world, however misleading this may be to judgement. The claim would be that pure hallucination is simply a failed attempt at any such perceptual access, to be characterized only derivatively by reference to the perceptible features of purely qualitatively described empirical things that would be accessible were the world to be as the subject quite mistakenly takes it to be.

## V

In final conclusion, then, I claim that the (OV) version of (P) provides the most promising account of the nature of perceptual experience in connection with vindicating our commonsense commitment to empirical realism. This account is in my view independently highly compelling and richly explanatory. So I recommend buying the whole package.

## Notes

1. The same choice at this point has recently also been urged by John Campbell (2002), Mike Martin (2002) and Charles Travis (2004). Travis firmly acknowledges Austin (1964).
2. This way of setting out the orthodoxy is very much indebted to John Campbell (1993). Like him, though, I myself reject the orthodoxy concerning secondary qualities. A third, 'no-priority', view may also be proposed (McDowell, 1981). I must confess myself quite unable to give any determinate content to that, though.
3. See Dretske (1971); and Nozick (1981, ch. 3).
4. Ch. 4 of my 1999 pursues this debate in a way which is critical of epistemic externalism of this kind. The source of the difficulties I find with it, though, is a

failure properly to account for the understanding of beliefs about empirical things rather than any purely epistemic requirement.

5. The difficulty here is very much the difficulty which Berkeley (1975a, 1975b) raises for his realist opponent (Locke, 1975), with his insistence that "an idea can be like nothing but an idea" (Berkeley, 1975b, § 8).

6. At least in the *Dialogues* (1975a). See Foster (1985), for discussion of the metaphysical variation in Berkeley's work; and see pp. 65–66 below for an account of where the phenomenalism of the *Principles* (1975b) fits into my own argument.

7. This is, I think, precisely the dilemma which Berkeley (1975b, § 8) offers his Lockean (1975) realist opponent, especially in objection to the claim that our ideas of the primary qualities at least *resemble* the real physical qualities of mind-independent things, and hence that they provide us with a sensory-based conception of the nature of such things. In Berkeley's terms the argument goes like this. Physical qualities are either perceptible or they are not. If they are, then they are ideas, and are therefore manifestly mind-dependent. If they are not, then they cannot possibly resemble our ideas, which are therefore incapable of providing any intelligible conception of the qualities of things in a mind-independent empirical world.

8. This is perhaps the metaphysics of Berkeley's *Principles* (1975b). See again Foster (1985).

9. Langton (1998) ascribes to Kant this very account of our epistemic relation with empirical things; and Lewis (2002) defends it as correct in itself.

10. These two challenges clearly raise a vast number of controversial issues that I cannot even begin to address here.

11. Many thanks to John Campbell for pressing me at various points in the development of my views here.

# References

Austin, J. L. 1964. *Sense and Sensibilia*. Oxford: Oxford University Press.

Ayers, M. 1991. *Locke*, vols. I & II. London: Routledge.

Berkeley, G. 1975a. *Three Dialogues Between Hylas and Philonous*. In M. Ayers (ed.), *George Berkeley: Philosophical Works*. London: Everyman.

———1975b. *A Treatise Concerning the Principles of Human Knowledge*. In M. Ayers (ed.), *George Berkeley: Philosophical Works*. London: Everyman.

Brewer, B. 1999. *Perception and Reason*. Oxford: Oxford University Press.

Bridgeman, B. 1997. 'Cognitive and Sensorimotor Maps of Visual Space'. *Perception and Psychophysics*, **59**, 456–469.

Campbell, J. 1993. 'A Simple View of Colour'. In J. Haldane and C. Wright (eds.), *Reality, Representation and Projection*. Oxford: Oxford University Press.

———2002. *Reference and Consciousness*. Oxford: Oxford University Press.

Dretske, F. 1971. 'Conclusive Reasons'. *Australasian Journal of Philosophy*, **49**, 1–22.

Evans, G. 1982. *The Varieties of Reference*. Oxford: Oxford University Press.

Foster, J. 1985. 'Berkeley on the Physical World'. In J. Foster and H. Robinson (eds.), *Essays on Berkeley*. Oxford: Oxford University Press.

Langton, R. 1998. *Kantian Humility*. Oxford: Oxford University Press.

Lewis, D. 2002. 'Ramseyan Humility'. Gareth Evans Memorial Lecture to Oxford University, delivered posthumously by Stephanie Lewis, 2.iii.02.

Locke, J. 1975. *An Essay Concerning Human Understanding*, ed. P. H. Nidditch. Oxford: Oxford University Press.

Martin, M. G. F. 2002. 'The Transparency of Experience'. *Mind and Language*, **17**, 376–425.

McDowell, J. 1981. 'Non-Cognitivism and Rule-Following'. In S. H. Holtzman and C. M. Leich (eds.), *Wittgenstein: to Follow a Rule*. London: Routledge.

Milner, D. & Goodale, M. 1995. *The Visual Brain in Action*. Oxford: Oxford University Press.

Nozick, R. 1981. *Philosophical Explanations*. Oxford: Oxford University Press.

Stratton, G. 1896. 'Some Preliminary Experiments in Vision Without Inversion of the Retinal Image'. *Psychological Review*, **3**, 611–617.

Travis, C. 2004. 'The Silence of the Senses'. *Mind*, **113**, 57–94.

*Philosophical Issues, 14, Epistemology, 2004*

# EXTERNALISM, INTERNALISM, AND SKEPTICISM

Earl Conee
University of Rochester

*Introduction.* Some skeptical arguments rely on remote possibilities, such as the possibility that one's experiences are deceptive effects of alien manipulations. The skeptical arguments assert that we have to do something about such possibilities, if we are to know anything about the external world. We have to exclude the possibilities, or eliminate them, or rule them out. The task appears to be beyond our capacities. The skeptical arguments assert that it is. The arguments conclude that we lack external world knowledge.

Externalism can seem to offer the best reply to this variety of skeptical reasoning. A robustly externalist account of knowledge provides for something in the external world to share the burden of dealing with the skeptical scenarios. With this assistance, we seem able to have external world knowledge when all else goes well enough.

Reliance on something external can seem to be the only promising approach. The skeptical scenarios are compatible with the existence of all that is internal to our minds. Our internal epistemic resources therefore seem incapable of narrowing down the possibilities so as to exclude the skeptical alternatives. Thus it can seem that we need external help if we are to have knowledge of the external world.

What distinguishes externalism about knowledge? The internalism/ externalism distinction concerning justification is comparatively straightforward. Internalism asserts that justification is internally determined, whether by evidence possessed, or by coherence among beliefs, or by some other internal condition. Externalism about justification is readily understood as the denial that internal factors are sufficient. Something external has an independent role in justifying beliefs. Justification does not supervene on the internal alone.[1]

In the matter of knowledge, the status of an internal sufficient condition is less useful for distinguishing internalism from externalism. Gettier cases involve internally adequate justification without knowledge. In response to the Gettier problem, multifarious epistemologists—dyed-in-the-wool internalists included—are committed to there being some external requirement for knowledge that solves the Gettier problem. Also, no matter what internal justification we have, any of our external world beliefs might still have been false. So on any non-skeptical account, truth is an independent external condition on knowledge. Thus, internalist accounts of knowledge include external conditions to provide for Gettier prevention and truth. What distinguishes externalist accounts?

Externalist accounts of knowledge are those that reach farther into the external world than is needed to provide for Gettier prevention and truth. Some externalist accounts of knowledge replace the justification condition with something external, or count something external as justification. This qualifies as externalist, since preventing the Gettier problem and providing for the entailment of truth do not require this additional externality. The other externalist views about knowledge require internal reasons while adding a supplemental external condition that does more than address the Gettier problem or imply truth. At least, this is how externalism about knowledge will be understood here.

Let us return to the skeptical arguments about possibilities. The anti-skeptical work for distinctively externalist conditions on knowledge is to make it true that the skeptic's possibilities need not be dealt with entirely in our minds. Rather, we are to be aided by some external condition such as a lawful connection between the known external world belief and a fact making it true, or by the causal history of the belief, or by the reliability of a mechanism by which the belief is acquired. Such proposals allow internal reasons for the belief to take on some seemingly more manageable assignment. Perhaps internal reasons must merely eliminate relevant possibilities, or they must merely contingently depend for their existence on the truth of the belief, or perhaps internal reasons are unnecessary for knowledge because the external conditions on their own do what needs doing about contrary possibilities.

It will be argued here that asserting a distinctively externalist condition on knowledge runs into trouble. The externalist conditions exclude knowledge where we otherwise seem to have it. After this problem for externalism is developed, it will be argued that the task of eliminating contrary possibilities does not need doing. Internalist conditions on knowledge are adequate for meeting the nearest counterpart genuine requirement.

*The Informational Constraint.* Fred Dretske provides us with a prime example of an externalist view of knowledge with anti-skeptical implications.[2] Dretske argues that the pertinent external requirement occurs in the belief condition. Naturally the view requires belief for knowledge. And naturally the view requires that if one's belief attributes a property to something, then one has some concept that enables one to attribute the property. Putting these things together, we are required to have concepts in order to know how things are. There is nothing controversial or externalist about that.

More importantly, Dretske holds that there is an epistemically significant constraint on having concepts. For example, suppose that someone does not have the concept of a dingbat.[3] Dretske argues that in order to possess this concept, it is not enough to be able to sort out dingbats from the rest of reality. One might be able to sort out the dingbats on the basis of some correlated characteristic, without having the concept of a dingbat. Dretske contends that in order to acquire the dingbat concept, one must be sensitized to dingbattiness itself. The only way to become appropriately sensitized to dingbattiness, in Dretske's view, is to receive information about dingbats. In particular, in acquiring the concept one must receive a message of some sort that carries information with the content that something is a dingbat.

By "informational content" Dretske means something he takes to be ordinary and pre-theoretical.[4] The idea is that for a message to a person to contain certain information, the information must be veridical and more. The message is to be something by which the person could learn that information.

This requirement of information reception is clearly an externalist requirement. In general, it is not a matter internal to the mind whether or not there is factual information to the effect that some sort of thing exists. Yet there must be such an external fact, in order for a signal to bear that information.

The anti-skeptical potential of this requirement seems to be considerable. If we believe that there are dingbats, or even so much as doubt that there are dingbats, we must have the concept of a dingbat. Manifestly, we do have this concept.[5] To have it, we must receive information about dingbats, prominently including the information that there are dingbats. And again, this sort of receiving of information requires that we are capable of learning that the information is true, which is to say that we are capable of knowing it.

Thus, we cannot even form a thought about dingbats, conceived of as such, without receiving information about dingbats that renders us capable of knowing about the existence of dingbats. Let us call the universal generalization of this purported epistemic implication of concept possession the "Informational Constraint," or "IC" for short.

A restriction should be immediately noted. Dretske intends the IC to apply only to *primitive* concepts. He tells us that these are concepts not composed of simpler conceptual elements. Our concept of a dingbat, for instance, seems in some way to contain the concept of throwing. So it may not be primitive. The argument for a capacity to know therefore may not apply to the dingbat concept. Dretske does not offer any examples of primitive concepts. So, in our consideration of the Informational Constraint, we have to proceed on our own to identify them.

This will soon be attempted. First though, the modal status of the knowledge that the IC is about should be clarified. The IC implies that one is capable of knowing some facts involving whatever primitive concepts are used in one's beliefs. Dretske does not say exactly what sort of possibility of knowledge this capability implies. If the capacity were a sort of possibility that we could turn out to lack any means to implement, say, a merely metaphysical possibility of knowledge, then it would be a possibility that a skeptic about our actual knowledge could consistently concede. Dretske seems to intend something stronger. He also describes the implication of the IC in terms of our "having the cognitive resources for knowing" by use of the concept. If we have such resources, then we acquire knowledge by simply exercising this capacity. The capacity renders us all set to know the external facts that the pertinent information conveys to us. Skeptical arguments about possibility do not give any grounds for denying that we can exercise any of our cognitive capacities. So it is a genuinely anti-skeptical implication that we have this capacity to know about the external world.

*Problems.* Disputing external world skepticism by appeal to the IC has costs. First, the IC implies that we cannot have knowledge to the effect that certain properties are not instantiated. These are properties for which our concept is primitive. If some property is not instantiated, then we do not receive information about instances of it. The IC tells us that we do not have any corresponding concept. So we are cannot know any proposition that we need these concepts to believe.

The range of properties that are subject to this limitation is not clear. First, perhaps there are multiple ways to conceive of the same property, and not all of the concepts are primitive. If so, still, we would be unable to know by a primitive concept that the properties were not instantiated. Also, perhaps some uninstantiated properties for which our concepts would be primitive are properties that we are able to render instantiated. That is, perhaps we are capable of producing instances of the properties, though we never produce them. If so, then the Informational Constraint does not imply that we are incapable of acquiring the corresponding primitive concepts. The IC does tell us that in order to acquire them, we would have to render it false that such properties are uninstantiated. Given that we never do so, it remains true that the IC implies that we are unable to know by primitive concepts the facts of their non-instantiation.

Is this limit on what we can know known a defect in the view? That partly depends on which concepts are primitive. Again, Dretske offers no examples of primitive concepts. He does give three examples of non-primitive concepts: that of a miracle, that of a random sequence, and that of a unicorn. There is one clear sort of complexity to these concepts. There is a conspicuous implication by the concept of a miracle of the property of being a natural law, a conspicuous implication of the concept of a random sequence of the property of being a sequence, and a conspicuous implication of the concept of a unicorn of the property of having a horn. So perhaps for a concept to be primitive is for it to have no conspicuous implications of other properties.

By the test of conspicuously implying no other property, virtually no concept is primitive. For instance, an apparently simple concept such as that of being curved conspicuously implies the properties of being extended and having shape. Perhaps the property of existing conspicuously implies no other properties, and perhaps all other properties conspicuously imply it.

If existence is our only genuinely primitive concept, though, the Informational Constraint has minimal anti-skeptical force. Our having that concept would imply only that we can know that something exists. That is not much to know, and it is of no help concerning the external world.

If we have more substantial primitive concepts, then the anti-skeptical force of the IC is more exciting. G. E. Moore's favorite example of a simple natural property is that of being yellow. For Moore, a property is simple in virtue of its being unanalyzable. Suppose that we apply this idea of simplicity to concepts. The concept of some determinate shade of color, say, canary yellow, does not seem to be analyzable as a combination of conceptual elements. Perhaps it is partly analyzed by the concept of being extended. But there seem to be no further elementary concepts that compose it. The "rest" of the concept of canary yellow seems to be the whole concept of that particular shade of color. So let us try out the supposition that this sort of concept is primitive.

If concepts like that of canary yellow are primitive, then the Informational Constraint has significant anti-skeptical implications. The IC implies that, in virtue of our having the concept of canary yellow, we are capable of knowing that canary yellow things have existed. The same would go for our other unanalyzable concepts.

If these are primitive concepts, then the IC has a definite defect. It might have been that we knew that nothing was canary yellow. We might have discovered some physical reason why that color could not be instantiated. In our having this knowledge, we would have been applying our concept of canary yellow, and so we would have to have had the concept. But clearly we could have had such a concept under the circumstances. We do not need instances of colors to have color concepts. All we need are the right chromatic phenomenal qualities, together with the right sort of inclination to make external attributions on the basis of experiencing such qualities. We could have had the relevant visual qualities and attributive inclinations in the absence of the corresponding colored things. Thus, having such concepts does not require that we receive messages derived from things that have the color. On present assumptions about primitives, the IC has the implication that this is not true, and that we could not have known that nothing canary yellow existed. This denial of the possibility of such knowledge is itself a sort of skeptical claim. It is quite doubtful. So if the IC applies to such color concepts, then the constraint is in trouble.

Again, the presence of this defect in Dretske's externalist view of knowledge depends on our current assumption about which concepts are primitive. Again, the Informational Constraint may turn out to have some very narrow application, say, applying only to the concept of existence. This would be more acceptable, but lacking in anti-skeptical utility. There is no secure middle ground. There is no informational constraint that both limits our ability to possess concepts in a defensible way and applies to concepts entailing a capacity for significant knowledge of the external world.

The second cost of the use of the IC against skepticism is a problem about what our reasons can do for us. In order for the IC to have direct utility against external world skepticism, some of our reasons have to have a certain remarkable weakness.

The IC asserts that, in order for us to have externally applicable concept C, we must be capable of knowledge about things to which C applies. Suppose that we make the natural further assumption that any concept which is apparently external in its application is genuinely external. That is, suppose we assume that when it seems to one as though one's concept is of something external, such as the concepts of a dingbat and an armchair, then the concept is indeed external, if one is thereby having a concept at all.

On this supposition, an eerie sort of possibility is implied. In combination with this supposition the IC implies the possibility of a perfect illusion of thought. With uncontroversial premises about thought, the IC implies that we are not thinking unless we are using concepts the primitives among which we possess in virtue of information derived from their instances. It is possible for us not to have received any external information. Some versions of standard skeptical scenarios provide for possibilities in which our minds are not attuned to any external kinds. For instance, all of our sensations might have arisen by chance, or that they might have arisen from disparate and disorderly origins. If so, then if we engaged in activities that were qualitatively the same as external concept acquisitions in a normal environment, our lack of a stable sensitivity to anything in our environment would prevent us from receiving any external information. The IC tells us that, had one of these possibilities obtained, we would not have managed to acquire primitive external concepts. We would have no composite external concepts either, since they must be composed at least partly of simple external concepts. Yet all concepts are primitive or composite, and all believing requires some concept attribution. It follows that no conscious states guarantee that we are ever thinking anything about the external world. All of our conscious states are implied to be compatible with our being victims of a massive doxastic illusion.

Fallibilist anti-skeptics deny that knowledge of a proposition requires its entailment by internal evidence. Fallibilist knowledge of our thinking remains possible. In any suitably cooperative environment, we might still know that we have external world thoughts, and we might still know what we think. The point is rather that on the present supposition about when we have an external concept if we have one at all, the IC implies that we must lack entailing evidence for something for which we would otherwise have thought that we had it. When we reflectively attend to consideration of what seems to be an external world proposition,[6] it is overwhelmingly plausible that we do have entailing evidence for the proposition that at least we are considering some thought or other. The problem is that on our current supposition about concept possession, the IC implies that our evidence that we are thinking some thought cannot be this strong.

It is noteworthy that anti-individualists about mental content can avoid this problem for that view. A content anti-individualist must hold that some concepts are externally determined. The concepts' identity depends on contingent environmental conditions. Where the external world provides a suitable causal or social basis, some of our concepts depend partly on their causes or their social environment. Different causal bases can give us different concepts, without any conscious difference. That much environmental dependency is enough for the view to count as anti-individualism about mental content. Yet that much leaves it open that, in possible circumstances where no suitable external basis exists, there is some default content that is determined by internal facts about conceptual roles, or some other internal factor.[7] This contingent sort of anti-individualism about content allows intro-spectable evidence to entail that one is considering some thought.

We can make this sort of accommodation to avoid the problem for the Informational Constraint. We can suppose that, when one seemingly has a concept with external application, one has such a concept when some proper sort of external information is received. When it is not received, one's seemingly external concept has some default internally determined content.[8]

Now the eerie possibility of illusory thought is not implied. When the environment is insufficiently cooperative in the apparent acquisition of an external concept, one still possesses some default concept. So one can know from introspectable conditions that one is thinking some thought or other.

This accommodation sharply curtails the anti-skeptical utility of the IC, however. If it does turn out that one has some genuinely external concept, then the IC tells us that one is capable of knowing about external things to which the concept applies. That is an interesting claim. But on current suppositions, the question of whether this antecedent about having an external concept is actually satisfied is a topic for skeptical doubts of precisely the sort that appeared to have been bypassed by use of the IC. One can focus on a seemingly external primitive concept, carefully ponder-ing one's understanding of it to find every available assurance that the concept is indeed applicable to things beyond one's mind. Nevertheless, it could be that one has some merely apparently external concept instead, a concept whose possession implies nothing about the external world even if the IC is true.

In our actual situation this possibility of non-external content is quite implausible. It is a possibility that we have no reason to believe. But the same is true of the skeptical scenarios themselves. The exciting anti-skeptical potential of the IC is its apparent capacity to take us directly from obvious facts of concept possession to conclusions about a capacity for substantial external knowledge. On present suppositions, that direct route is closed. The IC gains external implications only via non-obvious externally determined facts about what sort of concepts are actually possessed. This is irremediable. The assumptions involved in any use of the IC with exciting anti-skeptical implications are bound to conflict with our having entailing internal evidence for thinking any external thought.

*External Conditions in General.* Distinctively externalist conditions on knowledge all impose objectionable limits on knowledge. There may be no rigorous way to show this, particularly given the vagueness of "distinctively external" and "objectionable limits." Here is a sketch of an argument for it, followed by illustrative instances of the problem.

Whatever distinctively external conditions are supposed to provide for our having external world knowledge, there must be something that makes the conditions exist, something that implements them. Because the external conditions on knowledge do not supervene on the mental, their implementation accompanies any internal state contingently. So it is possible for us to be in any internal state while the implementation is not present.

Now the reasoning becomes more tentative. It appears that, for any external condition on knowledge, we might have known propositions entailing that the condition had no implementation. It was argued above that we might have known by use of a primitive color concept that the color was not instantiated. Yet the mechanism of primitive concept possession asserted by the Informational Constraint requires that we be informed of instances of the property. So requiring this mechanism precludes our knowing such negative facts in this way.

Here is another illustration of the problem. One sort of reliability theory asserts that knowledge of a belief requires the belief to be formed by a truth conducive belief forming mechanism. These mechanisms are to be stable cognitive structures with some variety to their doxastic outputs.[9] The problem arises for this sort of view because it is not impossible for us to have known that our belief forming mechanisms tended to produce false beliefs. We might have known this by its becoming evident to us that, although we sometimes get excellent grounds for regarding propositions as true, we are psychologically constituted so that these grounds are not our usual bases for belief. It might have become evident to us that when we believed something, it tended to be on the basis of weak evidence, bias, careless judgment, wishful thinking, or the like. Our evidence could also show us that these are unreliable grounds. Suppose that this was all evident to us. In spite of the non-verific tendencies of our belief forming mechanisms, this evidence might have been the basis on which we managed to judge that our belief forming mechanisms were unreliable. We would thereby know that the mechanisms were unreliable. Yet the assumed external requirement for knowledge that the belief-forming mechanism be reliable is incompatible with our knowing that none of them is reliable.

The same sort of trouble affects subject contextualism about justification, when subject contextualism is employed as a theory about the justification condition on knowledge.[10] David Annis's subject contextualism is roughly the view that justified belief consists in belief for which the subject is able to meet the objections that the individuals in an appropriate objector group are inclined to make.[11] In this view, one's having justification for any given belief implies the existence of an appropriate objector group whose objections to the belief, if any, one is able to meet.[12] This implication qualifies the view as externalist when it is offered as a proposal about the justification required for knowledge.

Again an external requirement yields a problematic result to the effect that certain things could not have been known. It seems clear that one might have known many things, while also knowing that no appropriate objector exists. Most simply, though tragically, one might have known that one was the last survivor of a cataclysm. One could have had excellent reason for believing this, from veridical perception, memory, and fully supported theory, and thereby one would have known it to be true. Yet according to this subject contextualist view of knowledge, there would then be no appropriate objector group, and hence no justification, and hence no knowledge.[13]

These are examples, not a general proof that a problematic limit on knowledge affects all distinctively externalist theories of knowledge. The basis on which the results seem to generalize is the appearance that we might have known that no implementation existed for any given external condition.

*An Internalist Alternative.* Even if is some such limitation of knowledge is unavoidable, it might be regarded as regrettable but necessary to provide for external world knowledge. In order to know, we have to deal somehow with the possibilities that skeptics identify. How else can we eliminate them?

The concept of elimination has pernicious implications here, as do allied concepts such as exclusion and ruling out. We cannot eliminate, exclude, rule out, or otherwise do away with contrary possibilities. They remain possible no matter what we do. Distinctively externalist conditions on knowledge cannot affect the metaphysical status of possibilities any more than can internalist conditions.

Of course no one thinks that any such impossible metaphysical alteration is required. Knowing a truth does not require that we render it metaphysically necessary. But then, precisely what do we have to do with contrary possibilities in order to have knowledge? Talk of "eliminating" contrary possibilities is not simply foolishness. Something in the vicinity must be highly plausible. The metaphorical terminology does not clarify the required task.

Some skeptical arguments have a premise that requires knowledge that contrary possibilities do no obtain. This might be thought of as requiring their "epistemic elimination." Is this what we have to do with the possibilities?

No. On reflection it is clear that knowledge of a proposition does not require us either to know, concerning each possibility contrary to it, that the possibility does not obtain, or to know the generality that none of them obtain. Let us consider an external world proposition, say, asserting one's perception of some item of ordinary dry goods—call the proposition "X". Leaving aside skeptical scenarios, for any such proposition there are endlessly many contrary possibilities like this: X is not so and one Patagonian perpetrates a peccadillo, X is not so and two Patagonians perpetrate a peccadillo, etc. Knowledge that these possibilities do not obtain is plainly superfluous. We need not have so much as a thought about Patagonian peccadilloes in order to know that we are perceiving some item of ordinary dry goods.

Similarly, in order to know about a perception of an item of ordinary dry goods, no one need have any thought to the effect that anything is not true, including the thought that all contrary propositions are not true. Again, belief on the topic seems quite unnecessary, much less is knowledge on the topic required. Thus, there is no sustainable intuitive support for any requirement of knowledge concerning contrary possibilities. They need not be "epistemically eliminated."[14]

Here is a better candidate for something that has to be "eliminated" in order to have knowledge. It is quite plausible that when someone knows a proposition, from the person's perspective there is no chance that the proposition is untrue.[15] It is such perspectival chances that must not exist, in order to know. So if internal reasons exclude this sort of chance, then they do not need external help to meet this requirement.

Suppose that one has strong enough support for an external world proposition to make it thoroughly reasonable, while one lacks any reason to think that a contrary possibility obtains. If so, then from one's perspective there is no chance that the proposition is untrue. This is all that needs doing about contrary possibilities.[16]

Internalists about knowledge can defensibly maintain that internal conditions often do this for us. There is every appearance that our evidence for external world beliefs often accomplishes this, even when the skeptical possibilities are duly noted. For example, you now have powerful evidence that you see something. Your perceptual experiences makes it apparent to you that you see something, and the rest of your perspective on the world fits quite well with the proposition that you see something. You have no reason to believe that you are deceived about anything essential to the truth of this proposition. In light of these aspects of your current internal condition, it has no credibility for you that you see nothing. The possibility of some aberrant funny business having you in your current internal condition is a mere possibility that you have no reason to believe obtains. Given the considerations that are available to you, from your perspective there is no chance that any possibility obtains on which you do not see something.[17] Contrary possibilities that have this status do not intuitively conflict with your knowing.[18]

Internal reasons of this character are not the exclusive prerogative of the internalist. Once again, externalism about knowledge is the view that some external requirement either replaces the justification condition or supplements it in some way that goes beyond truth and blocking Gettier cases. None of that limits the strength that internal reasons can be held to have. So an externalist can consistently hold that internal reasons do the anti-skeptical work that the current internalist view attributes to them. Internalists have no monopoly on that option.

While this is a fact about compatibility, a point in favor of internalism remains. If the internal reasons can do the work, distinctively external conditions become superfluous for responding to the skeptical argument about eliminating possibilities.

The internalist approach to knowledge has the advantage of avoiding the sort of limitations of knowledge that we have seen for externalist views. An internalist account requires nothing special by way of implementation. We need only sufficient mental apparatus to have true beliefs for adequate reasons while no Gettier problem arises. Thus, an internalist account both provides for our having external world knowledge and avoids an objectionable limit on what can be known.

## Notes

1. Timothy Williamson defends at length the thesis that knowledge is a mental state, in *Knowledge and Its Limits* (Oxford University Press, 2000), Chapters 1–4. If being internal is being internal to one's mind, then the truth of this thesis of Williamson's would complicate things. The known fact seems to be included in the state of knowing it, yet the known facts are generally external. The simplest way around this complication is to hold that internalism is restricted to purely internal states and that states of knowing external facts are not purely internal. It

would be worthwhile to have something beyond a pre-theoretical understanding of the purely internal, but this should suffice for present purposes.

2. Fred Dretske, "The Epistemology of Belief", *Synthese* 55 (1983) pp. 3–19.

3. The concept of a dingbat is Dretske's example. He does not say what he has in mind. We can think of "dingbat" in the sense of "small object suitable to hurl at something".

4. In his book, *Knowledge and the Flow of Information* (Bradford Books, 1983), Dretske offers a probabilistic definition of what it is for some signal to have a certain informational content. But that special notion of content is not presently at stake.

5. The facts of concept possession are not as straightforward as they seem at first. See the second problem for the IC discussed below.

6. To put the matter neutrally, it seems the same as an external world proposition seems when consciously considered in a normal environment

7. For a very helpful discussion of contingent anti-individualism about mental content, see Brian P. McLaughlin and Michael Tye, "Externalism, Twin Earth, and Self-Knowledge," in Crispin Wright, Barry Smith, and Cynthia Macdonald, editors, *Knowing Our Own Minds* (Oxford University Press, 1998), pp. 285–320.

8. Nothing in the paper by Dretske is committed either way about the contingency of external content.

9. This counts as externalism about knowledge when it is proposed as a replacement of the justification condition, or a supplement for it

10. Subject contextualists about the epistemic hold that some condition in the context of the subject of an epistemic evaluation helps to determine the epistemic status; attributer contextualists about the epistemic hold that some condition in the context of the attributer of an epistemic evaluation helps to determine the epistemic status.

11. David Annis, "A Contextualist Theory of Epistemic Justification," reprinted in Paul K. Moser, editor, *Empirical Knowledge: Readings in Contemporary Epistemology*, Second Edition (Rowman and Littlefield, 1996), pp. 205–217. The members of an appropriate objector group for a given belief are roughly the experts on the topic of the belief who aim principally at truth about the topic. Their objections must arise from real doubts born of their aim for truth. There is an important further detail in Annis's view. Annis holds that justification is relative to an issue context. The same belief can be simultaneously justified relative to the standard of some comparatively casual purpose and unjustified relative to the standard of some comparatively serious purpose. When this sort of justification is held to be required for knowledge, either some one standard must be selected as uniformly determining the justification required for knowledge, or knowledge itself must be likewise relativized.

12. It is clear that Annis intends the view to have this implication. The objector group has to exist in order to set the issue context relative to which a belief may be justified. (Ibid., p. 209) See note 11 above.

13. Other versions of subject contextualism need not require the existence of an objector group. If they are also versions of externalism about knowledge, then they will require something external to the subject that can vary with context. If

the requirement resembles that of Annis's theory, then we can expect it to be possible to have knowledge while what is required does not exist. Of course other possible versions of subject contextualism would stand or fall on their own merits.

14. Perhaps one has to be "in a position to know" that contrary possibilities do not obtain. Depending on how this is understood, either it adds no substantial requirement or it is as mistaken as a requirement of actual knowledge. See note 17 below.

15. John Hawthorne discusses similar principles about knowledge in Chapter Two of his book, *Knowledge and Lotteries* (Oxford University Press, 2003).

16. For further discussion of this approach to the justification needed for knowledge, and its impact on external world skepticism, see section IV of Richard Feldman and Earl Conee, "Making Sense of Skepticism" in *Evidentialism: Essays in Epistemology* (Oxford University Press, 2004), pp. 277–306.

17. Are you "in a position to know" e.g. that it is not the case that you see nothing while two Patagonians perpetrate peccadilloes? Well, when you know according to the current internalist view you have a good enough evidential basis to infer this conclusion, if you have the relevant conceptual and inferential equipment. If that is enough to make you "in a position to know" that such contrary possibilities do not obtain, then you are automatically in such a position when you have the internal justification needed for knowledge. If you are not so equipped, and this keeps you from being "in a position to know" that such contrary possibilities do not obtain, then knowledge does not require you to be in such a position.

    A closely related issue is that of whether or not you have to be justified in believing that the contrary possibilities do not obtain, in order to know. There is an extensive helpful discussion of this in Chapter 2 of Peter Klein's *Certainty: A Refutation of Skepticism* (University of Minnesota Press, 1981).

18. What about the possibility of your being in a Gettier case? Purely internal states never entail that one is not in a Gettier case. But this possibility bears the same relation to knowledge as the skeptical possibilities. If you are in an extraordinary situation where some undefeated consideration in your possession makes for some actual chance that you are in a Gettier case, then you do not know. In the usual circumstance where you possess no such consideration, the mere possibility of a Gettier case does not intuitively conflict with your knowing. For more about this, see section IVB of "Making Sense of Skepticism," op. cit.

*Philosophical Issues, 14, Epistemology, 2004*

# TRUTH CONSEQUENTIALISM, WITHHOLDING AND PROPORTIONING BELIEF TO THE EVIDENCE

Michael R. DePaul
University of Notre Dame

## I. Introduction

Truth consequentialism is a view regarding epistemic evaluation. The basic idea is that true belief is the fundamental epistemic good, and that cognitive practices are to be evaluated by determining how much of this good we would attain as a consequence of employing those practices.[1] But just as in ethics consequentialism requires a developed account of the good, or moral value, to generate specific evaluations, if truth consequentialism is to produce concrete results, it presumably must do more than simply tell us that true belief is good. It must specify the value of believing a true proposition, and perhaps the values of certain other states as well, e.g., the value of disbelieving a true proposition or the value of believing a false proposition.

Alvin Goldman has recently proposed a theory of epistemic value that has the requisite specificity.[2] He should be commended for doing so. Many people assert that truth is the epistemic good, but I am not aware of anyone else who has proposed a specific assignment of values. With such an assignment, we can really put truth consequentialism to work—and to the test.[3] So I am going to focus on the theory of epistemic value that Goldman has proposed, which he calls veritism, but because his proposal is so straightforward and intuitively plausible, I hope what emerges will be more than a narrow criticism of Goldman's view.

## II. Veritistic Value

The first thing to notice is that there is not only an epistemically good thing, truth, that we can attain or fail to attain when we form a belief. When we form a belief we might also end up with something epistemically bad, falsehood. The pattern is the same as in a typical form of hedonism, which takes pleasure to be the good but recognizes that there is also something bad, pain, that must be taken into account. The overall value of a state of affairs according to such a typical hedonism is not, therefore, equivalent simply to the amount of pleasure it contains. The value of the state of affairs is provided by its utility, which is a kind of sum of the (positive) amount of pleasure it contains and the (negative) amount of pain it contains. Similarly truth consequentialists might be expected to have their eyes not merely on truth, but on an amalgam of the good, truth, and the bad, falsehood. Goldman conforms to this pattern and labels the combined value "veritistic value" or "V-value." So on Goldman's view it is actually V-value, not merely truth, that truth consequentialists wish to maximize, and any plausible alternative to Goldman's value theory would have to define some similar value that somehow aggregates epistemic goodness and badness.

Strictly speaking, it is not truth and falsehood that truth consequentialists take to be epistemically good and bad. It is true *belief* that they take to be the epistemic good and false *belief* that they take to be epistemically bad. There are (at least) two different ways in which we can think about belief. According to the first way, there are three discrete stands one can take with respect to a proposition: one can believe it, disbelieve or reject it, i.e., believe the negation, or withhold belief, i.e., neither believe nor disbelieve the proposition. According to the second way of thinking about belief, beliefs come in a seemingly infinite number of degrees or strengths ranging from absolute certainty to total disbelief. These degrees of belief are sometimes thought of as equivalent to subjective probabilities and represented by points in the interval from zero through one. A normal person would likely believe a simple truth of addition to degree one, and if the person thought about it, he or she would believe the negation of such a truth to degree zero. A person who is very sure that a proposition is true, but not certain, might believe the proposition to something like degree .9. If such a person were to consider the negation of such a proposition, he or she would believe it to a low degree, ideally, to degree .1. In providing his account of veritistic value, Goldman does not choose between these two ways of thinking about beliefs, which he calls the trichotomous scheme and the degree of belief (DB) scheme. He instead describes how to assign veritistic values to the various possible belief states on each scheme.

Goldman employs a question answering model according to which "agent *S*'s belief states (of either the trichotomous or the DB kind) have value or disvalue when they are responses to a question that *interests S* (or, more generally, when other agents are interested in *S*'s knowing the answer)." (Goldman 1999, p. 88) Goldman assigns veritistic value only to beliefs that answer questions that interest the agent, or other relevant parties, because he does not feel that a person's belief system should be assigned a low V-value just because the person is ignorant of the answers to many uninteresting questions. Goldman opts for a broad understanding of 'interesting' that includes questions about which the agent "has an aroused curiosity or concern" as well as questions that the agent would find interesting "if he/she only thought of them, or considered them" or "if he or she knew certain facts." (Goldman 1999, p. 95)

Within the trichotomous scheme, Goldman assigns V-values to belief states taken towards a true proposition that answers an interesting question as follows: "If *S believes* the true proposition, the V-value is 1.0. If he *rejects* the true proposition, the V-value is 0. And if he *withholds judgment*, the V-value is .50." (Goldman 1999, p. 89) On the DB scheme, the V-value of a belief in a true proposition is simply equal to the degree of belief.[4] Goldman is able to avoid assigning V-values to believing, disbelieving and withholding false propositions because he assumes that when one believes a proposition P one disbelieves not P and that when one believes P to degree n one believes not P to degree 1-n.[5] Hence, when one believes or has a high degree of belief in a false proposition, this will impact the V-value of one's total cognitive state because one will disbelieve or have a low degree of belief in the true negation of the false proposition.

Goldman is most interested in changes in V-value over time. He usually evaluates practices applied to a range of cases, actual and hypothetical, and takes "the *average* (mean) performance of the practice across those applications as a measure of its V-value." (Goldman 1999, p. 92) Thus, as he deploys it, truth consequentialism is a kind of epistemic rule consequentialism. Individual acts of belief formation are not evaluated with reference to the amount of veritistic value they produce. Rather, we are to consider how much veritistic value we would secure by following various practices, which we can think of as rules for the formation of beliefs so long as we bear in mind that these may or may not be rules we could self-consciously apply to cases and follow. In some social cases, Goldman is interested in the *aggregate* level of knowledge in a community. The mean V-value for individuals in the community can be used as a measure in such cases, but there are other possibilities. Finally, where appropriate, Goldman allows certain factors not represented in the basic V-value system to influence epistemic evaluation of a practice, for example, the speed of information acquisition or the degree of interest in the questions the practice addresses.

One might initially balk at the values Goldman assigns on the trichotomous scheme. "Why," one might ask, "should the value of disbelieving a true proposition, or equivalently, believing a false proposition, be zero? This is a bad state to be in, so it would seem more natural to represent its value with a negative number. And why assign withholding a true proposition a positive value of .5? Surely this seems to be a neutral state of affairs, and should accordingly get a value of zero, not a positive value." There really isn't any substance to such worries. The numerical values assigned really do not matter, so long as the relation between the values assigned to the three belief states remains the same. We could use −1, 0, +1 or 0, 5, 10 or −100, −50, 0, or, as Goldman chooses, 0, .5, 1. Whichever of these systems one uses to evaluate alternative modes of belief formation, one will end up ranking alternative belief forming practices in the same way. The substantive idea being advanced here is that believing a truth is as good, epistemically, as believing a falsehood is bad, epistemically, and withholding is neither good nor bad. Or to put the idea another way, the value of withholding a truth stands midway between the value of believing it and the value of disbelieving it. Goldman captures this idea with the numbers 0, .5, 1, and this is a perfectly good way of capturing the idea. In addition, I think we would have to grant that the idea these numerical values captures *seems* highly intuitive. Suppose someone were to propose assigning different values, say −1, 0 and 2, to disbelieving, withholding and believing a truth respectively. This would be to assert that believing a truth is twice as good as believing a falsehood is bad. Surely if no more were said, such a choice would seem arbitrary. "Why not −1, 0, 1.5 or 2.5 or 3 or...?" we would want to ask. We would naturally demand some sort of justification for such an assignment in a way we are not led to demand one of Goldman's. His is the obvious default position, the natural place to begin. If you want to try something different, you are going to need a good reason for doing so.

Nevertheless, as natural and intuitively obvious as Goldman's proposal regarding veritistic value is, I think it runs into problems concerning withholding and apportioning degree of belief to the evidence. The first problem I will describe arises because the assignment of V-value is limited to interesting propositions. Since it does not turn on the most fundamental element of the scheme, it is not, perhaps, terribly significant. I will even be able to suggest what might be an easy fix. But the next two problems, which are related, just might challenge the basic idea behind Goldman's assignment of V-values, the idea I have just argued is so highly natural and intuitively plausible.

### III. Uninteresting Propositions

Goldman justifies limiting the assignment of V-values to interesting propositions on the ground that a person should not be penalized for being ignorant of the answers to questions that are of no interest. Let's agree. It does not immediately follow that it should not matter at all, epistemically, what stance a person takes with respect to uninteresting propositions. Yet this is what Goldman suggests when he fails to define V-values for uninteresting propositions.[6] What follows immediately from the idea that a person should not be penalized for ignorance of the uninteresting is that it does not matter epistemically if a person fails to have *true* beliefs about uninteresting propositions. Although it is a slightly different matter, perhaps we could also agree that a person should receive no veritistic credit for true beliefs in uninteresting propositions. But what if a person employs cognitive practices that lead him or her to disbelieve many uninteresting true propositions, or equivalently, to form many false beliefs in uninteresting propositions?[7] Surely such cognitive practices should be counted as epistemically and, one would think, vertistically inferior to practices that produce either true beliefs or no beliefs at all regarding uninteresting propositions. It seems to me that false belief is always epistemically bad, regardless of whether the proposition believed is interesting. Hence, although I can agree, at least for the sake of argument,[8] that uninteresting propositions should be treated differently from interesting propositions in terms of V-value assignment, I do not think it is correct never to assign a V-value in the case of an uninteresting proposition.[9]

I believe Goldman needs some mechanism for penalizing practices that yield false beliefs in uninteresting propositions. Simply assigning a V-value of 0 to disbelief in uninteresting true propositions might well do the trick.[10] Suppose practices $\pi_W$, $\pi_R$ and $\pi_U$ perform equally well with respect to the same range of interesting propositions, but $\pi_W$ produces no beliefs at all with respect to uninteresting propositions, while $\pi_R$ and $\pi_U$ frequently produce beliefs regarding uninteresting propositions. The difference between $\pi_R$ and $\pi_U$ is that when it comes to uninteresting propositions, $\pi_R$ produces true beliefs just as reliably as it does with respect to interesting propositions while $\pi_U$ is terribly unreliable about uninteresting propositions. One way this might happen is if $\pi_R$ produces beliefs about interesting and uninteresting propositions in the same way, while $\pi_U$ would have us take wild guesses about uninteresting propositions. If we assign a V-value of 0 to false beliefs in uninteresting propositions, but still define no V-value for true beliefs in or withholdings of uninteresting propositions, the mean V-value for $\pi_U$ would be driven lower than the mean V-values for $\pi_W$ and $\pi_R$ by the additional disbeliefs assigned a V-value of 0. The total V-values for $\pi_W$, $\pi_R$ and $\pi_U$ would be equivalent, since the totals were equivalent on Goldman's original assignment, and any additional disbeliefs assigned a value by my proposal would get a value of 0. But because it is unreliable about uninteresting propositions, $\pi_U$ would have a higher number of output beliefs with a defined V-value than either $\pi_W$ or $\pi_R$. Hence, the total V-value would be divided by a larger number in the case of $\pi_U$, thus yielding the smaller mean.

Notice, in addition, that unless $\pi_R$ is perfectly reliable with respect to uninteresting propositions, a person employing $\pi_R$ would be led to disbelieve some uninteresting true propositions. As a result, a person employing $\pi_R$ would have more beliefs with an assigned V-value than a person employing $\pi_W$. Hence the mean V-value for $\pi_R$ would be lower than the mean V-value for $\pi_W$. I think this is a happy result. If we accept the idea that a person who fails to believe all sorts of uninteresting truths is not epistemically worse off than a person who believes such truths, then there is nothing to be gained by forming such beliefs. But if I am right that it is always epistemically bad to hold a false belief, there is something to be lost by forming beliefs about uninteresting propositions—unless one is infallible when it comes to the uninteresting. Hence, it would seem the best epistemic policy is to withhold uninteresting propositions.

There is more to be said in behalf of withholding uninteresting propositions. Although we often ignore the fact, there is a cost to believing things. At the extreme, there is a cost because we are finite beings and can only have so many beliefs: each belief we form takes up resources, and if we reach the limit of our capacity, every uninteresting belief we hold will prevent us from holding some interesting belief. But one might reasonably think there are significant costs, some of which are properly epistemic, associated with uninteresting beliefs even when we are running far below maximum capacity, as all of us surely are. It is appealing to think of our doxastic systems as analogous, in some ways, to an office filing system or the hard disk on a computer. As I well know, if either is loaded up with useless clutter, all sorts of problems arise. The useless material continually gets in the way, making it difficult, and perhaps impossible, to access and use the important material. The analog for a doxastic system of being unable to locate an important file in a cluttered office would be inability to remember something, which would entail failure to form a belief in an interesting true proposition and the consequent loss of V-value. An analog of the slow processing one experiences with an overly full hard drive might be something like finding it difficult to concentrate on answering an interesting question because one is distracted by recalled trivial facts and incidents.[11] And even if such problems could be avoided, it surely is not a good thing to accumulate clutter, be it physical, electronic or mental. If nothing else, any process of information acquisition and management that fosters such accumulation is grossly inelegant. (For goodness sakes, even the IRS lets us destroy records after three years!)

Consider two practices that deal exclusively with uninteresting propositions. The first, $\pi_{GH}$, is a good housekeeping practice. If we were to employ it, we would withhold belief in any propositions we consider that are uninteresting now and unlikely ever to become interesting and we would also jettison beliefs once it becomes clear that they will no longer be of any interest. The second practice, $\pi_{PR}$, is a pack rat practice. Those who employ it are led to acquire and retain true beliefs in large numbers of uninteresting propositions and to do so in an absolutely reliable way. Because neither of the ways of assigning V-values considered so far assigns values to beliefs in or withholdings of uninteresting true propositions, neither $\pi_{GH}$ nor $\pi_{PR}$ will have any direct impact on the total V-values or even the mean V-values of the doxastic systems of those who employ them. Nevertheless, although I could not say I am certain about this, I do think we would want to say that $\pi_{GH}$ is superior to $\pi_{PR}$. It is not implausible to think that at least part of the superiority is epistemic, and hence that the veritistic evaluation of the practices should capture this difference.

Perhaps we can account for the difference between $\pi_{GH}$ and $\pi_{PR}$ by looking at the indirect effects of the practices on the interesting beliefs persons employing them are able to form. As the analogies with cluttered offices and hard drives suggest, a person who does not waste cognitive resources on uninteresting propositions will almost certainly be able to do much better with respect to interesting propositions. Moreover, since $\pi_{PR}$ involves infallibility regarding uninteresting propositions, it is not a practice any of us could in fact employ. Practices we really could employ, and perhaps some of us actually do employ, that allow for the pack rattish accumulation of uninteresting beliefs will obviously involve the formation and retention of some false beliefs. Hence, usable practices that are similar to $\pi_{PR}$ will have a direct negative impact on the mean V-values of the beliefs of those who employ them. Perhaps these indirect and direct effects are sufficient to account for the epistemic superiority of good mental house-keeping over the accumulation of mental clutter, and the sense that there is more to be said in favor of the former and against the later arises from a confusion of pragmatic and properly epistemic considerations.

## IV. Withholding

I have suggested that it is appropriate to withhold belief in uninteresting propositions. I also believe that withholding is very significant in the case of interesting propositions. It is, in my opinion, very often epistemically best for us to withhold belief. Failure to withhold when the circumstances call for it, as I think they often do, can wreak havoc with a person's system of belief. Just think of gullibility and jumping to conclusions. Both involve failures to withhold. I would not think there is the slightest question about the epistemic evaluation of either practice: both are epistemically bad. Any significant system of epistemic evaluation ought to allow us to criticize such practices.[12] More generally, any such system ought to yield a favorable evaluation of withholding in many situations.

Consider a class **C** of propositions such that each proposition in **C** interests a person S and S takes the evidence to count equally for and against the proposition's truth.[13] Let us suppose, for simplicity, that the members of **C** are logically independent. Finally, let's suppose that S is an accurate assessor of evidence, where S is an accurate assessor of evidence just in case the proportion of true beliefs in the class of propositions S takes to be supported by the evidence to degree n ($0 \le n \le 1$) is equal to n.[14] So in this case, since S is an accurate assessor of evidence, half the propositions in

C are true and the other half false. What sort of practice would be epistemically best for S to follow in forming propositional attitudes towards the propositions in **C**? What doxastic practice for situations like this should society teach or otherwise seek to inculcate in individuals? Here are two possibilities: The daring practice, $\pi_D$, says, "Let the fact that you take the evidence to be perfectly balanced be damned—go ahead and believe the propositions in **C**!" The cautious practice, $\pi_C$, is to withhold judgment on all the propositions in **C**. I am very strongly inclined to say that the cautious policy is epistemically better. I expect you agree. Unfortunately, truth consequentialism, at least when Goldman's assignment of V-values is taken to provide the epistemic value theory, cannot endorse $\pi_C$ in preference to $\pi_D$. The reason for this is simple: $\pi_D$ and $\pi_C$ have the same mean V-values!

Here is the proof: If S were to employ $\pi_C$, S would withhold each proposition in **C**. S would also withhold the negations of all these propositions.[15] Half of the propositions S would withhold are true, so S will earn a V-value of .50 for each of these propositions. Goldman's assignment does not define a V-value for attitudes taken towards false propositions, so S's withholdings of these propositions would not count one way or the other. Since S would get a V-value of .50 for every proposition that figures in the computation, the mean V-value for employing $\pi_C$ would be .50. If S were to employ $\pi_D$, S would believe each proposition in **C** and disbelieve the negation of each proposition in **C**. Half of the propositions in **C** are true, and S would believe all of these true propositions. Half of the propositions in **C** are false. The negations of these propositions will be true, and S would disbelieve each of these propositions. S would earn a V-value of 1 for each of the true propositions from **C** S would believe and a V-value of 0 for each true negation of a proposition from **C** S would disbelieve. The number of beliefs for which S would earn a V-value of 1 equals the number of disbeliefs for which S would earn a V-value of 0. Again, no V-value is defined for attitudes towards false propositions, so these don't figure in the computation. Hence, the mean V-value for employing $\pi_D$ would be .50, the same as the mean V-value for $\pi_C$.

If we took this sort of V-value assessment seriously, we would have to approve even more daring doxastic practices. On the assumption that S is an accurate assessor of evidence, the *only* time a cautious practice of withholding would not have a mean V-value lower than a daring practice would be when the practice applies to a class of propositions like **C**, i.e., a class of propositions S takes the evidence to support to degree .5. If S is an accurate assessor of evidence, no matter how little evidence S thinks there is or how nearly balanced S takes it to be between a proposition's being true and it's being false, if S takes the evidence to tilt the scales the tiniest bit one way or the other, the policy of believing or disbelieving in accord with the slightest indication will have a higher mean V-value than a policy of withholding. Of course, the mean V-value of a policy of believing propositions that S takes to have only very slight support will only be very slightly greater than the mean V-value of withholding such propositions, but it will be greater.

I'm not clever enough mathematically to construct a general argument, but it is simple to convince oneself by working out examples. Here's one. Consider the class $C^*$ of propositions that S, who is an accurate assessor of evidence, takes the evidence to support to degree .6. For simplicity, let's suppose that there are 100 propositions in $C^*$ and compare practices $\pi_D$ and $\pi_C$, analogous to the practices described above, applied to the propositions in $C^*$. If S were to employ $\pi_C$ to form beliefs about the proposition in $C^*$, S would withhold all the propositions in $C^*$ and all the negations of these propositions. Of the 200 propositions S would withhold, there would be defined V-values only for the 100 that are true (60 from $C^*$ and 40 of the negations). These V-values would all be .50, so the mean V-value for $\pi_C$ would be .50. If S were to follow $\pi_D$, S would believe all the propositions in $C^*$. 60 of these beliefs would be true, and S would earn a V-value of 1 for each of these. The other propositions from $C^*$ are false, so the beliefs in these propositions would have no defined V-value. S would also disbelieve all the negations of the propositions in $C^*$. 60 of these propositions are false, so the disbeliefs in these would have no defined V-values and would not figure in the computation. But S would also disbelieve 40 true propositions. Each would have a defined V value of 0, so they do not add to the total V-value secured by employing $\pi_D$, but they do figure in the computation of mean V-value, lowering it to .60, which is still greater than the V-value for the cautious policy.

## V. Apportioning Degree of Belief

Apportioning degree of belief in a proposition to the degree of evidential support for the proposition can be seen as a kind of analog on the DB scheme of withholding when there is insufficient evidence on the trichotomous scheme. Goldman discusses apportioning degree of belief to the evidence, but does so in the context of criticizing the view that apportioning belief to the evidence is the sole intrinsic epistemic value. (Goldman 2001, pp. 34–37.) He argues that apportioning cannot be the sole value because it is unable to account for the epistemic virtues of evidence gathering. If our evidence for and against some proposition is equally balanced, we could fully attain the value of apportioning belief to the evidence by believing the proposition to degree .5. If we were to go out and acquire very strong evidence in favor of the proposition, e.g., by designing a clever experiment and carefully conducting it, we could again fully attain the value of apportioning belief to the evidence by increasing our degree of belief in the proposition to the requisite degree. The odd thing is that by designing and conducting the experiment and then adjusting our degree of belief accordingly, we would not manage to improve our epistemic situation at all—if the only epistemic value is apportioning degree of belief to the evidence. Our belief in the proposition would be no better apportioned to the evidence after the experiment than it would have been before. Hence, we are left with no epistemic rationale for gathering evidence. Goldman concludes, correctly in my view, that apportioning degree of belief to the evidence cannot be the fundamental epistemic value.

The question he does not raise, but in my view should, is whether we can provide a rationale for apportioning degree of belief to the evidence on the assumption that veritistic value is the fundamental epistemic value. I'll now try to show that just as we cannot adequately account for the epistemic value of withholding in terms of Goldman's assignment of V-values on the trichotomous scheme, we cannot account for the epistemic value of apportioning degree of belief to the evidence in terms of Goldman's assignment of V-values on the DB scheme.

Let's once again compare a conservative belief forming practice with a daring practice. The conservative practice, $\pi_C$, simply has us apportion degree of belief to what we take the evidence to be. The daring policy, $\pi_D$, has one give whole hearted assent when one takes the evidence to support the truth of a proposition, even if one takes that support to be very weak. I will argue that assessment of $\pi_C$ and $\pi_D$ in terms of V-value favors $\pi_D$ by working through a couple of examples. I make two simplifying assumptions, as I did above: (i) all the propositions involved are interesting, and (ii) S is an accurate assessor of evidence.

Consider the class of logically independent propositions, $C^{.8}$, that S takes the evidence to support to degree .8. To simplify computation, suppose there are 100 propositions in $C^{.8}$. Now let's evaluate and compare the performance of $\pi_C$ and $\pi_D$ as employed by S with respect to the propositions in $C^{.8}$. Since S is an accurate assessor of evidence, 80 of these propositions will be true and 20 false. If S were to employ $\pi_C$, S would believe all these propositions to degree .8. S would attain .8 units of V-value for each of the true beliefs, which would produce a total V-value of 64. There is no defined V-value for the beliefs S would form in the 20 false propositions in $C^{.8}$. However, on the DB scheme S would believe the negation of each of the propositions in $C^{.8}$ to degree .2. 20 of these negations would be true, so S's beliefs in them would each have a V-value of .2. This adds an additional V-value of 4. S would also believe each of the 80 false negations of the true propositions in $C^{.8}$ to degree .2, but once again, these false beliefs would have no defined V-value. So if S were employing $\pi_C$, the grand total V-value for S's 100 true beliefs, the beliefs for which a V-value is defined, would be 68. The mean V-value for $\pi_C$ would be .68.

If S were to follow $\pi_D$ instead, S would secure a V-value of 1 for each of the 80 true beliefs. But S would secure no additional V-value from beliefs in the true negations of the 20 false beliefs in $C^{.8}$, since S would hold each of these beliefs to degree 0. These 20 beliefs would count in the computation of the mean V-value for $\pi_D$, however, since they would have a defined V-value. As in the case of $\pi_C$ S's beliefs in false propositions do not figure in the computation of the mean V-value because they have no defined V-value. So if S were to employ $\pi_D$, S would attain a grand total V-value of 80, and the mean V-value for the practice would be .8. The difference between mean V-values for $\pi_C$ and $\pi_D$ in this case comes to .12 in favor of $\pi_D$.

Imagine now that S applies $\pi_C$ and $\pi_D$ to the class of propositions, $\mathbf{C^{.51}}$, that S takes the evidence to support to degree .51. To simplify computation let's again assume there are 100 logically independent propositions in $\mathbf{C^{.51}}$. Here the difference in mean V-values for $\pi_C$ and $\pi_D$ would be smaller, but it would still support $\pi_D$. If S were to follow $\pi_C$, S would have 51 true beliefs of degree .51, one for each of the true propositions in $\mathbf{C^{.51}}$. The total V-value for these beliefs would be 26.01. S would also believe to degree .49 the negation of each proposition in $\mathbf{C^{.51}}$. 49 of these beliefs would be true, yielding a total V-value of 24.01. S's false beliefs again would not figure in the computation. So by employing $\pi_C$ S would secure a total V-value of 50.02, and the mean V-value for $\pi_C$ applied to the propositions in $\mathbf{C^{.51}}$ would be .5002. The mean V-value for $\pi_D$ would be .51, since S would secure a V-value of 1 for each of the 51 true propositions in $\mathbf{C^{.51}}$ that S would believe to degree 1 and a V-value of 0 for the 49 true negations of the 49 false propositions in $\mathbf{C^{.51}}$ that S would believe to degree 0. No V-value is defined for the beliefs S would have in false propositions, 51 to degree 0 and 49 to degree 1, so these beliefs would not figure in the computation. The difference in the mean V-values now would be only .0098, but it still favors $\pi_D$.

In my opinion these two cases suffice to establish the pattern. At least if we are accurate assessors of evidence, daring, or perhaps we might better say, reckless belief forming practices that would have us believe propositions to a degree that far outstrips the positive evidential support we have for the propositions turn out to be veritistically superior to the practice of apportioning degree of belief to evidential support. But we almost certainly are not absolutely accurate assessors of evidence. Perhaps apportioning degree of belief to the evidence can be shown to be veritistically superior to reckless practice on the assumption that we are not accurate assessors of evidence.

As it turns out, apportioning is veritistically better than reckless practice if we are so badly mistaken about the evidence that more of the propositions we take the evidence to positively support are false than true. But that is the only situation where apportioning is veritistically better than the reckless strategy. If there are an equal number of true and false propositions in the class of propositions we take the evidence to support to some positive degree, apportioning and the reckless strategy will be veritistically equivalent. But if we are accurate about the evidence in only the minimal sense that there are more true than false propositions in the class of propositions we take the evidence to support to a given positive degree, then apportioning will be veritistically inferior to the reckless strategy for the propositions in that class. If we think the evidence is strongly indicative of the truth of some set of propositions, and more of them are true than false, but far fewer than our assessment of the evidence would suggest, then the reckless strategy is veritistically superior. And if we take the evidence to be only weakly indicative of the truth of some set of propositions, and many more of the propositions in this set are true than our assessment of the evidence would suggest, the reckless strategy is again veritistically superior. Hence, I do not think a friend of veritistic evaluation will get much traction by challenging the assumption that we are accurate assessors of evidence. Consider just how bizarre the following endorsement of apportioning would be: If you are a very inaccurate assessor of evidence, so much so that when you think the evidence supports some proposition it is in fact more likely to be false than true, then, and only then, it is best, epistemically, for you to apportion your degree of belief to the evidence. But this is the extent of the endorsement veritism can give to apportioning, at least as far as I have been able to determine.

## VI. Responses

I can think of two general approaches one might take to try to respond to my criticisms of veritism.[16] (1) One might agree with me that cautious practices such as withholding in the absence of sufficient evidence and proportioning degree of belief to the evidence are epistemically better than doxastic swashbuckling, but deny that I have succeeded in showing reckless doxastic practices are veritistically better than conservative practices. Unless my arguments involve some mistaken presupposition or I have made some sort of stupid arithmetical mistake, one would have to do this by trying to identify veritistic costs and benefits of conservative and daring policies that I have missed. (2) One might accept the veritistic evaluations of cautious and daring policies that I have presented, and deny that there is anything wrong with these evaluations—surprising as it may seem, doxastic swashbuckling is epistemically best. We've made an interesting discovery, not uncovered a ground for objection. In ethics, consequentialists have been far from squeamish about swallowing the unintuitive results of applying their theory, so perhaps we should expect truth consequentialists to have similarly tough palates. Still it would be best if truth consequentialists who opt for this approach could find some way of undermining or explaining away the intuition that withholding and proportioning degree of belief to the evidence are the epistemically best policies in the sorts of cases I have been considering. I can think of two ways in which they might try to do this. (A) They might argue that the intuition involves a different concept of epistemic evaluation from the one truth consequentialism is trying to capture.

(B) They might try to show that the intuition is a manifestation of a certain sort of systematic irrationality to which human beings are subject that has been well documented by cognitive psychologists. I will address these three possible lines of response in the subsections that follow.

## 1. Hidden Costs and Benefits

To show that withholding can have veritistic benefits that I have missed, one might ask us to consider how we would expect people who have employed the cautious policy to go on with their lives. Persons who employ it will retain a motivation to uncover the truth about many of the propositions they withhold. They will be motivated to continue their inquiries until they find sufficient evidence to decide the truth of the propositions one way or the other. And since such people can be expected to have relatively high standards of evidence, or at least higher than those of the doxastic swashbucklers, when they finally do form beliefs, they are likely to be true. Hence, we can expect that, with sufficient opportunity to continue inquiry and a little luck, such persons will eventually secure additional veritistic benefits in the form of true beliefs. Persons employing the daring policy will miss out on these benefits. Having formed beliefs, they will lack motivation to continue their inquiries regarding the propositions believed. In addition, they will miss the opportunity to correct any mistaken beliefs they might have formed following the daring policy and thereby acquire additional V-value. Hence, while the mean V-value for the daring policy may be greater than or equal to that for the cautious policy *at the point where I stopped my analysis*, we can expect that over time the V-value secured by the cautious policy will slowly improve, while that secured by the daring policy will remain static.

A likely story, but the future certainly need not play out in this way. For example, a person who employed the daring policy would have the time, energy and other resources saved by stopping inquiry to devote to other inquiries which may be expected to yield veritistic benefits. Having formed beliefs, the person will use those beliefs in arguments for other beliefs. The true beliefs thus formed will secure additional veritistic benefits in the form of other true beliefs. Finally, it is not as though the person who follows the daring policy is stuck with her mistakes forever. Proceeding on the basis of beliefs that are false, we would expect that the person would eventually run into some sort of problem, which would provide an occasion for catching the error. And each time she does catch an error, she will secure an additional unit of V-value as compared with the half unit secured by a person who forms a true belief after withholding. Correcting errors has a big veritistic up-side.

We cannot, therefore, count on the cautious policy securing more V-value than a daring policy over the long run, although I suppose it is possible that it will. Becaue of the uncertainty, this line of argument cannot provide a very secure defense of truth consequentialism, so let's move on to consider whether it is possible to undermine the intuition that the cautious policies of withholding without evidence and proportioning degree of belief to the evidence are epistemically better than the daring policies. As I've already indicated, I'll consider two ways in which one might try to do this.

## 2A. Internalist Justification

The first approach questions whether the intuition that the cautious practices are epistemically better than the daring practices employs the right concept of epistemic evaluation.[17] If one thinks in terms of a traditional conception of justification, for example, an internalist, deontological or responsibilist conception such as that extensively analyzed by R.M. Chisholm,[18] then it will seem perfectly obvious that in many instances cautious practices such as withholding and apportioning are epistemically best. But it has become increasingly clear that there is more than one concept of epistemic evaluation,[19] and in many cases it is devilishly difficult to keep these concepts straight in one's thinking. Try as one might, it is possible to make intuitive judgments about cases that one takes to be employing one of these concepts when these judgments are in fact colored by a different concept. We cannot just assume that truth consequentialists like Goldman are trying to work out an account of the traditional notion of justification. Indeed, there plenty of indications that they are trying to develop a different, but in their eyes very significant, conception of epistemic evaluation. Thus, they might claim that cautious practices just are not better, in the sense that interests them, than daring practices. The thought that cautious practices are better arises only because one has unwittingly slipped back into thinking in terms of the old-fashioned concept of justification.

It is hard to know how to defend against this kind of charge. My aim has been to remain more or less neutral regarding the exact concept of epistemic evaluation that is in play. I wanted to avoid asking whether Goldman's conception of veritistic value captures some sort of epistemic evaluation that especially interests me, so that I could instead consider whether Goldman's specific version of veritistic evaluation succeeds in producing any reasonable, interesting type of epistemic evaluation. I intentionally set out to avoid the sort of profitless confrontation of intuitions that arises when people are using different concepts of epistemic evaluation without realizing it. And so the point I have been trying to make is something like this: Whatever concept of epistemic evaluation one is using, there is something awfully fishy about that concept if it sanctions reckless doxastic practices of the sort I have considered.

In support of my contention that I have not slipped into using the traditional conception of justification, I might point out that in presenting my examples I never used the term 'justified' or one of its cognates. I did not ask whether beliefs formed as a result of employing one or another practice would count as knowledge, since the answers to that kind of question often turn on whether one thinks the relevant beliefs are justified. It is true that I have characterized the practices I do not think acceptable as daring and reckless. Perhaps I have thereby illicitly drawn upon ideas about epistemic responsibility which are closely associated with the traditional internalist conception of justification. But I do not think so. If withholding is recognized as a distinct propositional attitude and withholding true propositions is assigned a V-value that is not the lowest, presumably withholding is sometimes the best thing to do. I would think that, in essence, my argument regarding the trichotomous scheme turns only on the idea that if withholding is ever the thing to do, one such time is when we accurately take the evidence to count equally for and against a proposition. Similarly, if we are willing to think of belief as coming in degrees rather than as being an all or nothing affair, it seems we should accept that there are some circumstances where it is best to believe to something other than the maximum or minimum degree. My argument regarding the degree of belief scheme is based on the idea that one circumstance where it is obviously best to believe a proposition to some degree greater than .5 but far less than 1 is where we accurately take the evidence to favor the truth of the proposition very weakly. And so I deny that my argument turns on the illicit importation of any notion of epistemic responsibility or traditional conception of justification. But you be the judge.

## 2B. Prospect Theory

The second strategy for undermining the intuition that a cautious belief forming practice is preferable to a daring practice appeals to prospect theory.[20] If we assume that people are rational and that utility accurately captures what they value, then we would predict that when faced with a choice, subjects would choose the option that would maximize their expected utility.[21] But they do not always make such a choice. Indeed the option subjects take to be the best very often is not the one that maximizes expected utility. It turns out that what seems intuitively best to subjects deviates, and deviates systematically, from what we would calculate to be the most rational choice. Prospect theory is a psychological theory of choice designed by Daniel Kahneman and Amos Tversky (1979) to predict the choices empirical investigation has established that subjects actually make.

There is a way of looking at the intuitive judgments about what is epistemically best on which my arguments are based so that they might be explained—or explained away—in the same way that prospect theory explains why subjects intuitively choose options that are not rationally best. If my analysis has been correct, we might say that according to Goldman's version of a truth consequentialist framework, when S takes the evidence regarding $P$ to be equally balanced between $P$ and *not* $P$, the expected V-value, or to be cute, the expected veritility, of believing $P$ for S is equal to the expected veritility of withholding $P$.[22] Hence, on the assumption that S is rational and V-value is the only value at issue, one would predict that S would be indifferent between believing and withholding. Goldman's epistemological theory accords with this expectation insofar as it says that neither believing nor withholding is preferable in such a case, just as traditional theories of economic rationality would say that, in a similar case where monetary value replaces V-value, S would be indifferent between the two options. But my intuitive judgment is that withholding is preferable to believing. And I am pretty sure that I am not alone in thinking that withholding is the preferable choice in such a situation. So we have a case where one choice seems best intuitively, but given certain assumptions, e.g., that Goldman's V-value assignments accurately capture the values at stake, that option can be shown not to be the most rational, since the expected veritility of the two options is equal. I obviously think we should respond by holding fast to the intuitive judgment and reject at least one of the assumptions needed to argue that this judgment is not rational, and I would pick the assumption that Goldman's V-value assignments accurately capture the epistemic values at stake.

Here's how prospect theory might be used to explain away my intuitive preference. Prospect theory is a descriptive theory, not a normative theory. It predicts the choices people actually make; it does not tell us which choice is best in terms of securing what we value. Suppose we are presented a case where the only thing of value at issue is money. Cases of this sort used in psychological research often involve presenting subjects with a choice between various wagers at various odds. In many cases of this type, subjects judge that one choice is best, and this is predicted by prospect theory, but this choice does not maximize expected monetary payoff. In such a case, we might plausibly maintain that the choice that maximizes expected monetary payoff nevertheless is obviously the best or the rational choice, and that the choice subjects actually make is not rational. Thus, one can see prospect theory as charting the way in which actual choices systematically deviate from what is rational. If it could be shown that the intuitive judgment that withholding is better than believing in the case I considered above is exactly the judgment one would predict that a person would make on the basis of prospect theory, one might take this to provide grounds for writing off that intuitive judgment as a manifestation of a systematic, predictable deviation from rationality to which human beings are subject. There would then be no pressure to conclude that Goldman's framework should be altered so that the evaluations it yields capture this intuition.

Prospect theory is complicated. At the risk of oversimplification, I will discuss only two elements, which I think are sufficient for the purposes of this argument. According to prospect theory, the first phase of the choice process involves editing "to organize and reformulate the options so as to simplify subsequent evaluation and choice." (Kahneman and Tversky 1979, p. 274) A crucial step in the editing process involves fixing a neutral reference point with respect to which gains and losses are defined. According to prospect theory, the values that help determine choice are assigned to these gains and losses. The second element of prospect theory we must consider concerns the nature of the function that assigns values to gains and losses. Two features of this function are significant: (i) it is "generally concave for gains and commonly convex for losses" and (ii) it is "steeper for losses than for gains." (Kahneman and Tversky 1979, p. 279) Hence, if we are talking about dollars and cents, because of (i) the value of gaining a certain number of dollars typically will be less than twice the value of gaining half that number of dollars. And because of (ii) the value of a gain of a certain number of dollars typically will not equal the disvalue of the loss of that same number of dollars. The value of gaining that number of dollars will be less than the disvalue of losing that very same number of dollars.

Consider now the "choice" between believing and withholding. There would seem to be two natural ways of setting the reference point: one might set it with reference to believing a falsehood, as is suggested by Goldman's assignment of 0 V-value to this state, or one might set it with reference to withholding. If the reference point is taken to be believing a falsehood, then one might use prospect theory to account for the intuition favoring withholding by pointing to the concavity of the typical value function for gains. Because the function is concave, the value of believing the truth will be less than twice the value of withholding the truth. Hence, one would expect people to choose withholding—and a sure .5 gain in V-value—over a 50/50 chance of a V-value gain of 1. If the neutral reference point is instead set in terms of withholding, then the fact that the value function slopes more steeply for losses than for gains does the work, since it will follow from this that the value of a V-value gain of 1 will be less than the disvalue of a V-value loss of one. Hence, the total value of forming a belief which has a 50/50 chance of being true will be less than .5. Either way the reference point is set, prospect theory predicts that people will tend to favor withholding over believing in the sorts of cases under consideration, just as I have, even though the expected "veritility" of believing is equal to that of withholding. If my intuitive preference for withholding can be adequately explained in this way, it provides no reason to think withholding really is epistemically better than believing. Hence there is no reason for Goldman to alter his scheme for assigning V-values. I suspect a similar argument could be developed with respect to proportioning degree of belief to the evidence.

I am not sure how to respond to this line of argument. I am inclined to dig in my heels on the side of my intuition. But how much sense does that make? I might be doing the same sort of thing as a gambler who continues to think that the slot machine he has been playing has just got to hit soon, even after he has been shown that it works so that that each play is independent. I am not, however, generally incapable of recognizing cases where my intuitions play me false. In a case where bets of relatively small amounts of money are at stake, I am quite confident that the dollar amounts of the various gains and losses correspond to the values that are at stake. Hence when I am shown that the bet that seems best intuitively is not the bet that maximizes expected gain in dollars, I have no problem accepting that my intuition is mistaken. I readily conclude that the best bet is the one that maximizes expected monetary gain. Why then don't I draw the corresponding conclusion just as readily in the epistemic case? Perhaps it is because whether Goldman's V-values accurately capture the epistemic values that are at stake is the very question at issue, while the similar question about monetary values is not open in the case of simple bets. Not having confidence that the numbers correspond to the important values in the epistemic case, I am less inclined to give up intuition and side with the result of a calculation. I just cannot help but think about how strange the evaluations supported by the calculations are. Can we really accept that withholding a proposition is epistemically no better or worse than believing it when the evidence equally supports the proposition and its negation? Can we agree that it is epistemically best to believe a proposition, or believe it to the highest degree, when the evidence favors its being true only to the very slightest degree? The answers to these questions seem very obvious, but they are based on nothing more than intuition. Are such intuitions not of dubious worth in responding to an argument that calls those very intuitions into doubt? Maybe, but maybe not, for in a sense these are not the same intuitions we began with. These are now intuitions that have survived, as strong as ever, in the face of the effort to explain them away. They survive in a way the intuitions about the best bets do not. And so perhaps they should count for something after all.

## VII. Conclusion

Let's suppose that my argument has succeeded, that I have shown Goldman's system of V-values does not produce epistemic evaluations we can accept. How important is this result? It might seem that it is a narrow problem with the particular assignment of values Goldman has presented, a problem that can be solved by tinkering a bit with his numerical values. I think not. To avoid the problems I have presented, in effect what one would have to do is assign a value to believing a truth that is less than the disvalue assigned to disbelieving a truth. But any such choice will seem arbitrary unless some sort of principled rationale can be provided for it, and it is not at all clear what such a rationale might look like. A different assignment can hardly be justified solely on the ground that it avoids the problems I have identified. In addition, it is hard to avoid suspecting that as soon as specific numerical values are chosen it will be easy to show that they give rise to problems of their own. Hence, although it is surely somewhat hasty to make it just yet, it does seem a good bet that truth consequentialism, or at least Goldman's veritism, goes astray simply because it assigns specific values at all. But without a specific assignment of values, it is not clear how truth consequentialism will generate specific evaluations of cognitive practices. And so my hunch is that the problem I have uncovered is not narrow after all.[23]

## Notes

1. Throughout this paper I use 'cognitive practice', 'belief forming practice' and 'doxastic practice' interchangeably. I sometimes use the term 'policy' rather than 'practice', but this variation is stylistic as well; I make no distinction between practices and policies. My use of either 'practice' or 'policy' might suggest to some readers methods of forming beliefs that we choose to employ and self-consciously follow. This is not what I have in mind. For one thing, I do not want to commit myself to our having voluntary control over all or even some of our beliefs. I do not mean to commit myself to thinking that we have voluntary control, at least of any very direct kind, over the ways in which we go about forming beliefs. I definitely want to count as practices or policies ways of forming beliefs that we consciously monitor, but I also want to include ways of forming beliefs that we normally are not conscious of but can become conscious of, and even ways of forming beliefs that we cannot bring to consciousness. I also want to count as practices or policies ways of forming beliefs that we have in some sense chosen and trained ourselves to employ, but also ways that others have inculcated in us, ways that we have just picked up in the courses of our lives, and ways that we were born with or automatically acquired in the normal course of human development.
2. Goldman 1999 develops the proposal at length in Chapter 3 and then applies it to the evaluation of various social belief forming practices in the subsequent chapters. Goldman 2001 does not provide as detailed a presentation of the account of epistemic value, but the basic view figures importantly in the argument for the thematic unity of the epistemic virtues.
3. Notice that one can formulate a version of truth consequentialism that does not seem to require specific assignments of values. One could, e.g., claim that the best cognitive practice is the one that maximizes the number of true beliefs. However, it seems to me that such proposals often involve implicit views regarding the values of various cognitive states. For example, one obvious thing that seems to be presupposed by a truth consequentialism that looks

only to maximize the number of true belief is that false beliefs have no disvalue. If this were not so, the practice that maximizes true belief might not be as good as some other practice if the maximizing practice also produces many false beliefs while the other practice produces nearly as many true beliefs but no false beliefs.

4. Goldman cautions, however, that there is no easy way of translating between the trichotomous and DB schemes. Thus, e.g., one should not be misled into equating withholding a truth, which gets a V-value of 0.5, and believing a truth to degree .5, which also gets a V-value of 0.5.

5. Another simplifying assumption Goldman makes is bivalence.

6. I may be oversimplifying Goldman's view here. He explicitly allows that truth is not the only valuable thing, and even that truth is not the only value that is relevant to the assessment of cognitive practices. But he does claim that veritistic evaluation is the special job of epistemology. It is not, therefore, entirely clear whether Goldman holds that veritistic evaluation, and specifically evaluation with respect to V-values, can capture all epistemic evaluation. It is clear, however, that Goldman holds veritistic evaluation to be the most central and fundamental sort of evaluation for epistemology. And I think this is enough for the argument I am about to offer, since the difference between belief forming practices I will point out is the sort that should underwrite a difference in the most central kind of epistemic evaluation.

7. For stylistic reasons, I will often formulate points in terms of 'false belief.' This should usually be interpreted to mean "disbelief of a true proposition," a state to which Goldman assigns a V-value, rather than "belief of a false proposition," a state to which Goldman assigns no V-value.

8. I can only agree for the sake of the argument because I do not have a settled view regarding the treatment of uninteresting propositions. I find Goldman's idea that a person's system of belief is not worse for failing to contain all sorts of uninteresting truths plausible. But on the other hand, I am also drawn to the thought that any well formed true belief or item of knowledge is epistemically good, in some cases as good as possible, regardless of whether the proposition believed is interesting.

9. On the assumption that any proposition a person believes or disbelieves interests that person to some, perhaps very small, degree, there is no real problem here. It is not as though this assumption has no initial plausibility. After all, if the proposition did not interest the person at all, why would he or she go to the trouble of believing or disbelieving it? I know of nothing, however, at least in Goldman 1999, that indicates he makes this assumption. And I do not think the assumption stands up to reflection. In the course of a normal day, most of us take note of and cannot help but form beliefs about many completely trivial, uninteresting things. (Thankfully, most of these beliefs are very short lived.) For example, I might be looking for someone's number in the phone book. In the course of doing so, I notice all sorts of names. I see that there is a George Malone and a Harry Malone in the Dowagiac phone book as I run my finger down to the number I want, for Sean Malone. I see no reason to deny that I would believe that there is a George Malone in the phone book, at least for a minute or two after I read the name. But surely the proposition does not thereby

become interesting to me. And similarly for all the other trivial bits of information we pick up and just as quickly discard as we go through the day.

10. In the argument I am about to offer, and the other arguments I offer in this paper, I work in terms of the mean V-values of belief forming practices. I simply consider the number of true and false beliefs produced by the practices. Goldman 1999 prefers analysis in terms of change in V-value. I do not believe that working things out in terms of V-value change would alter the conclusions I reach; it would simply complicate the arguments. I would add to the specifications of the practices I consider that one begin withholding the propositions in question, and then proceed as the practice directs.

11. Goldman allows that speed of processing can be taken into account in the veritistic analysis of cognitive practices, so even if such distractions do not prevent one from forming true beliefs about what interests one in the end, the delay is a properly epistemic cost.

12. I am not here implying that gullibility cannot be criticized on veritistic grounds. It can, at least in certain circumstances. As will become clear, I will be trying to show that a certain sort of jumping to conclusions ends up getting a positive veritistic evaluation.

13. I do not here mean to be picky about what counts as evidence, e.g., by limiting it to other beliefs. Hence, such things as ordinary visual beliefs which we form quite automatically in response to our experience, and do not form on the basis of propositional evidence or reasons, could be members of **C**, since for my purposes here, I would simply count the visual experience as evidence. I would say the same thing about various memory beliefs, where I would count the experience of remembering as evidence. And similarly for introspective beliefs, intuitive beliefs, and beliefs about the positions of our own bodies.

14. I want it to be perfectly clear that I am introducing the concept of accurate assessment of evidence and defining it in a purely stipulative way solely for the purposes of this argument. I am not out to capture any intuitive, commonsense notion of accurate evidence or accurate assessment of evidence, nor do I care whether the concept I here define corresponds or fails to correspond with the technical concepts epistemologists, philosophers of science, cognitive scientists, or any other community of specialists might have of accurate evidence or the accurate assessment of evidence. Perhaps it would have been better to avoid any possible prior associations and consequent misunderstandings by designating the property I here define in some arbitrary way, e.g., as property Q, but I decided against that because the presentation seemed to read more smoothly as it is.

15. Goldman explicitly states he assumes that persons who believe a proposition *P* automatically disbelieve the negation of that proposition, *not P*. (Goldman 1999, p. 88) I assume he makes the corresponding assumption about withholding, i.e., that persons who withhold *P* also withhold *not P*.

16. I'll ignore a third strategy: Attempting to identify some third kind of doxastic practice that seems to be epistemically superior to both the conservative and daring practices I have considered and that can be shown to be veritistically superior to both practices. While I admit I would be very interested to hear of such a third practice, I will leave it to the friends of veritisism to try to discover one. My excuse for this, aside from sheer laziness and the lack of any good ideas

about where to look for such a practice, is that the discovery of such a practice would not get veritism completely off the hook, since veritism could still be charged with producing the wrong ranking of the practices. Of course, I would have to admit that if veritism succeeded in identifying the best practice, many would find mistakes in rankings further down the list easy to overlook.

17. Goldman said some things in correspondence responding to an initial formulation of my concerns about withholding that suggested this line of argument to me.
18. See Chisholm 1989 for one of many places where he works with this concept.
19. See Alston 1993 and DePaul 2000.
20. When I suggested this approach to Goldman in correspondence, he was not inclined to take it. But I think it represents an interesting line of argument that might have broad implications for epistemology, so I will present it.
21. I am obviously assuming that a certain instrumentalist account of practical rationality is correct for the sake of this argument.
22. At the risk of belaboring the obvious: S takes the probability of $P$ being true to be .5. So from S's perspective, if S withholds $P$, S has a .5 probability of a V-value payoff of .5 and a .5 probability of a V-value payoff of .5 for an expected veritility of .5. If S believes $P$, S has a .5 chance of a payoff of 1 and a .5 chance of a payoff of 0 for an expected veritility of .5.
23. I have had the benefit of discussing an earlier version of this paper with the Philosophy Department at Michigan State University. I have also profited from the opportunity to consider the excellent comments made on an earlier draft by Stephen Grimm and Christian Miller.

## References

Alston, W. (1993). "Epistemic Desiderata," *Philosophy and Phenomenological Research*.
Chisholm, R. M. (1989). *Theory of Knowledge* (3rd ed.). Englewood Cliffs, NJ: Prentice Hall.
DePaul, M. (2000). "Value Monism in Epistemology," Matthias Steup (ed.). *Knowledge, Truth, and Duty: Essays on Epistemic Justification, Responsibility, and Virtue*. Oxford: Oxford University Press.
Goldman, A. (1999). *Knowledge in a Social World*. Oxford: Clarendon Press.
———. (2001). "The Unity of the Epistemic Virtues," A. Fairweather and L. Zagzebski (eds.), *Virtue Epistemology: Essays on Epistemic Virtue and Responsibility*. Oxford: Oxford University Press.
Kahneman, D., and A. Tversky. (1979). "Prospect theory: an analysis of decision under risk," *Econometrica*.

*Philosophical Issues, 14, Epistemology, 2004*

# TRUE ENOUGH*

Catherine Z. Elgin
Harvard University

Epistemology valorizes truth. Sometimes practical, or prudential, or political reasons convince us to accept a known falsehood, but most epistemologists deny that we can have cognitively good reasons to do so. Our overriding cognitive objective, they maintain, is the truth, preferably the whole truth, and definitely nothing but the truth (Goldman 1999, p. 5; Lehrer 1986, p. 6; Bonjour 1985, p. 9). If they are right, then at least insofar as our ends are cognitive, we should accept only what we consider true, take pains to insure that the claims we accept are in fact true, and promptly repudiate any previously accepted claims upon learning that they are false. I suggest, however, that the relation between truth and epistemic acceptability is both more tenuous and more circuitous than is standardly supposed. Sometimes, I contend, it is epistemically responsible to prescind from truth to achieve more global cognitive ends.

At first blush, this looks mad. To retain a falsehood merely because it has epistemologically attractive features seems the height of cognitive irresponsibility. Allegations of intellectual dishonesty, wishful thinking, false consciousness, or worse immediately leap to mind. But science routinely transgresses the boundary between truth and falsehood. It smoothes curves and ignores outliers. It develops and deploys simplified models that diverge, sometimes considerably, from the phenomena they purport to represent. Even the best scientific theories are not true. Not only are they plagued with anomalies and outstanding problems, but where they are successful, they rely on laws, models, idealizations and approximations that diverge from the truth. Truth-centered epistemology, or *veritism*, as Alvin Goldman calls it, easily accommodates anomalies and outstanding problems, since they are readily construed as defects. The problem comes with the laws, models, idealizations, and approximations which are acknowledged not to be true, but which are nonetheless critical to, indeed constitutive of, the understanding that science delivers. Far from being defects, they figure ineliminably in the success of science. If truth is mandatory, much of our best science turns out to be epistemologically unacceptable and perhaps intellectually dishonest. Our predicament is this: We can retain the truth requirement and construe science either as cognitively defective or as non-cognitive, or we can reject, revise, or relax the truth requirement and remain cognitivists about, and fans of science.

I take it that science provides an understanding of the natural order. By this I do not mean merely that an ideal science *would* provide such an understanding or that in the end of inquiry science *will* provide one, but that much actual science has done so and continues to do so. I take it then that much actual science is cognitively reputable. So an adequate epistemology should explain what makes good science cognitively good. Too strict a commitment to truth stands in the way. Nor is science the only casualty. In other disciplines such as philosophy, and in everyday discourse, we often convey information and advance understanding by means of sentences that are not literally true. An adequate epistemology should account for this as well. A tenable theory is a tapestry of interconnected sentences that together constitute an understanding of a domain.[1] My thesis is that some sentences that figure ineliminably in tenable theories make no pretense of being true, but are not defective on that account. If I am right, theories and the understandings they embed have a more intricate symbolic structure than we standardly suppose. Nevertheless, I do not think that we should jettison concern for truth completely. The question is what role a truth commitment should play in a holism that recognizes a multiplicity of sometimes conflicting epistemological desiderata.

Consensus has it that epistemic acceptability requires something like justified and/or reliable, true belief. The justification, reliability, and belief requirements involve thresholds. '[O]ne may need to be confident enough and well enough justified and one's belief must perhaps derive from a reliable enough source, and be little enough liable to be false'(Sosa 2000, p. 2). But truth, unlike the other requirements, is supposed to be an absolute matter. Either the belief is true or it is not. I suggest, however, that the truth requirement on epistemic acceptability involves a threshold too. I am not saying that truth itself is a threshold concept. Perhaps such a construal of truth would facilitate treatments of vagueness, but that is not my concern. My point is rather that epistemic acceptability turns not on whether a sentence is true, but on whether it is true enough—that is, on whether it is close enough to the truth. 'True enough' obviously has a threshold.

I should begin by attempting to block some misunderstandings. I do not deny that (unqualified) truth is an intelligible concept or a realizable ideal. We readily understand instances of the (T) schema:

'Snow is white' is true ≡ snow is white
'Power corrupts' is true ≡ power corrupts
'Neutrinos have mass' is true ≡ neutrinos have mass

and so on. A disquotational theory of truth suffices to show that the criterion expressed in Convention (T) can be satisfied. One might, of course, want more from a theory of truth than satisfaction of Convention (T), but to make the case that the concept of truth is unobjectionable, a minimalist theory that evades the paradoxes suffices. Moreover, not only does it make sense to call a sentence true, we can often tell whether it is true. We are well aware not only that 'Snow is white' is true ≡ snow is white, but also that 'Newly fallen snow is white' is true. The intelligibility and realizability of truth, of course, show nothing about which sentences are true or which truths we can discover. Nevertheless, as far as I can see, nothing about the concept of truth discredits veritism. Since truth is an intelligible concept, epistemology can insist that only truths are epistemically acceptable. Since truth is a realizable objective, such a stance does not lead inexorably to skepticism. I do not deny that veritism is an available epistemic stance. But I think it is an unduly limiting one. It prevents epistemology from accounting for the full range of our cognitive achievements.

If epistemic acceptance is construed as belief, and epistemic acceptability as knowledge, the truth requirement seems reasonable. For cognizers like ourselves, there does not seem to be an epistemically significant gap between believing that $p$, and believing that $p$ is true. Ordinarily, upon learning that our belief that $p$ is false, we cease to believe that $p$. Moreover, we consider it cognitively obligatory to do so. One ought to believe only what is true. Perhaps a creature without a conception of truth can harbor beliefs. A cat, for example, might believe that there is a mouse in the wainscoting without believing that 'There is a mouse in the wainscoting' is true.[2] In that case, the connection between believing that $p$ and believing that $p$ is true is not exceptionless. But whatever we should say about cats, it does not seem feasible for any creature that has a conception of truth to believe that $p$ without believing that $p$ is true. If epistemic acceptance is a matter of belief, acceptance is closely linked to truth. Assertion is too. Although asserting that $p$ is not the same as asserting that $p$ is true, it seems plain that one ought not to assert that $p$ if one is prepared to deny that $p$ is true or to suspend judgment about whether $p$ is true; nor ought one assert that $p$ is true if one is prepared to deny that $p$ or to suspend judgment about whether $p$. Assertion and belief, then, seem committed to truth. So does knowledge. Whether or not we take knowledge to be equivalent to justified or reliably generated true belief, once we discover the falsity of something we took ourselves to know, we withdraw the claim to knowledge. We say, 'I thought I knew it, but I was wrong,' not 'I knew it, but I was wrong'.

Being skeptical about analyticity, I do not contend that a truth commitment is part of the meanings of 'belief,' 'assertion,' and 'knowledge'. But whatever the explanation, because the truth commitment tightly intertwines with our views about belief, assertion, and knowledge, it seems best to retain that connection and revise epistemology by making compensatory adjustments elsewhere. Once those adjustments are made, knowledge and belief turn out to be less central to epistemology than we standardly think. I do not then claim that it is epistemically acceptable to *believe* what is false or that it is linguistically acceptable to *assert* what is false. Rather, I suggest that epistemic acceptance is not restricted to belief (Cohen, 1992). Analogously, uttering or inscribing seriously and sincerely for cognitive purposes —call it 'professing'—is not limited to asserting. Understanding is often couched in and conveyed by symbols that are not, and do not purport to be, true. Where such symbols are sentential, I call them felicitous falsehoods. I contend that we cannot understand the cognitive contributions of science, philosophy, or even our ordinary take on things, if we fail to account for such symbols. Let's look at some cases:

*Curve smoothing*: Ordinarily, each data point is supposed to represent an independently ascertained truth. (The temperature at $t_1$, the temperature at $t_2, \dots$) By interpolating between and extrapolating beyond these truths, we expect to discern the pattern they instantiate. If the curve we draw connects the data points, this is reasonable. But the data rarely fall precisely on the curve adduced to account for them. The curve then reveals a pattern that the data do not instantiate. Veritism would seem to require accepting the data only if we are convinced that they are true, and connecting these truths to adduce more general truths. Unwavering commitment to truth would seem then to require connecting all the data points no matter how convoluted the resulting curve turned out to be. This is not done. To accommodate every point would be to abandon hope of finding order in most data sets, for jagged lines and complicated curves mask underlying regularities. Nevertheless, it seems cognitively disreputable simply to let hope triumph over experience. Surely we need a better reason to skirt the data and ignore the outliers than the fact that otherwise we will not get the kind of theory we want. Nobody, after all, promised that the phenomena would accommodate themselves to the kind of theory we want.

There are often quite good reasons for thinking that the data ought not, or at least need not be taken as entirely accurate. Sometimes we recognize that our measurements are relatively crude compared with the level of precision we are looking for. Then any curve that is within some δ of the evidence counts as accommodating the evidence. Sometimes we suspect that some sort of interference throws our measurements off. Then in plotting the curve, we compensate for the alleged interference. Sometimes the measurements are in fact accurate, but the phenomena measured are complexes only some of whose aspects concern us. Then in curve smoothing we, as it were, factor out the irrelevant aspects. Sometimes we have no explanation for the data's divergence from the smooth curve. But we may be rightly convinced that what matters is the smooth curve the data indicate, not the jagged curve they actually instantiate. Whatever the explanation, we accept the curve, taking its proximity to the data points as our justification. We understand the phenomena as displaying the pattern the curve marks out. We thus dismiss the data's deviation from the smooth curve as negligible.

*Ceteris paribus claims*: Many lawlike claims in science obtain only ceteris paribus.[3] The familiar law of gravity

$$F = Gm_1m_2/r^2$$

is not universally true, for other forces may be in play. The force between charged bodies, for example, is a resultant of electrical and gravitational forces. Nevertheless, we are not inclined to jettison the law of gravity. The complication that charge introduces just shows that the law obtains only ceteris paribus, and when bodies are charged, ceteris are not paribus. This is no news. 'Ceteris paribus' is Latin for 'other things being equal', but it is not obvious what makes for equality in a case like this. Sklar glosses it as 'other things being normal'(Sklar 1999, p. 702), where 'normal' seems to cash out as 'typical' or 'usual'. Then a 'ceteris paribus law' states what usually happens. In that case, to construe the law of gravity as a ceteris paribus law is to contend that although there are exceptions, bodies usually attract each other in direct proportion to the product of their masses and in inverse proportion to the square of the distance between them.

This construal does not always work. Some laws do not even usually hold. The law of gravity is one. Snell's law

$$n_1 \sin i = n_2 \sin r$$

which expresses the relation between the angle of incidence and the angle of refraction of a light ray passing from one medium to another, is a second.[4] As standardly stated, the law is perfectly general, ranging over every case of refraction. It is not true of every case, though; it obtains only where both media are optically isotropic. The law then is a ceteris paribus law. But it is not even usually true, since most media are optically anisotropic (Cartwright 1983, pp. 46–47). One might wonder why physicists don't simply restrict the scope of the law: 'For any two optically isotropic media, $n_1 \sin i = n_2 \sin r$'. The reason is Gricean: expressly restricting the scope of the law implicates that it affords no insight into cases where the restriction does not obtain. Snell's law is more helpful. Even though the law is usually false, it is often not far from the truth. Most media are aniso-tropic, but lots of them—and lots of the ones physicists are interested in— are nearly isotropic. The law supplies good approximations for nearly isotropic cases. So although explanations and calculations that rely on Snell's law do not yield truths, they are often not off by much.

The law is valuable for another reason as well. Sometimes it is useful to first represent a light ray as conforming to Snell's law, and later introduce 'corrections' to accommodate anisotropic media. If we were interested only in the path of a particular light ray, such a circuitous approach would be unattractive. But if we are interested in optical refraction in general, it might make sense to start with a prototypical case, and then show how anisotropy perturbs. By portraying anisotropic cases as perturbations, we point up affinities that direct comparisons would not reveal. The issue then is what sort of understanding we want. Showing how a variety of cases diverge from the prototypical case contributes valuable insights into the phenomenon we are interested in. And what makes the case prototypical is not that it usually obtains, but that it cleanly exemplifies the features we deem important.

*Idealizations*: Some laws never obtain. They characterize ideal cases that do not, perhaps cannot, occur in nature. The ideal gas law represents gas molecules as perfectly elastic spheres that occupy negligible space and exhibit no mutual attraction. There are no such molecules. Explanations that adduce the ideal gas law would be epistemically unacceptable if abject fidelity to truth were required. Since helium molecules are not dimensionless, mutually indifferent, elastic spheres, an account that represents them as such is false. If veritism is correct, it is epistemically unacceptable. But, at least if the explanation concerns the behavior of helium in circumstances where divergence from the ideal gas law is negligible (roughly, where temperature is high and pressure is low), scientists are apt to find it unexceptionable.

*Stylized facts* are close kin of ceteris paribus claims. They are 'broad generalizations, true in essence, though perhaps not in detail' (Bannock, et al. 1998, pp. 396–7). They play a major role in economics, constituting explananda that economic models are required to explain. Models of economic growth, for example, are supposed to explain the (stylized) fact that the profit rate is constant.[5] The unvarnished fact of course is that profit rates are not constant. All sorts of non-economic factors—such as war, pestilence, drought, and political chicanery—interfere. Manifestly, stylized facts are not (what philosophers would call) facts, for the simple reason that they do not obtain. It might seem then that economics takes itself to be required to explain why known falsehoods are true. (Voodoo economics, indeed!) This cannot be correct. Rather, economics is committed to the view that the claims it recognizes as stylized facts are in the right neighborhood, and that their being in the right neighborhood is something economic models need to account for. The models may show them to be good approximations in all cases, or where deviations from the economically ideal are slight, or where economic factors dominate non-economic ones. Or the models might afford some other account of their often being nearly right. The models may differ over what is actually true, or as to where, to what degree, and why the stylized facts are as good as they are. But to fail to acknowledge the stylized facts would be to lose valuable economic information (for example, the fact that if we control for the effects of non-economic interference such as wars, epidemics, and the president for life absconding with the national treasury, the profit rate is constant). Stylized facts figure in other social sciences as well. I suspect that under a less alarming description, they occur in the natural sciences too. The standard characterization of the pendulum, for example, strikes me as a stylized fact of physics. The motion of the pendulum that physics is supposed to explain is a motion that no actual pendulum exhibits. What such cases point to is this: The fact that a strictly false description is in the right neighborhood is sometimes integral to our understanding of a domain.

*A fortiori arguments from limiting cases*: Some accounts focus on a single, carefully chosen case and argue that what holds in that case holds in general. If so, it does no harm to represent the phenomena as having the features that characterize the exemplary case. Astronomy sometimes represents planets as point masses. Manifestly, they are not. But because the distance between planets is vastly greater than their size, their spatial dimensions can safely be neglected. Given the size and distribution of planets in the solar system, what holds for properly characterized point masses also holds for the planets. Another familiar example comes from Rawls. *A Theory of Justice* represents people as mutually disinterested. Rawls is under no illusion that this representation is accurate. He recognizes that people are bound to one another by ties of affection of varying degrees of strength, length, and resiliency. But, he believes, if political agents have reason to cooperate even under conditions of mutual disinterest, they will have all the more reason to cooperate when ties of affection are present. I do not want to discuss whether Rawls is right. I just want to highlight the form of his argument. If what holds for the one case holds for the others, then it does no harm to represent people as mutually disinterested. That people are mutually disinterested is far from the truth. Conceivably, no one on Earth is wholly indifferent to the fates of every other person. But if Rawls is right, the characterization's being far from the truth does not impede its function in his argument.

The foregoing examples show that in some cognitive endeavors we accept claims that we do not consider true. But we do not indiscriminately endorse falsehoods either. The question then is what makes a claim acceptable? Evidently, to accept a claim is not to take it to be true, but to take it that the claim's divergence from truth, if any, is negligible. The divergence need not be small, but whatever its magnitude, it can be safely neglected. We accept a claim, I suggest, when we consider it true enough. The success of our cognitive endeavors indicates that we are often right to do so. If so, a claim is acceptable when its divergence from truth is negligible. In that case it is true enough.

In practical, political, or prudential contexts, both the acceptance and the acceptability of falsehoods are widely recognized. One can accept, and be right to accept, the dean's latest dictum, if what matters is that the dean hath said it, not that it is true. But epistemic contexts are supposed to be different. Many epistemologists contend that when our concerns are cognitive we should accept only what we consider true. I disagree. I suggest that *to accept* that *p* is to take it that *p*'s divergence from truth, if any, does not matter. *To cognitively accept* that *p*, is to take it that *p*'s divergence from truth, if any, does not matter cognitively. The falsehood is 'as close as one needs for the purposes at hand' (Stalnaker 1987, p. 93). In what follows, I take 'acceptance' to mean 'cognitive acceptance'.

This raises a host of issues. Perhaps the most pressing is to say something about what I mean by 'cognitive'. A familiar line is that for a consideration to be cognitive is for it to aim at truth or to be truth conducive. Plainly, I can say no such thing. I suggest rather that a consideration is cognitive to the extent that it figures in an understanding of how things are. This is admittedly vague, but I am not sure that it is any worse than untethered remarks about truth-conduciveness and the like.

It might seem that my characterization just postpones the evil day (and not for long enough!), since 'an understanding of how things are' must itself be explicated in terms of truth or truth-conduciveness. To see the problem, compare three concepts—belief, thought, and understanding. Belief aims at truth. Roughly, a belief fulfills its goal in life only if it is true (Wedgwood, 2002; Adler, 2002). Thought, however, can be aimless. Musings, fantasies, and imaginings can be fully in order whether or not they are true. Understanding, the argument goes, is more like belief than like thought. Since there is such a thing as misunderstanding, understanding is subject to a standard of rightness. It has an aim. Misunderstanding evidently involves representing things as they are not. This suggests that the aim of understanding is truth. If so, it may seem, divergences from truth, even if unavoidable, are always cognitive defects.

The argument goes too fast. That misunderstanding involves representing things as they are not does not entail that whenever we represent things as they are not, we misunderstand them. At most it indicates that understanding is not indifferent to truth. But it does not follow that every sentence—or for that matter, any sentence—that figures in an understanding of how things are has its own truth as an objective. Understanding involves a network of commitments. It is not obvious that an aim of the network must be an aim of every, or indeed any, sentential node in the network. A goal of the whole need not be a goal of each of its parts. 'Understanding' is a cognitive success term but, in my view, not a factive. I do not expect these sketchy remarks to persuade anyone that I am right to loosen the tie between understanding and truth. My hope is that they are enough to persuade you that the jig is not yet up, that a willing suspension of disbelief is still in order.

Let us turn then to acceptance. To accept that *p*, I said, is to take it that *p*'s divergence from truth, if any, is negligible. In that case, *p* is true enough. Whether this is so is manifestly a contextual matter. A sentence can be true enough in some contexts but not in others. A variety of factors contribute constraints. Background assumptions play a role. 'A freely falling body falls at a rate of 32 ft./sec.$^2$' is true enough, assuming that the body is within the Earth's gravitational field, that nothing except the Earth exerts a significant gravitational force on the body, that the effects of non-gravitational forces are insignificant, and so on. But even when these assumptions are satisfied, the formula is not always true enough, since gravity varies slightly with longitude. Sometimes it matters where in the gravitational field the freely falling body is. Whether '$G = 32$ ft./sec.$^2$' is true enough depends on what we want the formula for, what level of precision is needed for the calculation or explanation or account it figures in. There is no saying whether a given contention is true enough independently of answering, or presupposing an answer to the question 'True enough for what?' So purposes contribute constraints as well. Whether a given sentence is true enough depends on what ends its acceptance is supposed to serve.

Function is critical too. If to accept that *p* is simply to take it that *p*'s divergence from truth does not matter, it might seem that we accept all irrelevant propositions. None of my projects, cognitive or otherwise, is affected by the truth or falsity of the claim that Ethelred the Unready was a wise leader. So its divergence from truth, if any, does not matter to me. Since acceptance can be tacit, the fact that I have never considered the issue is not decisive. Nevertheless it seems wrong to say that my indifference makes the claim true enough. The reason is that the contention is idle. It performs no function in my cognitive economy. Owing to my indifference, there is no answer to the question 'True enough for what?'

Context provides the framework. Purposes fix the ends. Function is a matter of means. The sentences that concern us tend not to have purposes or functions in isolation. Rather, they belong to and perform functions in larger bodies of discourse, such as arguments, explanations, or theories that have purposes. In accepting a sentence, then, we treat it in a given context as performing a function in a body of discourse which seeks to achieve some end. Whether '$G = 32$ ft./sec.$^2$' is acceptable depends on whether the body of discourse it figures in serves its cognitive purpose— whether, that is, it yields the understanding of the domain that we seek.

A statement's divergence from truth is negligible only if that divergence does not hinder its performing its cognitive function. Hence whether a contention is true enough depends not just on its having a function, but on what its function is—on what role it plays in the account it belongs to. To determine whether a statement is true enough, we thus need to identify its function. It might seem that for cognitive purposes only one function matters. If the criterion for felicity is being true enough, one might think, the function of all felicitous falsehoods is to approximate. There is, as it were, a tacit 'more or less' in front of all such claims. This will not do.

One reason is that the proposal is not sufficiently sensitive. Not all approximations perform the same function. Some are accepted simply because they are the best we can currently do. They are temporary expedients which we hope and expect eventually to replace with truths. We improve upon them by bringing them closer to the truth. Such approximations are, in Sellars's terms, promissory notes that remain to be discharged. The closer we get to the truth, the more of the debt is paid. They are, and are known to be, unsatisfactory. But not all approximations have this character. Some are preferable to the truths they approximate. For example, it is possible to derive a second-order partial differential equation that exactly describes fluid flow in a boundary layer. The equation, being non-linear, does not admit of an analytic solution. We can state the equation, but cannot solve it. This is highly inconvenient. To incorporate the truth into the theory would bring a line of inquiry to a halt, saying in effect: 'Here's the equation; it is impossible to solve.' Fluid dynamicists prefer a first-order partial differential equation, which approximates the truth, but admits of an analytical solution (Morrison, 1999, pp. 56–60). The solvable equation advances understanding by providing a close enough approximation that yields numerical values that can serve as evidence for or constraints on future theorizing. The approximation then is more fruitful than the truth. There is no hope that future inquiry will remedy the situation, for it is demonstrable that the second-order equation cannot be solved numerically, while the first-order equation can.[6] That reality forces such a choice upon us may be disappointing, but under the circumstances it does not seem intellectually disreputable to accept and prefer the tractable first-order equation. One might say that acceptance of the first-order approximation is only practical. It is preferable merely because it is more useful. This may be so, but the practice is a cognitive one. Its goal is to understand fluid flow in boundary layers. In cases like this, the practical and the theoretical inextricably intertwine. The practical value of the approximation is that it advances understanding of a domain. A felicitous falsehood thus is not always accepted only in default of the truth. Nor is its acceptance always 'second best'. It may make cognitive contributions that the unvarnished truth cannot match.

Moreover, not all felicitous falsehoods are approximations. Idealizations may be far from the truth, without thereby being epistemically inadequate. Political agents are not mutually disinterested. They are not nearly mutually disinterested. Nor is it the case that most political agents are mutually disinterested. There is no way I can see to construe Rawls's model as approximately true. Nevertheless, for Rawls's purposes, the characterization of political agents as mutually disinterested is felicitous if the features it highlights are constitutive of fair terms of cooperation underlying the basic structure of a democratic regime. There is no reason to think that in general the closer it is to the truth, the more felicitous a falsehood.

I suggest that felicitous falsehoods figure in cognitive discourse not as mistaken or inaccurate statements of fact, but as fictions. We are familiar with fictions and with reasoning about fictions. We regularly reason within the constraints dictated by a fiction, inferring, for example, that Hamlet may not have been mad, but Ophelia surely was. We also reason (with more trepidation) from a fiction to matters of fact. We may come to see a pattern in the facts through the lens that a fiction supplies. For example, we might understand the contemporary youth gang conception of being 'dissed' by reference to the wrath of Achilles at Agamemnon's affront.[7] What is needed then is an account of how fictions can advance understanding.

David Lewis (1983) interprets fictional statements as descriptions of other possible worlds. We understand them in the same way that we understand ordinary statements of fact. For example, we understand the Sherlock Holmes stories in the same way we understand histories of Victorian England, the crucial difference being that the histories pertain to the actual world, while the stories pertain to other possible worlds. Lewis's realism about possible worlds is hard to countenance, but we need not enter into debates about it here. For even if we accept his metaphysics, a problem remains. It is puzzling how knowing what happens in another possible world can afford any insight into what happens in this world. Lewis measures the proximity of possible worlds in terms of similarity (Lewis 1973). The closest possible worlds are the ones most similar to the actual world. But even if one thinks that there is a non-question-begging way to assess the relative similarity of different possible worlds, the gap remains. It is hard to see how the knowledge that a nearby world is populated by rational economic agents should contribute to our understanding of the economic behavior of actual human agents.

Kendall Walton (1990) construes fiction as make-believe. To understand a fiction is to make believe or pretend that it is true. Stephen Yablo uses Walton's account to underwrite fictionalism in the philosophy of mathematics (1998, 2002). We can, Yablo maintains, avoid ontological commitment to mathematical entities by construing mathematics as an elaborate, highly systematic fiction. Then in doing mathematics, we make believe that there are such entities and make believe that they are related to one another in the ways the theorems say. Although at first glance this seems promising, it faces two serious problems. First, what it is to pretend is by no means clear. Exactly how one can pretend that power sets or cube roots exist if they do not, is not obvious. Second, the problem we saw with Lewis's theory also plagues Walton and Yablo. It is not at all clear how a pretense illuminates reality—how, for example, pretending that human beings are rational economic agents provides any insight into actual human economic behavior.

Philip Kitcher (1993) suggests that scientific idealizations are stories whose referents are fixed by stipulation. The scientific statements involving the idealizations are true by convention. The gap remains. If a story is to advance scientific understanding we need to know the connection between the story and the facts. Otherwise, the realization that certain relations among pressure, temperature, and volume are true by stipulation in the story of the ideal gas leaves us in the dark about the relations among pressure, temperature, and volume in actual gases.

The gap can be bridged by appeal to exemplification, the device by which samples and examples highlight, exhibit, display, or otherwise make manifest some of their features (Goodman 1968, pp. 45–67). To make this out requires a brief discussion of the device. A commercial paint sample consists of a patch of color on a card. The patch is not merely an instance of the color, but a telling instance—an instance that exemplifies the color. By so doing, the sample equips us to recognize the color, to differentiate it from similar shades. The sample then affords epistemic access to the color. Although the patch on the sample card has a host of other features—size, shape, location, and so on—it standardly does not exemplify them. Exemplification is selective. It brings out some features of an exemplar by overshadowing, downplaying, or marginalizing others. Nothing in the nature of things dictates that the patch's color is worthy of selection, but its shape is not. What, if anything, an item exemplifies depends on its function. The very same item might perform any of a variety of functions. The patch on the sample card could be used to teach children what a rectangle is. In that case, it would exemplify its shape, not its color. The sample card could be used as a fan. Then the patch would not exemplify at all. Exemplification is not restricted to commercial and pedagogical contexts. Whatever an item exhibits, highlights, or displays, it exemplifies. A poem might exemplify its rhyme scheme, its imagery, or its style. A water sample might exemplify its mineral content, its flavor, or its impurities. Exemplification, I have argued elsewhere, is ubiquitous in art and science (Elgin 1996, pp. 171–183).

Treating paint samples as paradigmatic exemplars may encourage the idea that exemplified features are all like expanses of color—homogeneous qualities spread out before us, lacking depth and complexity, hence able to be taken in at a glance. Many are not like that. Pick up a rock containing iron ore. It might serve as a sample of iron, or of hematite, or of something that bears a striking resemblance to your high school algebra teacher. It can exemplify such features only where certain background assumptions are in place. Not just anyone looking at the rock could tell that it exemplified these features.

Moreover, although in principle any item can serve as an exemplar and any feature can be exemplified, a good deal of effort may be required to bring about the exemplification of a recondite feature. Some of that effort is mental. Just as we ignore the shape of the paint sample and focus on the color, we can ignore the fact that the rock looks like your algebra teacher and focus on its hardness. This is a start. But some irrelevant features so intricately intertwine with relevant ones that more drastic measures are called for. If we seek to exemplify recondite features of iron, mental agility alone may not be enough to bracket the effects of other minerals in the rock. So we refine the ore and filter out the impurities. The result of our efforts is pure iron. It is a product of a good deal of processing[8] which eliminates complicating factors and brings to the fore characteristics that are hard to detect and difficult to measure in nature. To facilitate the exemplification of the feature of interest, we do not just mentally sideline features we consider irrelevant, we physically remove some of them.

Even then, we do not just contemplate the bit of iron as we might a paint sample. We subject it to a variety of tests. We seek to produce circumstances where the features of interest stand out. We not only investigate the iron's behavior in standard conditions, we study what happens in extreme conditions—very high or low pressure or temperature, in a vacuum, under intense radiation, and so forth. Although we recognize that the test conditions do not ordinarily (or perhaps ever) obtain in nature, we take it that the behavior of the refined metal in the test conditions discloses something about the natural order. If so, by understanding what happens in the lab, we can understand something of what happens in the world. The connection is, of course, indirect. It involves a complicated extrapolation from situations and materials that are highly artificial and carefully contrived. One might argue that the lab itself is a fictional setting and the conclusions we draw about nature on the basis of our laboratory findings are projections from fiction to fact. I don't quite want to say that (although I suspect that Nancy Cartwright does). But I do want to point out that experimentation involves a lot of stage setting.

There is a tendency to think of experiments as processes that generate information, hence as ways to find things out. This of course is true. But it is worth noting that an experiment is not like an oracle,[9] or an anchorman, or a fortune cookie. It does not just issue a report stating its results. It displays them. It shows what happens to the magnetic properties of iron in conditions near the melting point. The experiment exemplifies its results.

No matter how carefully we set the stage, irrelevancies remain. We do not and ought not read every aspect of the experimental result back onto the world. Not only are there irrelevant features, there are issues about the appropriate vocabulary and level of precision for characterizing what occurs. The fact that the experiment occurred in Cleveland is unimportant. The fact that the sample has a certain mass or lattice structure may or may not be significant. The fact that the temperature is above $770°$ C may matter, while the fact that it was above $790°$ C does not. Some features of the iron in the experimental situation are telling features. Others are not. The telling features are the ones that the experiment discloses or makes manifest. By exemplifying certain features, the experiment brings them to light and affords epistemic access to them. That is its cognitive contribution. Other features, though equally real, are not exemplified. The experiment embodies an understanding of the phenomenon in question through its exemplification of telling features. By making these features manifest, it affords an understanding of the phenomenon.

If the cognitive contribution of an exemplar consists in the exemplification of select features, then anything that exemplifies exactly those features can, in a suitable context, make the same contribution. Return for a moment to the paint sample. I spoke of it as though it is a sample *of paint*, a telling instance of the stuff you might use to paint the porch. This is not true. The sample on the card does not consist of paint, but of an ink or dye of the same color as the paint whose color it exemplifies. If the sample were supposed to exemplify the paint itself, or the chemical features of the paint, the fact that it is not paint or has a different chemical composition would be objectionable. But since it exemplifies only the color, all that is needed is something that is the same color as the paint. The exemplar need not itself be paint. Similarly in scientific cases. Consider a DNA molecule that exemplifies its molecular structure. Anything that exemplifies the same structure has the capacity to perform the same function in our understanding of DNA. No more than the paint sample needs to consist of paint, does the exemplar of DNA's molecular structure need to consist of DNA. A schematic model that exemplifies the same features but has a different material (or even immaterial) substrate could to the job.

Here is where felicitous falsehoods enter the picture. Something other than paint can serve as a paint sample, affording epistemic access to a color also instantiated by the paint. Something other than a molecule can exemplify molecular structure, thereby affording epistemic access to a structure also instantiated by the molecule. A felicitous falsehood then is a fiction that exemplifies a feature in a context where the exemplification of that feature contributes to understanding. The utility of such a falsehood is plain. It is sometimes inconvenient, difficult, or even impossible to bring it about that the phenomena exemplify all and only the features that interest us. (DNA molecules are very small, charged pions are short lived.) If we introduce a falsehood that exemplifies those features—a bigger, longer-lasting model, for example—we can highlight them and display their significance for the understanding of the phenomenon in question. By exemplifying features it shares with the phenomena, a felicitous falsehood affords epistemic access to how things actually are. The camel's nose is now officially inside the tent.

There is more than one role that such fictions can play. Some serve as points of reference. We understand things in terms of them. In the simplest cases, like the model displaying the helical structure of the DNA molecule, they are simply schemata that exemplify factors they share with the phenomena they concern. They qualify as fictions because they diverge from the phenomena in unexemplified properties. (DNA molecules are not made of tinker toys.) In other cases, the connection to the facts is less direct. No real gas has the properties of the ideal gas. The model is illuminating though, because we understand the properties of real gases in terms of their deviation from the ideal. In such cases, understanding involves a pattern of schema and correction. We represent the phenomena with a schematic model, and introduce corrections as needed to closer accord with the facts. Different corrections are needed to accord with the behavior of different gases. The fictional ideal then serves as a sort of least common denominator that facilitates reasoning about and comparison of actual gases. We 'solve for' the simple case first, then introduce complications as needed.

Acknowledging the role of corrections might seem to suggest that the detour through fictions is just a circuitous route to the truth. Rather than a simple true description of the behavior of neon, we get a complicated truth that makes reference to deviations from some ideal. But the full cognitive contribution of the exercise resides in the truth, not the fiction. I don't think this is right for several reasons. The first is that sometimes the corrections that would be needed to yield a truth are unnecessary or even counterproductive. A fortiori arguments from limiting cases succeed because the corrections are unnecessary. If a consideration holds for one case, even if that case is a fiction, it holds for all. The multiple and complicated ways actual cases diverge from the fictive ideal make no difference. If Rawls's argument is sound, 'correcting for' ties of affection just muddies the waters. Nor is this the only case where fidelity to the facts can prove a hindrance. It follows from the ideal gas law that as volume goes to zero, pressure becomes infinite. This would not happen. Given a fixed number of molecules, pressure increases as volume decreases—not to infinity, but only to the point where the container explodes. No one of course denies this. But to understand what would happen in the limit, we need to prescind from such material inconveniences and pretend that the walls of the container are infinitely strong. We need then to introduce not corrections that bring us back to the facts, but further idealizations. A second reason is that the requisite corrections often yield not truths, but more refined models. They supplant one falsehood with another. A third reason is that even where corrections yield truths, the fiction may be more than a *façon de parler*. It can structure our understanding in a way that makes available information we would not otherwise have access to. If, e.g., we draw a smooth curve that skirts the data, and construe the data as a complex of relevant and irrelevant factors (signal and noise), or construe a transaction in terms of an economic model overlaid with non-economic factors which skew the outcome, we impose an order on things, highlight certain aspects of the phenomena, reveal connections, patterns and discrepancies, and make possible insights that we could not otherwise obtain (Dennett 1991). We put ourselves in a position to see affinities between disparate occurrences by recognizing them as variations on a common theme.

Still, to say that felicitous falsehoods figure ineliminably in our understanding of certain phenomena is not to say that without them we would have no understanding whatsoever of those phenomena. Even without Snell's law, inspection and instantial induction would provide some insight into what happens when light passes between air and water, or between any other two specified media. What we would lack is a systematic understanding of how the several cases are alike. Felicitous falsehoods configure a domain, enabling us to characterize the phenomena in ways that would otherwise be unavailable. When, for example, we can construe seemingly divergent phenomena as variants of a common scheme, or as perturbations of a regular pattern, or as deviations from a simple norm, we see them and their relations to one another in a new light. We can discern systematic interconnections that direct inspection of the facts would not reveal. The fictions and the configurations of the domains that they engender provide conceptual resources for representing and reasoning about the phenomena in new and sometimes fruitful ways.

If I am right, not every theory is a conjunction of sentences, all of which are supposed to be true. Rather, a theory may be composed of both factual and fictional sentences, and the fictional sentences may play any of several different roles. This means that to understand what a theory conveys, and to understand the phenomena in terms of the theory requires sensitivity to the different roles the different sentences play. And to assess a theory requires determining whether the component sentences are true enough for the parts they are assigned to play. Yablo is investigating the metaphysical implications of the idea that fictions infuse even our most fundamental theories (Yablo 1998; 2002). I want to underscore the epistemological implications. One obvious consequence is that it is not plausible to think of an acceptable theory as a mirror of nature. Even if the goal of a theory is to afford an understanding of a range of facts, it need not approach or achieve that goal by providing a direct reflection of those facts.

I have argued that a variety of components of cognitively acceptable theories neither are nor purport to be true. Rather, they are fictions that shed light on the phenomena they concern. They thereby contribute to our understanding of those phenomena. Even if my account makes sense of models and idealizations in science, a worry remains. My position threatens to make the world safe for postmodernist claptrap. If truth is not required for epistemic acceptability, why isn't a flagrantly false account acceptable? What is the objection to claiming that a theory attesting to the healing powers of crystals is as acceptable as the theories constituting mainstream crystallography? We seem to lose a valuable resource if we can't simply say, 'Because it is false!' My seemingly wimpy requirement that an acceptable account must yield an understanding of how things are gives us what we need. An account that yields such an understanding must accommodate the facts in a domain. The accommodation may be indirect. Strictly false idealizations may be deployed. Detours through stylized facts may be made. The justification for the falsehoods is that they figure in accounts that make sense of the facts. A cognitively acceptable account sheds light on its subject. Where felicitous falsehoods are involved, the light may be oblique.

A theory can claim to make sense of a range of facts only if it is factually defeasible—only if, that is, there is some reasonably determinate, epistemically accessible factual arrangement which, if it were found to obtain, would discredit the theory. A felicitous falsehood is acceptable only if the theory or system of thought it belongs to accommodates the epistemically accessible facts. Exactly what this requires needs to be spelled out. The usual considerations about evidence, simplicity, scope, and so forth come into play. Even though some of the sentences in a theory are not supposed to be true, the way the world is constrains the acceptability of the theory they figure in. If, for example, evidence shows that friction plays a major role in collisions between gas molecules, then unless compensating adjustments are made elsewhere, theories that model collisions as perfectly elastic spheres will be discredited. An acceptable theory must be at least as good as any available alternative, when judged in terms of currently available standards of cognitive goodness. So such a theory would also be discredited by a theory that better satisfied those standards. Neither a defeated nor an indefeasible theory is tenable. Because it is indifferent to evidence, claptrap is indefeasible. Hence it is untenable. I said earlier that even in theories that include felicitous falsehoods truth plays a role. We see now what the role is. A factually defeasible theory has epistemically accessible implications which, if found to be false, discredit the theory. So a defeasible theory, by preserving a commitment to testable consequences retains a commitment to truth. My account then does not turn science into a genre of fiction. Quine said that the sentences of a theory face the tribunal of experience as a corporate body (Quine, 1961, p. 41). Although he recognized that not all the members of the corporation could be separately tested against experience, he probably believed that all were supposed to be fine, upstanding truths. I suggest that this is not so. An acceptable theory must make its case before the tribunal of experience. But the members of the corporation are more various and some a bit shadier than Quine suspected.

## Notes

* I would like to thank Jonathan Adler, Nancy Nersessian, Amelie Rorty, Robert Schwartz, Bas van Fraassen, Stephen Yablo, and members of my audiences at Bryn Mawr College, Tufts University, and the 2003 Rutgers Epistemology Conference for helpful comments on earlier drafts of this paper.

1. I use the term 'theory' broadly, to comprehend the ways mature sciences and other disciplines account for the phenomena in their domains. Under my usage, a physical theory would include its models rather than being distinct from them.
2. I do not have strong intuitions about this case, but I do not think it is clearly wrong to say that the cat has such a belief.
3. Whether so-called ceteris paribus laws are really laws is a subject of controversy. See, for example, *Erkenntnis* 57, 2002, for a range of papers on the issue. Although for brevity I speak of them as laws, for my purposes, nothing hangs on whether the generalizations in questions really are laws, at least insofar as this is an ontological question. I am interested in the role such generalizations play in ongoing science. Whether or not they can (in some sense of 'can') be replaced by generalizations where all the caveats and restrictions are spelled out, in practice scientists typically make no effort to do so. Nor, often, do they know (or care) how to do so.
4. $i$ and $r$ are the angles made by the incident beam to the normal and $n_1$ and $n_2$ are the refractive indices of the two media.
5. 'The profit rate is the level of profits in the economy relative to the value of capital stock' (Bannock et al. 1998, p. 397).
6. Conceivably, of course, the equations in question will be superceded by some other understanding of the subject, but the fact that the equation we consider true does not have an analytical solution provides no reason to think so. Nor does it provide reason to think that the considerations that supersede it will be mathematically more tractable, much less that in the long run science will be free of all such irksome equations.
7. I am indebted to Amelie Rorty for this example.
8. This is why Nancy Cartwright thinks the laws of physics lie. The laws are developed on the basis of, and are strictly true only of, the processed samples, not their naturally occurring counterparts.
9. Actually, of course, I don't know how oracles are supposed to operate. I have always assumed that they simply emit true sentences like 'Socrates is the wisest of men.'

## References

Adler, Jonathan. (2002) *Belief's Own Ethics*, Cambridge, MA: MIT.
Bannock, Graham, R.E. Baxter, Evan Davis. (1998) *Dictionary of Economics*, New York: John Wiley and Sons.
Bonjour, Laurence. (1985) *The Structure of Empirical Knowledge*, Cambridge, MA: Harvard.
Cartwright, Nancy. (1983) *How the Laws of Physics Lie*, Oxford: Oxford.
Cohen, L. Jonathan. (1992) *An Essay on Belief and Acceptance*, Oxford: Clarendon.
Dennett, Daniel. (1991) 'Real Patterns,' *Journal of Philosophy* 88: 27–51.
Elgin, Catherine Z. (1996) *Considered Judgment*, Princeton: Princeton.
Goldman, Alvin. (1999) *Knowledge in a Social World*, Oxford: Clarendon.
Goodman, Nelson. (1968) *Languages of Art*, Indianapolis: Hackett.
Kitcher, Philip. (1993) *The Advancement of Science*, Oxford: Oxford.
Lehrer, Keith. (1986) 'The Coherence Theory of Knowledge,' *Philosophical Topics* 14: 5–25.
Lewis, David. (1983) 'Truth in Fiction,' *Philosophical Papers I*, Oxford: Oxford, pp. 261–281.
———. (1973) *Counterfactuals*, Cambridge, MA: Harvard.

Morrison, Margaret. (1999) 'Models as Autonomous Agents,' *Models as Mediators*, ed. Mary S. Morgan and Margaret Morrison, Cambridge: Cambridge, pp. 38–65.

Quine, W. V. (1961) 'Two Dogmas of Empiricism,' *From a Logical Point of View*, New York: Harper & Row, pp. 20–46.

Sklar, Lawrence. (1999) 'Philosophy of Science,' *Cambridge Dictionary of Philosophy*, ed. Robert Audi, Cambridge: Cambridge, pp. 700–704.

Sosa, Ernest. (2000) 'Skepticism and Contextualism, *Skepticism*, ed. Ernest Sosa and Enrique Villanueva, Boston: Blackwell, pp. 1–18.

Stalnaker, Robert. (1987) *Inquiry*, Cambridge, MA: MIT Press.

Walton, Kendall. (1990) *Mimesis as Make-Believe*, Cambridge, MA: Harvard.

Wedgwood, Ralph. (2002) 'The Aim of Belief,' *Philosophical Perspectives* 16: 267–297.

Yablo, Stephen. (2002) 'Abstract Objects,' *Philosophical Issues* 12: 220–240.

———. (1998) 'Does Ontology Rest on a Mistake?' *Proceedings of the Aristotelian Society*, Supplementary Volume 72: 229–261.

*Philosophical Issues, 14, Epistemology, 2004*

# FOUNDATIONAL BELIEFS AND EMPIRICAL POSSIBILITIES

Richard Feldman
University of Rochester

Foundationalists differ about the subject matter of the beliefs they regard as basic or foundational. According to the traditional version of foundationalism, a person's basic beliefs are about the character or content of experience. In contrast, some contemporary foundationalists have argued that basic beliefs can be simple external world beliefs. In this paper I will defend an argument against traditional foundationalism. It suggests that the contemporary, non-traditional view is preferable. This argument appeals to possible results from cognitive science. I will then briefly extend the argument to some other epistemological disputes and then conclude by distinguishing successful versions of this style of argument from unsuccessful versions.

## I. Two Versions of Foundationalism

According to traditional foundationalism, a person's basic empirical beliefs must have as their content propositions about the character of the person's experience. The basic empirical beliefs are always about one's own psychological states. The qualifier "empirical" is included here because foundationalists may hold that there are basic beliefs about mathematical or conceptual matters whose content is not psychological. My interest here is in the basic beliefs involved in knowledge of the external world. The traditional foundationalist view holds that one has a set of basic beliefs about the character of one's experiences and on their basis one can have justified beliefs about the external world.

Laurence BonJour defends the traditional view in his contribution to the recent book *Epistemic Justification: Internalism vs. Externalism, Foundations vs. Virtues.*[1] He writes:

Despite much recent skepticism, we seem, if the argument of the previous chapter is correct, to have located a secure foundation for empirical justification more or less where traditional foundationalists have always thought it was to be found: in the form of beliefs about the content of conscious states and particularly of states of sensory experience.[2]

The details of BonJour's view about the exact character of basic beliefs and his detailed explanation of why they are justified is not central to the discussion that follows. The crucial point is just that his view illustrates the classical foundationalist view that the foundations involve basic beliefs about one's own psychological states, not beliefs about the external world.

A representative example of the other kind of foundationalism—non-traditional foundationalism—is the view recently defended by James Pryor. He writes:

> For a large class of propositions, like the proposition that there are hands, it's intuitively very natural to think that having an experience as of that proposition justifies one in believing that proposition to be true. What's more, one's justi-fication here doesn't seem to depend on any complicated justifying argument. An experience as of there being hands seems to justify one in believing that there are hands in a perfectly straightforward and immediate way...[T]*he mere fact* that one has a visual experience of that phenomenological sort is enough to make it reasonable for one to believe that there are hands. No *premises* about the character of experience—or any other sophisticated assumptions—seem to be needed.
>
> I say, let's take these intuitive appearances at face value. Let's say that our perceptual beliefs in these propositions are indeed justified in a way that does not require any further beliefs or reflection or introspective awareness. They have a kind of justification which is *immediate*, albeit defeasible.[3]

As Pryor notes, several other philosophers have defended a similar view.[4]

I believe that a much discussed distinction will be of some help in clarifying the difference between these two views. The distinction I have in mind is the distinction between its being the case that a particular propo-sition is justified for a person and the person justifiably believing that proposition. If a person has excellent reasons to believe some proposition, then that proposition is justified for the person. Believing is the justified attitude, whether the person actually believes the proposition or not. Equivalently, the person is justified in believing the proposition. This does not imply that the person does believe the proposition. I will call this "propositional justification." Propositional justification should be distin-guished from what is sometimes called "doxastic justification." This is most clearly brought out by noting that a person can believe a proposition for which she has propositional justification, but fail to believe the proposition on the basis of the supporting evidence. In other words, she believes the right thing for the wrong reasons. When a person does believe on the basis of supporting evidence, then the belief has doxastic justification. In other places I have said that such beliefs are "well-founded."[5] Thus, propositions are, or are not, justified for a person. In my view, this depends upon the evidence the person has that bears on the proposition. Beliefs are, or are not, well-founded. This depends upon whether the belief is based on evidence that supports it. It is not my goal to provide analyses of justification and well-foundedness here. I will assume that they are clear enough for us to proceed.

To clarify the difference between traditional and non-traditional foundationalism, it will be helpful to reconsider the points so far discussed in light of the distinction between propositional justification and well-foundedness. Although both BonJour and Pryor seem to be making claims about the justification of beliefs, i.e., about well-foundedness, I will first develop their theories as accounts of propositional justification.

The general idea underlying the traditional view of propositional justification is that experiences provide justification for propositions about the character of experience, and these propositions in turn serve to provide justification for beliefs about the external world. For example, traditionalists might endorse the following principle about foundational justification:

1. If S is appeared to redly, then the proposition that S is appeared to redly is justified for S.

The link between the foundationally justified proposition and the non-basic propositions about the external might be formulated in terms of principles illustrated by the following:

2. If the proposition that S is appeared to redly is justified for S, then, provided S has no defeaters, the proposition that S sees something red is justified for S.

The "no defeaters" clause is need here because one might have good reason to think that a particular experience is misleading. However, according to (2), in the absence of such defeaters, the external world proposition corresponding to the experience is justified. Principles (1) and (2), of course, are just instances of a general pattern. The key idea is that experiences justify propositions about experiences, and these in turn justify propositions about the world. We will see shortly that traditionalists may well deny (2).

A non-traditionalist holds that experiences justify propositions about the world. There need not be any detour through propositions about the character of experience. Thus, a non-traditionalist endorses something like this:

3. If S is appeared to redly, then, provided S has no defeaters, the proposition that S sees something red is justified for S.[6]

Here, the proposition justified by experience is an external world proposition.

If the principles just described do illustrate the difference between the two types of foundationalism, then the difference between the two views is less than some may think. Notice that (1) and (2) imply (3). Thus, any traditionalist who defends (1) and (2) is committed to the truth of (3), the principle embodying the non-traditional view. And the defender of (3) can admit that (1) and (2) are also true. In fact, there is no reason for non-traditionalists to say that experiences fail to justify propositions about experiences (i.e., no reason to deny (1)) and no reason to deny that when those internal propositions are justified, then the corresponding external world propositions are also justified (i.e., no reason to deny (2)). This makes it less than clear just what the difference between the two views amounts to.

There are, as always, complications. The problem of the speckled hen raises a question about which principles along the lines of (1) are true.[7] The problem arises because some experiences do seem to provide justification for corresponding beliefs about experience, but other (more complex) experiences do not. Having an experience of a 48 speckled hen does not (typically, at least) render justified the proposition that one is having such an experience. A principle about such experiences, analogous to (1), seems not to be true. A well worked out foundationalist theory will specify which such principles are true and which are not, and why. Comparable puzzles apply to the non-traditionalist's principle (3). Not all experiences provide justification for corresponding external world beliefs. While (3) is true, it seems not to be true that if one has an experience as of a bristlecone pine tree, one is then justified in thinking that there is a bristlecone pine present. This proposition is justified only if one is suitably expert about those trees. Similarly, a principle like (3) but about 48-spottedness would seem not to be true. A well worked out non-traditional view will clarify all of this in a suitable way. These are complications I will not address here.

It may be that the crucial differences between the two kinds of foundationalism will emerge from consideration of the problem of the speckled hen. However, I suspect that this is not the case. The reason is this. Traditional foundationalists and non-traditional foundationalists agree about examples. If they think that experiences are the ultimate source of justification, then they will agree that, given a certain sorts of experience, corresponding beliefs about the external world can be justified, whereas other experiences need not lead to justification for the corresponding beliefs about the world. Given that they can agree about all of this, there is no particular reason to think that what they say about the speckled hen issue will bring out more clearly just what they do disagree about.

What does seem to be the point of contention has to do with the need to "go through" beliefs about experience in order to get justification for external world propositions (or beliefs). The idea that justification for external world propositions requires that one "go through" beliefs about one's internal states may lead traditionalists such as BonJour to deny (3). And, since he does endorse something like (1), he must deny (2) if he is to deny (3). And perhaps the source of the denial of (2) would be the idea that merely being justified in believing (i.e., having a justification for the proposition) that one is appeared to redly, is not sufficient, in the absence of defeaters, to be justified in believing that one is seeing something red. He might hold that one needs, in addition, the belief that one is appeared to redly. That is, he might endorse not (2) but rather something like:

2a.  If S is appeared to redly and believes on this basis that S is appeared to redly, then, provided S has no defeaters, the proposition that S sees something red is justified for S.

By rejecting (2) and replacing it with (2a), the traditional foundationalist adds the requirement that one have the belief about experience in order to have a sufficient basis for believing that one does see something red.[8] The idea behind (2a) is that what's sufficient for justification for the external world belief is not simply the appropriate experience (and the absence of defeaters). What is required is (at least) the well-founded belief about the character of experience. And this belief about experience will be well-founded when it is properly based on that experience.

This difference between the two kinds of foundationalism can also be formulated in terms of a difference in the supervenience theses the theories imply. Both views imply that facts about which propositions are justified for a person supervene on descriptive facts about the person. One might have thought that traditional foundationalism is the view that what one is justified in believing about the world supervenes on one's experiences. However, the discussion so far suggests that this is not quite correct. On the view that replaces (2) with something like (2a), the facts about what one is justified in believing about the world supervene on the combination of the character of one's experiences and what one believes about those experiences. Non-traditional foundationalists, such as Pryor, seem to endorse the simpler supervenience claim. That is, they do think that these epistemic facts supervene on facts about experience. This, then, is one way to spell out the difference between the two types of foundationalists. The traditionalists, in effect, are denying that having an experience of red is sufficient, in the absence of defeaters, to justify the proposition that there is something red present. One needs additional evidence, evidence that comes in part from forming the belief that one is having an experience of red.

It is a bit easier to appreciate the difference between the two types of foundationalism when we turn to well-foundedness. For a belief to be well-founded, it must be based on justifying evidence. Principles (1)–(3) are about justification, not about well-foundedness. Revising the traditionalist's principles to include reference to the basis of belief yields principles such as:

1'. If S is appeared to redly, and believes that he is appeared to redly on the basis of being appeared to this way, then S's belief that S is appeared to redly is well-founded.

2'. If S's belief that S is appeared to redly is well-founded and S believes on the basis of this belief that S sees something red, then, provided S has no defeaters, S's belief that S sees something red is well-founded.

In contrast, the non-traditional foundationalist would hold something like this:

3'. If S is appeared to redly, and believes on the basis of being appeared to this way that S sees something red, then, provided S has no defeaters, S's belief that S sees something red is well-founded.

What seems clear is that traditionalists like BonJour would reject (3'). They presumably think that one cannot justifiably base a belief about the external world on experiences alone. They think that what can be justifiably based on experiences alone are (at most) beliefs about experiences. As BonJour puts it, one is in a position to compare directly the experience to the belief and thereby justify it.[9] No such direct comparison, and hence no justification, is available in the case of experiences and external world beliefs. The idea is that one does have in experience all one needs to justify the external world belief. But that belief is well-founded only if one gets to it via the belief about experience.[10]

The fundamental contrast between the traditional view and the non-traditional view is thus clear. While both views hold that the epistemic status of beliefs about the external world depends partly on our experiential states, the traditional view holds that beliefs about the external world are well-founded only if they are based on beliefs about experiential states while the non-traditional view denies this. It allows for well-founded external world beliefs even if we do not have any beliefs about experiential states. Formulated in terms of justification for propositions about the external world, the traditional view denies that experiential states of any degree of complexity provide sufficient justification for external world propositions. At the very least, beliefs about internal states are required as well.

It is worth noting that both foundationalist views can count as "internalist," at least on one account of what internalism is. This account holds that internalism is a supervenience thesis, according to which what one is justified in believing supervenes on one's internal states.[11] Both BonJour's traditional view and Pryor's non-traditional view hold that what's justified depends on one's internal states. The difference between the theories is over which internal states are in the supervenience base for the epistemic facts.

## II. An Objection to Traditional Foundationalism

In defending his preference for non-traditional foundationalism, Pryor relies mainly on judgments about what seems to him (and, he assumes, to others) to happen when he forms beliefs about the world. As the passage quoted previously shows, he appeals to the fact that he does not seem to form introspective beliefs about his experiences and use those beliefs as premises in arguments for propositions about the world. He takes things to be as they seem to be. I have no quarrel with this approach. However, I think that a stronger argument can be given for preferring a view that does not require these introspective beliefs. I turn next to that argument.

I will formulate the argument by means of a simple example of a person who sees a tree and comes to know that there is a tree before him. I assume for the sake of discussion that skepticism in general is false, and that people can have knowledge of the world around them. The person in my example is a typical knower.

*The Cognitive Scientists' Discovery Argument*
1. If traditional foundationalism is true, then S knows that there is a tree in front of him only if S believes that he is having a "treeish" experience.
2. Cognitive science could (in principle) show that S does not believe that he is having a treeish experience without thereby showing that S does not know that there is a tree in front of him.
3. S could know that there is a tree in front of him without believing that he is having a treesish experience. (2)
4. So, traditional foundationalism is not true. (1), (3)

I think that this simple argument is sound. The first premise is simply a consequence of what traditional foundationalism holds. The premise relies on the plausible assumption that well-foundedness is necessary for knowledge. It also relies on the assumption that the only available way to a well-founded belief in the example under discussion is via principles (1′) and (2′).[12] These assumptions are congenial to traditional foundationalism, and premise (1) appears to be beyond dispute.

The second premise is, perhaps, more controversial. It depends upon two ideas, both of which strike me as relatively obvious. The first is that whether a person believes a particular proposition is a contingent fact about that person's mind. Whether S goes through a belief about appearances on his way to his belief about the world is a contingent fact about how S's mind works. Cognitive science could, in principle, find out how S's mind works. It could discover that S, when he has the treeish experience, goes directly to the belief that there's a tree there, without passing through any belief about appearances. In fact, as Pryor notes, this is surely how it seems that our minds work. We do not seem to making any inferences of the sort traditional foundationalism requires. It is difficult to see why things could not be the way they seem.

Premise (2) depends upon a second idea. This second idea also strikes me as obviously correct. The second idea is that if cognitive scientists were to discover that we do not in fact reason through beliefs about our internal states, they would not thereby discover that we do not have knowledge of the world around us. In support of this, consider the following example. Suppose that two people with comparable vision are standing side by side looking at a tree in plain view. Suppose further that both are familiar with trees and that both believe that there is a tree before them. Suppose also that both are wearing brain scanner helmets enabling cognitive scientists to discover the beliefs they have at the time. Finally, suppose that the cognitive scientists report that only one of them forms a belief about the character of his experience. The other just directly forms the belief that there is a tree there on the basis of the visual experience. I take it as not credible that this result would show that only one knows that there is a tree there. Premise (2) is true.

If premise (2) is true, then so is (3). If cognitive science could show that a person could lack the beliefs about internal states but not thereby show that the person lacks knowledge, then it could be the case that a person has that knowledge without that belief.[13] And (4) follows from (1) and (3). The argument is valid and the premises are true. This simple argument is sound.

I should add that in itself the argument presented is not an argument for non-traditional foundationalism. It is not my goal in this paper to offer any such argument. BonJour contends that non-traditional foundationalism is unacceptable. I do want to mention one such argument. BonJour writes:

> Things would be far easier if it were plausible to hold, as some have, that non-conceptual content could somehow directly justify beliefs that are not immediately about it, e.g., beliefs whose content has to do with physical objects, without the experiential content needing to be itself formulated or formulable in conceptual terms. I believe, however, that any such view is pretty obviously untenable, that Davidson and the others are right in thinking that no intelligible relation of justification can hold between non-conceptual sensory content and conceptual beliefs in general.[14]

I think that BonJour intends to argue here against the sort of view Pryor defends. The topic is complicated by the fact that two related issues are involved. One is about whether experiences have propositional content— whether experiences should be characterized in propositional terms or in some other non-conceptual, purely qualitative way. The other issue is about whether experiences, whatever their content, can directly justify beliefs about the external world. BonJour takes experiences to be non-conceptual, and argues that "a special sort of justificatory relation can exist in the specific case where the conceptual belief is a purported description of the conscious, non-conceptual experiential content itself."[15] There are, then, four views under consideration here: (i) experiences are non-conceptual and they directly justify beliefs about experiences; (ii) experiences are non-conceptual and they directly justify beliefs about the external world; (iii) experiences are conceptual and they directly justify beliefs about experiences; (iv) experiences are conceptual and they directly justify beliefs about the external world. BonJour accepts (i). Pryor accepts (iv). (He also accepts (iii), though he thinks that we typically don't form the beliefs it mentions.) BonJour rejects (ii) in the passage just quoted. He does not directly address (iv) here. However, I am confident that he would reject it. It is worth noting that the argument in the passage quoted says that the problem with non-traditional foundationalism stems from the non-propositional content of experience, and that is something that non-traditionalists need not accept. Though I am less than clear about exactly what is at stake in the debate about whether experiences have propositional content, I lean toward (ii), the view BonJour rejects. In any case, both (ii) and (iv) can be constituents of non-traditional foundationalism. I have not here addressed arguments for them, or arguments about whether experience is conceptual.

## III. Implicit Beliefs

A non-skeptical defender of traditional foundationalism has available a fairly obvious reply to the cognitive scientists' Discovery Argument: people always do have the appearance belief, even if they do not explicitly formulate it. BonJour says something along these lines in the following passage:

> Many philosophers have questioned whether ordinary people in ordinary percep-
> tual situations normally or standardly have beliefs of *any* sort about the non-
> conceptual content of their sensory experience, even ones that are couched in
> physical-object appearance terms. But it is hard to see how a person who has, e.g.,
> a visual belief about a certain sort of physical object can fail to also have at least
> an implicit grasp of the character of his visual experience in physical-object
> appearance terms.[16]

I take it that this is supposed to deny (2) in the argument. Cognitive science could not show that we lack these beliefs.

Timothy McGrew has defended traditional foundationalism from an objection along the lines of the one proposed here. McGrew writes:

> A[n]... objection is that our typical empirical beliefs simply don't seem to be based on first-person foundations. In fact, it is difficult for most people to look out over a garden and "see it as" a patchwork of colors, a pure visual experience without any level of interpretation imposed on it.[17]

It is not clear to me whether McGrew here intends to be considering an objection according to which we don't ordinarily have beliefs about our experiences. His concern may be instead about an objection holding that we are not "aware" of our experiences. In any case, it will be useful to consider briefly his remarks to see if they will be helpful in replying to the present argument.

McGrew begins his response by saying:

> At one level this observation is perfectly legitimate, but to use it as an objection to strong foundationalism confuses psychological priority with epistemic priority. It is certainly true that the first explicit thought we have when looking at a garden is of the real, three-dimensional physical garden, and it may be very difficult for us, unless we are professional artists, to create a mind-set in which we can look out over the garden and be aware only of a collage of colors.... The answer to this challenge to strong foundationalism is that an adult's awareness of visual, tactile, and auditory stimuli is often subconscious but not therefore irrelevant to justification of empirical beliefs.[18]

The first sentence of McGrew's reply appeals to a distinction between psychological and epistemic priority. He does not elaborate upon this distinction, and I am unsure just what he had in mind. One possibility is that psychological priority has to do with the order in which things occur in the mind, while epistemic priority has to do with epistemic dependence relations. One might hold that the justification of propositions about external world propositions depends upon the justification of propositions about internal states, yet deny that one must actually form beliefs about those internal states. As noted earlier, however, defenders of non-traditional foundationalism need not deny that propositions about the external world are justified for a person only if propositions about internal states are also justified for that person. If this is what epistemic priority amounts to, then it is unclear that it brings out any point of disagreement between the two kinds of foundationalism. Perhaps McGrew has in mind some kind of epistemic priority which is not captured by any of the principles mentioned here. Since I lack any clear idea what that relation might be, and he does not develop the point, I will not attempt to address it here. I leave it to defenders of traditional foundationalism to spell out the relevant notion of epistemic dependence and show how it avoids the argument presented here.

The remainder of McGrew's response does not address matters of epistemic or psychological priority but instead claims that the required psychological states do occur, though sub-consciously. He says that the first "explicit thought" in the relevant cases is about external things. This suggests that his idea is that there is a non-explicit thought about something else, presumably an experience. If this is his point, then his response is similar to BonJour's. The idea is that people do believe that they are having experiences of the relevant kinds, though these beliefs are sub-conscious (or implicit or tacit).[19]

It is possible that people actually do have the required implicit beliefs and, perhaps, that they make implicit arguments. It is possible that traditional foundationalism should be understood as requiring no more than these implicit beliefs. Nevertheless, I think that the argument against traditional foundationalism is still sound. While it is true that our lack of awareness of the belief does not establish that we do not have it, the insistence that we do have such a (implicit) belief in all the relevant cases is an empirical assertion about our psychologies devised to rescue a philosophical thesis. I think that such rescues are ill-conceived.

Defenders of traditional foundationalism may claim that while cognitive scientists might somehow be able to identify occurrent beliefs, they cannot identify implicit beliefs by monitoring occurrences in the brain. I suspect, however, that this response rests on some obscurity in what counts as "implicit". Perhaps the relevant beliefs are supposed to be "sub-conscious" or "non-conscious". If there are such beliefs, then, of course, they could exist without our noticing them. Perhaps there is much that goes on behind the scenes in our minds, and perhaps this non-conscious mental processing is relevant to justification. Our not being aware of such events is, obviously, no reason to think they do not occur. But there is no reason at all to think that non-conscious events are not genuine events in the brain. There is no reason to think that, at least in principle, their physical manifestations in the brain could not be observed. So if implicit beliefs are just non-conscious occurrences, they do not help with the argument. Insisting that they occur in all the relevant cases amounts to insisting on the outcome of empirical research from the armchair.

A different idea, perhaps also suggested by the term "implicit", is that these beliefs about our internal states are dispositional. There are subtleties about just what this amounts to that could distract us at considerable length. There is a difference between already formed dispositional beliefs and dispositions to form a belief if the right circumstances arise. I do not now have the belief, not even dispositionally, that it is raining outside. But, were I to look outside and see rain, I would then consciously believe that it is raining. If it is now raining, then, perhaps, I have a disposition to believe that it is raining. I do not, however, have the dispositional, or non-occurrent, belief that it is raining. Perhaps people do have dispositions to form beliefs about their internal states. Were you to call their attention to them in the right way, perhaps they would form such beliefs. There is no reason at all to think that dispositions to believe play any role in determining whether occurrent beliefs are well-founded. My disposition to believe that it is raining (were I to see the rain) has no bearing at all on what well-founded beliefs I now have about the weather. So if implicit beliefs are dispositions to believe, they cannot affect what is well-founded.

Perhaps dispositional beliefs can affect justification. Without offering an analysis of dispositional beliefs, we can say that dispositional beliefs are, in some sense, stored beliefs. They are existing states. Maybe, for some reason, unexercised dispositions are relevant to justification. Of course, they presumably are in some way determined by existing states of my brain. And they are states that, again in principle, could be observed. And then it is possible that cognitive scientists will discover that some knowers just do not have the dispositional beliefs traditional foundationalism requires. This reinstates the argument.

One might think that this is an outlandish possibility. Perhaps, as BonJour said, "it is hard to see how a person" who has a treeish experience and believes that there is a tree before him could fail to have the dispositional belief that he has a treeish experience. However, this is, first of all, an empirical claim about the unnoticed goings-on in the minds of people. I do not understand the basis for thinking that they must have some such dispositional belief. Furthermore, it does take some work to get beginning philosophy students to focus on the beliefs in question. Perhaps this is because they have not been implicitly believing huge numbers of these things at virtually every moment of their lives since the time they became capable of knowledge of the external world. I do not think that epistemologists are in a position to judge that people do have the dispositional beliefs traditional foundationalism says they must have in order to have knowledge of the world around them. It is a mistake to do this sort of empirical psychology in one's armchair and it is a mistake to let one's philosophical view depend upon empirical speculation of this sort.

I conclude that appeal to implicit beliefs does not refute the argument against traditional foundationalism. Since this is the only potentially promising objection to the argument that I know of, I conclude that the argument is sound.

## IV. Extending the Argument to Other Cases

I think that the kind of argument offered here against traditional foundationalism also applies to some other theories. I will briefly offer one illustration. Alvin Plantinga has defended the view that beliefs have warrant (that which is needed to turn true beliefs into knowledge) when they result from the proper functioning of the segment of the cognitive system that produced them.[20] He notes that aspects of our cognitive system may have different goals or purposes. For example, we may be designed for self-deception in some circumstances, as when such deception will promote happiness or survival. His view is that when a belief results from a segment of our cognitive system that has such an end, the belief is not warranted. However, when the belief results from a segment of our design plan aimed at truth, then, given the satisfaction of other conditions, the belief is warranted.

It is not my purpose here to discuss the details of Plantinga's complex and sophisticated view. What is important for present purposes is the fact that the success of his view depends upon contingent empirical facts about the ends of segments of our cognitive design plan. Plantinga is no skeptic, and it is likely that he believes that our ordinary perceptual beliefs—such as a normal person's belief that there is an apple in front of him when he sees it clearly and knows what apples look like—results from a part of the perceptual system geared toward the production of true beliefs. But the ends of the parts of our perceptual systems are contingent empirical facts about us. Assuming (contrary to Plantinga) that we were not designed by a conscious designer, these are biological facts determined by events in our evolutionary history. Perhaps it will turn out that truth is not the proximate goal of the relevant sub-system, even in the case of obvious instances of knowledge. If we were designed, perhaps the goal of the designer was not truth. Maybe the designer was thinking mainly of how to get people to succeed in getting food, and designed the relevant portion of the cognitive system with that in mind. It surely would not follow that the person does not know that he sees an apple. The point can be made especially clear by considering cases of cognitive beings who were designed. Imagine two people whose designers gave them the same cognitive mechanisms, both of whom regularly get true beliefs about some domain. But imagine further the designer of one of them had truth as a goal, whereas the designer of the other had something else in mind. It is difficult to swallow the implication that only the former has warranted beliefs.[21] As it applies to us, then, Plantinga's theory depends upon empirical conjectures in an implausible way.

There are apparent applications of the same style of argument that I think would not be successful. This is not because there are *a priori* limitations on what cognitive science could show about our cognitive systems, but because there are limitations about what it could show without also showing that we lack knowledge. To illustrate this, consider a simple belief and a wildly implausible, yet possible, empirical result.

Suppose that you are standing in front of a table. Your eyes are open and you are facing the table. The lighting is good. You say that there is table before you. Any observer would normally agree that you know that there is a table there. Results from cognitive science could undermine this claim. Suppose investigation into your brain revealed a small transmitter and receiver. Further investigation showed that your visual information was sent to a remote location where it was randomly associated with a classification of the viewed object, and this result was then transmitted back to you. You then reported your belief. This, admittedly ridiculous, result would show that you lack knowledge. Thus, my claim is not that no empirical result could show that people lack knowledge in seemingly ordinary cases of knowledge. Rather, my claim is that certain results, such as the result that we do not ordinarily form beliefs about how we are appeared to, are possible and they would not show that we lack knowledge. Epistemological theories can be undermined by such results.

This last point has implications for the debate about "particularism" and "methodism" in epistemology.[22] Particularism is sometimes characterized as the view that our epistemological starting point is that certain cases are cases of knowledge. This can be taken to be the view that the seemingly clear cases of knowledge really are knowledge, come what may. That is, nothing could show that they are not cases of knowledge. If that is correct, then cognitive science cannot show that they are not cases of knowledge. However, if the point of the previous paragraph is correct, then particularism, at least construed in the way just described, is false.

I think, however, that the best version of particularism is not refuted by the argument here. The best version does not say that certain actual examples are knowledge, come what may. Rather, it says one or the other of two nearly equivalent things. It says that no *philosophical* argument will establish that a case is not a case of knowledge. Consider my current belief that I am sitting on a chair. The particularist idea may be that any philosophical argument that might tend to show that this is not a case of knowledge is less plausible than the proposition that I do have knowledge in such a case. This leaves open the possibility of empirical results showing that this is not a case of knowledge. And surely that possibility should be left open. In addition to the possibility that empirical results will show something odd about my psychology that makes me lack knowledge, empirical results could also show that I am not sitting on a chair. So, my belief could be false. Of course, this latter result would not show that my belief is not well-founded. In any case, particularism is distinctly implausible if it insists that this is a case of knowledge, or even of well-founded belief, come what may. Particularism may be on stronger ground if it claims that the proposition that I am sitting on a chair is justified for me, come what may.

An alternative way to develop a similar thought is this: the judgment about the particular case is not really a judgment about the actual case but rather a judgment about a possible case which is related to the actual one in a significant way. That relation is this: it takes all the obvious features of the actual case and embeds them in a possible world that has the key features we take the actual world to have. In judging that I know that I am sitting on a chair, I assume that my general beliefs about the world are true. I will not, and cannot, make precise just which general beliefs these are. The rough idea is that I assume that I am a normal perceiver who does have contact with external objects that are pretty much the way I take them to be. And the particularist idea is that such possible cases—which presumably includes the actual case—is a case of knowledge. No empirical information will refute that judgment about possible cases. Learning that the odd things described above are true would show that the actual case is not one of the possible cases judged to be knowledge. And the particularist contends that any philosophical argument designed to show that such possible cases are not cases of knowledge is less plausible than the view that they are cases of knowledge. Nothing I have said in this paper is intended to establish the truth of this kind of particularism. However, I think that my argument about empirical discoveries falsifying philosophical theories does not in any way jeopardize this kind of particularism.

There is one other potential application of the sort of argument presented here that I will discuss very briefly.[23] Some have thought that cognitive science may show that we do not have beliefs at all. If this is a possibility, one might wonder whether it refutes any theory of knowledge according to which knowledge requires belief. The correct answer is not clear to me. I think that if it turns out that we have no beliefs, then we have no propositional knowledge either. However, I am not sure that cognitive science could show that we have no beliefs. Much depends upon how much is read into the concept of belief. If "belief" is correctly interpreted in a way that makes it consistent with our experiences that we lack beliefs, then I think that arguments such as the one presented here may well work against theories according to which knowledge requires belief. Knowledge, perhaps, requires only that we do have those belief-like states that we can observe ourselves to have. Cognitive science cannot show that we lack those states. However, I think that the interpretation of "belief" that allows for the possibility that cognitive science could show that we have no beliefs is incorrect, and thus that the application of the argument to this case fails.

## V. Conclusion

My conclusion is that "The Cognitive Scientists' Discovery Argument" is a sound argument against the traditional version of foundationalism, which holds that knowledge of (and well-founded belief about) the external world requires beliefs about introspective states. If any kind of foundationalism is correct, it is the non-traditional kind, which imposes no such requirement. My argument depends essentially on the premise that empirical results could reveal that we lack such beliefs without thereby revealing that we lack knowledge. Similar arguments, invoking possible empirical results, also threaten to undermine some other epistemological claims. However, this is not to say that no empirical results could show that we lack knowledge or well-founded belief in some cases that we may antecedently take to be clear cases of knowledge or well-founded belief.[24]

## Notes

1. Laurence BonJour and Ernest Sosa, *Epistemic Justification: Internalism vs. Externalism, Foundations vs. Virtues* (Malden, MA: Blackwell, 2003). See especially Chapter 4.
2. P. 77.
3. James Pryor, "The Skeptic and the Dogmatist," *Noûs* 34 (2000): 517–549. The quotation is from p. 536. Italics in original.
4. He mentions William Alston, Robert Audi, John Pollock, and, possibly, Roderick Chisholm, as holding a similar view. See endnote 31 of "The Skeptic and the Dogmatist" for references.
5. See, for example, Richard Feldman and Earl Conee, "Evidentialism," *Philosophical Studies*, 48 (1985): 15–34. This paper is reprinted as Chapter 4 of Earl Conee and Richard Feldman, *Evidentialism: Essays in Epistemology* (Oxford: Oxford University Press, 2004).
6. Pryor is more apt to formulate the principle in the following way:

    If S has an experience as of it's being the case that there is something red, then S is justified in believing that there is something red.

    This makes the experience seem to have propositional content. The formulation in the text does not do that. I believe that nothing in the present paper turns on these two ways of understanding experiences.
7. For recent discussion of the problem, see Ernest Sosa's contribution to *Epistemic Justification*. See especially, Chapter 7. I have responded to Sosa's arguments in "BonJour and Sosa on Internalism, Externalism, and Basic Beliefs," forthcoming in *Philosophical Studies*.
8. And maybe even more is required. BonJour apparently thinks that one must realize that the proposition that there is something red present is part of the best explanation of one's basic beliefs. See *Epistemic Justification*, Chapter 5.
9. See *Epistemic Justification*, p. 73.
10. Notice that (1′) and (2′) do not imply (3′).
11. This view is defended in "Internalism Defended" in Earl Conee and Richard Feldman, *Evidentialism: Essays in Epistemology*.
12. I ignore here the fact that there are other ways S might come to know that there is a tree in front of him. For example, S might learn it by testimony.

13. There is room to quibble here. It is possible that cognitive science could show that there are cases in which people lack the relevant beliefs without *showing* that they lack knowledge in those cases. However, it might still be true that people do lack knowledge in all such cases. It's just that cognitive science does not show this. However, I think that there is no reason at all to think that all cases in which people lack the belief about their internal states, they must also lack knowledge about the world. So the example still undermines traditional foundationalism.
14. *Epistemic Justification*, p. 78.
15. *Epistemic Justification*, p. 78.
16. *Epistemic Justification*, p. 81.
17. "A Defense of Classical Foundationalism," in Louis P. Pojman, ed., *The Theory of Knowledge: Classical and Contemporary Readings 3$^{rd}$ Edition* (Belmont, CA: Wadsworth, 2003), pp. 194–206. The quotation is from p. 200.
18. P. 200.
19. I want to emphasize that McGrew's claim here is not clearly about whether one has a belief about one's experience. His point may be that we are "aware of" our experiential state. However, other things he says support the idea that he does think that the beliefs about experience are implicit. For example, he says that traditional foundationalists "are free to construe belief in a modest way that is separable from and does not entail the existence of explicit verbalized judgment." (p. 200) He goes on to suggest that perhaps having such a belief is identical with having an experience. I will not take up this last suggestion here.
20. Alvin Plantinga, *Warrant and Proper Function* (Oxford: Oxford University Press, 1993).
21. I am grateful to Michael Bergmann for helpful discussions of this point.
22. I believe that these terms were coined by Ernest Sosa in "The Foundations of Foundationalism," *Noûs* 14 (1980): 547–65.
23. This possibility was suggested to me independently by Ernest Sosa and Earl Conee.
24. I am grateful to Earl Conee, Andrew Cullison, and Daniel Mittag for helpful comments on a draft of this paper.

*Philosophical Issues, 14, Epistemology, 2004*

# EPISTEMIC PROBABILITY[1]

Richard Fumerton
The University of Iowa

In this paper I want to explore both the conceptual and epistemic place of epistemic probability within a foundationalist theory of justification. After arguing that one should take the relation of making probable holding between propositions to be one of the most important conceptual building blocks in epistemology, I examine different ways of trying to understand this key concept and explore the question of how our understanding of it will affect our prospects for finding a defensible version of inferential internalism.

**Regress Arguments for Foundationalism:**

As I indicated, I'm primarily interested in the place of probability within the framework of foundationalism. More specifically still, I'll focus on the way in which our understanding of probability is involved in the foundationalist's understanding of *inferential* justification. Before setting to that task, it might be helpful, however, to very briefly travel some familiar terrain and remind ourselves of the ways in which foundationalists typically argue for their view about the structure of justification. As we shall see later, the desire to avoid regress that so influences foundationalists might bear directly on the advantages that one particular theory of probability might have for certain versions of internalism.

The standard argument for foundationalism is the regress argument. But there are, however, two importantly different versions of that argument, an epistemic version, and a conceptual version.

## The Epistemic Regress Argument for Foundationalism:

The more familiar of the two regress arguments for foundationalism is probably the epistemic version. Let us say that S's belief that p is inferentially justified if S's justification for believing P is *constituted* in part by the fact that S is justified in believing some proposition other than P, a proposition on which S at least partially bases his belief that P. The following principle seems patently obvious to both externalists and internalists alike. For S to be justified in believing P by basing that belief on some other proposition believed, say E1, S must be justified in believing E1. But if all justification were inferential, then the only way for S to be justified in believing E1 would be for S to be justified in believing yet another proposition E2, and so on *ad infinitum*. Finite minds cannot complete an infinitely long chain of reasoning, so if all justification were inferential we would be forced to the absurd (and epistemically self-defeating) conclusion that no-one is justified in believing anything at all to any extent whatsoever.[2]

## The Conceptual Regress Argument:

The epistemic regress argument rests on a number of controversial presuppositions. As the coherence theorist points out, the foundationalist assumes that justification is *linear* in character and, as Peter Klein (1998) argues (in defending the view he calls infinitism), it also presupposes that having justification can only be constituted by a chain of reasoning that one *actually* completes, as opposed to one each link of which *could* be completed. If one allows that E's status as justifier requires only that one be capable of coming up with an appropriate argument for P having E as a premise, then even as finite epistemic agents we may have the potential to come up with an infinite number of different arguments, one for every link in an infinitely long chain of reasoning.

These sorts of responses to the regress argument presuppose that the problematic nature of the regress derives from the need to have an infinite number of different beliefs to serve as justifiers. As I have argued elsewhere (1995), there is another way of construing the problematic nature of the regress foundationalism seeks to avoid. Why *is* it a necessary truth that to be justified in believing P on the basis of E one must be justified in believing E? The most obvious answer, perhaps, is that one's inferential justification for believing P on the basis of E is partially *constituted* by one's justification for believing E. It is an *analytic* truth that one can be inferentially justified in believing P on the basis of E only if one is justified in believing E. But if this is correct, then the above account of *inferential* justification is viciously *circular* if it is intended to be an account of justification in general. Our understanding of inferential justification *presupposes* an understanding of the concept of justified belief (in just the way, for example, our under-standing of instrumental goodness presupposes an understanding of intrin-sic goodness). Put another way, reflection on the concept of inferential justification suggests that any plausible definition of inferential justification will be *recursive*. Our understanding of the recursive definition of inferential justification will require an understanding of some base clause that invokes a concept of justification that is not inferential.[3] My desire to end a threat-ening conceptual regress is the basis of one of my fundamental concerns with Klein's infinitism.

To be sure, the argument is not decisive. Klein would argue that one might have some generic understanding of justification that we could employ in our attempt to understand inferential justification. Perhaps, for example, we could try some deontic conception of justified belief as belief that one ought to have, given certain epistemic goals or ends.[4] Employing that generic concept one could still insist that all justification is inferential. But the virtue of a recursive analysis of justification is that one successfully completes two tasks at once. One shows how one ends vicious epistemic regress while analyzing the very concept of justification.

### The Principle of Inferential Justification:

S's having a justified belief in E might be a conceptually *necessary* condition for S's justifiably believing P on the basis of E, but it obviously isn't conceptually *sufficient*. At the very least S must *base* his belief that P on E. The analysis of the basing relation is problematic. Some insist that it is exhausted by causal connection between beliefs; others insist that it involves something else. In any event, it is again obvious that S's justification for believing P on the basis of E requires more than that S be justified in believing E and that S base his belief that P on E.[5] The most obvious candidates for the missing condition are the following:

1) There is a correct epistemic rule sanctioning the move from believing E to believing P
2) S is *aware of*, or has a *justified belief that* there is a correct epistemic rule sanctioning the move from believing E to believing P,
3) There is an appropriate logical or probabilistic connection between the propositions E and P, or
4) S is *aware of*, or has a *justified belief that* there is an appropriate logical or probabilistic connection between E and P.

Now on analysis there may be no difference between the contents of 1) and 3) (and therefore between 2) and 4)). One might argue that to claim that E makes probable P, for example, *in the sense relevant to epistemic justification*, is just a way of acknowledging that there is an epistemic rule licensing the move from believing E to believing P. Conversely, one might argue that all this talk about the correctness of epistemic rules is itself a convoluted way of talking about relationships between propositions. So, for example, there are rules of *deductive* logic that permit certain sorts of inferences, say modus ponens, but the most obvious answer to the question of what makes modus ponens a *correct* rule of inference is that there is a relation of entailment holding between the premises and conclusions of arguments having a certain form, where this entailment exists independently of any rule acknowledging it. Similarly, in the case of inductive reasoning, one might argue that to say that the premises of an inductive argument make probable its conclusion is just a way of pointing out that there is a correct rule licensing the inference to the inductive conclusion from the premises describing observed correlations. Conversely, one might argue that the rule itself merely acknowledges the relevant relation of making probable that holds between the premises and conclusion of the argument whether or not there exists some rule that takes account of that relation.

While 1) and 3) may be alternative ways of making a common claim, it is important, I think, to decide the direction of the reduction. We need to figure out what the relevant conceptual building blocks are in trying to understand inferential justification. I'll return to this issue later. But, however, one decides the issue of conceptual priority, one still needs to decide whether it is the *existence* of the probability connection/correct rule or our *awareness* of the relevant connection/rule that is crucial to the possession of inferential justification. It is disagreement on this last point, I have argued elsewhere (1995), that gives us one (though only one) way of isolating a point on which self-proclaimed internalists and externalists often disagree. One might label the view that insists that for one to be inferentially justified in believing P on the basis of E one must be *justified in believing* that E makes probable P (where entailment can be viewed as the upper limit of making probable) or, alternatively, that the inference from E to P is sanctioned by a correct epistemic rule, *inferential internalism*.

Leaving aside for a moment the correct analysis of probabilistic connection, what arguments can we offer for inferential internalism? It seems obvious that something like the view was simply taken for granted, explicitly or implicitly, by most of those in the history of philosophy who either argued for skepticism or took the problem of skepticism seriously. But given the enormous difficulties of meeting the skeptical challenge within the constraints of inferential internalism, why accept the view? We are surely rather liberal in our allowing that all sorts of people, including of course the philosophically unsophisticated (and the philosophically sophisticated with false views about justification) have all sorts of perfectly rational beliefs. Given that we seem not the least bit inclined to abandon the view that people have justified beliefs about the external world, the future, and the past, despite the difficulty they have coming up with any sort of reasons indicating the legitimacy of their inferences, should we not at least suspect that the ordinary understanding of justification requires nothing as strong as what is proposed by the inferential internalist?[6] Perhaps, but there also appears to be prima facie evidence to indicate widespread acknowledgement of the inferential internalist's requirements for inferential justification.

Consider the palm reader who predicts that I will have a long life based on the belief that I have the proverbial long "life line" on the palm of my hand. It seems obvious that a *sufficient* condition for rejecting the palm reader's inference as rational is that the palm reader has no reason to believe that the length of a line on one's palm has anything to do with the probability of one's living to a ripe old age. If my high priest predicts that the war I am planning will go badly based on the observation that the entrails of a recently dissected bird are bloody, an epistemically rational person will surely demand evidence for supposing that features of entrails are correlated with success in battle before conceding the rationality of the priest's prediction. These commonplace examples and indefinitely many others like them surely indicate that we do in fact embrace the inferential internalist's account of what is necessary for inferential justification. We may pick and choose when we decide to make an issue of someone's lacking reason to believe in a legitimate evidential connection. We do sometimes take for granted the justification of certain beliefs and the legitimacy of certain inferences when we are primarily concerned with the justification of other beliefs and inferential connections. But once we take seriously a skeptical challenge to a commonplace inference, we must apply the same standards that we insist on applying to astrologers and fortune tellers.

Mike Huemer (2002) objects to the above argument for inferential internalism. He argues that the examples I use to make initially attractive the principle are misleading in that they inappropriately characterize the evidence from which one infers the relevant conclusion. Even palm readers don't think that they can legitimately infer their predictions from propositions describing the character of a person's palm *and from that information alone*. I suspect that the priests at Delphi didn't think of themselves as inferring truths about battles from the appearance of entrails *and from that alone*. It should be a truism that much of the argument we actually give outside of a philosophical context is highly compressed, highly enthymematic. As we ordinarily use the term "evidence", we certainly do characterize litmus paper's turning red in a solution as evidence that the solution is acidic. The approach of very dark clouds is evidence that there will soon be a storm. Footprints on a beach is evidence that someone walked on the beach recently. But it is surely obvious upon reflection that one's evidence for believing that the solution is acidic, for example, is not the color of the litmus paper *by itself*. To legitimately draw the conclusion one would need an additional *premise*, most likely a premise describing a correlation between the color of litmus paper in a solution and the character of that solution.

Once one realizes that the reasoning in the examples I discussed above is enthymematic, one is positioned to respond to that appearance of an argument for inferential internalism. For the reasoning described above to be legitimate, it *is* indeed necessary to have some justification for believing that there is a connection between palm lines and life expectancy, the approach of dark clouds and storms, footprints on a beach and the recent presence of people; but *only* because propositions describing connections or correlations of the relevant sort are implicitly recognized as critical *premises* from which the relevant conclusions are drawn. As we saw earlier, internalists *and* externalists alike typically share the foundationalist's insight that inferential justification is parasitic upon the justification we possess for believing the relevant premises of our arguments. If the palm reader is relying on an unstated, but critical premise describing correlations between palm lines and length of life in reaching her conclusion, she will, of course, need justification for believing that *premise* (in exactly the same unproblematic sense that she will need justification for believing the premise describing the length of the palm line itself). But that in no way suggests that when we have fully described all of the relevant premises from which a conclusion is drawn, we should require that the person who draws that conclusion needs additional evidence for believing that the premises make probable the conclusion. The existence of the relevant connection between premises and conclusion is enough.

While Huemer is right, I think, in arguing that the examples discussed above do not support inferential internalism, it is not clear to me that one can't make just as strong a case for inferential internalism focusing on non-enthymematic reasoning. Consider the case of someone who infers P from E where E logically *entails* P. Is the inferential internalist right in maintaining that in order for S to believe justifiably P on the basis of E, S must be aware of the fact that (or at least have a justified belief that) E entails P (or alternatively, that the inference in question is legitimate)? The answer still seems to me obviously "Yes." We can easily imagine someone who is *caused* to believe P as a result of believing E where E does in fact entail P, but where the entailment is far too complicated for S to understand. Unless S "sees" that P follows from E, would we really allow that the inference in question generates a justified belief? Or to make my case a bit stronger, would we allow that the person who reaches the conclusion has philosophically relevant justification or ideal justification—the kind of justification one seeks when one searches for philosophical assurance.[7]

A great deal hinges on how we understand the critical concept of someone's believing one proposition on the basis of another. There is some plausibility to the claim that genuine inference involves more than mere causal connection. But the source of this intuition will, I think, provide little solace for the inferential externalist. In fact, I suspect that we may not concede that there has been a genuine inference unless there has been a veridical or nonveridical "perception" of a connection between that from which P is inferred and P. But, of course, this "perception" will be just what the inferential internalist claims is the awareness of connection that is necessary for inferentially justified belief.

There is at least some concern that inferential internalism will lead to regress. The view does at least remind one of Carroll's (1895) famous dialogue between the Tortoise and Achilles.[8] Paraphrasing liberally, the Tortoise admits at one point that P is true and also that if P is true then Q is true but doesn't see why that's a reason to believe Q. Obligingly, Achilles plays the game and adds an additional premise: If P is true and if it is true that if P is true then Q is true then Q is true. Even so, wonders the Tortoise, why does that premise coupled with P and (if P then Q) give one reason to believe Q. Isn't the inferential internalist in the position of the Tortoise who keeps insisting that even when one has in one's possession evidence that entails one's conclusion, epistemically rational belief in the conclusion requires yet additional reason for supposing that the entailment holds? Like the Tortoise the inferential internalist *does* require for justified belief in a conclusion something other than mere justified belief in premises which do, in fact, entail the conclusion. The inferential internalist does insist that the person possessing the justification be aware of the entailment. But that requirement for inferential *justification* does not, obviously, suggest that the *argument* needs additional premises in order to be good argument. But even if we make that distinction, we should recognize that to avoid vicious regress the inferential internalist may need to ensure that the relevant awareness of connection between premises and conclusion does not itself require *inference* from still additional premises. But we'll have more to say about that shortly.

I have dwelt on Huemer's argument against inferential internalism not just because I'm interested in the question of whether or not the argument succeeds. It seems to me that Huemer's insightful argument reminds us of certain features of our talk of evidence that will be important to keep in mind when we evaluate the plausibility of certain views about the nature of probability.

## The Analysis of Epistemic Probability:

Whether or not we adopt inferential internalism, we need an analysis of the probability connection that by itself or as the object of awareness is partially constitutive of inferential justification. Earlier we suggested two ways in which one might think of the epistemic claim that one proposition or conjunction of propositions makes probable another. We might think that the truth of the probability claim derives from the existence of a correct *rule* sanctioning the inference in question. Or we might think that our understanding of the probability connection is prior to and legitimizes our putting forth the rule that sanctions the relevant inference.

The rule-oriented approach itself can be thought of in quite different ways. On the most radical view, the rules of inference might be thought of as analogous to the rules of a game, rules that are themselves neither true nor false (though the claim that they are the rules of the game is either true or false). Rules thought of this way are more like imperatives that prescribe, permit, and prohibit certain inferential "moves." What we obviously need from the proponent of such a view, though, is some answer to the question of what makes a given rule "correct", or the right rule to employ.[9] There are many possible responses to this question. On one extreme one might advance a thoroughgoing subjectivist/relativist position, according to which there is no possible non-question-begging answer to the question of how to choose rules, since any answer would itself presuppose the legitimacy of certain rules. Such a view seems to lead inevitably to a kind of philosophical anarchy.

Chisholm and his followers are inclined to take as basic certain *epistemic* concepts that apply to beliefs and would employ these concepts in turn in defining the correctness of epistemic rules, and more generally the concept of epistemic probability.[10] So on Chisholm's view there are facts about what it is reasonable to believe that supervene on certain properties of believers. The noninferential justification of certain beliefs supervenes on non-epistemic features of various conscious states (such as what I seem to remember or seem to perceive). But once we get justified beliefs, there are additional synthetic necessary truths that tell us which other beliefs are justified provided that we have certain justified beliefs. We can, if we like, summarize these truths with rules that permit, require us, or prohibit us from forming certain beliefs when we have others.

The pragmatist might suggest that the legitimacy of a rule is a function of how well we get on employing the rule. But depending on how one understands getting along well, that view might collapse into a view I'll talk about shortly, a view that understands the critical concept of probability in terms of *frequency*. If, for example, a rule of inference is legitimate only in so far as it generates more true beliefs than false beliefs (when the input beliefs are true), then the theory that appears to take rules as its conceptual cornerstone is better understood as a version of the reliabilism that has become so popular primarily through the writings of Alvin Goldman.

Finally, one might take the legitimacy of a rule to be a function of internal relations of making probable (more about this shortly) that hold between propositions. But if one adopts this approach one will again be in a position to eliminate reference to rules in the analysis of inferential justification. It will be our understanding of the relations that hold between propositions that is key to our understanding inferential justification.

In what follows I want to focus on the last two approaches to understanding epistemic probability. I'm not sure many are willing to embrace the philosophical anarchy that accompanies a view in which arbitrary epistemic rules occupy center stage. And while there may be synthetic necessary truths about what one is justified in believing when one is justified in believing certain other propositions, it is hard for me to believe that the justificatory status of inferentially justified beliefs is not fundamentally derived from relationships between that which is believed. Put another way, it is surely a feature of the *arguments* whose premises and conclusions are believed that is key to understanding the justificatory status of the beliefs formed in the conclusions as a result of justified belief in the premises.

Suppose we agree that a key to understanding inferential justification is an understanding of the relation of making probable that holds between the premises and conclusions of arguments. What's the best way of understanding that relation? That debate has a long history, one that predates, but in many ways foreshadows, the now more familiar internalist/externalist controversies in epistemology.[11] Painting with a very broad stroke, one can attempt to analyze probability claims in epistemology on the well-known model of relative frequency that is offered as a way of interpreting claims about the probability of an individual or event having a certain characteristic. On a very crude interpretation of the frequency theory, to say of something that it is probably G is always elliptical for a more complex relativized claim of probability. One must refer the individual about which the probability claim is made to some reference class, say F. The more perspicuous statement of the probability claim is one about the probability of a's being G relative to its belonging to the class F. On the crudest and least plausible version of the view, the truth conditions for the claim of relative probability are determined by the percentage of F's that are G. The higher the percentage of F's that are G, the more likely it is that something is G relative to its being F. Of course, we very often don't *explicitly* supply the relevant reference class for a probability claim. A great deal of time and energy has been spent by philosophers trying to figure out what reference class is the appropriate *default* for ordinary probability claims. Is it a class that is ontologically homogeneous, or one that is epistemically homogeneous?[12] If epistemically homogeneous, with respect to *whose* knowledge is the homogeneity defined? I'm not sure that there are unambiguous answers to these questions, and in any event I'm not concerned with these questions now. It is also fairly obvious that the relative frequencies that constitute the truth conditions for probability claims are not actual frequencies—one will inevitably need to turn to counterfactuals with all of the problems that that move meets. My main concern, here, however, is the extent to which one can incorporate the alleged insight of a relative frequency theory of probability into an analysis of the *epistemic* probability that we are assuming holds between propositions.

One could borrow at least the spirit of the relative frequency interpretation of probability and apply it to relations between propositions in the following way. We could suggest that in claiming that P is probable relative to E we are simply asserting that E and P constitute a pair of propositions, which pair is a member of a certain class of proposition pairs such that, when the first member of the pair is true, usually the second is. Thus in saying that a's being G is probable relative to its being F and most observed F's being G, I could be construed as claiming that this pair of propositions is of the sort: Most observed X's are Y and this is X/This is Y, and most often it is the case that when the first member of such a pair is true, the second is. Similarly, if I claim that my seeming to remember eating this morning (E) makes it likely that I did eat this morning (P), I could be construed as asserting that the pair of propositions E/P is of the form S seems to remember X/X, such that most often when the first member of the pair is true, the second is.

The above view obviously resembles, at least superficially, the reliabilist's attempt to understand justified belief in terms of reliably produced beliefs. And it encounters many of the same difficulties. Just as the relative frequency theory of probability must inevitably move beyond actual frequencies in defining probability, so both the above account of epistemic probability and the reliabilist will inevitably be forced to move beyond actual frequencies in order to define the relevant epistemic probability/reliability. Just as reliabilism must deal with the generality problem, so the above approach to understanding epistemic probability as a relation between propositions must deal with the problem of how to choose from among alternative ways of characterizing the class of propositions pairs to which a given pair belongs. In evaluating the reliability of beliefs produced by memory, for example, the reliabilist must decide whether or not to lump together faint and vivid apparent memories, apparent memories of events in the distant past and events in the recent past, apparent memories of emotions and apparent memories of memories, vivid memories that occur in young people and vivid memories that occur in old people. A frequency approach to understanding epistemic probability can make the same sorts of distinctions between pairs of propositions, and consequently has the same sorts of decisions to make. Just as many reliabilists are troubled by the implications of their view for what to say about worlds in which demons consistently deceive epistemically "faultless" believers, so a frequency theory of epistemic probability must deal with similar alleged counterintuitive consequences about what is evidence for what in demon worlds. Lastly, both reliabilism and the frequency theory of epistemic probability will be anathema to the inferential internalist who is convinced that one needs *access* to probability connections in order to gain philosophically satisfying inferential justification. The inferential internalist who is a foundationalist will need to end a potential regress when it comes to gaining access to probabilistic connections. If one's model for foundational knowledge is something like knowledge of truths made true by facts with which one is directly presented, there seems no hope that one will get that kind of access to either the reliability of a belief-forming process or a probability relation (understood in terms of frequency) holding between propositions.

One of the historically most interesting alternatives to the frequency interpretation of epistemic probability is a view developed some eighty years ago by Keynes (1921). Keynes wanted to model epistemic probability on entailment. He held that just as one can be directly aware of entailment holding between two propositions, so one can also be directly aware of a relation of making probable holding between two propositions. There are, of course, obvious differences between entailment and making probable. From the fact that P entails Q it follows that the conjunction of P with any other proposition entails Q. From the fact that P makes probable Q, it doesn't follow that P together with anything else makes probable Q. But for all that, we could still take making probable to be an a priori internal relation holding between propositions (where an internal relation is one that necessarily holds given the existence and nonrelational character of its relata). P and Q being what they are it cannot fail to be the case that P makes probable Q. (It might also be true that P, R, and Q being what they are it cannot fail to be the case that (P and R) makes probable not-Q).

Which view of probability is correct? One might approach an answer to this question by looking at the most uncontroversial upper limit of making probable—entailment. But it quickly becomes apparent that entailment is a double-edged sword when it comes to serving as a paradigm for under-standing probability. The Keynesean will, of course, be right to stress the fact that entailment is an internal relation knowable a priori. But the frequency theorist (or the reliabilist) can equally stress that valid deduction is a paradigm of a conditionally reliable belief-producing process (a para-digm of pairs of proposition types such that when the first member of the pair is true, the second is as well).

Against the Keynesean, one might argue that it is patently absurd to suppose that making probable is an internal relation holding between propositions. Such a view yields the absurd consequence that claims about evidential connections are necessary truths knowable a priori. If *anything* is obvious it is that the discovery of evidential connections is a matter for empirical research. But while the objection might *seem* initially forceful, *one must remember the point we conceded in considering Huemer's objections to inferential internalism.* There is certainly no necessary connection between the litmus paper's turning red in a solution and the solution's being acidic, between dark clouds and storms, between footprints on a beach and the prior presence of people. But then, on reflection, we decided that it is misleading to characterize the litmus paper, dark clouds and footprints as *the* evidence from which we infer the respective conclusions. What we call evidence in ordinary parlance is just a *piece* of the very elaborate fabric of background information against which we draw our conclusions. So we shouldn't *expect* to find Keynesean probabilistic connections holding between, for example, the proposition that the litmus paper turned red and the proposition that the solution is acidic. Where *should* we look for a plausible example of Keynes's relation of making probable?

The obvious, though perhaps not all that helpful, answer is that we should look for it wherever we have what we take to be legitimate, *non-enthymematic* and non-deductive reasoning. One needn't, and probably shouldn't, insist that even if probability connections between propositions are know*able* a priori they are *easy* to know a priori. On some views, all mathematical truths are knowable a priori but as we painfully learned in math classes, their a priori character doesn't necessarily make the final for the course easy. Keyneseans have been given considerable grief for the fact that they may have come up with bad examples of alleged necessary truths about probability.[13] Various formulations of the principle of indifference, for example, are notoriously seductive but also notoriously problematic. The difficulty has always been to find the "right" way to characterize the continuum of alternative hypotheses whose probability can then be "divided" equally. If I know that something is either red or not-red, but don't have any evidence that bears on the thing's specific color one might suppose that it is just as likely relative to that evidence that it is red as that it is not-red. But a bit of reflection tells us that it is unreasonable to treat being red and being not-red the same way. There are many more ways of being not-red than there are ways of being red. The examples that give rise to paradox suggest, however, that there may be no unproblematic way of finding the appropriate way to divide up the properties along a continuum.[14] If it should turn out that there is no useful principle of indifference available to the epistemologist, it doesn't follow, of course, that a Keynesean conception of epistemic probability is doomed. The Keynesean should simply look elsewhere for plausible examples of propositions standing in the relation.

The trouble, of course, is that philosophers don't agree with each other about what constitutes legitimate but deductively invalid reasoning. Notwithstanding difficulties posed by Goodman's new (now not so new) riddle of induction, one might look at the relationship between the premises and conclusion of an enumerative inductive argument. Less plausibly, perhaps, one might think about the connection between the proposition that I seem to remember having an experience and the proposition that I had the experience. Still more problematically, we might suggest that there it is some sort of synthetic necessary truth that when I seem to see some physical object that is red and round that makes likely that there is some object that is red and round. How plausible is it to suppose that there are necessary truths asserting that our putative evidence in the above examples makes at least prima facie probable the conclusions?

Well how do we generally assess the plausibility of the claim that a certain proposition is necessarily true? We often start by asking ourselves whether we can conceive of a situation in which the proposition in question is false. And here, it seems we are in a position no more, but no less, plausible than that critic of externalist analyses of justification who invokes demon world scenarios in order to cast doubt on the externalist's view. The critic of reliabilism, for example, asks you to consider a possible world in which our sensory experiences have been produced by a demon bent on inducing in us a massively mistaken system of beliefs. The victim of the demon, the argument goes, surely has as much reason to believe propositions about the external world as do we with our phenomenologically indistinguishable sense experience. Because the reliabilist seems committed to the view that the unreliable belief-producing process in the demon world yields unjustified belief, while the reliable belief-producing process in the world as we take it to be yields justified beliefs, the reliabilist has an implausible view.

This objection to reliabilism is actually neutral with respect to the epistemic status of beliefs about the external world based on perception. It states only that *whatever* epistemic status such beliefs have in the world of veridical perception, they surely have that same status in the demon world. But if one adds the premise that both our beliefs and the beliefs of the demon's victims are *justified*, then one seems to be very close to endorsing the view that one can't *conceive of* having the kind of perceptual evidence we have without that evidence making probable the truth of what we believe, at least in the sense of "making probable" relevant to the possession of epistemic justification. Since many internalists (and even some externalists) have felt the force of the demon world objection to reliabilism, the view that making probable is an internal relation between propositions should be at least initially attractive to many epistemologists.[15]

At present, I am arguing only for the very modest conclusion that the Keynesean approach to understanding epistemic probability is a view worth considering seriously. When one distinguishes partial "evidence" from genuine evidence (the body of propositions in its *entirety* from which we infer conclusions), and when one keeps firmly in mind the ways in which making probable would differ from entailment (even if it is an internal relation between propositions), it is not that hard to take seriously the idea that one couldn't seem to remember having done X, for example, without that rendering probable having done X.

The view that there is an internal relation of making probable that holds between propositions is also just what the inferential internalist desperately needs in order to avoid vicious regress. While the classic foundationalist recognizes the need to cauterize the chain of reasoning that threatens to extend infinitely into the past, the inferential internalist needs to fear not one but an infinite number of infinite regresses. Just as one's inferential justification for believing P must be traced ultimately to something one is noninferentially justified in believing, so one must find evidential connections one can justifiably accept without inference. If one infers P from E one must not only be justified in believing E, but one must be justified in believing that E makes probable P. One might be able to infer that E makes probable P from some other proposition F, but then one must not only be justified in believing F, one must be justified in believing that F makes probable that E makes probable P. If inferential internalism and foundationalism are true, then unless we are to embrace a fairly radical skepticism, we must find *some* proposition of the form E makes probable P that we can justifiably believe without inference. Since most foundationalists will concede that there are at least some propositions of the form E entails P that one can know without inference, the closer we can make our analysis of making probable resemble our analysis of entailment, the more plausible will be the claim that we can know without inference propositions of the form E makes probable P.[16]

# Notes

1. I read a version of this paper at an APA symposium and profited greatly from the comments of Jim Van Cleve and James Joyce.
2. The conclusion of an argument can be said to be epistemically self-defeating if its truth entails that no-one could have justification for believing that it is true.
3. This is an argument Goldman made in "What is Justified Belief?" Both classic foundationalists and their newer externalist/reliabilist cousins hold very similar views about the need to embrace a foundationalist *structure* for justification.
4. Foley (1987) pursues a variation on this strategy.
5. As I'm using the locution, S can be justified in believing P on the basis of E even though S is not justified in believing P on the basis of his entire body of evidence.
6. Of course, one might argue that their difficulties reflect an implicit awareness that talk of inference in this context is highly misleading. One might also argue that one can "see" a probabilistic connection without being able to articulate it.
7. I argue in "Achieving Epistemic Ascent" that one might accommodate at least some externalist intuitions by allowing derivative concepts of inferential justification. Perhaps in certain contexts we will concede the justificatory status of a belief if it was inferred from premises that do make probable the conclusion, particularly if we think that the existence of the probability connection is causally connected to the person's willingness to form belief in the conclusion. Relaxing our standards still further, I suggest, we may even allow that a belief is justified if it is caused by a *fact* that is the truth-maker for a proposition that makes probable the proposition believed.
8. Jim Van Cleve suggested to me that inferential internalism might give rise to the regress.

9. There is an exactly analogous question that arises for rule utilitarians. One can perhaps define morally justified and morally unjustified action by reference to rules that require, permit, and prohibit certain sorts of actions, but we are in desperate need of a criterion for choosing between alternative rules.

10. So, for example, in Chisholm (1977), the primitive "more reasonable to believe than" is used to define "beyond reasonable doubt," "has some presumption in its favor," "is acceptable," "is certain," and "is evident."

11. One of the most interesting debates that has clear implications for the internalism/externalism controversy can be found in Keynes (1921) and Russell (1948) Part V.

12. Let us say that a reference class F is ontologically homogeneous with respect to some characteristic G when there is no way of dividing the class further such that the frequency with which things are G relative to membership in the subclass is different from the frequency with which things are G relative to F. A reference class F is epistemically homogeneous with respect to G when as far as we know the class is ontologically homogeneous.

13. Gillies (2000) seems to rely on counterexamples to putative probability connections to attack the Keynesean view.

14. Consider a well-known example. You know that I drove the mile between point A and point B traveling somewhere between 30 mph and 60 mph and thus taking somewhere between 1 minute and 2 minutes to make the trip. So what's the probability that I was going between 30 and 45 mph? It's surely just as likely as that I was going between 45 and 60 mph—the probability must be .5. And what's the probability that it took me somewhere between a minute and a minute and a half. Also the same as that I took between a minute and a half and two minutes—.5. But it turns out that you can't assign .5 probability to both the hypothesis that I was traveling between 30 and 45 mph and the hypothesis that it took me between a minute and a minute and a half.

15. Goldman himself was clearly troubled by the problem in his early paper on reliabilism (1979). Concern with the general problem led him first to "normal worlds" reliabilism (1986), and ultimately to bifurcate the concept of justification (1988).

16. Notice that the Keynesean approach to understanding probability does not require that for one to be inferentially justified in believing P on the basis of E one must know or be able to formulate *general* principles of probability. One might be able to see the connection between particular propositions without seeing how to generalize. An analogous point holds of entailment. One can see that P entails Q without being able to see that entailment as an instance of modus ponens, modus tollens, or any other general *kind* of entailment.

# References

Carroll, Lewis (1895). "What the Tortoise said to Achilles." *Mind*, 4, No. 14, 278–80.
Chisholm, Roderick (1977). *Theory of Knowledge*, 2nd Edition. Prentice-Hall.
Foley, Richard (1985). *The Theory of Epistemic Rationality*. Harvard University Press.
Fumerton, Richard (1995). *Metaepistemology and Skepticism*. Rowman and Littlefield.

———— (Forthcoming). "Achieving Epistemic Ascent" in *Ernest Sosa and His Critics.* Blackwell.

Gillies, Donald (2000). *Philosophical Theories of Probability.* Routledge.

Goldman, Alvin (1979). "What is Justified Belief?" in *Justification and Knowledge,* ed. George Pappas. Dordrecht.

———— (1986). *Epistemology and Cognition.* Harvard University Press.

———— (1988). "Strong and Weak Justification." Pp. 51–69 in *Philosophical Perspectives.* Ed. James Toberlin. Ridgeview Publishing.

Huemer, Mike (2002). "Fumerton's Principle of Inferential Justification." *Journal of Philosophical Research,* 27, 329–40.

Keynes, John (1921). *A Treatise on Probability.* Macmillan.

Klein, Peter (1998). "Foundationalism and the Infinite Regress of Reasons." *Philosophy and Phenomenological Research,* LVIII, 919–26.

Russell, Bertrand (1948). *Human Knowledge: Its Scope and Limits.* Simon and Schuster.

*Philosophical Issues, 14, Epistemology, 2004*

# CLOSURE MATTERS: ACADEMIC SKEPTICISM AND EASY KNOWLEDGE*

Peter Klein
Rutgers University

## Introduction

Epistemic closure matters because it seems to be responsible for much mischief in matters regarding local and global skepticism and in matters related to "easy knowledge." If closure holds, then, every circumspect knower of the fact that she has hands also knows that she is not being deceived by a highly powerful, malevolent demon hellbent on making it only appear that way. And how can we know that? Also, if closure holds, every circumspect knower of the fact that the table is red would also know that it is not a white table being illuminated by a red light. In such a case, it appears that our knowledge has been amplified too much for it seems that we can come to know that the table is red by looking at it, but how could we come to know that it is not white being illuminated by a red light by looking at the table?[1]

Nevertheless, closure seems intuitively plausible. If I know that all men are mortal and Socrates is a man, then it seems that I know, or at least am in a position to know, that Socrates is mortal because I know, or at least am in a position to know, the logical consequences of what I know. Every student of Euclidean Geometry implicitly employs closure when she claims she knows a high numbered theorem because she derived it from some lower numbered theorems. In general, it seems that we can always expand our knowledge by deduction.

What to do?

These are rough and ready intuitions and we need to get clear about what is really at stake and what is really informing the intuitions. I think if we do that, it will be clear that closure does not lend any credence either to any form of academic skepticism (i.e., the view that holds that we lack knowledge) or to the claim that we can gain knowledge too easily. Indeed, just the opposite is true. Closure, properly understood, helps to remove the power of a standard argument for academic skepticism, and it provides a basis for recognizing that the knowledge we have is very far from an ill-gotten gain.

## 1. What Epistemic Closure Is and Is Not

A property of propositions, $\Phi$, is closed under entailment just in case for every proposition, $x$, if $x$ has $\Phi$ and $x$ entails $y$, then $y$ has $\Phi$. Some properties clearly instantiate closure: truth, for example. If $x$ is true and $x$ entails $y$, then $y$ is true. Some properties clearly do not support closure: belief, for example. If $x$ is believed and $x$ entails $y$, it does not follow that $y$ is believed. Some properties seem *close* to being closed: knowledge, for example. Since $x$ can be believed and $x$ can entail $y$ without $y$ being believed, knowledge is not closed (on the reasonable assumption that the other necessary and jointly sufficient conditions of knowledge are such that when combined with the belief that x do not entail the belief that y).[2] Nevertheless, knowledge is at least *close* to being closed—or so one set of intuitions goes. If $x$ is known by S and $x$ entails $y$, then, even if S does not believe that y, S is at least in a position to know that y; that is, all of the necessary conditions for knowledge that y obtain, with the possible exception of the belief condition.

Further, "justified belief" is ambiguous. In one sense, justified belief appears closed; in another sense, it appears only *close* to being closed. On the one hand, when we say that a belief is justified, we could be referring to the propositional content of a belief (which may or may not be actually held). A proposition, $p$, is justified for S *iff* S has adequate reasons available for $p$ which are not ultimately overridden by other available reasons.[3] Following Firth, let us call this *propositional justification*.[4] This form of justification appears closed. For if I have adequate reasons available for $x$ and $x$ entails $y$, it appears that I have adequate reasons available for $y$—although, of course, we will have to examine this intuition carefully to determine just what it entails. On the other hand, when we say that a belief is justified, we could be referring to the justificatory status of the belief state itself. Again, following Firth, let us call this *doxastic justification*. We can say that a belief that p is doxastically justified for S *iff* S is acting in an epistemically responsible way in believing that p. Doxastic justification is only *close* to being closed because belief is not closed. I think the context will make clear which form of justification is at stake, but occasionally I will make explicit reference to one form or another in order to avoid confusion.

What is crucial to note here is that S need not do anything for a proposition to be justified for her. All that is required is that there be adequate evidence *available* to her. On the other hand, in order for a belief state to be doxastically justified, S must gather evidence and employ it properly.

With this distinction in mind, and employing propositional justification, the relevant form of the closure principle regarding justification is:

> CJ: If *x* is propositionally justified for S and *x* entails *y*, then *y* is propositionally justified for S.

The close-closure principle with regard to knowledge is:

> CK: If *x* is known by S and *x* entails *y*, then S is in a position to know that y.

Even these principles are obviously false unless we restrict the range of the variables to contingent propositions because, otherwise, "*y*" could stand for a necessary truth. So, we will make that restriction from now on. Most of the discussion regarding academic skepticism will be about CJ, because the issues there concern whether we possess adequate justifications for our beliefs; and for obvious reasons most of the discussion concerning easy *knowledge* will be about CK. I will assume that knowledge—at least of the sort that academic skepticism and the so-called easy knowledge problem is about—requires its possessor to have the right sort of adequate reasons for her beliefs. Although it is true that in some environments, dogs, small children and security devices are good detectors of hands and, thus, have some sort of knowledge, this rudimentary type of knowledge is not the type of knowledge at stake here.[5] For what matters here is whether we have adequate reasons available for our beliefs, whether we base our beliefs on those reasons, and whether those reasons are Gettier-proof, i.e., whether they are not defeated.[6] I will take knowledge to be true belief that is based upon reasoning that is not defeated.

Given those constraints, CJ would be true just in case, necessarily, whenever there are adequate reasons available for S to believe that x and *x* entails *y*, there are adequate reasons available for S to believe that y. I take good reasons for *p* to be the premises in a good argument which has *p* as its conclusion.[7] CK would be true just in case, necessarily, whenever *x* is known by S, all of the conditions for knowledge are satisfied for *y* with the exception of the belief condition.

Before turning to what makes a reason available to S, it is crucial to see what CK and CJ do ***not*** say. They do not specify any epistemic priority between *x* and *y*. In particular, 1) they do not require that the adequate reason available for the entailed proposition, *y*, be the entailing proposition, *x*. Further, 2) they do not require that an adequate reason, say *r*, for *x* be the reason for *y*. And finally, 3) they do not require that the adequate reasons for *x* include *y*.

1) To see that the closure principles cannot lead to the requirement that the adequate reason for the entailed proposition be the entailing one, consider this: If S knows that p, then S is in a position to know that p; and if S is justified in believing that p, then S is justified in believing that p. But it is clear that *p* cannot be an adequate reason for *p* because the argument '*p, therefore p*' begs the question and, hence, is not a good argument.

Nevertheless, we have to be careful here for it might also seem that any argument that contains an inference from *(A&B)* to *A* begs the question. For example, the following argument seems clearly to beg the question:

I.  1. *p & q*
    Therefore, *p*.

But not all arguments that contain the suspect step in **I** beg the question. Consider this argument:

II.  1. Sally says "*p & q*."
     2. Whatever Sally says is true.
     3. Therefore, *p & q*.
     4. Therefore, *q*.

The relevant difference between **I** and **II** is that in **I** what serves as an unchallenged reason—something taken as given for the purposes of this argument—is a proposition, one conjunct of which is the conclusion, whereas in **II** the unchallenged reasons (1 and 2) do not contain a conjunction one conjunct of which is the conclusion. Hence, in order to determine whether an argument begs the question, we have to trace the reasoning back to the unchallenged premises.

The crucial point here is that there are some clear cases in which CJ and CK would fail if the entailing proposition were required to be the reason for the entailed proposition because arguments employing the entailing proposition as a reason for the entailed proposition would beg the question.

There are other cases that are somewhat harder to detect which beg the question and in which *x* (in CJ and CK) has the form *[A & (A->B)]* and *y* is *B*. Suppose S gives this argument for God's existence:

1. The Bible says that God exists.
2. If the Bible says God exists, then God exists.
   Therefore, God exists.

That argument appears to be a good one until S gives her reason for believing premise 2. Suppose S's reason for believing 2 is that the Bible was written by God and whatever God writes is true. Such an argument would beg the question. Whereas, if S were to give as the reason for 2 that one thousand claims chosen at random from the Bible proved to be true, the argument would seem not to beg the question.

The crucial point here is, once again, that $x$ can entail $y$ without $x$ being able to provide S with a good reason for $y$ when, for example, S's reasons for $x$ happen to include $y$.

2) To see that neither CK nor CJ requires that the reason for the entailing proposition be the same reason for the entailed proposition, consider this case: Suppose that S is considering whether a certain hypothesis, $h$, is true and her argument for $h$ is that either $h$ is true or some contrary of $h$, say $c$, is true, but that $c$ is not true. So, in this case $\sim c$ serves as one of the reasons for $h$ for S. Consequently, S could not use the reasons for $h$ (which include $\sim c$) as the reason for $\sim c$ even though $h$ entails $\sim c$ because doing so will be begging the question. (S would be arguing from $\sim c$ to $\sim c$ through $h$.) Thus, even though $h$ entails $\sim c$, S could not employ her reason for $h$ as her reason for $\sim c$ because doing so will beg the question.

But we must be very careful not to succumb to a foundationalist bias here. Whatever is an available good reason for believing $x$ on one occasion, i.e., whatever is epistemically prior to $x$ on that occasion, might not be epistemically prior for the same person or a different person on another occasion. I might employ $\sim c$ as part of my reason for thinking that $h$ and, hence, I could not use $h$ as a reason for $\sim c$. However, you might not employ $\sim c$ as part of your reason for $h$ and you could then use $h$ as your reason for $\sim c$. And on some other occasion, I might follow your example and, then, I could use $h$ as my reason for $\sim c$ even were I first to have come to know $h$ by reasoning from $\sim c$.

Foundationalists will think that some propositions, for example, first person sensation reports, are necessarily epistemically prior to material object propositions. For foundationalists, propositional epistemic priority is pre-established before the concrete process of reasoning begins. They will hold that the concrete process must be modeled on the pre-established epistemic priority. But that flies in the face of what we take to be good reasoning. For there are occasions on which I can employ *there is a red object before me* as my reason for thinking that I am seeing redly (as opposed to, for example, seeing greenly). I could be wondering whether I'm remembering what seeing redly is like and on such an occasion a reason for believing that I am seeing redly could be that there is a red patch of cloth before me (perhaps the patch is so labeled and others tell me it is red). The point here is simply that closure does not dictate the epistemic priority among reasons for beliefs because even if I were to come to know a proposition, $p$, by reasoning to it from $q$, it does not follow that on some occasions I could not give $p$ as my reason for $q$, when $q$ is what is being challenged and $p$ is taken for granted.

3) To see that neither CJ nor CK requires that the entailed proposition, $y$, be one of the reasons for the entailing proposition, consider a simple case

in which $x$ and $y$ are mutually entailing. If $x$ were required to be in the evidential ancestry of $y$ and $y$ were required to be in the evidential ancestry of $x$, then the closure principles would require circular reasoning.

The crucial point to keep in mind is that neither of the closure principles specifies any *sui generis* evidential relationship between the entailing and the entailed proposition.

## 2. Availability of Reasons

What does it mean for a reason to be "available" to S? Consider a case: Suppose S believes that silver is more dense than copper. In order for that belief to be knowledge, we have said that there must be good reasons available to S for that belief. And the question is this: How readily available must they be? Must they be armchair available, such that on mere careful reflection, *ceteris paribus*, S will produce them? Put another way, must a proposition be entailed or otherwise implied by the content of S's current beliefs in order for that proposition to be available? In the case under consideration here, that requirement would be fulfilled if, for example, S believed that a cubic centimeter of silver weighs approximately 10.5 grams and that a cubic centimeter of copper weighs about 8.3 grams. But requiring armchair availability might strike some as too strict.

One could take a more lenient view and hold that a proposition, $x$, is available to S just in case there is an epistemically credible way of S's coming to believe that $x$ given S's current epistemic practices.[8] In the case under consideration, one could hold that if S's epistemic practices are such that she would consult a reliable source of information about relative densities and if that reliable source were to list silver as more dense than copper, then one could deem that there are adequate reasons available for S to believe that silver is more dense than copper. This might seem too lenient until it is remembered that the mere availability of reasons is not sufficient for knowledge. The reasons must be deployed by S.

It is not easy to determine the appropriate standards for "availability of reasons." But luckily we need not solve that problem here so long as we employ the same standards in both the antecedent and consequent of CJ.

I argued earlier that closure does not dictate an epistemic priority among reasons. On one occasion, $x$ could be available as a reason for $y$, and on another occasion, $y$ could be available as a reason for $x$. What is ruled out is that there is an occasion on which each is available as a reason for the other. Otherwise, the rules would permit begging the question.

What differentiates one occasion from another? My answer is neo-Wittgensteinian. Being able to provide reasons requires that some propositions are occasion-relative up-for-grabs (the ones requiring the reasons) and others are occasion-relative bedrock propositions (the ones that serve as reasons and are not up-for-grabs). Of course the occasion can change and something that was bedrock relative to one occasion can be up-for-grabs relative to another occasion. If, for example, on one occasion I am asked what reason I have for believing that Socrates is mortal, I could answer that all humans are mortal and Socrates is a human. On another occasion, if I were asked why I believe that all humans are mortal, I could give *Socrates is human and mortal* among my reasons.

A crucial question to ask in a discussion of global academic skepticism is this: Is there some occasion on which everything is up-for-grabs? I think the answer is clearly "no," if what would be required on such an occasion is that no reasons are available to provide a good argument for the propositions that are up-for-grabs. For if everything were up-for-grabs, nothing could be available as a reason because nothing could qualify as an occasion-relative bedrock proposition. On the other hand, if what is meant is that once a reason is given, it can be challenged, and the reason then offered can be challenged, etc., then that seems perfectly possible.[9] Put another way, the question "Is there a reason for everything I believe?" is ambiguous. If it means "Is there some reason or other available for each thing I believe?", the answer could be "yes." If it means "Is there one reason for all the things I believe?", the answer is "no."

## 3. Academic Skepticism

Using the following abbreviations, here is the *standard argument* for academic skepticism employing CJ:

m: any Moorean proposition (e.g., I have hands, there are other people, the earth has existed for many years)

sk: S is in a skeptical scenario in which *m* is false but it appears just as if *m* were true

Jsx: S has good reasons that are available and not ultimately overridden for *x*

1. If Jsm, then Js$\sim$sk.
2. $\sim$Js$\sim$sk
Therefore, $\sim$Jsm

In giving this argument, the skeptic is making two claims: First, if there are good enough reasons available for S to believe that m, then there are good enough reasons available for S to deny that sk. Second, there aren't good enough reasons available for S to deny that sk. The first claim is taken to be true because CJ is true and *m* and $\sim$*sk* are substitution instances in the general principle. If CJ is true, then *necessarily* whenever there is a good set of reasons available for $x$ (and $x$ entails $y$), then there is a good set of reasons available for $y$. We have already seen that CJ (and CK) do not dictate the epistemic priority between the entailing and entailed propositions, but taking a clue from that discussion, it becomes clear that there are only three possible arrangements of reasons that would satisfy the requirement that *on any given occasion* when there are adequate, available reasons for $x$ and $x$ entails $y$, there are adequate, available reasons for $y$:

I.   $x$ is epistemically prior to $y$ and is available as a reason for $y$; or
II.  $x$ and $y$ are epistemically on par and there is some reason, say $r$, that is available and epistemically prior to both $x$ and $y$, and serves as a reason for either $x$ or $y$; or
III. $y$ is epistemically prior to $x$ and is available as a reason for $x$.

We can schematize those three arrangements as follows by thinking of available reasons as steps along an inference path from premises to a conclusion as follows:[10]

Path I    $r \ldots x \ldots y$

Path II   $r \diagup^{x}_{\diagdown y}$

Path III  $r \ldots y \ldots x$

Although I argued above that CJ does not dictate the epistemic priority between the entailing and entailed propositions, CJ does require that on any occasion there be at least one of the three paths available that includes the entailing and the entailed proposition. That there are such paths is clear.

Path I reasoning is employed whenever we can use a justified proposition, $x$, that entails another, $y$, as our reason for $y$. Suppose I have good reasons to believe the five Euclidean postulates. Maybe they strike me as "clear and distinct" or maybe a highly trusted teacher has told me that they are true. On such an occasion I could use the conjunction of those axioms as my reasons for believing the theorems that they entail. What better argument could there be for the theorems? Further, if I had reasoned that way on a particular occasion, then on pain of circular reasoning, on that same occasion the theorems could not be available as reasons for thinking the axioms are true.

Nevertheless, one could imagine occasions in which Path III type reasoning could be employed: Suppose that I was ignorant of the five postulates but that I had measured the legs and the hypotenuse of many right triangles and concluded on inductive grounds that the sum of the squares of the legs is equal to the square of the hypotenuse. I could then reason that the postulates (or the subset of them that entails the Pythagorean Theorem) are true because by assuming them, the appearances can be saved. On such an occasion, the entailed proposition serves as evidence for the entailing one.

Path II cases are those when there is a proposition, $r$, that is a good reason for both $x$ and $y$. For example, if I have a good reason to believe that Anne has two brothers, that reason would be a good reason for believing that Anne has one brother. In such a case, the entailed and the entailing proposition are on an epistemic par because the very same reason, $r$, that provides an inference path to $x$ also provides the path to $y$.

So much for the abstract characterization of the closure principles. How would they apply to the argument for academic skepticism under consideration here? Given premise 1 in the standard argument for academic skepticism, the skeptic must think that one of the three paths just described correctly depicts the evidential priority between $m$ and $\sim sk$ on the occasion when $\sim Jsm$ is up-for-grabs. My argument will be i) that if the skeptic thinks that either Path I or Path II is the correct depiction, closure is playing no role in the standard argument because the conclusion would be reached without employing Premise 1 and ii) that the skeptic cannot provide a basis for thinking that Path III is the correct portrayal.

Suppose the skeptic held that the appropriate evidential priority is portrayed by Path I. Then, in giving her argument for premise 2 (i.e., $\sim Js\sim sk$) in the standard argument, she would have to show that there is no reason, $r$, that is available for $m$ because it is granted (in premise 1) that there is a path from $m$ to $\sim sk$ on the occasion when $\sim Jsm$ is up-for-grabs. But whatever argument she provides for the claim that there are no adequate reasons available for $m$ would show that $m$ is not justified. That, however, is the conclusion to which this argument is aimed. In other words, the conclusion would have to be established in giving the argument for premise 2. Thus, premise 1—closure—is useless. It plays no role in the standard argument. I am not claiming that there is no such an argument for premise 2. The point is that closure is not useful in motivating the conclusion, because such an argument for premise 2 would not employ closure and that argument would be sufficient to establish the conclusion.

Suppose the skeptic held that the proper evidential priorities are depicted by Path II, that is, that $m$ and $\sim sk$ are epistemically on a par. Two propositions, $m$ and $\sim sk$, are epistemically on a par on some occasion just in case for every reason, $r$, $r$ is an adequate reason for $m$ iff $r$ is an adequate reason for $\sim sk$. In arguing for premise 2 in the standard argument, the skeptic must provide a basis for thinking that there is no such reason for $\sim sk$. The skeptic cannot argue that there is an adequate reason for $m$ that is not an adequate reason for $\sim sk$, because that would be inconsistent with the conclusion. The skeptic cannot argue that there is an adequate reason for $\sim sk$ that is not an adequate reason for $m$, because that would be inconsistent with premise 2. What the skeptic must claim is that there is no adequate reason for $\sim sk$ since there is no adequate reason for either $m$ or $\sim sk$. But if there is such an argument for premise 2, once again closure is useless to the academic skeptic because the conclusion would have been reached without employing premise 1 in the standard argument.

Finally, suppose the skeptic thinks that the proper epistemic priority between $\sim sk$ and $m$ is that depicted by Path III. Here the skeptic would be claiming that $\sim sk$ must be among the reasons for believing that $m$. Unlike the two other options just considered in which CJ was not needed by the skeptic, here—and only here—is closure potentially useful in the skeptic's argument.

But on what basis can the skeptic claim that we are required to have evidence available against the skeptical scenario's obtaining as part of our reasons for believing that we have hands? In general, when must we have evidence against a contrary of a proposition as part of our evidence for believing the proposition?

That's not an easy question to answer, but we can begin by showing that one can't be required to do so with regard to every contrary. Let $m$ be the proposition for which we are seeking adequate reasons. Here are two contraries of $m$: $\sim m$ & $p$, $\sim m$ & $\sim p$. If it is required that our reasons for $m$ include the denial of both contraries, then we are requiring that our reasons for $m$ entail $m$, since $\{\sim(\sim m$ & $p)$, $\sim(\sim m$ & $\sim p)\}$ entails $m$. So, on pain of requiring that even for contingent, empirical propositions we have adequate evidence for $m$ only if our evidence entails $m$, the skeptic cannot require that our evidence include the denial of every contrary of $m$.

So what contraries of $m$ need to be included in the adequate available evidence for $m$?

Consider a case with a long history—the case of identical twins. Cicero considered such a case of the twins Publius Geminus and Quintus Geminus who looked exactly alike—at least from the distance and perspective from which we normally identify people.[11] If we believed there were such twins, then *that looks like Publius* will not provide the basis for doxastically justifying the belief that the person we are seeing from the normal distance and perspective is, indeed, Publius. In such a case, adequate reasoning would seem to require including *it's not Quintus* among the reasons.

Contrast this case with one in which we think we see Publius but an incredulous bystander claims that in order to have an adequate reason for believing it is Publius we must first eliminate the possibility that it is Magicus's dog that Magicus has transformed into an exact duplicate of Publius. Presumably, we would not have to include the denial of that alternative among the available reasons because there is absolutely no reason to think it is true—unless, of course, we have a reason to think Magicus has that ability, a suitable motive, and an opportunity.

My suggestion is that we are required to include the denial of an alternative to $m$ as part of the evidence for $m$ only when there is some reason, however slight, for thinking that the alternative is true. And that requires that it is *logically possible* for there to be some reason, however slight, that it is true. But if *sk* were true, there could not possibly be any reason for thinking it to be true. Put another way, if there were a reason for thinking that *sk* is true, then *sk* would not be true.

To see that, suppose that there were some phenomenon that necessarily obliterates all traces of its existence. I mean *all*! If it exists, there is no evidence that it does. A global skeptical scenario is like that. If it were true, there could be no reason for thinking it to be true. For there are only two types of reasons: *a priori* reasons and empirical reasons. I assume that there can be no *a priori* reason for thinking that *sk* is true. There could be a reason for thinking it is logically possible that *sk* is true, but that isn't a reason for thinking it is true. There could be no empirical reason for thinking that *sk* is true, for if *sk* were true, all (I mean *all*!) so-called empirical *reasons* would be nothing but pseudo-reasons. If, for example, I were a BIV, everything would look just as it does—that is, everything would look just as though I am not a BIV but rather had hands (and all the other nice accouterments!). That's the way the skeptic typically presents the consequence of being a BIV. But it is also true that the BIV hypothesis, like any *global* switched-world hypothesis, is designed to discredit all (I mean *all*!) empirical reasons. Thus, the BIV hypothesis also discredits all reasons for thinking that we are BIV's. All so-called evidence about the "external world" is really pseudo-evidence and completely worthless if the BIV hypothesis is true. Thus, it is not logically possible for *sk* to be true and for there to be empirical evidence of its truth.

So, if the academic skeptic were to suggest that I had better eliminate *sk* as an alternative to *m* prior to believing that *m*, I should respond by saying "I am under no obligation to do so because either there is no reason to believe *sk* or *sk* is false. If there is no reason to believe that *sk*, then I need not eliminate it as an alternative to *m*. So, either I need not eliminate *sk* or *sk* is false. Take your choice. In neither case, is *sk* a serious rival of *m*."

That strikes me as a perfectly good response to an academic skeptic who holds that Path III depicts the appropriate evidential priorities. Hence, the mere mentioning or considering an alternative (even in a serious manner) does not make it a relevant alternative. In order to know that there is a hand, I do not first have to provide evidence against BIV—even were someone to seriously mention that possibility. (I should note parenthetically, that if I am right about this, contextualist responses to skepticism are misguided. But that's a story for another occasion.)

If the argument up to this point is correct, closure can provide no help to the academic skeptic in her pursuit of an argument for global skepticism because either i) the correct depiction of the epistemic priority between *m* and ~*sk* is displayed by Path I or Path II and in that case the conclusion of the argument will have been reached without employing closure or ii) the skeptic is simply wrong in thinking that Path III correctly depicts the epistemic priority because there cannot be a reason for thinking that *sk* is true.

But, you say, what about less global, less all encompassing skepticisms that don't require that all reasons be discounted? Consider dreaming, for example. Isn't there some evidence for the claim that I am now dreaming? After all, we sometimes dream and sometimes when dreaming it seems as though we are sitting by the fire and looking at our hands. So, isn't there some reason—however slight—for thinking that we are now dreaming? Yes, there is. But we can and do have further reasons for eliminating that hypothesis. For as Descartes said in the "Sixth Meditation" we find that our dreams don't cohere well with the rest of our experience:

> ...I ought to set aside all the doubts of these past days as hyperbolical and ridiculous, particularly that very common uncertainty respecting sleep, which I could not distinguish from the waking state: for *at present* [emphasis added] I find a very notable difference between the two. Inasmuch as our memory can never connect our dreams one with the other, or with the whole course of our lives as it unites events which happen to us while we are awake. And, as a matter of fact, if someone, while I was awake, quite suddenly appeared to me and disappeared as fast as do the images which I see in sleep, so that I could not know from whence the form came nor whither it went, it would not be without reason that I should deem it a spectre or a phantom...[12]

The point here seems to be that while dreaming, we might not be doxastically justified in believing that we are dreaming because we might fail to appreciate the evidence that we are dreaming. Nevertheless, after we awake, we can be doxastically justified in believing that we had been dreaming and that we are not dreaming now.[13]

## 4. Easy Knowledge

The problem of easy knowledge has been developed by Stewart Cohen. Cohen imagines what I call an epistemist (a person who claims that we have knowledge) arguing that we know we are not brains-in-a-vat by employing what I have called Path I as follows:

> ...if I know that the table is red, then it follows, by closure, e.g., that I know I am not a brain-in-a-vat being deceived into believing that the table is red. Now some proponents of evidentialism... openly embrace this as a way of responding to the skeptical argument that relies on the closure principle. They concede that I cannot come to know I am not a brain-in-a-vat being deceived into thinking the table is red, by inferring it from the table looks red. But I *can* come to know the table is red on the basis of its looking red. And once I know

the table is red, I can infer and thereby come to know that I am not a brain-in-a-vat being deceived into thinking that the table is red.[14]

While not directly challenging this line of reasoning attributed to the epistemist, Cohen does think that it leads, by parity of reasoning, to a clearly unacceptable consequence, namely that in some cases of less than global skepticism we can acquire knowledge all too easily. Here is what he says:

> For example, if I know the table is red on the basis of its looking red, then it follows by the closure principle that I can know that it's not the case that the table is white but illuminated by red lights. Presumably, I cannot know that it's not the case that the table is white illuminated by red lights, on the basis of table's looking red. So, the evidential foundationalist will have to treat this case analogously to the global deception case: I can know the table is red on the basis of its looking red, and once I know the table is red, I can infer and come to know that it is not white but illuminated by red lights. But it seems very implausible that I could in this way come to know that I'm not seeing a white table illuminated by red lights.[15]

What are we to say about this problem posed for the evidential foundationalist who i) accepts closure and ii) reasons against the global skeptic as Cohen envisions? Is she committed to the all-too-easy acquisition of knowledge?

First, since we are here concerned with knowledge, I take it that the relevant closure principle is CK. The issue is whether we can come to know (or at least be in a position to come to know) that the table is not white illuminated by a red light in this fashion. Now it might be thought that this issue is equivalent to whether the belief that the table is not white illuminated by a red light can be doxastically justified by the table's looking red through an intermediary doxastically justified belief that the table is red. But as we will see, I think those two issues are not equivalent and keeping them distinct will help to dissolve the problem of too easily obtained knowledge.

There is one readily available response, namely give up foundationalism.[16] In fact, I have argued against foundationalism on other occasions.[17] And I have already suggested a reason in this paper for rejecting foundationalism—namely that foundationalism holds, illegitimately, that there is a fixed epistemic priority among propositions which on every occasion must be mirrored in what leads to a belief being doxastically justified. But I don't think there really is a problem for foundationalism here because the problem of easy knowledge is orthogonal to the issue of whether there are foundational propositions. For the basic question is this: Regardless of whether *the table looks red* is foundational in this case, have we gained knowledge too easily?

To begin to answer that question, we should be very clear about what knowledge would have been gained through employing closure. From, *(t)* *the table is red*, I cannot infer anything about the lighting conditions in which I am seeing the table. In particular I cannot deduce that the table I am seeing is not white *and* being illuminated by a red light where the "and" is not within the scope of the "not." In other words, I could not infer from t that *(∼w & r)*, where "w" stands for *the table is white* and "r" stands for *the table is being illuminated by a red light*. What I can infer is that ∼*(w & r)*. But that, of course, is not a claim about the lighting conditions. I could just as easily have inferred that the table is not white while **not** being illuminated by a red light. That is, I could just as easily have inferred ∼*(w & ∼r)*. The English sentence "the table is not white but illuminated by red lights" might seem to indicate that I had gained some knowledge of the perceptual circumstances by employing closure on *the table is red*. But the scope of the negation has to include the conjunction if this is to be a case of the application of closure.

The same comments hold for Dretske's famous zebra-in-the-zoo case.[18] In that case I know that the animals are zebras but it is claimed that I don't know that they are not cleverly disguised mules. But once again we must be careful here. I cannot infer anything about whether the animals I'm observing are or are not disguised. All that I am entitled to infer from the *animals are zebras* is that it is not the case that both (the animals are mules and the animals are cleverly disguised). Indeed I can infer from what I know that it is not the case that both (the animals are mules and Cincinnati is not the capital of Ohio). But, of course, I didn't gain any knowledge about state capitals in this way. That *would be* too easy!

So, I must admit to not feeling the bite of the example. The inference to *the table is not white while being illuminated by red lights* has not amplified our knowledge at all. Nothing has been "gained" by inferring *the table is not white but illuminated by red lights* from *the table is red*. If there is a problem with too easily gained knowledge it must have arisen prior to that inference.

So, why does Cohen think that there has been some ill-gotten gain? Here is what he says:

> Suppose my son wants to buy a red table for his room. We go in the store and I say, "That table is red. I'll buy it for you." Having inherited his father's obsessive personality, he worries, "Daddy, what if it's white with red lights shining on it?" I reply, "Don't worry—you see, it looks red, so it is red, so it's not white but illuminated by red lights." Surely he should not be satisfied with this response.[19]

I agree. The son should not be satisfied with this response because what the son is challenging is not the move from *the table is red* to *the table is not white being illumined by a red light*, but rather the son is challenging the move from *the table looks red* to *the table is red*. The son is questioning whether his father is entitled to move from a claim about how the table looks to a claim about how the table is.

Put another way, just as closure was not useful to the academic skeptic, it does not help to explain why the inquisitive son should not be satisfied with the putative response. The problem of easy knowledge, if indeed there is a problem, arises before closure is employed by the father to arrive at ~*(w & r)*. The son's requirement that Cohen produce some reason for thinking that in this situation the table's apparent color does not provide an adequate basis for coming to know its "real" color does not challenge the step at which closure becomes relevant.

Let's be clear what the issue is here. The issue isn't whether Cohen could offer to his son *the table looks red* as a reason for thinking that the table is red when what's up-for-grabs is whether how things look in this circumstance has any probative value concerning how things are in this circumstance. The issue is, or rather should be, whether the *father* could have come to know the "real" color of the table by reasoning from *the table looks red* to *the table is red*. And this case doesn't show or even tend to show that he couldn't.

Now, if what Cohen means is that the father could not come to know that the table is not white illuminated by a red light *solely* because it looks red, then he is clearly correct—given that knowledge—at least the kind requiring non-defeated reasoning—cannot arise simply on the basis of how things look. Detector knowledge could. But our target here, presumably, is knowledge that requires that our beliefs be doxastically justified. So, our question is this: Can someone *come to know* that the table is not white illuminated by a red light solely by reasoning from *the table looks red* to *the table is red* and then to *the table is not white illuminated by a red light*? Since the problematic step is the first one, not the second one, that question becomes: Can someone come to know *the table is red* by reasoning from *the table appears red*?

For our purposes, we can say that S *comes to know p at t* just in case S did not know that p prior to t, and *p* is true, and S has located good enough reasons for believing that p, and S believes *p* on the basis of those reasons, and there are no genuine defeaters of the reasons on which S bases her belief that p.[20] So, the issue becomes: Can S come to know *the table is red* simply by reasoning from *the table looks red*?

I think that question is ambiguous and once the ambiguity is exposed, the so-called problem of easy knowledge will dissolve.

1. The question could mean this: Is *the table looks red* a good enough reason, on some occasions, for satisfying one of the necessary conditions for knowing *the table is red*? In our terminology: On some occasions, does the former make the latter propositionally justified? Or, equivalently: On some occasions, does the belief that the table looks red make the belief that the

table is red doxastically justified? If those are the questions, then I think the answer to each is clearly "yes." I take it that a mark of empirical knowledge is that the justification condition can be satisfied by defeasible reasoning. Further, I take it as given that *the table looks red* provides an adequate defeasible reason for *the table is red*—at least on some occasions. On what occasions? Occasions on which the probative value of how things look is not up-for-grabs.[21]

What makes something up-for-grabs? That's a difficult question, and for our purposes an answer is not required. I think we can assume that prior to Cohen's son's having questioned the lighting conditions, the probative value of how the table appeared was not up-for-grabs and that during the conversation it did become up-for-grabs. Hence, there are some occasions when *the table looks red* is a good enough reason for satisfying one of the necessary conditions for knowing *the table is red*.

2. The question could mean this: On the occasions when *the table looks red* is a good enough reason for rendering *the table is red* propositionally justified and S comes know that the table is red, does S's knowledge owe its existence only to that reasoning? If that is the question, then I think the answer is clearly "no." We have said that knowledge is true belief based upon defeasible, *but undefeated* reasoning. So, if the lighting conditions are misleading or if S's perceptual equipment is not working properly, then S would not have gained knowledge that the table is red even if the belief is doxastically justified on that occasion. More generally, if the circumstance is not propitious for obtaining the truth, then evidence about how things look is defeated evidence. In other words, when reasoning is defeated by a proposition describing the infelicitous circumstance, the reasoning cannot produce knowledge. The crucial point is that knowledge does not arise merely on the basis of adequate defeasible reasoning, it arises on the basis of such reasoning that is not defeated.

Nevertheless, Cohen thinks that we cannot come to know *the table is red* by reasoning from *the table looks red* because if we could, then we could come to know that the table is not white being illuminated by a red light on the basis of the table's looking red. Here is what he says in defense of that claim:

> ... It seems implausible that we could come to know [that the table is not white but illuminated by a red light] in this way. And if we cannot come to know that it is not white illuminated by red lights in this way, then given the trivial entailment and the closure principle, it follows that we can't know that it is red simply on the basis of its looking red.[22]

I have agreed that we cannot come to know that the table is red "simply on the basis of its looking red" because more is required than merely possessing the reason that the table looks red for us to gain knowledge that the table is red. The table's looking red is a good, albeit defeasible, reason for believing that the table is red. We don't need additional *reasons* on those occasions when the reasoning is not defeated but—and here's the crucial point— having a good, defeasible reason for believing that the table is red is not sufficient for possessing or gaining knowledge that the table is red. The belief that the table is red owes its status as knowledge to more than the mere possession of an adequate, defeasible reason. The belief is doxastically justified on the basis of the inference but it owes its status as knowledge to the fact that there are no defeaters of the justification of the proposition that the table is red.[23] In other words, we can't *come to know* a true proposition *solely* on the basis of defeasible reasoning. Our knowledge also owes is status to the fact that there are no defeaters.

Further, *pace* Cohen, the so-called case of easy knowledge is not really parallel to the situation posited by the academic skeptic. The son might have a reason for thinking that the appearances are not to be taken at face value in this circumstance. Perhaps he's heard that lighting in stores is not designed to illuminate things in a way that their apparent color is their "real" color. Or perhaps he has overheard his father saying that he intends to buy a white table. Of course, if what prompts the son to raise the possibility of the table's being white illuminated by a red light is merely that he is obsessive (as Cohen says), then (perhaps) he has no reason at all for doubting the probative value of the table's appearance. In that case, it strikes me that Cohen could reasonably respond "You don't have any reason for distrusting the appearances in this case. You're just being obses- sive like your old man. And unless you have a reason for thinking that the appearances might be deceiving on this occasion, the table's looking red provides a good enough basis for believing that it is red. Now, if you're asking me whether my knowledge that it is red arises solely on the basis of how it appears, then the issue becomes more complex and I will have to explain how knowledge arises only when the reasoning is undefeated."

Let us, however, suppose that the son really does have a reason for thinking appearances might be deceiving on this occasion. A proper response from the father would be to provide evidence which removes the son's doubts. And that is possible. For example, the father could simply point out that there are no red lights in the store.

This case can be used to underscore the crucial disanalogy between ordinary incredulity and global skepticism. Only in former *can* there be reasons available i) for thinking the alternative possibility obtains and ii) for adequately overriding that thought. By contrast, global skeptical sce- narios are constructed so that no reasons for thinking that they are true *can* be provided and no reasons for removing the doubt *can* be provided.

The "solution" to global skeptical worries is quite different from the "solution" to ordinary incredulousness. In the latter case, the doubt can be removed by locating more evidence. In the former, careful reflection about the standard argument shows that either it begs the question or that it is impossible for the skeptical hypothesis to be true and for there to be evidence for its truth. Such hypotheses need not be ruled out. Thus, Hume was wrong to claim that inattention alone would provide relief from global academic skepticism; careful attention to the standard arguments can provide a remedy.[24]

To sum up the discussion about the so-called problem of easy knowledge: Cohen knew that the table was red before the doubts were raised because he could come to know that the table is red without first knowing that the table was not white illuminated by red lights. The belief that the table is not white illuminated by a red light is doxastically justified by the belief that the table is red *but* the belief that the table is not white illuminated by a red light owes is epistemic status as knowledge to its being based upon an undefeated justification.

Knowledge would be too easily obtained if it were merely true, doxastically justified belief. More is required. Each time our reasoning amplifies our empirical knowledge it must be resistant to defeat.[25] And such reasoning is much harder to come by.

## Summary

Closure neither provides any solace to the academic skeptic nor contributes to the so-called problem of easy knowledge. Indeed, a proper understanding of closure shows that the academic skeptic cannot provide a good argument for her view and helps to show that there is no genuine problem of easy knowledge.

## Notes

* I would like to thank Anne Ashbaugh and Ernest Sosa for their many discussions about the issues in this paper.

1. The problem of easy knowledge was developed by Stewart Cohen in his "Basic Knowledge and the Problem of Easy Knowledge," *Philosophy and Phenomenological Research*, 65.2, 2002, 309–329. There is the related issue of bootstrapping developed by Jonathan Vogel in "Reliabilism Leveled," *Journal of Philosophy*, 2000, and employed by Cohen as another purported instance of knowledge too easily obtained. This paper is concerned only with the problem of easy knowledge as it is related to closure. (But see endnote 25.)
2. Ted Warfield has correctly pointed out that the failure of closure of one of the necessary and jointly sufficient conditions of a property, Φ, is not sufficient for Φ to fail to be closed. See his "When Epistemic Closure Does and Does Not Fail: A Lesson from the History of Epistemology," *Analysis*, forthcoming.
3. "Ultimately" is needed since the overridder could itself be overridden, etc.

4. As far as I know, this distinction was first introduced by Roderick Firth in "Are Epistemic Concepts Reducible to Ethical Concepts?" in *Values and Morals* (Dordrecht, Holland: D. Reidel Publishing Co., 1978), edited by Alvin Goldman and Jaegwon Kim.

5. Ernest Sosa has discussed a similar but not identical distinction in *Knowledge in Perspective* (Cambridge: Cambridge University Press, 1991), especially p. 95. As I understand it, reflective knowledge arises only after reflection about the probative value of our reasons. While I agree that this is often an appropriate topic for rational inquiry, the knowledge I take to be at stake here does not require that one have examined the probative value of the reasons for *p*. It merely requires that S's belief that p be based upon adequate, undefeated, reasons for *p*.

6. See my "A Proposed Definition of Propositional Knowledge," *Journal of Philosophy*, 67 (16), 1971, 471–482 and a more recent defense of the defeasibility theory in "Knowledge is True, Non-defeated Justified Belief," *Essential Knowledge* (New York: Longman Publishers, 2004) ed. Steven Luper, 124–135. We can define a defeater of the propositional justification of *x* as a *true* proposition such that when conjoined with the propositions in *x*'s evidential ancestry render *x* not justified. That account of defeaters is not able to handle the problem of misleading defeaters but it is unnecessary to take a detour into that esoteric domain for our purposes here.

7. By a "good" argument, I mean one that does not beg the question and which, if it is deductive, it is valid, and if it is non-deductive, it is sufficiently strong.

8. Further, it seems plausible to suggest that S might even develop new concepts when seeking reasons. But a discussion of that would take us too far afield. I have discussed that elsewhere, most recently in "Human Knowledge and the Infinite Regress of Reasons," *Philosophical Perspectives*, 13, J. Tomberlin (ed.), 1999, 297–325 and "Human Knowledge and the Infinite Progress of Reasoning" (forthcoming).

9. See endnote 8 for a list of some articles in which I have defended such a view. In addition it is defended in "When Infinite Regresses Are *Not* Vicious," *Philosophy and Phenomenological Research*, 66.3, 2003, 718–729, "What *IS* Wrong with Foundationalism is that it Cannot Solve the Epistemic Regress Problem," *Philosophy and Phenomenological Research*, 68.1, 2004, 166–171 and in "Infinitism is the Solution to the Regress Problem" and "Response to Ginet" *Contemporary Debates in Philosophy*, (Blackwell), ed. Matthias Steup, forthcoming.

10. I have discussed this elsewhere. See "Skepticism and Closure: Why the Evil Genius Argument Fails," *Philosophical Topics*, 23.1, 1995, 213–236; "Skepticism," *The Oxford Handbook of Epistemology* (Oxford: Oxford University Press, 2002), Paul Moser (ed.), 336–361 and in "Skepticism," *Stanford Encyclopedia of Philosophy*, http://plato.stanford.edu/entries/skepticism/

11. *Academica* II, xxvi, 84.

12. Descartes, "Meditations on First Philosophy," *Philosophical Works of Descartes* (Dover Publications, 1931), Elizabeth S. Haldane and G.R.T. Ross (eds.), p. 198–9.

13. One more quasi-historical point seems worth mentioning here. In the "First Meditation," Descartes might seem to be providing a reason for thinking that our epistemic equipment is not reliable, thus seeming to discredit all reasons for belief. His argument is that since we do fall into error and error seems to be an

imperfection, there is some basis for believing that our epistemic equipment might not be reliable. As he says:

> ...in whatever way they suppose that I have arrived at the state of being that I have reached – whether they attribute it to fate to accident, or make out that it is by a continual succession of antecedents or by some other method – since to err and deceive oneself is a defect, it is clear that the greater will be the probability of my being so imperfect as to deceive myself ever as is the Author to whom they assign my origin less powerful. (Descartes, *op. cit.* p. 147)

But note that even this argument depends implicitly upon not doubting the following propositions: I have made errors; there are events that are causally related; an effect cannot be more perfect than its cause.

My point here is merely that even in this argument—the very one used in the "First Meditation" to provide a reason for thinking that the skeptical hypothesis is true, namely, that perhaps the author of our being is insufficiently epistemically benign—Descartes leaves some wiggle room for removing the doubt. For if he could show that error is not a basis for calling into question the perfection of our "author," he would have removed this reason for thinking the skeptical hypothesis is true. And, of course, that is exactly the purpose of the "Fourth Meditation." In other words, the skepticism of the "First Meditation" isn't so global after all because he could have reasoned as he did in the "Fourth Meditation" without first having "proved" God's existence and epistemic benevolence. Indeed, I think the truly genuine global skeptical hypothesis does not appear until early in the "Third Meditation."

14. Cohen, *op. cit.*, p. 313.
15. *Idem.*
16. That is Cohen's solution.
17. See endnotes 8 and 9.
18. The zebra-in-the-zoo case was first present by Fred Dretske in "Epistemic Operators," *Journal of Philosophy*, 67 (1970), 1015–16. I have discussed it elsewhere—see the articles listed in endnote 10.
19. Cohen, *op. cit.*, p. 314.
20. See endnote 6.
21. Peter Markie has argued a similar point. See his "Easy Knowledge," *Philosophy and Phenomenological Research*, forthcoming.
22. Cohen, *op. cit.*, 314.
23. There being no defeaters in this case entails that the table is red because if *the table is not red* were true, it would be a defeater. Generalizing: The truth condition for knowledge is satisfied whenever the reasoning is not defeated. Put another way, it is not an accident that non-defeated reasoning leads to the truth.
24. Hume wrote that skeptical worries "arise naturally" within a philosophical context and that "carelessness and in-attention alone can afford us any remedy." David Hume, *Treatise of Human Nature*, (Oxford: Oxford Clarendon Press, 1978), second edition, L. A. Selby-Bigge (ed.), p. 218.
25. I said in endnote 1 that this paper would only be concerned with the problem of easy knowledge as it is related to closure and not to it as it is related to the bootstrapping problem. But my hunch is that recognizing that reasoning that produces knowledge must be resistant to defeat will help in resolving the bootstrapping problem as well.

*Philosophical Issues, 14, Epistemology, 2004*

# DOES RELIABILISM MAKE KNOWLEDGE MERELY CONDITIONAL?[1]

Hilary Kornblith
University of Massachusetts, Amherst

Reliabilism is the view that knowledge is reliably produced true belief. It is a form of externalism. According to the reliabilist, it is the fact that a true belief is reliably produced which makes it a case of knowledge; this fact need not be known, or believed, or epistemically accessible to the knower. Thus, on this view, if Andrew is looking at a table in standard conditions and comes to believe that there is a table in front of him, then, so long as this belief is reliably produced, it is a case of knowledge. Andrew needn't know that his belief is reliably produced; the question of the reliability of the belief acquisition process need never have crossed Andrew's mind. The fact which makes Andrew's belief a case of knowledge may be, in a word, external to Andrew's epistemic perspective.

But how, one might wonder, could such facts external to Andrew's epistemic perspective turn his true beliefs into knowledge? If Andrew doesn't know that his belief about the table is reliably produced, if he doesn't even have any reason to believe that it is reliably produced, then surely the fact that his belief is reliably produced is epistemically impotent: it can't do the work of turning his true belief into knowledge because it cannot do any epistemic work at all. Or so it has seemed to many philosophers.

Thus, Laurence BonJour presents the following problem for reliabilism:

> If, for example, an epistemologist claims that a certain belief or set of beliefs, whether his own or someone else's, has been arrived at in a reliable way, but says this on the basis of cognitive processes of his or her own whose reliability is merely for him or her merely an external fact to which he or she has no first-person access, then the proper conclusion is merely that the belief or beliefs originally in question are reliably arrived at (and perhaps thereby are justified or constitute knowledge in externalist senses) *if* the epistemologist's own cognitive processes are reliable in the way that he or she believes them to be ... But the

only apparent way to arrive at a result that is not ultimately hypothetical in this way is for the reliability of at least some processes to be establishable on the basis of what the epistemologist can know directly or immediately from his or her own first-person perspective.[2]

Reliabilism, according to this criticism, makes knowledge merely hypothetical or conditional: we have knowledge *if* we have a belief which is reliably produced. But the antecedent of this conditional, according to BonJour, cannot be discharged. Externalism is thereby revealed as "a very powerful and commonsensically unpalatable version of skepticism..."[3]

BonJour is not alone in making this kind of argument. A similar point is developed by Barry Stroud. Stroud considers the status of the externalist's avowed belief in externalism itself.

> The scientific "externalist" claims to have good reason to believe that his theory is true. It must be granted that if, in arriving at his theory, he did fulfill the conditions his theory says are sufficient for knowing things about the world, then if that theory is correct, he does in fact know that it is. But still, I want to say, he himself has no reason to think that he does have good reason to think that his theory is correct. He is at best in the position of someone who has good reason to believe his theory if that theory is in fact true, but has no such reason to believe it if some other theory is true instead. He can see what he *would* have good reason to believe if the theory he believes were true, but he cannot see or understand himself as knowing or having good reason to believe what his theory says.[4]

The externalist cannot legitimately claim to know that his theory of knowledge is true; his avowed knowledge of his own theory is merely conditional. Moreover, what is true of the externalist's avowed belief in externalism itself is also true of his avowed beliefs about the physical world. The externalist may not legitimately claim to have any knowledge at all; all such claims are merely conditional.

If BonJour and Stroud are right, then one point long thought to count in favor of externalism is fully undercut. Historically, internalism has consistently been faced with skeptical problems. Internalist foundationalists have had tremendous difficulties showing how beliefs about the physical world might meet their stringent standards for justification. Internalist coherentists have found themselves in a similar bind. Internalism seems to lead, both inexorably and quickly, to a radical skepticism. Externalism, whatever its other problems, seemed to be clearly superior in this respect. Thus, consider reliabilism. While internalism leads to the result that knowledge of the physical world is impossible, reliabilism tells us that we have knowledge of the physical world if we have true beliefs about it which are reliably produced. Such a condition is not impossible to meet. There are, beyond doubt, possible worlds in which creatures form true beliefs about their environments by way of reliable cognitive mechanisms. So reliabilism seems to make knowledge possible while internalism makes it impossible. More than this, reliabilism seems to do far more than make knowledge possible. Surely our world is a world containing creatures many of whose beliefs are both true and reliably produced, and surely we are among those creatures. So reliabilism explains not only how knowledge is possible, but how it is that we have a great deal of knowledge. This seems to be a significant advantage of externalism over internalism.

BonJour and Stroud seek to undermine this advantage, for if they are right, reliabilists may make no legitimate claims to knowledge at all. As Stroud remarks, this issue is tied to "the very sources of the epistemological quest."[5] In this paper, I argue that BonJour and Stroud are mistaken. Reliabilism does not make knowledge merely conditional, nor does it force us to make knowledge claims which are merely conditional. Instead, reliabilism properly explains the phenomenon of human knowledge and, indeed, of knowledge in general.

I

The issues involved in this debate are complex, and they involve not only questions about the nature of knowledge (and justified belief as well), but also questions about the relationship between knowing and knowing that one knows (as well as questions about the relationship between being justified and being justified in believing that one is justified). In order to pin these issues down, it will be especially useful to begin with some examples.

Consider Jack. Jack is a know-it-all. In saying this, I don't mean, of course, that Jack is omniscient. Rather, Jack is someone who claims, and sincerely believes, that he has an extraordinarily wide range of knowledge. Whenever an issue arises as to whether some proposition p is true, whether p concerns abstruse matters of geography, history, politics or quantum mechanics, Jack not only has opinions as to whether p is true, but he sincerely claims, and with great confidence, to know whether p is true. Jack is quite bright and quite knowledgeable, though not nearly so bright or knowledgeable as he takes himself to be. Many of the claims Jack makes are false, and some are downright absurd. Others sometimes try to correct Jack in his mistaken claims, but they have little effect. Jack is utterly self-confident, both in his claims about various abstruse matters and in his claims to know about these matters.

Mary, on the other hand, has an intellectual temperament altogether different from Jack's. Mary is at least as bright, and at least as knowledge-able, as Jack, but she is not given to the wild claims and overconfidence which typify Jack. Instead, Mary is quite circumspect. When a question arises as to whether some proposition p is true, more often than not, Mary will sincerely claim that she doesn't know, although her friends sometimes suspect that she does. At the same time, Mary does not disclaim all knowledge. There are certain areas, and certain sorts of questions, about which Mary is quite confident, and if she is asked about these, she will answer forthrightly and she will say that these are things about which she does indeed know.

What should the reliabilist say about Jack and Mary? When it comes to Jack, the reliabilist will allow that there are many things that Jack knows, though not nearly as many as he takes himself to know. This is in part because many of the things Jack claims to know are false, and so on any account of knowledge Jack doesn't know those things; but it is not only for this reason. Many of Jack's beliefs are formed in utterly unreliable ways. Whatever subject might be under discussion, Jack has an opinion on it, and these opinions seem to pop into Jack's head out of nowhere, although this is not how it seems to Jack. I will simply stipulate, for purposes of discussion, that the mental mechanism at work in Jack which produces the majority of his beliefs is unreliable, and so, on the reliabilist view, the beliefs which result from this mechanism, even when true, do not constitute knowledge. At the same time, this is not the only mechanism responsible for Jack's beliefs. In standard perceptual circumstances, Jack's beliefs are formed in much the same ways as yours and mine are, and I will suppose that these perceptual mechanisms are extremely reliable. Jack has a good deal of perceptual knowledge.

What, according to the reliabilist, does Jack know that he knows? This depends, of course, on the reliability of the mechanisms by which Jack's beliefs that he knows are produced. For most individuals, there are probably many such mechanisms, but in Jack's case I want to make a simplifying assumption. Let us suppose that whenever the issue arises as to whether Jack knows something, whether that issue is raised by someone else or by Jack himself, Jack comes to believe that he does in fact know. This mechanism produces far more false beliefs than truths, precisely because Jack forms beliefs on such an extraordinarily wide range of topics and in such a haphazard way. The one mechanism by which Jack's beliefs about what he knows are formed is thus unreliable, and the reliabilist must thus say that Jack does not know that he knows anything. Although Jack has a good deal of first-order knowledge, he has no second-order knowledge.

The reliabilist will rightly see Mary as quite different in this respect. She has a good deal of first-order knowledge, since many of her beliefs about the world are reliably produced, but she has a good deal of second-order knowledge as well, for the mechanisms which produce her beliefs that she has knowledge are themselves reliable as well. For the reliabilist, Mary need not be in a position to cite reasons for her beliefs; the reasons she has need not be cognitively accessible to her. Mary may simply say, quietly yet confidently, that this is something which she knows, when asked about some particular issue, and if her belief that she knows is reliably arrived at, and if it is also true, the reliabilist will say that Mary knows that she knows. What the reliabilist says about Mary and Jack is not, I believe, altogether unreasonable.

The internalist, on the other hand, sees reliably formed true belief as neither necessary nor sufficient for knowledge. Knowledge requires justification, according to the internalist, and justification requires reasons "available within a first-person epistemic perspective," as BonJour puts it.[6] The reliabilist sees the formation of beliefs on the basis of such reasons[7] as one kind of reliable process among many: reliability is just a matter of attunement to the facts, and such attunement may involve reasons available from the first-person perspective or not. But since the internalist insists that there is no knowledge without reasons available from the first-person perspective, the internalist will have to insist that Mary, like Jack, is wholly lacking in second-order knowledge if the attunement she has to her first-order knowledge is not achieved by way of resources available from the first-person perspective. This is, I believe, quite counterintuitive.

Let us look at what is going on in this case in more detail. BonJour and Stroud wish to argue that externalists are not entitled to make unconditional claims to knowledge. Now both Jack and Mary make unconditional knowledge claims. Jack will insist that he knows such things as that Addis Ababa is the capital of Burkina Fasso, and Mary will claim that she knows, for example, that George Washington was born in 1732. We all agree that Jack is not entitled to the knowledge claims he makes. What should we say about Mary? Is she entitled to claim that she knows when George Washington was born, or must her claims to knowledge be qualified by some conditional?

According to BonJour, externalists are entitled to make the conditional claim that Mary knows when Washington was born *if* her belief was reliably produced, but neither the externalist nor Mary is entitled to the unconditional claim that Mary knows when Washington was born. Reliabilism tells us that whether Mary knows depends on the reliability of the process by which Mary's belief was produced. But Mary does not have first-person access to the process which produced her belief about the year of Washington's birth, nor does she have such access to the reliability of that process, and so, BonJour concludes, the reliabilist must say that Mary is entitled to nothing more than the claim that *if* her belief is reliably produced, *then* she knows. And the same is true of the externalist himself, contemplating Mary's epistemic situation, unless the externalist has some way of establishing, from his own first-person perspective, that Mary's belief was reliably produced.

If this argument is an attempt to show that, by their own standards, externalists are not entitled to make any unconditional knowledge claims nor are they in a position to view others as entitled to make unconditional knowledge claims, then the argument surely fails. According to reliabilism, Mary knows that p if and only if her belief that p is both true and reliably produced; Mary knows that she knows that p if and only if her belief that she knows that p is both true and reliably produced. Nothing about the first-person perspective is epistemically essential to knowledge, according to the reliabilist.

As far as what Mary is entitled to claim, or what the externalist is entitled to claim about Mary, similar considerations apply. I don't know exactly what conditions are required for an individual to be entitled to make a claim. Perhaps an individual is entitled to claim that p if and only if he or she is justified in believing that p. Or perhaps more than this is required: perhaps an individual is entitled to claim that p if and only if he or she knows that p. Let us assume, for the sake of argument, that the stronger of these two requirements gets things right. Then according to the reliabilist, Mary will only be entitled to claim that p if she knows that p, that is, if her belief that p is both true and reliably produced. And Mary will be entitled to claim to know that p if and only if her belief that she knows that p is both true and reliably produced. The reliabilist, of course, does not believe that anything about Mary's first-person epistemic perspective is relevant here, and BonJour's insistence that it is does not show a problem within the externalist position; it only shows what we already knew, that externalists will attribute knowledge in a variety of situations where internalist conditions are not met.

## II

While BonJour does not pursue this argument further, Stroud anticipates exactly this reply. After arguing that externalists are not entitled to claim to have knowledge unconditionally, but only subject to conditions, Stroud remarks,

> I am aware that describing what I see as the deficiency in this way is not really satisfactory or conclusive. It encourages the "externalist" to re-apply his theory of knowing or having good reason to believe at the next level up, and to claim that he can understand himself [to know or] to have good reason to believe ...because [he knows that he knows or] he has good reason to believe that he does have good reason to believe...That further belief...is arrived at in turn by fulfilling what his theory says are the conditions [for knowing or] for reasonably believing something.[8]

The externalist will be encouraged to make this response, of course, because externalism is not a theory about first-order knowledge only, holding that internalist conditions must be met for higher-order knowledge; externalism is a theory about propositional knowledge generally, whether the propositions concern tables and chairs, or knowledge about tables and chairs, or anything else. So this is not some ad hoc move on the part of the externalist to dodge an unattractive consequence of the theory. The externalist is here simply insisting that his theory be consistently applied across the board, and that internalist conditions not be smuggled in when the subject of discussion moves from knowing to knowing that one knows.

After acknowledging that the externalist is encouraged to make just this response to his argument, Stroud comments,

> It is difficult to say precisely what is inadequate about that kind of response, especially in terms that would be acceptable to an "externalist." Perhaps it is best to say that the theorist has to see himself as [knowing or] having good reason to believe his theory in some sense of ["knowing" or] "having good reason" that cannot be fully captured by an "externalist" account.[9]

So Stroud's objection, and perhaps BonJour's as well, is not a problem within externalism. The objection is not that when the externalist theory is consistently applied to cases, it generates results about when individuals know which are different from those advertised by externalists. Rather, the suggestion is that there is some important sense of "knowledge," or "justified belief," or "having a good reason," which externalism cannot capture. And this suggestion, if true, would certainly still present a serious problem for externalism.

Applying this understanding of the problem to the externalist's belief in his own theory, Stroud now formulates the problem in this way:

> So even if it is true that you can know something without knowing that you know it, the philosophical theorist of knowledge cannot simply insist on the point and expect to find acceptance of an "externalist" account of knowledge fully satisfactory. If he could, he would be in the position of someone who says: "I don't know whether I understand human knowledge or not. If what I believe about it is true and my beliefs are produced in what my theory says is the right way, I do know how human knowledge comes to be, so in that sense I do understand. But if my beliefs are not true, or not arrived at in that way, I do not. I wonder which it is. I wonder whether I understand human knowledge or not." That is not a satisfactory position to arrive at in one's study of human knowledge—or of anything else.[10]

Stroud is surely right that this is not a satisfactory position in which to find oneself. But externalists are not in this position.

Let us return to cases. Once again, consider Mary. Mary does not have internalist reasons for believing that Washington was born in 1732, nor does she have internalist reasons for believing that she knows that Washington was born in 1732. In spite of that, her belief about the year of Washington's birth is true and it was reliably produced, and the same, we may suppose, is true of her belief that she knows the year of Washington's birth. Mary claims, with a quiet confidence, "I know that Washington was born in 1732," and if she is challenged on this and asked to provide some justification for the claim, she will acknowledge that she is unable to do so. But this will not diminish her confidence that she knows the year of Washington's birth. "This is simply something I know," Mary will say. Looked at in isolation, this attitude of Mary's will look like hubris or dogmatism, but those who know Mary will not see it that way. Mary does not often claim to know things, and when she does, she is almost invariably right. Mary should not be confused with Jack.

So Mary will not say, as Stroud seems to suggest she must, "I don't know whether I know the year of Washington's birth. If what I believe about it is true, and my belief about it is produced in the right sort of way, then I do know when Washington was born. But if what I believe is false, or if my belief was produced in an unreliable way, then I don't know. I wonder which it is." Mary won't say any of this because she confidently believes that Washington was born in 1732, and she confidently believes that she knows that Washington was born in 1732. She does not wonder whether she knows these things or not.

Now perhaps this is unfair to Stroud, and for two different reasons. First, in the quoted passage, Stroud specifically discusses neither ordinary individuals nor their garden variety beliefs, but the externalist epistemologist's belief in his own theory of knowledge. So perhaps Mary's belief about Washington is not relevant. And second, Stroud focuses, in that passage, on issues having to do with understanding, and not merely on questions about knowledge. This complicates things considerably.

As far as Stroud's focus on understanding goes, it is important to recognize that the externalist and the reliabilist offer accounts of knowledge, or, in some views, justified belief; they have nothing to say about understanding. I don't know exactly what understanding dogs, or chemistry, or human knowledge comes to, but someone who has propositional knowledge of, say, a handful of propositions about dogs, or chemistry, or human knowledge probably doesn't count as understanding these things; it surely takes more than that. I don't know whether understanding something can be fully explained in terms of propositional knowledge, for example as knowing a great many truths about that thing, or knowing the most important truths about it, or whether understanding something instead requires more than just propositional knowledge.[11] But if Stroud's remarks are meant to apply to understanding but not to propositional knowledge or justification, then they are simply irrelevant to externalism and reliabilism, and I very much doubt that Stroud intends his remarks to be taken in that way.

So how does the situation of the externalist epistemologist's belief in his own theory differ from that of Mary's belief that Washington was born in

1732? We supposed that Mary was not in a position to cite any reasons for her belief, and we supposed this in order to provide a clear case of an individual who satisfies externalist conditions for knowledge without, at the same time, satisfying internalist conditions for knowledge. A perfectly parallel case would thus require an externalist epistemologist who claims to know that externalism is true, and yet, at the same time, insists that he is in no position to offer any reason whatever to believe that externalism is true. Like Mary, he would have to say, "This is simply something that I know." There would, admittedly, be something very odd about such a case. Epistemologists tend to be fairly reflective individuals, and their beliefs, at least about epistemological theories, tend to be formed only after a good deal of self-conscious consideration. This self-conscious consideration typically puts them in a position to offer a fairly elaborate set of reasons for their epistemological views, and there is considerable professional pay-off in being able to remember and articulate these reasons. An epistemologist who could offer no reasons for his views at all—someone who simply stated, "I know this to be true"—would find himself at a considerable professional disadvantage. These reasons alone make it hard to imagine an externalist epistemologist whose belief about externalism is exactly parallel to Mary's belief about Washington. This is not to say that the externalist epistemologist will inevitably have good *internalist* reasons for believing externalism. After all, there are substantial reasons for wondering whether anyone could have good internalist reasons for believing that the sun will rise tomorrow, or that the sun rose yesterday, or even that $2 + 2 = 4$ or that there is a table in front of me now, let alone for a philosophical theory.[12] Nevertheless, it must be granted that there are substantial impediments to constructing a case involving an externalist's belief in externalism which exactly parallels Mary's belief about Washington.

There is no reason, however, to think that the difficulty of constructing such a parallel case tells us anything about human knowledge in general rather than about epistemologists and the character of their professional practice. Our externalist epistemologist may claim, with perfect consistency, that knowledge does not require having good internalist reasons or arguments, while simultaneously allowing that he himself can present a good many reasons and arguments in favor of that very view. Externalism, after all, is not the absurd view that knowledge precludes being in a position to offer reasons or present arguments. The externalist may go on to argue that his own view accounts quite naturally for cases like Mary's, involving individuals who have no internalist reasons for their beliefs, unlike internalism, which must see Mary as epistemically on a par with Jack. The externalist might even argue that internalist conditions on knowledge are rarely, if ever, satisfied,[13] and that internalists thereby fail to capture the very phenomenon of human knowledge, or knowledge in general, which they seek to characterize. There would be no internal inconsistency in any of this.

And perhaps, in the end, we may construct cases in which epistemologists form beliefs about epistemological theories which do fully parallel the case of Mary. There is, after all, the famous case, in mathematics, of Srinivasa Ramanujan, the self-taught Indian number theorist.[14] As a young man, Ramanujan wrote a long letter to the Oxford mathematician G. H. Hardy, filled with page upon page of number theoretic claims, but entirely devoid of proofs or even proof sketches. Hardy found that some of the claims were well-known truths; some were mildly interesting extensions of familiar results; and some were extremely interesting claims about which Hardy could not tell, at least immediately, whether they were true or false. Hardy spent a good deal of time working on these claims, and found that he could prove many of them to be true, although, unsurprisingly, some of the claims were mistaken. On the basis of this letter, Hardy arranged for Ramanujan to go to Oxford, and a lengthy collaboration resulted. At first, Hardy tried to teach Ramanujan how to construct a proof, but he soon gave up. Although Hardy was a first-rate mathematician in his own right, his partnership with Ramanujan saw him in a crucial but merely supporting role: Ramanujan was a fount of important results, and Hardy, as he modestly put it, provided the "gas," that is, the proofs.

Reliabilists will say, not implausibly, that Ramanujan had a great deal of mathematical knowledge, in spite of the fact that he could provide neither proofs nor proof sketches for his results; he simply could not provide an appropriate internalist justification for his claims. There is no doubt that one could achieve a far greater degree of mathematical understanding by reading the papers resulting from Ramanujan's collaboration with Hardy than by looking at nothing more than Ramanujan's lists of mathematical results. For this reason, the reliabilist will certainly want to allow that Hardy was being overly modest in describing his own contribution as "gas." This does nothing, however, to undermine the claim that Ramanujan had genuine mathematical knowledge. Hardy's work is a source of additional knowledge, including knowledge of why Ramanujan's results are true. But it would surely be a mistake to insist that Hardy's proofs account for the difference between knowledge and true belief. Such a suggestion not only undervalues Ramanujan's cognitive achievements; it also overestimates the importance of Hardy's proofs.

It is surely tempting to say that Ramanujan's claims—even if one knows his track record, his ratio of true mathematical claims to false ones— provide one with nothing more than the likelihood that the given claim is true, while Hardy's proofs provide one with certainty. Even if certainty is not required for knowledge, this shows that Hardy's knowledge of these claims is, at a minimum, superior to that of Ramanujan's, if Ramanujan's cognitive achievements deserve the name of 'knowledge' at all.

But this way of seeing things is surely mistaken. Ramanujan's track record was not perfect: he sometimes made mathematical claims which were false. But if Hardy was like any other human mathematician I've ever spoken with, his track record in producing proofs was not perfect either. Hardy must surely have had occasions on which he took himself to have proven a certain result, but later discovered that his would-be proof contained an error. So when Hardy produced what he took to be a proof of a mathematical claim, this could not have been a source of certainty to Hardy or to anyone else. Lengthy and complicated mathematical "proofs" may contain errors which evade detection by even the greatest of mathematical minds. When we acknowledge that Ramanujan's track record in producing true mathematical claims was less than perfect, we should add that Hardy's record in producing genuine mathematical proofs was almost certainly less than perfect as well.

Indeed, for all we know, it could be that Ramanujan's track record was better than Hardy's. We may imagine two mathematicians, R and H, this time working independently of one another. R produces a series of claims entirely devoid of proof; H produces a series of what he tells us are proofs. The results which R and H produce overlap a good deal: R frequently makes claims which H takes himself to have proven. But now let us suppose that R is right 99% of the time, whereas H is only right 97% of the time.

One could take a hard line here and insist that neither R nor H have mathematical knowledge since they both have imperfect track records, but this line would commit one to the claim that human mathematicians are all utterly lacking in mathematical knowledge since they have all made mistakes at one time or another. I won't explore this view further.

The reliabilist may claim that both R and H know a great many mathematical claims to be true, and there are certain respects in which R's knowledge of these claims is superior, and others in which H's knowledge is superior: R is more likely to be right when he makes a claim, while H is often in a position to explain why various claims are true, something R cannot do. Depending on one's purposes, one may gain more either from talking to R or to H, but they both have a great deal of knowledge.

The internalist, if he is not a complete skeptic, will need to claim that in this case, H has a great deal of knowledge while R has none, in spite of the fact that R is more reliable than H. This seems to me quite implausible.

I originally brought up the case of Hardy and Ramanujan because Stroud claims that the externalist epistemologist is in an untenable position if his knowledge of his own theory fails to satisfy internalist standards. But what may plausibly be said of Hardy and Ramanujan may plausibly be said of epistemologists as well. Imagine a self-taught philosopher, let us call him Philo, who makes a long list off oracular pronouncements on philosophical topics, none of which are provided with supporting argumentation. Let us further suppose that many of these claims are widely agreed upon results in the literature, although Philo has never read the relevant literature, and some of these claims are interesting extensions of these results, extensions which no one else had ever thought of. In addition, there are many claims which go far beyond anything currently available in the literature. Philo writes to a prominent philosopher, Discursis, who is, among other things, particularly skilled in constructing arguments, and a collaboration results, with Philo providing the results and Discursis providing the arguments, arguments which are generally found to be utterly convincing by other professional philosophers.

If Philo should one day offer an externalist account of knowledge, and claim to know that his account is correct, he is guilty of no inconsistency nor has he committed any intellectual impropriety. Philo, like Mary, and like Ramanujan, may have a quiet confidence in his ideas. He may reasonably say, "I know this theory to be true." He would certainly not say, as Stroud says he must,

> I don't know whether I understand human knowledge or not. If what I believe about it is true and my beliefs about it are produced in what my theory says is the right way, I do know how human knowledge comes to be, so in that sense I do understand. But if my beliefs are not true, or not arrived at in that way, I do not. I wonder which it is. I wonder whether I do understand human knowledge or not.

Philo does not wonder whether he understands human knowledge or not, for he is confident that he does understand it, and he has every right to say so. Philo may in the end turn out to be mistaken, for he is not infallible, but in this respect, he differs from no one. Certainly internalists are not infallible in their beliefs, and yet neither Stroud nor BonJour think that they are prohibited from making unconditional knowledge claims.[15] If what is required for making legitimate knowledge claims is infallibility, then no one may make them, and there is no special problem about externalism.

While Stroud and BonJour both argue that externalist knowledge claims must be understood as merely conditional, BonJour focuses on the fact that the reliability of the process by which a person's beliefs are produced is external to that person's "first-person epistemic perspective"; Stroud not only focuses on this, but also on the fact that the truth of a person's belief is external to that person's epistemic perspective. Thus, in the passage just quoted, Stroud insists that the externalist must say, "If what I believe... *is true* and my beliefs... are produced in... the right way, I do know... But if my beliefs *are not true*, or not arrived at in that way, I do not." [emphasis added] Stroud is right that the truth of a person's belief is just as external to that person's first-person epistemic perspective as is the reliability of the process which produced it. But in noting this, Stroud undermines not only the point he is trying to make, but BonJour's point as well. After all, the truth of a person's belief is a necessary condition for knowledge on all views, not just externalist accounts. Internalists too recognize that knowledge requires true belief. So if the mere fact that the truth of a person's belief is external to their epistemic perspective thereby requires that all knowledge claims be merely conditional, then the problem which Stroud and BonJour have unearthed is not a problem *about externalism* at all; it is instead a problem for all views. There is no special problem about externalism.

But surely the real conclusion we should all draw here is that there is no problem about externalism because there is no problem here at all. Externalists as well as internalists may make unconditional knowledge claims without fear of thereby coming into conflict with their own views.[16] Neither Stroud nor BonJour believe that knowledge requires infallibility, and so long as it does not, fallible yet unconditional knowledge claims are perfectly legitimate. Externalists need not qualify each of their knowledge claims with the proviso "if my belief is reliably produced" any more than internalists need to qualify their knowledge claims with the proviso "if I'm not mistaken." Reliabilism does not make knowledge merely conditional.

## III

Thus far, we have been treating reliabilism, and externalism more generally, as a theory of knowledge, but there is also a reliabilist, or externalist, theory of justified belief, and BonJour and Stroud present their objections not only against the former, but against the latter as well. While they each argue, as we have seen, that reliabilism, or externalism, makes knowledge merely conditional, they also argue that these views make justified belief merely conditional. The point is also sometimes put in terms of what the externalist has "good reason to believe."[17] So we will need to consider whether this objection is any more effective against reliabilist or externalist theories of justification than it proved to be against reliabilist or externalist theories of knowledge.

Indeed, at least in the case of BonJour, there is reason to think that he regards the objection to externalist theories of justification as the more fundamental point. "The concept of knowledge," BonJour tells us,

> Though it provides a necessary starting point for epistemological reflection, is much less ultimately important in relation to the main epistemological issues than it has usually been thought to be . . . the main issues [in epistemology] will be whether and how we have reasons or justification for our beliefs of various kinds and just how strong such reasons or justification in fact turn out to be.[18]

Questions about knowledge, BonJour holds, fall "very much into the background."[19] So the important question, on this view, is not so much whether externalists about knowledge may make unconditional knowledge claims, but whether externalists about justified belief may make unconditional claims to have justified beliefs.

There can be little doubt that the objection against externalist theories looks far more plausible when it is couched as an objection against externalist theories of justification rather than an objection against externalist theories of knowledge. As was just pointed out, everyone is an externalist about knowledge to the following extent: because knowledge that p requires the truth of p, and truth, at least in the typical case, is a fact external to the individual's epistemic perspective, whether an individual in fact knows some claim to be true will not typically be directly available from the individual's first-person perspective. Justification, however, is different. Internalists hold that the facts in virtue of which a belief is justified must be available from the first-person perspective, while externalists deny this. So internalists will hold that whether an individual is justified in his belief is something to which he must have direct first-person access, unlike externalists. And this is the basis of the suggestion that externalists, therefore, cannot make unconditional claims to have justified beliefs; they can only claim that their beliefs are justified *if* they are reliably produced.

But once again, the objection fails. Externalists do not in any way fail to meet their own standards; they merely fail to meet internalist standards. And this does not show a problem with externalism—that they cannot make unconditional claims to have justified beliefs—unless there is an independent argument that externalism is an inadequate theory of justified belief. There have, of course, been numerous arguments to that effect, but this is not the place to examine them. The suggestion that externalism makes all claims to have justified beliefs merely conditional was supposed to be an independent argument against externalism, not one which piggybacked upon some other, and independent, criticism.

The worry internalists have seems to come down to this: since externalists, by their own admission, do not have direct first-person access to the justificatory status of their beliefs, it would, in every case, be sheer dogmatism for an externalist to claim that one of his or her beliefs is justified. Any such claim to be justified, it might seem, would be an utter shot in the dark: perhaps the belief is, as a matter of fact, reliably produced, and so, according to the externalist, fully justified, but so long as the individual has no direct access to this fact from his first-person perspective, the individual is in no position to claim that the belief is justified. All that can reasonably be claimed, it seems, is that the belief is justified *if* it is reliably produced. If externalists are to avoid the charge of dogmatism, then, it seems that they will need to stop making unconditional claims to have justified beliefs.

But this objection is no more successful when directed against an externalist theory of justified belief than it was when directed against an externalist theory of knowledge. Mary, as we saw, is not dogmatic, and she is entitled not only to claim that she knows when Washington was born; she is entitled to claim that she is justified in her belief about when he was born. Her knowledge claims, and her claims to have justified beliefs, are not mere shots in the dark, as her track record in making such claims amply shows. She has a very good sense of when she knows, and when she is justified in believing, and when she isn't. The internalist assumes that if one doesn't have some sort of direct first-person access to the facts which determine justifiedness, then one is in no position whatever to assess whether one is justified. But Mary is well-calibrated; she doesn't just shoot from the hip. Such calibration requires that one's judgments be regulated by the facts which determine whether one is justified; it does not require that this calibration be achieved in ways which are recognizable from the first-person perspective.

## IV

There is thus no good reason to think that reliabilism, or externalism in general, make knowledge, or justified belief, merely conditional. Good reasons to reject these views will need to come from some other quarter.

## Notes

1. Thanks to Earl Conee for comments on a draft of this paper.
2. "The Indispensability of Internalism," *Philosophical Topics*, 29(2001), 64. BonJour presents this argument again in *Epistemology: Classic Problems and Contemporary Responses*, Rowman and Littlefield, 2002, 236–7.
3. *Epistemology: Classic Problems and Contemporary Responses*, 237.
4. "Understanding Human Knowledge in General," reprinted in H. Kornblith, ed., *Epistemology: Internalism and Externalism*, Blackwell, 2001, 142. (This paper originally appeared in 1989.)
5. *Op. cit.*, 145.
6. For example in "The Indispensability of Internalism," 64.
7. Assuming, of course, that proper sense can be made of the idea of the first-person epistemic perspective.
8. "Understanding Human Knowledge in General," 142–3.
9. *Ibid.*, 143.
10. *Ibid.*, 143.
11. Catherine Elgin has useful and interesting things to say about these issues in *Considered Judgment*, Princeton University Press, 1996.
12. Thus, even BonJour, who is as ardent a defender of internalism as one can get, allows that memory beliefs cannot be justified on internalist grounds. (See *Epistemology: Classic Problems and Contemporary Responses*, 184: "But if I am right that memory cannot in this way be treated as part of the foundation, are we not then left after all with skepticism? In a way, I think we are.") And when he acknowledges that his "conditions on cognitive sanity" require an

"externalist dimension" (*In Defense of Pure Reason*, Cambridge University Press, 1998, 128), he thereby commits himself to the view that internalists are incapable of justifying any a priori claims. By his own account, this results in radical skepticism, a kind of "intellectual suicide" (*In Defense of Pure Reason*, 5). For further discussion of this issue, see my "Conditions on Cognitive Sanity and the Death of Internalism," in R. Schantz, ed., *The Externalist Challenge: New Studies on Cognition and Intentionality*, de Gruyter, forthcoming.

13. Indeed, some internalists are committed to this view. See note 12 above.

14. The story of Ramanujan and Hardy is told briefly by Hardy himself in *A Mathematician's Apology*, Cambridge University Press, 1967, and, at greater length, in Robert Kanigel, *The Man Who Knew Infinity: A Life of the Genius Ramanujan*, Scribners, 1991.

15. It is thus odd that BonJour should insist that externalist claims to knowledge are "merely hypothetical *and insecure* as long as they cannot be arrived at from the resources available within a first-person epistemic perspective" ["The Indispensibility of Internalism," 64, and also *Epistemology: Classic Problems and Contemporary Responses*, 236; emphasis added], since internalist knowledge claims are no more secure on BonJour's view.

16. More precisely, the present argument shows no such problem, either for externalists or for internalists. As pointed out in note 12, there is reason to think that internalists, or at least internalists such as BonJour, lay down standards for justified belief which, on their own theory, they cannot meet. But this is a different problem.

17. See passages quoted above.

18. *Epistemology: Classic Problems and Contemporary Responses*, 49.

19. *Ibid., loc. cit.*

*Philosophical Issues, 14, Epistemology, 2004*

# NOZICKIAN EPISTEMOLOGY AND THE VALUE OF KNOWLEDGE

Jonathan L. Kvanvig
University of Missouri, Columbia

Epistemology involves reflection on cognitive achievements of a theoretical sort, the primary example of which is knowledge. The history of epistemology has focused primarily on questions concerning the nature and extent of human knowledge, but there is another question in epistemology's history that is equally important though little addressed, which is the question of the value of knowledge. Knowledge, we assume, is valuable, and more valuable than mere belief, mere true belief, and even more valuable than mere justified true belief. The problem I will here address is how to explain this value.

The question of the value of knowledge arises first in Plato's Meno, where Socrates queries Meno concerning the value of knowledge over that of true belief. Meno first proposes that knowledge is more valuable because of the practical benefits to which it contributed, but upon seeing counter-examples to this claim, Meno entertains two thoughts. First, he wonders whether knowledge really is valuable, and second, he ponders whether knowledge is different from true belief. Socrates does not pursue the first issue but devotes some attention to the second, citing as metaphor the statues of Daedelus. The moral of the story, according to Socrates, is something he claims to know: that knowledge is different from true opinion.

The direction of the discussion leaves open the possibility that Socrates is willing to abandon the idea that knowledge is more valuable than true belief, but such a path should not be viewed as initially attractive (and it is surely implausible to think that Socrates or Plato would ever propose such an idea). Knowledge may not be all that we legitimately seek from an intellectual point of view, but it ought to take powerful arguments to move us to give up on the idea that knowledge is one such thing. Another way to put this point is that there is a presumption in favor of the idea that knowledge is valuable, and any adequate epistemology should, in the absence of countervailing considerations, be able to provide a good answer to Socrates's questions. The ideal would be for one's epistemology to contain an explanation or account of the value of knowledge, but at the very least, a good epistemology should not (without argument) rule out the value of knowledge or imply that it is all-things-considered very unlikely to be valuable.

The difficulty is that it is not an easy task to answer the Socratic queries concerning the value of knowledge. In section 1 below, I explain the difficulty. Once we see what is needed for an adequate explanation of the value of knowledge, I turn in section 2 to the merits of Nozickian epistemology for addressing the problem of the value of knowledge. In section 3, however, I argue that such hope disappoints. Truth-tracking epistemology is not able to navigate successfully between the dual difficulties of explaining the nature and extent of knowledge on the one hand and the value of knowledge on the other.

## I. The Swamping Problem

Let us begin by asking with Socrates what the difference in value is between knowledge and true belief. Though the possible answers here are manifold, two come to mind immediately. The first is Meno's pragmatic theory: knowledge is valuable as a means to getting what you want, whether it is getting to Larissa or becoming a millionaire. Socrates' reply undermines this account, for true belief works every bit as well for getting what you want as does knowledge—if you want to get to Larissa, a guide with true beliefs will work just as well as a guide with knowledge. The second, and more plausible, attempt proceeds in terms of the constituents of knowledge: knowledge is more valuable than true belief because it involves additional elements which are themselves valuable.

Thus enter into the picture concepts such as justification, certainty, reliability, infallibility, incorrigibility, having the right to be sure, being probably true, and other such concepts. What is distinctive about each of these properties, it is claimed, is that they are valuable properties for a belief to have: in each case, the value of a belief with that property exceeds the value of a belief lacking that property.

These properties can be divided into two groups: those that are conceptually stronger than truth and those that are conceptually weaker than truth. Among the former category are concepts that imply, but are not implied by true belief: infallibility, incorrigibility, and (objective) certainty. Among the latter category are concepts compatible with false belief: reliability, justification, having the right to be sure, probability of truth, and subjective certainty.

Concepts in the latter category face severe difficulty in addressing Socrates's concerns about the value of knowledge. Since each such concept is weaker than truth, each must find an answer to what I will call the swamping problem, which can be illustrated most clearly using the concept of probability. The difficulty encountered by appeals to this concept arises from the fact that the value of truth and the value of probability interact in a certain way. Socrates's question concerns the value of knowledge over that of true belief, so the proposed theory must hold that true beliefs that are likely to be true are more valuable than true beliefs that are not likely to be true. This value judgement has little to commend it, however. Once we have stipulated that a belief is true, adding that it is also likely to be true fails to enhance its value. Beautiful people are not more beautiful because they have beautiful parents; a good-tasting apple tastes no better because it comes from a tree that usually produces good-tasting apples; and well-functioning furniture functions no better because it is made by a factory likely to produce such. In general, where P is a good-making characteristic of a thing T, T does not become more valuable by being likely to have P when T already has P.

We should be careful not to confuse this point with a related, but distinct, issue. The claim here is not the claim that likelihood of truth is not valuable, nor that a belief likely to be true is not more valuable than one that is unlikely to be true. These claims, I assume, are true, but they are not the point in question here. Instead, the view I am arguing is false is that a *true* belief is not more valuable in virtue of being likely to be true.

The above examples may be too cryptic to convince, so consider the following more careful example. Suppose I like chocolate and wish to have some within the next few minutes. Being new to the area, I consult the web, searching for places that sell chocolate and are within walking distance of my present location. My search turns up three sites. The first site is a list of places that sell chocolate and are within walking distance. The second site is a list of places that are likely to sell chocolate and are within walking distance. The third list is the intersection of the first two: it is a list of places that both sell chocolate and are likely to sell chocolate and are within walking distance. Given that the only relevant interest at hand is my interest in having chocolate soon, two points are true. First, the second list is inferior to the other two lists: given my interest in chocolate, a list of places that actually sell it is preferable to a list of places that are likely to sell it. Second, and more important, the first list is every bit as good as the third: however likelihood of selling chocolate is measured, it adds nothing of interest in the present context to know of a place that actually sells chocolate that it is also likely to sell chocolate.

This phenomenon is the swamping problem. The problem is that when a property is valuable by being instrumentally related to another property, the value of the instrumental property is swamped by the presence of that for which it is instrumental. This fact alone does not undermine every attempt to explain the value of knowledge over true belief in terms of some property conceptually weaker than truth, for a property conceptually weaker than truth might be valuable on grounds unrelated to its relationship to truth. This possibility, however, offers little hope, for it immediately faces the problem of the truth connection. That problem is this: any property that distinguishes knowledge from true belief must bear some significant connection to the truth of belief, on pain of being irrelevant to the distinction between knowledge and true belief. A common expression of the truth connection is that whatever closes the gap between true belief and knowledge must make for likelihood of truth. If so, however, any property conceptually weaker than truth which has any hope of satisfying the truth connection will have to be conceived as instrumentally related to truth. As soon as this feature is included, the swamping problem appears.

Let me make clear here that I am not endorsing this entire line of reasoning. Instead, I only wish to display its plausibility. In my view, such reasoning contains important mistakes, but this is not the place for such a discussion. Instead, I only want to point out the plausibility of this line of reasoning in order to explain why it will be difficult to sustain the theory that properties weaker than truth and instrumentally related to it are up to the task of answering Socrates's queries.

As soon as this point is appreciated, it is easy to see why a vast majority of the history of epistemology focuses on the other category, the category including concepts stronger than truth. Not that the problem of the value of knowledge is the only, or even the primary, force behind this predilection, for such a thesis ignores the pervasive and dominant influence of skepticism on the history of epistemology. Yet, a point remains, even if we grant the primary influence of skepticism, for no property conceptually weaker than truth and only instrumentally related to it appears to have much hope of escaping the swamping problem.

This latter point is especially important once we move into the post-Moorean period in which the falsity of skepticism is assumed. Even if we make this assumption, the problem of the value of knowledge still motivates us to look beyond the category of concepts conceptually weaker than truth in attempting to distinguish knowledge from true belief. It is here that Nozickian epistemology is instructive and helpful.

## II. Nozickian Epistemology and the Value of Knowledge

If we adopt the Moorean assumption that skepticism is false, but also heed the lesson above concerning the swamping problem, we will be led to favor accounts of knowledge that clarify the difference between knowledge and true belief in terms of properties conceptually stronger than truth. Such an approach, however, will make it difficult to keep skepticism at bay for long. Consider the property of infallibility, for example. Since it is conceptually stronger than truth, an infallible true belief is clearly more valuable than a mere true belief—it is better to be incapable of error regarding a particular subject than merely to avoid error. The problem is that if knowledge requires infallibility, then we know (nearly) nothing. Skepticism reenters the picture, not because the skeptic gets to dictate the agenda of epistemology, but because the problem of the value of knowledge leads us to focus on concepts stronger than truth, and infallibility is a paradigm example of such a property.

The same result occurs when we consider other properties that are assumed to be conceptually stronger than truth, such as Descartes' concept of metaphysical certainty. False metaphysically certain beliefs are not possible, according to Descartes, and because they are not, metaphysical certainty is conceptually stronger than truth. But it is so strong that it is doubtful that anything but the most modest of successes can be achieved in avoiding skepticism on a theory of knowledge maintaining that such certainty is required for knowledge.

It is here that Nozickian epistemology has an advantage. According to Nozick, knowledge is a factive doxastic state that is counterfactual supporting, so that if one knows that it is raining, then if it weren't raining one would not believe that it is raining and if it were raining one would believe that it is raining. Nozick's truth-tracking theory thus presents a condition for knowledge that is stronger than truth in the following sense: a condition C is stronger than truth if and only if (a) it is possible to have a true belief even though one's belief does not satisfy condition C, but (b) necessarily, when a belief satisfies condition C, it is a true belief. To see that Nozick's truth-tracking condition is stronger than truth, consider a particular example. Suppose that one believes that it is raining. Clause (a) is obviously true, since one could be doxastically promiscuous, being convinced by any sincere utterance by a completely untrustworthy source. To see that clause (b) is true, we assume that the belief is false. If the belief is false, the first counterfactual, usually called the sensitivity claim, will be false as well: it would be false that if it weren't raining, one wouldn't believe that it is raining (since by hypothesis it isn't raining and one believes that it is raining).

Because truth-tracking is stronger than truth, it offers hope of explaining the value of knowledge and not only its nature. It implies that knowledge is more valuable than mere true belief since being a truth-tracker is better than merely being a true believer. Thus even in the presence of the truth of a belief, adding the property of truth-tracking adds something to the composite that is not swamped by the value of truth itself.

## III. Sensitivity and Safety

Nozickian epistemology thus passes a test for an adequate theory of knowledge not passed by many popular contemporary approaches to knowledge, such as process reliabilism of the sort Goldman proposes[1] (which, when considered from the perspective of the question of the value of knowledge, offers nothing more than the probabilistic theory used to explain the swamping problem). The harder question is whether this theoretical virtue can co-exist with a defense of the adequacy of such a Nozickian approach to the nature of knowledge. I will argue that the simpler versions of Nozickian epistemology are not promising at all, and that refinements that offer some hope of a more adequate account of the nature of knowledge force the loss of this theoretical virtue regarding the value of knowledge.

There are four counterfactuals on which a theory might focus in giving a counterfactual-based account of knowledge. Where 'p' is a sentence, 'B' is the operator 'S believes that', and '$\square\rightarrow$' the symbol for counterfactual implication, the four candidates are, with identifying descriptions:

1. $p \square\rightarrow Bp$ (the transparency condition)
2. $Bp \square\rightarrow p$ (the safety condition)
3. $\sim p \square\rightarrow \sim Bp$ (the sensitivity condition)
4. $\sim Bp \square\rightarrow \sim p$ (the idealism condition)

Neither the idealism condition nor the transparency condition have been popular in recent epistemology, and for good reason. The transparency condition would limit what we know to things that wouldn't be true unawares. Yet, there is good reason to think that much of what we know requires attention on our part. The fact that we don't know what is going on around us when we are asleep doesn't imply that we don't know what is going on around us when we are awake and attending to the features of our immediate environment.

A similar problem affects the idealism condition. We can know what is going on around us when we are awake and attending to the features of our immediate environment, and yet the idealism condition limits what we can know to what would be false when not believed. That would require that anything about our immediate environment that is unchanged when we are asleep would fail to be a candidate for knowledge.

Equally instructive is the fact that neither of these conditions yield a condition on knowledge stronger than truth. A false belief can satisfy either the idealism condition or the transparency condition (or both), implying that a belief can meet these conditions without being a true belief. Given our starting point that identifies the promise of Nozickian epistemology in terms of an ability to explain the value of knowledge in virtue of adverting to conditions for knowledge that are stronger than truth, this failure gives a reason independent of those above for rejecting counterfactual approaches that focus on these two conditions.

Such considerations explain the focus of recent epistemology on the other two conditionals, the safety and sensitivity conditions. Nozick uses the sensitivity condition, while epistemologists such as Sosa and Williamson prefer the safety condition. Both approaches are Nozickian in the sense that they distinguish knowledge from true belief on the basis of subjunctive conditionals. Moreover, the use of such conditionals offers some promise of accounting for the value of knowledge over that of true belief, but this promise is hollow if these approaches provide inadequate accounts of the nature of knowledge. One ground on which such approaches have been criticized concerns the question of whether knowledge is closed under known deduction. Exploring this issue will reveal that both conditions encounter problems on this score.

## A. Closure

A theory of knowledge respects closure when it adopts some version of the idea that we know the logical consequences of what we know. This rough closure claim is certainly false; otherwise, we'd all be logically and mathematically omniscient. Theories that wish to respect closure defend the view by restricting this rough form of the view. One way to restrict it is to hold that when we know p and know p entails q, then we know (or are in a position to know) q.

The project of refining the closure claim so that it is defensible is not a simple and easy project, but there is intuitive plausibility to the general idea, for we often appeal to some kind of closure condition in order to explain why a claim to knowledge is mistaken. When identifying a particular SUV as a Ford Explorer, my assertion may be challenged by one of my children with the question, "How do you know it's not a Nissan?" The point of the question is that Nissan makes an SUV with the same body style as the Ford Explorer, and the presupposition of the question is that I could only know that it was an Explorer if I knew it was not a Nissan. This presupposition involves some sort of closure principle about knowledge, one that I accepted in the context when I reply that I saw the Ford logo on the front hood. Closure is initially attractive precisely because it provides a plausible explanation of the type of discussion this example illustrates.

Nozick noticed and embraced the fact that the sensitivity requirement does not preserve closure with respect to knowledge, using this feature of his account to respond to skepticism. For example, on Nozick's view, it is possible to know that some object is a hand, know that if that object is a hand then no deception by a Cartesian evil demon is occurring, and yet not know that no such deception is occurring. Not many have been impressed with this aspect of Nozick's view, and some have claimed that replacing sensitivity conditions with safety conditions gives hope for upholding closure.[2]

Consider the following two arguments:

| | |
|---|---|
| 1. Bp | 1. Bp |
| 2. p | 2. p |
| 3. p entails q | 3. p entails q |
| 4. ~p □→ ~Bp | 4. Bp □→ p |
| 5. So, ~q □→ ~Bq | 5. So, Bq □→ q |

The first two premises of each argument are not needed for the points that follow, but since the context is one of attempting to ascertain the difference between knowledge and true belief, I include them to serve as a reminder of the context. We know that the first argument fails, on the basis of the example given above about hands and Cartesian demons. If I had no hands, I wouldn't believe that I do, so the belief that I have hands is sensitive to the facts. My having hands entails that no demon is active who makes it always and everywhere false that anyone has hands. But if there was such a demon, I wouldn't believe that there was, so this belief is not sensitive to the facts even though it is entailed by one that is.

Notice that this example provides no counterexample to safety, thereby lending support to the idea that safety might preserve closure even though sensitivity does not. If one were to believe one has hands, one would have hands, so this belief is safe. Furthermore, if one were to believe that there is no demon, there would be no demon, so this belief is safe as well. So the standard examples used to show that sensitivity is not closed under entailment lend support to the idea that safety is so closed.

Still, concluding that safety is closed under entailment would be incautious. First, note that it would an amazing coincidence if every case in which sensitivity fails the closure test constitutes a counterexample to transposition on counterfactual conditionals, and yet it is precisely that to which defenders of closure for safety are committed. This intuitive point against the claim that safety involves closure can be further supported using the standard semantics of possible worlds and similarity relations for counterfactuals, for this apparatus makes it very easy to construct a countermodel to both arguments above. Stipulate that in the actual world α the following is the case:

**True-in-α:** p, Bp, q, ~Bq, p entails q.

This stipulation guarantees the truth of the first three premises of the above arguments. Further stipulate that in all worlds **W** most similar to α, we have:

**True-in-W:** ~p, ~Bp, ~q, Bq.

This stipulation does not conflict with any reasonable interpretation of the closeness relation on worlds, so it is a model for the above two arguments. On this model, the premises of both arguments are all true, and each conclusion is false. For the first argument, the conclusion is false since in the most similar world where q is false, Bq is true. For the second argument, the conclusion is false as well, since in the closest world in which Bq is true, q is false.

This result should not surprise us. We know that transposition fails for counterfactual conditionals, but that fact is compatible with such transpositives nearly always having the same truth value. So it shouldn't surprise us if the transpositives defining safety and sensitivity have the same truth value in some special context, unless we had reason to think that such a context was one where counterexamples to transposition were likely to occur. It is hard to find any basis for such a suspicion in the special context of closure issues, so we shouldn't expect safety to be immune from whatever closure failures bear on sensitivity.

One may still resist such a conclusion by pointing out general difficulties with the standard semantics for counterfactuals, and claiming that more intuitive readings of subjunctive conditionals on a case-by-case basis fail to produce counterexamples. The upshot of such a position is that, even though we can't see some intuitive connection between closure difficulties for sensitivity and counterexamples to contraposition, the case-by-case examination shows that there is nonetheless a connection between them. If these claims were true, that would give some reason for maintaining the closure claim about safety and blaming the inadequacy of the standard semantics for formal failures such as the one described above.

The problem is that the case-by-case claim made above is false. Suppose Bill is in fake barn country. The residents of this locale have changed the ordinary landscape in the following way. They have made a decision for each barn whether to replace it with a fake barn or paint it green. We may imagine the decision-making to proceed in any number of ways, but let us suppose that they draw a card from a fair deck, and they replace if the card is black and paint if the card is red. Suppose that, in this area, Bill is asked whether the object in question is a green barn, and Bill answers, "Yes," believing that the object in question is a green barn. His belief is safe: anytime he forms such a belief in an environment relevantly like the present one, he will be correct. Bill believes also that the object in question is a barn. This belief, however, is not safe: If he were to form such a belief in an environment relevantly like the present one, he would be mistaken, for it is a matter of chance whether he'd be correct (depending on whether the drawn card is black or red).[3] Hence, safety does not preserve closure.

So safety theorists have no more right to claims about closure than do sensitivity theorists. The difference is that defenders of sensitivity have admitted failure of closure and safety theorists such as Sosa deny that their view has this implication. We can explain this difference in terms of a confusion between two closely related alternatives to sensitivity. I think defenders of closure using the language of safety have confused safety with a closely related view that is best expressed using the language of reliable indication. If one begins by thinking about sensitivity and safety in terms of subjunctive conditionals, one may be tempted to think of reliable indication as expressible in terms of a subjunctive conditional where the reliable indicator is the belief itself. Thinking in this way generates the following closure argument, which I juxtapose with the failed safety closure argument:

| | |
|---|---|
| 1. p entails q | 3. p entails q |
| 2. Bp □→ p | 4. Bp □→ p |
| 5. So, Bp □→ q | 5. So, Bq □→ q |

Notice that this first argument, the argument representing closure of reliable indication, has no counterexamples, either intuitive or formal. For the second premise to be true, we must consider a situation in which both Bp and p are true, and the first premise requires that in any such situation q will be true as well. Thus, such a situation cannot be one where Bp is true while q is false.

Reliable indication, however, is a different condition from the safety condition, and defenses of closure under reliable indication do not support closure under safety. So no mere substitution of a safety condition for Nozick's sensitivity condition will save the view from the untoward failure of closure. Instead, what will be needed is a replacement of the kind of theory Nozick favors with a version of reliabilism. In doing so, one might attempt to highlight the resemblances between the two views by clarifying reliable indication in terms of counterfactuals, but one will be hard-pressed to rely on the resemblances for long. For example, if believing that p is a reliable indicator of p, why think that it is the only kind of reliable indicator that can function in one's theory of knowledge? Why not any reliable indicator, whether a belief or not? For example, perhaps sensory experience itself is a reliable indicator of the truth of certain propositions. If so, why should the theory rule out this kind of reliable indicator as suitable in the account of knowledge?

Reliable indicator theorists may respond by claiming that the reliable indicator view is simply the deeper explanation of the truth of the safety view, in the following way. They may say, "If something is a reliable indicator of p, then believing p is also a reliable indicator of p, so reliable indication explains what is correct about the safety view." The idea behind such a claim is to keep the counterfactual relationship between beliefs and propositions central to the view, so as to maintain in some form an analogy between the safety view and the reliable indication view. The problem is that such a response generates a new violation of closure, for it commits the reliable indicator theorist to the following argument form:

---

1. p entails q
2. X □→ p
3. So, X □→ q
4. So Bp □→ p (using "if X is a reliable indicator of p, then so is believing p.")
5. So, Bq □→ q (again using "if X is a reliable indicator of p, then so is believing p.")

---

This argument implies a restricted form of closure for safety: it says that if you have a reliable indicator for p, then the belief that p is safe and so is any belief entailed by the belief that p. The barn example above shows that one cannot endorse such a view.

So if an interest in preserving closure leads one to endorse a reliable indication theory, the best thing to do is simply to embrace reliabilism and stop trying to pretend that one is defending a view of the same family as Nozick's. Restricting the reliable indicators to beliefs makes the theory insufficiently general, and once one generalizes, no basis is left for maintaining that the reliable indicator view is some small variant of the safety view.

From the perspective of the problem of the value of knowledge, this latter point is easy to appreciate. The characteristic feature of a Nozickian approach to the value of knowledge centers on finding a condition for knowledge that is stronger than truth. It is in virtue of this feature that transparency and idealism conditions are not promising counterfactual approaches to the question of the value of knowledge. It is noteworthy, then, that a counterfactual reliable indication theory fails to offer a condition for knowledge that is strictly stronger than truth. To offer such a condition requires offering a condition for knowing *p* which implies that a belief with content *p* satisfying this condition must be true. When the reliable indicator is the belief itself, as is the case with the safety condition, this condition is clearly met: the result is obtained by an application of counterfactual *modus ponens*. No such inference is available, however, for the more general reliable indication theory. The only way such an inference could work is if the identity conditions on belief included its grounding in terms of the reliable indicator in question, but that view of belief is implausible. So the conclusion to draw is that the reliable indication theory is as impotent in addressing the problem of the value of knowledge as are the transparency and idealism counterfactual conditions dismissed earlier.

## B. Probability and Closure

A natural move at this point is to wonder whether closure can be rescued by inserting talk of probabilities into these approaches. Instead of the above conditions, a theorist might say that a belief is safe when the claim in question is usually true in the presence of belief,[4] and one might say that a belief is sensitive when one would typically not hold the belief if the claim were false.

Both of these claims contain a scope ambiguity, depending on whether the probability operator is taken to govern the entire conditional or only the consequent of the conditional. Disambiguating gives us the following:

Wide scope probable safety: $Pr(Bp \;\square\rightarrow\; p)$
Wide scope probable sensitivity: $Pr(\sim p \;\square\rightarrow\; \sim Bp)$
Narrow scope probable safety: $Bp \;\square\rightarrow\; Pr(p)$
Narrow scope probable sensitivity: $\sim p \;\square\rightarrow\; Pr(\sim Bp)$

The first thing to notice is that closure fares no better on the narrow scope probabilistic readings than on the non-probabilistic versions of safety and sensitivity. If Bill were to believe that the object in question is a barn, in all likelihood he'd be wrong—after all, the real barns in the area are extremely rare. So if our goal is to preserve closure, neither the move from sensitivity to safety, nor the move from narrow scope probabilistic sensitivity to narrow scope probabilistic safety will help.

What about wide scope readings? Such readings generate the following arguments:

| | |
|---|---|
| 1. $Bp$ | 1. $Bp$ |
| 2. $p$ | 2. $p$ |
| 3. $p$ entails $q$ | 3. $p$ entails $q$ |
| 4. $Pr(\sim p \;\square\rightarrow\; \sim Bp)$ | 4. $Pr(Bp \;\square\rightarrow\; p)$ |
| 5. So, $Pr(\sim q \;\square\rightarrow\; \sim Bq)$ | 5. So, $Pr(Bq \;\square\rightarrow\; q)$ |

These arguments are harder to assess in large part because of the variety of interpretations proposed for the Pr operator, and the accompanying difficulties for each. For example, if we take a frequency approach to probability, these arguments will fail since it will be a contingent matter whether the claim within the scope of the probability operator in the conclusion is true most of the time when the premises are true. A similar point holds for other interpretations of probability, such as subjective theories and nomological ones, namely that the truth of the conclusion in face of the truth of the premises will be contingent at best.

The only approach that might allow the validity of these arguments is also one of the more mysterious ones, the logical theory, which maintains that any true probability judgment is necessarily true. If the conclusions are true, the above arguments will be valid since any argument with a logically necessary conclusion is valid.

Even so, there is cause for concern here. Recall that the defender of safety is claiming superiority for that view over the sensitivity view on the basis of closure results. So even if the second argument above is valid, that will not be a reason to favor safety over sensitivity unless the first argument is invalid. How would a defender of safety show that the first argument is invalid (assuming the logical theory of probability)? The best that can be done, I think, is to show that the information in the premises leaves the likelihood of the embedded sentence of the conclusion utterly inscrutable, i.e., they provide us with no information from which we can obviously conclude that the conclusion must be true. The same holds, however, for the second argument. So the challenge to the defender of safety is that it is not enough to maintain that the second argument is valid. Some difference must be found between it and the former argument if the superiority of safety is to be sustained.

Moreover, the move to any probabilistic reading raises a further problem for the idea that some safety condition explains the difference between knowledge and true belief. Consider how beliefs in lottery cases can be probabilistically safe. No adequate theory of knowledge can imply that we know that our ticket in a fair lottery will lose, no matter how large the lottery is, but if some probabilistic safety condition distinguishes knowledge from true belief, then such knowledge is possible.[5] In the case of a relatively large lottery where one believes that one's ticket will lose, one's belief is, if not safe, at least probably safe. The lesson is that probabilistic safety theorists will need some further condition to give an adequate account of the nature of knowledge.

Furthermore, the move to a probabilistic understanding of safety removes the primary virtue of counterfactual approaches to the nature of knowledge. Recall the initial attraction of such theories: the capacity to explain the value of knowledge in virtue of citing a condition strictly stronger than truth. Once a probability operator is introduced, either of wide or narrow scope, the new condition is no longer strictly stronger than truth. In particular, no such condition guarantees that a belief that meets such a condition must be true. Believing a false claim is compatible both with it being likely that the belief counterfactually implies its content and with the belief counterfactually implying the likely truth of its content.

We must judge, therefore, that the probabilistic move is a non-starter. There is no reason to think it will do better on the closure issue, and it raises additional problems not faced by non-probabilistic approaches. In the context of our discussion, the worst of these problems is that such a move eviscerates the safety approach of its promise of accounting for the value of knowledge.

## IV. Deeper Problems for Safety and Sensitivity Conditions

Two responses might blunt the force of the above discussion of varieties of counterfactual approaches in epistemology. First, one might find some way of preserving closure for one of the two views in some way I have not considered. Given the variety of considerations above, I think it is highly doubtful that any such approach can be found, but I've given no decisive proof against the idea. Second, even if no rescue is possible, it may be possible to preserve Nozick's central contention that denies closure while restricting the failures in such a way that the denial is more palatable. For example, it is hard to defend the view that one can know that something is a green barn, but not that it is a barn. Such a position is truly deserving of DeRose's appellation, "the abominable conjunction."[6] My own intuitive response is not nearly as hostile to the suggestion that we can know we have hands even though we do not know that we are not brains-in-a-vat being stimulated to experience the world in precisely the way we are actually experiencing it. I am not saying that I find the latter conjunction unproblematic. I am saying, though, that I find it less problematic than the former conjunction. So perhaps there is a way to develop safety or sensitivity to reduce the kinds of failures of closure to those that are the least problematic kind, and to argue that the virtues of the approach are sufficient to outweigh the disvalue of this negative aspect of the theory.

Furthermore, I don't think the issue of closure gets to the heart of the matter of what is troublesome about these approaches to the nature of knowledge, for recent epistemology has found it extremely difficult to formulate a correct account of closure.[7] In light of the difficulties in formulating an acceptable closure condition, we should be suspicious of categorical rejections of a theory based only on closure considerations.

I will argue, however, that there are deeper problems with Nozickian approaches to the nature of knowledge. I will argue that neither sensitivity nor safety approaches are suited to explaining the nature of knowledge, but instead are suitable only for explaining part of what we know. The limited roles I will argue for are these: sensitivity is more naturally suited to explaining perceptual knowledge, whereas safety is more naturally suited for explaining statistical or inductive knowledge, and neither is well-suited for explaining the other category.

Sosa argues against the sensitivity requirement and in favor of the safety requirement in just this way. He imagines a case where a person has dropped one's garbage down a chute in an apartment building, and that person believes that the garbage will soon be in the basement. The long track record of correlation between the two events makes the belief safe: if one believes, in this situation, that the garbage will soon be in the basement, it would be true. Notice, however, that the belief is not sensitive. If the garbage would not soon be in the basement, it likely would somehow have gotten caught in the chute, in which case one would still believe that the garbage will soon be in the basement.

What is instructive here is that Sosa's defense appeals to a case of inductive knowledge, and sensitivity is not well-suited to such contexts. It is equally instructive to notice that things go in the other direction in perceptual cases. Suppose one is color blind to the extreme: everything looks brown. Suppose also that in one's local environment, everything is a shade of brown. Then, when looking at a brown thing, one's belief is safe: if one believes it is brown, it would be brown. But one's belief is not sensitive, and its insensitivity is the important point here, for such a person does not know the color of the thing he is looking at even if the environment is so unbelievably friendly to him that he is always right.

In perceptual cases, our attention generally focuses on powers of discrimination, and here sensitivity is central. A substantial track record of truth may show that a belief is safe, but it won't show that it counts as knowledge when one lacks the discriminatory capacity to differentiate truth from error. Lacking such a capacity makes one's beliefs insensitive, and this feature dominates the safe character of the belief, for in such cases, knowledge is lacking.

If I am right, neither sensitivity nor safety, as formulated in 2 and 3 above, are conditions for knowledge. Sensitivity is more at home in the realm of perceptual knowledge and safety in the realm of inductive or statistical knowledge.[8] Of course, it is open to a theorist to opt for one of the two, and simply deny that there is knowledge of the other sort. Such a route would be a very difficult one for a defender of the safety condition, for that would require holding that inductive knowledge is possible even though perceptual knowledge isn't. More likely is the other route: to hold that perceptual knowledge is possible, but statistical or inductive knowledge is not. I will not pursue either line here, except to point out what I take to be the severest counterexample to the idea that inductive knowledge is not possible. One of the deepest aspects of the human condition is coping with our own impending death, and among the most important items of self-knowledge that we have is that we will die. Only theory-clouded judgment can maintain that I can know what color the sky is but not that I will die.

The other option is to bifurcate one's theory of knowledge, maintaining that one of the two counterfactual conditions we've examined always explains the difference between knowledge and true belief. Not so, as is shown by a central example in the Gettier literature. You see Tim steal a book from the library, and believe as a result that Tim stole the book. You report Tim to the police, and when they go to Tim's home to arrest him, Tim's mother swears his innocence. She says that Tim has a twin brother, Tom, who is a kleptomaniac, and that Tim is on a safari expedition in Africa. Where is Tom? She has no idea, of course.

This case splits into two. In one case, the police have no past history with Tim's mother. Her claims are persuasive and she appears honest, so the police must check out her story before proceeding with their plans to find Tim and arrest him. In the other case, the police have a long history of acquaintance with Tim's mother, knowing that she has lied repeatedly to save Tim from trouble. In fact, she has used this precise lie in the past, and the police have investigated the story and learned that Tim does not have a twin but that he is an only child. In such a case, they laugh off the tale and carry on with their plans to arrest Tim.

In the second case, both you and the police have knowledge about who stole the book that is unaffected by the mother's testimony, but not in the first case. In both cases, the mother's testimony is a defeater of your evidence that Tim stole the book, but it has differential significance in the two cases. In the first case, it undermines your knowledge, since it is a possibility that the police cannot rule out. But in the second case, it doesn't undermine your knowledge.

If this particular case isn't convincing, imagine different contexts for the mother to say what she says. Imagine, for example, that the mother's testimony is part of a theater production in which she was acting. Or imagine her saying it in her sleep, as part of a dream, or saying it to convince herself: "He *has* a twin brother! He really does! Tim's in Africa, he *really* is!" And imagine any of these possibilities with no one around at all to hear what she says. Knowledge can't be so fragile that it disappears just because a normally competent speaker denies what we believe.

Notice that neither safety nor sensitivity can explain the difference between the two cases. In both cases, the mother is failing to tell the truth, and whatever is the proper account of the relevant difference in the two cases, that difference cannot be explained in terms of safety or sensitivity.

Furthermore, notice that there will be cases like this one for any type of belief one wishes to consider. The above case involves a perceptual belief, but it could just as easily have been a statistical or inductive belief, a belief based on memory, or a testimonial belief. Safety and sensitivity may be part of the story of what distinguishes knowledge from true belief, but they are not enough of the story to fulfill the promise of Nozickian epistemology to account for the value of knowledge over that of true belief.

## Conclusion

These results are deeply disappointing. We began with an intuitive account of how Nozickian approaches to epistemology might help us understand the value of knowledge over that of true belief. Nozickian approaches have a virtue not possessed by other contemporary theories of knowledge, for such accounts impose a condition on knowledge logically stronger than truth. This feature endows these theories with the same resources for explaining the value of knowledge over that of true belief as are possessed by historically prominent infallibilist theories of knowledge while avoiding the nearly universal skepticism implied by the latter. Given this strong promise of Nozick's approach, it is regrettable that we must conclude it to be a failure. This failure raises a larger question that deserves careful investigation. That question is the question of whether any approach to the theory of knowledge can successfully explain the value of knowledge over that of its subparts (without encountering other problems such as implying the truth of wholesale skepticism). Our discussion can be read as providing significant evidence for a negative answer to this question,[9] thereby robbing the theory of knowledge of one argument for its centrality in a proper conception of the tasks of philosophy.[10]

### Notes

1. See, e.g., Alvin Goldman, "What is Justified Belief?" in G. Pappas, ed., *Knowledge and Justification*, (Dordrecht: D. Reidel, 1979), pp. 1–25.
2. A clear and helpful discussion of these issues can be found in Steven Luper, "The Epistemic Closure Principle," in the *Stanford Encyclopedia of Philosophy*.
3. I thank Stew Cohen for this point, who noted that the example is borrowed from what are now referred to as Saul Kripke's "Nozick-bashing" lectures at Princeton.
4. It is interesting to note that Sosa makes such a move in "The Place of Truth in Epistemology," in Zagzebski and DePaul, eds., *Intellectual Virtue: Perspectives from Ethics and Epistemology*, (New York: Oxford University Press, 2003).
5. There are contexts in which no criticism is warranted for an assertion that one knows that one's ticket will not win (e.g., if one has to choose between waiting to receive the prize for winning and attending to some emergency). My view of such cases is that a careful account of the pragmatics/semantics distinction applied to the concept of knowledge will count such assertions as pragmatically acceptable even though semantically false.
6. Keith DeRose, "Solving the Skeptical Problem," *The Philosophical Review* 104 (1995), pp. 1–52.
7. For a comprehensive account of the issues involved in this problem, see John Hawthorne's forthcoming book *Knowledge and Lotteries*, (Oxford: Oxford University Press).
8. What I am claiming does not imply that there are no counterexamples to sensitivity in cases of perceptual knowledge, nor that there are no counterexamples to safety in statistical or inductive cases. I am only pointing out the natural fit between sensitivity considerations and perceptual knowledge, on the one hand, and safety considerations and statistical knowledge, on the other.
9. For further argument for this conclusion, see my *The Value of Knowledge and the Pursuit of Understanding*, (New York: Cambridge University Press, 2003).

10. For helpful discussion of these issues and comments on earlier drafts, I wish to thank Peter Markie, Matt McGrath, Peter Vallentyne, and Paul Weirich. I also wish to thank audiences at the University of Arkansas, St. Louis University, and North Carolina State University for useful and provocative discussion of these issues.

*Philosophical Issues, 14, Epistemology, 2004*

# ON JUSTIFYING AND BEING JUSTIFIED

Adam Leite
Indiana University

We commonly speak of people as being "justified" or "unjustified" in believing as they do. These terms describe a person's epistemic condition. To be justified in believing as one does is to have a positive epistemic status in virtue of holding one's belief in a way which fully satisfies the relevant epistemic requirements or norms. This requires something more (or other) than simply believing a proposition whose truth is well-supported by evidence, even by evidence which one possesses oneself, since one could entirely miss the relevance of this evidence and hold the belief as a result of wishful thinking or for some other bad reason. My topic in this paper is the notion of being justified which precludes beliefs flawed in this way. I will take the notion of something's telling in favor of the truth of a proposition—that is, the notion of evidential support—for granted.

In addition to being (or not being) justified in holding beliefs, we also engage in the activity of justifying: we sincerely articulate what we take to be good reasons for our beliefs, commit to holding our beliefs for those reasons, and attempt to meet objections, all in order to establish our right to hold our beliefs. This activity is often conversational, though it can also take place in private meditation. Either way, if one is taken to have performed successfully, then one's interlocutor (who may be oneself) will conclude that one is justified.

It would seem, at first blush, that the state of being justified can't be fully distinguished from considerations pertaining to the activity. In particular, many people find it natural to think that if you can't justify a belief, then you aren't justified in holding it. Imagine, for instance, a case in which your interlocutor insists upon a surprising claim. He offers some reasons which manifestly fail to support the truth of his belief, and he has no satisfactory reply when this shortcoming is pointed out to him. His belief isn't justified, or so it would seem; he really shouldn't be so certain about the matter. Consequently, it seems that he is faced with two choices: give up his belief, or find better reasons for it. It would be outrageous dogmatism for him simply to insist upon its truth even though he can't satisfactorily defend it. Thus his epistemic status with regard to this belief appears to be tied to his poor performance in the activity of justifying.

Many epistemologists would disagree. Robert Audi, for instance, writes,

> It would seem that just as a little child can be of good character even if unable to defend its character against attack, one can have a justified belief even if, in response to someone who doubts this, one could not show that one does.[1]

William Alston agrees.

> We must clear out of the way a confusion between one's *being* justified in believing that p, and one's *justifying* one's belief that p, where the latter involves one's *doing* something to show that p, or to show that one's belief was justified, or to exhibit one's justification. The first side of this distinction is a state or condition one is in, not anything one does *or any upshot thereof*.[2]

He adds that one's belief may be justified even if one is *incapable* of justifying it.[3] Audi and Alston are quite orthodox in this regard. The tendency in most recent epistemology has been to treat epistemic status as being completely independent from the person's performance in the activity of justifying.[4]

My aim in this paper is to argue for an opposing view. Being justified, I will propose, is ordinarily a matter of being able to justify one's belief—that is, of being able to develop and provide an appropriate and adequate defense of one's belief when asked to do so under appropriate conditions. As will become apparent, this proposal amounts to a reconceptualization of the basic framework for understanding epistemic justification.

My topic also raises an issue of fundamental philosophical orientation, for it promises a deeper lesson about what kind of creatures we are—in particular, about what it is to be an appropriate subject of epistemic evaluation. The justificatory status of people's beliefs carries a great deal of normative weight. For instance, if we find that someone is not justified in holding a particular belief, then we demand that he give it up or find better reasons upon which to base it. If he maintains his belief without basing it upon better reasons, we will quite appropriately cease to take him seriously if he asserts its truth. I will argue that such normative evaluations and responses are appropriate precisely because we human beings are able to make particular considerations our reasons by undertaking certain commitments in the course of our conscious deliberative and justificatory activity. So one point which I ultimately want to urge is that because the common view misunderstands our justificatory activities, it misses precisely what is distinctive about us in virtue of which we are appropriately evaluated in epistemic terms.

My argument will proceed somewhat indirectly. In the first two parts I articulate and reject a view of the relation between being justified and being able to justify which has structured much recent epistemological thought. Seeing this view's failings will help reorient our basic approach to the issue. However, rejecting this view does not suffice to establish a link between being justified and being able to justify. In part 3 I pursue issues initially broached in part 2 regarding the epistemic basing relation, the relation between a belief and the reasons for which it is held. Roughly, the upshot is that basing relations must be established through, or be capable of being appropriately manifested in, the person's explicit deliberative and justificatory activity. Finally, in parts 4 and 5, I elaborate and defend my proposal for the core of an account of justification.

## I. The Spectatorial Conception

A certain conception of the relation between justification and the activity of justifying has been presupposed by much of the discussion over the past 25 or so years. To get it clearly in view, it will be helpful to look briefly at two recently influential theories.

According to William Alston, a belief is justified just if it is based upon an adequate ground, such as an appropriate perceptual experience or memory state.[5] Alston holds that whether a given belief is based upon a particular ground is a causal matter: a particular psychological state, say a particular perceptual experience, is the ground upon which a belief is based just if the state served as an input to the processes through which the belief was formed.[6] A belief's ground is "adequate," according to Alston, just if it is a highly reliable indication of the truth of the belief (given how the world usually is).[7] For Alston, then, a belief is justified in virtue of two sets of facts: (1) facts about what states served as inputs in the process of belief formation, and (2) facts about the degree to which those states indicate the truth of the belief. The activity of justifying thus does not enter into Alston's account of the nature of justification. As he puts it, "the *state* concept is the more basic one, since the activity of justifying is an activity directed to showing that a belief is in the *state* of being justified."[8] Justifying, according to Alston, is a secondary and optional activity of trying to report the antecedent facts in virtue of which one's belief is justified.

This conception of the activity of justifying is shared by the many theories of justification which take a belief's justificatory status to be determined simply by the adequacy of the psychological states or processes which causally give rise to or sustain it. For it is commonly assumed that the correct causal story about one's beliefs is prior to, and not determined by, whatever one might happen to say when asked to justify them. Since the causal view is a main tenet of recent "naturalized" theories of justification, I take these views to be committed to the conception articulated by Alston.[9]

The causal view is not a necessary feature of this conception, however. To see this, consider another example: Laurence BonJour's former coherentist view. On one plausible interpretation, BonJour held that positive justificatory status accrues to each belief in a system of beliefs in virtue of features of the whole system such as logical consistency and wide-ranging relations of mutual inferability.[10] A given system of beliefs will possess or fail to possess these features quite independently of its possessor's attempts to justify his or her beliefs. Consequently, BonJour held that though justification requires that there *be* an acceptable inference from other things one believes, and that the acceptability of this inference not be undercut by other things which one believes, one need not have made the inference or its acceptability explicit in an attempt to justify the belief.[11] In fact, BonJour allowed that one's belief will be justified even if one is incapable of making the justification explicit at all. One might, he wrote, be too stupid.[12]

The fundamental idea shared by these views is that being justified is something which *happens to you*. According to these theories, the justificatory status of a person's belief is determined by certain facts which obtain prior to and independently of the activity of justifying. The activity itself plays no role in determining justificatory status; it is simply a secondary and optional matter of attempting to determine and report, as far as is conversationally necessary, the prior and independent facts which determine the justificatory status of one's belief. Consequently, even if things go badly wrong in the course of the activity, that will not determine one's actual justificatory status. On this conception, one stands in a primarily theoretical or epistemic relation to the justificatory status of one's beliefs: positive justificatory status is something which one finds out about, not something which one brings about. I therefore call this view *the Spectatorial Conception*.

It may seem that to question the Spectatorial Conception is simply to urge a familiar form of epistemological internalism. However, this impression is incorrect.

Two distinct issues are commonly debated under the rubric of "epistemological internalism." The first concerns the extent to which the factors which determine a belief's justificatory status must be "internal" to the psychology of the individual. An externalist view on this issue allows factors external to the individual's psychology, such as the real-world reliability of a particular belief-forming mechanism, to affect the justificatory status of his or her beliefs. Denial of the Spectatorial Conception is compatible with any position on this issue. I myself hold a view which combines denial of the Spectatorial Conception with an externalist account of the goodness of reasons. Since I hold that being justified requires having good reasons, my view is externalist, in this sense of "externalism."

The second issue concerns the cognitive accessibility of the justificatory status of one's beliefs or of the factors determining their justificatory status. A strong accessibility internalist holds that one can't be justified unless one is aware of the justificatory status of one's beliefs or of the factors determining their status, while a more moderate view requires only that one be able to become aware of these matters through introspection and a priori reflection. By contrast, thoroughgoing accessibility externalism maintains that a belief can be justified even if its possessor currently has no good way of finding out about these matters.[13]

Two points should be made here. First, accessibility internalism and the Spectatorial Conception are perfectly compatible. In fact, the current disagreement over accessibility externalism does not concern the Spectatorial Conception at all, but rather proceeds entirely within its terms. For as it is currently conducted, the debate presupposes that a belief's justificatory status is primarily determined by facts which obtain independently of what goes on when the person justifies the belief; the question is simply whether, and to what extent, being justified also requires epistemic access to these prior and independent facts. BonJour, for instance, advocated a moderate form of accessibility internalism, holding that the inference which justifies a belief must be "available" to the person, so that the person "would be able *in principle* to rehearse it if the belief should be called into question, either by others or by himself..."[14] This requirement is perfectly compatible with the spirit of the Spectatorial Conception. BonJour's internalism is simply an additional, supplementary requirement that one must be able, in principle, to find out about the acceptable inference in virtue of which one's belief is justified.

The Spectatorial Conception allows for an even stronger form of accessibility internalism. One could supplement the basic Spectatorial model with the additional requirement that one must *in fact* be able to find out about and report the prior, independent facts which are primarily responsible for the justificatory status of one's belief. This additional requirement would allow a proponent of the Spectatorial Conception to hold that a belief can't be justified unless its possessor is actually able to justify it. But even on this modified view, one's relation to the facts which determine the justificatory status of one's beliefs would still be theoretical or quasi-perceptual, merely a matter of epistemic access. The activity of justifying still wouldn't play any significant role in shaping the facts which determine justificatory status.

The second point about accessibility internalism is this: rejection of the Spectatorial Conception does not force one to accept accessibility internalism. If we already accept the Spectatorial Conception, then it will appear that the question of the justificatory significance of the activity of justifying simply amounts to a question about the acceptability of a very strong accessibility requirement. But if we challenge the Spectatorial Conception itself, then we open the door to a reconceptualization both of the nature of the facts which determine justificatory status and of the activity of justifying. We allow for the possibility that the activity of justifying is not simply a matter of reporting prior and independent facts which determine justificatory status, but is instead an attempt to secure and defend a positive justificatory status by offering reasons in defense of one's belief and responding to challenges. On this alternative view, the facts which determine justificatory status would depend, at least in part, upon what one does and says when one sincerely attempts to justify one's beliefs. Such a view is not equivalent to any standard form of internalism, though it provides what, I believe, accessibility internalists really want: a view which allows the person some measure of involvement in, and hence responsibility for, the justificatory status of his or her beliefs.[15]

Since any view along these lines requires that one possess and be able to offer reasons in support of one's belief, it might seem that it will also involve a familiar form of accessibility internalism: namely, epistemic access to one's reasons. In a sense, this is correct. But we have to be very careful here. If the act of offering a reason is interpreted simply as a matter of reporting a prior and independent psychological relation which holds between the belief being justified and one's other beliefs (or other psychological states), then the suggested view would indeed require some form of epistemic access to that relation. But, as I will urge, this interpretation is incorrect: in many cases we should instead understand the link between one's belief and one's reasons as being constituted through one's deliberative and justificatory activity. If this view is correct, then in at least many cases there will be no prior fact about the reasons upon which one bases one's belief. Consequently, the activity of justifying will not require epistemic access to any such facts. What will be required, instead, is nothing more than the ordinary ability to utilize beliefs in reasoning and express them in speech. I leave open whether such abilities are appropriately understood as depending upon some form of epistemic access. Even if so, this is hardly the issue standardly debated under the rubric of accessibility internalism. It is rather an issue concerning the nature of our relation to our own minds.

## II. The Failure of the Spectatorial Conception

I will now attempt to bring out a fundamental incoherence in the Spectatorial Conception. My argument will depend upon considerations about the epistemic basing relation, the relation between a belief and the belief(s) or other psychological state(s) which are its ground, or between a belief and the reasons for which it is held. This relation's role is primarily normative: it ties the person's justificatory status regarding the belief to the adequacy of certain reasons for holding it. (I'll say more about this point later on.)

Any Spectatorialist account of justification needs to appeal to basing relations. Here's why. The Spectatorial Conception is a view about what it is for persons to be justified in believing as they do. As previously noted, a person who believes *p* and who possesses evidence which adequately indicates *p*'s truth, or who believes things which enable an acceptable inference to it, may still not have a justified belief, since he may believe *p* for some ridiculous reason and not for the good reasons which he possesses. The trouble is not that he lacks good grounds for his belief, but that his belief is not appropriately related to those grounds. Any Spectatorialist account of justification must capture this difference without appealing to considerations about the person's justificatory activity. To do so, it will appeal to the epistemic basing relation.[16]

Now the key idea behind the Spectatorial Conception is that all factors relevant to justificatory status are in place independently of and not directly affected by what goes on when the person attempts to justify the belief. Since basing relations are among these factors, the Spectatorial Conception must hold that they too are determined independently of the person's justificatory activity and not directly affected by it. So the fundamental idea is this: a person's belief is justified only if it is located within an appropriate system of basing relations, a system which is in place independently what goes on when the person attempts to formulate a justification for her belief and which is not directly affected by anything involved in that attempt. As we will see, this conception provides the basis for a fundamental criticism of the Spectatorial Conception itself.

Recent work on the basing relation has remained squarely within the terms of this picture. The dominant view is that basing relations are determined, somehow, by the factors causally responsible for originating or sustaining the belief.[17] And even those theorists who reject this approach have mainly conceived of basing relations as being established independently of the subject's justificatory activity.[18]

In a paper which established the framework for the debate about the basing relation over the past three decades, Gilbert Harman offered a particularly clear instance of this Spectatorial conception of the basing relation.[19] On Harman's view, we come to have beliefs as a result of processes of reasoning which are largely subconscious or unconscious. Our reasons are the considerations which, by figuring in these reasoning processes, lead us to have the beliefs that we have.[20] Thus, according to Harman, the reasons upon which a belief is based are the considerations which figure in a correct psychological explanation of why the person believes as he does. This explanation is distinct from what the person says when asked to justify his beliefs; what a person appeals to or offers when attempting to justify a belief are, at best, merely those aspects of the

responsibilities by sincerely declaring that one holds one's belief for particular reasons.[25] (It may be helpful to clarify the first requirement slightly.
By "directly determine," I mean a role of the sort we ordinarily play in
establishing our intentions when we seriously and sincerely declare
"I intend..." Barring fundamental irrationality, such a declaration of
intention precludes one's not so intending unless one changes one's mind;
nothing more need happen in order for one so to intend. However, I do not
claim that one can establish basing relations at will. Again, the declaration
of intention provides a helpful analogy. I cannot now, simply by an act of
will, intend to jump out of the window of my third-floor office.[26] Nor can
I seriously and sincerely declare that I intend to do so. Nonetheless, my
declarations of intention often directly determine my intentions.)

The Spectatorial Conception does not meet the first condition. According
to the Spectatorial Conception, basing relations obtain independently of,
and are not directly determined by, either what one says or the thinking that
is involved when one sincerely offers reasons in justification of one's belief.
And this means that basing relations will *never* be directly determined by the
conclusions of one's explicit evaluations of reasons. Even barring irrationality, it will always be a further question whether one has thereby succeeded
in making those considerations the reasons for which one holds one's belief.
For instance, recall Harman's view. Suppose that one currently holds a
certain belief. According to Harman, the correct cognitive-psychological
explanation of why one holds this belief determines the reasons for which
one currently holds it. One now engages in some conscious deliberation
about one's reasons and concludes, "I base this belief on ____." On
Harman's view, one might very well be wrong about this; one's explicit
deliberations will determine the reasons for which one holds the belief only
if the reasons arrived at actually explain why one holds the belief. Suppose
they weren't the reasons which previously explained the belief. Then something further has to happen: the actual relations between one's beliefs have
to be made to line up with one's explicit reflections. A similar point applies
even when it seems, from the first-person perspective, that one has arrived at
a belief through a course of explicit inference and reasoning. Thus, for
Harman, whenever one sincerely declares, after explicit reflection upon the
available reasons, "*these* are my reasons for holding this belief," one must
either be issuing a hypothesis about what explains one's belief or giving
oneself a recommendation. One is not, then and there, doing something
which directly determines what one's reasons are.

Of course, Harman can give an explanatory role to explicit reasoning
and inference, since he can allow that it is a (contingent) psychological fact
that when we explicitly infer a conclusion from particular considerations,
the corresponding beliefs ordinarily figure in the correct explanation of our
belief in the conclusion. On his view, however, basing relations would still
be in place even if our explicit reasoning and inference *never* affected the

correct explanation of our beliefs. And the explanatory role which he allows to our explicit deliberations falls short of the role which these activities ordinarily play in determining basing relations.

Just as the Spectatorial Conception fails to allow for the possibility of directly establishing basing relations through one's explicit deliberations, it also fails to allow for the obligations and vulnerability to criticism which are ordinarily incurred when one sincerely declares that one holds one's belief for particular reasons. If one's statement of the reasons for which one holds a belief is merely a recommendation or hypothesis about what one's belief is independently based upon, then one could take comfort if the reasons which one states are met with decisive criticism. One could say, "Well, I might be wrong, those might not actually be the reasons upon which my belief is based, and so my belief might be justified nonetheless . . . " Thus even if one acknowledges that the reasons one has offered are inadequate or false, one could always beg off any responsibility either to give up the belief or to come up with better reasons for holding it. The Spectatorial Conception thus prevents us from directly evaluating a person purely on the basis of what she sincerely says about the reasons for which she holds her beliefs.[27]

This point brings us to the Spectatorial Conception's fundamental failing. For the flip side of the problem just canvassed is that, as I will discuss in a moment, the Spectatorial Conception also fails to allow for epistemic evaluation or criticism of a person on account of the reasons upon which her beliefs are (according to the Spectatorial Conception) *actually based*. As a result, it fails to do justice to the basing relation's normative role.

To see this point, consider first the role we expect basing relations to play. If a person holds a belief on the basis of particular reasons, then her justificatory status with regard to the belief is thereby tied to the adequacy of those reasons. Basing relations thus open the person to epistemic evaluation, and to further normative consequences, on account of the adequacy of the belief's grounds, and they engender an obligation to give up the belief or seek better reasons if its grounds prove inadequate. We thus expect the basing relation to span the space between a person, a belief, and particular reasons, so that the person's attitude of belief becomes linked to those reasons in such a way that their adequacy or inadequacy can provide a fair basis for epistemic evaluation of the person and can engender further obligations and responsibilities.[28]

Now the facts which the Spectatorial Conception treats as determining basing relations do not establish the right sort of link between the person and the reasons upon which her beliefs are putatively based. According to the Spectatorial Conception the facts which determine basing relations are in place independently of the person's explicit deliberation, reasoning, or declaration of reasons and are not directly determined by any of the person's explicit deliberative or justificatory activity. On this view, your relation to the bases of your own beliefs is fundamentally like your relation to the bases of someone else's beliefs: in both cases, your task is to find out what they are and, perhaps, to attempt to influence them. The only difference is that the facts which determine the grounds of your beliefs are "in you"—they concern your psychology. Consider, then, that having found out the reasons upon which someone else's belief is based, you might conclude that they are inadequate or even false. If the Spectatorial Conception is correct, there is no reason why your own case should be any different. Hence, after determining the correct explanation of your own belief, you should be free to conclude, "$q$ is the reason upon which the belief that $p$ is based, but $q$ is a lousy reason for believing that $p$." Now, if you determine that $q$ is a poor reason for believing that $p$, then you are ordinarily entitled to repudiate it as a reason for believing that $p$. So insofar as the Spectatorial Conception is intended to account for our ordinary notion of holding a belief for a reason, it must allow one to say, "$I$ don't base $p$ on $q$, because $q$ is an entirely inadequate reason." (It is, after all, incoherent to say, "I base my belief that $p$ on $q$, but $q$ is an entirely inadequate reason.") But according to the Spectatorial Conception, one's explicit evaluation and endorsement or rejection of reasons does not directly determine the reasons upon which one's belief is based. So if the Spectatorial Conception is correct, there should be situations in which it would be intelligible to say (putting the two together), "My belief that $p$ is based upon $q$, but I don't base $p$ upon $q$, since $q$ is an inadequate reason." But this is incoherent. Of course, one can discover or conclude that one has held a belief for bad reasons. But to state the reasons my belief is *now* based upon is to state the reasons $I$ base it upon, the reasons for which I hold it. And I cannot simultaneously declare that I both do and do not hold a given belief for given reasons.[29]

The Spectatorial Conception runs into trouble here because of a fundamental bifurcation which it forces within our thinking about a person: on one side are the facts which determine basing relations, on the other is the person's overt deliberative and justificatory activity, and the latter does not ever directly determine the former. Once we clearly recognize this division, we can see that the Spectatorial Conception of the basing relation does not do the necessary work: it does not provide an adequate basis for epistemic evaluation of the person, at least not for the forms of evaluation which are my concern here—forms of evaluation connected with the notions of entitlement, responsibility and fair criticism of the person. The crucial question here concerns the appropriateness of treating a person as responsible for a certain condition and hence as an appropriate subject of normative evaluation and criticism on its account. We must distinguish, on the one hand, sub-personal states and processes (such as the states and processes which result in perceptual beliefs) as well as states and processes to which the person is merely passively subject and, on the other hand, states and reasoning processes *of the person*. Only the latter will form a proper basis for normative evaluation of the person. So to enable the relevant sorts of epistemic evaluation—and the normative consequences thereof—basing relations must be attributable to the person and not merely to some process which takes place "in" him or her. But the Spectatorial Conception prevents this. The problem is not that the Spectatorial Conception places basing relations outside the person's voluntary control; basing relations, on any plausible view, can't be modified simply at will. The problem is rather that according to the Spectatorial Conception basing relations are never directly determined through the person's explicit evaluation of reasons in the course of her deliberative and justificatory activity. In this regard, they are no more an appropriate ground for evaluation of her than is her heart rate. States of a sort which are never directly determined by a person's conscious deliberation, the commitments incurred through her conscious deliberation, or her best explicit evaluation of reasons are not attributable to her in the relevant sense.[30]

It might be suggested that it is enough for purposes of attributability and evaluation that basing relations be reliably caused by the conclusions of a person's explicit deliberations. The proposal doesn't succeed, however, because reliable causal control isn't sufficient to make a state "mine" in the relevant sense. Suppose, for instance, that I am an excellent hypnotist. As a result, I have a great deal of causal control over the beliefs of my victims. (We might even imagine that I have perfect causal control.) I may justly be held responsible for bringing it about that they have certain beliefs rather than others. That is something which is attributable to me. But their beliefs are not thereby mine: their beliefs are not attributable to me in the relevant sense, since I may not believe what they believe. And one part of the explanation of this fact is that their beliefs are not open to direct determination through my first-personal deliberations about what I should believe.[31] Similarly, on a version of the Spectatorial Conception which allows me reliable causal control over (so-called) basing relations, I may justly be held responsible for bringing it about that there are certain relations and not others. But that alone does not make the basing relations in question mine in the relevant sense; it is not enough to establish that *I* hold the beliefs for those reasons. Imagine, for instance, that there is a systematic derangement of the causal processes. Suppose that we human beings were such that when we arrived at conclusions through explicit processes of deliberation, this causally affected the relations amongst our beliefs in a systematic and predictable way, but in such a way that certain beliefs *other* than our beliefs in the premises took on the causally sustaining role. In that case, too, we would have reliable causal control over the relations in question. But it would be perverse to take the resultant relations to fix one's reasons for holding one's beliefs and to evaluate one on their basis. They are not attributable to one in the right sort of way.

In sum, by discounting our ordinary deliberative and justificatory activities the Spectatorial Conception loses sight of the person, the locus of epistemic evaluation and criticism. This spells disaster. The Spectatorial Conception needs basing relations in its account of justification, but whatever the Spectatorial Conception calls a "basing relation" will not be the relation which is involved when a person holds a belief for a particular reason.

### III. The Basis of Basing Relations

The demise of the Spectatorial Conception does not entail that being justified requires the ability to justify. However, it clears the way for a defense of this requirement. This section begins such a defense by sketching an account of the basing relation just far enough to make it plausible that if someone holds a belief on the basis of particular reasons, then (to put it roughly) she must be able to acknowledge or appropriately express those reasons in the course of her explicit deliberative and justificatory activity. If this claim is correct, then in order for someone's belief to be justified in virtue of being based upon certain reasons, she must be able to justify it by appealing to those reasons.

As our consideration of the Spectatorial Conception revealed, the normative significance of ordinary epistemic evaluation places certain constraints on accounts of the basing relation. It must be possible for basing relations to be directly established by one's conscious reasoning, decision to hold one's belief for particular reasons, or sincere declaration that one holds one's belief for given reasons. And in order for a person to hold a belief on the basis of particular considerations, she must at least have the *capacity* to directly establish her reasons for holding the belief through her explicit deliberation and reflection about reasons for belief.

By themselves, these points are logically compatible with the view that once a basing relation is in place, there is no need for one to be able to express or manifest it in any way in one's explicit thought or attempts to justify one's belief. For instance, it might be said that so long as the above requirements are met, basing relations are always in place prior to one's explicit deliberative or justificatory activity simply in virtue of causal or other explanatory factors which one may not be in any position to find out about. (On this view, causal or other explanatory factors would establish default basing relations, subject to overriding by links established through one's explicit deliberative or justificatory activity should one ever engage in it.) Or it might be claimed that once one has put a basing relation in place through one's explicit deliberations, there is no need for one later to be able to articulate that basing relation in order for it to persist. On such views, one could be justified in virtue of holding a belief for adequate reasons even if one is incapable of justifying it.

However, though these suggestions are logically compatible with the above points, we can't make good sense of them once we've put *the person* at the center of our thinking about what's involved in holding a belief for a reason. Consider an example of the first suggestion. We are supposed to imagine that certain good reasons play a causal or explanatory role which suffices for a person's belief to be based upon those reasons, but that when the person attempts to justify the belief he can only come up with bad reasons even though he hasn't forgotten anything and there is no other special condition which explains this failing. I don't think that we can see this as a case in which he ever held his belief on the basis of the good reasons. Admittedly, there is a sense in which he had (and continues to have) good reasons for believing as he does. But what he does when he attempts to justify his belief reveals that *he* does not appreciate their force. Consequently, though there are many favorable things which we can say about his belief and its provenance, he doesn't hold his belief on the basis of those reasons. At most, those reasons affected him.

Consider, now, the second suggestion. A person has established a basing relation through her explicit deliberation and reasoning. We are supposed to imagine that she continues to hold her belief for this reason even though she cannot now manifest it either in her explicit thinking or when she attempts to justify the belief in optimal circumstances. And we are supposed to imagine that there is no special condition which explains this inability. I must admit that I can make no sense of this. Certain cases are perfectly intelligible: she can't articulate the relevant reasons because of absent-mindedness, temporary amnesia, exhaustion, neurosis, anxiety, repression, etc. But none of that is what is supposed to be going on here. We're simply supposed to imagine that in virtue of her previous explicit deliberative activity she now bases her belief upon certain reasons which are brutely unavailable to her explicit thinking. No good sense can be made of that suggestion.

Both suggestions present a dissociated picture analogous to that arising from the Spectatorial Conception. They grant that one can directly establish basing relations through one's explicit thinking and activity, but they deny that one must be able to appropriately manifest or express previously established basing relations in one's explicit thinking and activity. This view must be rejected. It neglects, as does the Spectatorial Conception, that basing relations involve a kind of *commitment* on the part of the person. Holding a belief for particular reasons is an attitude of the person—a matter of taking up a certain normative position—in virtue of which the belief and the reasons are linked in such a way that evaluation of the person on their basis becomes legitimate. It involves, in particular, endorsement of certain considerations as adequate reasons for holding the belief and a commitment to give up the belief (or appropriately hedge one's conviction and seek better reasons) if those reasons prove inadequate.

This is not to say that explicitly stating that one undertakes these commitments always suffices to establish basing relations. I will say more about this below. The crucial point here, however, is that a person's commitments, however established, must be capable of being manifested, expressed, or acknowledged in certain characteristic ways in the person's explicit thought, conversation, and other conduct. This requirement is defeasible. Someone may hold a commitment which, because of irrationality or forgetfulness, he cannot currently manifest in his explicit thinking and conduct or acknowledge even when he is speaking sincerely. In such cases, the failure is intelligible in terms of other features of his mental life. If there is no such special circumstance, however, and if a person in appropriate circumstances cannot manifest or express a given commitment in his explicit thought, conversation or conduct and does not acknowledge it when speaking sincerely, then he does not hold it.

Because basing relations depend upon the person's commitments, a similar requirement holds in their case as well. One must be able to appropriately manifest, express, or acknowledge one's reasons in one's explicit thinking or attempts to justify one's belief unless there is some special circumstance (such as absentmindedness, temporary amnesia, anxiety, exhaustion, or repression) which hinders one's ability to do so. And what is required, in the absence of such conditions, are some appropriate instances of behavior such as the following: giving up one's belief (or appropriately hedging it while seeking further reasons) if one stops believing one's reasons for it or recognizes good evidence against them; appealing to those reasons when sincerely attempting to justify one's belief; otherwise treating them as good reasons in one's sincere conversations and explicit reasoning; refusing to reason from the belief to the truth of one's reasons (or else recognizing the need for new reasons for holding the belief); acknowledging one's reasons when reminded. If one is not speaking sincerely, then one will not manifest or acknowledge one's reasons in some of these ways. But insincerity, too, constitutes a special circumstance, rendering one's behavior intelligible in a way consistent with the attribution of a basing relation.

As we have seen, recent discussions of the basing relation have emphasized an essential link between basing relations and psychological explanation. I have argued that the common view is incorrect: etiological or other explanatory considerations do not suffice to establish basing relations. Still, there is something right in the common view. Basing relations are bound up with explanatory considerations, in particular with commonsense, person-level psychological explanation, in three ways.[32]

First, if one holds, or has held, a belief for particular reasons, that fact can explain certain features of one's thought and conduct, such as why one accepts certain arguments or reasoning, why one refuses to argue in certain ways, or why one has given up a certain belief upon discovering that certain other considerations are false. In this regard, basing relations are like other commitment-related states of the person, such as having promised, which play a role in commonsense psychological explanations.

Second, commonsense explanatory considerations can sometimes fix basing relations even if one has not engaged in any explicit deliberative or justificatory activity. For instance, suppose that you are walking across a snowy meadow. You remark that someone has been there recently. I look where you are looking and see footprints in the snow ahead. I don't take you to have any other relevant information. Accordingly, I take your belief to be explained by your belief that there are footprints ahead, which is in turn explained by your having seen footprints. And I take it that your reason for believing that someone has been there recently is that there are footprints ahead.

This verdict about your reasons depends upon considerations about your commitments. You have the ability to make certain considerations your reasons by explicitly taking on relevant commitments. Given this background capacity, and given your basic rationality, it is reasonable to take you to have undertaken the relevant commitments by believing as you do in the described circumstances. You believe that there are footprints ahead and that this is a good reason for thinking that someone else was here recently, and you are committed to giving up your belief that someone else was here recently (or to doing something else appropriate) if it turns out that these things aren't so. So when a mature human being with appropriate background abilities forms a particular belief in an appropriate way in an appropriate setting, that can constitute undertaking the commitments necessary for the establishment of basing relations. If one were to request the person's reasons in such a case, his reply (assuming he is sincere and there is no other special circumstance) would manifest the commitments which he has undertaken. And if, despite the correct explanation of his belief, he is incapable of appropriately manifesting any such commitments and there is no explanation of the right sort for this inability, then he does not now hold the belief on the basis of the reasons in question.

Finally, it is constitutive of belief and the basing relation that if one holds a belief for particular reasons, then those reasons figure in an adequate commonsense psychological explanation of one's belief. For this reason, Harman is quite right when he comments, "it is difficult to see how to imagine a difference in the reasons for which people believe as they do without imagining a difference in the explanation of why they believe as they do."[33] It doesn't follow, however, that a correct causal or other psychologically explanatory account of a belief always suffices, merely as such, to establish that the person holds the belief on the basis of given reasons. For one thing, explanatory factors will fix basing relations only in appropriate circumstances and against a background of appropriate capacities on the person's part. And this means that we can't hold that a basing relation is established merely in virtue of the fact that a cognitive-psychological process went on which we want to model as reasoning, since these processes can go on even in creatures which lack any ability to make the relevant endorsements and commitments.[34] Moreover, in some cases it would be quite ludicrous to ascribe commitments to the person corresponding to the elements figuring in the explanation. Consider, for instance, the sophisticated representations regarding motion which figure in a cognitive-psychological explanation of a person's visually-prompted belief about where a ball will land. Finally, even an adequate commonsense psychological explanation of a person's belief will not always suffice to establish that the person holds the belief on the basis of particular reasons, since such an explanation can be had even when the person is not committed to anything in particular regarding reasons for the belief. Just consider the case in which there is no straightforward reasons-based explanation of the belief and the person believes many things which could constitute good reasons for believing as he does.

It may be helpful to expand on this last point in order to remove any residual feeling that explanatory or causal factors must always suffice to establish basing relations. Consider, for instance, my belief that I live in the United States. I believe many things which tell in favor of its truth. But it is implausible to suppose that I currently hold this belief on the basis of specific reasons. (What are they?) Granted, this belief can be explained: it was formed and reinforced as a result of many and various experiences (including being told things repeatedly and by various sources), and it fits well with all my other relevant beliefs. But this explanation is not the right sort to fix the reasons for which I now hold the belief. A proponent of the view that causal or other explanatory factors always suffice to fix basing relations will claim that the difficulty here arises simply from our ignorance of the details of the causal story. But it is hard to make good sense of the suggestion that beliefs such as this one are already part of a structure of basing relations. The propositions constituting one's basic standing view of the world form a tangled web of reciprocal relations of evidential support. If we suppose that there are basing relations tracking all of these relations of evidential support, then many of these beliefs will be caught up in justificatory circles. Since this is epistemically unacceptable, we will need to conceive of the network of basing relations as having a directional structure, and we will need to find a principled ground for thinking that the basing relations go in one direction rather than another. But this isn't to be expected. Consider, for instance, my beliefs that my wife loves me and that she would not lie to me about matters concerning our relationship. Given appropriate background considerations, each of these beliefs could function as a premise in a cogent argument to the other. Counterfactual tests won't tell us which belief is currently based on the other; both beliefs are such that (given my basic rationality) if I stopped believing one I would stop believing the other. Perhaps it will be suggested that both beliefs are based on some shared ground. But what? My belief that she has sincerely told me she loves me? This won't do. It could equally well be suggested that this latter belief is based, in part, on my belief that she wouldn't lie to me. Other suggestions are possible here, but I won't pursue the matter further.[35] It suffices to note the difficulty. It is quite plausible that there is no structure of epistemic basing relations which is currently in place regarding these beliefs. The same goes for many of one's beliefs. As we will see, this is not to say that they are unjustified.[36]

Returning now to the main thread, the explanatory role of basing relations has an important consequence. Sincerely declaring one's reasons, or engaging in conscious reasoning, does not always make it the case that one holds one's belief on the basis of the given reasons. Such activities establish the reasons for which one holds a belief only if one's rationality is not impaired. This point is clearest in cases of rationalization. A rationalizer may sincerely offer certain reasons in defense of his belief and make use of them in his solitary deliberations about why he should believe as he does. But they are not in fact his reasons for believing as he does, and in appealing to them in these ways he does not make them his reasons for believing as he does. This is because they do not explain why he believes as he does. But this is a very special kind of case. Given that one is functioning rationally, one's consciously adopted commitments *do* explain one's beliefs, and consequently one can directly establish basing relations through one's conscious deliberations or explicit declarations of one's reasons.[37]

In sum, I suggest the following basic approach to the epistemic basing relation. To be in the business of holding beliefs for reasons, one must have the ability to make considerations one's reasons by making certain endorsements and taking on certain commitments. Against this background of abilities, a proposition $q$ is a reason upon the basis of which one believes that $p$ just when (1) one believes $q$, endorses its adequacy as a reason for believing that $p$, and is committed to responding in appropriate ways if $q$ proves to be an inadequate reason, and (2) these endorsements and commitments play appropriate roles in commonsense psychological explanations of one's belief, thinking and conduct. In many cases, condition (1) is met in virtue of one's explicit deliberative or justificatory activity. In some cases, however, one can make the relevant endorsements and commitments simply by forming a belief which has the right sort of commonsense psychological explanation. Either way, however, one must be able to express, manifest, or acknowledge one's reasons in one's conscious thinking or sincere conversation, provided there are no special conditions preventing exercise of this ability. For if one sincerely appeals to some other consideration(s) when attempting to justify one's belief, or doesn't know what to say, then, unless there is some special explanation, one can no longer be viewed as having maintained the relevant commitments.

I should stress that I have *not* claimed that the reasons for which one now holds a belief are the reasons which one would sincerely offer in defense of it when asked. Like the view that merely declaring that one holds a belief for certain reasons always makes it so, this claim conflicts with the manifest facts about the explanatory role of basing relations and the ways in which we can lose rational authority over our mental lives. What I have claimed is that basing relations can be directly established through a person's consciously adopted commitments, and that if a basing relation is already in place, then the person must be able to appropriately manifest or express the relevant reasons in his explicit deliberative and justificatory activity unless something of an appropriate sort prevents him from doing so. Consequently, if someone is justified in believing as he does in virtue of basing his belief upon good reasons, then, in the absence of any special circumstances preventing him from doing so, he must be able to provide those reasons in defense of his belief. He must be able to justify holding it.

## IV. Justifying and Being Justified: A Proposal

I now want to propose a basic framework for understanding epistemic justification, where (to repeat) my concern is what it is for a mature human being to be justified in believing as she does. My aim here is to motivate an approach. Its detailed development must await another occasion.

Let me begin by taking stock. In order to be susceptible to epistemic evaluation in the way that adult human beings are, a creature must be able to hold beliefs for reasons. As we have seen, this requires in turn that it have certain background abilities and capacities necessary for engaging in the activity of justifying, such as the abilities to evaluate reasons and to undertake the commitments involved in basing relations. So, in general being justified in holding any beliefs at all requires that one have some justificatory abilities. Furthermore, if one's belief is justified in virtue of being held for adequate reasons, then, as I have argued, one must be able to justify it. Once we've come this far, two plausible options remain if we want to say that beliefs which are not (yet) held for any reasons can be justified even if one is unable to justify them. We can say that one can be justified in holding beliefs of this sort, even if one cannot justify holding them, in virtue of etiological or other explanatory facts which do not establish basing relations.[38] Or we can hold that one can be justified in holding some such beliefs in virtue of their privileged position in one's inquiries or in the epistemic practices in which one is engaged.[39] However, both views conflict with our ordinary expectations. We expect mature adults to be able to say *something* in defense of their justified beliefs, even if we don't think it worthwhile or appropriate to ask them to do so. Moreover, both views strike me as unmotivated. Once we have accepted a general link between being justified and being able to justify one's beliefs, why stop short of holding that the ability is required in each case? So far as I can see, the only significant motivation is fear that this requirement generates a vicious justificatory regress. As I explain below, however, this fear is unwarranted. I propose, therefore, that we should accept the requirement.

What does this requirement come to? It will be helpful here to reconsider the nature of the ordinary activity of justifying. According to the Spectatorial Conception, when one justifies a belief one attempts to show that one possesses a status which is independent of this activity. As we have seen, however, this interpretation is fundamentally incorrect in many cases. The basic point of the ordinary conversational activity of requesting and offering reasons in defense of beliefs is to provide a setting within which entitlements to hold beliefs can be challenged, defended, established, and shared. To develop a justification for one's belief is to attempt to establish or secure a positive normative status by offering reasons in one's defense, and successfully justifying a belief is more like achieving a checkmate than like showing or reporting that one has won the game. So we can put the requirement this way: in order to be justified in holding a particular belief, one must be able to succeed in this activity, so understood. In particular, one must have an adequate set of justified background beliefs (including beliefs about what is a good reason for what), and sufficient rational capacities, to be able to successfully defend holding the belief by coming up with and committing to adequate reasons and responding adequately to objections.

Several further clarifications may be helpful.

First, the requirement is not that one must actually succeed in justifying one's belief whenever one is asked to do so, but rather that one must succeed when one has adequate time, is not under undue stress, and is not too tired or otherwise cognitively impaired. As with any standing ability, one can possess the ability to justify even when its exercise is blocked on a particular occasion by interfering factors. This consideration undermines putative counterexamples drawn from cases of temporary amnesia, neurotic fear, and the like, since such conditions only involve blockage of the exercise of the ability to justify, not loss of the ability itself. (Compare the case of a sprinter who has the ability to run a four-minute mile but currently has a hurt toe.)

Second, the requirement does not demand verbal articulateness. Any practice which allows for the establishment of propositionally contentful commitments of the sort involved in basing relations will do. For instance, an inarticulate but expert mechanic may be justified in believing that the trouble is with your fuel pump, if he can defend this assessment by making manifest some considerations which support it (for instance, by pointing, or by saying "Listen to that" while tapping on something appropriate with a screwdriver). I take no stand here on the difficult question of whether a completely non-linguistic being could engage in such practices.

Third, the proposed requirement speaks of "adequate reasons" without specifying what counts as "adequate." This is as it should be. The question is a large and difficult one, and I cannot decide it here. Still, the proposal is specific enough to be worth debating, since it counters the widespread view that one can be justified even if one cannot do anything at all to justify one's belief. It should be noted, too, that the proposal need not be interpreted in an overly stringent way. It is sometimes urged that a requirement along these lines has unacceptable skeptical consequences because most people are incapable of justifying many of their beliefs. For instance, one might think that in order to justify a perceptual belief, one would have to provide or deploy a philosophical theory of perceptual justification, which most people obviously cannot do.[40] However, this worry evaporates once we abandon the Spectatorial Conception of our justificatory activities. In ordinary life we often accept assertions such as, "Well, I see that it is so," "I've studied the matter quite thoroughly," or even, "There is no reason to doubt it," as quite enough to justify a belief, so long as we aren't aware of any reason for doubt which the person is unable to overcome. I think that we should take this fact at face value. In appropriate settings, such considerations can constitute adequate reasons. It is not easy to specify under what circumstances, exactly, such a consideration is in fact adequate.[41] My claim here is simply that there can be some such circumstances. This does not trivialize the requirement, since (again) the pertinent alternative view is that one need not be able to justify one's belief at all.

Many prominent accounts which emphasize the ability to justify also relativize justificatory success to what is accepted, or would be accepted, by some relevant social group.[42] However, I find such relativization implausible. Even if one's reasons are good, one's interlocutors (or the members of the relevant social group) may be stubborn, dense or confused. Likewise, one might be silver-tongued but benighted. I therefore hold that justificatory success depends instead upon objective relations of evidential support.[43] A successful justification requires objectively good epistemic reasons for one's belief, that is, reasons which actually provide strong support for the truth of one's belief given how the world actually is. And the set of objections which one must be able to defeat is likewise determined, at least in part, by what is the case which defeasibly tells against the truth of one's belief or against the truth or adequacy of the reasons one has offered in its favor. Three considerations support this view. First, it gives us a straightforward way to accommodate the familiar thought that being justified, though not truth-entailing, is "truth-conducive" in the sense of making it objectively likely that one's belief is true. Second, I take the notion of epistemic justification to be correlative with judgments regarding whether or not someone *should* hold a given belief, where such judgments have an epistemic basis and are not based on the truth-value of the belief in question. The proposed view accords well with our judgments about whether or not people should believe as they do, in this sense of "should." Third, the proposed view accords well with our actual justificatory practice. When you attempt to justify holding a particular belief about the world, you offer other considerations about the world which you take to constitute good reasons for holding the belief, and you attempt to offer good reasons for dismissing objections which you take to have some reason in their favor. You thus attempt to offer what are in fact good reasons, not merely what you take to be reasons sufficient to convince or satisfy any particular group of interlocutors.

With these clarifications in place, let us now consider the many justified beliefs which we have never actually attempted to justify. If one succeeds in justifying a belief, then one establishes one's right to hold it. If one did not previously hold it for bad reasons, then one can also thereby establish that one previously had the right as well. Consequently, a belief which one has not attempted to justify can be justified in virtue of one's ability to successfully justify it, so long as one does not hold it for bad reasons. This is not to say that being in a position to equip oneself to justify a belief at a later time is sufficient for being justified in holding it now. What is sufficient is not the ability to find a justification by gaining new information or insight, but rather the ability to provide an adequate justification using the resources which one already has in one's possession. It is difficult to formulate a precise characterization of this difference, but we draw the distinction well enough in practice and there is no reason to expect (or demand) a sharp line.[44]

It should be emphasized that the claim here is not that someone is justified merely in virtue of being able to state a good argument in defense of his belief. He must be sincere, and he must not already hold his belief for bad reasons or on an irrational basis (such as wishful thinking). This appeal to sincerity can be cashed out by adverting to the person's intentions and the fit between his assertions and his larger background sense of what is the case and what would constitute a good reason for believing as he does. It does not require that he have already held his belief for the reasons which he arrives at in the course of his justificatory activity, or indeed that there already have been any basing relation in place at all. This point has an important implication. We do not need to appeal to basing relations already in place in order to draw the familiar distinction between someone who is justified in believing as she does in part because of the good reasons she possesses and someone who has the same good reasons but isn't justified because she holds her belief on an irrational basis. The relevant difference may simply be that the former person, unlike the latter, does not already hold the belief on the basis of bad reasons or out of wishful thinking, self-deception, or anything of the sort, and is currently in a position to justify her belief by basing it upon her good reasons.[45]

I propose, then, that we take the following thought as the basis for the attempt to understand epistemic justification: in the case of normal adult human beings, to be justified in holding a belief is to be able to justify holding it. Or, to put it slightly more fully, to be justified is to be able to draw upon one's background conception of the world in order to defend one's belief by basing it upon objectively adequate reasons and providing objectively good reasons against certain objections.[46] On this view, to be justified is to have a sufficient grasp of how the world is (including both the relevant facts and the relevant relations of evidential support), and sufficient rational capacities, to enable one to recognize good reasons which one possesses for believing as one does, to make them one's reasons for holding the belief, and to respond adequately to objections. Whether one is justified in holding a particular belief in particular circumstances is thus a product of the interplay between what is the case in the world and one's ability to deploy one's overall conception of the world to provide reasons in defense of believing as one does.

### V. Two Worries

Any proposal along these lines can give rise to two important worries. The first concerns the threat of vicious regress, the second young children and animals. I will address each in turn.

Here's how the threat of vicious regress can seem to arise. The ability to justify seemingly can't do one any good unless one is justified in believing the considerations which one offers in defense of one's belief. Given this thought, a vicious regress of basing relations results if one conjoins the requirements (1) that one must be able to justify one's belief and (2) that one can't be justified unless one holds one's belief for adequate reasons. In order to avoid this regress, some epistemologists who otherwise link being justified and the ability to justify have claimed, in effect, that there must be at least some beliefs which are justified though they are not based upon other beliefs and one can't justify holding them.[47] But this is overkill. To avoid a regress of basing relations it is sufficient to deny, as I have, that being justified requires that one already hold one's belief for adequate reasons.

This solution may not seem to avoid all threat of vicious regress, since I grant that one must also be justified in believing whatever considerations one might appeal to in defense of one's belief. But no problematic regress arises from this point, once we have rejected the requirement that one must already hold one's belief for adequate reasons. One is justified in believing the justifying considerations because one is able to justify believing them.

Thus being justified in holding a particular belief requires being able to justify many other beliefs as well. However, the requirement that one be able to justify *each* belief is not equivalent to the requirement that one be able (even in principle) to satisfactorily justify all of them at once. And there is nothing inherently problematic in the thought that possession of one ability requires possession of a whole set of interlocking abilities. One may still have worries at this point concerning the dialectical regress familiar from Pyrrhonian skepticism. Such worries can be assuaged, however, by considering the structure of the activity of justifying: a particular justificatory attempt can appropriately terminate, on a particular occasion, with claims which one does not *have* to defend in order to be justified, though one must be able to justify them.[48]

One other regress may seem relevant here. It is sometimes urged that an account of justification built around the activity of justifying generates an infinite regress of higher-order epistemic beliefs because it requires that in order to be justified, one must have justified beliefs about the justificatory status of one's beliefs. This result can seem unavoidable if one is thinking about the issue from within the Spectatorial framework. However, my proposal does not in fact have this consequence. The ability to justify requires the abilities to reflectively evaluate reasons, make use of them in defense of one's convictions, and respond appropriately to one's evaluations: the abilities constitutive of epistemic agency. Full possession of these abilities may require possession of the concepts of *reasons, responsible belief,* and *justified belief.* But none of this entails that one can't be justified in believing that *p* unless one has justified higher-order epistemic beliefs about one's belief that *p.* I do hold that if one believes that *p* and believes, with what one takes to be good reason, that one is *not* justified in believing that *p,* then one is not justified in believing that *p,* since one's belief is not responsible. But to require the absence of certain higher-order beliefs is not to require the presence of any higher-order beliefs.

I turn now to the second worry. Given the plausible assumption that non-human animals and very young children cannot justify their beliefs, my proposal implies that they are not justified in believing as they do. Experience has shown me that this implication can seem troubling. I don't think it should be, however, so long as one is clear about just what status I mean to be picking out by the term "justified."[49]

Several points are relevant here. First, my view does not imply that animals and very young children have *unjustified* beliefs. Rather, it implies that such terms of appraisal (and the larger normative structure of obligations and entitlements which they invoke) don't appropriately apply to them. A similar point is familiar from the moral realm: animals and very young children are not aptly charged with *immorality*; rather, they are not appropriate candidates for moral evaluation at all. In the epistemic case, the crucial issue concerns basing relations. As I have argued, a creature can't be an appropriate candidate for normative epistemic evaluation and criticism unless it is able to base its beliefs upon particular reasons. This requires having the conceptual and reasoning abilities requisite for evaluating reasons and mastery of the skills and practices through which the commitments establishing basing relations are made. Very young children have not yet attained such skills and abilities, and most (if not all) animals lack even the capacity for them. They therefore do not hold beliefs on the basis of reasons and are not appropriately subjected to the forms of epistemic evaluation with which I am concerned. There is admittedly room for debate regarding particular types of animals. But to argue that any animals are justified in just the way that adult humans are, one would have to show that they are capable of holding beliefs for reasons—with all that that involves.

Second, I do not deny that an importantly related notion of justification may pertain to animals and very young children. For instance, an animal or small child can believe something in a way that involves and is sensitive to considerations which constitute good evidence for its truth. I have no opposition to using the word "justified" to describe this situation. It is important, however, not to be misled into thinking that there must be something in common between the "justified" dog's belief and the justified adult human's belief which suffices to make both beliefs justified, so that in order to determine what it is for an adult human to have a justified belief one could just as well investigate dogs. The dog enjoys an epistemic status which is importantly different from that enjoyed by a mature human being who bases a belief upon good reasons.

This difference shows up in our interactions with very young children and animals. As I have emphasized, the notion of epistemic justification with which I am concerned involves significant normative demands: if one is not justified in holding a particular belief, then one must either give it up or find better grounds for holding it. This larger normative structure is missing in the dog's case. If we judge that a dog has no good reasons for a belief, we might say, "Stop barking, you dumb dog!" But we will not feel that the dog is rationally obliged to give up the belief. Dogs are not appropriately subjected to such obligations. The same goes for my 18-month-old son's belief that airplanes flying overhead are geese. Nor, moreover, do dogs or very young children have the corresponding entitlements when all goes as well as it can for them. A dog cannot be entitled to tell you how things are and to invite you to believe him on the strength of his assurance. This is not to deny that we might rely on a dog as on an instrument. But this kind of reliance is fundamentally different from our relation to the speaker in many cases where we rely on someone's say-so.[50] The difference isn't just that a dog can't speak, as the case of very young children shows. It is that a dog lacks the rational abilities which enable a creature to enter into these practices. The same is true of young children, though we do something *like* impose this larger normative structure on them from a very early age. This is part of how we turn them into mature epistemic agents.

## VI. Coda

I have argued that the justificatory status of our beliefs is determined by what we are able to do when we attempt to defend our beliefs. It can be tempting to think that this view is itself an instance of something like the Spectatorial Conception. Isn't positive justificatory status still something which "happens to you"? And if our overt rational abilities in some sense consist in or arise from facts captured by cognitive psychology (or perhaps even by neurophysiology), then won't the same be true for the ability to justify? Take the latter question first. I have not quarreled with the view it suggests. However, I have attempted to show that a description of these facts, if there are such, would not provide us with an adequate reflective understanding of what it is for a person to be justified. For it is only in virtue of their connection with the activity of justifying that those facts would have whatever epistemological significance they have. They would suffice to render a person justified in holding a given belief only in virtue of what they enable to the person *to do*, namely, successfully justify the belief. And if a person were to report such facts in response to a request for justification, this by itself would not amount to justifying the belief. A mere description (as if from a third-person perspective) of one's psycho-logical or neurophysiological situation is not a justification or defense of believing as one does. For it to be a justification or defense, one would have to offer it in a spirit which would tie the justificatory status of one's belief to the adequacy of that answer as a reason for holding the belief. One would have to establish it as the basis of one's belief. The mere description of one's psychology does not do that.

Consider now the charge that on my view, too, justification is just something which "happens to you." This is certainly how matters look from a third-person standpoint. Consider, however, how they look from the vantage-point of the person who is doing the justifying. Here, what goes on during a justificatory episode, and hence the status of his belief, appears to be relevantly up to him, his doing, something for which he is properly held accountable. This provides a marked contrast with views of justifica-tion which embrace the Spectatorial Conception, insofar as they render the person's justificatory activity incoherent from his own point of view. There is a parallel here with issues relating to moral responsibility (in the sense of accountability). According to a familiar line of roughly Kantian thought, the first-personal standpoint of the deliberating agent is fundamentally different from the standpoint of the external observer attempting to con-struct a scientific prediction or explanation. What may appear ineluctably "up to the agent" from the former standpoint, may appear to be something which "just happens to the person" from the latter. Still, the former standpoint is itself inescapable, and in responding to an agent in morally-evaluative terms we respond from a stance which is the other-person counterpart of that first-person standpoint, a stance in which we treat the person as an autonomous, accountable agent. Something similar, I would suggest, takes place in the epistemological sphere as well. There is a point of view, shared by both the evaluator and the person under evaluation, from which the person's justificatory activity is "up to" the person in the relevant sense, not something which merely happens to the person—whatever its natural explanation might be. The task is to get a description of our epistemic lives which does not render that point of view incoherent. That is what my proposal aims to do.

It is an interesting question whether the ability to justify is underwritten by specific facts discoverable in any science of the mind or brain. That question, however, concerns what it is about us, as natural creatures, which makes it possible for us to evaluate reasons, engage in certain practices, and make the normative moves constitutive of making certain considerations our reasons. It is a question about the explanation of our abilities. It is a different question from the question of *what it is* for a rational being to be justified in holding a particular belief. The latter question has been my concern here. As I have proposed, an adequate answer appeals to the ability to justify.[51]

## Notes

1. "The Foundationalism-Coherentism Controversy," in Audi, *The Structure of Justification* (Cambridge University Press, 1993), p. 145.
2. "Concepts of Epistemic Justification," in Alston, *Epistemic Justification* (Cornell University Press, 1989), p. 82, final italics added.
3. *Ibid.*, p. 83, fn. 3.
4. In addition to Audi and Alston, this tendency can be found in the writings of Laurence BonJour, Alvin Goldman, Hilary Kornblith, Susan Haack, Alvin Plantinga, Roderick Chisholm, John Pollock, and James Pryor. I discuss Alston and BonJour below.

   Opposition can be found in Wilfrid Sellars' remark, "In characterizing an episode or a state as that of *knowing*, we are not giving an empirical description of that episode or state; we are placing it in the logical space of reasons, *of justifying and being able to justify what one says*" (Sellars, "Empiricism and the Philosophy of Mind," in his *Science, Perception and Reality* (Routledge and Kegan Paul, 1963), p. 169, second italics added). However, many epistemologists who have drawn inspiration from Sellars accept the dominant view. Robert Brandom, for instance, writes: "A fundamental point on which broadly externalist approaches to epistemology are clearly right is that one can *be* justified without being *able* to justify"

("Knowledge and the Social Articulation of the Space of Reasons," *Philosophy and Phenomenological Research* 55 (1995), pp. 895–908, at p. 904, italics in the original). Michael Williams agrees, since he maintains that on pains of vicious regress being justified cannot always require the ability to justify ("Skepticism," in *The Blackwell Guide to Epistemology*, J. Greco and E. Sosa (eds.), Blackwell Publishers, 1999, pp. 35–69).

5. "An Internalist Externalism," in *Epistemic Justification*, p. 227.

6. *Ibid.*, pp. 228–31, in particular 228–9.

7. *Ibid.*, pp. 231–3.

8. *Epistemic Justification*, p. 7. Italics in original.

9. One could supplement such views with the requirement that one must also be able to determine and correctly report the facts in virtue of which one's belief is justified, but such an addition would not repudiate the conception articulated by Alston, as I argue below.

10. BonJour, *The Structure of Empirical Knowledge* (Harvard University Press, 1985), p. 24. Cf. p. 90.

11. *Ibid.*, p. 19.

12. P. 20. BonJour is not always perfectly consistent on this point elsewhere in the text or in subsequent discussion, and at times he appears to favor a view of the sort which I advocate here. In this regard, his view may not be a perfect example of the conception which is my target. As I explain below, however, BonJour's "accessibility internalism" is perfectly compatible with this conception. Consequently, one could endorse an internalist form of coherentism, deny the causal view, and still accept this conception.

13. Finer-grained positions are possible here, since one could impose accessibility requirements on some of the factors relevant to justificatory status but not others. See, for instance, Alston's "An Internalist Externalism," in *Epistemic Justification*.

14. *Op. cit.*, p. 19.

15. See, for instance, BonJour's attempt to motivate accessibility internalism by appealing to the requirements which one must meet in order to hold a belief in a responsible way (*op. cit.*, chapt. 1).

16. I don't claim that the Spectatorial Conception logically or conceptually entails an appeal to basing relations, but rather that this appeal is needed in order to work out the Spectatorial Conception in a plausible way. This need has been widely recognized. See, for instance, Roderick Firth, "Are Epistemic Concepts Reducible to Ethical Concepts?" and lecture II of his 1978 Schneck Lectures (both in *In Defense of Radical Empiricism*, J. Troyer (ed.), Rowman and Littlefield, 1998), and Hilary Kornblith, "Beyond Foundationalism and the Coherence Theory," *Journal of Philosophy* 77 (1980), 597–612. Indeed, the need to appeal to basing relations provides a crucial part of a standard argument for "naturalizing" the theory of justification (see Kornblith, *op. cit.*, pp. 601–3, Philip Kitcher, "The Naturalists Return," *Philosophical Review* 101 (1992), pp. 53–114, esp. p. 60). (BonJour, too, acknowledges this need when he requires that in order for a person's belief to be justified, the acceptable inference must be "in the final analysis and in a sense most difficult to define precisely, *his actual reason for holding the belief*" (*op. cit.*, p. 19, italics added).

17. For representative statements, see Alston, *Epistemic Justification*, pp. 228–9; Audi, "Psychological Foundationalism," in *The Structure of Justification*, p. 54, and "Belief, Reason, and Inference," *ibid.*, pp. 233–73; Pollock, *Contemporary Theories of Knowledge* (Rowman and Littlefield, 1986), p. 37. See also Swain, "Justification and the Basis of Belief," in George Pappas (ed.), *Knowledge and Justification* (D. Reidel, 1979), pp. 25–50. For a survey of recent work on the basing relation in this broad tradition, see Keith Korcz, "Recent Work on the Basing Relation," *American Philosophical Quarterly* 34 (1997), pp. 171–91. Gilbert Harman rejects the causal view on the grounds that reasons-explanations of people's beliefs are not, strictly speaking, *causal* explanations, but he defends an etiological account of the basing relation, as I discuss below.

18. Keith Lehrer denies the causal view and, it seems, etiological views as well (*Theory of Knowledge* (Westview Press, 1990), p. 171). Nonetheless, he maintains that the reasons upon which a belief is based are determined by the correct answer to the question, "How do you know that *p*?", and he insists that the answer to this question "need not be anything S would be able to produce" ("How Reasons Give Us Knowledge," *Journal of Philosophy* 68 (1971), p. 312).

19. Harman's paper, "Knowledge, Reasons, and Causes" (*Journal of Philosophy* 67 (1970), pp. 841–55), offered arguments against an earlier characterization of basing relations offered by Lehrer, according to which a belief is not based upon particular reasons if the person would not appeal to those reasons to justify his belief ("Knowledge, Truth, and Evidence," 1965, reprinted in L. Galis and M. Roth (eds.), *Knowing: Essays in the Analysis of Knowledge* (University Press of America, 1984), at p. 56). Lehrer's suggestion is the last instance of an earlier tradition which took the person's justificatory activity to be centrally important in establishing basing relations. Lehrer accepted Harman's criticisms (see "How Reasons Give us Knowledge," p. 311), and the subsequent discussion has proceeded entirely within the terms of the framework laid out by Harman (though later writers have rejected Harman's restrictive conception of causal explanation).

20. Compare Alston's description of the grounds of a belief as "those features of the input to the formation of the belief that were actually taken account of in the belief formation" (*op. cit.*, p. 231).

21. "People often believe things for good reasons, which give them knowledge, even though they cannot say what those reasons are . . . . In most cases a person is unable to state his reasons in any sort of detail. At best he can give only the vaguest indication of the reasons that convince him. It is only in rare cases that we can tell a person's reasons from what he can say about them. Indeed, it is doubtful that a person can ever fully identify his reasons" ("Knowledge, Reasons, and Causes," p. 844).

22. *Ibid.*, p. 845.

23. I am grateful to Dick Moran for this example.

24. One significant exception is the case in which the person arrived at a belief through an explicit process of inference and is now attempting to remember precisely how the inference had gone. I'm grateful to Fred Schmitt for pointing this out.

25. As will become apparent, these two requirements are linked: in order for an account to meet the second requirement, it must meet the first.

26. C. Ginet, "Contra Reliabilism," *Monist* 68 (1985), pp. 175–87, at p. 183.

27. The argument of this paragraph uses an assumption which is not strictly speaking essential to the Spectatorial Conception, namely, the thought that if stating one's reasons is a matter of offering a report about prior and independent causal or etiological relations between one's beliefs, then statements of one's reasons will have to be construed as *fallible*. In principle, one could combine the Spectatorial Conception with the claim that barring irrationality (such as rationalization or self-deception), we are guaranteed to be right about what our beliefs are based upon whenever we make a judgment about the matter. Robert Audi suggests such a view—a (more or less) causal account of the basing relation plus a *ceteris paribus* infallibility condition—in "Belief, Reason, and Inference," in Audi, *op. cit.*, pp. 233–73, especially pp. 250 ff. The resulting view seems implausible. Why think that barring irrationality we have infallible access to the correct causal explanations of our beliefs? Surely we don't! (This is not to deny that people *do* speak with authority about their reasons when they are not suffering from irrationality. But this fact cannot really be rendered intelligible within the terms of the Spectatorial Conception.)

28. It might be urged that the basing relation does not play this normative role. It seems undeniable, however, that if there is such a thing as the epistemic evaluation of persons with the normative consequences I have in mind, then we must postulate a relation playing the role I describe. And it seems plain that we do engage in epistemic evaluation of people and place normative epistemic demands upon them. (One might doubt that such evaluation is really appropriate or really makes sense, e.g., on the grounds that we lack voluntary control over our beliefs, but that is another issue. As I explain below, I do not think that these forms of evaluation presuppose or require voluntary control.)

29. One can say, without incoherence, "q is my reason for believing that p, but I admit that it is a rotten reason." However, though not incoherent, this utterance is irrational; it marks a failing on the part of the agent. Another way to put the problem with the Spectatorial Conception is to note that if it were correct, such a statement would not mark any failing by *the person*, but only a failing in the causal processes within him which produce or sustain the belief.

30. For an important recent discussion of when it is appropriate to treat a condition as attributable to a person for the purposes of normative evaluation of that person, see T. M. Scanlon, *What We Owe to Each Other* (Harvard University Press, 1998), pp. 17–25 and 267–90. Scanlon argues, correctly in my view, that normative appraisal of the person does not require the person's voluntary control over the condition in question, but rather that the condition be responsive to the person's evaluations of reasons. A full discussion of these issues is beyond the scope of this paper. However, the need for such discussion points towards a potentially fruitful interaction between epistemology, philosophy of mind, and ethics (particularly, the literature on "moral responsibility") and reveals one of the many ways in which epistemology is part of the larger philosophical project of understanding the normative aspects of our lives.

31. For an important discussion of the role of first-personal deliberation, particularly in relation to self-knowledge, see Richard Moran, *Authority and Estrangement* (Princeton University Press, 2001).

32. One may doubt whether the concept *holding a belief for a reason* can have the features I have described and also be genuinely explanatory. Since this concept is part of the network of concepts of commonsense psychology, this is an instance of the familiar, and more general, puzzle regarding the relation between person-level commonsense psychological explanation and explanations in scientific psychology (or, indeed, neurophysiology). This difficult topic is beyond the scope of this paper.

33. *Thought* (Princeton University Press, 1973), p. 29. Lehrer has offered putative counterexamples to this requirement (his well-known example of the Gypsy Lawyer in "How Reasons Give Us Knowledge" and the slightly different example of Mr. Raco in *Theory of Knowledge*). With slight modifications, the account sketched here can deal with these examples.

34. A note on non-human animals. Cognitive-psychological explanations of animals' beliefs might show that these beliefs arise through processes usefully termed "reasoning," and for certain purposes we might talk as though these explanations provide reasons for which these creatures hold these beliefs. But this talk must be taken with a grain of salt. If we fail to recognize that it is an extension to the more primitive case of notions which apply in the first instance to the more sophisticated adult case, then we might be tempted to treat the adult case as being merely the more primitive case along with something added (the ability for explicit reflection, deliberation, etc.) But then we will think that in the adult case, too, basing relations have no fundamental connection with the commitments and endorsements taken on by the person, and as a result we will lose sight of precisely what makes it possible for basing relations to play their normative role. So to retain the normative role of the basing relation in the epistemic evaluation of persons, we must treat the adult case as central. The animal case is a derivative version of the case in which we attribute basing relations to an adult human being in virtue of the commitments which the person has undertaken. In both cases, a certain sort of explanation of the belief is possible; what is missing in the animal case is the larger background of abilities (e.g., to make the appropriate commitments) which enables full-fledged attribution of basing relations in the first place. (In section V (below) I discuss animals in relation to my account of justification.)

35. Perhaps it will be suggested that both beliefs are based on some body of experiences or memories. But now we return to the first problem. Precisely *which* experiences or memories are the relevant ones? Furthermore, if the memories or experiences are described in a way that is noncommittal as to whether she loves me, then basing the belief that she loves me on those experiences or memories arguably requires believing that she isn't misleading me through her behavior; for if I didn't believe that, then I couldn't plausibly be said to take my experiences (or memories) of her behavior to be a reason to believe she loves me. But then the problem of the structure of basing relations recurs. For what is my

reason for believing that she wouldn't mislead me? These puzzles are dissolved if we simply allow that these beliefs aren't (yet) epistemically based on any particular reasons at all.

36. This point has important implications for traditional debates about the "structure of justification." It is often assumed that the traditional debate over foundationalism concerns the structure of a system of basing relations which encompasses all of one's justified beliefs. If the debate is understood in this way, however, then it is based upon a false presupposition. At any given time, there is no system of basing relations encompassing all of one's justified beliefs. An adequate account of justification must allow for this fact.

37. Harman appeals to rationalization as support for a purely explanatory or etiological account of the basing relation and against the suggestion that one must be able to express one's reasons (*Thought*, p. 28.). In his example, a person holds a belief for certain reasons which, because of repression, he cannot acknowledge even in his own private deliberations. It appears possible for someone to get into such a fix. However, this does not tell against my proposals. In such cases, the correct explanation of the person's belief shows that he holds the commitments necessary for making the repressed considerations his reasons for believing as he does. However, because he has repressed the relevant beliefs they are not available to his conscious thought when he reflects upon the grounds for and against the belief in question. Consequently, he cannot acknowledge his commitments in his explicit thinking, nor can he currently change the reasons for which he holds this belief in the usual way. But it remains the case that *if* the repression were lifted, then he would both be able to acknowledge these commitments and modify them in the usual way. Such a case is thus a highly derivative one; it depends upon the person's background ability to explicitly undertake the relevant commitments, his having the relevant commitments in the particular case, and his possession of the psychic structures necessary for repression and self-deception. Consequently, even if (as I am willing to grant) such examples are intelligible, they do not show that explanatory factors alone always suffice to establish basing relations or that basing relations are ordinarily in place even if one can't acknowledge them. Nor is it appropriate to take such a case as central for an account of the basing relation, as Harman in effect does.

38. This is roughly the position of Robert Brandom (*Articulating Reasons* (Harvard University Press, 2000), chapter 3, and *Making It Explicit* (Harvard University Press, 1994), esp. chapter 4) and Michael Williams ("Skepticism," *op. cit.*).

39. Michael Williams urged this sort of view in *Unnatural Doubts* (Princeton University Press, 1996). On one common interpretation of *On Certainty* (Blackwell, 1969), so did Wittgenstein.

40. Alston, "Concepts of Epistemic Justification," in *Epistemic Justification*, pp. 82–3 fn.

41. One might hold, for instance, that standards of adequacy depend in some way upon social or conversational factors. Though I am not inclined to accept such views, I take no official stand on them here.

42. Richard Rorty once claimed that a person is justified just if he is able to convince his conversational partners (*Philosophy and the Mirror of Nature* (Princeton University Press, 1979)). David Annis makes a similar claim, emphasizing

instead a relevant group of experts ("A Contextualist Theory of Epistemic Justification," *American Philosophical Quarterly* 15 (1978), pp. 213–9).

43. I take no stand here on the metaphysical nature of relations of evidential support, except to rule out the crudest subjectivist or relativist views, which would hold that x supports y just if, and in virtue of the fact that, some relevant group of people take (or would take) x to support y.

44. Consider, for instance, Andrew Wiles' success in developing a proof of Fermat's last theorem. He was able to find a justification for his belief, but he wasn't in possession of that justification from the beginning. Finding it required making discoveries. This is so even though his proof was a priori.

45. This point undermines a standard argument for a certain form of "psychologistic epistemology" articulated by Kornblith, Harman, and Kitcher. Kitcher puts it this way:

> Take any set of favored logical relations among propositions that a subject believes. It is nonetheless possible that the subject lacks knowledge and lacks justification because the *psychological* connections among her states of belief have nothing to do with the logical relations. . . . Apsychologistic epistemology can struggle to accommodate such examples by invoking ever more complicated conditions on knowledge and justification, but the accumulation of epicycles serves only to disguise the fundamental point that the epistemic status of a belief state depends on the etiology of the state, and consequently, on psychological facts about the subject ("The Naturalists Return," p. 60, italics in original).

The problem with the argument is this. While a person's justificatory status regarding a particular belief does indeed depend upon something about the person, it is not true that what is crucial are always psychologically explanatory connections mirroring the logical relations amongst her beliefs. Of course, someone is not justified if she currently holds a belief for bad reasons, regardless of whether she also believes things which constitute good reasons for her belief. But someone may be justified who does not (yet) base her belief on *any* reasons, and this is not because of the etiology of her belief but rather because of her justificatory abilities. In this sort of case, etiological considerations are only negatively relevant.

46. These formulations assume that one does not already hold the belief on the basis of bad reasons.

47. See, for instance, Michael Williams, "Skepticism," *op. cit.*

48. This issue is discussed at length in my unpublished manuscript, "A Localist Solution to the Regress of Epistemic Justification."

49. In what follows, I grant for the sake of discussion that animals and very young children have determinate beliefs. Though I have reservations on this score, they are not pertinent here.

50. For important discussions of this large and difficult topic, see Tyler Burge, "Content Preservation," *Philosophical Review* 102 (1993), pp. 457–88 and "Interlocution, Perception and Memory," *Philosophical Studies* 86 (1997), 21–47, and Angus Ross, "Why Do We Believe What We are Told?" *Ratio* 28 (1986), pp. 69–88. I have been helped here by unpublished work by Dick Moran.

51. Many people have helped, encouraged, and challenged me regarding the ideas in this paper. I'd especially like to thank Luca Ferrero, David Finkelstein, Warren Goldfarb, Mark Kaplan, Hilary Kornblith, Dick Moran, Ram Neta, James

Pryor, Fred Schmitt, Angie Smith, Jonathan Weinberg, and audiences at Pomona College, Indiana University (Bloomington), Harvard University, and UCLA. Thanks, especially, to James Pryor for asking the question that got the whole project started.

*Philosophical Issues, 14, Epistemology, 2004*

# EPISTEMIC CIRCULARITY AGAIN

Noah Lemos
The College of William and Mary

Does epistemic circularity prevent us from knowing that our ways of forming beliefs are reliable? Some philosophers say "yes". Others say it doesn't. Ernest Sosa, for example, argues that epistemic circularity is ultimately unavoidable, but that it does not preclude our knowing that our ways of forming beliefs are reliable. In this essay, I examine some objections to Sosa's view. In the first section, I begin with William Alston's discussion of the problem of epistemic circularity and consider briefly Sosa's view. In the second section, I turn to Richard Fumerton's objections to epistemically circular ways of supporting the reliability of one's ways of forming beliefs. In the third, I consider some interesting criticisms that Jonathan Vogel makes concerning bootstrapping procedures and the "neo-Moorean argument". I will argue that neither Fumerton's nor Vogel's criticisms should lead us to reject the use of all epistemically circular arguments.

## The Problem of Circularity: Alston and Sosa

The problem of knowing whether one's faculties are reliable has been addressed with care and subtlety by Alston. Let us consider his discussion of the following "track record" argument for the reliability of perception.

(1) At $t_1$, I formed the perceptual belief that $p$, and $p$.
(2) At $t_2$, I formed the perceptual belief that $q$, and $q$.
(3) At $t_3$, I formed the perceptual belief that $r$, and $r$.
(And so on)
Conclusion: Perception is a reliable source of belief[1]

In a track record argument for the reliability of perception, we reason inductively from a wide sampling of perceptual beliefs, noting that the vast majority have been true, and conclude that perception is reliable. Now, in this argument the conclusion does not appear as a premise in the argument. So, the argument is not logically circular. Still, Alston says that the argument is "epistemically circular". According to Alston, epistemic circularity "consists in assuming the reliability of a source of belief in arguing for the reliability of that source. That assumption does not appear as a premise in the argument, but it is only by making that assumption that we consider ourselves entitled to use some or all of the premises."[2] How in this track record argument are we "assuming" the reliability of perception? Consider the second conjunct of each premise. How do I know that it is true? On the basis of sense perception itself. It is only by *using* sense perception or *relying* upon it that I can know the truth of the premises.

Alston, however, does not think epistemic circularity renders an argument epistemically useless. He writes, "contrary to what one might suppose, epistemic circularity does not render an argument useless for justifying or establishing its conclusion. Provided that I can *be* justified in certain perceptual beliefs without already being *justified* in supposing perception to be reliable, I can legitimately use perceptual beliefs in an argument for the reliability of sense perception."[3] To see how this is so, suppose that our perceptual beliefs are immediately evident. They might be evident in virtue of the character of our sensory experience as the foundationalist suggests or perhaps they are evident in virtue of their origin in a reliable faculty of perception. If our perceptual beliefs are immediately evident, then the second conjunct of each premise in the track record argument is immediately evident. But if they are immediately evident, then they are not epistemically dependent on any other justified belief, including the belief that sense perception is reliable. Our justification and knowledge of the premises would not epistemically depend, therefore, upon our knowing or being justified in believing the conclusion. We may grant that any argument in which knowledge of the premises is epistemically based on prior knowledge of the conclusion is worthless as a way of gaining knowledge of the conclusion. But that is not how track record arguments must be construed. If knowledge of the premises is epistemically independent of knowledge of the conclusion, such as when the premises are immediately evident, then a track record argument won't have *that* flaw. Of course, we may also note that the argument won't have that flaw even if knowledge of the premises is not immediate, provided, of course, that knowledge of the premises is not epistemically dependent upon the conclusion.

Still, in spite of this concession, Alston thinks that epistemically circular arguments including track record arguments are not satisfactory ways of discriminating between reliable and unreliable sources of belief. But why not? What is the problem that he sees with epistemically circular arguments? Alston tells us,

If we are entitled to use beliefs from a certain source in showing that source to be reliable, then any source can be validated. If all else fails, we can simply use each belief twice over, once as testee and once as tester. Consider crystal ball gazing. Gazing into the crystal ball, the seer makes a series of pronouncements: p, q, r, s . . . Is this a reliable mode of belief formation? Yes. That can be shown as follows. The gazer forms the belief that p, and using the same procedure, ascertains that p. By running through a series of beliefs in this way, we discover that the accuracy of this mode of belief formation is 100%! If some beliefs contradict others, that will reduce the accuracy somewhat, but in the absence of massive internal contradiction the percentage of verified beliefs will be quite high. Thus, if we allow the use of mode of belief-formation M to determine whether the beliefs formed by M are true, M is sure to get a clean bill of health. But a line of argument that will validate any mode of belief formation, no matter how irresponsible, is not what we are looking for. We want, and need something much more discriminating. Hence the fact that the reliability of sense perception can be established by relying on sense perception does not solve our problem.[4]

One can support the reliability of sense perception through track record arguments and by using sense perception. In this respect, we may say that sense perception is "self-supportive". However, the problem with such epistemically circular arguments in Alston's view is that clearly unacceptable procedures, such as gazing, can also be supported *via* a track record argument. So a track record argument is not, he thinks, a satisfactory way of discriminating between reliable and unreliable ways of forming beliefs. Alston thinks we need to find a better way of discriminating between reliable and unreliable ways of forming beliefs.[5]

Let us turn to consider Sosa's approach to the problem of circularity. To appreciate Sosa's approach we need to introduce some important distinctions he makes. First, Sosa distinguishes between the "aptness" of a belief and its "justification". He writes,

The "justification" of a belief B requires that B have a basis in its inference or coherence relations to other beliefs in the believer's mind—as in the "justification" of a belief derived from deeper principles, and thus "justified," or the "justification" of a belief adopted through cognizance of its according with the subject's principles as to what beliefs are permissible in the circumstances as viewed by that subject.

The "aptness" of a belief B relative to an environment E requires that B derive from what is relative to E is an intellectual virtue, i.e., a way of arriving at beliefs that yields an appropriate preponderance of truth over error (in the field of propositions in question, in the sort of context involved.)[6]

Sosa suggests that we distinguish between the "justification" of a belief B, which he treats as matter of B's cohering with other beliefs, including beliefs about what it is permissible or reasonable to believe, and the "aptness" of B, which is a matter of the intellectual virtue that yields B. Conceivably, a belief might have much in the way of justification and fail to be apt. Consider the victim of the evil demon to whom nothing seems amiss. He forms perceptual beliefs and believes (mistakenly) perception to be a reliable source. He may even reason brilliantly from his false perceptual beliefs to mistaken conclusions about the world around him and about the nature of his own perceptual faculties. But although his perceptual beliefs might have much in the way of justification, they fail to be apt, since relative to his demonic environment, perception is no virtue, failing to yield much that is true. Conversely, a belief might be apt and yet fail to be justified.

Sosa also introduces a distinction between "animal knowledge" and "reflective knowledge". He says, "For animal knowledge one needs only belief that is apt and derives from an intellectual virtue or faculty. By contrast, reflective knowledge always requires belief that not only is apt but also has a kind of justification, since it must be belief that fits coherently within the epistemic perspective of the believer."[7] On Sosa's view we may attribute animal knowledge to small children and animals who lack the concept of reliability and who are incapable of forming a perspective on their own intellectual powers and lack the capacity to evaluate their beliefs against standards of what are permissible or acceptable ways of forming beliefs. Animal knowledge does not require a knowledge or justified meta-perspective about one's way of forming beliefs. Reflective knowledge, in contrast, requires reasons which support and sustain one's belief. These reasons must be beliefs of the subject, though they may be largely implicit and not consciously entertained. They form the subject's meta-perspective about his beliefs and support the beliefs in question. The notion of a meta-perspective must, I think, allow for degrees of complexity. There is no reason to insist that reflective knowledge requires the sort of deep and detailed view to which philosophers may aspire. The web of beliefs that forms a perspective can grow and become more complex over time, increasing in sophistication with reflection and experience.

Let us return to Sosa's views on epistemic circularity. Sosa concedes that any reasoning for the reliability of our ways of forming beliefs will, if reflection is pushed far enough, exhibit epistemic circularity. This is so if only because any reasoning for the reliability of our faculties must rely on or use reason itself. Epistemic circularity seems inescapable. But must our inability to give arguments free of epistemic circularity preclude our knowing that our ways of forming beliefs are reliable? Sosa thinks not. Suppose, he suggests, that W is our total way of forming beliefs. Suppose we use W, and W assures us that it is reliable. Suppose also:

(a) "W *is* reliable (and suppose, even that, given our overall circumstances and fundamental nature, it is the *most* reliable overall way we could have.)"

(b) "We are *right* in our description of W; it *is* exactly W that we use in forming
beliefs; and it is of course (therefore) W that we use in forming the belief
that W is our way of forming beliefs."

(c) "We *believe* that W *is reliable* (correctly so, given *a* above), and this belief,
too, is formed by means of W."[8]

In this situation, what more do we need for an epistemically satisfactory
understanding of ourselves and our own reliability? Of course, our belief
that W is reliable is itself formed by means of W. We have not, therefore,
avoided epistemic circularity. But our belief that W is reliably formed is (i)
true, (ii) reliably formed by our best intellectual procedures, and (iii) fits
coherently in our view of ourselves and our intellectual endowments.
Though we have not avoided epistemic circularity, Sosa asks, in what way
do we fall short? He concludes that the mere presence of epistemic circularity would not preclude our knowing ourselves to be reliable. We can achieve
an epistemically satisfactory understanding of the reliability our ways of
forming beliefs in spite of it.

Again, Sosa asks, what exactly is the problem with epistemically circular arguments? Why should we think that they are epistemically unacceptable ways of supporting the reliability of our faculties? Recall Alston's
complaints about track record arguments. Alston objects that someone
with decidedly unreliable ways of forming beliefs might be able to support
the reliability of his ways of forming beliefs with a coherence equal to our
own. The ball gazer, it is urged, might be able to reach a view of his powers
that is as well supported by such an inference as our view about the
reliability of our powers of perception, memory, and the like. However,
Sosa argues that though the ball gazer might be able to achieve a coherent
view about the reliability of gazing, we need to distinguish justification that
is merely a matter of internal coherence from the aptness of beliefs. The
gazer's beliefs, based as they are on gazing, fail to be *apt*. We need not hold,
therefore, that the gazer's beliefs, though supported from his perspective by
a track record argument, are epistemically on a par with our own. Though
enjoying the internal justification of coherence, the gazer's conclusions fall
short insofar as they rest on reasoning from premises that fail to be apt.
Consider the cartoon character, Mr. Magoo, whose perceptual faculties are
terribly unreliable. Magoo might reason brilliantly from his flawed perceptual beliefs, and his beliefs might enjoy a level of coherence comparable to
our own. But Magoo's view of the world is flawed by epistemic vice and fails
to manifest overall virtue. The point is that while coherence is a good thing
epistemically, it is not the only epistemic virtue. We should not hold that if
two bodies of belief enjoy equal coherence, then they enjoy equal epistemic
status or conclude that if someone can support the reliability of his flawed
ways of forming beliefs through arguments which mirror our own in terms
of structure and coherence, that his premises or conclusions are as good

epistemically. So, Alston's fear that the use of epistemically circular arguments by the gazer will yield a view epistemically on a par with our own is unfounded once one takes into consideration the aptness of one's ways of forming beliefs. We are not forced to accept the view that the gazer's conclusion about the reliability of gazing is epistemically on a par with our beliefs about the reliability of perception and memory.


### Fumerton on Circularity

Sosa finds that epistemic circularity is ultimately unavoidable, but he does not think that it prevents us from knowing that our ways of forming beliefs are reliable. Many philosophers disagree. Consider the following reaction by Richard Fumerton:

> You cannot *use* perception to justify the reliability of perception! You cannot *use* memory to justify the reliability of memory! You cannot *use* induction to justify the reliability of induction! Such attempts to respond to the skeptic's concerns involve blatant, indeed pathetic, circularity.[9]

But what really is wrong with such a view? Fumerton tells us:

> If a philosopher starts wondering about the reliability of astrological inference, the philosopher will not allow the astrologer to read in the stars the reliability of astrology. Even if astrological inferences happen to be reliable, the astrologer is missing the point of a *philosophical* inquiry into the justifiability of astrological inference if the inquiry is answered using the techniques of astrology... If I really am interested in knowing whether astrological inference is legitimate, if I have the kind of philosophical curiosity that leads me to raise this question in the first place, I will not for a moment suppose that further use of astrology might help me to find the answer to my question. Similarly, if as a philosopher I start wondering whether perceptual beliefs are accurate reflections of the way the world really is, I would not dream of using perception to resolve my doubt. Even if there is some sense in which the reliable process of perception might yield justified beliefs about the reliability of perception, the use of perception could never satisfy a *philosophical curiosity* about the legitimacy of perceptual beliefs.[10]

We might compare Fumerton's complaint with that leveled against someone checking the reliability of a newspaper against other reports from that same paper. One finds that the paper reports that *p* and then checks that report against back issues and finds that they also report that *p* and then one concludes that the paper is reliable. Would this not be an unacceptable procedure? And would not relying upon astrological readings to support their reliability be similarly unsatisfactory? If so, then would not the same complaint be appropriately raised against using perceptual reports to support the reliability of perception?

With respect to the newspaper case, Sosa suggests "What is wrong in the newspaper case, even as a case of simple reasoning is, it now appears, the narrowness of one's purview in judging the newspaper reliable simply on the basis of a set of data one knows to be remediably and relevantly too narrow; namely, the reports of that very newspaper accepted at face value."[11] We know that appealing only to the newspaper reports is not our only option, though, Sosa notes, it might be the only option for someone in jail. We know that we can move beyond the narrowness of our limited data, bringing in other sources that seem to us relevant to the matter at hand. Here we might also think of the detective who has available to him a dozen eye witnesses to a crime, but chooses to interview only one. We would not think that the detective's procedure satisfactory since he fails to take into account further relevant and easily accessible evidence.

Might not the same be said for the astrological case? Fumerton is right in thinking that no philosopher would be content to rest simply with the reports of astrology that confirm its own reliability. But what is wrong with such an approach need not be the appeal to that very source. We might fault such an approach because we can make use of other sources such as perception, memory, and reason in evaluating the reliability of astrology. We can widen the body of data against which the claims of astrology might be judged, seeing how astrological reports fare against these other sources. The appeal to the reports of astrology alone is, we know, remediably too narrow and for us poor intellectual procedure. In contrast, in assessing the reliability of memory, sense perception, introspection, and reason we can consider the extent to which the testimony of these sources conflicts with the others. Our assessment of their reliability need not display that sort of unacceptable narrowness.

Still, I think Fumerton would object not merely to the narrowness of appealing *only* to astrological readings, but to one's appealing to a source to support the reliability of that source. But here I think Fumerton leaves himself open to a *tu quoque*. Fumerton, for example, defends the view that "acquaintance" is a source of noninferential justification. Acquaintance, according to Fumerton, is a *sui generis* relationship that holds between a self and a thing, property, or relation. It is not, in his view, another intentional state, like belief, to be construed as a nonrelational property of the mind. Fumerton writes, "My suggestion is that one has noninferentially justified belief that $P$ when one has the thought that $P$ and one is acquainted with the fact that $P$, the thought that $P$, *and* the relation of correspondence holding between the thought that $P$ and the fact that $P$."[12] For Fumerton, a belief that $P$ can be noninferentially justified on the basis of a complex set of several relations of acquaintance, such as being acquainted with the thought that $P$, the fact that $P$, and the correspondence between the thought that $P$

and the fact that *P*. The details of this account need not concern us. But suppose we ask two questions. First, suppose we ask how we know that the belief that *P* is likely to be true when we have this complex set of relations of acquaintance? Second, we might ask how do we know that we ever bear this set of relations of acquaintance to anything? With respect to the first question, Fumerton writes, "If my being acquainted with the fact that *P* is part of what justifies me in believing that *P* and if acquaintance is a genuine relation that requires the existence of its relata, then when I am acquainted with the fact that *P*, *P* is true."[13] According to this view, the complex state of acquaintances that is the source of one's noninferential justification for believing that *P* is an *infallible* source of justification for believing that *P*. But how do we know that it is thus infallible and thus perfectly reliable? How do I know that when I am acquainted with *P*, *P* is true? Would not our answer be that we are acquainted with the relation of acquaintance itself? Would not this knowledge about the perfect reliability of this source rest ultimately upon noninferentially justified belief about the nature of acquaintance? But where would such justification come from if not through acquaintance itself? As for our second question, how do we know that we ever bear the complex set of relations of acquaintance that would, in Fumerton's view, be a source of noninferential justification? Fumerton answers, "If I am asked what reason do I have for thinking that there is any such relation as acquaintance, I will, of course give the unhelpful answer that I am acquainted with such a relation. The answer is question-begging if it is designed to convince someone that there is such a relation, but if the view is true it would be unreasonable to expect its proponents to give any other answer."[14]

The point I wish to make is not that there is no such relation as acquaintance. It is rather to note that Fumerton himself appeals to acquaintance as his source of justification for believing that he is acquainted with things and, I think, he must appeal to acquaintance ultimately as his source of justification for believing that acquaintance is reliable. Yet that fact does not prevent Fumerton from taking acquaintance to be a source of noninferential justification. Why, then, should we object *in principle* to one's using memory and perception to support the view that memory and perception are reliable?[15]

Fumerton objects that we cannot satisfy a "philosophical" curiosity about perception and memory by using perception and memory. If what is required to satisfy such a curiosity is an argument free of epistemic circularity then such a curiosity cannot be satisfied. But that would imply as well that we cannot satisfy a philosophical curiosity about reasoning itself. As Laurence BonJour points out, it is obvious that any argument to show that reasoning is reliable must make use of reasoning itself.[16] Satisfying the demands of what Fumerton calls a philosophical curiosity about the reliability of reasoning is impossible. Moreover, we could not satisfy a philosophical curiosity about the reliability of direct acquaintance either. If a philosophical curiosity about the reliability of our faculties could only be satisfied by an argument free of epistemic circularity, then it would seem to be a mark of philosophical wisdom to accept the fact that that cannot be done. But why think that the only way to satisfy a philosophical curiosity about the reliability of our faculties requires arguments free of epistemic circularity? As Sosa argues, epistemic circularity does not prevent us from knowing that our faculties are reliable. Could not a curiosity, even a philosophical one, about the reliability of our faculties be satisfied by the knowledge that they are? The fact that we cannot support the reliability of our faculties except ultimately by using them does not commit us to skepticism about their reliability. And it does not imply that one's use of those sources must exhibit the same flaws exhibited in the newspaper case or the narrow appeal to astrological readings.

## Vogel, Roxanne, and the Neo-Moorean Argument

Jonathan Vogel gives an interesting argument against what he calls "neighborhood reliabilism" (NR). The neighborhood reliabilist holds that a belief is reliable "just in case it turns out to be true whenever it is held in a neighborhood $N$ of worlds not too far away from the actual world; a process is reliable just in case it yields (mostly) true beliefs in a neighborhood of worlds not too far away from the actual world."[17] Roughly, according to NR, S knows that $p$ just in case S's belief that $p$ is true and S's belief that $p$ is reliable or produced by a reliable process. Vogel's argument calls into question what he calls a "bootstrapping" procedure for defending the reliability of one's way of forming beliefs. Vogel asks us to consider an example first suggested by Michael Williams.

> Williams describes himself driving a car with a working, highly reliable gas gauge. Williams does not know, however, that the gauge is reliable. Let us stipulate that he has never checked it, he has never been told anything about its reliability, and he does not even have any background information as to whether gauges like his are likely to be working. He never takes any special steps to see whether the gauge is going up or down when it ought to be. Rather, without giving the matter a second thought, Williams simply goes by what the gauge says. The gauge reads 'F', and Williams believes that his gas tank is full. According to NR, he *knows* that his tank is full. He has this knowledge because his belief results from a reliable process, that is, going by a well-functioning gas gauge. But Williams does not *know that he knows* that his tank is full. To have this higher-level knowledge, he would need to know that the gauge reliably registers the level of gas in his tank, and we have stipulated that he has no such information.[18]

In this example, we are to assume that Williams "does not even have any background information as to whether gauges like his are likely to be working." As Vogel notes, it is hard to imagine how Williams could fail to have *any* background information about the reliability of his gas gauge or gas gauges like his. Are we to assume, for example, that Williams does not know that there are tens of millions of cars that do have reliable gas gauges, that there are thousands of other cars of the same model as his that do have reliable gauges, that tens of millions of people successfully operate their cars using their gas gauges, that if gas gauges were generally unreliable, then there would be widespread consumer complaints and many stranded motorists? If Williams had these sorts of background beliefs, which I assume the typical driver has, then it seems Williams would have reasons to believe that his gas gauge is reliable. In any case, Vogel suggests that we should not be distracted by the details of the case.

Vogel then asks us to consider another driver, Roxanne, similarly situated to Williams in the previous example. Roxanne has a well-functioning gas gauge, believes implicitly what her gas gauge says without knowing that her gas gauge is reliable. We may also assume she lacks any background beliefs about the reliability of gauges like hers and has never taken any special steps to see whether the gauge is going up or down as it ought. She looks at the gauge often and forms a belief about how much gas is in her tank. She also, however, takes note of the state of the gauge itself. So when the gauge reads 'F' she believes the tank is full, *F*, and she also believes that the gauge reads 'F'. Roxanne combines these beliefs and accepts,

(1) On this occasion, the gauge reads 'F' and *F*.

Vogel says that the perceptual process by which Roxanne forms the belief that the gauge reads 'F' is a reliable one. Moreover, we are assuming that her belief that the tank is full is also reached by a reliable process. So, Vogel says, according to NR, Roxanne knows (1). From (1), Roxanne deduces,

(2) On this occasion, the gauge is reading accurately.

Since deduction is a reliable process, it seems that NR would imply that Roxanne knows (2) as well. Now suppose that Roxanne repeats this procedure many times. She reads that the gauge says 'X' and forms the belief that the tank is *X*. Given NR, she comes to know on each of these occasions that the tank was reading accurately. Then, putting these bits of information together, she concludes by induction that,

(3) The gauge reads accurately all the time.

As Vogel notes, reliabilists generally hold that induction is a reliable process and so they should concede that Roxanne knows (3). From (3), Roxanne infers,

(4) The gauge is reliable.

Vogel suggests that NR is committed to the view that Roxanne knows (4). But Vogel claims Roxanne does not know (4). So, he concludes that NR is false. He concludes this because NR in conjunction with various steps of inductive and deductive reasoning imply incorrectly that Roxanne knows that her gas gauge is reliable. But note that Vogel writes,

> This extraordinary procedure, which I shall call *bootstrapping*, seems to allow one to promote many, if not all, of one's beliefs that were formed by reliable processes into *knowledge* that those beliefs were formed by reliable process. I assume that bootstrapping is illegitimate. Roxanne cannot establish that her gas gauge is reliable by the peculiar reasoning I have just described. The challenge to NR is that it may go wrong here. On the face of things, it does improperly ratify bootstrapping as a way of gaining knowledge.[19]

Vogel says that he assumes that bootstrapping is illegitimate.[20] He is convinced that Roxanne's way of forming the belief that her gauge is reliable is unsatisfactory. But he also thinks that the case of Roxanne poses a problem for what has been called "the neo-Moorean argument". The neo-Moorean argument has been suggested and defended by Sosa as a way of illustrating how one might support the reliability of perception. Here is roughly Sosa's version of the argument:

(1) Datum: I know I have a hand.
(2) I can see and feel that here is a hand, and that is the only, or anyhow the best account of the source of my knowledge that here is a hand.
(3) So, my perception that here is a hand explains why or how it is that I know here's a hand.
(4) But my perception could not serve as a source of that knowledge if perception were not a reliable faculty.
(5) So, perception must be a reliable faculty.[21]

In this argument, one accepts (3) because it is the best explanation of how it is that one knows one has a hand. One then notes that perception would not yield that knowledge if perception were generally unreliable, so one concludes it must be reliable. Sosa admits that such reasoning is epistemically circular insofar as one knows the first premise only if perception is indeed reliable. But Sosa denies that such circularity is vicious. Now, one might go on to reason further that since one knows that perception is a reliable faculty and knows that one has a hand, one knows that one is not being deceived by an evil demon to believe falsely that one does have a hand.

Vogel suggests that the neo-Moorean argument resembles Roxanne's poor reasoning. He suggests that we might reformulate the former as:

(A) You know you have a hand.
(B) You know that it appears to you as though you have a hand.
(C) Therefore, you know that your appearance of having a hand is veridical.
(D) Therefore, you know that you are not a deceived brain in a vat.

Vogel suggests that we can compare the neo-Moorean reasoning with:

(A′) Roxanne knows her tank is full.
(B′) Roxanne knows the gas gauge reads 'F'.
(C′) Therefore, Roxanne knows that, on this occasion, her gas gauge is reading accurately.

Vogel thinks that since Roxanne's bootstrapping procedure is unacceptable, so too is the bootstrapping procedure that we find in the neo-Moorean argument.[22]

If we reject Roxanne's reasoning, must we reject the neo-Moorean argument as well? More generally, must we reject the view that one can use a source of belief to support the reliability of that source? In considering these matters, I think we should agree with Vogel that NR is false. NR says,

NR  S knows that *p* if and only if S's belief that *p* is true and S's belief that *p* is reliable or produced by a reliable process.

There are, I think, good reasons for rejecting NR quite apart from Vogel's argument. First, suppose that one forms the belief that *p* on the basis of a reliable process and *p* is true. Yet suppose that one has defeating evidence for *p* and yet ignores this evidence. In such a case, one does not know that *p* is true. Suppose, for example, that Jones perceives a red object before him and suppose that there is in fact a red object before him. But suppose further that Jones is told that the object is really white and that there is a red light shining on it. Still, Jones ignores this piece of defeating evidence and persists in believing that the object before him is red. In such a case, it does not seem that Jones knows the object is red even though his belief has been formed on the basis of a reliable process and is true. The mere fact that one has a true belief reliably produced is not therefore sufficient for knowledge. Jones's ignoring defeating evidence would seem to preclude his knowing that the object before him is red even though his belief that it is red is formed by a reliable process. Second, it would seem that not just *any* reliable process is sufficient for turning a true belief into knowledge. Suppose that my colleague, Marcia, has lost her dog. She looks for the dog and far in the distance sees something she takes to be her dog, and forms the belief, "That's my dog." Let us suppose Marcia's belief is true, but the dog is just too far away for her perceptual experience to justify her belief. But now consider a process of belief formation that makes reference to the identity of the perceiver, the precise time, and the location at which she spots her dog: *Marcia visually perceiving a dog at 3:15 pm on June 15, 2001 next to the water tower*. This process type has only one instantiation, and it turns out to be perfectly reliable. But though Marcia has a true belief that is produced by a reliable process, her belief is not an instance of knowledge.[23] So we have good reasons for rejecting NR.

Still, we need to distinguish Sosa's virtue account from NR. Sosa's virtue account is *not* committed to the view that just any reliable way of forming beliefs is a source of knowledge, animal or reflective. A virtue-based approach need not hold that every true belief that is formed by a reliable process manifests an intellectual virtue. The narrowly defined process that Marcia uses in forming her belief about the whereabouts of her dog does not count as a virtue. For one thing, a virtue must be some way of forming beliefs that is repeatable, and the process that Marcia follows is not. Moreover, the subject who ignores or "blinks at" defeating evidence might have beliefs produced by a reliable source, but in ignoring defeating evidence fails to manifest overall intellectual virtue. One can fail to know because one has ignored defeating evidence even when one's belief is aptly formed.

I do not think that a virtue based approach to knowledge, such as Sosa's, is committed to endorsing Roxanne's procedure. In particular, I think that a virtue-based approach may deny that Roxanne has knowledge of her first premise and thus Roxanne has no bootstraps on which to pull. It may deny that Roxanne's knows (1) because she does not know that her gas gauge is reliable and, furthermore, she fails to manifest the overall intellectual virtue expected of someone capable of monitoring and assessing her beliefs by failing to make use of other epistemically significant options available to her. Let us consider these points more closely.

First, a defender of a virtue-based approach may argue that the competent use of instruments like gas gauges in a way that yields knowledge is for creatures like us a *derived* virtue or competence. A derived virtue is acquired and sustained through the use of more fundamental virtues such as perception, memory, testimony, and inductive inference.[24] The virtue or competence involved in reading a text, understanding a language, or using an instrument such as a gas gauge is a derived virtue. In order for the use of instruments to yield knowledge, one must have certain background beliefs about the reliability of those instruments, including beliefs about their reliability in the environment in which they are employed. One's knowledge that *p* formed on the basis of using an instrument, *I*, would depend on one's knowing that *I* was indeed reliable. Now, in Roxanne's case, she lacks this sort of background knowledge concerning the reliability of gauges like hers and for this reason we may hold that she does not know (1), she does not know that her tank is full. She thus has no bootstraps on which to pull and thus to reach the conclusion that her gauge is reliable.

Of course, from the fact that knowledge based on the virtuous use of instruments depends on various background beliefs about the reliability of the instruments employed, it does *not* follow that all knowledge must depend on background beliefs about the reliability of one's way of forming beliefs. Indeed, Vogel himself makes a similar point concerning justification.

> Suppose, in general, justification for believing that *X* always requires justification for the belief that the process by which you came to believe that *X* is reliable. It apparently follows that justification for believing any belief will require an endless hierarchy of further beliefs of level (*N* + 1) as to the reliability of the way one's belief at level *N* was formed. But to say that justification *sometimes* requires reason to believe that one's belief-forming process is reliable, as it does in Roxanne's situation, does not imply that justification *always* requires such higher-level support or supplementation. It is this second stronger claim that creates the regress, and one can refuse to agree to it.[25]

Vogel points out that we can avoid the problematic regress by denying that justified belief that *p* always requires a meta-belief to the effect that one's way of forming the belief that *p* is reliable. By the same token, it seems open to the proponent of a virtue-based theory to hold that the beliefs based on the basic virtues of perception, memory and the like do not require such meta-beliefs about the reliability of those ways of forming beliefs in order to have at least animal knowledge. For animal knowledge of the perceptual and mnemonic variety, true belief aptly formed on the basis of a basic or fundamental intellectual virtue is enough. This is so even if for reflective knowledge we do require more by way of justification in terms of a supporting coherent framework.

Second, we might hold that Roxanne's belief that her gas gauge is reliable is epistemically flawed and does not amount to knowledge insofar as she ignores other epistemically significant options readily available to her. She does not check to see if the gas gauge is moving as it ought. She does not check to see if the gauge moves closer to "E" the longer she drives or whether it takes more gas to fill her tank when it says "E" than when it says "F". These procedures would offer independent support for the reliability of her gauge. But also, these procedures offer the possibility of defeating evidence for her belief that her gauge is reliable. If, for example, her gauge did not move down as she drove, then she would have reason to believe that her gauge is not reliable. Because she fails to consider these possible defeaters when it is easy to do so, her procedure and conclusion seem epistemically unsatisfactory and a failure of overall intellectual virtue. Our assessment of the excellence of someone's reasoning depends not simply on whether they have good reasons to support their conclusion, but also on whether they have considered possible defeaters or reasons to the contrary when it is easy to do so. As we noted above, we might object to the astrologer who relies solely upon the outputs of his astrological readings, ignoring whatever conflicts such readings present with perception and other sources. We would also object to the detective who interviews only one of the many witnesses available to him. By her failure to check her beliefs against these procedures available to her, Roxanne's procedure exhibits a similar flaw. Her procedure seems too narrow in way that is for her not necessary. But again, the problem is not relying upon a source to show that that source is reliable, but is rather reasoning in a way that exemplifies a remediable narrowness.

I conclude, then, that a virtue-based approach such as Sosa's may plausibly deny that Roxanne knows in the first instance that her gas tank is full. She has no bootstraps on which to pull in her version of the track record argument. Moreover, the first premise of Roxanne's version of the neo-Moorean argument is false. In contrast, however, a virtue-based approach need not hold that the first premise of the neo-Moorean argument is false. Even if knowledge based on the use of instruments depends on knowledge that the instrument is reliable, we need not impose that requirement on knowledge based on the operation of fundamental virtues such as perception and memory. If this is so, then perceptual knowledge that here's a hand does not depend epistemically upon knowing that perception is a reliable source of knowledge. But what is more, we need not hold that Moore has mere animal knowledge of hand that here's a hand. We may assume that Moore's beliefs, both that here's a hand and that he knows here's hand, have the backing of reasons from within his own perspective and that they fit coherently within his epistemic perspective. Moore, for example, believes that he has known for a long time that he has hands, that other people know he has hands, and that other people like him know similar things about themselves. Moore could thus have much in the way of background beliefs that support his beliefs that here's a hand and that he knows here's a hand. Moore's beliefs fit, even initially, into a coherent perspective, but one that rises to even greater coherence through the neo-Moorean argument. Moore, unlike Roxanne, might have a some degree of reflective knowledge of his first premise, but a degree of reflective knowledge further enhanced by the neo-Moorean argument. The upshot is that a proponent of a virtue account like Sosa's could explain why the neo-Moorean argument does not face the same problem as Roxanne's. Consequently, even if bootstrapping when conjoined with NR seems unacceptable, it does not follow that we must reject bootstrapping in general or the neo-Moorean argument. Moore, unlike Roxanne, has bootstraps on which to pull.

It seems to me, therefore, that a virtue-based approach such as Sosa's can agree with Vogel that NR is false, and, more to the point, it can also deny that Roxanne's bootstrapping procedure is acceptable. Roxanne's procedure is unacceptable because she does not know her first premise. But in agreeing that Roxanne's bootstrapping procedure is unacceptable, a virtue based approach need not reject all bootstrapping or the neo-Moorean argument. More importantly, we are not led to the conclusion that epistemically circular arguments such as the neo-Moorean argument are unsatisfactory ways of supporting the reliability of perception.

**Notes**

1. Cf. William Alston, "Epistemic Circularity" in *Epistemic Justification: Essays in the Theory of Knowledge* (Ithaca, NY: Cornell University Press, 1989), p. 327.
2. William Alston, "A 'Doxastic Practice' Approach to Epistemology" in *Empirical Knowledge* 2nd edition edited by Paul Moser (Lanham, MD: Rowman and Littlefield Publishers, 1996), p. 271.
3. *Ibid.*, p. 271.
4. *Ibid.*, pp. 271–72.
5. Alston's views on how to deal with the problem of epistemic circularity are developed in "A 'Doxastic Practice' Approach to Epistemology" and in *The Reliability of Sense Perception* (Ithaca, NY: Cornell University Press, 1991). For a criticism of this approach see Ernest Sosa, "Philosophical Scepticism and Epistemic Circularity" in *Empirical Knowledge* 2nd edition, pp. 303–29.
6. Ernest Sosa, "Reliabilism and Intellectual Virtue" in *Knowledge in Perspective* (Cambridge: Cambridge University Press, 1991), p. 144.
7. *Ibid.*, p. 145. Cf. Ernest Sosa, "Knowledge and Intellectual Virtue" in *Knowledge in Perspective*, p. 240.
8. Ernest Sosa, "Philosophical Scepticism and Epistemic Circularity", p. 318.
9. Richard Fumerton, *Metaepistemology and Skepticism* (Lanham, MD: Rowman and Littlefield Publishers, 1995), p. 177.
10. *Ibid.*, p. 177.
11. Ernest Sosa, "The Coherence of Virtue and the Virtue of Coherence" in *Knowledge in Perspective*, p. 202.
12. Richard Fumerton, *Metaepistemology and Skepticism*, p. 75.
13. *Ibid.*, p. 76.
14. *Ibid.*, p. 77.
15. I believe that Michael Bergmann makes this point in his "Externalism and Skepticism", *The Philosophical Review*, vol. 109, April 2000, pp. 171–72.
16. Laurence BonJour, *The Structure of Empirical Knowledge* (Cambridge, MA: Harvard University Press, 1985), p. 195. BonJour writes, "obviously, no *argument* can be used to show that reasoning is trustworthy without implicitly begging the question."
17. Jonathan Vogel, "Reliabilism Leveled", *The Journal of Philosophy*, vol. 97, Nov. 2000, p. 604.
18. *Ibid.*, p. 612.

19. *Ibid.*, pp. 614–15.
20. It is not entirely clear what Vogel means by "bootstrapping". Does bootstrapping presuppose a commitment to NR? Or is bootstrapping to be thought of more generally as a procedure that uses the output of some way of forming beliefs to support the belief that that way of forming beliefs is reliable? Vogel writes, "For definiteness, let us say that bootstrapping is the procedure that leads to beliefs like [the gauge is reliable], about the underlying reliability of its process. Bootstrapping may require that one be able to identify appropriately the underlying process by which one has arrived at a particular belief, and sometimes one may not meet that condition." *Ibid.*, p. 615. Unfortunately, this comment doesn't really tell us whether "the procedure" is one that presupposes the truth of NR or whether it is the more general procedure of using the outputs of some way of forming beliefs to support the view that that way of forming beliefs is reliable.
21. Ernest Sosa, "Reflective Knolwedge in the Best Circles" in *Knowledge, Truth, and Duty* edited by Matthias Steup (Oxford: Oxford University Press, 2001), p. 192. Sosa suggests that one can find a similar argument in the second paragraph of Descartes's third mediation.
22. He writes, "Thus, the reliabilist version of Moore's refutation of skepticism sanctions the same kind of inference that created problems in connection with the gas-gauge case. Suppose we grant that the reliabilist is able to evade those problems by denying, either for principled reasons or by fiat, that bootstrapping can lead to knowledge. The upshot will be that reliabilism cannot provide a satisfactory response to skepticism along the lines provided." Jonathan Vogel, "Reliabilism Leveled", p. 619.
23. This example is taken from Mattias Steup, *Contemporary Epistemology* (Upper Saddle River, NJ: Prentice-Hall Publishing, 1996), p. 166.
24. Ernest Sosa, "Intellectual Virtue in Perspective" in *Knowledge in Perspective*, p. 278.
25. Jonathan Vogel, "Reliabilism Leveled", p. 622.

*Philosophical Issues, 14, Epistemology, 2004*

# EPISTEMIC RELATIVISM

Steven Luper
Trinity University

Epistemic relativism rejects the idea that claims can be assessed from a universally applicable, objective standpoint. It is greatly disdained because it suggests that the real 'basis' for our views is something fleeting, such as "the techniques of mass persuasion" (Thomas Kuhn 1970) or the determination of intellectuals to achieve "solidarity" (Rorty 1984) or "keep the conversation going" (Rorty 1979). But epistemic relativism, like skepticism, is far easier to despise than to convincingly refute, for two main reasons. First, its definition is unclear, so we cannot always tell where relativism leaves off and other views, such as skepticism or subjectivism, begin. Consequently, it can be difficult to tell when a criticism has done enough. Second, the grounds for relativism are unclear, which can make it hard to know how to attack it or whether we have dismantled all of the ways of supporting it.

As I see it, the case for epistemic relativism involves (one form of) skepticism, and cannot be defeated satisfactorily unless we simultaneously deny it the skeptical resources upon which it draws. And that is not something we can do unless we challenge beliefs lying deep in the heart of mainstream epistemological thought. To defend epistemic absolutism, I will argue, we must move closer to skepticism and relativism, without succumbing to either.[1]

I'll start by clarifying epistemic relativism and its relation to some allied doctrines.

## Epistemic Relativism Defined; Subjectivism and Skepticism

Relativism is best defined in contrast to absolutism, which comes in two forms. The first, *ontological* or *truth* absolutism, says there is a single, objectively true characterization of reality, at least in its broadest outlines. Of course, different aspects of reality will receive different accounts: the color of the proverbial elephant is one thing, while its shape is quite another. But at least one of two substantially distinct accounts of (the whole elephant or) the whole of reality must be false. It is likely, let us add, that no existing person's account of reality fully coincides with the true and complete account. The second form of absolutism, *epistemic* absolutism, says there is only one correct or authoritative fundamental standard (comprised, perhaps, of component standards) for assessing epistemic merit (although possibly no existing person has adopted it in its entirety). Ultimately, this standard determines the epistemic appropriateness of beliefs and of rules for adopting beliefs. However, quite possibly two competing beliefs (or rules) will be equally justified, or equally unjustified, according to the authoritative standard, leaving us unable to settle some disputes on a rational basis.

Relativism is the denial of absolutism. In one form, it denies ontological absolutism; in another, it denies epistemic absolutism. *Ontological relativism* denies that there is but one objectively correct characterization of reality, while *epistemic relativism* denies that there is only one correct epistemic standard. Ontological relativism can appear in a *subjectivist* form, denying that there is any correct account of reality, or in a *pluralist* form, averring that there are many correct accounts. Ontological relativism is not the claim that any account of reality is made using, or relative to, the concepts involved in the account itself—that claim is a mere truism that everyone, including absolutists, grants. Similarly, epistemic relativism should be distinguished from the truism that assessments of the merit of claims must be made relative to some standard or another.

I will say nothing further about the ontological variety of relativism. My target is the *epistemic* variety.[2]

Epistemic relativism can take either of two forms, since there are two camps of people who deny that there is only one authoritative fundamental epistemic standard. Those in the first camp, *subjectivist* epistemic relativists, say that there is *no* correct (authoritative) epistemic standard, and that epistemic merit is always assessed relative to standards that are entirely subjective. Those in the second camp, *pluralist* epistemic relativists, say that there is *more than one* correct (authoritative) fundamental epistemic standard: the assessment of epistemic merit is relative to a range of competing standards, each applied in exclusion of the others (to avoid an incoherent hodgepodge), and each objectively correct (in some sense which the pluralist must eventually supply).

The relationships among epistemic relativism, subjectivism and skepticism are complicated because each view comes in various varieties. Consider some points of contact.

*Relativism and subjectivism.* subjectivist relativism is closely related to s*tandard subjectivism*, which denies that any epistemic standards are objectively correct. Subjectivism says that an epistemic standard's claim to acceptability is wholly contingent upon the features of an individual subject. Epistemic standards are like the 'guidelines' for matters of taste: they apply only to those who accept them. Subjectivist relativists accept standard subjectivism, adding only that accepted subjective standards vary from person to person or from group to group. However, subjectivism is incompatible with pluralist relativism.

*Skepticism and subjectivist relativism.* Standard subjectivism (and hence subjectivist relativism) implies the *radical* skeptical position that no beliefs are justified. At the same time, however, subjectivism undercuts the *strong* skeptical view that all claims are irrational and should be abandoned, for an assessment of the *epistemic* merit of a view, pro or con, can be made only against the backdrop of an authoritative standard; if none exists, as subjectivists say, then no view is defensible, but neither can any view be condemned as irrational. Neither form of skepticism implies standard subjectivism: radical and strong skepticism are compatible with the possibility that some epistemic standard is correct. Radical skepticism is equivalent to the conditional claim that strong skepticism is true *if* there are authoritative standards. This conditional claim, in turn, is equivalent to the assertion that either standard subjectivism is true or strong skepticism is true.

*Pluralist relativism and skepticism.* Either (a) no epistemic standards are authoritative, or (b) one is, or (c) many are. Pluralist relativism is consistent only with (c). But if (c) holds, standard subjectivism does not, so radical (and strong) skepticism is true only if every authoritative standard condemns all claims as irrational. Therefore pluralist relativism is compatible with skepticism only if there is more than one authoritative epistemic standard, and each one of them condemns all claims as irrational. Presumably not every standard recognized by a pluralist will be so demanding, and hence the pluralist will reject skepticism as ordinarily understood. However, pluralism is consistent with views related to skepticism, namely *skepticism relative to a given person S*, or the contention that the epistemic standard authoritative for S condemns all claims as irrational, and *pluralist skepticism*, or the view that *an* authoritative epistemic standard condemns all claims as irrational. The former implies the latter but not vice versa. Clearly, neither is traditional skepticism, for each is consistent with the possibility that there are authoritative epistemic standards that *endorse* many claims as rational. Pluralist relativists will accept skepticism relative to S so long as S's standard is too demanding to be met by any claim, and they will accept pluralist skepticism if they accept skepticism relativized to at least one person.[3]

## The Argument for Epistemic Relativism

Theorists disagree about how best to defend relativism. Thomas Kuhn suggests that fundamental scientific theories are on a par in that any argument for one against another will inevitably be circular.[4] David Bloor and Barry Barnes (1982) write that relativism "requires what may be called . . . an 'equivalence' postulate. Our equivalence postulate is that all beliefs are on a par with one another with respect to the causes of their credibility."[5] And Harvey Siegel (1987), a resourceful critic, says epistemic relativism is (or is based on) the view that alternative standards for epistemic evaluation are on a par in the sense that there is no neutral way of choosing among them.[6] Instead of assuming that epistemic relativists develop a single line of argument, I will borrow from (and elaborate) various discussions and attempt to put together the strongest case possible. I take ontological absolutism for granted.

I think epistemic relativism is best defended on the basis of the *parity thesis*, which holds that (nearly) all epistemic standards are on a par in that none of them is more defensible than the next. In its broadest outlines the case for relativism looks like this:

1. Many (if not all) epistemic standards can be provided defenses that are as good as the best defense of an epistemic standard: they are on a par (the *parity thesis*).
2. So absolutism is false: there is no one correct (authoritative) standard for assessing the rationality of believers and beliefs (*epistemic relativism*).

Obviously, this initial argument needs development: the parity thesis is unclear and undefended; worse, it does not entail relativism. Let us see what we can do in behalf of the parity thesis. We can worry about deriving relativism later.

The parity thesis admits of two interpretations. On the one hand, standards might be on a par since none are defensible at all. This first option is a form of skepticism directed at epistemic standards. (Of course, skeptics will go on to say that the indefensibility of standards leads to the indefensibility of beliefs). On the other hand, standards would be on a par, even though there is a standard that can be defended well, if the others could be defended equally well. This second option takes a credulous attitude toward standards—an attitude that is just the opposite of skepticism, even though it is usually conflated with skepticism.

In effect, then, the parity thesis is a disjunctive claim, asserting that there is no way to defend any epistemic standard as authoritative (*standard skepticism*), or that virtually any standard can be given a defense that is not only fully adequate, but as good as the defense of any competitor (*standard credulism*). Therefore, whether this *disjunctive parity thesis* is justifiable depends on whether its disjuncts are defensible. Let us examine each.

The first—asserting standard skepticism—has been embraced by skeptics as far back as the Pyrrhonians on the grounds that any argument we provide for an epistemic standard will involve arbitrariness, circularity, or dialectical deadlock, and that no such defense is any good. They conclude that no standard is adequately defensible, as in the *standard skeptic's argument*, below:

(1) It is rational to use a standard only if it is defensible, and an adequate defense cannot involve circularity, arbitrary assumptions, or dialectical deadlock

(2) No standard can be defended without circularity, arbitrary assumptions, or dialectical deadlock.

(3) So no standard can be adequately defended as authoritative.

Premise (1) can be called the *defense tenet*. Consider three points about it: first, if pressed to justify it, skeptics would likely say it is implicit in the ordinary notion of rationality—that the opponents of skepticism understand rationality in a way that implies that the tenet is correct, so skeptics need take no steps to make their tenet palatable. Second, the tenet does not require that a standard actually be defended in order for its use to be rational: it must be defens*ible*, not necessarily defend*ed*. Third, the term 'arbitrary' applies to a person's assumption when that person cannot, even after some reflection, associate with it any reason that suggests it is true. A fourth remark clarifies the notion of dialectical deadlock: a *claim* is in dialectical deadlock if it is disputed for intelligible reasons and the controversy has not been resolved on grounds common (or acceptable) to all sides. (E.g., it is deadlocked if one side depends on grounds the other side is committed to rejecting.) An *argument* involves deadlock if it appeals to a deadlocked claim. Such arguments are said to beg the question. Sometimes deadlock (and question begging) cannot be overcome, as in a dispute between a critic and a resourceful solipsist: neither can argue on grounds the other will grant.

The standard skeptic's argument might be attacked on the grounds that its second premise is false, since the skeptic's demands, as stated in their tenet, can be met. We will discuss this strategy later. For now let us suppose that the skeptic's demands cannot be met. Then the only remaining line of attack is to reject the defense tenet. This brings us to standard credulism, whose advocates reject that tenet. They say that, whatever else is true of a conception of rationality that is *correct*—whatever else is true of *the*, or *a*, correct standard of rationality—the one and only adequate way to defend *that standard itself* involves an argument that is circular, or an argument that relies on assumptions that are arbitrary (or both). And then credulists claim that the same sort of defense is available for a wide range of epistemic standards, each taken in exclusion of all others. The authoritativeness of each is, therefore, equally defensible. (Upon further thought, credulists might insist that a standard have other qualifications to be fully defensible; surely, for example, it must not endorse contradictions. But the additional qualifications cannot be onerous without precluding our defending a standard by arguing circularly or on the basis of arbitrary grounds.) The *credulous argument* spelled out:

1. An epistemic standard that is authoritative can be adequately defended using an argument that is circular or whose premises are arbitrary.
2. If an authoritative epistemic standard can be adequately defended on the basis of an argument that is circular or that invokes arbitrary assumptions, then any standard that can be provided such a supporting argument will be adequately defended.
3. The authoritativeness of virtually any epistemic standard can be supported with an argument that is circular or that invokes arbitrary assumptions.
4. So the authoritativeness of virtually any epistemic standard can be adequately defended.

But if the case for each of a great many standards is as powerful as the next, shouldn't we conclude that we are in no position to select *any* of those standards as authoritative? Indeed, shouldn't we conclude that in the final analysis none is truly defensible, which brings us back to standard skepticism, so that credulism supports skepticism? We should indeed accept this conclusion, if we assume the following *no-ties* principle: if the defense of the authoritativeness of standard T is not better than the defense of the authoritativeness of an alternative to T, then there are inadequate grounds for accepting the authoritativeness of T. However, credulists will not accept this principle, nor the resulting argument that reduces their view to skepticism. Their main position is that a standard resting on arbitrary or circular grounds *is* defended, even though another standard resting on such grounds is defended just as well, so credulists accept defenses that violate the no-ties principle. For similar reasons, they allow for the adequacy of defenses that are in dialectical deadlock: the dispute between advocates of self-supporting standards cannot be settled on grounds common to (or neutral among) all sides. The credulist's view is that a wide range of epistemic standards can be given adequate defenses even though these defenses involve circularity, arbitrariness, dialectical deadlock, or even ties in force.

When we combine the considerations in favor of the skeptical and credulist versions of the parity thesis, and maintain our assumption that the demands skeptics lay out (in their defense tenet) cannot be met, we find ourselves in the following dilemma: either the conception of rationality most people accept—a conception that entails the defense tenet—is correct or it is not. If it is correct, we cannot defend any standards, since we cannot meet the tenet's demands. But if we alter the commonsense view of rationality so as to sustain the conclusion that some standard—say the one with which we are operating—is defensible, we must conclude that many competing standards are defensible. So we must accept either standard skepticism or standard credulism. To review:

1. Either the defense tenet is correct or not.
2. If it is, no standard is defensible (standard skepticism).
3. If the defense tenet is incorrect, then defenses that are circular, arbitrary or in dialectical deadlock are acceptable, and virtually any epistemic standard is defensible (standard credulism).
4. So standard skepticism or standard credulism is true (the disjunctive parity thesis).

Let us call this argument the *preliminary dilemma.*

Now that we have a defense of the parity thesis, it is time to see whether we can use it to derive relativism. Surprisingly, perhaps, we can come close. Choosing between standard skepticism and standard credulism is much like choosing between subjectivist and pluralist relativism, for the (standard skeptic's) claim that no standard is adequately defensible is much like the subjectivist relativist claim that no standard is authoritative, and the (standard credulist's) claim that any standard can be adequately defended is closely allied to the pluralist relativist claim that all standards are authoritative. The disjunctive parity thesis has placed us at the brink of epistemic relativism.

To get us over the edge, we need grounds for saying two things. The first is that if no standard is defensible, as standard skepticism says, then no standard is authoritative, which is what subjectivist relativism claims. The second is that if nearly any standard is defensible, as standard credulism suggests, then nearly any standard is authoritative, as pluralist relativism says. But what would entitle relativists to make these two claims? The answer, I suggest, is a form of verificationism: implicitly or explicitly, relativists assume that the mark of the correctness of a standard is its defensibility. Perhaps, they reason, we can imagine some authoritative standard that cannot be supported, but if *no* standard can be adequately defended, then no standard is authoritative. Perhaps we can also imagine some epistemic standard that can be justified even though it is not authoritative, but if *many* (or all) standards can be given defenses that are adequate and even as good as the best defense (as good as the defense of an admittedly authoritative standard), then each of those standards is authoritative. The relativists' version of verificationism holds that the indefensibility of all standards entails that no standard is authoritative, and the defensibility of nearly any standard entails the authoritativeness of those standards.

Hence verificationism converts the choice between standard skepticism and credulism into the choice between subjectivist and pluralist relativism, and we can defend epistemic relativism by supplementing the preliminary dilemma with verificationism, as in the following *pincer argument*:

1. Either the defense tenet is correct or not.
2. If it is, no standard is defensible (standard skepticism).
3. If the defense tenet is incorrect, then defenses that are circular, arbitrary or in dialectical deadlock are acceptable, and virtually any epistemic standard is defensible (standard credulism).
4. So standard skepticism or standard credulism is true (the disjunctive parity thesis).
5. If no standard can be adequately defended, then no standard is authoritative; if virtually any standard can be adequately defended, then any of these defensible standards is authoritative (verificationism).[7]
6. So either no standard is authoritative (subjectivism), or nearly any standard is authoritative, and the correct assessment of epistemic merit varies depending on the standard in play (pluralism). Either way, absolutism is false.

(I will not argue the point here, but Pyrrhonian skeptics[8] seem to have used something like the preliminary dilemma to prepare the way to a pseudo-relativist decision to live "by the appearances." The disjunctive parity thesis does not select between standard skepticism and standard credulism, so Pyrrhonians were not precisely skeptics, not even standard skeptics. Their position resembles relativism, since the disjunctive parity thesis is allied to and consistent with the claim that relativism is true. "Appearances" was their term for what they found themselves inclined to accept, sometimes so forcefully as to be involuntary. Finding themselves so inclined, they adopted their society's customs and beliefs, while acknowledging the epistemic parity of these with ways in other lands.)

One loose end needs attention: is there a case for the verificationist thesis on which relativists rely? Perhaps. Relativists might offer verificationism as the best explanation of the parity thesis—of the fact that either standard skepticism or credulism is correct. Consider standard skepticism. Why, they might ask, is it impossible to show that any standard is authoritative? Certainly it is theoretically possible that some standard is authoritative even though there is no way to tell that it is, but the best explanation of the fact that we cannot find good grounds for saying that a standard is authoritative is that no standard *is* authoritative. Now consider standard credulism. Why can we give many standards an extremely, and equally, compelling defense? Possibly, none of them is really authoritative, even though we have good grounds for thinking otherwise; possibly, too, only one is authoritative, even though what can be said on its behalf can be said (*mutatis mutandis*) on behalf of alternatives. But the best explanation is that the entire set of standards is authoritative. This defense of verificationism has at least prima facie plausibility.[9]

We now have a strong case against absolutism.[10] Yet absolutism is held in high esteem, and relativism is widely rejected. Are these assessments warranted? There are two main strategies for criticizing relativism. The strategy nearly every critic follows (e.g., Plato in *Theaetetus*) is to argue that it is self-defeating. Now that we have laid out the pincer argument for relativism, we also know there is a second way to assail relativism: we can attack the skeptic's prediction, whose reliability we have been taking for granted, that defending a standard invariably involves circularity, arbitrariness or deadlock. A successful attack would allow us to undermine the pincer argument by rejecting its second premise. In the following section I propose that we continue to accept the skeptic's prediction, and focus on the familiar strategy of criticizing relativism by showing it is self-defeating. Let us ask whether it can succeed on its own, without help from a simultaneous attack on the skeptic's prediction.

### The Traditional Argument Against Epistemic Relativism

To show relativism is self-defeating we must argue that it is incoherent, or that the very claim it makes implies that it is not defensible, much like the following statement: This statement cannot be justified. However, the first option is a nonstarter: subjectivist relativism makes the entirely intelligible (if false) claim that no standard is authoritative, while pluralist relativism says, again intelligibly, that many standards are authoritative. How about the other option? Here the strategy is to catch relativists on the horns of the *antirelativist dilemma*, as follows: Relativists must support their view either relatively (i.e., in a way that presupposes the truth of relativism) or non-relatively. However, they cannot support it relatively, since that would (a) beg the question and (b) violate the no-ties principle. Nor can they support it on a non-relative basis, since doing so requires giving it up. They must give up their view to defend it, so relativism is self-defeating. Consider each prong of attack.

*First prong: relativist defense of relativism.* Consider the relativist's dialectical context. An argument for relativism amounts to an argument against absolutism. So to engage with their opponents, relativists must argue on grounds absolutists take seriously. But absolutists will reject as question-begging the assertion that epistemic merit can be assessed subjectively, as well as the idea that this assertion can be defended using subjective considerations, which have no bearing on epistemic merit as the absolutist understands it. Hence a subjectivist case for subjectivist relativism fails. Nor will absolutists accept the standards by which pluralism is defensible. Suppose, for example, that, to support their view, pluralists point out that it is not self-contradictory. Perhaps by *that* standard pluralism is justifiable, but absolutists will reject the idea that mere consistency is adequate support for a view. So a pluralist case for pluralism fails too. Indeed, the absolutist will not be satisfied with anything short of a non-relativist defense of relativism, so that is what is required. In sum:

1. To successfully defend their view relativists must honor the no-dead-lock principle that each side in a dispute must argue on the basis of claims acceptable to the opposing side.
2. They cannot meet this principle if they argue on relativist grounds.
3. So a relativist case for relativism is no case at all.

To reject this argument, it suffices for relativists to defeat its first premise, as follows: like anyone else who adopts the no-deadlock principle, absolutists must apply it to themselves. Since no one can defeat relativism or defend absolutism on grounds acceptable to determined relativists, absolutists must conclude that *neither* relativism nor absolutism is defensible. As for relativists, they do not face this difficulty, since they need not rely on the no-deadlock principle in a relativist case for relativism. Nor is the absolutist positioned to show that relativists *have* to honor the no-deadlock principle, for absolutists must, by that very principle, argue on grounds acceptable to relativists. Relativists, however, find that principle antithetical to their case, and reject anything that supports it. Thus accepting the no-deadlock principle bars absolutists from insisting that relativists follow suit!

Recall that the first prong of the antirelativist dilemma consisted of the charge that relativism cannot be supported relatively, since that would (a) beg the question and (b) violate the no-ties principle. We've dealt with (a); now let us consider (b).

Admittedly, in arguing for *anything* subjectivist relativists are greatly hobbled by their position that no standard is authoritative. If they are correct, there is no authoritative point of view from which to defend any view, including the assertion that no standard is authoritative. Still, claims can be 'supported' subjectively, in the same sense that assertions of taste and related matters are 'defensible.' Thus its proponents might say it would be a bummer if subjectivism were false. However, by their own admission, the subjectivist's 'defense' of a view A does not show that it is preferable to an alternative position B, for proponents of B can easily 'support' B and 'criticize' A subjectively. In particular, subjectivist-style grounds cannot be adduced to show that subjectivist relativism is better than absolutism, since absolutists can easily 'support' *their* view subjectively, say on the grounds that people who deny absolutism are irritating.

Like subjectivists, pluralist relativists can offer a relativist defense of their view: if each standard (applied in exclusion of all others) is authoritative (or if many are), then whether a view is defensible depends on the standard in play, and pluralism is defensible relative to standards that support it. For instance, it is endorsed by a standard that approves of any view that is not self-contradictory. However, pluralists must admit that a pluralist-style 'defense' of a view A does not show that it is preferable to an alternative B, whose advocates might defend B and attack A relative to their own standards. So a pluralist defense of pluralism does not show it is superior to absolutism.

Absolutists will be ready to reject a relativist defense of subjectivism as well as a relativist case for pluralism upon concluding that both violate the no-ties principle: a 'defense' of relativism that does not contend—let alone establish—that relativism is superior to absolutism is not a defense at all. But will relativists have the same response? Not at all, since they reject the no-ties principle! They will admit that, on their view, by some 'valid' standards relativism is not justifiable. For people who embrace those standards, relativism *is* indefensible. But there are also 'valid' standards by which relativism can be supported. For anyone who accepts the no-ties principle, relativism is indefensible, but it does not follow that, 'for the relativist,' relativism cannot be supported.

Mightn't absolutists *insist* on the no-ties principle? Suppose they appeal to the no-deadlock principle, and say that relativists are not really engaging with absolutists unless they honor the no-ties principle. We have already seen that the no-deadlock principle bars absolutists from insisting that relativists adopt the no-deadlock principle. Obviously that same principle bars absolutists from arguing that relativists should adopt the no-ties principle, too. This is not to say that the no-ties principle is false, however; the point is that the no-deadlock principle bars absolutists from expecting relativists to argue on the basis of *any* principle antithetical to relativism.

*Second prong: non-relativist defense.* According to the second prong of the antirelativist dilemma, relativists cannot press their case on a non-relative basis, since doing so requires that they give up relativism. Can the relativist escape this prong, too?

It is true that a defense of relativism acceptable to its proponents will not automatically count as a case against absolutism compelling to *its* proponents. It does not follow, however, that relativists cannot set forth a case against absolutism that is compelling to absolutists, nor that they must abandon relativism in doing so. Relativists can attack absolutism using the absolutist's own style of argumentation. To do this without embracing absolutism in the process, relativists can pursue a strategy skeptics have always adopted: turn the tables and argue that their opponents hold assumptions that undermine their own view. Let's spell this out.

Like relativists, skeptics are often criticized on the grounds that they are in no position to defend their view if it is correct. But there is also a familiar response: skeptics have no need to justify or adopt their premises, since these are claims their opponents make; the skeptic is developing a *reductio ad absurdum* argument, pointing out dire implications of the antiskeptic's own position. Thus, it is the antiskeptic who needs to worry about whether the skeptic's premises are defensible.

Similarly, relativists may lay the pincer argument at the doorstep of the absolutist. It is a *reductio* based on views absolutists take seriously. Assuming that absolutists cannot wriggle out of the skeptic's claim that the defense tenet cannot be met, *they* must accept the reasoning of the preliminary dilemma, which commits them to the disjunctive parity thesis. *They* have to accept either standard skepticism or, after lowering the bar, standard credulism. This choice is not quite the same as the choice between subjectivist and pluralist relativism, which absolutists would be forced into only if they followed relativists in accepting verificationism (and not all will, so absolutists can escape the full force of the pincer argument), but it is certainly a horror for the absolutist. For if the disjunctive parity thesis is true, it is impossible to defend absolutism. Standard skepticism implies that no standard can be defended. Standard credulism, on the other hand, implies that many standards can be supported, and if that is true, we are in no position to show that only one standard is authoritative even if it is true. Either way, the absolutist is defenseless.

For relativists, the situation could scarcely be better. They can 'defend' their view in their own way. They cannot support it to the satisfaction of the absolutist, but this hardly matters since absolutists cannot defend their own view to their own satisfaction. Apparently it is absolutism that proves indefensible.

We now have the answer to the question we posed in this section: absolutism cannot be supported merely on the grounds that relativism is self-defeating. But there are other ways to defend absolutism, including a strategy that, until now, we have suppressed: denying the skeptic's prediction that the terms of the defense tenet cannot be met. It is time to consider this approach.

**The Skeptic's Prediction**

Recall the argument for standard skepticism:

1. It is rational to use a standard only if it can be given a defense that does not involve arbitrary assumptions, circularity, or dialectical deadlock (the defense tenet).

2. No standard's authoritativeness can be defended without arbitrary assumptions, circularity, or dialectical deadlock (the skeptic's prediction).

3. So no standard's authoritativeness can be adequately defended (standard skepticism).

When confronted with this argument, many epistemologists will want to accept the first premise and deny the second. Indeed, one of the most important and enduring strands of endeavor in epistemology has been the attempt to demonstrate, in a way that is consistent with the defense tenet, the authoritativeness of an epistemic standard. Many will want to take the same traditional approach when it comes to relativism. By successfully attacking the skeptic's prediction, absolutists would position themselves to show that there is an authoritative epistemic standard, and, simultaneously, would undermine the relativist's pincer argument, by knocking away its skeptical prong. The relativist could no longer force the absolutist to conclude that absolutism is indefensible. Nothing relativists could say, in self-defense, would have any merit to the absolutist.

However, there is a problem with the traditional approach: there are no good grounds for denying the skeptic's prediction. Certainly there is no consensus on any strategy for denying the prediction; in all likelihood, the hostility among epistemologists towards it is not based on the *case* against it. Instead, I suggest, the hostility is based on the belief that, of the two possible ways to counter the argument for standard skepticism, it is the only viable approach. To attack the skeptic's argument, we must deny the prediction or the defense tenet. But epistemologists have long suspected that the credulist leg of the argument for the preliminary dilemma is correct: unless the tenet is true, then defenses that are circular, arbitrary or in dialectical deadlock are acceptable, and virtually any epistemic standard is defensible. Epistemologists want to refute skepticism, but in doing so they don't want to embrace an uncritical credulist view. They fear that the price of abandoning the defense tenet is that, as Feyerabend (1975; cf. Moser 1993, p. 1) proclaimed, *anything goes*. They see only one way out: denying 2, the prediction, and not 1, the tenet.

I think it is time to give up on the traditional approach to criticizing skepticism. Attempts to deny 2 have proven to be a fruitless dead end. It is time to respond to standard skepticism (and its offshoots) by rejecting 1 instead. Indeed, we should reject 1 *because* 2 is true: the tenet blocks the way to our defending an epistemic standard, so it must be mistaken.

Admittedly, my claim that no one has found a way to refute the skeptic's prediction is not a case for endorsing that prediction. But I won't try to prove that the prediction is true. I will assume it is. What I want to do is remove the barrier, just described, against accepting the skeptic's prediction. I want to show that even if the prediction is true, the skeptic cannot stop us from supporting absolutism, and our case need not devolve into uncritical credulism or relativism. Even theorists who are convinced that the skeptic's prediction can be shown false might find this project interesting. It is no small matter that we can give skeptics their prediction and still argue convincingly for absolutism.

## How to Defend Absolutism

My contention is (a) there is an argument that, even though it violates the defense tenet, provides adequate support for the authoritativeness of an epistemic standard, yet (b) not just any epistemic standard can be supported in the same way, so we need not fall into some form of credulism or relativism. To defend (a), I must define 'standard', clarify the conditions under which a standard is 'correct' or 'authoritative', and, finally, sketch how, on a suitably weakened defense tenet, the authoritativeness of such a beast can be adequately defended. To support (b), I must argue that the weakened tenet does not make it possible to underwrite the authoritativeness of wholly counterintuitive standards.

*First task: clarify 'standard'.* Epistemic standards come in different kinds. There are *warrant standards*, which are rules or criteria by which we assess how probable it is that a claim is true. There are also *management standards*, which are rules (or policies, methods, procedures and so forth) of two sorts: rules that tell us whether to (begin, continue, or cease to) believe claims, and whose purpose is to enable us to develop and maintain a worldview that is as complete and accurate as possible, and rules that tell us whether to maintain (or revise) these rules, again with verisimilitude as the final purpose. For convenience, we can treat warrant standards as a kind of management standard, and call the one type of rule a *belief management rule* and the other a *rule management rule*. The latter are, in effect, standards for managing standards.

*Second task: clarify the conditions under which a standard is authoritative.* An epistemic standard is authoritative or 'correct' insofar as it is truth-*conducive*; that is, to the extent that its application in a wide range of the circumstances in which people sometimes are placed facilitates our reaching (and retaining) the truth. The greater the truth-conduciveness of a management rule (including a rule for authoritativeness) in a broad range of people's circumstances, the more authoritative it is.

But if authoritativeness is a matter of degree, as just said, then it is not immediately clear what absolutists mean when they claim that *one* standard is authoritative. Presumably their main claim is something like the following: a unique core standard is not only truth-conducive, it is the *most* truth-conducive, hence most authoritative, core standard we might adopt. But this claim requires qualification, since, however helpful a standard T is, there might be any number of variations on T, each as truth-conducive as the next. I take the absolutist's claim to mean that one standard T is not only truth-conducive enough to give us a good chance of arriving at an accurate view of the world, it is the *core part* of all of the highly truth-conducive standards we might adopt, so that any highly truth-conducive standard will be a development of T. Thus absolutism is compatible with the view, which we might call *pluralist absolutism*, that by augmenting one core epistemic standard in competing ways we can create a range of equally authoritative standards.

*Third task: show how to defend a standard.* To defend the authoritativeness of some standard T, our main job is to establish that applying T will help us reach the truth. A complete defense of absolutism as I have understood it will also require showing that T is the heart of any of the most truth-conducive standards we might employ. Let us sketch how we can achieve the first objective, leaving the second for another occasion.

Defending our standard's truth-conduciveness will require that we take for granted our worldview, our depiction of the truth about the world. We'll have to argue that, in a world that takes the shape we assume it to take, people who adhere to our standard have a good chance of arriving at an accurate view of the world. Now, I will not attempt to sketch out a complete epistemic standard in all its detail, or its defense. My claim is just that many of the belief management practices by which people (implicitly) steer themselves fit together as components of one overall standard whose authoritativeness is adequately defensible given the worldview we take for granted. These practices, which, taken together, we can call the ordinary standard, include four belief management rules and two rule management rules:

(1) Do not reason in ways that violate rules of deductive logic.
(2) Other things being equal, retain beliefs prompted by your senses.
(3) Other things being equal, believe the best explanation of your data (cf. Harman 1986).
(4) Continue to believe what you do unless you have good reason to stop (Peirce 1877, Popper 1959, Harman 1984, 1986).
(5) Other things being equal, prefer (as more authoritative) one management rule over a competitor when you have good reason to believe it is more truth-conducive.
(6) Continue to operate by these six management rules unless you have good reason to stop.

In the commonsense world of tables, pumpkins and people, adhering to these principles gives us a good chance of reaching the truth. No doubt, they need a good deal of clarification, and they can be improved with refinement. Our expectations for an epistemic standard should not be overly great: there are no algorithms for cranking out the truth about the world (Feyerabend

1975). It is especially unrealistic to think that wholly general principles such as (1)–(6) will suffice in every domain of inquiry. They will have to be supplemented with specialized principles in specific areas of investigation. Our expectations in some domains should be even lower than our expectations in others. Deductive logic does not tell us what to think about the empirical world; still, rules of deductive argument must always preserve truth and they must do so in every possible world. Rules of non-deductive, or inductive or 'ampliative' argument cannot be expected always to preserve truth even in the actual world.

Consider two of the points just made, one of which is (relatively) uncontroversial, while the other is not. The uncontroversial point is the conditional claim that *if* the world is shaped the way commonsense beliefs say it is, the ordinary epistemic standard is truth-conducive. The controversial point is that this conditional claim constitutes a *defense* of the ordinary epistemic standard. The problem is obvious: the kind of argument I just sketched violates the defense tenet! It involves circularity or arbitrariness.

In effect, this objection says that the skeptic's defense tenet must be a part of any epistemic standard that is to count as authoritative—that a truly authoritative standard must include, and cohere with, the following rules (which are counterparts of our rules 4 and 6):

(S4) Adopt or retain a belief only if you can provide an adequate justification for it, a justification that does not involve circularity, arbitrariness or dialectical deadlock.

(S6) Adopt or retain a management rule only if you can provide an adequate justification for it, a justification free of circularity, arbitrariness or dialectical deadlock.

However, the objection is mistaken, and the skeptic's characterization of rationality is false. Adhering to (S4) precludes our having any beliefs at all about the world, and operating with (S6) deprives us of any standard at all—including itself. These rules leave us rudderless (having no policies for managing our beliefs) and blind (having no view of the world, and no chance for arriving at the truth about the world). Only if we retain (4) and (6), or versions thereof, do we have any chance whatever of arriving at an accurate view of the world, while at the same time avoiding the credulist position that nearly any standards and nearly any worldview is warranted. So it is rational to retain (4) and (6) and irrational to replace them with (S4) and (S6). The history of philosophy is replete with attempts to replace the components of the ordinary epistemic standard with rules that appear to be better guides to the truth but that end up restricting us to an overly narrow conception of reality. The skeptic's defense tenet is the most radical example. A less extreme example is the empiricist's version of (3) (rarely adopted in this uncompromising form): believe only what is empirically verifiable.

Another is the positivist's rule: believe only what is analytic or empirically verifiable.

Only against the backdrop of a worldview can we assess how truth-conducive a standard is, and only with an epistemic standard can we assess the truth of a worldview. So we must either argue, circularly, from our worldview to our standard and back again, or, arbitrarily, take one or the other for granted. Such an argument is part of (what we must count as) an adequate defense even though it involves circularity or arbitrariness (or both: circularity *is* a form of arbitrariness). And this sort of argument is endorsed by (4) and (6). Let us add that the argument is adequate even though it involves inescapable dialectical deadlock: it is not always true that, if an argument between two disputants cannot be resolved on common grounds, then neither side's view is defensible; if it were, we could not resist solipsism. Nor could we resist the extreme form of skepticism that insists on the defense tenet. Skeptics could veto any case we offer.

I have argued that the ordinary epistemic standard is defensible. However, it is important to see that, from the standpoint of rationality, there is no *need* to provide such a defense. That is, being able to justify the ordinary standard (1)–(6) is not a precondition for its rational use. Nor is being able to defend our worldview a condition for its rational acceptance. In line with (4) and (6), it is rational to retain our worldview as well as the ordinary epistemic standard unless we come to have good grounds to stop.[11] This consequence aligns our view with pragmatism (Peirce 1877) and reliabilism (Ramsey 1931, Armstrong 1973, Goldman 1979).

*Final task: avoiding credulism and pluralist relativism.* We can now consider whether our strategy for defending the ordinary epistemic standard commits us to credulism or relativism.

One reason for optimism is that many conceivable standards are patently indefensible. When we assess the authoritativeness of a standard we are assessing its truth-conduciveness; obviously, many conceivable standards do not facilitate our reaching the truth. Hence we can rule out the authoritativeness of many kinds of standards from the outset. For example, a policy of believing only false claims obviously is indefensible. The same goes for the policy of believing anything tasteful, or whatever makes us happy. A standard that is too impractical or too vague to apply is also indefensible.

Unfortunately, these fairly obvious points only get us so far, and there remain several challenges to overcome.

*First challenge.* On our account, the claim that the ordinary epistemic standard is authoritative is only contingently true. Hence, each of a great many standards might have been authoritative, since there is a possible world in which it is (more) truth-conducive (than any competitor). Even wishful thinking may be part of an authoritative standard in a world where wishes come true. Doesn't it follow that many standards are authoritative, as pluralist relativism says?

No. The claim that many standards *might have been* authoritative (i.e., for each of many standards, there is a possible world in which it is authoritative), which is correct, is much weaker than, and fails to entail, the false claim that many standards *are* authoritative (i.e., many standards are each authoritative in the actual world). (For similar reasons, a case for subjectivist relativism cannot be based on the grounds that there are worlds in which the ordinary epistemic standard is not truth-conducive.)

Admittedly, it seems intuitively false that authoritativeness is a contingent matter. Platonic-Cartesian rationalism, which shaped the intuitions of most (Western) epistemologists, suggests that deductive and mathematical logic, whose rules can be worked out a priori since valid in any possible world, is the paradigm for rational thought. The rationalist legacy suggests that, a priori, we can identify each authoritative belief management practice (each component of a complete authoritative standard), something we could do only if authoritativeness were wholly a matter of necessity—that is, only if each of the practices comprising our standard were authoritative in every possible world if authoritative at all. If authoritativeness were a matter of necessity, there would be hope that, using unaided reason, we could satisfy ourselves that each belief-management practice is authoritative, in much the same way that we can satisfy ourselves that $2 + 2 = 4$. Since the authoritativeness of some of the practices that go to make up a complete standard is a contingent matter, we have to rely on experience. There it is: the intuitions are misleading. Intuitions sometimes can serve as prima facie evidence for or against theories (Bealer and Strawson 1992), but intuitions are not sacrosanct, and when we identify intuitions that have been molded under false assumptions we must revise them. There is no such thing as a complete standard that is truth-conducive in every possible world; hence it is clearly false that a complete standard is authoritative in every possible world. The correct standard might not have been correct.

*Second challenge.* On our view of authoritativeness, we can imagine a situation in which people believe things that are epistemically inappropriate even though there is no way they can be expected to discover this shortcoming, and are, in this sense, blameless. Suppose that Fred accepts epistemic standard D, that D says unequivocally that D is truth-conducive given Fred's worldview, and that D would indeed be truth-conducive if Fred's worldview were true. Unfortunately, in Fred's world D is wholly misleading. (Maybe Fred is plagued by a demon who undermines the truth-conduciveness of D and Fred cannot detect the demonic manipulation.) Worse luck, an alternative standard T really is truth-conducive yet nothing in Fred's beliefs about the world suggests that this is so. Then T, not D, determines what is epistemically appropriate for Fred to believe, yet Fred's worldview suggests that D determines what is appropriate. Isn't this result counterintuitive? If so, we must adopt a different notion of authoritativeness. Let us say that *actual* authoritativeness is truth-conduciveness in the world as it is, and *apparent* authoritativeness is truth-conduciveness given the worldview we accept. The view we need is that *real* authoritativeness is apparent authoritativeness—then Fred's standard D determines what is appropriate for him to believe in spite of its being a bad guide to the truth. And then we can conclude, with pluralist relativists, that standards are authoritative only relative to worldviews.

Admittedly, it seems counter to our intuitions that everything we believe can point to the authoritativeness of one standard, yet another determines what counts as a rational belief. I suggest that two errors are responsible for these misleading intuitions.

First error: once again our rationalist legacy, discussed earlier, is partly to blame. Our intuitions and expectations are shaped under the influence of the view that a standard is authoritative in every possible world if authoritative at all, which fosters the view that we can identify authoritativeness a priori. This view, in turn, suggests that if a standard really is authoritative, we will always have good reason to think it is, no matter what our circumstances are like. It cannot happen that everything we believe suggests that some standard is authoritative when it is not. However, as we have said, these intuitions must be revised now that we reject the rationalist legacy.

Second error: It seems that (a) everything we believe will be epistemically appropriate so long as we follow the dictates of the epistemic standard by which we manage our beliefs. And (a) suggests (b) if our standard is self-supporting given our worldview—if our standard says of itself, on the strength of our view of the world, that it is authoritative—then there can be no epistemic objection whatever to our concluding that our standard is authoritative. Yet (b) is incompatible with the assumption that a standard is not an authoritative guide to rational belief if not truth-conducive. Indeed, (b) implies that authoritativeness is nothing more than self-support relative to our worldview (this is much like Richard Foley's (2003) view of rationality as immunity to self-criticism). So (a) suggests that our view of authoritativeness is mistaken, and that there is no way that everything we believe can suggest that some standard is authoritative when it is not. We are led to reduce real authoritativeness to apparent authoritativeness, and our intuitions are influenced accordingly.

There *is* a sense in which (a) is true. However, it is misleading, and (a) does not support (b). The rationality of a belief involves two things: a person S has met the *external* requirement for rational belief that *p* if and only if the standard guiding S in believing *p* is authoritative. S has met the *internal* requirement for rational belief that *p* if and only if S believes *p* in accordance with the dictates of S's standard. Rational belief is created through the joint efforts of the world, on the one hand, and epistemic agents, on the other.[12] The world's contribution is the external component: only if the world takes a certain shape will our standard be truth-conducive. Our contribution is the internal component: it is up to us to apply our standard in accordance with its dictates. We exhaust our part in the bargain when we satisfy the internal component—in this sense (a) is true. But the world has to do its part—in this sense (a) is misleading. Thus even if we have done our part in concluding that our standard is authoritative, there still can be an epistemic objection to our reasoning, contrary to (b). For (through no fault of ours) the standard guiding our reasoning might not be truth-conducive.[13]

Advocates of *internalism*, the view that epistemic merit depends wholly on factors accessible from within the perspective of the agent (BonJour 1997, Earl Conee and Richard Feldman 2001) will resist our responses to the first and second challenges. It is worth emphasizing, however, that internalists rely heavily on appeals to the very intuitions that, we have argued, are forged under the influence of errors. According to some, internalism just is the rationalist doctrine that a standard is authoritative in every possible world if authoritative at all (Luper 1988, Coney and Feldman 2001). This position is unworkable, and internalists cannot defend it by arguing solely on the basis of the intuitions it inculcates.

*Third challenge.* My defense of the ordinary epistemic standard took the commonsense view of the world for granted. But if taking this worldview for granted is epistemically permissible, may we not take any view of the world for granted? If so, can't we defend the authoritativeness of nearly any standard? As we have already said, for nearly any standard there is a possible world in which it is truth-conducive. So to support the authoritativeness of a standard, all we have to do is take for granted a worldview in which it is properly truth-conducive.

This objection is based on the permissive assumption that it is rational to *adopt* a belief for which we have no grounds. If this assumption were correct, it would be rational to adopt, arbitrarily, an entire worldview, and with the right worldview, nearly any epistemic standard will be defensible. This reasoning supports standard credulism, if not pluralist relativism. Fortunately, nothing in our defense of the ordinary epistemic standard commits us to the permissive assumption. For the very reason that this assumption leads to credulism we should reject it. What we are committed to is the Peircean principle that it is rational to *retain* a belief unless we have positive reason to think it false—even if we also lack reason to think it true. On this principle, it is not rational arbitrarily to *adopt* a worldview and any standard it favors. Given the Peircean principle, it is true that if we *had* a different worldview we *could have* defended some other standard. But here there is no support for standard credulism or relativism. The fact that we *might have been able to* defend some standard does not imply that we *can* defend that standard. We can only defend a standard from the point of view of one worldview, namely our own, and the only standard we can defend is the one that is most truth-conducive from the vantage point of that worldview. Let us add that even if we did have a different worldview, we still could not defend just any standard, but only one that, arguably, is truth-conducive from the vantage point of that different worldview. For *no* one, in *any* possible world, is it the case that nearly any standard is justifiable.

*Fourth challenge.* Among people in the actual world, there is a wide range of worldviews, so there is a wide range of defensible standards. For no one is it the case that nearly any standard is justifiable, but for each of a great many standards there will be someone relative to whom that standard will be defensible. In this sense a great many standards are defensible—each by different groups of people. Granting verificationism, pluralist relativists are back in business: relative to each of many separate groups, a different epistemic standard is authoritative.

This challenge is based on the assumption that there are groups of people committed to worldviews that are so widely divergent from each other as to support entirely different epistemic standards. But this assumption is not plausible. Take any worldview that is actually accepted, at least by sane people. In the world as it would be if that worldview were correct, the ordinary epistemic standard is truth-conducive. I cannot fully defend this claim; I will try to make it plausible with an example. Consider that there are people who believe that incantations will produce certain effects magically. I claim that, in a world in which magic occurred, the ordinary epistemic standard would help people reach true beliefs. For experience would bear out the efficacy of the spells, and lead people to a host of accurate relevant beliefs. We can conclude that the authoritativeness of the ordinary standard is defensible for every actual person in spite of the differences in their specific beliefs. Hence for everyone it is reasonable to think that the ordinary standard is the correct one, and that absolutism is true.

None of this is to deny that there is a good deal of divergence among people's beliefs about the world. Some people have sophisticated views about theoretical physics, while others have very confused ideas in this area. Some people are well positioned to observe the behavior of distant nebulae or furtive woodland creatures, and can speak knowledgeably about these matters, while others do not know a star from a planet or a wood-chuck from a chipmunk. Given these differences, some variations of the ordinary epistemic standard are defensible, each by different groups of people. Moreover, the rationality of belief is relative in the following sense: beliefs are not rational *simpliciter*; the rational status of a belief varies relative to people's evidence and circumstances. The astronomer's belief about some twinkling heavenly body is warranted where the layperson's is not; indeed, my belief as to whether I am sitting on April 30, 2003 at 5 pm is warranted, while your belief about my position, if you have one, is not. These familiar points do not imply that epistemic relativism is true. They are straightforward consequences of the fact that the one authoritative standard yields different assessments of epistemic merit (assessments as to a belief's status as rational, or justified, and so forth) depending on a person's evidence and circumstances. Epistemic absolutists will certainly grant that rationality is relative to these factors—this is an innocuous, derivative form of relativity. What they insist upon is that, for all actual people, one core standard is the appropriate one for making assessments of epistemic merit.

*Fifth challenge.* I have said that an epistemic standard is authoritative insofar as it is truth-conducive. This amounts to the assertion that the *standard* (or metastandard) for the authoritativeness of an epistemic standard is truth-conduciveness. But other metastandards are possible, and people manage their beliefs in accordance with a variety of criteria; it is rational for us to consider our own metastandard authoritative only if we can show it to be rationally preferable to the alternatives (Stephen Stich 1988 argues roughly this way). However, either no (meta)standard is defensible, or a great many are, as the reasoning involved in the preliminary dilemma shows. Hence, we cannot single out some metastandard as rationally preferable, and in that case there is no way to defend the rational preferability of an epistemic standard.

My view is that epistemic standards at *any* level are authoritative insofar as they are truth conducive. The fifth challenge is that either this view cannot be supported (the skeptical charge), or, if it can, then similar defenses favor taking a wide range of criteria as the mark of the authoritativeness of epistemic standards at whatever level (the credulist charge). However, those of us who identify authoritativeness with truth conduciveness can meet the challenge.[14] The justification for continuing to take truth-conduciveness as the mark of authoritativeness is that doing so is truth-conducive. Indeed, unless our epistemic standard takes truth-conduciveness to determine authoritativeness, it will not be truth-conducive. Such a defense is circular. As already noted, however, it is rational to tolerate circularity at certain fundamental junctures. But if we accept this defense, aren't we committed to saying that it is rational to adopt any criterion as the mark of authoritativeness, so long as it is self-supporting in the way that truth-conduciveness is?[15] No, what we are committed to is rule (6) of the ordinary standard—the (Peircean) principle that it is rational to retain our standard for authoritativeness unless we have positive reason to alter it—and rule (5), which says, of the discovery that we can improve the reliability of our standard, that this is reason to alter it. These principles do not condone the decision, based on nothing, to replace our criterion of authoritativeness with a fresh one, even one that is self-supporting.

## Notes

1. This essay elaborates upon Luper 1990 and 2001, refining some arguments and correcting defects in others.

2. The literature concerning relativism is vast. An excellent (critical) overview is Siegel 1987. Many relativists defend both ontological and epistemic relativism, using the former to help with the latter. But some (Field 1982, Stich 1988) reject the former and defend the latter. I mean to criticize the epistemic relativist who does not assume the truth of ontological relativism.

3. Later I will suggest that proponents of relativism draw upon a restricted form of skepticism, namely *standard skepticism*: the position that no epistemic standard is defensible. The route from standard skepticism to relativism is perforce indirect, however, since the two views are not fully compatible. Standard skepticism is implied by subjectivist relativism, but the former does not imply the latter.

4. Kuhn (1987), p. 94.

5. "Relativism, Rationalism and the Sociology of Knowledge," p. 22. In Hollis (1982) 21–48.

6. 1987, p. 6. Siegel seems to define epistemic relativism in terms of the claim about parity, but he may mean to say, as I do, that the claim is part of the argument for relativism.

7. Alternatively: If no standard can be adequately defended, then no standard is authoritative; if virtually any standard can be defended as well as a standard that is admittedly authoritative, then any of these standards is authoritative.

8. See the excerpts in Annas and Barnes (1985).

9. Relativists, we have said, apply verificationism to standards, saying the mark of the correctness of a standard is its defensibility. Suppose they apply verificationism to truth itself, saying that (ideally) defensible claims are true (Putnam 1978). Then, by altering the pincer argument in obvious ways, they can derive ontological relativism. (And why apply verificationism to standards and *not* to truth? It is hard to take our route to epistemic relativism without then accepting ontological relativism.) But the kind of response we offer, below, against the original pincer argument is effective against this defense of ontological relativism, too.

10. Strikingly, pluralism has the advantages adduced in favor of (speaker-centered) contextualism by its recent proponents (e.g., Lewis 1996, Cohen 1987), namely, the possibility of claiming that skepticism is avoidable if, but only if, weak enough standards are in play. The claim can also be defended by an absolutist who accepts the skeptical principle, rejected below, that an adequate defense of a claim cannot involve dialectical deadlock, but then it is self-defeating. This spurious skeptical principle is a salient source of the facial plausibility contextualist accounts of knowledge and rationality enjoy. Deadlock is wholly a matter of context: whether deadlock exists depends on what disputants take for granted. Thus it can happen that *I* am warranted in believing *p* until *you* come along and reject my mode of defending *p*, say by pointing out that I might be a brain in a vat, a possibility I do not know how to rule out. Then, whether I take the possibility seriously or not, I am no longer justified in believing *p*, unless you go away, and I ignore your doubts.

11. The previous points constitute my response to the view Peter Klein (1999) calls "infinitism".

12. I make similar points about the division of epistemic labor in Luper 1985, 1988.

13. Something else contributes to the impression that real authoritativeness is apparent authoritativeness: as we have said, we may arrive at rational beliefs about the world even if we never check our standard for authoritativeness or truth-conduciveness. (We have to check for self-support only if we are asking specifically whether it is rational to believe that our standard is self-supporting.) This can foster the illusion that the authoritativeness of our standard is not a requirement for rationality. In fact, however, authoritativeness is part of the external component of rational belief.

14. Our claim that the authoritativeness of our standard can be defended is consistent with the fact that people could be *prudentially* rational even if they do not manage their beliefs in an epistemically appropriate way. Prudential behavior is dependent upon our final goals. Someone whose highest and sole priority is (say) to live by the tenets of a cult may well find epistemic rationality inconvenient.

15. Cf. Peter Achinstein's 1962 response to Max Black 1958 in the debate over induction.

# References

Achinstein, Peter (1962). "The Circularity of a Self-supporting Inductive Argument," *Analysis* **22**: 138–141.

Annas, Julia, and Barnes, Jonathan (1985). *The Modes of Scepticism*. Cambridge: Cambridge University Press.

Armstrong, D. M. (1973). *Belief, Truth and Knowledge*. Cambridge: Cambridge University Press.

Bealer, George and Strawson, P.F. (1992). "The Incoherence of Empiricism," *The Aristotelian Society* **LXVI**: 99–137.

Black, Max (1958). "Self-Supporting Inductive Arguments," *Journal of Philosophy* **55**: 718–725.

BonJour, Laurence (1985). *The Structure of Empirical Knowledge*. Cambridge: Harvard University Press.

—— (1997). *In Defense of Pure Reason*. Cambridge; New York: Cambridge University Press.

Cohen, Stewart (1987). "Knowledge, Context, and Social Standards," *Synthese* **73**: 3–26.

Conee, Earl and Feldman, Richard (2001). "Internalism Defended," *American Philosophical Quarterly* **38**: 1–18.

Dretske, Fred (1971). "Conclusive Reasons," *Australasian Journal of Philosophy* **49**: 1–22.

—— (2003). "Skepticism: What Perception Teaches," in Luper 2003a, 105–119.

Feyerabend, Paul (1975). *Against Method*. London: Verso Press.

Field, Hartry (1982). "Realism and Relativism," *Journal of Philosophy* **79**: 553–567.

Foley, Richard (2003). "Epistemic Rationality as Immunity to Self-Criticism," *Essential Knowledge*. Steven Luper, ed. New York: Longman Press.

Goldman, Alvin (1979). "What Is Justified Belief?" in *Justification and Knowledge*. George Pappas, ed. Dordrecht: Reidel.

Harman, Gilbert (1984). "Positive versus Negative Undermining in Belief Revision," *Noûs* **18**: 39–49.

—— (1986). *Change in View*. Cambridge: MIT Press.

Hollis, Martin and Lukes, Steven (1982), eds. *Rationality and Relativism*. Cambridge: The MIT Press.

Klein, Peter (1999). "Human Knowledge and the Infinite Regress of Reasons," *Philosophical Perspectives* **13**: 297–325.

Kuhn, Thomas (1970). *The Structure of Scientific Revolutions*. Chicago: Chicago University Press, 2nd ed.

Lewis, David (1996). "Elusive Knowledge," *Australasian Journal of Philosophy* **74**. Reprinted in Luper 2003a, 183–203.

Luper, Steven (1985). "The Reliabilist Theory of Rational Belief," *The Monist* **68**: 203–226.

—— (1988). "The Knower, Inside and Out," *Synthese* **74**: 349–367.

—— (1990). "Arbitrary Reasons." *Doubting: Contemporary Perspectives on Skepticism*. Michael Roth and Glenn Ross, eds. Dordrecht: Kluwer Academic Publishers.

—— (2001). "Skepticism, Relativism, and the Sociology of Knowledge," *Facta Philosophica* **3**: 197–211.

—— (2003a). *The Skeptics*. Steven Luper, ed. Ashgate Publishing.

—— (2003b). "Indiscernability Skepticism," in Luper 2003a.

Moser, Paul (1993). *Philosophy After Objectivity*. New York: Oxford University Press.

Peirce, C.S. (1877). "The Fixation of Belief," *Popular Science Monthly* **12**: 1–15.

Popper, Karl (1959). *Logic of Scientific Discovery*. New York: Basic Books.

Putnam, Hilary (1978). *Meaning and the Moral Sciences*. London: Routledge and Kegan Paul.

Ramsey, F. P. (1931). *The Foundations of Mathematics and Other Logical Essays*. London: Routledge and Kegan Paul.

Rorty, Richard (1979). *Philosophy and the Mirror of Nature*. Princeton: Princeton University Press.

—— (1984). "Solidarity or Objectivity?" in *Post-Analytic Philosophy*. John Rajchman and Cornel West, eds. New York: Columbia University Press.

Siegel, Harvey (1987). *Relativism Refuted*. Dordrecht: D. Reidel Publishing Company.

Stich, Stephen (1988). "Reflective Equilibrium, Analytic Epistemology and the Problem of Cognitive Diversity," *Synthese* **74**: 391–413.

*Philosophical Issues, 14, Epistemology, 2004*

# SKEPTICISM, ABDUCTIVISM, AND THE EXPLANATORY GAP

Ram Neta
University of North Carolina, Chapel Hill

## I. Introduction: The Skeptical Problem and its Proposed Abductivist Solution

Since at least the time of Descartes, many epistemologists have presupposed a certain conception of the relation between the individual mind and the world around it. On this conception, the mind is known to itself in an especially intimate way. But there are things that exist independently of the mind—things like tables and chairs, say—and these "external" things are not known to the mind in this same intimate way. The mind's knowledge of these external things can be achieved, if at all, solely on the basis of its intimate knowledge of itself. Theoretical reason is the engine that converts the latter into the former. A central problem of epistemology, then, is to spell out how such reasoning operates, i.e., how the mind can acquire knowledge of external things given that it has only its intimate knowledge of itself from which to work.

We can offer a sharper characterization of this problem if we define "Cartesianism" as the conjunction of the following three theses.[1]

(1) Our knowledge of the contingent facts of the external world is justified *solely* by inference from our knowledge of our perceptual experiences.[2]

(2) Our knowledge of our perceptual experiences is non-inferential.

(3) It is possible for the very same perceptual experience to occur whether we are hallucinating or enjoying veridical perception.[3]

There are many different versions of Cartesianism, corresponding to the different ways of spelling out these three theses. But we needn't be concerned at present to distinguish the different versions of Cartesianism, for our aim is to examine a skeptical problem that can be raised within *any* version of Cartesianism; more specifically, we aim to examine one popular line of solution to that problem. The skeptical problem at issue is the problem of understanding how our perceptual experiences can furnish us with epistemic access to the contingent facts of the external world.[4] If (1) is true, then our knowledge of our own perceptual experiences provides us with the only premises we have by means of which we can come to know inferentially how things are in the external world. If (2) is true, then the range of these premises is restricted within the narrow scope of what we can know without inference. And if (3) is true, then the premises within this narrow scope do not entail the conclusions that we draw from them. And so how can we know these conclusions to be true? How can we achieve any knowledge of the external world? To answer these questions is to solve what I shall call "the problem of Cartesian skepticism".

This problem has proved difficult to solve. This is because there is no well-understood form of reasoning that will take us from introspectively known premises to our beliefs about the external world. From (3), it follows that deductive reasoning won't do the job: it is logically possible for the external world to be different without any difference in our perceptual experiences. And from (1), it follows that reasoning by induction won't do the job either: since we never have non-inferential access to the external world, we cannot directly compare our perceptual experiences with the external world, and so we cannot have the data necessary for any inductive inference from claims about our perceptual experiences to claims about the external world.[5] But if neither deductive nor inductive reasoning can justify our beliefs about the external world on the basis of introspectively known premises, then what kind of good reasoning can do so?

Philosophers have often sought to understand the epistemic situation of the ordinary person by assimilating it to the epistemic situation of the scientist. The scientist is faced with the task of developing a theory that can, among other things, explain the data. Typically, the theory posits unobservable entities or properties, and so the truth of that theory cannot be ascertained by observation alone. Rather, it can be ascertained only by inference from the data, and the inference in question will be better or worse depending, at least in part, on how well the theory explains the data. Let's call all such inferences "abductive". The whole practice of abductive inference has been subject to criticism,[6] and I do not intend to defend it here. But in what follows, I will examine and criticize a commonly proposed solution to the problem of Cartesian skepticism—a solution that presupposes that there are at least some good abductive inferences. For the sake of argument then, I intend to concede this presupposition to the proponent of this solution. If the presupposition is false, then so much the worse for the position that I will be criticizing.

Now to describe that target position. Many philosophers have attempted to solve the problem of Cartesian skepticism by assimilating our ordinary epistemic situation with respect to the external world to the epistemic situation of the scientist with respect to unobservables. Just as the scientist must draw inferences from the data in order to ascertain the truth of her theory, so too (it is alleged) we must ordinarily draw inferences from our perceptual experiences in order to form justified beliefs about the external world. The premises of the relevant inferences are just those propositions that are about our own perceptual experiences and that we know to be true in the non-inferential way mentioned in (2) above. Let's use the term "introspection" to designate this non-inferential way that we allegedly have of knowing things about our own perceptual experiences. Then, the premises of the relevant inferences are just those propositions that we know by introspection. And the rules of inference governing the relevant inferences include whatever non-deductive principles of inference scientists can reasonably employ when they draw inferences from data to theory. Such principles are generally thought to license what we have called abductive inferences, and so I'll call this the "abductivist" solution to Cartesian skepticism.[7] The abductivist claims that all of our knowledge of the external world is *ultimately* justified by abductive reasoning from introspectively known premises.[8] In other words, without any good abductive reasoning from introspectively known premises, we could have no knowledge of the external world.

Many philosophers have criticized abductivism. These critics typically make one or more of the following three points. First, we can categorize our perceptual experience only by appeal to their characteristic causes in the external world. So unless we already know their causes in the external world, we cannot know how to categorize the perceptual experiences that we're having. But the premises of the relevant abductive inference must involve categorizing the perceptual experiences that we're having. Therefore, we cannot know the premises of the relevant abductive inference unless we already have some knowledge of the external world.[9] Second, we can have no reason to regard one explanation as better than another, in any epistemically interesting sense of "better", unless we already know something about which explanations are more likely to be true than which others. But that in turn requires that we have some knowledge of how the external world works, and so our knowledge of the external world cannot all be grounded on abductive inference from our introspective knowledge.[10] And third, even if we could form our beliefs about the external world by abductive inference from our introspective knowledge of our own perceptual experiences, that is not actually how we form those beliefs. Thus their being so formed cannot be what justifies them.[11]

The abductivist can respond to all three of these criticisms. She can grant that we do not know how to formulate the premises of the relevant abductive inference, that we do not know how to formulate the criteria of explanatory goodness at work in the relevant abductive inference, and that we are not aware of making any such inference. Nonetheless, the abductivist will claim, it is an obvious fact that we have knowledge of the external world. And *the best explanation of that epistemic fact* is that our beliefs about the external world are conclusions of immensely complicated unconscious inferences to the best explanation of our perceptual experiences—inferences that begin from tacitly known premises about our perceptual experiences, and that follow hard-wired rules of abductive reasoning.[12] This explanation is not invalidated by the fact that it posits cognitive events and mechanisms of which we were not hitherto aware: positing unobservable events or mechanisms is just part of what good explanations typically do. Thus, the abductivist can appeal to an abductive inference in order to reply to all three of the main objections to abductivism.

The critic of abductivism might challenge the abductivist to specify the alleged unconscious inferences in our cognitive machinery. But I believe there is a problem with abductivism that no amount of cognitive science can fix. No matter what inferences the cognitive scientist discovers us to be making, those inferences cannot do the work that the abductivist needs them to do. Or so I'll argue here. More specifically, I'll argue that abductivism is bound to fail because it runs up against the problem of "the explanatory gap". The problem is not that our beliefs about the external world are not clearly the *best* explanation of our sensory data. The problem, rather, is that our beliefs about the external world *cannot provide any explanation at all* of our sensory data—at least not given the way in which the abductivist must conceive of our sensory data.

I can briefly outline the structure of the coming argument as follows: For a proposition p to serve as a statement of the abductivists's explanandum, it must meet these two conditions:

(a) It is introspectively known to be true, and
(b) It can be explained by a theory that comprises our beliefs about the external world.

I argue in section III below that if (a) obtains with regard to p, then thinking that p involves conceiving of the explanandum in such a way that there can't be any difference between how the explanandum is and how it appears. But, I go on to argue in section IV, "the explanatory gap" consists precisely in the fact no objective facts can explain any such explanandum. Thus, (a) and (b) are not jointly satisfiable with regard to any proposition, and no proposition can serve as a statement of the data in the abductivist's explanation.

In order to argue for this conclusion, I'll first have to provide an account of precisely what the abductivist is committed to. I'll do that in section III. I'll also have to provide an account of precisely what the problem of the explanatory gap is. I'll do that in section IV. But before undertaking either of those tasks, I'll first spend section II addressing a concern that some devoted abductivists may have, namely, that abductivism is just plain common sense, and so no complicated philosophical argument could possibly serve to refute it.

## II. Abductivism and Common Sense

The abductivist solution says that the best explanation of our having the perceptual experiences that we have is that the external world is roughly the way we believe it to be. This might seem to be mere common sense. When I look out my window at the ocean on a cloudy day, I have a certain visual experience, and the best explanation of my having that particular visual experience is not that I am being deceived by an evil genius, or that I am being electrochemically stimulated by neuroscientists. Rather, it is that I am looking out my window at the ocean on a cloudy day. Isn't this just common sense? Well, it depends upon what we mean when we speak of "visual experience", or more generally, of "perceptual experiences". On some interpretations of that term, it is just common sense to say that the best explanation of our having the perceptual experiences that we have is that the external world is roughly the way we believe it to be. But on those same interpretations, I'll argue, we can't have introspective knowledge of what our perceptual experiences are. On other interpretations of the term "perceptual experience", we can have introspective knowledge of what our perceptual experiences are. But on those same interpretations, common sense is silent on the issue of how to explain the occurrence of such experiences. Either way, the abductivist solution receives no support from common sense. I'll devote the present section to spelling out this argument. I should make it clear that I will *not* attempt to argue against abductivism in this section. The only conclusion that I will attempt to defend in this section is that abductivism is not mere common sense.

What do we mean when we speak of "perceptual experiences"? Could we mean to be denoting whatever things make true such sentences such as "I see the ocean", "she heard the doorbell", "he tasted the curry", and so on? These sentences all ascribe a certain kind of perceptual success to the subject. For me to see the ocean, the ocean must really be there. For her to hear the doorbell, the doorbell must really have rung, and so on. Such things then, don't satisfy the Cartesian constraint (3), i.e., that it is logically possible for our perceptual experiences to occur just as they do occur whether we are hallucinating or enjoying veridical perception. Could we then be using the term "perceptual experience" to mean whatever things make true such sentences as "the ocean looks blue to me", "the doorbell sounds broken to her", "the curry tasted good to him", and so on? Again, this won't do. For although such sentences do not ascribe perceptual success to the subject, they imply that she enjoys such success. For the ocean to look blue to me, I must see the ocean, and so the ocean must really be there. For the doorbell to sound broken to her, she must hear the doorbell, and so the doorbell must really have rung, and so on. And so again, such things don't satisfy the Cartesian constraint (3).

It may seem that we can avoid these problems by agreeing to use the term "perceptual experiences" to mean whatever things make true such sentences as the following: "It looks to me as if there is a blue ocean before me", "it sounds to her as if a doorbell has rung", "it tastes to him as if there is curry here", etc.[13] These sentences do not ascribe any perceptual success to the subject, nor do they imply that the subject enjoys such success. It can look to me as if there is a blue ocean before me even if there are no oceans, and no blue objects, anywhere. It can sound to her as if a doorbell has rung even if there are no doorbells anywhere. Are these the perceptual experiences of which the Cartesian speaks?

Here the answer is a bit more complicated. To use our introspective knowledge of our own perceptual experiences in reasoning to our beliefs about the external world, we must at least understand the premises of that reasoning: If we don't understand the premises of some bit of reasoning, then, whether that reasoning is conscious or not, we cannot be justified in believing the conclusion of that reasoning. Being justified in believing the conclusion of our reasoning requires at least that we understand the premises. In this case, understanding those premises requires understanding which perceptual experiences we're having. And if our understanding of which perceptual experiences we're having is captured in sentences of the form "it looks as if . . ." and "it sounds as if . . .", then the blanks in those sentence forms must be filled in using clauses that we understand. For if we don't understand the embedded clauses, then of course we won't understand the sentences that embed them. But if the sentences that result by filling in these blanks with those embedded clauses are *true*, then the embedded clauses express (at least some of) the content of the perceptual experiences mentioned by these sentences. That's just how the operators "it looks as if . . .", "it sounds as if . . ." are supposed to work: they function to attribute those perceptual experiences (at least part of) the content of which is expressed by the embedded clauses. And if we can understand the content expressed by the embedded clauses, then that content is conceptual.[14] In short, if our perceptual experiences are the experiences that we ascribe to ourselves using such sentence forms as "it looks as if . . ." and "it sounds as if . . .", and we can use our knowledge of those premises in reasoning to justified beliefs about the external world, then those experiences must have at least some conceptual content (whether or not they also have any non-conceptual content). And this fact generates a problem for the present way of trying to understand the abductivist's use of the term "perceptual experiences".

To see what the problem is, consider the difference between what happens to me when I taste a 1995 Woodbridge Riesling and what happens to an expert wine taster as she tastes the same wine. It tastes to her as if this is a 1995 Woodbridge Riesling, but it doesn't taste that way to me. It tastes to me as if I'm drinking white wine, or at best Riesling, but it doesn't taste to me as if I'm drinking 1995 Woodbridge Riesling, since I can't gustatorily discriminate 1995 Woodbridge Riesling from other Rieslings—probably not even from other white wines. My powers of gustatory discrimination are capable of improvement in this respect: I could come to acquire the relevant gustatory discriminatory power. But to acquire this power I would at least need to know what 1995 Woodbridge Riesling tastes like. And to know that fact is to know a contingent fact about the external world. So, in order for it to taste to me as if this is 1995 Woodbridge Riesling, I would have to know a contingent fact about the external world. But then from the premise "it tastes to me as if this is 1995 Woodbridge Riesling", I can deduce that 1995 Woodbridge Riesling tastes like *that* (ostending the same thing that I was ostending in the premise). And it is a contingent fact about the external world that 1995 Woodbridge Riesling tastes like that. Thus, if my knowledge of this premise were introspective, then I could use this bit of introspective knowledge to deduce a contingent conclusion about the external world. But recall that the abductivist is committed to denying the possibility of our having any knowledge of contingent facts of the external world solely on the basis of deduction from introspectively known premises. The abductivist is thereby committed to *not* using the term "perceptual experiences" to denote those things that make true sentences of the form "it looks as if . . . ", "it sounds as if . . . ", "it smells as if . . . ", etc.[15]

The same problem affects various other proposals on behalf of the abductivist. Consider the proposal that the abductivist is using the term "perceptual experience" to denote those things that make true sentences of the form "this looks like . . . ", "this sounds like . . . ", and so on. This proposal runs into the same problem: what can look like what to me depends in part upon what I know about the external world. I cannot know that this looks like quartz unless I know what quartz looks like. I cannot know that this tastes like Kashkaval cheese unless I know what Kashkaval cheese tastes like. And so on.[16]

I propose the following admittedly controversial diagnosis of what's gone wrong in each of the last two proposals. In each case, we're trying to interpret "perceptual experience" as denoting mental events that have conceptual content. But what concepts a person has—and so what conceptual contents their mental events can have—depends in part upon what that person knows. And more specifically, it depends upon what she knows about the external things that she perceives. That, I suggest, is why conceptually contentful perceptual experiences cannot provide the basis for all of my knowledge of the external world.

But we need not accept this controversial diagnosis of what's gone wrong in the last two proposals in order to accept the general lesson of the preceding survey of failed proposals. The general lesson of that survey was the following: the abductivist is *not* using the term "perceptual experiences" to denote those things that make true the sentences that we ordinarily use to ascribe perceptual states. (Either that is because the abductivist is using the term to denote things that cannot be ascribed in ordinary terms, or else it is because she is using the term to denote things that can be ascribed in ordinary terms only by means of sentences so complicated that they could not express the content of any of our ordinary beliefs.) And why should we have thought otherwise? Ordinary language is designed for ordinary purposes, and there's no reason why we should expect philosophically interesting categories to be captured therein. Better for the abductivist not to worry about finding ordinary language that ascribes just the kinds of occurrences that she means to include in the extension of her term "perceptual experiences". Let the abductivist pursue this strategy then.

But in that case her claim that the best explanation of our having the perceptual experiences that we have is that the external world is roughly the way we believe it to be is unmasked as something other than mere common sense. That claim seems to be mere common sense if we think that the abductivist is using the phrase "perceptual experience" to denote things that we ordinarily talk and think about. But now it turns out that the abductivist is best understood as using the phrase "perceptual experience" in a theoretical way. And if we have to use theoretical terms just to *state* the abductivist thesis, then abductivism cannot be mere common sense. Rather, it's a philosophical thesis in need of defense. But, as I will argue in the next three sections, abductivism cannot receive the defense that it requires.

### III. Appearance and Reality; Objectivity and Subjectivity

So far, the only thing that I have argued for is this: abductivism is not a piece of common sense, but rather a philosophical thesis in need of defense. Specifically, it is a philosophical attempt to solve the problem of Cartesian skepticism without rejecting any of the tenets of Cartesianism. In this section, I'll begin to consider whether abductivism can actually work.

Let's begin by trying to figure out why the abductivist, or anyone else for that matter, is concerned to solve the problem of Cartesian skepticism. Why not just give up one or more of the Cartesian tenets that generate that skeptical problem? Why should anyone be willing to endorse the tenets of Cartesianism in the first place? Evidently, Cartesianism has seemed plausible to many generations of philosophers, and there must be a reason why it has seemed so. In this section, I will suggest an explanation of the plausibility of Cartesianism. I will do so in order to show what it is that the Cartesian must want from a solution to the problem of Cartesian skepticism. It will eventually turn out that what the Cartesian must want from such a solution is something that the abductivist cannot give her.

I will suggest here that the best explanation for the fact that a philosopher finds Cartesianism plausible is that she accepts certain philosophical assumptions (to be specified below). I take it that the abductivist finds Cartesianism plausible, else why would she be committed to solving the problem of Cartesian skepticism without rejecting any of the tenets of Cartesianism? And so, I conclude that the abductivist accepts the philosophical assumptions at issue. I will now begin to spell out just what these assumptions are.

Cartesianism tells a particular story about what gives us knowledge of the external world. This story says that our knowledge of the external world is inferentially justified by our introspective knowledge of our own perceptual experiences, whereas our introspective knowledge of our own perceptual experiences is not inferentially justified by anything else. But what explanation can the Cartesian offer for the putative fact that there is this difference between our epistemic access to the external world and our epistemic access to our own perceptual experiences? If our knowledge of the external world is inferential, then why, according to the Cartesian, isn't our introspective knowledge of our own perceptual experiences *also* inferential? If I can have non-inferential knowledge of my own perceptual experiences, then why can't I also have non-inferential knowledge of the tables and chairs around me?

To answer these questions, let's begin by noting that there's a sense in which the external world can vary independently of any variation in how it appears to us. The sense in which it "can" so vary is the following. Let S's belief that p be a belief about some contingent fact of the external world. Then, normally, "p" does not imply "it appears to S as if p", nor does the latter imply the former. To illustrate, consider the following two lists:

| | |
|---|---|
| John is running down the street | It appears to me as if John is running down the street |
| I have hands | It appears to Sally as if I have hands |
| There is a tree in the backyard | It appears to Harry as if there is a tree in the backyard |

None of the propositions expressed in the first list implies the corresponding proposition in the second list, nor do any of the propositions expressed in the second list imply the corresponding proposition in the first list. We might put this point by saying that external things are "objective": how they are is logically independent of how they appear.

But this way of putting things is not entirely clear. For what do we mean when we speak of how external things "are", as opposed to how they "appear"? Suppose there is a tomato in front of me. There are lots of true propositions about the tomato. For instance, it's true that the tomato is red. It's also true that the tomato looks red, whether or not there's any observer around for it to look red to. And it's also true that the tomato looks red to me now. Intuitively, the first of these three propositions counts as fact about how the tomato is. But does the second proposition count as a fact about how the tomato is, or how it appears? And if the third proposition counts as a fact about how the tomato appears, then why doesn't it also count as a fact about how the tomato *is*? How do we draw the reality/appearance distinction with respect to the tomato, or with respect to external things in general?

Any way of drawing the distinction is going to involve a lot of complexity. To illustrate, suppose we pick this simple way of drawing the distinction: a proposition about how a thing x *appears* is a proposition expressed by a statement of the form "it appears to S as if p", where "p" expresses a proposition about x. (I can spell out what I mean by saying that "p" expresses a proposition *about* x as follows: "p" is a clause that contains a term referring to x in referentially transparent position and in logically ineliminable occurrence.) If this is how we demarcate the class of propositions concerning how things appear, then it seems that some propositions about how external things *are* do imply propositions about how they appear. For instance, consider the proposition "the tomato is seen by me to be red". Given how we've just chosen to explicate the appearance/reality distinction, this does not count as a proposition about how the tomato appears. But it implies that the tomato appears red to me. So this is a case in which a proposition about how an external thing is implies a proposition about how it appears. Any attempt to draw the appearance/reality distinction in such a way as to sustain our claim that external things are objective is going to be complicated.

Still, there is obviously *some* truth to the claim that external things are objective. What the last two paragraphs have shown is that it's not entirely clear how to spell out the truth in this claim in a precise and yet general way. But for purposes of this paper, this doesn't matter very much. Rather than fix on a precise way of specifying the truth in the claim that external things are objective, I propose that we rest content with the following vague claim: the propositions that we *normally* entertain about how external things are do not logically imply any of the propositions that we *normally* entertain about how they appear to us, or vice-versa. Rather than say that external things are "objective", we will instead say that we normally "*conceive of them* objectively", i.e., we entertain propositions about how they are which do not entail any propositions about how they appear to us, and vice-versa. I will henceforth use the term "objective" to refer to this feature of our way of thinking about external things. To put the point in terms provided by Williamson 2000: normally, when we think about external things, we are not cognitively "at home".[17]

To say that we conceive of external things objectively is then to say at least this much: it is conceivable for us that external things are not the way that they appear to us to be. But then, in order for us to have knowledge of the external world, it may seem that we must have some epistemic basis for preferring our actual beliefs about the external world to alternative hypotheses on which the external world is not the way that it appears to us to be. (I say *it may seem* this way because I do not want to be committed to its actually being this way. I will return to this point in the last section, when I attempt to locate the error in the present line of thinking.) The abductivist appeals to abductive inference to provide such a basis: we have an epistemic basis to prefer our actual beliefs about the external world to alternative hypotheses because the contents of our actual beliefs provide a better explanation of our perceptual experience than do the contents of the alternative hypotheses.

There is a role for abductive inference to play here only because our beliefs about external things involve our conceiving of external things objectively. In contrast—according to the Cartesian—we do not conceive of our perceptual experiences objectively. In other words, on the Cartesian view, the following is not conceivable: our own perceptual experiences are not the way they appear to be.[18] Knowing how our perceptual experiences appear to us is not a different state than knowing how they are, assuming that it even makes sense to speak of their "appearing" to us at all. And so there is no conceivable skeptical hypothesis that is such that we need to have some epistemic basis to disprefer it to our actual introspective beliefs in order for us to have introspective knowledge of our own perceptual experiences.[19] Thus, although the abductivist takes herself to have a reason to appeal to abductive inference to explain our knowledge of the external world, she cannot have that same reason to appeal to abductive inference to explain our introspective knowledge of our own perceptual experiences. Absent some other reason to appeal to inference in order to explain our introspective knowledge of our own perceptual experiences, the abductivist has no reason to claim that our introspective knowledge of them is inferential.[20]

Thus, on my interpretation, the abductivist thinks of the difference between our epistemic access to the external world and our epistemic access to our own perceptual experience as resulting from the following two facts. First, when we form our beliefs about external things on the basis of perception, we conceive of those things objectively. In other words, our perceptual beliefs about how they are don't imply any of the propositions that we normally entertain about how they appear, or vice-versa. In contrast, when we form our beliefs about our own perceptual experiences on the basis of introspection, we do not conceive of those experiences objectively. To mark this difference, I'll say that we normally conceive of our perceptual experiences "subjectively".[21] Or, to adopt once again the vocabulary of

Williamson 2000, when we think about our perceptual experiences, we are cognitively "at home".

I do not say that the abductivist *must* claim all this. It would not be *inconsistent* with the basic tenets of abductivism to give an alternative answer to the question of what it is that accounts for the difference between our epistemic access to external things and our epistemic access to our own perceptual experiences. But what alternative is there? Since I don't know of any plausible answer to this question, I take it that the abductivist accepts the view that I have attributed to her.

In this section, I have offered an interpretation of the abductivist's philosophical motivations, and this interpretation will be crucial to my argument against abductivism. For what my argument will show is that, given this motivation, there is no abductive argument that can do what the abductivist wants it to do: there is no abductive argument that can solve the problem of Cartesian skepticism. That is precisely what I go on to argue in section IV.

## IV. The Explanatory Gap (between Objectively Conceived Causes and Subjectively Conceived Effects)

On my interpretation, the abductivist claims that the difference between our epistemic access to the external world and our epistemic access to our own perceptual experience results from the following fact: we conceive of external things objectively (so that there is a possible gap between how they appear and how they are), but we conceive of our own perceptual experiences subjectively (so that there is no such possible gap). The abductivist also claims that the contents of our beliefs about the external world provide a better explanation of our own perceptual experiences than do the contents of various conceivable skeptical hypotheses. *A fortiori*, the abductivist is committed to claiming that the content of our beliefs about the external world provides *some* explanation of our own perceptual experiences. In this section, I will argue that the abductivist cannot consistently claim all of this. And the reason that she cannot consistently claim all of this has to do with what philosophers of mind have called "the explanatory gap". In spelling out this argument, I will have to spell out what I take the explanatory gap to be. In order to do this, let's begin with some general and familiar points about the nature of explanation.

Note that there may be many ways to explain the same effect. This is partly because the same effect may have many different causes. But it is also partly because we can ask many different questions about the same effect. For instance, say that the hurricane knocked down the house. Now we may ask different "why?" questions about the effect, the knocking down of the house. For instance, "why did the hurricane knock down the house (as opposed to the tent)?" or "why did the hurricane knock down the house (as opposed to lifting it up into the air)?" Each of these questions requires a different answer than the other, but each of these answers is an explanation of the same effect, namely, the knocking down of the house.[22]

So we can ask different "why" questions about the same effect. But one specific way in which "why?" questions about the same effect can differ is that they can involve different ways of conceiving of that effect. Thus, I might conceive of a particular effect as *Jones's* sitting down, or as the tallest person in the room sitting down. Then, I might ask "why did Jones sit down?", and the answer to this question does not, by itself, answer the question "why did the tallest person in the room sit down?" To answer the latter question, we should at least have to add this bit of information to our answer to the former question: that Jones *is* the tallest person in the room. To explain an effect is always to explain it *as conceived in one or another way*.[23]

Now what does all this have to do with abductivism? The abductivist claims that the contents of our beliefs about the external world collectively constitute an explanation of our perceptual experiences. But the premises of the abductivist's inference—the statements of the effects to be explained by the abductive inference—are all supposed to be known by introspection. Thus, the abductivist is committed to claiming that the content of our beliefs about the external world can explain our perceptual experiences *as conceived by introspection*. Now, we have already said (in section III) that we introspectively conceive of our perceptual experiences subjectively. But can we explain our perceptual experiences *so conceived*?

Keep in mind what such an explanation would involve. If our perceptual experiences were non-physical phenomena, then it would be quite mysterious how they could be explained by appeal to contingent facts about the external world. The abductivist should not, then, allow that our perceptual experiences are non-physical phenomena. So let's grant, for the sake of argument, that our perceptual experiences are physical phenomena, and let's also grant, for the sake of argument, that we know how to explain those physical phenomena. This still wouldn't be the kind of explanation that the abductivist needs. For recall, the kind of explanation that the abductivist needs is an explanation of perceptual experiences conceived in such a way that there can't conceivably be any difference between their actually being that way and their merely appearing to be that way. That is, the abductivist needs an explanation of perceptual experiences conceived *subjectively*.

Is it possible to give an explanation of phenomena *so conceived*?[24] According to the Cartesian, our knowledge of the explanans propositions of our explanation is *inferential* knowledge: we gain knowledge of the external world *only* by means of inference to the best explanation of our perceptual experience. If we were to conceive of our explanans (i.e., the external world) subjectively, then we should be able to know our explanans non-inferentially, just as know our explanandum (i.e., our perceptual experiences) non-inferentially. Since the Cartesian claims that we cannot know our explanans non-inferentially, she is committed (on the interpretation that I've advanced in section III above) to claiming that we do not conceive of our explanans subjectively. Thus, we must conceive of our explanans objectively. That is, we conceive of our explanans (i.e., the external world) in such a way that there is a potential gap between how it appears and how it is, although we conceive of our explanandum (i.e., our perceptual experiences) in such a way that there is no such potential gap. But now we must ask: *is it possible to explain a subjectively conceived effect by appeal to an objectively conceived cause?*

Let's consider what light can be shed on this question by contemporary philosophical accounts of explanation. There are many different accounts available, but most of these accounts fall into two broad schools of thought: according to one school, explanation involves locating effects within causal processes;[25] according to the other school, explanation involves unification of natural phenomena.[26] (I leave aside, for the moment, the old Hempelian account of explanation, according to which explanations are arguments.[27] In section V, I will consider an objection to the present line of argument, an objection which appeals to such Hempelian accounts of explanation.) On the "causalist" account, explanation involves conceiving of the explanandum as a part of a causal process in nature; on the "unificationist" account, it involves conceiving of the explanandum in a hierarchy of more or less general regularities in nature. But on either account, to explain an explanandum involves conceiving of that explanandum as part of a process or a regularity that is *objectively conceived.* That is, we conceive of how the process or the regularity is in such a way as to imply nothing about how it appears to us, or vice-versa.

To locate an explanandum within an objectively conceived order of processes or regularities involves conceiving of that explanandum objectively. And this is something that we do not do when we conceive of that explanandum subjectively, e.g., through introspection. We can conceive of something objectively or we can conceive of it subjectively, but these are necessarily different ways of conceiving of that thing. Explanation, I've just argued, necessarily involves conceiving of the explanandum objectively; introspection, according to the abductivist, involves conceiving of it subjectively. So, while we can explain a phenomenon objectively conceived, we cannot explain that same phenomenon introspectively (i.e., subjectively) conceived. If the phenomena that we conceive of subjectively are identical to phenomena that we conceive of objectively, then we can explain those same phenomena conceived of objectively. But we cannot introspectively know those phenomena under their objective description, and so the truths that we explain are not identical with the truths that we intro-spectively know. This seems to me to be the best way of spelling out the point that recent philosophers of mind have been gesturing at when they speak of the "explanatory gap".[28] Thus, I will say that the explanatory gap results from the impossibility of explaining phenomena subjectively conceived.

This argument against the abductivist should immediately provoke the following objections:

*Objection 1.* If that's what the explanatory gap is, then it should be easy to overcome it. If we already have an explanation of our phenomenon objectively conceived, then we can simply conjoin to our explanans the claim that the phenomenon objectively conceived (as, say, the firing of C-fibers) is identical to the phenomenon subjectively conceived (as, say, this particular quale). Won't that give us an explanation of the phenomenon subjectively conceived?

*Reply.* Conjoining our explanans with the identity claim in question will give us the desired explanation only if the "explanatoriness" of our expla-nans is preserved by conjoining the identity claim. *But conjoining an identity claim will preserve explanatoriness only if we can understand how that identity claim could itself be true.* If we take a perfectly good explanans, and conjoin it with a completely baffling identity claim (e.g. aluminum is identical to little purple dinosaurs), then the resulting conjunction is no longer explana-tory. Now what's involved in understanding how an identity claim can be true? For us to understand how it can be true that water is identical to $H_2O$, we need to understand how it is that $H_2O$ can produce the characteristic appearances of water. For us to understand how it can be true that tem-perature of a gas is identical to its mean molecular kinetic energy, we need to understand how it is that mean molecular kinetic energy can produce the characteristic appearances of temperature in a gas. Analogously, for us to understand how a particular phenomenon objectively conceived (as, say, the firing of C-fibers) could be identical to a particular phenomenon subjectively conceived (as, say, a particular quale), we would have to under-stand how the phenomenon objectively conceived could give rise to the appearances of the phenomenon subjectively conceived. Why does the firing of C-fibers feel that way, rather than some other way? Why does eating a peach produce that taste sensation, rather than some other?[29] But, by the argument just given, these are questions that we cannot answer—at least, not if feels and sensations are subjectively conceived (so that there can be no gap between how they appear and how they are). We cannot have an explanation of appearances so conceived, because explanation involves conceiving of its explanandum objectively, whereas we conceive of appear-ances subjectively when we conceive of them *as appearances.*

*Objection 2.* It may be objected that I have been placing unreasonably high demands on explanation.[30] Suppose that we have a perfectly good causal explanation of all of our neurochemical activity, and furthermore we somehow come to know that certain neurochemical processes constitute, or are identical with, certain perceptual experiences. Wouldn't this supply us with a perfectly adequate explanation of our perceptual experiences? Couldn't a perfectly adequate explanation appeal to constitutive claims or identity claims which are such that we do not understand how they could be true? Couldn't there be some mechanisms—however mysterious they may be to us—whereby certain neurochemical processes produce one perceptual experience rather than another? And couldn't we somehow come to know what those mechanisms are? Maybe God tells us about them.

*Reply.* I leave it open, for the sake of argument, that this is possible. Maybe God will one day reveal to us the mechanisms whereby certain neurochemical processes produce certain perceptual experiences, and then we will know the correct answer to the question "why do we have these perceptual experiences, rather than some others?" But notice that, in the scenario that I've just described, we gain knowledge of these mechanisms in some way *other than* by inference to the best explanation of our perceptual experiences. The explanatory virtues of the divinely-revealed causal story are not what justify us in believing that causal story, for by hypothesis that causal story *has no explanatory virtues*. If we come to know the truth of that causal story, our knowledge cannot be acquired by inference to the best explanation. And so, even if there is a true and knowable story about how our perceptual experiences (subjectively conceived) are produced by our neurochemical processes (objectively conceived), our knowledge of this story—our justification for believing it—cannot be based on abductive inference. And so this possibility is, once again, of no help to the abductivist.

*Objection 3.* It may be objected that the problem that I'm raising for the abductivist is really a problem for any explanation whatsoever, and so not really a problem at all. Whenever we explain any phenomenon, our explanation will itself invite further "why?" questions that we don't know how to answer. When Newton explained the motions of the planets by appeal to gravity, he was positing one mystery (gravity) to explain another (celestial and terrestrial motions). When Darwin explained the origin of species by appeal to natural selection, he was positing one mystery (the heritability of traits) to explain another (the origin of species). How is the abductivist's proposed explanation any worse than Newton's or Darwin's?

*Reply.* I am *not* claiming that the abductivist's "explanation" invites futher "why?" questions that we don't know how to answer. That much is of course true of many excellent explanations. Rather, I am claiming that the abductivist's "explanation" is not an explanation at all, because it doesn't locate its subjectively conceived explanandum within any objectively conceived explanans (be it a causal process or a natural regularity). While Newton left us with plenty of questions about gravity, at least he gave us the inverse square law of gravitational attraction, thereby locating the effects of gravity within an objectively conceived order. While Darwin left us with plenty of questions about the mechanisms of heritability and of variation, at least he gave us reason to predict that heritability and variation would alter species, and thereby located the effects of heritability and variation within an objectively conceived order. For the abductivist to do something analogous, she'd have to locate our subjectively conceived perceptual experiences within an objectively conceived order. But that's exactly what she cannot do, *while she conceives of those experiences subjectively*. And if she conceives of them objectively instead, then she can't know them introspectively under that description. Either way, she can't explain the very same truths that she introspectively knows. She can explain one set of truths. She can introspectively know another set of truths. But she cannot explain the same truths that she introspectively knows.

*Objection 4.* Apart from what philosophers tell us about the nature of explanation, aren't there obviously good explanations of our introspectible experiences? To illustrate: I am now feeling nervous *because* I just had a mental image of falling from a great height. Isn't this a perfectly good explanation, whether or not it fits into the mold described by any of the current philosophical accounts of explanation? If it is a perfectly good explanation (as it seems to be), then doesn't this tell against my "explanatory gap" argument against abductivism?

*Reply.* In the example that I've just described, either my knowledge of the explanans is inferential knowledge or it is not. If it is inferential knowledge (gained, say, through some form of psychological theorizing about myself), then I am not conceiving of the explanans subjectively, and the explanans can appear to be other than it is: my inference could have led me to the wrong conclusion. If it is not inferential knowledge (if, say, it is gained directly through introspection), then I am conceiving of the explanans subjectively, and the explanans cannot appear to be other than it is. Either way, I am not bridging the gap between subjectively conceived explanandum and objectively conceived explanans by appeal to inference to the best explanation. And so the perfectly good explanation above cannot serve as a model for the kind of explanation that the abductivist needs to offer: an explanation in which a subjectively conceived explanandum is explained by appeal to an objectively conceived explanans.

Here's a modification of the case just described: I acquire knowledge of the explanans inferentially at first, and then I am able to retain that knowledge introspectively, since my powers of introspection are improved by the initial inference. In this modified case, the abductivist story still cannot be right about either stage of the process. In the first stage, I conceive of the explanans objectively. If, however, I conceive of the explanandum subjectively, then my initial knowledge of the explanans cannot be based on inference to the best explanation, but must be gained by means of some other inference. In the second stage, my knowledge of the explanans is non-inferential. Either way, my knowledge of the explanans is not based on inference to the best explanation. And so this new case also cannot be of any use to the abductivist.

*Objection 5.* If explanation is contrastive, then there's a difference between explaining why I'm having this experience *now* (as opposed to some other time) and explaining why I'm now having *this experience* (as opposed to some other experience). Even if the explanatory gap argument shows that the second kind of explanation is impossible, it still doesn't show that the first kind of explanation is impossible.[31]

*Reply.* We can grant this, but it doesn't help the abductivist. For it shows only that the abductivist can appeal to hypotheses about the external world in order to explain why our experiences happen at the times at which they happen. It doesn't show that the abductivist can appeal to hypotheses about the external world in order to explain anything else about our experiences. But if *all* that the abductivist seeks to explain is why our experiences happen at the times at which they happen, and there's nothing else about our experiences that the abductivist seeks to explain, then the abductivist's explanandum obviously massively underdetermines her explanans. In fact, the situation is even worse than this. For according to the present objection, the fact that we have perceptual experiences *with various intrinsic qualities* is completely irrelevant to what the abductivist seeks to explain. The abductivist's explanandum could just as easily be stated as follows: "something is happening *now* (ostending a particular moment), and something else is happening *now* (ostending a later moment), and something else is happening *now* (ostending a still later moment)," and so on. If that's all that we want to explain, then we could explain it in countless different ways, and without resorting to all the explanatorily useless detail of our beliefs about the external world. Most of our beliefs about the external world would turn out to be explanatorily useless if this were all that the abductivist sought to explain.

Of course, the explanatory gap, as I have described it, is a gap that obtains only between phenomena objectively conceived and phenomena subjectively conceived. I have assumed that there are some phenomena of which we can conceive subjectively, but I have made this assumption only because, as I argued in section III, this assumption is part of the only motivation to be a Cartesian, and so I infer that the Cartesian must be committed to this assumption. And I have granted this assumption to the Cartesian for the sake of argument. Now, I don't see any compelling reason to believe that there are phenomena of which we can conceive subjectively (as I've defined the phrase above), and so I don't see any reason to think that there is any real explanatory gap. Nevertheless, I shall not try to argue for that controversial claim here. For now, my conclusion is just this: *if* the Cartesian's assumptions are granted, *then* there is an explanatory gap. But *if* there is an explanatory gap, *then* the abductivist solution to Cartesian skepticism won't work. In sum, if the Cartesian's assumptions are granted, then the abductivist solution won't work. And so abductivism cannot do the work that it was designed to do—namely, to solve the problem of Cartesian skepticism without rejecting any of the tenets of Cartesianism.

## V. Can the Abductivist Avoid the Problem of the Explanatory Gap?

Here is a summary of my argument so far:

For a proposition p to serve as a statement of the data to be explained by the abductivists's explanation, it has to meet at least these two conditions:

(a) It is introspectively known to be true, and
(b) It can be explained by a theory that comprises our beliefs about the external world.

But if (a) obtains with regard to p, then thinking that p involves conceiving of an effect subjectively, and so there's an explanatory gap between p and our beliefs about the external world. Thus, (a) and (b) are not jointly satisfiable with regard to any proposition, and no proposition can serve as a statement of the data in the abductivist's explanation. Thus, no abductive inference can do what the abductivist needs for it to do.

There are two ways in which the abductivist may wish to avoid the problem posed by this argument. Let's consider each of them in turn:

(1) It may seem that the abductivist can bypass the problem of the explanatory gap by adopting an alternative account of explanation, an account according to which for a theory to explain some data is just for that data to be inferable from the theory. How might this help the abductivist? It might help if the abductivist claims that our theory of the external world includes not just propositions about contingent features of that world, but also bridge principles connecting features of the external world with subjectively conceived features of our perceptual experience. These

bridge principles would state that certain features of the external world cause the occurrence of such-and-such perceptual experiences, subjectively conceived. The total theory that comprised such bridge principles, along with other claims about the external world, might be thought to explain our introspectively known data by virtue of entailing or probabilifying the content of that introspective knowledge. Thus, the abductivist might claim to have constructed a schema for a theory of the external world that explains our perceptual experiences, subjectively conceived.

Let's set aside whatever worries we might have about this inferentialist account of explanation, and ask whether, granting such an account of explanation, this maneuver can save the abductivist. It may at first seem that it can't, since, by varying our theory of the external world and making compensating adjustments in our bridge principles, this very same maneuver can be employed to construct infinitely many mutually incompatible explanations of the same body of introspected data. And since the abductivist claims that our only source of evidence about the external world is our introspected data, she cannot appeal to any other evidence to favor any one of these theories to any other. But this is just to level at the abductivist the general problem of underdetermination of theory by data, and that seems unfair since the underdetermination problem is everyone's problem.

Or is it? We normally avoid the underdetermination problem in our explanatory practice by appealing to non-evidential standards of explanatory goodness (e.g., simplicity, elegance, plausibility) to favor one explanation over empirically equivalent alternative explanations. Can the abductivist avail herself of this strategy? In order to answer this question, let's recall the familiar point that the application of such non-evidential standards in comparing theories may produce different results depending upon our choice of primitive vocabulary.[32] Let T1 and T2 be two empirically equivalent and empirically adequate theories that differ in their ontology: T1 posits stuffs but not objects, whereas T2 posits objects but not stuffs. And let C1 and C2 be two scientific communities. C1 has a primitive vocabulary that includes no referring devices other than mass nouns. Since the scientists of C1 do not employ logically primitive referring devices, they tend to be not so much interested in minimizing their ontological commitments as in minimizing the number of logically independent principles of their theories. C2, on the other hand, has a primitive vocabulary that includes no referring devices other than count nouns. The scientists of C2 are not so much interested in minimizing the number of logically independent principles of their theories as they are in minimizing their ontological commitments. In this case, the scientists of C1 might be entitled to regard T1 as simpler, more elegant, or more parsimonious than T2, whereas the scientists of C2 might be entitled to regard T2 as simpler, more elegant, or more parsimonious than T1. In general, which of two empirically equivalent theories we are entitled to regard as better than which other depends upon which primitive vocabulary we use, and which non-empirical virtues we look for in a theory. Thus, if the abductivist says that our theory of the external world enjoys non-evidentiary advantages over those empirically equivalent alternative theories, she is committed to using her own primitive vocabulary in applying non-evidentiary standards to our theory of the external world.

Now, when we use certain terms in thinking or speaking, we presuppose that those terms are meaningful. But most of the terms that we use have the following property: they can have a certain meaning only if the non-linguistic world is a certain way. For instance, when we use a term "F" as a count noun, we presuppose the coherence of certain principles of identity and individuation for F's. When we use a term "D" as a demonstrative, we presuppose the existence of D. And when we use a substance term X, we presuppose that there is an essence common to various samples to which the term "X" applies. If we discover that these presuppositions are false, then we must either stop using the terms in question or else use them in a different way (e.g., use the term in question as a mass noun rather than a count noun, or as a description rather than a name, etc.).[33] Thus, when we use certain terms in theorizing, or in appraising our theories, we presuppose that the world is the way that it would have to be in order for those terms to mean what we are trying to mean by them.

Now, as I said above, if the abductivist appeals to non-evidentiary standards of explanatory goodness to favor our theory of the external world over its alternatives, she is committed to using her own primitive vocabulary in the application of those standards. But using the terms of her primitive vocabulary involves presupposing that the non-linguistic world is just the way that it would have to be in order for those terms to mean what she's trying to mean by them. Is the abductivist entitled to presuppose that the non-linguistic world is this way?[34] Since the abductivist is committed to regarding all our knowledge of the external world as inferentially justified by our introspective knowledge, she cannot, by her own lights, justifiably commit herself to presuppositions about the external world unless those presuppositions are themselves inferentially justified by her introspective knowledge. But we have already granted that her introspective knowledge, by itself, cannot justify any one theory of the external world over the infinitely many alternatives to it that equally well entail or probabilify the content of that introspective knowledge. Thus, the abductivist cannot appeal to non-evidentiary standards of explanatory goodness to favor our theory of the external world over its alternatives. And so she is committed to claiming that we have no epistemic basis to favor our actual beliefs about the external world over the infinitely many incompatible alternatives to it. We normally avoid the underdetermination problem in our scientific practice by relying on what we take to be our background knowledge of the external world, but this is precisely what the abductivist cannot do.

Can the abductivist avoid the underdetermination problem by claiming that these various explanations are only *apparently* incompatible, and that their empirical equivalence reveals that they are actually just different ways of saying the same thing? This reply implies that empirically equivalent explanations are also semantically equivalent. Now, for two explanations to be empirically equivalent is for them to have all the same implications for our experience. And since our explanations posit an external world to explain our experiences, for two of these explanations to be semantically equivalent is at least for them to have all the same implications about the external world. Thus, the present reply assumes that explanations that have all the same implications for our experience have all the same implications for the way the external world is. But how could this be? Part of what makes external things *external* is just the fact that we can correctly conceive of them objectively, i.e., we can conceive of how they are in such a way as to leave it logically open how they appear to us in our experience. So the proponent of the present reply must give up the very idea that the explanations in question posit an *external* world at all. This is incompatible with Cartesianism generally, and so incompatible with abductivism specifically.

(2) The abductivist might attempt to avoid the problem of the explanatory gap by claiming that what has to be explained by the external world hypothesis are not our introspectible data, but rather *patterns* in our introspectible data. These patterns cannot be discerned solely by introspection, but only with the help of memory. That's because we must rely on memory of past introspectible data in order to discern the diachronic patterns in such data. And so the patterns to be explained by the external world hypothesis are patterns known only by the combined use of introspection and memory. Thus, the data to be explained needn't be introspectible. On this proposal, the abductivist isn't committed to there being any facts that jointly satisfy (a) and (b), since she's given up on (a). And so the preceding argument is ineffective against this new kind of abductivism.

Now let's ask the proponent of this new kind of abductivism the following question: can facts about one's own experiential past vary independently of how they now appear? For instance, can it now appear to you as if you had a particular experience yesterday, whether or not you actually did? Obviously, it can: we are frequently subject to illusory memories concerning our own experiential past. It now seems to me as if I enjoyed the taste of a Merlot yesterday, and it can seem this way to me even if I had a cold yesterday and so was unable to enjoy any gustatory experiences at all. So we conceive of our experiential past objectively. More generally, we conceive of the past objectively. Since, as we saw in section III, such objectivity in our way of conceiving of external things is what gives the Cartesian grounds for claiming that our knowledge of the external world is inferential, it should equally well give her grounds for claiming that our memory knowledge is inferential.

But then by what kind of inference are our memory-based beliefs justified? What are the premises of that inference, and what is the rule of inference? If the premises of the relevant inference are themselves known by memory, then we can raise the same question about how we have memory knowledge of them. If memory knowledge of our own experiential past is inferential, then there must be some memory knowledge that is not justified by inference from other memory knowledge, but is rather justified by inference from non-memory knowledge. But the inference in question cannot be deductive, since what we can know about the present without the help of memory does not entail any contingent facts about the past. Again, the inference in question cannot be inductive: for us to inductively infer anything about the past from what we can know about the present without the help of memory, we would need to know something about the correlation between past and present facts. But we cannot have such knowledge without already having some memory knowledge. So the same considerations that led the abductivist to say that our knowledge of the external world is abductive might now lead us to say that our memory knowledge is abductive.[35]

But now the abductivist has not avoided the problem of the explanatory gap: she has only relocated it. For now she is committed to the claim that there are good abductive inferences from introspectively known premises to conclusions about the past. The premises of such inferences must state facts that satisfy constraints (a) and (b) above. But recall the argument of the previous section: the problem of the explanatory gap implies that no fact can satisfy (a) and (b) simultaneously. And so there can be no good abductive inferences from introspectively known premises to conclusions about the past. Our memory knowledge is not abductive.[36] And so the present attempt to rescue abductivism from the problem of the explanatory gap fails. There is, it now seems, no way to save abductivism from the problem of the explanatory gap.

## VI. Conclusion

It turns out to be no accident that the abductivist cannot spell out in any detail the abductive inferences to which she appeals: it is impossible for any inferences to satisfy the constraints that the abductivist needs them to satisfy. Abductivism can't solve the problem of Cartesian skepticism.

But then how to solve the problem? The solution becomes clear if we draw a lesson from the discussion of memory knowledge in section V. We argued that memory knowledge cannot be deductively, inductively, or abductively justified by appeal to non-memory knowledge. In fact, it is utterly implausible to suppose that memory knowledge is inferential. Why should we have thought otherwise? Recall that we were led to think of memory knowledge as inferential by noticing that we conceive of the past objectively. If this is the case, then isn't it a requirement of having memory knowledge at all that we be able, without appealing to any other memory knowledge, to rule out conceivable skeptical hypotheses about the past? If the answer to this question were "yes", then we couldn't have any memory knowledge whatsoever. If we have any memory knowledge, then our knowledge of how things are, objectively conceived, needn't be inferential.

But if that's the case, then there is something wrong with the line of thinking that makes Cartesianism plausible. Recall from section III, that line of thinking goes as follows:

> It is conceivable that the external world is not the way it appears to be, but it is not conceivable that our own perceptual experiences are not the way they appear to be. So, in order for us to have knowledge of the external world, we must have some epistemic basis for preferring our actual beliefs about the external world to alternative hypotheses on which the external world is not the way it appears to be. But this is not something that we must have in order to have knowledge of our own perceptual experiences. Thus, our knowledge of our own perceptual experiences can be non-inferential, but our knowledge of the external world can only be inferential.

But we can consistently accept the premises of this reasoning without accepting the conclusion. This is just what epistemological externalists typically do: they reject the conclusion of this argument on the grounds that our epistemic basis for preferring our actual beliefs about the external world to alternative hypotheses is not an argument that we have available to us, but is rather some fact about us (say, about the reliability of our belief-forming processes, or about the counterfactual co-variation of our beliefs with the facts) of which we needn't be aware.

The point for now is that the line of thinking that makes Cartesianism plausible is not compelling. (I have elsewhere addressed the diagnostic question why has it seemed compelling to so many generations of philosophers.[37]) Cartesianism creates an insoluble skeptical problem, but there's no good reason to accept Cartesianism, and so no good reason to undertake the futile task of solving that problem. In short, the non-skeptical solution to the problem of Cartesian skepticism lies in rejecting Cartesianism altogether, and allowing that our knowledge of the external world can be as non-inferential as our introspective knowledge. We can have non-inferential knowledge even when we conceive of the objects of our knowledge objectively, i.e., even when we are not cognitively "at home".[38] We can have direct knowledge of a world that can appear to be other than it is.[39]

## Notes

1. I treat this as a *definition* of "Cartesianism" in order to avoid interesting but difficult issues concerning the correct interpretation of Descartes, or of his influence upon subsequent epistemology. Of course Descartes thought that we could have knowledge of extended substance by deduction from first principles, but then we could only know the necessary features of extended substances not its contingent features. Such issues are not relevant for present purposes.
2. It may be thought that this claim was refuted when Kripke 1980 showed that we have *a priori* knowledge of contingent facts (e.g., the length of the meter stick). But this is not true. To have the *a priori* knowledge that Kripke describes, we must already have various bits of *a posteriori* knowledge (e.g., that a particular stick has been established as the standard meter).
3. A worry: It may seem that perceptual experience A can be "the same" as perceptual experience B only if there are principles of identity for perceptual experiences. But what are these principles of identity? I will not attempt to answer this question on behalf of the Cartesian; it is her problem and not mine.
4. Henceforth, I will speak of our epistemic relations to the external world when I mean to indicate our epistemic relation to *the contingent facts* of the external world.
5. For a classic statement of the preceding argument, see Ayer 1956.
6. See van Fraassen 1980, Hacking 1982, Cartwright 1983, van Fraassen 1983. For a defense of inference to the best explanation, see Lipton 1991.
7. One or another version of abductivism is propounded in Brandt 1955, Ayer 1956, Russell 1959, Mackie 1969, Slote 1970, Harman 1973, Jackson 1977, Cornman 1980, Watkins 1984, BonJour 1985, Goldman 1988, Moser 1989, Vogel 1990, and BonJour 1999.
8. The abductivist should not be confused with Quine 1960, Sellars 1963b, or Lycan 1988, all of whom she superficially resembles. Quine takes all our knowledge of physical objects to be abductively achieved, but he also takes our knowledge of our own perceptual experiences to be abductively achieved. And so, unlike the abductivist, Quine rejects the basic tenets of Cartesianism. Sellars and Lycan take much of our knowledge of physical objects to be abductively achieved, but accept that not all such knowledge is so achieved.
9. See Sellars 1963a and Williams 1977. (Sellars uses this point in criticism of phenomenalism rather than abductivism, but the point can be adapted to work against the abductivist.) The point is also implicit in Strawson 1959, Evans 1984, Long 1992, and Cassam 1997.
10. See Chisholm 1989, Lehrer 1990, Alston 1993, Fumerton 1995, and Butcharov 1998. The point is also implicit in the attack on "the causal theory" in Price 1932.
11. See Strawson 1985.
12. Cf. Harman 1973.
13. The proposal to use such sentences to ascribe perceptual experiences (of the sort that the Cartesian wants to speak of) is in Firth 1952.
14. I've found philosophers who refuse to assent to this. But the claim strikes me as true by the definition of "conceptual". Of course, the term "conceptual" is to some extent a term of art, and we're free to use it as we like. So maybe I should

say that I'm using the term as follows: the content of a mental state is *conceptual* if and only if the possessor of that mental state has (at the time of being in the state) the ability to understand that content.

15. Chisholm 1957 would have tried to avoid this problem by saying that we might use "appears" talk "noncomparatively". But I don't have any reason to believe that we so much as understand the alleged "noncomparative" use of "appears" talk. In any case, even if we could understand it, it's clear that we do not *ordinarily* use "appears" talk noncomparatively. And so any claim that we express using "appears" noncomparatively cannot be part of the content of common sense. That is all I need for my present argument.

Burge 1979 argues that the contents of our thoughts and experiences generally depend upon factors outside the individual. If we accept this form of anti-individualism about content, then we have another argument for the conclusion that the abductivist cannot be using the term "perceptual experience" to denote events that are ordinarily ascribed by sentences of the form "it looks as if p", "it sounds as if p", etc. For if the abductivist were to use the term that way, then from my knowledge that I have such-and-such perceptual experiences I could deduce various claims about the external world.

16. What about this case: I know that a particular thing I'm seeing looks like a unicorn. Then, on the present reasoning, I must know what unicorns look like. But how can unicorns look like anything if there are no unicorns? This question doesn't pose a problem for my argument, for there *is* something that unicorns look like—namely, like horses with straight horns coming out of the middle of their heads. But since unicorns aren't real animals, the fact that this is what they look like is made the case by our standard depictions of unicorns. Analogously, there is something that Santa Claus looks like, but his looking that way is the result of our depictions of him.

17. See Williamson 1996 and Williamson 2000, ch. 4.

18. Price 1932: "in the sphere of the given (as in that of pleasure and pain), what seems, is." (10)

19. This does not imply that we are infallible, incorrigible, or omniscient about our perceptual experiences. But it does imply this: *if* we form false beliefs about our perceptual experiences, that is *not* because they appear to us to be some way that they are not.

20. The view developed in this paragraph on the abductivist's behalf is suggested by Ayer 1940, 117–34.

21. Some philosophers might claim that this is because our perceptual experiences *cannot* be thought of objectively; to think of them at all is to think of them subjectively. I take no stand on this issue here.

22. The contrastiveness of explanation has been made very familiar in the literature on explanation. See, for instance, Van Fraassen 1980 and Lipton 1991.

23. At least this is true if the effect is an event, and if events are individuated more coarsely than the propositions that state that they occurred. For more on this issue, see Davidson 1967. On the intensionality of "explains", see Williamson 2000 (195).

24. We can understand the request for such explanation in three different ways: First, we may want an explanation of why there is anything at all that has the

following property: it can't conceivably vary independently of any variation in how it appears. Why are there these subjective facts in the world? Second, we may want an explanation of why there are just these particular subjective features instantiated in the world, rather than some alternative set. For instance, what explains the fact that our perceptual experiences have qualitative features within this range, rather than some other? And third, we may want an explanation of why these particular subjective facts obtain just when they do. Why does coffee taste like *this* (referring to the taste of coffee) rather than like pizza? I don't distinguish these questions in the text, since I need not appeal to the distinction in my argument.

25. The most influential and well-developed exposition of this view is in Salmon 1984.
26. See, e.g., Friedman 1974, Kitcher 1976, and Kitcher 1993.
27. See, e.g., Hempel 1965b and the other essays in Hempel 1965a for the most influential defense of this inferentialist account of explanation.
28. See Nagel 1974, Levine 1983, McGinn 1989, Loar 1990, Searle 1992, Levine 1993, Sturgeon 1994, and Levine 2001. But the insight long antedates these philosophers. We read in Locke 1975: 'Tis evident that the bulk, figure, and motion of several Bodies about us, produce in us several Sensations, as of Colours, Sounds, Tastes, Smells, Pleasure and Pain, etc. These mechanical Affections of Bodies, having no affinity at all with those Ideas, they produce in us, (there being no conceivable connexion between any impulse of any sort of Body, and any perception of a Colour, or Smell, which we find in our Minds) we can have no distinct knowledge of such Operations beyond our Experience; and can reason no otherwise about them, than as effects produced by the appointment of an infinitely Wise Agent, which perfectly surpass our Comprehensions. (Book IV, iii. §28)
29. See Kripke 1980, Searle 1992, and Sturgeon 1994 on this point.
30. I am grateful to an anonymous referee for raising the objection in response to which the present paragraph was written.
31. Let's recall that the abductivist's explanandum must be subjectively conceived. That is, there must be no possible difference between how the explanandum is and how it appears. If the whole explanandum proposition "I'm having this experience now" is to fit this description, then the temporal indicator "now" must also fit this description. There must be no possible difference between its being now and its appearing to be now. But if that's the case, then wouldn't the explanatory gap argument given above show that it's impossible to explain why I'm having this experience now? Not quite. If we can explain why it is that e takes place now, and it's true that now = 6:48 PM on Tuesday, and adding this identity claim to our explanans preserves the explanatoriness of the explanans, then we can explain why it is that e takes place now. So, for all I've shown, it is possible for us to explain why I'm having this experience *now* (as opposed to some other time).
32. Cf. Goodman 1983 on the relative epistemic merits of the "green" and "grue" hypotheses.
33. The preceding points have been made familiar in the literature on semantic externalism. See, for instance, Putnam 1975, Burge 1979, and Kripke 1980.

34. If we regard her entitlement to this presupposition as deriving from the fact that the presupposition is built into her language, then her abductive inference from introspectively known premises to her conclusions about the external world is only justified relative to her linguistic community. But if justification relative to her linguistic community was all that the abductivist wanted, then why did she need to bother finding an abductive inference from introspectively known premises in the first place? Why couldn't she simply have appealed to the fact that, in her linguistic community, some beliefs about the external world count as justified?

35. This abductivist position concerning memory is explored in Harman 1973 and Peacocke 1986.

36. For arguments against the view that memory knowledge is, in general, inferentially justified by non-memory knowledge, see Pollock 1986, Burge 1993, Plantinga 1993, Huemer 1999, and Owens 2000.

37. See Neta 2002, Neta 2003, Neta 2004 and Neta manuscript.

38. Williamson 1996 and Williamson 2000, ch. 4 argue that we are *never* cognitively at home. His argument relies on an assumption that is criticized in Neta and Rohbaugh forthcoming.

39. I am grateful to Dorit Bar-On, Jonathan Cohen, Mark Greenberg, Thomas Hofweber, Michael Huemer, Adam Leite, William Lycan, Ron Mallon, Eric Marcus, Elijah Millgram, and Jonathan Schaffer for their very helpful comments on earlier drafts of this manuscript.

## References

Alston, William. 1993. *The Reliability of Sense Perception*. Cornell University Press: Ithaca, NY.

Ayer, A. J. 1940. *The Foundations of Empirical Knowledge*. MacMillan: London.

———. 1956. *The Problem of Knowledge*. Hammondsworth: London.

Berkeley, George. 1975. *Philosophical Works*, ed. P. H. Nidditch. Everyman's Library: London and Melbourne.

BonJour, Laurence. 1985. *The Structure of Empirical Knowledge*. Harvard University Press: Cambridge, MA.

———. 1999. "Foundationalism and the External World" in Tomberlin 1999.

Brandt, R. B. 1955. "The Epistemological Status of Memory Beliefs." *Philosophical Review* **64**: 78–95.

Burge, Tyler. 1979. "Individualism and the Mental" in French, Uehling, and Wettstein 1979.

———. 1993. "Content Preservation." *Philosophical Review* **102**: 457–88.

Butcharov, Panayot. 1998. *Skepticism About the External World*. Oxford University Press: Oxford.

Cartwright, Nancy. 1983. *How the Laws of Physics Lie*. Clarendon Press: Oxford.

Cassam, Quassim. 1997. *Self and World*. Oxford University Press: Oxford.

Chisholm, Roderick. 1957. *Perceiving: A Philosophical Study*. Cornell University Press: Ithaca, NY.

———. 1989. *Theory of Knowledge*, Third edition. Prentice-Hall: Englewood Cliffs, NJ.

Cornman, James. 1980. *Skepticism, Justification, and Explanation*. Reidel: Dordrecht.

Davidson, Donald. 1967. "Causal Relations." *Journal of Philosophy* **64**: 691–703.

Earman, John., ed. 1983. *Minnesota Studies in the Philosophy of Science, vol. 10: Testing Scientific Theories*. University of Minnesota Press: Minneapolis, MN.

Evans, Gareth. 1984. *The Varieties of Reference*. Oxford University Press: Oxford.

Firth, Roderick. 1952. "Phenomenalism." *Proceedings and Addresses of the American Philosophical Association*.

French, P. A., Uehling, T. E., and Wettstein, H. K. 1979. *Midwest Studies in Philosophy 4: Studies in Metaphysics*. University of Minnesota Press: Minneapolis, MN.

Friedman, Michael. 1974. "Explanation and Scientific Understanding." *Journal of Philosophy* **71**: 5–19.

Fumerton, Richard. 1995. *Metaepistemology and Skepticism*. Rowman and Littlefield: Lanham, MD.

Goldman, Alan. 1988. *Empirical Knowledge*. University of California Press: Berkeley and Los Angeles.

Goodman, Nelson. 1983. *Fact, Fiction and Forecast*, 4th edition. Harvard University Press: Cambridge, MA.

Gunderson, Keith, ed. 1975. *Language, Mind, and Knowledge*. University of Minnesota Press: Minneapolis, MN.

Hacking, Ian. 1982. "Experimentation and Scientific Realism." *Philosophical Topics* **13**: 111–222

Harman, Gilbert. 1973. *Thought*. Princeton University Press: Princeton, NJ.

Hempel, Carl. 1965a. *Aspects of Scientific Explanation and Other Essays in the Philosophy of Science*. Free Press: New York.

———. 1965b. "Aspects of Scientific Explanation" in Hempel 1965a.

Huemer, Michael. 1999. "The Problem of Memory Knowledge." *Pacific Philosophical Quarterly* **80**: 346–57.

Jackson, Frank. 1977. *Perception: A Representative Theory*. Cambridge University Press: Cambridge.

Kitcher, Philip. 1976. "Explanation, Conjunction, and Unification." *Journal of Philosophy* **73**: 207–12.

———. 1993. *The Advancement of Science*. Oxford University Press: Oxford.

Kripke, Saul. 1980. *Naming and Necessity*. Harvard University Press: Cambridge, MA.

Lehrer, Keith. 1990. *Theory of Knowledge*. Westview Press: Boulder, CO and San Francisco, CA.

Levine, Joseph. 1983. "Materialism and qualia: The explanatory gap." *Pacific Philosophical Quarterly* **64**: 354–61.

———. 1993. "On Leaving Out What It's Like" in Davies and Humphreys 1993.

———. 2001. *Purple Haze*. Oxford University Press: Oxford.

Lipton, Peter. 1991. *Inference to the Best Explanation*. Routledge: London.

Loar, Brian. 1990. "Phenomenal States" in Tomberlin 1990.

Locke, John. 1975. *Essay Concerning Human Understanding*, ed. P.H. Nidditch. Oxford University Press: Oxford.

Long, Douglas. 1992. "The Self-Defeating Character of Skepticism." *Philosophy and Phenomenological Research* **52**: 67–84.

Lycan, William. 1988. *Judgment and Justification*. Cambridge University Press: Cambridge.

Mackie, J. L. 1969. "What's Really Wrong with Phenomenalism?" *Proceedings of the British Academy* **55**: 113–27.

McGinn, Colin. 1989. "Can We Solve the Mind-Body Problem?" *Mind* **98**: 349–66.

Moser, Paul. 1989. *Knowledge and Evidence*. Cambridge University Press: Cambridge.

Nagel, Thomas. 1974. "What Is it Like to be a Bat?" *Philosophical Review* **83**: 435–50.

Neta, Ram. 2002. "S knows that p." *Nous* **36**: 663–81.

———. 2003. "Contextualism and the Problem of the External World." *Philosophy and Phenomenological Research* **66**: 1–31.

———. 2004. "Perceptual Evidence and the New Dogmatism." *Philosophical Studies* **119**: 199–214.

———. Manuscript. "How to Raise and Lower the Veil of Ideas."

Neta, Ram and Rohrbaugh, Guy. Forthcoming. "Luminosity and the Safety of Knowledge." *Pacific Philosophical Quarterly*.

Owens, David. 2000. *Reason without Freedom*. Routledge: London and New York.

Peacocke, Christopher. 1986. *Thoughts: An Essay on Content*. Basil Blackwell: Oxford.

Plantinga, Alvin. 1993. *Warrant and Proper Function*. Oxford University Press: Oxford.

Pollock, John. 1986. *Contemporary Theories of Knowledge*. Rowman and Littlefield: Savage, MD.

Price, H. H. 1932. *Perception*. Methuen: London.

Putnam, Hilary. 1975. "The Meaning of 'Meaning'" in Gunderson 1975.

Quine, W. V. O. 1960. *Word and Object*. MIT Press: Cambridge, MA.

Russell, Bertrand. 1959. *The Problems of Philosophy*. Oxford University Press: Oxford.

Salmon, Wesley. 1984. *Scientific Explanation and the Causal Structure of the World*. Princeton University Press: Princeton, NJ.

———. 1990. *Four Decades of Scientific Explanation*. University of Minnesota Press: Minneapolis, MN.

Searle, John. 1992. *The Rediscovery of the Mind*. MIT Press: Cambridge, MA.

Sellars, Wilfrid. 1963a. "Phenomenalism" in Sellars 1963c.

———. 1963b. "Some Reflections on Language Games" in Sellars 1963c.

———. 1963c. *Science, Perception and Reality*. Ridgeview: Atascadero, CA.

Slote, Michael. 1970. *Reason and Scepticism*. George Allen and Unwin: London.

Strawson, P. F. 1959. *Individuals*. Methuen: London.

———. 1985. *Skepticism and Naturalism: Some Varieties*. Columbia University Press: New York.

Sturgeon, Scott. 1994. "The Epistemic View of Subjectivity." *Journal of Philosophy* 91: 221–35.

Tomberlin, James, ed. 1990. *Philosophical Perspectives 4: Action Theory and Philosophy of Mind*. Ridgeview: Atascadero, CA.

———, ed. 1999. *Philosophical Perspectives 13: Epistemology*. Blackwell: Cambridge, MA and Oxford.

Van Fraassen, Bas. 1980. *The Scientific Image*. Oxford University Press: Oxford.

———. 1983. "Glymour on Evidence and Explanation" in Earman 1983.

Vogel, Jonathan. 1990. "Cartesian Scepticism and Inference to the Best Explanation." *Journal of Philosophy* 87: 658–66.

Watkins, J. W. N. 1984. *Science and Scepticism*. Hutchinson: London.

Williams, Michael. 1977. *Groundless Belief: An Essay in the Possibility of Epistemology*. Yale University Press: New Haven, CT.

Williamson, Timothy. 1996. "Cognitive Homelessness." *Journal of Philosophy* 93: 554–73.

———. 2000. *Knowledge and its Limits*. Oxford University Press: Oxford.

*Philosophical Issues, 14, Epistemology, 2004*

# THE EPISTEMOLOGY OF TESTIMONY

Duncan Pritchard
University of Stirling

## 1. The Epistemology of Testimony—*Scylla and Charybdis*

As the title of this piece indicates, my interest here is the epistemology of testimony, or, more precisely, testimony-based belief. What I will be canvassing is a certain form of pessimism about the justification we have for this sort of belief.

Let us focus on what I take it is the paradigm case of testimony—the intentional transfer of a belief from one agent to another, whether in the usual way via a verbal assertion made by the one agent to the other, or by some other means, such as through a note.[1] So, for example, John says to Mary that the house is on fire (or, if you like, 'texts' her this message on her phone), and Mary, upon hearing this, forms the belief that the house is on fire and consequently exits the building at speed. Clearly, a great deal of our beliefs are gained via testimony, and if the epistemic status of our testimony-based beliefs were to be called into question *en masse*, then this would present us with quite a predicament. It is thus essential that we have some plausible account of the epistemology of testimony. Our primary focus will be on the *justification* for our testimony-based beliefs, though along the way we will say a little about other relevant epistemic notions like epistemic entitlement as well.

In what follows, we will call a 'testimony-based belief' (TBB) any belief which one reasonably and directly forms in response to what one reasonably takes to be testimony and which is essentially caused and sustained by testimony. A few remarks about this characterisation of a TBB is in order.

To begin with, it is worth noting that whilst this formulation of a TBB is quite permissive in that it allows that one can gain a TBB from a merely apparent instance of testimony (so long as the agent's judgement that it is an instance of testimony is reasonably made), it is also somewhat restrictive in that it insists that the agent forming the belief must regard the belief as testimony-based.[2] In order to simplify matters, in what follows we will take it for granted that the testimony in question is genuine and not merely apparent, unless the discussion demands otherwise.

Second, the purpose of the clause "reasonably and directly" is to allow that someone might legitimately draw a direct consequence from a testimonial assertion and that direct consequence still be regarded as a TBB. For example, if you assert "P, and if P then Q", but do not also assert "Q", I want to allow that one can legitimately form a belief not only in the proposition asserted but also in Q and that this latter belief should also be treated as a TBB. The belief needs to be directly formed since otherwise other factors will inevitably be brought into play, such as memory.[3]

In contrast, third, the clause "essentially" is being used to put some pressure in a more restrictive direction by ruling out cases where other (non-testimonial) factors are playing a substantive role, either in the formation of one's belief or in the sustaining of that belief. For example, if I know from my previous experience of dealings with you that you are a pathological liar, and I hear you assert "P", then I might reasonably form the belief that not-P. Such a belief would not be a TBB on this view because it essentially rests not only on the instance of testimony in question but also on further collateral information gained via observation.[4]

Fourth, the point that the belief must be sustained by testimony is meant to rule out cases in which a belief is originally gained via testimony but is later sustained by some other source of knowledge, such as observation. For example, once Mary sees for herself that the house is on fire we would expect her belief that the house is on fire to be sustained by her observation of the fire rather than by John's testimony in this regard. By the lights of the characterisation just offered, therefore, this belief would no longer be a TBB.

Finally, it should be noted that this characterisation of TBBs allows that a TBB might be based on more than one instance of testimony, and that it might even be sustained by different instances of testimony over time. That said, for the sake of simplicity our focus in what follows will be on the basic case in this regard in which the agent forms a TBB on the basis of a single instance of testimony.

The contemporary discussion of the epistemology of testimony has tended to cluster around two opposing positions. On the one hand, there are the *reductionists* who argue, roughly, that the justification of an agent's TBB is always dependent upon that agent possessing further independent grounds—i.e., at the very least, grounds that are independent of the instance of testimony in question.[5] The standard story goes that this camp of theorists gets their inspiration from Hume.[6] In effect, the idea is that the epistemic status of one's TBBs can always be reduced to the epistemic status of one's non-TBBs, and this is why the bold formulation of the reductionist thesis is often known as *global reductionism*. We can formulate global reductionism roughly as follows:

*Global Reductionism*
For all of one's TBBs, if one's TBB is justified, then one is able to offer sufficient non-testimonial grounds in support of that TBB.

This formulation is rather vague of course, especially in its use of the qualifier "sufficient", but it will do for our present purposes.

One can see the attraction of the view. Plausibly, the mere fact that someone testifies that P is not a reason—or at least not a reason sufficient for justification at any rate—for believing P. Instead, one must be in the possession of further justifying grounds that are independent of this instance of testimony. The problem is, of course, that if those further grounds are themselves simply additional instances of testimony—e.g., someone else saying that one can trust the person making the original assertion—then the issue of one's justification for holding the original TBB, far from being resolved, simply gets moved one stage back on to the issue of one's justification for believing this further supporting TBB. The only way out of this chain of justification is, it seems, to find adequate supporting grounds which are non-testimonial, such as, say, one's observation over time of the testimonial reliability of the agent making the original assertion when it comes to the target subject matter. Thus, if we are to have justification for our TBBs, then that justification had better be reducible to a non-testimonial set of grounds.[7]

On the other side of the contemporary divide are the *defaultists*, or *credulists*, who maintain that the epistemic status of a TBB need not depend upon the agent possessing any independent grounds in favour of that belief. Just so long as there are no grounds for doubt in this regard, then one can acquire a justified TBB even whilst lacking independent grounds in favour of that belief. The standard story goes that this camp of theorists gets their inspiration from Reid.[8] In its starkest formulation this thesis is more than just the denial of global reductionism. Instead, it maintains something like the following claim:

*Bare Credulism*
For all of one's TBBs, one's TBB can be justified even though one is unable to offer any supporting grounds in favour of that TBB.

By allowing that one's TBBs can be justified even in the absence of any supporting grounds in their favour, the credulist is proposing quite a radical thesis. After all, one's TBBs don't seem to be the sort of beliefs that one would typically regard as forming part of one's basic beliefs, at least on any classical conception of that notion at any rate. They are not, for example, the kinds of beliefs that are typically infallible, self-evident, or incorrigible. And note that if they were, then we wouldn't need a credulist thesis to explain their epistemic status since we could then simply appeal to one of the classical foundationalist models of justification instead. The idea behind credulism is that even despite being fallible, non-self-evident and corrigible, nevertheless TBBs can have an epistemic status which does not depend upon any further grounds that the agent possesses. Furthermore, this epistemic status is meant to be robust enough to be worthy of the title 'justification'. This is a bold thesis indeed.[9] In what follows, we will call any TBB that is justified because, at least in part (the reason for this qualification will become apparent below), it enjoys a default epistemic support a *T-basic TBB*.

Essentially, then, the worry that reductionists have is that without independent evidence there is no reason for thinking that a particular instance of testimony is true—more precisely, there is nothing in an instance of testimony which of itself indicates that it tends towards the truth. On this picture, the credulists are simply offering a recipe for widespread gullibility. In contrast, the credulists maintain that the reductionist model unduly intellectualises TBB by denying even the possibility that such beliefs might posses an innate epistemic status. By setting the hurdle for testimonial justification so high, they argue, the reductionist walks right into the trap set by the sceptic.

Of these two motivations, it is probably the reductionist rationale that fares better on initial inspection. The claim that reductionism overly intellectualises testimonial justification is not all that compelling given that the reductionist demand that agents must possess further grounds in favour of a TBB does not require any explicit inference on the part of the subject, nor even any great intellectual sophistication (the claim is not, for example, that one should run through an inference prior to forming any particular TBB).

The related claim made by the credulists regarding the scepticism-friendly nature of reductionism is more cogent, but is also only of ambiguous import. This objection emphasises our widespread cognitive dependence on testimony, especially as children, to highlight the implausibility of the reductionist model and show how it is congenial to a general scepticism about justification.[10] After all, if the reductionist thesis is that any justification for a TBB must ultimately rest upon non-testimonial foundations, then it is hard to see how the vast majority of our beliefs could ever be justified. Most of our beliefs seem to be ultimately or largely testimony-based, and this means both that the reductionist demand constrains the epistemic status of a large number of our beliefs and also that there are very few non-TBBs which could serve the required supporting role. Together, these two factors ensure that only a very restricted class of our beliefs is justified.

Take, for example, my belief that the earth is round. Although this might not initially seem to be a TBB, since one isn't typically aware of one explicitly being told that this is the case, a moment's reflection reveals that it is almost certainly a TBB since it could hardly have been gained in any other way (by going into outer space to determine that this is the case for oneself, for example).[11] The problem is, of course, that it is hard to see how one could go about acquiring non-testimonial grounds for believing this proposition, since whatever further support one sought (e.g., from textbooks, or from photographs that purport to have been taken from outer space) would itself owe its epistemic status, whether directly or indirectly, to instances of testimony.[12] The same goes for many of our TBBs. But if that is right, and if it is also right that a good many of our beliefs in general are TBBs, then a fairly broad and disconcerting scepticism appears to immediately ensue.

Opting for the credulist position enables us to evade this problem by allowing our TBBs a positive epistemic status even in the absence of supporting grounds, but now one has to deal with the very different worry that afflicts this stance—*viz.*, how could it be that one could be justified in holding a TBB even in the absence of supporting reasons? Perhaps more pertinently, the worry is in what sense we can call the default epistemic status of these TBBs a 'justification' when there doesn't seem to be anything *justifying* the belief at all?[13] In any case, it is hardly much of an objection, in and of itself, to a particular epistemological view that it leads to scepticism, since such scepticism could well be *warranted*.

On the face of it, then, it seems that the choice is between either an epistemology of testimony (global reductionism) that makes plausible demands on what counts as a testimonial justification, but which leads directly to a form of scepticism about the epistemic status of our TBBs; or an alternative view (bare credulism) that can avoid the scepticism, but only at the cost of allowing us to be justified in holding TBBs even in the absence of supporting grounds.[14] The motivation for some sort of midway account is thus very strong. We will begin by examining the prospects for compromise from the reductionist side of the debate.

## 2. The Search for a Hybrid View (I)—Reductionism

One way in which one might qualify the reductionist thesis is to 'localise' the central reductionist claim that it makes. That is, whilst one retains the core reductionist requirement that one's justification for one's TBBs must always be dependent upon additional independent grounds (i.e., grounds which are independent of the target instance(s) of testimony), one drops the further demand that those independent grounds should be non-testimonial. So, for example, one cannot be justified in forming a TBB that P solely on the basis of hearing someone's testimony that P, but neither does one need to find epistemic support for that belief which goes beyond additional testimonial grounds (such as the testimonial ground from another testifier that the original testifier can be trusted in this regard). One can find an influential version of this view in recent work by Elizabeth Fricker (1987; 1994; 1995).[15]

We can roughly formulate such a position as follows:

*Local Reductionism*
For all of one's TBBs, if one's TBB is justified, then one is able to offer sufficient independent grounds in support of that TBB.

The attraction of such a view is that it lessens the counterintuitive consequences of global reductionism. In particular, by dropping the demand that one's TBBs should always be supported by further non-testimonial grounds we both weaken the intellectualism that is held to be inherent in the view whilst also reducing its potential to generate sceptical consequences.

The problem with such a position, however, is that insofar as one is impressed by the considerations that led us to take the global reductionist thesis seriously, then one will not be satisfied by this weakening of the view. After all, for a wide class of our TBBs, the 'independent' support in question will simply consist of further TBBs which require independent support and which, moreover, will be 'independently' supported by further TBBs, and so on. In all likelihood a circle of justification will form here, in that the original TBB will at some point figure in one of the supporting classes of TBBs, but even if this does not happen, we are still left with a regress of justification, and that is hardly any better.[16] It seems, then, that if one is to motivate a suitable hybrid view then one is going to have to allow some of one's TBBs to have a default epistemic status.

One possibility in this respect, which retains at least the spirit of local reductionism, is to allow that TBBs have a default epistemic status, but only in the initial stages of our intellectual development. As noted above we largely gain our beliefs—and our picture of the world in general—from the testimony of others, and to insist on an unqualified version of reductionism appears to make this kind of knowledge acquisition epistemically problematic. One might contend, however, that one could consistently allow a default epistemic status to one's TBBs in this regard without thereby conceding the core claim behind the reductionist thesis as regards the beliefs of the intellectually developed. On this model, in offering independent support for one's TBB when one has passed the developmental stage, one may adduce TBBs gained whilst in the developmental stage and which as a result possess a default epistemic status. Accordingly, the chain of justification can come to an end with a TBB that requires no further epistemic support because of its default epistemic status.[17]

We thus get a thesis of roughly the following sort:

*Local Developmental Reductionism*
For all of one's TBBs gained in the non-developmental stage, if one's TBB is justified, then one is able to offer sufficient independent grounds in support of that TBB.

On the face of it, this seems to meet some of the problems facing both global and local reductionism. On the one hand, we can account of our intellectual development in a way that does not epistemically problematize our widespread acquisition of knowledge via testimony during this stage. And, on the other, we can also insist that once this stage has passed then one's TBBs must be placed under the scrutiny required by the reductionist model. Accordingly, the kind of epistemic dispensation licensed by the credulist, and which appears to allow widespread gullibility as an epistemic policy, is avoided.

Crucially, however, local developmental reductionism is not really a form of reductionism at all but a species of credulism, in that, in keeping with the spirit of credulism, it grants some TBBs a default epistemic status. With this in mind, it is better to situate this position amongst other credulist positions rather than with reductionist accounts. This is what we will now do.


## 3. The Search for a Hybrid View (II)—Credulism

There are several ways in which one might modify the bare credulist thesis. The most straightforward way is to weaken it by noting that in coming by an instance of testimony, understanding it (or seeming to at any rate), and recognising it as an instance of testimony, one thereby gains some epistemic support for one's TBB, even if that support is not in itself sufficient for justification (so that further default support is also necessary).[18] After all, the mere fact that someone would be willing to go to the trouble of asserting P at all is a *prima facie* reason for thinking that P is true.

With this in mind, we can formulate a modest credulism as follows:

*Modest Credulism*
For all of one's TBBs, one's TBB can be justified even though one is unable to offer any independent supporting grounds in favour of that TBB.

The credulist claim therefore comes down to the thesis that one's TBBs are able to possess a default epistemic status which, along with the grounds one gains for a TBB in virtue of it being a TBB, enables them to be justified even in the absence of further independent grounds—provided, of course, that there are no grounds for doubt in this regard.

A second way in which one might modify the bare credulist thesis, which is in the spirit of the local developmental reductionism that we have just considered, is to place a restriction on the kind of TBBs that can be granted a default epistemic status. For whilst it might well be true that there is a standing presumption in favour of, say, a child's reliance on testimony, it is not nearly so plausible that such a default epistemic status should transfer to very different cases where TBBs are involved, such as in murder trials.[19] This then motivates the idea that it is not all TBBs that have a standing default epistemic status but only, at best, a specific sub-class of them.

Moreover, it is not as if one needs to allow that all of one's TBBs could potentially be T-basic TBBs in order to ensure that one can evade the kind of sceptical worry at issue in the debate about global reductionism. Just so long as a sufficiently large class of one's TBBs are justified in the absence of independent supporting grounds, then, at a formal level at any rate, the possibility remains that the chain of justification that is in play in favour of one's non-T-basic TBBs, whilst it might not sufficiently go outside of one's other TBBs, nevertheless does ultimately end with T-basic TBBs which do not stand in need of any further independent epistemic support for their justification. In the case of the TBBs gained in the developmental stage, and where no subsequent grounds for doubt in this regard have been raised, this seems very plausible. I need to offer independent support for my non-T-basic TBBs and, whilst at least a large part of this additional support will be itself testimonial, just so long as it incorporates T-basic TBBs (such as those TBBs gained in the developmental stage) in the appropriate way, then this can suffice to support a justification for my non-T-basic TBBs.

We can formulate such a restricted credulist thesis as follows:

*Modest Restricted Credulism*
For at least some of one's TBBs, one's TBB can be justified even though one is unable to offer any independent supporting grounds in favour of that TBB.

Note that this formulation leaves it open as to which class of TBBs is to be privileged in this regard. Moreover, this characterisation of restricted credulism is also consistent with the point made earlier as regards modest credulism that any TBB brings with it some supporting grounds, even if those grounds are not independent of the instance of testimony in question and even though they are not in themselves sufficient to support a justification (which is why I have called it a '*modest* restricted credulist' thesis).

Now one might argue that the difference between modest credulism and modest restricted credulism is rather limited, in that even by the lights of the former proposal the claim is only that there is a *default* epistemic standing for one's TBBs, and thus it is implicitly incorporated into the view that there may be a wide class of TBBs for which this default status is overridden. Accordingly, one could treat, say, a developmental version of modest restricted credulism as being simply a modest credulist thesis on the grounds that there are always overriding considerations in play when it comes to the TBBs of those who are no longer in the developmental stage.

This may well be true, although I still think that such a view would be best expressed as a modest restricted credulist position. After all, the spirit of modest credulism is that the grounds for doubt come from defeaters that are specific to that particular belief, as when one is in possession of counter-evidence against the target proposition. In the case we are imagining, however, the defeaters are standing defeaters which apply to beliefs of a certain type rather than being specific to that belief.[20] It is thus more transparent to formulate the position as a modest restricted credulist thesis rather than simply as a modest credulist thesis. That said, we do not need to decide on this matter here, since we can treat both of these formulations of the modest credulist thesis as plausible ways in which one might refine the bare credulist account.

Nevertheless, this talk of defeaters does direct us towards a further modification that we should make to the bare credulist thesis. The issue relates to how it is part of the credulist view that one's TBBs only have the relevant default epistemic status provided that there are no grounds for doubt in this regard. With this in mind, however, there *is* an additional supporting ground in favour of the TBB which the agent does not gain in virtue of receiving the instance of testimony at issue—*viz.*, the ground that there are no grounds to doubt this TBB. This 'meta' ground is 'negative' in the sense that it is a ground for not doubting this TBB, as opposed to being a 'positive' ground in favour of belief in this TBB.

With this consideration in mind, we can re-formulate the two credulist theses just described as follows:

*Modest Credulism\**
For all of one's TBBs, one's TBB can be justified even though one is unable to offer any independent positive supporting grounds in favour of that TBB.

*Modest Restricted Credulism\**
For at least some of one's TBBs, one's TBB can be justified even though one is unable to offer any independent positive supporting grounds in favour of that TBB.

Note that in order to maintain the credulist thesis it is going to be essential that this independent ground is, as one would expect, insufficient to justify one's

TBB, even when combined with the non-independent grounds that one gains for one's TBB in virtue of it being a TBB. If this were not so then the core credulist claim that these beliefs have a default epistemic status would be lost.

We now have two fairly plausible renderings of what a compromise position might look like in the debate regarding the epistemology of testimonial beliefs, at least where the notion of justification is concerned. We have moved away from the austerity of the bare credulist thesis by acknowledging the fact that agents will always have some grounds in favour of their TBBs, even some independent grounds of a limited and negative sort. Nevertheless, we have also retained the key anti-global reductionist claim that there is a default epistemic status that accrues to at least some of our TBBs in virtue of them being TBBs, and hence rejected the analogous austerity of the global reductionist demand that our TBBs always be justified by appeal to non-testimonial grounds.

## 4. Internalist Versions of Credulism

We are not quite home and dry yet, however, since we still need to identify what sort of epistemological thesis these credulist accounts are. In particular, we need to decide whether they should be understood along epistemological internalist or externalist lines. As we will see, this is easier said than done. We will begin by considering the prospects for these accounts when they are read as internalist theses.

We will define epistemological internalism about justification in the following way:

> *Internalist Justification*
> An agent's belief is internalistically justified if, and only if, the facts which determine that justification are knowable by the agent via reflection alone (i.e., through *a priori* reasoning, introspection of her own mental states, or memory of knowledge gained via either of these means).[21]

Specifically applied to the issue of testimonial justification, we thus get the following formulation of the internalist thesis:

> *Internalist Testimonial Justification*
> An agent's TBB is internalistically justified if, and only if, the facts which determine that justification are knowable by the agent via reflection alone.

And we will take epistemological non-internalism—i.e., *externalism*—about justification to consist in the denial of this thesis, such that it allows that an agent can be justified without being able to know the facts which determine that justification by reflection alone.

Although there will always be a certain amount of debate about how best to draw this distinction, I think this characterisation is relatively uncontroversial in that it captures the key sense in which an internalist theory of justification demands a special kind of cognitive access on the part of the agent to the relevant justifiers. Moreover, it also accounts for how externalist theories, like reliabilist views, are externalist precisely because they allow facts to count as determining an agent's justification for her belief (such as facts about the reliability the agent's belief–forming process) which are not knowable by that agent by reflection alone.[22]

Consider how the two versions of the credulist thesis that we have just formulated fare if they are understood along internalist lines. To begin with, note that all internalist versions of the credulist account face an immediate problem regarding what the relevant reflectively accessible facts which determine justification are. When it comes to the bare credulist thesis this problem is particularly pressing since it seems as if there just are no reflectively accessible justification-determining facts that are applicable to T-basic TBBs. Moreover, since such T-basic TBBs are not usually of their nature self-justifying in any way—they are not typically of their nature self-evident, for example—it is not as if the relevant reflectively accessible facts could simply concern the epistemic properties of the T-basic TBB itself. Accordingly, it is hard to see how, on an internalist construal of bare credulism, one could regard T-basic TBBs as justified at all.

On the face of it, the modest versions of credulism that we have formulated fare better in this regard since they do make appeal to some supporting grounds in their account of the default epistemic status of T-basic TBBs. On the internalist view, these grounds will be understood in the standard way as being reflectively accessible to the agent. Thus we have an account here of how the epistemic support one has for one's T-basic TBBs can be dependent upon reflectively accessible facts which determine that epistemic support.

The problem, however, is that the relevant reflectively accessible facts here *only* suffice to determine a positive epistemic status for the T-basic TBBs. That is, they do not suffice, even by the lights of the credulist (indeed, *especially* by the lights of the credulist), to determine a *justification* for the T-basic TBBs. Accordingly, there is a lacuna in the justificational story on the internalist construal of the modest credulist model, one that parallels the lacuna in the internalist rendering of bare credulism that was just noted. Put starkly, the worry about internalist construals of the credulist thesis is that it looks as if nothing, or nothing sufficient at any rate, is doing the work of justifying one's T-basic TBBs, and if this is right then the justification for most of one's TBBs is lacking.

Moreover, even if one were able to adequately respond to this concern, further problems would remain. In particular, note that one of the facts which is determining justification on the credulist account would be that there are no grounds for doubt—i.e., defeaters—available. On the face of it, this might not seem like a particularly problematic demand to make in that it is quite plausible to suppose that this would be a fact that is reflectively available to the subject. The problem, however, is that intuitively it is not enough merely to be of the *opinion* that there are no grounds for doubt— rather one also needs to be *competent* in forming judgements of this sort. That is, if one were completely incompetent when it comes to assessing whether grounds for doubt are present (one lacks skills for detecting obvious deception, for example), then one could meet this constraint on default epistemic status even though there are manifest grounds for doubt at issue in that situation (perhaps, for example, the testifier is making a very serious set of claims whilst dressed in a clown costume and tooting a horn after each statement).

This worry is structurally similar to a problem posed by Matthew Weiner (2003) regarding any local reductionist thesis that allows TBBs formed in the developmental stage a default justification, which is unsurprising given that we have already noted that such a position is, in effect, a form of restricted credulism. Weiner argues that this model of testimonial justification will not work because it generates the counterintuitive result that an adult and a child could hear the same piece of testimony and form a TBB solely on the basis of that testimony which is, respectively, justified in the latter case but not in the former. He claims that this is counterintuitive because if these two beliefs are to be accorded different epistemic evaluations at all, then it should be the *adult's* belief that is privileged and not the child's. His reason for this is that adults will typically have acquired a discriminative capacity to evaluate testimony that children will usually lack and he notes in this respect that the child in this case would be likely to believe in the existence of Santa Claus on the basis of an isolated instance of testimony (Weiner 2003, 261). It takes experience to be good at detecting defeaters, and this is something that children lack.

Accordingly, when it comes to the 'no defeater' condition for internalist testimonial justification it is not enough for the agent to merely meet this condition by her own lights alone, no matter how incompetent her ability to detect grounds for doubt may be. Instead, what we require of the agent is that she is competent in this regard and thus, on the internalist account, this will mean that she must have adequate grounds for believing that she is competent. And since this is an additional fact which determines justification, on the internalist account it will be necessary that these grounds are also understood, in the usual way, as being reflectively accessible to the agent.

Once one has imposed this further restriction on internalist testimonial justification, however, then, as suggested by Weiner's complaint against local developmental reductionism, a problem immediately emerges for any version of the modest local credulist thesis that is cast along developmental lines. After all, the whole point of this sort of position is that those in the developmental stage lack adequate grounds for thinking that they are competent in this regard—this is part of what contributes to the fact that they are in the developmental stage. At the very least, then, internalism about justification does not sit well with a modest local credulism under-stood along developmental lines. Given that part of the attraction of credu-list views is that they can explain how we can come to (legitimately) acquire a wide set of beliefs about the world on the basis of testimony without being in a position, at least initially, to offer independent grounds in favour of those beliefs, this result is very worrying for the credulist.

Moreover, the problem at issue here extends beyond developmental versions of the modest local credulist position. In order to see this, all one needs to recognise is that the kind of reflectively accessible grounds that one has in favour of one's belief in one's competence in this regard had better not simply consist of further TBBs if they are to play the required supporting role. For suppose for a moment that the only grounds one possessed in this respect were themselves simply further TBBs. The question would then arise as to one's reflective access to the facts which justify these TBBs, and this will include facts concerning one's grounds for regarding oneself as competent at detecting defeaters in the situations in which these TBBs were acquired. Furthermore, it is not as if an appeal to further T-basic TBBs would help in this respect, since even in this case one would still need to have reflectively accessible grounds for regarding oneself as being competent at detecting defeaters in the situations in which they were acquired, and so the chain of justification would simply continue.

A regress of justification—or, failing, that, a *circle* of justification—is thus starting to loom which is structurally akin to that in play when we considered reductionist views. Indeed, as with reductionist views, one pos-sible way of preventing this regress is to justify one's TBBs by appeal to one's non-TBBs, but then one would be faced with the equally disastrous prospect of the kind of limited scepticism that we saw above to be entailed by reductionist accounts. It seems, then, that a limited scepticism faces us either way. The moral is clear: insofar as one interprets this 'competence' constraint in a manner that is robust enough to make the epistemic status that results when one forms one's TBBs in ways that meet this constraint a type of justification then one is presented with the sort of worries about regresses of justification that the move to credulism was meant to avoid.

An internalist version of the credulist thesis is thus faced with two key problems. The first is to account for how one's TBBs can be justified at all by the lights of this thesis given that there appears to be a lacuna in the reflectively accessible grounds that are supposed to determine justification in this respect. The second problem comes in the form of a dilemma regarding how we understand the 'no defeater' condition. Either we understand that condition robustly, such that it demands adequate reflectively accessible grounds on the part of the agent for thinking that she is competent in this regard, in which case we are presented with the same kinds of worries about circularity and regress that the credulist thesis was meant to help us avoid; or else we interpret the 'no defeater' condition liberally such that adequate grounds for competence in this respect are not demanded, but then it looks as if there is now good cause to doubt whether what we are proposing here is a theory about epistemic *justification* at all.

It is worth pausing for a moment to consider this last point further, since there does seem to be an epistemic notion available here which is weaker than justification that might be what we are left with on the liberal reading of the 'no defeater' condition. Consider again the child and the adult in the scenario that Weiner envisaged. Furthermore, suppose that there are clear grounds for doubt present in this case—say, the 'testifier' is finding it hard to suppress laughter whilst making the 'assertion' in question. It is a defeater of this sort that the adult should be taking into account when she forms her TBBs, and if she doesn't give it due weight in this case—perhaps because she just isn't paying attention to the speaker, for example—then this would count against her possessing a justification for her TBB. We can account for this on the internalist credulist account of testimonial justification by contending that she lacks the necessary reflective accessible grounds for thinking that she has formed her TBB competently in this respect.

Now consider the case of the child faced with the same instance of testimony. As Weiner points out, if either of these agents is justified then it will be the adult, and so it is implausible to suppose that the child's TBB is justified in this case. Nevertheless, there does seem to be an epistemic status that is applicable to the child's TBB that is lacking in the case of the adult, and this is that we would regard the child as being *epistemically blameless* in forming her TBB even whilst not taking into account this defeater. Unlike the adult, who we think should have been more careful in the formation of her TBB, we recognise that the child does not know any better and cannot be expected to have known any better. She is doing the best she can, by her lights, which is more than can be said of the adult, and in this sense she has an *epistemic entitlement* to her belief. Nevertheless, since, *ex hypothesi*, neither agent is justified in forming her TBB, the epistemic blamelessness or entitlement that is accruing to the child's TBB is a weaker epistemic status than that at issue in a justification. At most, then, all an internalist construal of the credulist thesis can offer is an account of the epistemic blamelessness or entitlement of forming T-basic TBBs; it does not establish a justification for those beliefs. Since it was the latter that was the goal of the credulist project (at least as we have understood it here), this is not enough.[23]

## 5. Externalist Versions of Credulism

So if we are to make sense of the credulist account of justification, it is essential that we interpret it along externalist lines. This conclusion will not come as a surprise to many involved in this debate, since it is often just taken for granted that a credulist thesis is tied, whether explicitly or implicitly, to an externalist epistemology. Rather than get drawn into the details of specific externalist renderings of the credulist thesis, we will just say that what is common to all of them is the idea that, broadly speaking, the *reliability* of the relevant belief-forming process can contribute to the epistemic status of the agent's TBB, regardless of whether the agent has reflectively accessible grounds for thinking that this reliability is being exhibited. We will leave it an open question how this 'reliability' is to be understood, whether in terms of a modal condition, such as the sensitivity or safety condition, or in terms of some kind of proper functionalist or virtue-theoretic thesis, or in some other way.

Note that this externalist brand of credulism can allow that there will be certain grounds that one will gain in forming a TBB simply in virtue of that belief being a TBB, and it is consistent with this sort of view that these grounds are understood internalistically as being reflectively accessible to the agent. Nevertheless, the point remains that such grounds are, in themselves at any rate, insufficient to justify a TBB. On the externalist account, what additional epistemic support is required to justify a TBB can come from non-reflectively accessible factors, such as the reliability of the belief-forming mechanism that is in operation.

For example, if I am in fact forming my TBB in an (externally) appropriate way then, even if I have no good independent reflectively accessible grounds in favour of my belief—such as grounds for thinking that I am forming this belief appropriately—my belief could still be justified. Thus, the first problem raised above against internalist versions of the credulist thesis, regarding the apparent lacuna in epistemic support, is met, since there is no gap to fill on this view. That my reflectively accessible grounds do not suffice to ensure a justification for my TBB is neither here nor there on this picture, since non-reflectively accessible factors, such as the reliability of the process by which I formed my TBB, can contribute to the epistemic status of this belief.

Moreover, the second issue raised above regarding how one is to understand the 'no defeater' condition can also be dealt with on this model. As we saw, it is necessary that such a condition is understood relatively robustly if it is to perform the required role in helping to establish a *justification* for one's T-basic TBBs rather than just the mere epistemic blamelessness of these beliefs. It was hard to see how this demand could be met on the internalist construal of the credulist thesis since insofar as this condition is understood as robustly as it needs to be then a regress (or a circle) of justification quickly opens up that undermines the prospects for establishing the widespread justification of our TBBs. On the externalist rendering of the thesis, however, no such regress (or circle) presents itself because the additional feature supporting the justification need not be specified in such a way that the agent must have reflective access to it, and it was this element of the view that was creating the regress (/circle). Accordingly, the second key problem with internalist versions of the credulist thesis that we noted is also met.

We do not need to get into the details of specific externalist renderings of the credulist thesis in order to recognise, however, that such a view faces some fairly pressing problems of its own. To begin with, note that an externalist version of the credulist thesis will be unable to do any better when it comes to our TBBs formed in the developmental stage than its internalist rival. This is because, as we noted above, agents in such a stage of development will lack the competency in evaluating testimony (and, relatedly, defeaters) that comes with repeated exposure to instances of testimony within a social milieu, and this is bound to undermine their reliability in forming TBBs. At best, then, all we will be able to say about the TBBs formed by agents in this stage is that these agents are epistemically blameless in holding them, not that they are justified in holding them, whether by the lights of an externalist *or* an internalist account of testimonial justification.

This is not the only problem facing externalist treatments of the credulist thesis either, since there are pressing concerns about whether we can even make sense of the notion of externalist justification when it comes to testimony. Of course, there are many who think that an externalist rendering of the notion of justification is *never* possible, as regards *any* kind of subject matter, but that is not the issue that I wish to raise here. After all, externalist treatments of justification do seem (or so I would argue at any rate) very plausible in a wide range of cases, especially when it comes to our basic perceptual beliefs. Here what is most important is, I would argue, that the belief was formed in the right kind of way, regardless of whether the agent is able to offer sufficient reflectively accessible grounds in favour of that belief (such as grounds for thinking that the belief was formed in the right kind of way).

Moreover, it is not as if in the case of testimony the externalist is offering a 'pure' treatment of the justification of TBBs such that reflectively accessible grounds play no role whatsoever (as occurs in the more problematic cases on which the externalist/internalist debate focuses, such as regarding the so-called 'chicken-sexers'). In particular, on the view sketched here some reflectively accessible grounds accrue to the agent's belief just in virtue of the belief in question being a TBB. Instead, the crux of the thesis proposed by the externalist credulist is simply that, at least for some TBBs, the justification one possesses for one's TBBs will be at least partly determined by 'external' factors (such that these TBBs would be unjustified without the contribution of these 'external' factors).

Nevertheless, even if we grant the general plausibility of externalism about justification and also note the 'mixed' nature of the externalist thesis in this respect, there are still worries remaining about this particular use of externalism. The worry concerns how TBBs are not obvious candidates to be subject to the kind of externalist treatment that is needed in this regard. In short, the worry is that the 'mixed' externalist treatment on offer does not contain a robust enough internal component, but that if we were to enhance the internal component to the justification then we would be back facing the very same problems that afflicted the internalist versions of credulism.

In order to see this, it is worth contrasting a case in which an agent forms a TBB with a scenario in which that same agent forms the same belief, though this time via perception. Moreover, in order to keep the examples constant, we will stipulate in each case that the epistemic support for the belief is 'mixed' in the same way. That is, the 'internal' component will solely consist of those reflectively accessible grounds that the agent gains in virtue of acquiring the belief in the relevant manner, with the 'external' component making up the rest of the rest of the total epistemic support that the agent has for this belief.

Imagine, for instance, that the proposition in question is that the agent's car is outside on the driveway. In the perceptual case, this belief is formed via the agent looking outside and seeing what looks to be her car on the driveway. In the testimonial case, in contrast, the belief is formed by the agent hearing an apparent instance of testimony to this effect. In both cases, we will stipulate that the agent has no other reason for thinking that her car is, or isn't, on the driveway. (Suppose, for example, that our agent's car has been away at the garage and she has no expectation that it will be delivered back today, but no expectation either that it won't be delivered back today—she just has no idea when it is due to be returned).

In the perceptual case, it does seem entirely plausible to suppose that the agent is justified in forming this belief just so long as this belief was indeed formed in an appropriate way. If, say, the agent's perceptual faculties are functioning correctly within an environment for which they are suited (the lighting is good and so forth), then this will (depending on the details of the externalist theory under consideration) suffice for the agent to have a justified belief in this respect. We would expect (and we may even insist) that the agent also comes by some reflectively accessible grounds in favour of her belief in virtue of gaining her belief in this way (the fact that it looks as if one's car is parked outside on the driveway is, after all, a *prima facie* reflectively accessible ground for thinking that it is parked outside), but we would not demand any further reflectively accessible grounds before we would count this belief as justified. In particular, it seems unnecessary to insist that the agent has *independent* reflectively accessible grounds in favour of this belief, such as grounds for thinking that she is indeed employing reliable cognitive faculties in appropriate circumstances, or (in normal circumstances at least) grounds for thinking that there are no defeaters present.

The situation is very different, however, when it comes to the corresponding TBB in this proposition. In this case we are to suppose that the agent forms her TBB simply in response to hearing an apparent instance of testimony to the effect that her car is on the driveway. Moreover, we are to suppose that the epistemic support for this belief is due only to those reflectively accessible grounds that the agent acquires in virtue of forming that TBB along with the relevant 'external' facts demanded by whichever externalist version of the credulist thesis is under consideration. The crux here is that, intuitively, without independent reflectively accessible grounds this TBB is not justified. If the only grounds available to the agent for thinking that this belief is true are the grounds gained in virtue of the belief being a TBB, then reliability in the method of belief-formation, however that is to be specified, will not be enough to ensure that the belief is justified.

One way to see this point is to consider what each of these agents would say if asked why they believe what they do. Whilst it seems unproblematic for an agent to say that she believes that her car is on the driveway simply because it looks as if it is there, it does seem highly problematic for that same agent to say that that she believes this proposition simply because someone told her that this was the case. Part of the point here is that, unlike the perceptual case, it is hard to see what the testimonial reliability in question could consist in if it did not manifest itself in further independent reflectively accessible grounds. Whilst we can conceive of an agent exhibiting a perceptual reliability without thereby acquiring any reflectively accessible grounds for thinking that such reliability is being exhibited, how would one exhibit a testimonial reliability without having such additional grounds? Here the reliability is constituted by the agent's ability to make sound judgements about, for example, the testifier's authority to make the assertion in question, the plausibility of the assertion made, and the appropriateness of the testifier making this assertion in this context (an instance of testimony that is *apropos* nothing in particular is usually a cause for suspicion, for example). It is hard to see how these recognitional capacities could be in play in the formation of a TBB without this resulting in the agent acquiring additional independent reflectively accessible grounds to back up the belief in question.

The testimonial example that we have just described is thus immediately puzzling in that the absence of such grounds itself calls into question our stipulation that these reliable testimonial belief-forming traits are present. This is reflected in the fact that whilst an adequate response to why one believes what one does in the perceptual case can sometimes be simply that this is way things look, it is hard to see how the equivalent response in the testimonial case (i.e., that this is what I was told) would ever be acceptable. In the perceptual case, such a defence doesn't in any way call into question whether one is forming one's belief in an appropriate fashion, whilst in the testimonial case, in contrast, it does.

Of course, we need to remember here that the apparent exception to this are those TBBs that are formed in the developmental stage, which seem to be unobjectionable even in the absence of supporting reflectively accessible grounds. Here it *can* be appropriate to say that the only reason one believes what one does is because this is what one was told. Crucially, however, in this case it is taken as given that the reliability in question is *not* being exhibited, since this is part of what constitutes an agent being in the developmental stage. Accordingly, there is no question here (at least on the externalist account at any rate) of the agent's belief being justified, and thus no issue regarding how this relatively ungrounded assertion could call into question a presupposed testimonial reliability. All we have here, as noted above, is mere epistemic blamelessness, not justification.

If one is to advance a plausible externalist credulist thesis, it is thus going to be essential that one insists on further independent reflectively accessible grounds being possessed by the agent, and thus one must abandon the key credulist claim that there are T-basic TBBs. When it comes to such 'local' beliefs regarding the location of one's car, then one may well be able to adduce independent grounds which are not themselves, at least ultimately at any rate, TBBs. Perhaps, for example, one has personal experience of the authority of this informant as regards assertions of this sort. The difficulty, however, is that most of our TBBs do not concern such 'local' beliefs in this way, and hence we are back to the familiar reductionist problem regarding how supplying adequate justificatory support for one's TBBs requires one to cite further TBBs, leading to a regress (or circle) of justification. The sceptical worry that results here does not afflict all of one's TBBs, but it will afflict enough of them to ensure that the scope of our testimonial justifications is far more limited that we might have otherwise supposed.[24]

So there are also problems with conceiving of the credulist account along externalist lines. And given that internalism and externalism are exhaustive options in this respect, this means that there is a standing challenge present to the justification for a wide class of our TBBs.[25]

## Notes

1. This way of putting matters sets to one side those types of 'testimony' that raise distinctive problems, such as, for example, insincere or unintentional 'testimony'. Although the type of testimony that will be the focus here is to a certain degree a restricted class, it is more inclusive than the dominant account of testimony in the literature that is offered by Coady (1992). This incorporates

the requirements that the agent is authoritative about the proposition asserted and that the assertion in question is relevant to the conversational context. See Coady (1992, 42). This view is criticised and slightly amended in Graham (1997); see also Fricker (1994).

2. For a contrasting view in this regard, see Audi (2002, 79). Note, however, that by 'reasonably' here I only have epistemic blamelessness in mind, rather than the stronger notion of epistemic justification (this contrast will be explained further below), and so this feature of the characterisation of TBBs is not as restrictive as it might at first appear. Indeed, on this way of understanding reasonableness, this formulation of TBBs is consistent with the possibility that small children are able to form TBBs.

3. That said, the use of memory in forming one's TBBs may not be problematic in this regard just so long as it does not contribute any additional information, or at least any additional information which is not itself testimony-based. In order to keep matters simple, however, we will set this possibility to one side.

4. What if my belief that you are a pathological liar is itself testimony-based? Even here it would be problematic to regard the resulting belief as a TBB, because of the essential role of memory in the formation of the belief. (Nevertheless, as noted in the last footnote, there may be grounds to be more permissive where memory is concerned). In general, it is worth noting that there is a continuum here. At the one end of the continuum there is the drawing of obvious logical inferences from what has just been said, which I maintain is consistent with this restriction. At the other end, in contrast, there is the employment of a substantive degree of collateral non-testimonial information, which I maintain is inconsistent with this restriction. In between there will be some 'grey' areas, especially given the fact that what is an immediate logical inference from a testimonial assertion when it comes to the Sherlock Holmes's of this world may not be an immediate logical inference when it comes to us mere mortals.

5. Reductionist views are also often refereed to as being 'inferentialist', but I won't be employing this terminology here because it tends to be misleading, implying that the reductionist position goes hand-in-hand with the view that the epistemic status of our TBBs must be understood in terms of the agent concerned making an actual inference.

6. The passage that tends to be quoted in this respect is Hume (1748, 111), though there are actually good textual grounds not to take this passage at face-value in the way that it is often taken. For more on the Humean position, see Coady (1992, chapter 2).

7. Or at least, reducible to grounds which the agent reasonably holds to be non-testimonial. For some recent (and qualified) versions of the reductionist thesis, see Adler (1994), Fricker (1994) and Lyons (1997).

8. See, for example, Reid (1970, 240–1).

9. In the contemporary literature, the credulist thesis is most often associated with the work of Coady (1973; 1992) and Burge (1993; 1997), though in neither case is the position stated quite as starkly as we have formulated it here. See also Stevenson (1993), Foley (1994), Audi (2002) and Weiner (2003).

10. This worry about how dependent we are on testimony in our acquisition of knowledge connects up with the point often made against global reductionism

that it is unclear how we could ever learn a language and so understand the instances of testimony in play if we were to pursue the epistemic policy that this thesis lays down. This is one of the key claims made by Coady (1992) in favour of a credulist model of the epistemology of testimony. The more general claim that a good deal of what we believe is ultimately based on testimony is widely noted. See, for example, Stevenson (1993, 437) and Sosa (1994, 59). This claim is also a recurrent motif of Wittgenstein (1969).

11. Of course, one might have reasonably inferred this belief from other beliefs one holds. Crucially, however, the 'other beliefs' in question here will almost certainly be themselves TBBs. Accordingly, this belief would also have been brought about via testimony and hence, although it is moot whether this belief would count as a TBB by the lights of the characterisation of that notion set forth here (it would depend on how immediate the inference was from those instances), it would be akin to a TBB in the key respect of being causally dependent on testimony.

12. In the case of the textbook the testimonial support is direct in that this is itself a form of testimony. In the case of the photograph the testimonial support is indirect in that, intuitively at any rate, one can only regard the photograph in question as showing that the earth is round provided one is also entitled to certain further claims which will be inevitably testimony-based—e.g., amongst other things, that it was taken from outer space and has not been interfered in any way.

13. I think it is telling that proponents of this sort of position often express the point not in terms of justification but in terms of the weaker notion of *entitlement*. My interest here, however, is in the credulist thesis as a theoretical alternative to reductionism, and thus as a view about justification. Accordingly, I will set those construals of the thesis that drop the reference to justification to one side. I comment further on the contrast between justification and entitlement below.

14. For more on the main contours of the debate between reductionists and credulists, see Fricker (1987; 1995) and McDowell (1994), though note that the main focus for McDowell's discussion, unlike ours, is testimonial *knowledge* rather than justification.

15. See also, Fricker (2004). For two useful and recent discussions of Fricker's local reductionism, see Insole (2000) and Weiner (2003).

16. For a development of this general line of argument against local reductionism, see Weiner (2003). For a critique of both local and global reductionism, see Insole (2000).

17. Fricker herself expresses sympathy with this sort of proposal. See, for example, Fricker (1995, 402–3). For recent discussion of this distinction between the 'developmental' and 'mature' stages in the light of the epistemology of testimony, see Insole (2000) and Weiner (2003).

18. Of course, if one allows, with Audi (2002, 79), that one could gain a TBB without recognising the instance of testimony in question *as* an instance of testimony, then this variety of modest credulism would be unavailable.

19. I discuss the specific epistemological demands placed on testimony in the legal context in Pritchard (2005).

20. Moreover, note that the class of beliefs at issue is defined non-epistemically. That is, we are considering a case where the relevant class of TBBs which lack

the default epistemic status in question is defined in terms of how they were acquired in the developmental stage rather than, for example, in terms of how they were acquired in epistemically sub-optimal environmental conditions. Where the target class of beliefs is understood in the latter epistemic fashion, then it may well be that nothing would be gained by characterising one's modest credulist thesis in restricted, rather than unrestricted, terms, but this consideration does not apply here.

21. In both this characterisation of epistemological internalism and reflective access, I follow the account given by Pryor (2001) in his extremely useful survey of recent trends in epistemology.

22. For more on the externalism/internalism distinction, see the papers collected in Kornblith (2001).

23. The thesis that justification should not be identified with mere epistemic blamelessness is commonly made by the leading epistemological internalists. For two recent examples of this, see Pryor (2001) and Bonjour in Bonjour & Sosa (2003, §10.1). The reader should note that I am not suggesting here that the notions of epistemic blamelessness and epistemic entitlement are synonymous or even co-extensive, only that there is no important difference between them in this particular case because they are both clearly weaker epistemic notions than justification.

24. Note that the further question of whether this limited scepticism will have ramifications for our testimonial knowledge is moot on the externalist account, since it is an open question on this view whether justification is necessary for knowledge (although, for some of the reasons just given, it is more plausible, I take it, to suppose that justification is necessary for knowledge in the testimonial case than it is in other cases).

25. I'm grateful to the organisers of *The Trial on Trial* project—Antony Duff, Lindsay Farmer, Sandra Marshall and Victor Tadros—for inviting me to address their workshops at the Universities of Edinburgh and Glasgow on the topic of 'Testimony', since it was this stimulus that got me working on this issue in the first place. Thanks also to Tony Pitson for discussions on the historical background to this debate, and to Lizzie Fricker, Axel Gelfert and Alan Millar for all their help. Finally, I am grateful to The Leverhulme Trust for the award of a Special Research Fellowship which has enabled me to conduct research in this area.

## References

Adler, J. (1994). 'Testimony, Trust, Knowing', *Journal of Philosophy* **91**, 264–75.

Audi, R. (2002). 'The Sources of Knowledge', *The Oxford Handbook of Epistemology*, (ed.) P. Moser, Oxford University Press, Oxford.

Bonjour, L., & Sosa, E. (2003). *Epistemic Justification: Internalism vs. Externalism, Foundations vs. Virtues*, Basil Blackwell, Oxford.

Burge, T. (1993). 'Content Preservation', *Philosophical Review* **102**, 457–88.

Burge, T. (1997). 'Interlocution, Perception, and Memory', *Philosophical Studies* **86**, 21–47.

Coady, C. A. J. (1973). 'Testimony and Observation', *American Philosophical Quarterly* **10**, 149–55.

Coady, C. A. J. (1992). *Testimony: A Philosophical Study*, Clarendon Press, Oxford.

Foley, R. (1994). 'Egoism in Epistemology', *Socializing Epistemology*, (ed.) F. Schmitt, Rowman & Littlefield, Lanham, Maryland.

Fricker, E. (1987). 'The Epistemology of Testimony', *Proceedings of the Aristotelian Society* (supplementary volume) **61**, 57–83.

Fricker, E. (1994). 'Against Gullibility', *Knowing from Words: Western and Indian Philosophical Analysis of Understanding and Testimony*, (eds.) B. K. Matilal & A. Chakrabarti, 125–61, Dordrecht, Holland, Kluwer.

Fricker, E. (1995). 'Telling and Trusting: Reductionism and Anti-Reductionism in the Epistemology of Testimony', *Mind* **104**, 393–411.

Fricker, E. (2004). 'Testimony: Knowing Through Being Told', *Handbook of Epistemology*, (ed.) J. Wolenski, chapter 2, Dordrecht, Holland, Kluwer.

Graham, P. J. (1997). 'What is Testimony?', *The Philosophical Quarterly* **47**, 227–32.

Hume, D. (1972). *Enquiries Concerning Human Understanding and Concerning the Language of Morals* (1777), (ed.) L. A. Selby-Bigge, 2$^{nd}$ ed., Oxford University Press, Oxford.

Insole, C. (2000). 'Seeing Off the Local Threat to Irreducible Knowledge by Testimony', *The Philosophical Quarterly* **50**, 44–56.

Kornblith, H. (2001). *Epistemology: Internalism and Externalism* (ed.), Basil Blackwell, Oxford.

Lyons, J. (1997). 'Testimony, Induction and Folk Psychology', *Australasian Journal of Philosophy* **75**, 163–78.

McDowell, J. (1994). 'Knowledge by Hearsay', *Knowing from Words: Western and Indian Philosophical Analysis of Understanding and Testimony*, (eds.) B. K. Matilal & A. Chakrabarti, 195–224, Kluwer, Dordrecht, Holland.

Pritchard, D. H. (2005). 'Testimony', *The Trial on Trial: Truth and Due Process*, (eds.) R. A. Duff, L. Farmer, S. Marshall & V. Tadros, Hart Publishing, Oxford.

Pryor, J. (2001). 'Highlights of Recent Epistemology', *British Journal for the Philosophy of Science* **52**, 95–124.

Reid, T. (1970). *An Inquiry into the Human Mind* (1764), (ed.) T. Duggan, Chicago University Press, Chicago, Illinois.

Sosa, E. (1994). 'Testimony and Coherence', *Knowing from Words: Western and Indian Philosophical Analysis of Understanding and Testimony*, (eds.) B. K. Matilal & A. Chakrabarti, 59–67, Kluwer, Dordrecht, Holland.

Stevenson, L. (1993). 'Why Believe What People Say?', *Synthese* **94**, 429–51.

Weiner, M. (2003). 'Accepting Testimony', *The Philosophical Quarterly* **53**, 256–64.

Wittgenstein, L. (1969). *On Certainty*, (eds.) G. E. M. Anscombe & G. H. von Wright, (tr.) D. Paul & G. E. M. Anscombe, Basil Blackwell, Oxford.

*Philosophical Issues, 14, Epistemology, 2004*

# WHAT'S WRONG WITH MOORE'S ARGUMENT?

James Pryor*
Princeton University

## 1 Some Diagnoses

Moore looked at his hands and argued:

(1) Here are two hands.
(2) If hands exist, then there is an external world.
(3) So there is an external world.[1]

*Something* about this argument sounds funny. As we'll see, though, it takes some care to identify exactly what Moore has done wrong.

I will assume that Moore knows premise (2) to be true. One could inquire into *how* he knows it, and whether that knowledge can be defeated; but I won't. I'll focus instead on what epistemic relations Moore has to premise (1) and to his conclusion (3).

It may matter which epistemic relations we choose to consider. Some philosophers will diagnose Moore's argument using Contextualist machinery. They'll say:

> In some contexts, it'd be true to count Moore as knowing he has hands and that there is an external world. In more restrictive contexts, it would not. Moore's argument sounds funny because Moore plays fast and loose with the context. His straightforward assertion "Here are two hands" invites us to occupy a lax context; but one would only be *concerned to argue* that there's an external world in a more restrictive context, where the existence of the external world is an open question.

If these philosophers are right to count 'knows' as context-sensitive,[2] then they're probably right in their complaint that Moore's performance plays fast and loose with the context. However, I don't think that can be a full account of the epistemology of Moore's argument. Why? Because some epistemological predicates resist Contextualist treatment. Even if you think 'knows' is context-sensitive, you'll probably grant that predicates like:

... gives Moore some justification to believe...
... makes Moore more justified in believing... than he was

are not. And the funny epistemic qualities of Moore's argument are manifest even when we confine ourselves to those predicates. Pre-reflectively, it seems like Moore's perception of his hands should give him more justification to believe he has hands than he'd have without it. And we grant that hands are external objects (and that Moore knows them to be so). Yet many are reluctant to accept that Moore's perception of hands gives him more justification to believe there's an external world. Why do we hesitate? If something gives you justification to believe P, and you know P to entail Q, then shouldn't it give you justification to believe Q, too?

Some philosophers will say that Moore's argument just illustrates that Closure is false: you can have justification to believe P, know that P entails Q, and yet fail to have justification to believe Q. But recent years have seen vigorous defenses of Closure; and my sympathies lie largely with the defenders.[3] Minimally, I'll assume that if Moore has some justification to believe he has hands, he also has (at least as much) justification to believe there's an external world. We need to say more about this, but for the moment let's press on.

Three diagnoses of why Moore's argument sounds so unconvincing remain.

One diagnosis is the skeptic's. He'll agree that *if* Moore's perceptual experiences gave him justification to believe he has hands, they'd also give him justification to believe there's an external world. But he denies that Moore's perceptual experiences give him any justification to believe *either* hypothesis. That's why Moore's argument generates no conviction.

A second diagnosis has been advanced by Martin Davies and Crispin Wright. They say that Moore *does* acquire perceptual justification to believe he has hands, but this justification doesn't "transmit" across the entailment from (1) to (3).[4] Davies' and Wright's point is not that Moore *lacks* justification to believe (3). They'll allow that the relation of *having some* justification is closed across known entailment. But they'll point out that *not every* epistemic relation is so closed. (For instance: you might *know* P *non-inferentially*, and know that P entails Q, without knowing Q non-inferentially.) So it's a good question whether the relation of *giving you more* justification is closed across known entailment.

As it turns out, it's not. Suppose you start with its being 80% likely for you that Clio's pet is a dog. Then you're informed that Clio's pet has no hair. One effect of this information is to raise the likelihood that her pet is an

American Hairless Terrier, which hypothesis *entails* that it's a dog. But the information also *decreases* the total likelihood that Clio's pet is a dog. It makes it more likely that she owns a fish or a bird. So: evidence can give you more justification to believe P than you had before, you can know P to entail Q, and yet your evidence make you *less* justified in believing Q than you were before.

That being noted, I doubt that this example provides a useful analogy for thinking about Moore. Moore's situation seems rather different from our situation regarding Clio's pet. (Moore doesn't learn that he has hands in an unexpected way that makes it *less* likely that there's an external world.) Davies and Wright will argue, though, that there's *something* about the structure of Moore's justification for (1) and (3) that prevents his evidence for the former from adding credibility to the latter. They'll argue that Moore's experiences of hands are *only able to* justify him in believing (1) to the extent that *he has antecedent reason* to believe (3). And they'll say this is why Moore's argument sounds so unconvincing. We'll examine this diagnosis closely in sections 3 and 4.

I will be defending a third diagnosis. I think that Moore *does* have perceptual justification to believe he has hands, and I think his justification to believe that *does* transmit to the hypothesis that there's an external world. So Moore *can* acquire justification to believe there's an external world by having experiences of hands and reasoning in the way he does. The challenge is to explain our squeamishness about his argument in some way that respects these claims.


## 2 Theory of Justification

It's essential for insight to these issues to get clear about what we're evaluating. Are we evaluating *the proof* Moore rehearsed? *The reasoning* he engaged in? or what?

In all, I discern five targets of evaluation. They are importantly different. I'll identify two of them now, and introduce the others at later stages in our discussion.

First, there is the **proof** Moore rehearsed: a sequence of propositions and derivation-rules. There doesn't seem to be anything objectionable about this. The proof is clearly valid, and all but the skeptic will grant that its premises are true.

A second, and more interesting target of evaluation is the **justificatory structure** that Moore seems to be endorsing. Does Moore's argument articulate a structure your justification genuinely can have? Can the credibility of (3) really be *enhanced by* your perceptual justification to believe (1)?

Wright, Davies, and the skeptic agree that justification *cannot* be structured in that way. I'll be arguing that it can. I think you genuinely *do* get justification to believe the external world exists from your perceptual justification to believe hands exist. So if what we're evaluating is the justificatory structure that Moore proposed, I think that there is nothing objectionable here, either. Defending this will be my first task.

I'll begin with some groundwork in the theory of justification. I understand **justification** to be the quality that hypotheses possess for you when they're epistemically likely for you to be true, and so epistemically appropriate for you to believe. That's not meant as an *explanation*: if you're not already familiar with the quality I'm talking about, then you won't understand talk about epistemic likelihood, either. Rather, I'm trying to *specify which of various uses* of 'justification' I'm employing. Some philosophers use "X has justification to believe P" or "X is justified in believing P" to mean merely that X is epistemically blameless for believing P.[5] Some use it to mean that X has a reflective appreciation of *why* P is appropriate for him to believe, and so can offer arguments for P. Given the way I'm using 'justification,' those are all substantive claims; and as it happens, I think they're false. I think you can be careful and blameless in managing your beliefs, and still believe things that aren't well-supported by your evidence—and so aren't epistemically likely for you to be true. The mistakes you're making may be too subtle and well-entrenched for you to recognize. So being blameless for believing P doesn't guarantee genuinely having *justification* to believe P. Neither does having justification to believe P require you to *have some argument* you could present for P. Justification need not be that sophisticated and reflective.[6]

I said that justification is a quality that *hypotheses* can possess for you: they can be hypotheses you have *justification to believe*. It doesn't matter whether *you do* believe them. This is sometimes called "propositional justification." We also have a notion of *doxastic attitudes* being justified. I will return to that notion in section 5. For now, let's keep thinking about propositional justification.

Justification comes in degrees and it can be defeated. It can be defeated in different ways. Suppose my brother tells you that his landlord is shifty-looking. That gives you some justification to believe that his landlord is dishonest. One way for that justification to be defeated is for my brother's roommate to tell you that their landlord is *not* shifty-looking. That evidence *opposes* my brother's testimony. It gives you some justification to believe the opposite. Another way for your justification to be defeated is for you to learn that my brother's landlord is an active member of his church and donates generously to charity. This evidence *narrows the reference class*. Shifty-looking people are in general likely to be dishonest, but shifty-looking people who are active in their church and so on tend not to be. A third way for your justification to be defeated is for me to tell you that my brother never met his landlord, and just has a prejudice against him because of a disagreement over the rent. This evidence attests to my brother's *not being in a position to know* what his landlord looks like. So it *undermines* the justification my brother's testimony gave you to believe that the landlord is dishonest. It doesn't give you any special reason to believe the landlord *is* or *looks honest*; he *may very well* look shifty and be dishonest. My testimony just gives you less reason to rely on my brother's word for it.

Of course, since justification comes in degrees, all these varieties of defeating evidence will come in degrees too. And they may themselves be defeated or undermined by further considerations.

Since justification to believe P can be defeated in these ways, we need to distinguish prima facie justification from all things considered justification. By "prima facie justification" to believe P, I *don't* mean merely that at first glance, *it seems like* you have justification to believe P. You really must have a body of justification for P. That justification can at the same time *be defeated or undermined* by further evidence you possess; but *in the absence of* such further evidence—and when the further evidence *itself* gets defeated— your prima facie justification to believe P must constitute some degree of *all things considered* justification to believe P.[7] That's what I mean by "prima facie justification" to believe P.

There are several different roles a theory of justification can assign a hypothesis H. To begin with, the theory needs to identify conditions whose *truth* is what *makes you* have prima facie justification to believe P. Let M be those conditions: conditions the mere satisfaction of which is supposed to make you justified. (You don't need to be *aware* that you satisfy them—unless that too is one of the conditions included in M.) One role a theory of justification can assign a hypothesis H is to include *H's being true* in M. That is, in order for you to have a given kind of prima facie justification to believe P, H has to be true. I'll call this a **truth-requiring** treatment of H.

Various hypotheses U will be such that evidence for them *undermines* the prima facie justification that satisfying M gives you to believe P. Hence, in order to be *all things considered* justified in believing P, you'll need to *lack* (undefeated) justification to believe that U obtains.[8] In the example I gave several paragraphs ago, what made you prima facie justified in believing the landlord is dishonest included hearing my brother testify that he's shifty-looking, and knowing that shifty-looking people are likely to be dishonest. One undermining hypothesis U for that justification is that my brother has never seen his landlord and so doesn't know what he looks like. My testimony gave you some justification to believe U, and thus (to some degree) undermined the prima facie justification you got from listening to my brother.

We're now ready to distinguish two further roles a theory of justification can assign a hypothesis H. A theory treats H **conservatively** when it says that you need some justification to believe H *in order to* have a given kind of prima facie justification to believe P. That is, the conditions M that *make you* have that prima facie justification include your having this justification to believe H. The justification to believe H has to come from sources *other than* the justification to believe P that we're considering, since it needs to be in place as a precondition of *your having* that justification to believe P. I'll put this by saying that your justification to believe H needs to be **antecedent to** this justification to believe P.[9] (It's *allowed* to derive from justification to believe P you have by other routes.)

A theory that treats H **liberally** *denies* that having prima facie justification to believe P requires you to have antecedent justification to believe H. But it does count not-H as an *undermining* hypothesis: evidence against H undermines your prima facie justification to believe P.[10]

Conservative and liberal treatments of H may or may not also assign H a truth-requiring role. If a theory assigns H a truth-requiring role, but *neither* of the other roles, I'll call that a *merely* truth-requiring treatment of H.[11]

A typical theory of justification will choose different options for different hypotheses. It might be conservative about some hypotheses, liberal about others, and merely truth-requiring about still others.

Let's consider some examples.

Suppose you're reading some proof of the Pythagorean Theorem. H1 is the claim that you *understand* and *correctly follow* the proof. Presumably, for you to be justified in believing the theorem, H1 does have to be true. But you don't need to have *evidence that* H1 is true. It's the proof itself that justifies you in believing the theorem. H1 is just some condition that *enables* this to happen.[12] It's not itself one of the premises that your justification for believing the theorem rests on—not even a suppressed, background premise. So the right treatment of H1 seems to be a non-conservative one.[13]

A second example. You remember parking your car in Lot 15. After you finish teaching, you intend to walk to Lot 15 and drive your car home. Presumably, having this intention gives you some justification to believe *you will* walk to Lot 15 and drive your car home. However, that assumes that your car is *still located* in Lot 15, and hasn't been stolen or towed away. Let H2 be the hypothesis that your car is still there. In this case, a conservative treatment seems most plausible. Having the intention to go drive your car home is not enough *by itself* to give you prima facie justification to believe you'll succeed in doing it. You also need some antecedent justification to believe H2 is true—that your car will still be there when you arrive.

A third example. You have visual experiences of your car. H3 is the claim that those experiences are reliable. A *reliabilist* will take H3 to have a status like H1's: it has to *be true*, for your experiences to justify you in believing your car is present, but you don't need to have *evidence or justification to believe* it's true. Internalists, on the other hand, deny that H3 needs to be true. Either they'll treat H3 liberally, and say it's enough that you *lack* reason to believe your experiences are *unreliable*. Or they'll treat it conservatively, and say you do require antecedent reason to believe your experiences are reliable. But in neither case does *the truth* of H3 make an epistemological difference. It's only *your epistemic situation concerning* H3 that is important.

As we can see, one will likely handle different cases differently.

## 3 Perceptual Justification

It seems to Moore that he's perceiving his hands. There are various things he could learn that would entail he's not. I'll call these **non-perceiving hypotheses**: they're hypotheses that are (known to be) incompatible with his experiences being genuine perceptions. For instance, the hypothesis that Moore is hallucinating his hands is a non-perceiving hypothesis. It's compatible with Moore's *having* hands; but it denies that he's perceiving them. Evidence for non-perceiving hypotheses will tend to *undermine* any justification Moore's experiences give him to believe he has hands.[14]

What role should we assign these hypotheses? Should we treat them conservatively, and say that Moore needs to have antecedent justification against them, as part of the conditions that *make him* have any prima facie perceptual justification? Or should we treat the hypotheses liberally, and say they *just count as underminers*?

A **conservative about perception** treats all non-perceiving hypotheses conservatively.[15] In my 2000, I defend a view that treats all such hypotheses liberally. I call that view **dogmatism about perception**. Intermediate views are also possible, but I will focus on these two.

I understand Wright to be a conservative about perception. This attribution is a bit complicated, though. One difficulty is that he uses different terminology than I use. The epistemic quality I call "justification" includes what he calls "entitlements" and "warrants."[16] A second difficulty is that I'm presently discussing propositional justification—justification *to believe* certain hypotheses—whereas Wright is often concerned whether you really have *justified beliefs*, and if so, what processes were involved in your acquiring them. I want to reserve questions about doxastic justification for later. Doxastic justification is complicated. It will pay to get clear about propositional justification first. A third difficulty is that Wright sometimes shifts to higher-order questions: not what it would take for you to justifiably believe *P*, but what it would take for you to justifiably believe that *you have justification* for P, or that *you're perceiving* that P. These higher-order questions are difficult, too. Some of our discussion will bear on them (see note 33 and section 7). But mostly, I'll stay focused on questions about your first-order justification to believe P, and I'll interpret Wright's views as directed to those questions, too.[17] A final difficulty is that Wright's position has evolved recently, in ways that complicate the dialectic between us (see his 2004). To keep our discussion manageable, I'll ignore the latest developments.

If we translate Wright's pre-2004 views into our present framework, this is what he says: In order for Moore's experiences to give him any justification to believe he has hands, Moore does need to have antecedent justification to believe that he's not hallucinating, that he's not a brain in a vat, that there's an external world, and so on.[18] As it happens, Wright thinks that Moore *has* that justification. It's not justification that Moore did anything special to earn. It didn't require him to engage in any a posteriori (or a priori) inquiry. He gets it by default. We all have defeasible default justifications to believe that we're not hallucinating, that there's an external world, and so on.[19] Our perceptual beliefs about hands aren't typically *inferred from* or based on prior beliefs that we're not hallucinating; and they don't *need* to be. We may just tacitly *assume* we're not hallucinating. But Wright thinks we *do* need antecedent *justification* for that assumption, before our experiences will even prima facie justify our perceptual beliefs.[20]

My view is that when Moore's experiences represent there to be hands, that *by itself* makes him prima facie justified in believing there are hands. This justification doesn't rest on any *premises about* Moore's experiences: whether they constitute perceptions, how reliable they are, or anything like that. It's in place so long as he *merely has* experiences that represent there to be hands. There are things Moore could learn that would undermine this justification. But it's not a condition for having it that he *first* have justification to believe those undermining hypotheses are false.

That is the view I defended in Pryor 2000. I emphasized there how simple and intuitively appealing the view is; I said the main work for systematic epistemology should be to defend the view against challenges. I think I was overly modest. But systematic epistemology can do more. One way it can do more is by highlighting how *un*convincing other answers to skepticism are. In fact, I suspect we'll have *no* prospect of avoiding skepticism unless we agree to be liberal to *some* degree, about *some* kinds of hypotheses. This puts pressure on any non-skeptic to say what's wrong with *the particular kind* of liberalism that the perceptual dogmatist espouses.

Another way for systematic epistemology to do more is to give a *positive* account of why our perceptual experiences should have the epistemic powers the dogmatist says they have. What I've said so far is compatible with a variety of such accounts. Some will argue that experiences as of P justify you in believing P because they make that belief *irresistible*, and it can't be the case that you ought not believe what you can't help believing.[21] Others will argue there's something distinctive about *the concepts* we employ in our perceptual beliefs, which makes those beliefs epistemically appropriate responses to our experiences.[22] I'm not sympathetic to either of those approaches. My view is that our perceptual experiences have the epistemic powers the dogmatist says they have because of what the *phenomenology* of perception is like.

I think there's a distinctive phenomenology: the feeling of *seeming to ascertain* that a given proposition is true. This is present when the way a mental episode represents its content makes it feel as though, *by* enjoying that episode, you can *thereby just tell* that that content obtains. We find this phenomenology in perception and in memory. When you have a perceptual experience of your hands, that experience makes it feel as though you *can just see* that hands are present. It feels as though hands are being shown or revealed to you. This phenomenology may be present in other mental episodes, too. But it's not present in *every* representational mental episode. When you daydream or exercise your visual imagination, you represent propositions (the same propositions you represent when you perceive), but it does not feel as though you can thereby just tell that those propositions are true.[23]

My view is that our perceptual justification comes from that phenomenology. Having the phenomenology of seeming to ascertain P is *what makes us* have prima facie justification to believe P. (You really need *to have* the phenomenology. It's not enough to think you do.)

Often, our perceptual experiences will move us to believe *more* than just what is presented in the phenomenologically distinctive way I described. For example, you may enjoy the phenomenology of seeming to ascertain that a blue-uniformed man is present, and unreflectively believe in response that the police have arrived. As I'm imagining this case, you *don't* have the phenomenology of seeming to ascertain that the police have arrived.[24] In such a case, I don't think your experiences are enough, *by themselves*, to give you prima facie justification to believe the police have arrived. They only justify you in believing the propositions they give you the phenomenology of seeming to ascertain.[25] To get justification to believe that the police have arrived, you'd need further justification to believe that blue-uniformed men are likely to be members of the police.

It's not easy to discern what propositions we "seem to ascertain," and what propositions we merely unreflectively infer. Our *perceptual reports* don't track the difference very closely. When you have the right kinds of background evidence, you'll unhesitatingly *say* things like "It looks as if the police have arrived" and "I see that the Smiths have already left for Australia." But I think there is a real difference. And my theory is that what we seem to ascertain, we thereby have immediate prima facie justification to believe. We don't need to have antecedent justification to believe we're not hallucinating, and so on.

## 4 Some Different Types of Epistemic Dependence

I've described two epistemologies of perception: the conservative and the dogmatist. They disagree about Moore's justification to believe (1).

According to the conservative, Moore's experiences give him justification to believe (1) only if he has antecedent justification to believe (3). According to the dogmatist, Moore's experiences immediately justify him in believing (1) and don't require him to have antecedent justification to believe anything else.

In particular cases, a conservative like Wright and I will largely agree about *which* subjects have justification. Wright says subjects need antecedent justification against undermining hypotheses, but they get it by default. I say they don't need it. We'll disagree about some details. For example, we'll disagree about when subjects have justification to believe the undermining hypotheses are false. But our central disagreement isn't about *who has* justification; it's about *the structure* of their justification. (Compare: the central disagreement between modal realists and ersatzists is not about *which* propositions are possible; it's about what their possibility consists in.) As we'll see now, this disagreement about justificatory structure drives further disagreement about which arguments count as objectionably question-begging.

Moore's justification for (1) is often said to "presuppose" or already "epistemically depend" in some way on his conclusion (3). This is thought to prevent his justification for (1) from lending any additional credibility to (3). He can't *get* any justification to believe (3) from his perceptual justification to believe (1). In Wright's and Davies' terminology, Moore's justification for (1) doesn't **transmit to** his conclusion (3).

Let's figure out what kind of "epistemic dependence" Moore's argument really exhibits, and whether that dependence really does have the claimed effect. I'll canvas five types of dependence; only the fourth and fifth will hold our interest.

**Type 1.** One way for an argument's premise to epistemically depend on its conclusion is that, in order for the premise to be true, it's necessary that the conclusion is true too. But there can't be anything epistemologically objectionable about *that*; if there were then deductive arguments would never be legitimate.

**Type 2.** Another way for a premise to epistemically depend on a conclusion is that, in order for you *to have justification to believe* the premise, it's necessary that the conclusion is true.[26] One problem here is that, again, it's not clear there's anything epistemologically objectionable about it. Suppose you're wondering whether people have justification to believe *anything*. You persuade yourself that if nothing else, at least cogito judgments are justified. That is, you reason:

(4)  Whoever believes he exists is justified in so believing, since his belief must be true.

(5)  I believe I exist.

(6)  So I'm justified in believing I exist.

(7) So there are at least some cases of people having justification.

This argument exhibits the type of epistemic dependence we're considering. It's necessary for you to have justification to believe *any* of its premises that its conclusion be true. But—setting aside controversies about why premise (4) should be true—this argument seems perfectly respectable. It seems like a perfectly good way to argue that at least some beliefs are justified.[27]

Furthermore, it's not clear that this type of epistemic dependence is one that Moore's argument even *exhibits*. Many epistemologists would allow Moore to be justified in believing he has hands even if *he were* an immaterial spirit, and the external world a mere hallucination. So he could have justification for his premises, even if his conclusion were false.

Let's keep looking, then.

**Type 3.** What about arguments where for you to have justification to believe the premise, it's necessary that *you have justification to believe* the conclusion? Once more, this seems to include some arguments that are perfectly respectable. It includes arguments where the connection between premise and conclusion is *so obvious* that understanding the premise well enough to be justified in believing it *requires* you to take any justification for the premise to also justify you in believing the conclusion.

A difficulty common to the proposals we've considered so far is that they characterize the premise's dependence on the conclusion as some kind of **necessary condition**. That doesn't seem to be what we need. Let's try a different approach.

**Type 4.** Another type of dependence between premise and conclusion is that the conclusion be such that evidence *against it* would (to at least some degree) undermine the kind of justification you purport to have for the premises.[28] Moore's argument clearly *does* exhibit this type of dependence. So long as we maintain the assumption that hands are external objects, any evidence that *there is no external world* will (to some degree) undermine Moore's perceptual justification for believing he has hands.

But is this type of dependence, in itself, a bad thing?

That's a difficult question, because many arguments that exhibit it will also exhibit a further type of epistemic dependence.

**Type 5.** We have this type of dependence when having justification to believe the conclusion *is among the conditions that make you* have the justification you purport to have for the premise. That is, whenever you need *antecedent* justification to believe the conclusion, as condition for having that justification for the premise.

Type 5 dependence does clearly seem to be an epistemic vice. Consider an example we discussed before:

(8) I intend to walk to Lot 15 and drive home.
(9) So *I will* walk to Lot 15 and drive home.

(10) So my car will still be in Lot 15 when I get there.

This argument sounds bad to us because we think your intention is not enough, by itself, to justify you in believing you'll succeed in driving your car out of the lot. We think you also need antecedent justification to believe your car is still *in* the lot. Wright and Davies argue that any Type 5 argument will **fail to transmit** the kind of justification you have for its premises to its conclusion.[29] Your justification for (9) *relies on* antecedent justification to believe (10); and for that reason, it can't *make* (10) any more credible for you.

I agree that Type 5 dependence ruins an argument. But what about Type 4 dependence?

There are several questions to address:

Q1.  Is it *possible* for an argument to exhibit Type 4 dependence while failing to exhibit Type 5?

Q2.  If so, are arguments that *merely* exhibit Type 4 dependence epistemologically objectionable?

Q3.  In which group does Moore's argument fall?

Let's take Q1 first. If you insist on treating *all* undermining hypotheses conservatively, then you can maintain that the two types of dependence coincide. Whenever evidence against a conclusion would undermine your justification to believe its premise, you'll think your justification for the premise must already rest on, and require antecedent justification for, the assumption that the conclusion is true.

But if you're willing to be liberal about *any* undermining hypotheses, then you think there can be undermining hypotheses that you don't need to be antecedently able to eliminate. This opens up room for arguments that have Type 4 dependence but not Type 5.

Which arguments *exhibit* that dependence will depend on what hypotheses you're willing to be liberal about. But here's a plausible example. Your introspective beliefs about what sensations you're having are fallible. You can be primed to expect sensations of cold and actually be given sensations of heat. In such cases you'll believe that you're having sensations you're not having.[30] So the hypothesis that you're making a priming mistake looks like an underminer for your introspective justification for believing you feel cold. Evidence that *you are* making a priming mistake ought to diminish the credibility of your introspective belief by at least *some degree*. At the same time, it's not plausible that your justification to believe you're having a given sensation requires you to have antecedent justification to believe you're not making any priming mistakes. *Sophisticated* subjects may know that they're reliable about their sensations. But I think you can have justified beliefs about your sensations long before attaining that degree of epistemic sophistication. So the hypothesis that you're making a priming mistake is not one you need antecedent justification to rule out.

Suppose that's all correct. Now consider a case where you *genuinely have* a cold sensation, are aware of having it, and you believe you have it. On the basis of your introspective awareness of your sensation, you judge that you're really having the sensation you think you're having, so you're not making a priming mistake right now.[31]

That piece of reasoning seems to exhibit Type 4 dependence, without exhibiting Type 5. It also sounds to me like an *epistemologically respectable* piece of reasoning. I think your introspective awareness of your sensation does make the hypothesis that you're not making a priming mistake *somewhat* more credible. You needn't be a dogmatist about perception to agree. You only need to be willing to treat this one undermining hypothesis for introspective justification in a liberal way.

In answer to Q1, then, I think yes, there can be arguments that exhibit Type 4 dependence without exhibiting Type 5. I think any liberal should be open to this possibility. I also think such arguments can be epistemologically respectable.[32] I hope the reasoning I just described gives a useful example; but I'll need to do a lot more to make the claim fully plausible. The next three sections will try.

Since I'm a dogmatist about perception, I think Moore's argument is another case where we have Type 4 dependence without Type 5. Here are a few more. Suppose you're watching a cat stalk a mouse. Your visual experiences justify you in believing:

(11) The cat sees the mouse.

You reason:

(12) If the cat sees the mouse, then there are some cases of seeing.
(13) So there are some cases of seeing.

Evidence against (13) would undermine your visual justification to believe (11); but I don't think you need antecedent justification to believe (13), before your experiences can give you justification to believe (11). I *also* think it's plausible that your perceptual justification to believe (11) contributes to the credibility of (13).

Suppose you look at a wall that's been painted red. Your visual experiences justify you in believing:

(14) The wall is red.

You reason:

(15) If the wall is red, it's not white but lit by tricky red lights that make it appear red.

(16) So the wall is not white but lit by tricky red lights.

Here too I think your visual justification to believe the premise makes the conclusion more credible for you. Your justification to believe the wall is red contributes to the credibility of the claim that the wall isn't white but lit by tricky red lights.[33]

I think all of these arguments are *epistemologically* respectable: that is, they articulate structures your justification genuinely can have.

When people learn this is my view, they complain that I'm giving away too cheaply justification to believe we're not in undermining scenarios. Stewart Cohen has argued this forcefully in Cohen 2002. One of his arguments involves a dialogue with his son. His son asks whether a certain table is red, and Cohen replies, "Yes I can see that it's red." The son asks whether Cohen knows that it's not white but lit by tricky red lighting, and Cohen imagines replying with an argument like my Red Wall argument (14)–(16). Cohen complains: "Surely [my son] should not be satisfied with this response."[34]

I agree that there are *some* respects in which these arguments are persuasively crippled, and so can fail to satisfy. I'll try to characterize those respects in the remaining sections of this paper. In terms of their justificatory structure, though, I think these arguments have nothing to be ashamed of.

## 5 Reasoning and Doubt

I've argued that there's nothing wrong with the justificatory structure that Moore's argument articulates. It's a structure that your justification genuinely can have.

Let's now take up a new target of evaluation: the **reasoning** that Moore engaged in.

We have justification to believe many things that we don't yet believe. Reasoning is a process by which we actively try to bring ourselves around. We try to believe what we have justification to believe. Usually this will involve recognizing that some beliefs you already have make a conclusion likely to be true, and believing the conclusion in response.

What does it mean to believe a conclusion "in response"? That depends. Sometimes reasoning just aims to "tease out" implications of things you already believe,[35] and undertakes no commitment about the epistemic priority of premises and conclusion. For example, suppose you see Joey emerge from a classroom with a big smile on his face. You believe that he's performed well on his Latin exam. *Your justification* to believe this will come in part from your having justification to believe that *he had* a Latin exam today. But *your first explicit recognition* that Joey had a Latin exam today may come by inferring it from your belief that he just performed well on it. You may be thinking: "Look how happy Joey is. He must have aced the Latin exam I see him emerging from. Wait a second! If Joey *just aced* the Latin exam, that means he *just took* the Latin exam! Damn it, I thought that exam was on Thursday...!"

We sometimes do reason in that "teasing-out" way. But I think often our reasoning aims to do more: it aims to reconstruct *the structure* of our justification. It aims to make explicit the justificatory relationships *by virtue of which* we have justification to believe a conclusion. When you reason from P to Q in *this* way, your resulting belief in Q will be (at least in part) *based on* your belief in P, and your recognition that P supports Q.[36] For the rest of our discussion, I'll understand "reasoning" to mean reasoning that has this aim.

I've argued that Moore's *justification can have the structure* he presents it as having. Let's now consider whether *the piece of reasoning* that Moore engaged in can be epistemologically legitimate, too.

One complaint often charged against Moore's argument—and my Red Wall argument—is that anyone who had doubts about its conclusion couldn't *use* the argument to rationally overcome those doubts. I think this complaint is correct. Let's see if we can respect it, while still maintaining that your justification has the structure the dogmatist says it has.

We need to get clear about what "doubting" an argument's conclusion involves. The dogmatist will agree that *having evidence against* the conclusion of Moore's argument undermines your perceptual justification to believe the premise. To get a disputed case, we need to consider examples where you lack such evidence. One possibility is that you start out believing—or at least suspecting—the conclusion is false, without having justification for doing so. (There are other ways to understand "doubt," too. We'll consider them later.)

If you *recognize* that your belief or suspicion about the argument's conclusion is unjustified, but can't help having it, I'll say you have a "pathological doubt." Otherwise your doubt is non-pathological. Let's set the pathological doubts aside for now. I assume you can have doubts that are unjustified without being pathological. Can such doubts affect what you're justified in believing? For example, if you *believe* without evidence that there is no external world, does that belief undermine the justification your experiences give you to believe you have hands? If you *believe* without evidence that the wall is lit by tricky red lighting, does that undermine your justification to believe the wall is red?

To answer these questions, we need to keep two epistemological contrasts firmly in mind.

The first contrast is between what you have justification to believe, and what you're **rationally committed** to believe by beliefs you already have. A rational commitment is a hypothetical relation between your beliefs; it doesn't "detach." That is, you can have a belief in P, that belief can rationally commit you to believe Q, and yet you be under no categorical requirement to believe Q. Suppose you believe Johnny can fly. This belief rationally commits you to the belief that someone can fly. If you're not *justified* in believing that Johnny can fly, though, you need not have any *justification* for the further belief. You may even have plenty of evidence and be fully justified in believing that *no one* can fly. But your belief that Johnny can fly still rationally commits you to the belief that someone can fly. Given your belief about Johnny, if you refrain from believing that someone can fly, you'll thereby exhibit a rational failing.[37]

I think we can understand rational commitments like this. Take a belief the subject happens to have, e.g., his belief in P. Consider what would be the epistemic effects of his *having (decisive) justification for* that belief. (It will be important what *other* parts of the subject's evidence we also suppose changed; but I won't try to sort that out here.) If one of the effects is that the subject has decisive justification to believe Q, then his belief in P counts as rationally committing him to the belief in Q—regardless of whether he *really does* have any justification to believe P. (Notice: although from the facts that you believe P, and that belief commits you to believe Q, we can't infer that you have any justification to believe Q, we *can* infer that when we add the further premise that you have justification to believe P.)

For our purposes, it will be useful to weaken and generalize this notion. We can do that by considering the effects of having *degrees* of justification to believe P, and considering *a broader variety* of effects. That lets us introduce the following normative relations. We can say that a subject's belief in P **rationally supports** those beliefs that *justification* for P would lend some credibility to (even if it doesn't decisively commit the subject to them). We can say that a subject's belief in P **rationally opposes** those beliefs that justification for P would tell against. Most interestingly, we can say that a subject's belief in P **rationally obstructs** him from believing Q on certain grounds, when justification for P would undermine the justification those grounds give him for Q. For example, the mere belief that your color vision is defective—whether justified or not—would rationally obstruct you from believing the wall is red on the basis of your color experiences. It would rationally pressure you to place less trust in those grounds on that question.

Because the epistemic effects we're considering are non-monotonic and matters of degree, so too will be the relations of rational obstruction, rational support, and rational opposition. To keep our discussion simpler, though, I will mostly suppress the complications that introduces. But I will allow myself to talk about partial doxastic attitudes—attitudes like doubt, suspicion, and disbelief—standing in these various relations.

I will count a belief as **rational** when it's a belief that none of your other beliefs or doubts rationally oppose or rationally obstruct you from believing.

This makes "being rational" a different quality than having justification. A subject can *have some justification* to believe P, but be unable to *rationally* believe P on the basis of that justification, because of some (unjustified) beliefs and doubts he also has. Consider again your belief that your color-vision is defective. Suppose that this belief is unjustified (but you don't realize it). Because you don't have *justification* to doubt your color vision, I don't think the justification you get from your color experiences will be *undermined*. You'll still *have justification* to believe the wall is red. But your actual doubt will *rationally obstruct you* from relying on your color experiences. It'll prevent you from rationally accepting that justification.

I said we need to keep two contrasts firmly in mind. The second contrast is between having *justification to believe* something, and having *a belief* that is justified or well-founded. Unjustified beliefs and doubts may have no undermining effect on what propositions you have justification to believe; but for your beliefs to be well-founded, it's *not enough* that they be beliefs in propositions you have justification to believe. They also have to be *based on* that justification, and they have to be *rational* beliefs. Suppose you believe P, on the basis of what are in fact good reasons for believing P. But you also have doubts that rationally oppose P, or rationally obstruct you from believing P for the reasons you do. Those doubts will render your belief in P *irrational* even if they don't affect your justification *to* believe it. And if your belief in P *is* irrational, then it can't be a justified or well-founded belief. In this way, then, even unjustified doubts can affect what justified beliefs you're able to have.[38]

Let's suppose you doubt whether the premises of some argument are true. Or you doubt whether the argument really justifies you in believing its conclusion. Or perhaps you believe something that rationally commits you to doubting those things. In all of these cases, it *won't be rational* for you to accept the argument's conclusion. (At least, not on the basis of that argument. You might have other, independent reasons for believing it.) It doesn't matter whether your doubts are justified. Even unjustified doubts will make it irrational for you to accept the conclusion. Those doubts will prevent the argument from rationally persuading you, until you give them up.

But none of that should cast epistemic discredit on *the argument*. For all I've said, the argument could be any standard proof of the Pythagorean Theorem. You may *in fact have* justification to believe its premises, and just have unjustified doubts about them. The proof would then *still give you* justification to believe its conclusion. Your doubts would prevent you from *rationally accepting* that conclusion, until you gave them up. But this is no fault of the proof's. The fault lies with you, for having doubts you have no good reason to have.

The same holds for any argument that exhibits only Type 4 dependence. A subject doesn't need antecedent justification for the conclusion; but if she *acquires reason to doubt* the conclusion, that will undermine her justification for the premises. It follows that if the subject *just happens to* doubt the conclusion, without having any reason for doing so, her doubt will rationally obstruct her from believing the argument's premises. Hence, her doubt will make it irrational for her to accept the argument's conclusion (at least, on the basis of that argument). So the argument can't "rationally overcome" her doubt. It doesn't give her a piece of reasoning she can *rationally* accept, while starting from a position of having that doubt. To be sure, that's *some* kind of failing. But it's a deficiency in the argument's *persuasive* power, not in its justificatory structure. We just saw that unjustified doubts can make it irrational for you to accept the conclusions of *perfectly respectable* arguments, like standard proofs of the Pythagorean Theorem. These Type 4 arguments are a special case, where your doubts happen to be about the very proposition that is the argument's conclusion. But that makes no epistemological difference. In both cases, you may very well *be justified* in believing the argument's premises, and the argument may very well *give you justification* to believe its conclusion. Given your doubts, it may not be rational for you to accept the premises, or the conclusion. But that won't be the argument's fault. It'll be your fault, for having doubts where no doubt is justified.[39]

## 6 Other Varieties of Doubt

Up to this point, I've been understanding "doubt" as some degree of *disbelief*. However, sometimes doubt is a matter of mere *agnosticism* or *suspended judgment*. We might regard the skeptic's hypotheses as equally likely true as false. That's not enough to count as *believing* those hypotheses.

In some cases, I think agnosticism will be compatible with rationally accepting Moore-type reasoning. (If you do accept the reasoning, that will rationally commit you to give your agnosticism up: it's irrational to believe you have hands on the basis of your experiences while *retaining* agnosticism about whether those experiences count as perceptions.) In other cases, I think agnosticism will have the same effects as positive disbelief (albeit to a lesser degree). I'll have to explain and defend this contrast elsewhere.[40]

There is still another way to understand "doubt" about an argument's conclusion. Sometimes we "entertain doubt" about a hypothesis in a sense that's compatible with *continuing to believe* the hypothesis. This is what goes on when we read Descartes' First Meditation. We don't *really* suspend our beliefs about our surroundings; we just *entertain the hypothesis* that those beliefs are false, and think about what epistemic relations we bear to that hypothesis, and what follows. Call this **hypothetical doubt**. (In conversation, Cohen insists this is the only kind of doubt his son has when he asks whether Cohen knows the table isn't white but lit by tricky red lights.)

Are hypothetical doubts enough to undermine or take away our perceptual justification? Some philosophers say they are. For instance, Wright says that:

> Once *the hypothesis is seriously entertained* that it is as likely as not, for all I know, that there is no material world as ordinarily conceived, my experience will lose all tendency to corroborate the particular propositions about the material world which I normally take to be certain.[41]

I on the other hand want to treat hypothetical doubt along the same lines I sketched in the previous section.

Let me say a little to set my account up. Suppose you do in fact possess some prima facie justification to believe P. Then a trustworthy philosophical authority tells you you *don't* have any justification (even prima facie justification) to believe P. Now you have negative higher-order justification: justification to believe you *don't* have (even prima facie) justification to believe P.

What will the effect of that higher-order justification be on your first-order prima facie justification? Will there be no effect? Will it undermine that first-order justification (at least to some degree)? Will it mean that you no longer satisfy the conditions *making you* have even prima facie justification to believe P? I'm inclined to say the second; but I've encountered sympathy for each of these answers.

Now suppose that, instead of higher-order *justification*, you merely acquire a negative higher-order *belief*. What then will the effect be? I think the most plausible answer here is that the higher-order belief will rationally obstruct you from believing P.[42]

So, now, consider: You have a visual experience of your hands. That experience gives you some prima facie justification to believe you do have hands. Initially, you're *inclined to believe* you have hands, on the basis of your experiences.

Then along comes a skeptic. He starts presenting various undermining hypotheses $U_1$, $U_2$, ... He argues that since you have no antecedent justification *against* those hypotheses, your experiences don't really give you justification—even prima facie justification—to believe you have hands. He argues that if *you did* have justification to believe there's an external world, you ought to be able to rationally persuade him that there is, but you can't.

As it happens, the skeptic's arguments are flawed. Before you encountered him, you *did* have justification to believe you have hands and so on, contrary to what he's claiming. But the skeptic is a smooth dialectician. His arguments sound pretty compelling to you. You don't discern their flaws. When a flawed argument sounds compelling to you, we might say *you're justified* in believing its conclusion—at least until further reflection reveals the flaws.[43] If we do say that, then you'll be *justified* in believing what the skeptic tells you. You'll be justified in believing your experiences don't give you any perceptual justification. In my view, that has the result of *undermining* your first-order perceptual justification. Listening to the skeptic will have undermined some prima facie perceptual justification you really have.[44]

Alternatively, perhaps we should *deny* that you're justified in believing the conclusions of flawed but compelling arguments. The skeptic's arguments merely *persuade* you. They don't persuade you that any of $U_1$, $U_2, \ldots$ are true; but they do persuade you to believe, or at least give some credence to, the negative higher-order claim that your experiences don't give you perceptual justification. (Or perhaps they just persuade you to believe some things that *rationally commit you* to that conclusion.) In that case, I think the skeptic will have succeeded in rationally obstructing you from believing you have hands on the basis of your experiences. So you'll no longer be able to *justifiably believe* you have hands.

Neither of these outcomes means that the skeptic *was right*. The skeptic makes claims about *all subjects*, even subjects who haven't heard his argument. On the story I just told, those claims are false. But subjects who *do* hear the skeptic's arguments, and are partly taken in by them, do really end up with some of the epistemic difficulties the skeptic says we all suffer from.

Skepticism isn't the truth about all of us, then. It's just a disease that some of us catch. The way to cure the disease is to realize that skepticism *isn't* the truth about all of us: the skeptic's arguments are flawed. So our negative higher-order beliefs are false. When we give those negative higher-order beliefs up, then the prima facie justification our perceptual experiences gave us all along will be undefeated and unobstructed.

## 7 Persuading the Skeptic

Let's revisit the different targets of evaluation I've identified so far.

It was clear from the beginning that the **proof** Moore rehearsed is perfectly respectable.

I argued in sections 3–4 that the **justificatory structure** Moore was endorsing is a genuine one. Perceptual justification to believe you have hands doesn't require antecedent justification to believe there's an external world; and it can make the latter hypothesis more credible for you.

Sections 5–6 gave us the following results:

- It was already agreed that if you *have evidence* that you're in a skeptical scenario, it will (to some degree) undermine your perceptual justification to believe Moore's premise (1).
- If you *believe or suspect* without evidence that you're in a skeptical scenario, that won't *undermine your justification* for Moore's premise (1). But it will (to some extent) *rationally obstruct you* from believing

that premise on the basis of your experiences. So you won't be able to use Moore's argument to rationally overcome your suspicions.[45]

• I think some cases of agnosticism work the same way. Others don't. I'll argue for this elsewhere.

• In the happy case where you neither *have* nor *have reason to have* the kinds of doubts the skeptic wants to induce, then the justification your experiences give you for Moore's premise (1) will be undefeated and unobstructed. Having that justification for the premise *will* make Moore's conclusion more credible for you; and that justificatory relationship is one that you can rationally endorse in your reasoning.

If Moore's psychological and epistemic situation was the last one, then I claim the reasoning he engaged in was perfectly legitimate.

Let's now consider a fourth target of evaluation. Instead of Moore's own reasoning, let's consider the **dialectical power** of his argument.

Arguments are dialectical creatures, in a way that proofs and pieces of reasoning are not. Arguing involves *offering* pieces of reasoning *to audiences*. (You can argue with yourself. I think of that as arguing with a *hypothetical* audience.) An argument *succeeds* for a given audience to the extent that it presents the audience with a piece of reasoning they can rationally accept. I call arguments that do that **dialectically effective**. (I don't care whether the audience *really does* accept the presented reasoning.)

Of course, different audiences come to the table with different commitments and doubts, and we've just seen that those attitudes can affect what pieces of reasoning one can rationally accept. So how dialectically effective an argument is will depend on *who* its audience is. (I imagine this will affect how pragmatically appropriate it is *to give* the argument in different conversational contexts.)

Moore's argument is directed at a skeptic. We've focused on the skeptic who doubts whether our perceptual experiences give us any justification at all for our perceptual beliefs. Clearly Moore's argument is not very dialectically effective against that skeptic. But it should be clear by now why that's so. The skeptic *has doubts* that prevent Moore's argument from rationally persuading him. There's nothing wrong with the justificatory structure the argument articulates, or with Moore's own reasoning. What's wrong is that the skeptic has doubts he ought not to have.

We just discussed *how dialectically effective* Moore's argument will be against a skeptic. A separate question, and a fifth target of evaluation, is how good of a **philosophical response to skepticism** Moore's argument constitutes. Moore had a variety of anti-skeptical ideas, including his claim that we're reasonably more confident that we have hands than we are of the premises in the skeptic's arguments.[46] But let's just consider Moore's argument from (1) and (2) to (3). Our question is: how satisfying a philosophical response to skepticism does *that argument* constitute?

Nowadays, it's commonly agreed that an adequate *philosophical response* to the skeptic need not be capable of rationally *persuading* the skeptic that the external world exists, or that we have justification to believe it exists.[47] Nor need it be capable of persuading someone who's seized by skeptical doubts. What it *does* have to do is diagnose and explain the flaws in the skeptic's reasoning. It has to explain away the intuitions that the skeptic draws support from. These are *not* responsibilities that one has as an ordinary believer. The ordinary believer who's never heard the skeptic's arguments—or who's heard them but rationally believes they've got to be flawed somehow—doesn't need to to do anything more, before he can believe with justification that the world is the way it looks to him. But they are responsibilities we have when we're doing philosophy. That's *the business* of philosophy: to diagnose and criticize arguments like the skeptic's.

Clearly Moore's argument, by itself, does little to discharge those responsibilities. I think it *does* offer us a piece of reasoning by which we can acquire justification to believe the external world exists. But it takes a lot of supporting argument—only some of which I've given here—to establish that. If we're to have a satisfying philosophical response to skepticism, it will consist in that supporting argument, not in the reasoning that Moore's argument articulates.

## Notes

* Versions of this paper have been circulating since 2001. Many thanks to Robert Audi, Jake Beck, Helen Beebee, Karen Bennett, Alex Byrne, Stew Cohen, Annalisa Coliva, Juan Comesaña, Martin Davies, Greg Epstein, Miguel Fernández, Mark Greenberg, Patrick Hawley, Richard Heck, Tom Kelly, Adam Leite, Christian Piller, Mark Schroeder, Nico Silins, Jonathan Vogel, Ralph Wedgwood, Tim Williamson, Crispin Wright, my spring 2004 graduate seminar, and audiences in Arizona, Mexico City, Paris, Seattle, and Wake Forest, for all their useful comments and feedback.

1. In Moore 1939.
2. Contextualism has come under heavy fire recently: see Sosa 2000; Kornblith 2000; Feldman 1999; Williamson forthcoming; Stanley 2004; Hawthorne 2004, Ch. 2; and Richard 2004.
3. For instance, see Hawthorne 2004, Ch. 1 and forthcoming.
4. See Wright 1985, 2000a, 2002, 2003, 2004; and Davies 1998, 2000, 2003, and 2004.
5. Consider e.g., Plautinga 1993, Ch. 1; and Goldman 1988's notion of "weak justification."
6. For more on these issues, see my 2001, §4.2.
7. Matters would be more complicated if we were talking of justification to *fully believe* P. You can have a degree of justification to believe P that's not yet enough to justify an attitude of full belief. However, I propose to work always with a notion of justification to *partially* believe P: justification to believe P to a

given degree. When I omit mention of degrees (as I often do), it's just for expository convenience.

8. As I said in the previous footnote, this all needs to be understood in terms of degrees. Additionally, I'm assuming you don't *also* have prima facie justification to believe P from further sources that *aren't* undermined by U.

9. For more on this relation of antecedent justification, see my 2000. I argue there that it plays an essential role in the most powerful skeptical arguments. See also Klein 1981, §§2.13–15; Klein 1995, n. 16; and Wright's papers cited in note 4, above.

10. A conservative about H may also count evidence *against* H—that is, evidence that *opposes* the antecedent justification you have to believe H—as undermining the prima facie justification you have (and retain) to believe P. When your antecedent justification to believe H is *undermined*, though, the conservative will claim you cease to meet the conditions necessary *to have prima facie justification* to believe P.

11. Such a theory assigns H's truth an essential role in *giving* you prima facie justification to believe P; but says that evidence against H has no *intrinsic* undermining potential. It can undermine your prima facie justification for P only indirectly, by raising the likelihood of other hypotheses that *do* have undermining potential. The clearest way for this to obtain would be that *you don't recognize* the role H plays in justifying P. If *you do* recognize that role, then acquiring evidence against H should *at least* justify you in believing *you don't have justification* to believe P. I think that negative higher-order justification does undermine the first-order justification you get from H's really obtaining; but this is controversial. We'll discuss the question in section 6, below.

12. Compare BonJour's discussion of "background conditions" for a priori justification in BonJour 1998, pp. 126ff. and 137.

13. Suppose you *do* understand the proof in our example, but you acquire misleading evidence that you don't. That is, you get evidence against H1. I'm inclined to think this evidence would undermine the justification that your (actual) understanding of the proof gives you. If so, then we should treat H1 in the liberal (and truth-requiring) way. If on the other hand we think the hypothesis that not-H1 has no intrinsic undermining potential, then we should treat H1 in the merely truth-requiring way.

14. Hypotheses can undermine without being non-perceiving hypotheses. For example, consider the hypothesis that Moore *tends to* hallucinate hands, and the hypothesis that his visual experiences *aren't generally reliable*. It's compatible with these hypotheses that, on some particular occasion, Moore is perceiving his hands. So they're not non-perceiving hypotheses. But plausibly, if Moore were to acquire evidence for them, it would undermine his perceptual justification to believe he has hands. Perhaps that's because evidence for them *makes it more likely* that Moore is not perceiving right now. In any event, I will for simplicity confine my discussion to just those undermining hypotheses that are also non-perceiving hypotheses.

15. BonJour 1985 and Cohen 2002 are good examples. Note that one can be conservative about perception without being conservative across the board.

16. Burge, Peacocke, Davies, and Dretske also prefer the terms 'entitlement' and 'warrant' to 'justification.' I insist on 'justification.' It ought not to have the

undesired associations they hear it to have. Plus, 'entitlement' has bad associations of its own, and 'warrant' is already used in too many different ways.

17. The higher-order questions are most prominent in Wright's 2004.

18. See, e.g., Wright 1985, pp. 435–8 and Wright 2002, pp. 336–8.

19. See Wright's 1985, pp. 449ff.; 2000a, pp. 152–3, 156–7; 2000b, pp. 212–13; 2003, pp. 66, 68; and 2004. Compare Cohen's 1999 and 2000, which claim that certain skeptical hypotheses are a priori irrational, so we're entitled to reject them without evidence.

20. I understand Martin Davies to be a lapsed conservative. He used to express sympathy for a view like Wright's, which said that Moore's perceptual justification to believe he has hands rests against "background assumptions" that Moore needs antecedent "entitlement" for (see Davies 2000, p. 401). Davies stresses that normally one won't *believe* those background assumptions; it's enough merely to *not doubt* them. But it does seem that you need *justification* to believe a proposition, for it to play the role of a background assumption. Davies characterizes background assumptions as propositions B where the epistemic probability of H for you, given some evidence E, is $p(H|E\&B)$ (p. 396). B can only play that role when it itself has some epistemic probability for you.

   In his most recent paper (Davies 2004), Davies drops the requirement that Moore have "positive entitlement" to any background assumptions. His new view is near, or the same as, the view I favor.

21. See, e.g., Hume's *Treatise* I.IV.2; Reid's *Inquiry* V.7, VI.20; Strawson 1985; and Dretske 2000.

22. This includes Pollock 1986, pp. 142–8; Brewer 1999; and Peacocke 2004. The details of their accounts are quite different.

23. In Pryor 2000, n. 37, I called this the "phenomenal force" of perceptual experience, thinking of it on analogy with the assertoric force of a public utterance. See also Heck 2000, pp. 508–9; Thau 2002, §2.3; and Burge 2003, p. 543.

24. I imagine there *could* be subjects who represent that the police have arrived in the phenomenologically distinctive way I described. They would seem to ascertain that the police have arrived. But in my example, you do not.

25. That's somewhat over-stated. I think your experiences also justify you in believing that *you are ascertaining* those propositions, and that *you're having* those experiences. See note 33, below.

26. Compare McLaughlin's criterion for question-beggingness in McLaughlin 2000, pp. 104–5. That criterion should probably be amended to require that the subject *recognize* she has justification for the premise only if the conclusion is true. Even so amended, though, McLaughlin's criterion would still wrongly count the argument (4)–(7), and the argument in the next note, as question-begging.

27. Davies 1998, p. 352 also makes this point.

   Here's another example. I attend to my occurrent mental life, and observe:

   (i) I am conscious.

   from which I conclude:

   (ii) So somebody is conscious.

Here too, the truth of the conclusion seems a necessary condition for having the justification I do to believe the premise. Yet once again, the argument sounds perfectly respectable.

28. The reference to *what kind* of justification you purport to have for the premises is essential. Suppose your conclusion is "I ingested no memory-altering drugs recently" and your premises concern your activities over the past few days. If your grounds for believing those premises consist of other people's present testimony, then the case is unremarkable. Evidence that you *did* ingest memory-altering drugs may oppose, but it wouldn't undermine your grounds for believing the premises. However, if your grounds consist of *your memories* of the past few days, then your grounds would be undermined by evidence that you ingested memory-altering drugs recently. In this second case, we have an example of the type of epistemic dependence we're considering.

29. As with Type 4 arguments, the reference to a *kind* of justification for the premise is essential. Arguments may transmit some kinds of justification for their premises but fail to transmit others. See Wright 2000a, p. 141 and Wright 2003, p. 58.

30. Some will claim that you genuinely do feel cold, but only for a second. I think that's incorrect. Of course there's *some* qualitative difference between your entire phenomenology when you think you're having a sensation of cold, and when you *realize* you're having one of heat. But this difference is a difference in how you *recognize* or classify your sensation. When you decide that your initial classification was wrong, it doesn't feel like you're trying to keep up with a sensation whose intrinsic quality is changing. You feel like you're recognizing the true character of a sensation that has remained the same. See Feldman 2003, pp. 55–6.

31. Thanks to Jonathan Vogel for help constructing this example.

32. It's unclear to me what Wright's view is. Clearly he thinks Type 5 dependence suffices for transmission-failure. On the simplest reading, he thinks transmission-failure *coincides with* Type 5 dependence. Matters are complicated, though, in several ways.

(1) Wright sometimes seems to be saying that Type 4 dependence also suffices for transmission-failure. (For example, in some passages on pp. 342–3 of his 2002. These passages also occur in his 2000a and 2003.) However, when he says that he *seems* also to be thinking that Type 4 dependence entails Type 5 dependence. I hesitate because in the crucial passages he shifts to talking about higher-order justification. He *may* think that what transmission-failure coincides with is your needing antecedent justification for the conclusion in order to have justification to believe *that you have justification* for the premises.

(2) Wright talks about "information-dependent" and "inferential" warrants, and his characterization of these makes them sound like justification that relies on antecedent justification to believe something else. Wright *definitely* thinks arguments can exhibit transmission-failure even when your justification for their premises isn't "information-dependent" (see his 2002, pp. 344ff. and 2003, pp. 60–63). This suggests that we can have transmission-failure even when your justification to believe the premise *doesn't* require antecedent justification to believe the conclusion (or anything else). But there's also evidence that Wright understands "information-dependence" more narrowly than my relation of needing

antecedent justification to believe something else, and that he thinks all cases of transmission-failure *do* involve what I'd call Type 5 dependence. (See e.g., Wright 2002, p. 346 and 2000b, pp. 212–13.)

Davies is also difficult to interpret. He first says we have transmission-failure when your justification for an argument's premises "presupposes" or requires a "prior commitment" to the argument's conclusion, or when the conclusion's truth is a "precondition" of your justification for the premises (see his 1998, pp. 350–1, 354). He doesn't specify what those relations amount to. On one interpretation, he too should be read as saying that transmission-failure coincides with Type 5 dependence. But other interpretations are also possible.

Later Davies says we have transmission-failure when your justification for the premises has "background assumptions" that you could not rationally accept while doubting the conclusion (Davies 2000, pp. 402ff.). We'll discuss questions about what you can rationally accept while doubting below.

Davies' most recent account (Davies 2004) comes close to my own. He now grants that Moore's argument *can* transmit justification to its conclusion. He just thinks it cannot "settle the question" whether that conclusion is true. "Settling the question" is supposed to be analogous to convincing a doubter (see Davies 2003, pp. 41–3). So Moore's failure to settle the question is only a dialectical or persuasive failing.

Alston 1986 and Bergmann forthcoming also think that Type 4 arguments can give us justification to believe their conclusion. They do regard them as "epistemically circular" arguments, but they say in this case the circularity is benign. A Type 4 argument's weakness is just that it cannot persuade doubters.

33. As I mentioned in note 25, above, I think your experiences will *also* justify you in believing that *you're seeing* the wall to be red. You're visually ascertaining that *it is* red. From that premise you can infer the simpler conclusion that the wall is not lit by tricky red lights. (If it were so lit, then even if it were red, you wouldn't be ascertaining its redness.) I think this inference is just as good as the inference I cite in the text.

34. Cohen 2002, p. 314. See also Wright 2002, p. 342. The next few sections give the start of a response to Cohen's argument. My full response requires the non-classical system of epistemic probability I set out in Pryor forthcoming. Cohen also gives a second argument, concerning "bootstrapping." I'll have to respond to that argument elsewhere.

35. Compare Jackson 1987, Ch. 6 on the "teasing-out" role of argument.

36. When I talk of a subject's "trying" to believe what he has justification to believe, or "recognizing" that some premises support his conclusion, I'm not imagining him to have explicit attitudes. In normal cases, these will just be tacit commitments of his reasoning, commitments that are manifested in how ready he is to revise or retract that reasoning in response to different sorts of defeating evidence. There are difficult and important issues here, but we can't pursue them now.

37. Sometimes it can be *practically rational* to deliberate with, and act on, attitudes from which you haven't managed to purge all such flaws. (See Harman 1986, Ch. 2.) Nonetheless, believing in this way still constitutes a rational failing.

Relations like the one I'm calling "rational commitment" have been much discussed in moral philosophy. They play a central role in recent work by Broome and Dancy. (See Broome 1999; Broome 2003; and Dancy 2000, Ch. 2–3.) Broome and Dancy explicate the idea in terms of "wide-scope oughts," whose normative force attach to a conditional or disjunctive attitude, rather than to a particular attitude. As Broome would put it, you ought to: *believe Johnny can fly only if you believe someone can fly.* From that, and the fact that you actually do believe Johnny can fly (perhaps without reason), it does not follow that you ought to believe someone can fly: $O(Bp \supset Bq)$ and $Bp$ don't entail $OBq$. This explication is formally neat, and it makes the non-detachability of the ought vivid. However, Mark Schroeder has persuaded me that it shoulders controversial commitments not required by the core idea of a non-detachable relation between states (some of his argument is set out in Schroeder). These include a questionable semantics for the English auxiliary 'ought,' and predictions of more symmetries than our intuitions validate. The explication I give in the text avoids some of those further commitments.

38. Perhaps *pathological* doubts wouldn't have that power. Suppose you have a nagging belief that you're a brain in a vat, which you recognize to be unjustified, but which you just can't get rid of. But you go ahead and form perceptual beliefs on the basis of your experiences, just like everyone else. Then you'd be exhibiting a kind of irrationality. But in this case it's not clear we should attribute any irrationality to your perceptual beliefs. They might arguably count as well-founded.

39. Like me, Bergmann forthcoming also thinks that having doubts about Moore's conclusion will take away your doxastic justification for believing Moore's premise. Bergmann doesn't discuss what effects doubts have on propositional justification.

40. My account of agnosticism requires the non-classical system of epistemic probability I mentioned in note 34.

41. Wright 1985, p. 347, my italics. See also Davies 1998, p. 351; and Davies 2000, p. 404.

42. Compare Harman's Principle of Positive Undermining in Harman 1986. See also Goldman's account of undermining in Goldman 1986, Ch. 4–5.

43. I hesitate to say that *the argument* justifies you in believing its conclusion—after all, it's flawed. Perhaps we should say your present *understanding* of the argument justifies you. It *does* at least seem to justify you in the higher-order belief that the argument gives you justification for its conclusion. In the same way that I allowed negative higher-order justification the power *to undermine* first-order justification, I'm tempted to also allow *positive* higher-order justification the power *to supply* first-order justification. (Broome defends a practical analogue of this; see his 1999 and 2001, §4.) Notice that if we say this, then we need to posit some opacity about where one's justification is coming from. The subject will think it comes from the argument itself. In the case we're considering, it doesn't.

44. In Pryor 2000, I thought that we should not count a priori skeptical arguments as introducing "defeating evidence" (p. 354). On the current proposal, though, they do. (This *isn't* how the skeptic conceives what he's doing; see below.)

45. Wright's definition of a "cogent argument," in Wright 2002, p. 331 equates:

> (i) being an argument that could move someone *to rationally overcome doubt* about its conclusion

with:

> (ii) being an argument that could move someone *to rational conviction* in its conclusion.

See also Davies 2000, pp. 388, 397ff.. Our discussion in sections 5–6 shows that an argument can have virtue (ii) without having virtue (i). Davies now agrees: see his 2004. Beebee 2001 similarly distinguishes between arguments that "fail to convince" in the sense of not persuading someone who doubts their conclusion, and arguments that "fail to convince" in the sense of not giving one justification for their conclusion.

46. See Moore 1909 and Moore 1918/19.
47. See, e.g., Cohen 1988; DeRose 1995, §17; Pryor 2000; and Byrne 2004.

# References

Alston, William. 1986. Epistemic circularity. *Philosophy and Phenomenological Research*, **47**.

Beebee, Helen. 2001. Transfer of warrant, begging the question, and semantic externalism. *Philosophical Quarterly*, **51**, 356–74.

Bergmann, Michael. forthcoming. Epistemic circularity: malignant and benign. *Philosophy and Phenomenological Research*. Available online: http://philosophy.rutgers.edu/EVENTS/EPIS2003/Bergmann.pdf.

BonJour, Laurence. 1985. *The Structure of Empirical Knowledge*. Cambridge, Mass.: Harvard University Press.

BonJour, Laurence. 1998. *In Defense of Pure Reason*. Cambridge: Cambridge University Press.

Brewer, Bill. 1999. *Perception and Reason*. Oxford: Oxford University Press.

Broome, John. 1999. Normative requirements. *Ratio*, **12**, 398–419.

Broome, John. 2001. Normative practical reasoning. *Aristotelian Society Supplement*, **75**, 175–93.

Broome, John. 2003. Practical reasoning. In: Bermúdez, José Luis, & Millar, Alan (eds.), *Reason and Nature*. Oxford: Oxford University Press.

Burge, Tyler. 2003. Perceptual entitlement. *Philosophy and Phenomenological Research*, **67**, 503–48.

Byrne, Alex. 2004. How hard are the skeptical paradoxes? *Noûs*, **38**, 299–325.

Cohen, Stewart. 1988. How to be a fallibilist. *Philosophical Perspectives*, **2**, 91–123.

Cohen, Stewart. 1999. Contextualism, skepticism, and the structure of reasons. *Philosophical Perspectives*, **13**, 57–90.

Cohen, Stewart. 2000. Contextualism and skepticism. *Philosophical Issues*, **10**, 94–107.

Cohen, Stewart. 2002. Basic knowledge and the problem of easy knowledge. *Philosophy and Phenomenological Research*, **65**, 309–29.

Dancy, Jonathan. 2000. *Practical Reality*. New York: Oxford University Press.

Davies, Martin. 1998. Externalism, architecturalism, and epistemic warrant. Pages 321–61 of Wright, Crispin, Smith, Michael, & Macdonald, Cynthia (eds.), *Knowing Our Own Minds: Essays in Self-Knowledge*. Oxford: Oxford University Press.

Davies, Martin. 2000. Externalism and armchair knowledge. Pages 384–414 of: Boghossian, Paul, & Peacocke, Christopher (eds.), *New Essays on the A Priori*. Oxford: Oxford University Press.

Davies, Martin. 2003. The problem of armchair knowledge. Pages 23–55 of: Nuccetelli, Susana (ed.), *New Essays on Semantic Externalism and Self-Knowledge*. Cambridge, Mass.: MIT Press.

Davies, Martin. 2004. Epistemic entitlement, warrant transmission, and easy knowledge. *Aristotelian Society Supplement*, **78**, 213–45.

DeRose, Keith. 1995. Solving the skeptical problem. *Philosophical Review*, **104**, 1–52.

Dretske, Fred. 2000. Entitlement: epistemic rights without epistemic duties? *Philosophy and Phenomenological Research*, **60**, 591–606.

Feldman, Richard. 1999. Contextualism and skepticism. *Philosophical Perspectives*, **13**, 91–114.

Feldman, Richard. 2003. *Epistemology*. Upper Saddle River: Prentice-Hall.

Goldman, Alvin. 1986. *Epistemology and Cognition*. Cambridge, Mass.: Harvard University Press.

Goldman, Alvin. 1988. Strong and weak justification. *Philosophical Perspectives*, **2**, 51–69.

Harman, Gilbert. 1986. *Change in View*. Cambridge, Mass.: MIT Press.

Hawthorne, John. 2004. *Knowledge and Lotteries*. Oxford: Oxford University Press.

Hawthorne, John. forthcoming. The case for closure. In: Steup, Matthias, & Sosa, Ernest (eds.), *Contemporary Debates in Epistemology*. Oxford: Blackwell.

Heck, Richard G., Jr. 2000. Non-conceptual content and the 'space of reasons'. *Philosophical Review*, **109**, 483–523.

Jackson, Frank. 1987. *Conditionals*. Oxford: Blackwell.

Klein, Peter. 1981. *Certainty: a refutation of skepticism*. Minneapolis: University of Minnesota Press.

Klein, Peter. 1995. Skepticism and closure: why the evil genius argument fails. *Philosophical Topics*, **23**, 213–36.

Kornblith, Hilary. 2000. The contextualist evasion of epistemology. *Philosophical Issues*, **10**, 24–32.

McLaughlin, Brian. 2000. Self-knowledge, externalism, and skepticism. *Aristotelian Society Supplement*, **74**, 93–117.

Moore, G. E. 1909. Hume's philosophy. *The New Quarterly*.

Moore, G. E. 1918/19. Some judgments of perception. *Proceedings of the Aristotelian Society*, **19**.

Moore, G. E. 1939. Proof of an external world. *Proceedings of the British Academy*, **25**, 273–300.

Peacocke, Christopher. 2004. *The Realm of Reason*. New York: Oxford University Press.

Plantinga, Alvin. 1993. *Warrant: The Current Debate*. New York: Oxford University Press.

Pollock, John. 1986. *Contemporary Theories of Knowledge*. Totowa, NJ: Rowman & Littlefield.

Pryor, James. 2000. The skeptic and the dogmatist. *Noûs*, **34**, 517–49.

Pryor, James. 2001. Highlights of recent epistemology. *British Journal for the Philosophy of Science*, **52**, 1–30.

Pryor, James. forthcoming. Uncertainty and undermining.

Richard, Mark. 2004. Contextualism and relativism. *Philosophical Studies*, 215–42.

Schroeder, Mark. forthcoming. The scope of instrumental reason. Available online: http://www.princeton.edu/~mschroed/papers.html.

Sosa, Ernest. 2000. Skepticism and contextualism. *Philosophical Issues*, **10**, 1–18.

Stanley, Jason. 2004. On the linguistic basis for contextualism. *Philosophical Studies*, 119–46.

Strawson, P. F. 1985. *Skepticism and Naturalism: Some Varieties*. New York: Columbia University Press.

Thau, Michael. 2002. *Consciousness and Cognition*. Oxford: Oxford University Press.

Williamson, Timothy. forthcoming. Knowledge and skepticism. In: Jackson, Frank, & Smith, Michael (eds.), *The Oxford Handbook of Analytic Philosophy*. Oxford: Oxford University Press.

Wright, Crispin. 1985. Facts and certainty. *Proceedings of the British Academy*, **71**, 429–72.

Wright, Crispin. 2000a. Cogency and question-begging: some reflections on McKinsey's paradox and Putnam's proof. *Philosophical Issues*, **10**, 140–63.

Wright, Crispin. 2000b. Replies. *Philosophical Issues*, **10**, 201–19.

Wright, Crispin. 2002. (Anti-)sceptics simple and subtle: Moore and McDowell. *Philosophy and Phenomenological Research*, **65**, 330–48.

Wright, Crispin. 2003. Some reflections on the acquisition of warrant by inference. Pages 57–77 of: Nuccetelli, Susana (ed.), *New Essays on Semantic Externalism and Self-Knowledge*. Cambridge, Mass.: MIT Press.

Wright, Crispin. 2004. Warrant for nothing (and foundations for free)? *Aristotelian Society Supplement*.

*Philosophical Issues, 14, Epistemology, 2004*

# WHAT IS WRONG WITH EPISTEMIC CIRCULARITY?

Frederick F. Schmitt
Indiana University

The problem of epistemic circularity may be posed this way.[1] I believe that sense perception (SP) is reliable—tends to produce true beliefs. Intuitively, my belief that SP is reliable (my "reliability belief," as I will call it) is epistemically justified. If my reliability belief is justified, it is so on the basis either of other beliefs or of nonbelief reasons. It turns out, however, that in either case my reliability belief is justified on the basis of SP. For if my reliability belief is justified on the basis of other beliefs, the latter must include beliefs themselves based on SP (call these "SP beliefs"). If, by contrast, my reliability belief is justified on the basis of nonbelief reasons, then these reasons include sensory impressions, and my reliability belief is again justified on the basis of SP. To keep the discussion manageable, I will assume (as seems likely) that my reliability belief is justified (if at all) on the basis of SP beliefs. The simplest model of such justification is a *track-record* model: I am justified in my reliability on the basis of, and by inference from, the track-record of my SP beliefs. More exactly, I infer my reliability belief in this way: for each of my current and past SP beliefs, I judge whether the belief is true by relying on my current SP beliefs; as it happens, I judge most of these beliefs to be true; I then infer that SP is reliable. On a track-record model, it is patent that my reliability belief is justified on the basis of SP beliefs. Of course, a track-record model is not the only possible model of the justification of my reliability belief. But as William Alston (1993) has persuasively argued, all plausible models of the justification of my reliability belief share with the track-record model the feature of tracing the justification of my reliability belief to SP beliefs. The trouble, however, is that such a basis for my reliability belief is circular. It is circular, so the problem of epistemic circularity goes, in a way that prevents me from being justified in my belief that SP is reliable. We can see the problem if we assume, for the sake of exposition, that I am justified in a belief on a basis only if this basis answers any legitimate doubt that pertains to the task of justifying the target belief. Among these doubts is presumably a doubt as to whether the proposition believed is true. Thus, my reliability belief is justified on the basis of SP beliefs, and ultimately on the basis of SP, only if this basis answers a doubt as to whether SP is reliable. The basis (ultimately, SP) answers such a doubt (if at all) only in virtue of the reliability of SP. But, so the problem of epistemic circularity continues, the basis cannot answer a doubt as to whether SP is reliable in virtue of the reliability of SP. Such an answer would be circular in appealing to the reliability of SP to answer a doubt as to whether SP is reliable. Hence, a doubt as to whether SP is reliable left unanswered by the basis for my reliability belief prevents the justification of my reliability belief. My SP beliefs, though they may be justified by SP, are not justified in such a way that my reliability belief can be justified on the basis of these SP beliefs. This reasoning is supposed to show that my reliability belief cannot be justified on the basis of any SP belief. Thus, the circularity prevents my reliability belief from being justified. So goes the problem of epistemic circularity applied to SP.[2]

The problem generalizes to all epistemically circular sources. These apparently include most of our other intuitively justifying sources of belief—memory, deduction, induction, and inference to the best explanation. We may say that a *justification* (or basing) of the belief that SP is reliable is epistemically circular when the basis of the reliability belief is SP. We may say that a *source* is epistemically circular when the only justification of the belief that the source is reliable available to us (assuming there is any justification) is epistemically circular. The broader problem of epistemic circularity, then, is that most, if not all, of our intuitively justifying sources of belief are epistemically circular, but the epistemic circularity of a source deprives us of justification for the belief that the source is reliable.

Epistemic circularity is rightly regarded as a serious prima facie threat to the justification of our beliefs about the reliability of our most important sources of belief. It is not initially clear what to say in response to it. And if we cannot respond adequately, we must accept disastrous consequences. At the very least, we must accept that I am not justified in beliefs about the reliability of sources that are infected by epistemic circularity. Since these beliefs lie at the core of my evaluation of my cognitive capacities and achievements, epistemic circularity, left unresolved, deprives me of a justified assessment of my own cognition.

More disastrous than this is another consequence one could draw from epistemic circularity. One might hold that my SP beliefs are justified only if they are based on reasons that answer a doubt as to whether SP is reliable, and this is so apart from whether my reliability belief is justified on the basis of my SP beliefs. (Note that this is a stronger claim than the one employed in the case that epistemic circularity prevents my reliability belief from being justified, according to which my reliability belief is justified on the basis of my SP beliefs only if my SP beliefs can answer a doubt as to whether SP is reliable.) And one might also hold that any reasons for my SP beliefs that answer a doubt as to whether SP is reliable must be such as to make my SP beliefs justified on the basis of my reliability belief. Since, by epistemic circularity, my reliability belief is justified (if at all) only on the basis of my SP beliefs, it follows that my SP beliefs are (logically, as I will put it in section I) circularly justified (if justified at all). Since (logically) circular justification is impossible, epistemic circularity entails that my SP beliefs are no more justified than my reliability belief is. Thus, epistemic circularity entails the disastrous consequence of *SP skepticism*—that none of my SP beliefs is justified.[3]

I will assume in this paper that epistemic circularity does not pose a genuine threat of SP skepticism involving logical circularity. I dismiss this threat for three reasons. First, I do not find plausible the initial assumption on which the case for SP skepticism rests, that my SP beliefs are justified only if they are based on reasons that answer a doubt as to whether SP is reliable. The basis of my SP beliefs need answer such a doubt (if at all) only when the task is to justify the reliability belief, not when the task is merely to justify a particular SP belief. Second, I do not find obvious the second assumption on which the case for SP skepticism rests, that any reasons for my SP beliefs that answer a doubt as to whether SP is reliable must be such as to make my SP beliefs justified on the basis of my reliability belief. So it is not obvious to me that a (logical) circularity must arise in the justification of my SP beliefs, even given that their justification requires a basis that answers a doubt as to whether SP is reliable. My third reason for assuming that epistemic circularity poses no threat of SP skepticism involving logical circularity is that the alleged logical circularity does not even arise for a version of epistemic circularity on which the justification of my reliability belief (if any) is based on SP directly, without being based on SP beliefs. So logical circularity of the sort threatened here does not arise from epistemic circularity per se, but only from a particular version of it. Since it is unclear which version of epistemic circularity holds for SP, the case for SP skepticism involving logical circularity is hostage to the outcome of an undecided issue. Of course, if epistemic circularity does prevent the justification of my reliability belief, and my SP beliefs are justified (if at all) on the basis of my reliability belief, then epistemic circularity will entail SP skepticism even if there is no logical circularity. But this case for SP skepticism from epistemic circularity per se, apart from logical circularity, clearly presupposes that epistemic circularity prevents the justification of my reliability belief even granted the justifiedness of my SP beliefs; otherwise it would beg the question in favor of SP skepticism. This case is therefore no more plausible than its presupposition that epistemic circularity prevents the justification of my reliability belief. Indeed, the case is considerably less plausible than its presupposition if, as I say, it is not obvious that my SP beliefs are justified (if at all) on the basis of my reliability belief. In any event, the case for SP skepticism from epistemic circularity fails if its presupposition that epistemic circularity prevents the justification of my reliability belief fails. For this reason, my focus in this article is on this presupposition of the per se case for SP skepticism, rather than on the view that epistemic circularity entails SP skepticism. In short, I assume that epistemic circularity is compatible with the justifiedness of my SP beliefs, and I devote my attention to the narrower question whether epistemic circularity prevents the justification of my reliability belief.

The threat posed by epistemic circularity, as I take it, is that my SP beliefs, though justified, are not justified in such a way as to justify my reliability belief. In terms of answering doubt, the question is whether the basis for my SP beliefs can answer a doubt as to whether SP is reliable, a doubt that pertains specifically to the task of justifying the reliability belief. One suggestion is that we can reconcile epistemic circularity with the justifiedness of my reliability belief, but only by divorcing justifiedness from an ability to answer legitimate doubts. I want to argue that no such extreme reaction is needed to fend off the threat epistemic circularity poses to the justification of my reliability belief.[4] We may recognize epistemic circularity without denying that the justification of my reliability belief requires answering a doubt about reliability. For epistemic circularity does not prevent the basis for my reliability belief from answering a doubt about reliability.

## I. Epistemic Circularity and Logical Circularity: Is Indiscrimination Really a Problem?

To get a handle on epistemic circularity, it helps to contrast it with *logical* circularity, as several writers have done. Logical circularity is a feature of an argument, in which the conclusion of the argument, *p*, is identical with one of its premises. Logical circularity evidently prevents an argument from being used to support its conclusion. There are two properties of adducing a logically circular argument with intent to support its conclusion that might be thought to prevent the successful support of the conclusion.[5] One is that adducing such an argument in support of the conclusion *begs the question*. We may put the problem posed by begging the question this way. We accept what I will call the *Independence Requirement*: adducing an argument in support of its conclusion succeeds in supporting the conclusion only if adducing it supports the conclusion (to some degree, at least) *independently* of support the conclusion receives in any other way (e.g., from adducing other arguments in support of the same conclusion). But adducing a logically circular argument in support of its conclusion violates the Independence Requirement. For its support for the conclusion depends on the conclusion's being supported in some other way. This is because the conclusion is identical with one of the premises of the argument. But adducing an argument supports its conclusion only if its premises are already supported prior to this adducing. So adducing a question-begging argument supports its conclusion only if its premises are already supported prior to this adducing, and hence only if one of the premises, identical with the conclusion, is supported in some other way. Thus, begging the question runs afoul of the Independence Requirement, and this prevents adducing a logically circular argument from supporting its conclusion.

There is a second property of adducing a logically circular argument in support of its conclusion that might be thought to prevent support. The problem this time is that adducing such an argument is in a certain sense *indiscriminate*. If merely adducing a logically circular argument succeeded in supporting its conclusion, then any proposition *p* whatever could be supported merely by adducing a logically circular argument with conclusion *p*. But then any conclusion whatever could be supported.[6]

Fortunately, both the problem of begging the question and the indiscrimination problem are easily avoided simply by abstaining from adducing a logically circular argument in support of its conclusion. Regrettably, we cannot similarly abstain from an epistemically circular basis for our belief in the reliability of SP.

Epistemic circularity falls short of logical circularity in an important respect: an epistemically circular inference to the reliability of SP does not involve basing the output of the inference on an input belief that SP is reliable, as would be required for logical circularity. However, as Paul Boghossian has observed, epistemically circular inferences face prima facie problems analogous to the problems of begging the question and indiscrimination that afflict the attempt to adduce a logically circular argument in support of its conclusion.

Epistemically circular inferences beg the question in a certain sense. Suppose I infer my reliability belief from my SP beliefs (e.g., by a track-record inference). My reliability belief is justified on the basis of such an inference only if the inference answers a doubt as to whether SP is reliable. But the inference answers a doubt as to whether SP is reliable only if my SP beliefs are justified, and thus (since my SP beliefs are justified on the basis of SP) only if there is an answer to a doubt as to whether a given SP belief is true, for each of my SP beliefs. But there is no answer to such a doubt by appeal to SP as long as there is a doubt as to whether SP is reliable. So my reliability belief cannot be justified on the basis of an inference from my SP beliefs. This is the problem for epistemically circular inferences analogous to begging the question for logically circular arguments.

Some epistemically circular inferences may also seem to suffer from a problem analogous to the indiscrimination problem for logically circular arguments. In particular, *track-record* inferences of the sort mentioned at the outset of this article may seem to do so. Suppose I use SP to form SP beliefs. I then use my current SP beliefs to judge the truth of each SP belief, past as well as current. That is, I infer from my current beliefs that my current or past SP belief $q$ is true (or false, as the case may be), for each of my current and past SP beliefs. Suppose I judge that my SP belief $q$ is true, for most of my SP beliefs $q$. I then infer that SP is reliable. If I also accept certain assumptions, the latter inference is *deductive*. This is so if I accept that the beliefs $q$ I judge with respect to truth are all and only my current and past SP beliefs, and I also accept that the reliability of SP is the frequency of true beliefs among my current and past SP beliefs. (The inference will require nondeductive—inductive or counterfactual—reasoning if reliability is defined in terms of the total, including future, output of SP, or in terms of the frequency of true beliefs in the counterfactual output of SP.) The former inference, from my current SP beliefs to the truth or falsity of each of my past and current SP beliefs, is a nondeductive inference. Putting the two inferences together, we obtain a nondeductive track-record inference from my SP beliefs to a belief that SP is reliable.

Such a track-record inference to the reliability of SP may seem to suffer from a problem analogous to the indiscrimination problem for logically circular arguments. For if such an inference can justify the belief that SP is reliable, then, it would seem, a similar, artificially created track-record inference can justify a reliability belief for a great many sources. Suppose $T$ is a source that may be used to form beliefs about the future by reading tea leaves. Stipulate that the beliefs produced by $T$ do not conflict with other beliefs that I hold.[7] I may use $T$ to form $T$ beliefs until I have a sufficient basis for a track-record inference to the reliability of $T$. I may then infer the reliability of $T$. I can run a similar track-record inference to justify a belief in the reliability of any source I use persistently enough, so long as its output does not conflict with other beliefs I hold. Let us note that the apparent indiscrimination problem here applies to epistemically circular *track-record* inferences to reliability; it does not obviously apply to other epistemically circular inferences to reliability. Thus, the apparent indiscrimination problem for epistemically circular inferences is much narrower than that for logically circular arguments, all uses of which are indiscriminate in the relevant sense.[8]

Track-record inferences, I have said, may *seem* to suffer from the indiscrimination problem. Clearly they do have a feature structurally analogous to the property of indiscrimination in logically circular arguments. However, I believe that indiscrimination in track-record inferences does not pose the fatal problem that indiscrimination poses for logically circular arguments. In the case of logically circular arguments, there is no way to avoid indiscrimination, short of abstaining from using the arguments for purposes of supporting their conclusions. But in the case of epistemically circular inferences, there is a way to restrict the inferences so as to avoid the harmful consequences of indiscrimination. The problem is supposed to be that I can simply use any source $R$ I choose to form $R$ beliefs and then make the track-record inference to the reliability of $R$, so long as the outputs of $R$ do not conflict with my other beliefs. And this is objectionable because I should not be able to become justified in believing that an arbitrarily chosen source $R$ is reliable merely by forming $R$ beliefs and making the track-record inference. It is true that I should not be able to become justified in believing that $R$ is reliable in this way. But the obvious response is that the mere use of an arbitrary source $R$ to form $R$ beliefs does not necessarily give me justified inputs for the track-record inference. And I need justified inputs if the inference is to give me a justified belief in the reliability of $R$. There is a distinction between sources that lead to justified reliability beliefs and sources that lead to unjustified reliability beliefs. For there is a distinction between sources that lead to justified input beliefs and those that do not. The mere exercise of an epistemically circular track-record inference does not by itself justify a reliability belief. Thus, there is no real problem of indiscrimination for epistemically circular inferences, despite the fact that they are discriminate as a class.

Of course, one might object to the restriction to sources that are justifying on the ground that my SP beliefs are justified only if I am able to discriminate justifying sources from unjustifying ones, and I am able to do this only if there is available to me a justification of the belief that SP is reliable that is not epistemically circular. Since there is no such justification of the belief that SP is reliable, I cannot discriminate justifying from unjustifying sources, and so my SP beliefs are unjustified. But, in addition to its appeal to a dubious requirement of ability to discriminate justifying sources, this objection challenges epistemic circularity by adverting to the claim that epistemic circularity entails SP skepticism. And as I explained at the outset, any such claim presupposes that there is another objection to the justifying power of an epistemically circular inference to my reliability belief independent of an entailment of SP skepticism. So the objection is parasitic on some other, as yet unspecified, objection to the justifying power of an epistemically circular inference to my reliability belief.

This response to the indiscrimination problem leaves begging the question as the sole obstacle that might prevent epistemically circular inferences from justifying reliability beliefs. How, then, should we respond to the problem of begging the question? As I noted above, we cannot respond in the way we do to logical circularity, by avoiding the use of epistemically circular inferences. For the recent literature on epistemic circularity has shown that these inferences are indispensable for the justification of some important reliability beliefs.

There are studies showing that our main intuitively justifying sources of belief are embroiled in epistemic circularity. William Alston (1993) has made a detailed and persuasive case that the only justifying inferences to the reliability of SP are epistemically circular. Paul Boghossian (2000) has done the same for deduction. Memory seems obviously epistemically circular: I must consult my memory to judge which of my memory beliefs is true, if only because I must do so to judge which memory beliefs I have had in the past, and which of my current beliefs is a memory belief. In addition to these sources, induction is likely to be epistemically circular.[9] Almost all noncircular attempts to justify the reliability of induction have been shown to fail.

Granted, there remains some prospect of justifying the reliability of induction by inference to the best explanation (BonJour, 1998, pp. 187–216). This would suffice to show that induction is not epistemically circular. But there are three points against the significance of this conclusion. First, it would not show that lay beliefs (as opposed to those of epistemologists like BonJour) that induction is reliable are justified on the basis of inference to the best explanation. To the contrary, lay beliefs that inference to the best explanation is reliable are likely justified on the basis of induction. Induction seems to be a psychologically more primitive form of inference than inference to the best explanation. Second, if we are seeking an order of justification that where possible justifies the reliability of sources that are less obviously reliable by using those that are more obviously reliable, we will seek to justify the reliability of inference to the best explanation by using induction, rather than conversely. For inference to the best explanation is less obviously reliable than induction.[10] Third, inference to the best explanation may well be epistemically circular. We have no obvious inference to its reliability besides a track-record inference. So in arguing that induction is reliable by using inference to the best explanation, BonJour may well be trading one epistemically circular source for another. In sum, SP, deduction, and memory are certainly epistemically circular, while induction and inference to the best explanation may very well be epistemically circular. These observations mount a convincing case that most if not all of our major intuitively justifying sources of belief are epistemically circular.[11] We have no option of avoiding epistemically circular inferences, as we do of avoiding logically circular arguments.

With these thoughts about the inevitability and obnoxiousness of epistemic circularity in mind, let us turn to proposals for defusing the problem.

## II. The Coherentist Response

Let us consider first whether a *coherence* theory of justified belief can respond to the problem of epistemic circularity. The point of coherentism is not merely to tolerate but to celebrate circularity. So coherentism is a promising platform for a response to epistemic circularity. Alston (1991) suggests that coherentism, if otherwise plausible, could resolve the problem of epistemic circularity. On coherentism, at least in the version I will entertain here, my reliability belief is justified not by being *based* on my SP beliefs, but in virtue of a relation of *mutual support* between the belief and my SP beliefs (see, e.g., Goodman 1965, pp 66–7).[12] Mutual support is a relation of fit among beliefs. On one view, my reliability belief and my SP beliefs enjoy mutual support when there is an available inference of an appropriate kind (e.g., a track-record inference) from my SP beliefs to my reliability belief, and, conversely, there are also available appropriate inferences (e.g., instantiation) from my reliability belief to each SP belief. For convenience, I will assume here that mutual support is exhausted by the availability of inferences along these lines. The coherence theory might be able to avoid epistemic circularity because it prescinds justifiedness from basing on SP. My reliability belief is not justified on the basis of my SP beliefs. So it is not justified in an epistemically circular fashion. Rather, it is justified in virtue of a relation of mutual support between my reliability belief and my SP beliefs. In particular, my reliability belief is justified because it fits my SP beliefs. It is not justified in virtue of the fact that legitimate doubts about my SP beliefs are answered prior to the answering of doubts about my reliability belief. Either the justification of my reliability belief does not require that doubts about reliability be answered, or it allows doubts about the reliability belief and SP beliefs to be answered simultaneously in virtue of the fit between the beliefs. In either case, the justification of the SP beliefs is not prior to the justification of the reliability belief. I will address here only a version of coherentism on which the justification of my reliability belief requires answering doubts about reliability.

There are three objections to the coherentist response to epistemic circularity, for such a version of coherentism. First, it is not at all clear why a mere fit between the reliability belief and the SP beliefs would be enough to answer such a doubt. On the contrary, the coherence theory seems to have a worse circularity problem than does a theory on which justified belief answers any legitimate doubt in virtue of being based on reasons—a *basing theory*, as we might call it. On a basing theory, a doubt about reliability is answered in virtue of the fact that the SP beliefs are based on SP. Whatever the difficulties with this approach, it has the advantage of proposing that the doubt is answered by something in addition to a mere relation to the reliability belief itself. This holds out the prospect of stemming the doubt. But on coherentism, the doubt is answered merely because there is an available appropriate (track-record) inference from the SP beliefs to the reliability belief, and there are available appropriate (instantiating) inferences in the opposite direction. It is hard to see how the availability of such inferences could answer the doubt. On the one hand, the doubt is a doubt about reliability, so the availability of an inference from the reliability belief to each SP belief obviously goes no distance toward answering the doubt. On the other hand, the doubt is (nearly enough) a doubt that most SP beliefs are true, so the availability of an inference from all of the SP beliefs to the reliability belief also obviously goes no distance toward answering the doubt. Nor does it help to put the two available inferences together: if neither goes any distance toward answering the doubt, the two together cannot answer the doubt. The fact that SP itself is left out of the justificatory story prevents coherentism from allowing the doubt about reliability to be answered in such a way that the reliability belief is justified.[13]

A second objection to the coherentist response to epistemic circularity is that it is not a *fully general* response to the problem. The inferences the availability of which constitutes the relation of mutual support are deductive inferences, inductive inferences, or inferences to the best explanation. The availability of these inferences is supposed to answer a doubt about the reliability of SP or other target sources. So the availability of these inferences must be sufficient for answering the doubt about reliability. The doubt must not call them into question in such a way that their availability does not answer the doubt. This is no problem when SP is the target source. But when the target source is deduction, induction, or inference to the best explanation, then it would seem that the availability of the inference ceases to answer the doubt. If so the coherentist response is not a fully general response to the problem of epistemic circularity; it does not respond to the problem for the inferences that *constitute* mutual support.

The third objection to the coherentist response is the most serious. According to coherentism, a belief's bearing a relation of mutual support to other beliefs is a justifiedness-making characteristic of that belief. But we take beliefs with a justifiedness-making characteristic to tend to be true in somewhat the way we take sources to be reliable. And we take ourselves to be justified in believing that beliefs with a justifiedness-making characteristic tend to be true. So if coherentism is correct, then I am, so we take it, justified in believing that beliefs bearing a relation (call it $M$) of mutual support to other beliefs tend to be true, in somewhat the way I am justified in believing that SP is reliable. But a problem of epistemic circularity arises for my belief that $M$ beliefs (i.e., beliefs that bear the relation of mutual support) tend to be true, just as it does for beliefs about the reliability of SP. To be justified in believing that $M$ beliefs tend to be true, a condition must be satisfied that answers legitimate doubts as to whether $M$ beliefs tend to be true. But on coherentism, it is the relation of mutual support in virtue of which doubts are answered. So it is the relation of mutual support in virtue of which any legitimate doubt as to whether $M$ beliefs tend to be true must be answered. But unfortunately, such a doubt prevents it from happening that this very doubt is answered in virtue of the relation of mutual support (for the same reason that a doubt about the reliability of SP prevents SP from answering a doubt about the reliability of SP). So coherentism does not offer the resources to stem the doubt. With regard to answering the doubt, and thus with regard to epistemic circularity, I am in no better shape on a coherence theory than I am on a basing theory.

These three objections seem to me sufficient for rejecting the coherentist approach to epistemic circularity, for a version of coherentism on which the justification of my reliability belief requires answering a doubt about reliability. Of course, I am not claiming here that the problem of epistemic circularity poses any greater objection to coherentism than it does to other theories of justification, only that coherentism has no *special* resources for responding to the problem.

### III. Is Begging the Question Really A Problem for an Epistemically Circular Inference to the Reliability of SP?

I have rejected the coherentist response to the problem of epistemic circularity. Is there a better way to respond? I believe we may do so without invoking any particular substantive theory of justification. I have observed that indiscrimination is not a genuine problem for epistemically circular inferences; it does not prevent them from justifying reliability beliefs. I wish now to argue that begging the question is also not a genuine problem for epistemically circular sources like SP, deduction, or induction. Begging the question turns out to prevent epistemically circular inferences from justifying reliability beliefs only for sources that are not epistemically circular.[14]

The problem of begging the question, as I have formulated it, assumes a tie between justifiedness and doubt: one is justified in a belief *p* only if one's basis for the belief answers any legitimate doubts, and in particular a doubt as to whether *p*. We could defuse the problem of begging the question by divorcing justifiedness from answering doubts. Paul Boghossian (2000), on one reading, suggests just this response (for the case of deduction). As he puts it, we should divorce justifiedness from *suasiveness*. On the reading of Boghossian I have in mind, a suasive basis for belief *p* is one that answers a doubt as to whether *p*. The suggested response, then, is that my reliability belief can be justified on the basis of my SP beliefs even though my basis provides no means of answering a doubt as to whether SP is reliable.[15] But I do not think that we are forced to respond by divorcing justifiedness from suasiveness. For we can allow that the justification of my reliability belief requires answering a doubt as to whether SP is reliable, but deny that my basis for my reliability belief is unable to answer such a doubt for reasons of epistemic circularity.

I take it that, for purposes of judging whether epistemic circularity prevents the justification of my reliability belief, we may divide the inference into two legs. If epistemic circularity is to prevent my reliability belief from being justified on the basis of my SP beliefs, it must either prevent my SP beliefs from being justified, or it must prevent a justifying inference from my SP beliefs to my reliability beliefs. For, we may assume, a justifying inference is simply one that yields a justified belief as output given justified beliefs as inputs. From this it follows that if my SP beliefs are justified, then my reliability belief is justified unless the inference fails to be justifying. Thus, we may distinguish the first leg of the inference, in which I form my SP beliefs, from the second leg, in which I infer my reliability belief from my SP beliefs. Epistemic circularity must either deprive my SP beliefs of justifiedness or deprive my inference of justifying power.

I have assumed that epistemic circularity does not deprive my SP beliefs of justifiedness. Nevertheless, I will consider here whether a doubt as to whether SP is reliable could lead to SP skepticism. This will have the advantage of uncovering responses to the problem of begging the question additional to those I mentioned earlier in explaining why I assume that epistemic circularity does not entail SP skepticism.

There are two models of justification on which a legitimate doubt as to whether SP is reliable could lead to SP skepticism.

(a) *Second-Order Justification*: Let me begin with a relatively weak requirement, one that does not by itself entail that an epistemically circular inference prevents my SP beliefs from being justified:

> *Propositional Second-Order Justification Requirement*: My SP belief is justified only if I am propositionally justified in believing that SP is reliable.

I have labeled this a "propositional" requirement because it requires only that I am *propositionally* justified in believing that SP is reliable, not that I am *doxastically* justified in believing this. Propositional justification for the belief *p* differs from doxastic justification in not entailing that one has engaged in an inference to the belief *p*, or even that one believes *p*. The Propositional Requirement does not by itself prevent my SP beliefs from being justified despite the epistemic circularity of SP. On the contrary, an epistemically circular inference of the sort we have considered, such as the track-record inference, may well be *conditionally justifying*: it may well justify me in believing that SP is reliable conditional on my SP beliefs being justified. Where a conditionally justifying epistemically circular inference is available to me, it follows from the fact that my SP beliefs are justified that I am (propositionally) justified in believing that SP is reliable. In this case, my SP beliefs satisfy the Propositional Requirement in virtue of the availability of a conditionally justifying epistemically circular inference. Plausibly, then, the Propositional Requirement poses no obstacle to my SP beliefs being justified, despite the epistemic circularity of SP.

The Propositional Requirement can, however, be strengthened in such a way as to deprive my SP beliefs of justifiedness, given the epistemic circularity of SP. First, the Requirement might be strengthened from propositional to doxastic:

> *Doxastic Second-Order Justification Requirement*: My SP belief is justified (at a time $t$) only if I am doxastically justified (at $t$) in believing that SP is reliable.

This Doxastic Requirement entails SP skepticism, given that SP is epistemically circular and that my belief that SP is reliable is justified (if at all) on the basis of an inference. This is for temporal reasons. Under epistemic circularity, my belief that SP is reliable must be justified (if at all) by inference from my SP beliefs. But an inference takes time to justify a belief, so that my belief that SP is reliable becomes justified at time $t_1$ on the basis of an inference from my SP beliefs only if the latter beliefs are justified at a time $t_0$ prior to $t_1$. Yet, by the Doxastic Requirement, my SP beliefs are justified at $t_0$ only if my belief that SP is reliable is justified at $t_0$. Thus, the Doxastic Requirement entails that my SP beliefs are unjustified, given the epistemic circularity of SP, assuming that my reliability belief is justified (if at all) on the basis of an inference.

A second way to strengthen the Propositional Second-Order Require ment is to convert it to a basing requirement:

> *Basing Second-Order Justification Requirement*: My SP belief is justified (if at all) at least partly on the basis of my reliability belief.

By the epistemic circularity of SP, my reliability belief is justified (if at all) on the basis of my SP beliefs. But by the Basing Requirement, my SP beliefs are justified (partly) on the basis of my reliability belief. So my reliability belief is justified partly on the basis of itself. This circularity in the justification of my reliability belief is a logical circularity and objectionable for that reason (i.e., because it exhibits begging the question and indiscrimination). So the Basing Requirement also entails that my SP beliefs are unjustified, given the epistemic circularity of SP.

Despite this, neither the Doxastic nor the Basing Second-Order Requirement presents a serious case against begging the question in epistemically circular inferences. For both requirements should be rejected for a reason independent of their bearing on epistemic circularity: they lead to global skepticism quite apart from whether any source is epistemically circular. For they yield global skepticism if, as is inevitable, all of our sources form a cycle in which, for each source $S$, the justification of my belief that $S$ is reliable depends on outputs of the next source. A cycle of justified reliability beliefs of this sort is temporally impossible if justifiedness is governed by the Doxastic Requirement, and such a cycle exhibits logical circularity if justifiedness is governed by the Basing Requirement. Yet, as I say, a cycle of this sort is inevitable. For such a cycle follows from the fact that our sources are finite in number. Thus, the mere finitude of our sources rules out the Doxastic and Basing Requirements, on pain of global skepticism. These requirements yield global skepticism quite apart from whether there are any epistemically circular sources. Hence, they provide no good ground for inferring SP skepticism from the epistemic circularity of SP. So far, then, we have no reason to say that the epistemic circularity of the inference to the reliability belief prevents my SP beliefs from being justified.

(b) *Undermining*: We have another model of how a doubt about reliability might prevent SP beliefs from being justified. On this second model, the doubt *undermines* the justifiedness of my SP beliefs. It is an established principle in epistemology that the justifiedness otherwise supplied by a source is undermined by a justified belief (or by my being propositionally justified in believing) that the source is *unreliable*. According to this principle, a subject is justified in a belief on the basis of SP only if she is not justified in believing that SP is unreliable. Someone might propose, along similar lines, that the justifiedness supplied by SP is undermined by a *doubt* as to whether SP is reliable.

This last proposal is, however, less than compelling. True, if I had a doubt as to whether SP is reliable that also provided justification for believing that SP is *un*reliable, then the justifiedness of my SP beliefs would be undermined (by my being propositionally justified in believing that SP is unreliable). But I have no such doubt. At best I have a doubt that gives me good reason to suspend judgment as to whether SP is reliable. But this does not undermine the justification of my SP beliefs. We lack any compelling reason to think that a doubt as to whether SP is reliable prevents the use of SP from making my SP beliefs justified.

So much for the first leg of the inference. Let us, then, turn to the second leg of the inference—from my SP beliefs, via deduction or induction, to my belief that SP is reliable. Does a doubt about the reliability of SP prevent the inference from justifying my reliability belief, given the epistemic circularity of the inference?

Clearly, given the justifiedness of my SP beliefs, such a doubt cannot prevent the inference from justifying my reliability belief by *undermining* the justifiedness the inference would otherwise supply. For it cannot undermine the conditional justifying power of the inference. That is, it cannot prevent it from being the case that my reliability belief is justified on the basis of the inference, given the justifiedness of my input SP beliefs. For the doubt is not a doubt about the conditional reliability of this inference, as would be required for such undermining. It is not a doubt about the conditional reliability of deduction or induction, but merely about the reliability of SP.[16]

Is there another way the doubt about reliability might prevent the inference from justifying my reliability belief? There are two ways this might happen. One is that the character of the output belief in a deductive or inductive inference might impose a special demand on the input beliefs beyond justifiedness, and this demand might not be satisfied even though the input beliefs are justified. For example, it is sometimes thought that mathematical beliefs require an especially high degree of justifiedness to count as justified, and a mathematical belief might fail to be justified by an inference from a justified belief because the latter falls short of the degree of justifiedness needed in the basis for a mathematical belief. But I take it that no such problem applies here. For my SP beliefs have enough justifiedness to support my reliability belief at whatever level is required; at any rate, most of my SP beliefs have as much justifiedness as my reliability belief itself.

The problem, if there is one, must rather be that the character of the output belief, that SP is reliable, imposes a special demand on the input beliefs (other than a high degree of justifiedness) in virtue of exposure to a doubt as to whether SP is reliable, and this demand is not satisfied by my SP beliefs, despite their being justified. But what might this special demand be? I do not know, but I think there is a prima facie case that my SP beliefs can satisfy any plausible demand that might be imposed. For on the face of it, the situation with the deductive or inductive inference to my SP reliability belief is much like that of an inductive basis for a generalization, say, that most ravens are black. The output belief might be said to impose a demand on the justifiedness of the input beliefs (that raven *a* is black, etc.) over and above mere justifiedness—namely, that each be justified in a way that escapes a doubt as to whether most ravens are black. But the justification of the input beliefs does escape this doubt, and I take it that this would be so even if the input beliefs were justified in virtue of the reliability of a perceptual process that produces only beliefs as to whether particular ravens are black. The doubt raised by the output belief raises a doubt about the reliability of the perceptual process, since it is a doubt that the frequency of truths in the output of the process is high. But no one thinks that this doubt prevents the process from endowing the input beliefs with a kind of justifiedness sufficient to justify the generalization. The inductive justification of the generalization that most ravens are black does not impose any such debilitating demand. Neither does a deductive or inductive inference to the reliability of SP. A doubt as to whether SP is reliable does not deprive the input SP beliefs of whatever kind of justifiedness they need to justify my reliability belief deductively or inductively. No special demand on the input beliefs stands in the way of the justification of my reliability belief.

There is one last way in which a doubt about the reliability of SP might prevent the inference from justifying my reliability belief. It might prevent all of my input beliefs from being justified at once in such a way as to justify my reliability belief, even though each input belief is justified; for it might prevent all of my input beliefs together from answering a doubt about reliability. In discussing this last difficulty, I will assume that the inference is a deductive track-record inference. Nearly the same points apply to an inductive track-record inference. In a deductive inference, recall, the inputs include all of my SP beliefs. The difficulty to be discussed is this: A given SP belief is justified in such a way as to justify my reliability belief only if, under a doubt about reliability, the basis for the belief answers doubts about the belief. But the basis for the given belief answers doubts about the belief only if doubts about sufficiently many of the other SP beliefs are suspended. Unfortunately, given a doubt as to whether SP is reliable, doubts about sufficiently many of the other SP beliefs are not suspended. For a doubt as to whether SP is reliable entails a doubt as to whether any sufficiently large set of SP beliefs is true. And this doubt raises a doubt as to whether $p$ is true, for each belief $p$ in any sufficiently large set of SP beliefs. In effect, SP answers a doubt about a given SP belief only *conditional* on sufficiently many of the other SP input beliefs being doubt-free. But answering a doubt about a given SP belief under a doubt about reliability prevents sufficiently many other SP beliefs from being doubt-free. For this reason, the inference cannot answer the doubt about reliability.

On inspection, however, we can see that this objection does not work. The charge is that SP answers a doubt about a given SP belief only conditional on sufficiently many other SP beliefs being doubt-free; yet, under a doubt as to whether SP is reliable, sufficiently many of these other SP beliefs are *not* doubt-free. Evidently, this objection assumes that the doubt about reliability has prevented SP from rendering each SP input belief doubt-free for members of each sufficiently large set of SP beliefs. But this assumption would seem to entail that, for each member of each such set, and hence for all SP beliefs, a doubt about reliability undermines the power of SP to answer a doubt about that SP belief. Such undermining, however, entails the undermining of the justifiedness of each SP belief. But then the objection merely returns to the *first* leg of the inference and claims that the doubt about reliability does undermine the justifiedness of my SP beliefs. Yet we have, for various reasons, already rejected this way of attacking the justification of my reliability belief.

To be sure, one might raise a puzzle about how SP can answer a doubt about each of its outputs concurrently in virtue of its reliability. For SP is not *perfectly* reliable. So, one might ask, how can it answer a doubt in virtue of its reliability for more than a *portion* of its output equal to its reliability? There is some puzzle here closely related to the question how ampliative inference can justify a belief or answer doubt. I am inclined to say that the answering of doubt is somehow distributed over the output of SP. To answer a doubt about any one output, it is enough if sufficiently many (or most) of the outputs of SP are true. We need not retreat to the claim that a doubt has been answered only for some unspecified portion of the outputs equal to the reliability of SP. If answering a doubt required certainty, then we would succeed in answering it only by using a perfectly reliable source. A doubt would not be answered for *any* portion of the output of a less than perfectly reliable source. But as it happens, a doubt is answered when a threshold is met, and this affords answering a doubt for each output of an imperfectly reliable source like SP. But however this may be, the puzzle here is one that pertains to the first leg of the inference, not to the second leg. So we may safely set it aside as irrelevant to our present concerns.

We have not seen any obstacle to the second leg of the inference. Once the justifiedness of SP beliefs is accepted, the justifiedness of the reliability belief follows, given that I infer reliability via deduction or induction. I conclude that begging the question is not a genuine problem for an epistemically circular inference to the reliability of SP.

## IV. For Which Sources Do We Need an Inference to Reliability That Is Not Epistemically Circular?

To say that begging the question presents no genuine problem for an epistemically circular inference to the reliability of SP is not of course to say that I can become justified in believing that just any source is reliable by an epistemically circular inference (say, a track-record inference). I can do so for a given source $S$ only if I can form justified $S$ beliefs before making the inference. This requires that I have no legitimate doubt as to whether $S$ is reliable sufficient to undermine the justifiedness of my $S$ beliefs. Plausibly, what is required is that I lack good reason to suspect that $S$ is unreliable. I will assume that this is what is required. Rejecting SP skepticism entails rejecting the idea that I have good reason to suspect that SP is unreliable. Cases in which the inference does go through (as with SP) and cases in which it fails differ in whether I have good reason to suspect unreliability, not in whether the inference begs the question. It could be that our knee-jerk antipathy to begging the question in epistemically circular inferences results from confusing these two issues.

Suppose, for example, that I wish to find a formula for the volume of a cone—for, say, the practical purpose of using the formula to find the volumes of particular ice cream cones. I know that most individuals, including myself, are not very good at discovering reliable formulas for the volumes of geometrical figures (where reliability is tendency to compute the true volume of a given cone, to an approximation).[17] So if someone advertises a certain formula $V$ as computing the volume of a cone, I have good reason to suspect that $V$ is unreliable, unless I have reason to believe the person is unusually good at discovering such formulas. Similarly, if I myself devise the formula $V$, I have good reason to suspect that $V$ is unreliable, unless I check it for reliability. These doubts are sufficient to undermine my $V$ beliefs. Of course, I could arbitrarily use $V$ to form beliefs about the volumes of particular cones and infer that $V$ is reliable by an epistemically circular track-record inference. But this inference would not justify my belief in the reliability of $V$, since I would not be justified in my $V$ beliefs. To be justified in such beliefs, I would need to infer the reliability of $V$ from beliefs based on sources other than $V$ itself.

The case here contrasts with cases like SP, in which I have no good reason to suspect the unreliability of the source. I have no good reason to suspect that my sensory perception of the shapes and colors of medium-sized bodies in broad daylight is unreliable. To be sure, SP differs from $V$ in that I do not select or devise my perceptual sources de novo as I do a formula for the volume of a geometrical figure. Nevertheless, I do select some modifications of my innate perceptual resources. My use of perception has a developmental history in which I gradually refine my innate perceptual apparatus in the direction of greater reliability. This developmental system seems to be successful in selecting reliability-enhancing modifications of perceptual resources. At any rate, I have no good reason to suspect that SP is unreliable.

I have argued that epistemically circular inferences may justify the belief that SP is reliable in such a way as to answer doubts about the reliability of SP, despite begging the question. I am now pointing out that epistemically circular inferences are not justifying for sources like $V$ for which I have good reason to suspect unreliability, since there is a legitimate doubt about the reliability of $V$, and this doubt undermines the justifiedness of $V$ beliefs, preventing the epistemically circular inference from justifying the belief that $V$ is reliable. For these sources, only an inference that is *not* epistemically circular can justify the reliability belief. The problem does not stem from the fact that these sources beg the question but merely from the fact that the justification of my $V$ beliefs is undermined until I have good reason to believe that $V$ is reliable.

It is natural at this point to ask what our discussion implies about the requirements for justified $S$ beliefs, for a given source $S$, if skepticism about $S$ beliefs is to be avoided. For which sources $S$ do justified $S$ beliefs require a (non-epistemically circularly) justified reliability belief? According to our discussion so far, beliefs for which I lack good reason to suspect the unreliability of the source (such as SP beliefs) do not require any justified reliability belief, whereas beliefs for which I have good reason to suspect the unreliability of the source (such as $V$ beliefs) do require a non-epistemically circularly justified reliability belief. It is possible, however, to take a different view and think that the distinction between beliefs for which a justified reliability belief is required and beliefs for which it is not required differs from the distinction between beliefs for which I have a good reason to suspect unreliability and beliefs for which I lack such a reason. Alvin Goldman (1986, pp. 93–5, 115–6) has proposed that the former distinction is that between *native processes* (e.g., SP) and *acquired methods* (such as $V$). These sources differ in their powers of justification. The exercise of a native process like SP is sufficient for the justifiedness of SP beliefs. But the use of $V$, or other such acquired methods, is not sufficient for justifiedness. I cannot become justified in a $V$-belief merely by applying the reliable formula $V$ to a particular cone. That would be compatible with having luckily selected the correct formula $V$ at random from a hatful of candidates, and having selected in this way clearly would not suffice for justifiedness. I must have selected the formula in an appropriate way. One can question whether for *every* acquired method $M$, a $M$ belief is justified only if the method is selected in a certain way (Schmitt 1992, pp. 163–74; 2000, pp. 364–9, 374–9). But Goldman's proposal is surely at least roughly correct.

Our discussion suggests two points about this proposal. One is that what is crucial for justification by an acquired method is not the manner of selection of the method but the basis on which the beliefs that result from the method are justified. The basis requires a justified belief that the method is reliable because I have good reason to suspect that acquired methods are unreliable, and the justification that the method would otherwise provide is undermined unless I am justified in believing that the method is reliable.

Our discussion also suggests a second point about Goldman's proposal: that the key distinction is not that between a native process and an acquired method, as Goldman has it, but between a source for which I lack good reason to suspect unreliability and one for which I have such reason.[18] A native process would require a justified reliability belief if I had good reason to suspect that it is unreliable. And an acquired method would not require a justified reliability belief if I lacked good reason to suspect that the method is unreliable. It so happens that the distinction between sources for which I lack good reason to suspect unreliability and those for which I have such reason roughly coincides with that between native processes and acquired methods.

There could be native processes that are reliable but not justifying because I have good reason to suspect that they are unreliable, and I do not infer their reliability by an inference that is not epistemically circular. For example, it is possible for there to be people who are natively clairvoyant. Their clairvoyance about future events could be reliable, but it is not justifying in the absence of an inference to reliability that is not epistemically circular, if the subjects have good reason to suspect that such a process is unreliable. Conversely, there could be, and perhaps are, acquired methods that need not be appropriately selected to be justifying. For example, it may be that I acquire my method of adding numbers, but I never have any good reason to suspect the unreliability of this method. People are successful in coming up with reliable ways to add numbers, even though not in coming up with formulas for volumes. So I do not need to infer the reliability of the method by an inference that is not epistemically circular. We can, then, assimilate Goldman's insight about the need for selecting acquired methods if we shift his distinction from native processes vs. acquired methods to sources for which I lack good reason to suspect unreliability and sources for which I have such reason.

In this paper, I have proposed a way to reckon with the fact that for certain important sources—SP, deduction, induction—there is no potentially justifying available inference to reliability that is not epistemically circular. This fact threatens the justifiedness of the belief that SP is reliable because epistemically circular inferences suffer from two apparent deficiencies —begging the question and indiscrimination. I have argued that, on close inspection, neither begging the question nor indiscrimination prevents an epistemically circular inference from justifying a reliability belief—not if SP beliefs are justified. This is because I have no good reason to suspect the unreliability of SP. For sources $S$ for which I do have good reason to suspect unreliability, I am justified in my reliability belief, and indeed in my $S$ beliefs, only if there is an available inference to reliability that is not epistemically circular. But this is not because an epistemically circular inference begs the question. Rather, it is because some justifying inference to reliability is needed in order for $S$ beliefs to be justified, and an epistemically circular inference cannot justify $S$ beliefs until $S$ beliefs themselves are justified. For many such sources, like the formula for the volume of a cone, we do have available inferences that are not epistemically circular.

In sum, on close inspection the phenomenon of epistemic circularity does not force us to abandon the traditional connection between justifiedness and answering legitimate doubts. An epistemically circular inference can justify a belief in the reliability of SP even if justified belief requires answering legitimate doubts. Can we learn anything, then, about the nature of justifiedness from reflection on the phenomenon of epistemic circularity? Our discussion suggests that we can learn only what can also be learned by another route: examining the necessary conditions for avoiding SP skepticism. Epistemic circularity does not lead to skepticism about the belief that SP is reliable if SP skepticism is mistaken. Epistemic circularity avoids skepticism about the reliability belief only if the justifiedness of SP beliefs is not undermined when we have no good reason to suspect unreliability. So to avoid skepticism about the reliability belief stemming from epistemic circularity, we must deny undermining by a good reason to suspect unreliability. But we already had to deny this to avoid SP skepticism. So from epistemic circularity we learn nothing new about the conditions of justifiedness.[19]

## Notes

1. For important discussions of epistemic circularity, see Alston (1989) and Sosa (1994).

2. Alston (1989) has argued that the epistemic circularity of SP really does entail that no one is *fully reflectively justified* in any SP belief—i.e., justified not only in the belief, but in believing that the belief is justified, and in believing that the beliefs on the basis of which one is justified in believing that the belief is justified are justified, etc. Alston is right about this if what is required for fully reflective justifiedness of a belief is the temporally prior justifiedness of each belief in the hierarchy, or otherwise the basing of the belief on the beliefs in the hierarchy (entailing a logical circularity in the justification). But it is not clear how troubled we should be by the fact. For, plausibly, the requirement of fully reflective justifiedness for a SP belief would also not be satisfied if neither SP nor any other sources were epistemically circular. The requirement imposes either a cycle or an infinite regress of justification even if no sources are epistemically circular. But the cycle is temporally impossible if temporal priority is assumed, and logically circular if basing is assumed. And the infinite regress is not feasible for any but a being with infinite cognitive powers. So the requirement of fully reflective justification does not seem to be satisfiable, whether there are epistemically circular sources or not. However this may be, I focus in this paper on the bearing of epistemic circularity on whether the belief that SP is reliable is justified and skip its bearing on fully reflective justifiedness.

3. *Global* skepticism follows if, as seems likely, beliefs about the reliability of sources not infected by epistemic circularity are based in part on beliefs in the reliability of infected sources.

4. Alston (1991, pp. 146–83) has charged that epistemic circularity deprives us of what we seek from cognitive evaluation—a nonarbitrary basis for preferring our own sources to other possible sources. Alston proposes that we respond by turning from the evaluation of justifiedness to that of practical rationality. But I argue elsewhere (Schmitt, 2003) that practical rationality does not satisfy the demand for a nonarbitrary basis for preferring our own sources. See also Sosa (1994). If this is so, we must seek an alternative response to the charge of arbitrariness. I believe the right response is to deny that epistemically circular inference is arbitrary in a worrisome sense. My discussion in this paper provides oblique support for that response.

5. Here I adopt a distinction in Boghossian (2000), though I alter his terminology. I discussed a related distinction between circularity and rubberstamping in (1992, ch. 3).

6. One might propose this difference between the problems of begging the question and indiscrimination. The problem of begging the question, one might say, attaches to a *specific use* of a logically circular argument to support a belief. By contrast, the indiscrimination problem attaches to a *general strategy* of supporting beliefs by appeal to logically circular arguments, rather than to a specific use of an argument to support a belief. The problem with begging the question has to do with the way the particular argument manages support. The problem with indiscrimination, by contrast, arises from the fact that the strategy of using a logically circular argument of a certain kind would support arbitrarily chosen conclusions, if any at all. If this is the right description of the difference between the problems, then we could get around the indiscrimination problem in a way we cannot get around the problem of begging the question—by

forswearing the general strategy. At least, we could do so if some specific uses of a logically circular argument to support a conclusion are not instances of the general strategy of using a logically circular argument to support a conclusion. However, I do not think that an objection to the general strategy exhausts the indiscrimination problem. So forswearing the general strategy is not enough to stanch the problem.

7. There is a question whether the absence of a belief that $T$ is reliable will not set up a conflict among my beliefs, by producing the belief that I have no belief that $T$ is reliable, this belief in turn conflicting with the outputs of $T$. But I take it that the same situation obtains in the case of a track-record inference to the reliability of SP; so I am in no worse position in the case of $T$ than in the case of SP.

8. In (1992, ch. 3) I discussed an apparent fault of track-record inferences related to indiscrimination—the fault of rubberstamping. A track-record inference to the reliability of SP rubberstamps SP if it necessarily yields the belief that SP is reliable when used to judge whether SP is reliable. (Rubberstamping would be equivalent to indiscrimination if saying that an inference relying on a source $T$ necessarily yields the belief that $T$ is reliable is just saying that the inference is of a type for which any instance relying on a source $S$ yields the belief that $S$ is reliable.) I argued that suitably sophisticated track-record inferences are not in fact bound to validate the source on which they rely, hence do not rubberstamp. My remarks in the text show that even those track-record inferences that do rubberstamp are not for that reason prevented from justifying the inferred reliability belief.

9. For defenses of a circular, inductive justification of the reliability of induction, see Braithewaite (1953, pp. 264–92), Black (1958, pp. 718–25), Rescher (1980, ch. 7), and Van Cleve (1984). Hume (1974, p. 173) appears to have offered a circular, inductive justification of induction. For a case in favor of this interpretation, see Beauchamp and Rosenberg (1981).

10. Fumerton (1980) argues that induction is more basic than inference to the best explanation. For critical discussion of Fumerton's argument, see Thagard (1988, pp. 139–41).

11. There is no *logical* case that there must be an epistemically circular source. As Alston (1993, pp. 118–19) has argued, what is inevitable is that *either* some source is epistemically circular *or else* our sources form a cycle such that for each source $A$, I am justified in believing that $A$ is reliable (if at all) on the basis of $B$ beliefs, where $B$ is the next source in the cycle. For any belief in the reliability of a given source must either be based on that source—in which case the source is epistemically circular—or else based on another source, in which case there is a regress. If the regress is finite, it either terminates in an epistemically circular source, or it circles around. And the regress must be finite, since we individuate sources in such a way that we use only finitely many sources. This leads to the result that either there is at least one epistemically circular source, or there is a cycle. Alston seems to think that a cycle faces a problem of begging the question as troubling as the problem faced by epistemically circular sources, but I am not convinced of this. This would be so if a doubt about the reliability of $B$ had to be answered for me to be justified in believing that $A$ is reliable on the basis of $B$. It is not clear to me that this is so. At any rate, it is not obvious that there is any urgency here comparable to

the case of epistemically circular inference, where I am justified in believing that *A* is reliable (if at all) on the basis of *A*.

12. For a Bayesian coherentist attempt to avoid circularity, see Shogenji (2000). Shogenji employs the technique of partitioning background knowledge into perceptual and nonperceptual components and conditionalizing only on the nonperceptual component. The difficulty with this technique is that, once the perceptual component is added to the reliability hypothesis to be tested, the probabilities can be expected to shift downward to an extent that prevents justification. An analogous point is made by Alston (1991, ch.4, sec. v) in his discussion of justifying the reliability of perception by inference to the best explanation.

13. The coherentist might reply that we must see my reliability belief and my SP beliefs in the broader context of my entire system of beliefs: a doubt about the reliability of SP is answered only by mutual support between my SP beliefs and my beliefs from sources other than SP; the latter relation of mutual support affords an answer to doubts about the truth of SP beliefs and hence about whether most SP beliefs are true. But even granting the assumption that there is substantial mutual support among SP beliefs and beliefs from other sources, this reply faces the response that any mutual support must be strong enough to overcome the doubt as to whether most SP beliefs are true. It is hard to see how mutual support could overcome such a sweeping doubt unless the supporting non-SP beliefs constituted the overwhelming majority of beliefs (or, more generally, had overwhelming cumulative strength of whatever kind is relevant to support). Thus, the reply assumes that SP beliefs are (in the relevant way) swamped by non-SP beliefs. This assumption is implausible. For these reasons, I am inclined to reject this coherentist reply to my first objection.

14. I note that epistemically circular inferences are ruled out on *logical* grounds when judgments of the reliability of sources are used for a certain practical purpose—to enable us to decide whether to make use of a source for the first time. For this purpose, we cannot employ an epistemically circular inference, since we have never used the source before. Here we consider what beliefs the source would produce and rely on other sources to check whether those beliefs tend to be true. But this shows only that, as a matter of logic, we are barred from an epistemically circular inference when we make such judgments of reliability. It does not show that we are barred from such an inference because it is question-begging.

15. There are alternative readings of Boghossian's response. Perhaps he intends only to agree with Alston (1989, p. 334) that one cannot appeal to an epistemically circular argument to convince someone rationally of the reliability of a source who does not practically accept the use of that source. But this point offers no help in responding to the charge that epistemic circularity prevents the justifiedness of my reliability belief. Alternatively, Boghossian may be suggesting that justified belief does not entail fully reflective justification, in Alston's (1989) sense (see note 3). Alston argues that, under epistemic circularity, fully reflective justification turns into a sort of logical circularity and thus entails SP skepticism. But again, denying that justified belief entails fully reflective justification does not explain how I can be justified in my reliability belief under epistemic circularity. Charity thus requires interpreting Boghossian in the way I do in

the text, as denying that justifiedness requires answering a doubt as to whether my source is reliable.

16. Of course, in the special case where the source in question is deduction or induction, there might be such undermining. But pressing this point in the special case would, again, run afoul of my proviso against skepticism—here, skepticism about deduction or induction.

17. A formula for the volume of a cone is not a belief-forming source or process, but we can speak of a standard way of using the formula cognitively to form a belief that a given cone has a certain volume.

18. An alternative suggestion is that the relevant distinction is between sources of a sort I tend to use only if they are reliable even without my selecting them in light of my reliability beliefs and sources not of this sort (Schmitt 2000).

19. I would like to thank Kevin Kimble and Adam Leite for help on this article.

# References

Alston, William. 1989. "Epistemic Circularity." In William Alston, *Epistemic Justification: Essays in the Theory of Knowledge.* Ithaca, NY: Cornell University Press, pp. 319–49.

———. 1991. *Perceiving God.* Ithaca, NY: Cornell University Press.

———. 1993. *The Reliability of Sense Perception.* Ithaca, NY: Cornell University Press.

Beauchamp, Thomas and Alexander Rosenberg. 1981. *Hume and the Problem of Causation.* Oxford: Oxford University Press.

Black, Max. 1958. "Self-Supporting Inductive Arguments," *The Journal of Philosophy* 55: 718–25.

Boghossian, Paul. 2000. "Knowledge of Logic." In Paul Boghossian and Christopher Peacocke, eds., *New Essays on The A Priori.* Oxford: Oxford University Press, 2000, pp. 229–54.

BonJour, Laurence. 1998. *In Defense of Pure Reason.* Cambridge: Cambridge University Press.

Braithewaite, Richard. 1953. *Scientific Explanation.* Cambridge: Cambridge University Press.

Fumerton, Richard. 1980. "Induction and Reasoning to the Best Explanation," *Philosophy of Science* 47: 589–600.

Goldman, Alvin. 1986. *Epistemology and Cognition.* Cambridge, MA: Harvard University Press.

Goodman, Nelson. 1965. *Fact, Fiction, and Forecast.* Indianapolis: Bobbs-Merrill.

Hume, David. 1974. *A Treatise of Human Nature.* Oxford: Oxford University Press.

Rescher, Nicholas. 1980. *Induction.* Pittsburgh: University of Pittsburgh Press.

Schmitt, Frederick F. 1992. *Knowledge and Belief.* London: Routledge.

———. 2000. "Social Epistemology." In John Greco and Ernest Sosa, eds., *The Blackwell Guide to Epistemology.* Oxford: Blackwell, pp. 354–82.

———. 2003. "Epistemic Circularity and Practical Rationality," manuscript.

Shogenji, T. 2000. "Self-Dependent Justification without Circularity," *British Journal for the Philosophy of Science* 51: 287–98

Sosa, Ernest. 1994. "Philosophical Skepticism and Epistemic Circularity," *Aristotelian Society Supplementary Volume* 68: 263–90.

Thagard, Paul. 1988. *Computational Philosophy of Science.* Cambridge, MA: MIT Press.

Van Cleve, James. 1984. "Reliability, Justification, and the Problem of Induction." In Peter French, T. Uehling, Jr., and H. Wettstein, eds., *Midwest Studies in Philosophy* IX. Minneapolis: University of Minnesota Press, 1984, pp. 555–67.

*Philosophical Issues, 14, Epistemology, 2004*

# INTERNALIST RELIABILISM

Matthias Steup
St. Cloud State University

## The Question

When I take a sip from the coffee in my cup, I can taste that it is sweet. When I hold the cup with my hands, I can feel that it is hot. Why does the experience of *feeling* that the cup is hot give me justification for *believing* that the cup is hot? And why does the experience of *tasting* that the coffee is sweet give me justification for *believing* that the coffee is sweet? In general terms:

Why is it that a sense experience that P is a source of justification—a reason—for believing that P?

Call this *the Question*. I will discuss various answers to the Question, and defend the one I myself favor.

The way I have put the Question assumes that sense experiences have propositional content.[1] This assumption makes it easy to articulate the issues I wish to discuss. However, what I'm going to say can be recast so as to avoid commitment to propositional content. Nothing essential is going to hinge on this matter, and thus there is no need to dwell on it.

The kind of justification of which sense experience is a source is *prima facie*, or defeasible. For example, the experience of feeling that my cup of coffee is hot will typically justify me in believing that it is. But it won't when I know that I have ice cold hands, for then a cup will feel hot even if it is merely lukewarm. Since the defeasibility of sense experience is a rather obvious matter, I trust I will not be misunderstood when henceforth I will not attach the qualifier 'prima facie' to the word 'justification' every single time I use it, but instead simply speak of justification.

The Question should be distinguished from a different one, namely:

> Under which conditions does a sense experience that P justify me in believing that P?

The two questions are obviously closely related. Nevertheless, it is one thing for a sense experience that P to give me a reason for believing that P, and another for such an experience to remain undefeated, that is, to *succeed* in justifying my belief. Suppose you're before a wall that looks red to you. Your sense experience gives you justification—a reason—for believing that the wall is red. But you notice that red light illuminates the wall. Thus all things considered you are not justified in believing that the wall is red. Nevertheless, you still have a reason for thinking it is. But why? Why is it that the wall's looking red to you gives you a reason for believing that the wall is red? That's the issue I will be concerned with.

## Justification

Which answers to the Question are plausible and which are not depends on what the term 'justification' is supposed to mean. There are four main options to choose from. We can understand 'justification' as denoting the kind of epistemic status that:

(1) turns a true belief into knowledge;
(2) makes a belief objectively probable;
(3) is as well denoted by the locutions 'having adequate evidence' and 'having good reasons';
(4) is as well denoted by deontological locutions such as 'entitlement,' 'responsibility,' and 'permissibility,' understood in a specifically epistemic sense.

(1) and (2) yield an *externalist* concept: whether or not a belief is justified in that sense might be something utterly hidden from the subject, as Evil Demon and brain-the-vat scenarios illustrate. (3) and (4), on the other hand, yield an *internalist* concept (at least on a standard understanding of the relevant terms). When I use the term 'justification' in this essay, I will have (3) in mind. I will understand 'justification' in a sense that is generically internalist, and thus remains neutral with regard to (4). Thus the Question could equally well be put by asking, Why are sense experiences evidence, or reasons, for our beliefs about the world?

The relevant sense of internality can be pinned down either metaphysically, by saying that nothing can be a justifier for S's beliefs unless it is one of S's mental states,[2] or epistemically by imposing the constraint that justifiers must be accessible in a way that is suitably privileged.[3] The difference between the internalist and the externalist understanding of justification is nicely exhibited when we consider a victim of Descartes's Evil Demon.[4] Such a victim has mental states like our own, but her perceptual beliefs are (presumably unlike our own) mostly false. On an internalist conception of justification, the victim's perceptual beliefs are no less justified than our own; on an externalist conception, they are not justified even though our own are.

Until further issues are raised, choosing an internalist understanding of 'justification' is a mere terminological stipulation. Things become controversial only when substantive claims are made about the significance of justification thus understood. At the extreme end, there are those who claim that internalist justification is of no interest in epistemology.[5] From that point of view, the Question will be one worth debating only if we adopt a different sense of 'justification.' Then there are those who think that internalist justification, although not required for knowledge, is nevertheless an independently interesting concept.[6] To philosophers who hold this view, the Question will be of epistemological interest, but divorced from issues having to do with knowledge. Finally, there are those—and I count myself among them—who view internalist justification to be of epistemological interest, perhaps not exclusively but certainly primarily, because it is a necessary condition of knowledge. Such philosophers would say that the correct answer to the Question is also, at least in part, the correct answer to the question of why sense experience is a source of knowledge.

### Externalist Reliabilism

It should be reasonably clear, then, how the Question is to be understood. Let's proceed and examine various answers to it. Here is a radically externalist answer:

**Radical Externalist Reliabilism (R-EXREL)**
Sense experiences are a source of justification iff they are reliable.[7]

Reliabilism, as understood here, is a theory of, not justified belief,[8] but rather sense experience as a source of justification. Nevertheless, the kind of reliabilism I'm going to discuss is a close relative of reliabilism about justified belief, and thus succumbs to analogous objections.

According to R-EXREL, the reliability of sense experience is sufficient to make it a source of justification. That doesn't seem right. Imagine a possible world whose inhabitants have reliable perceptual faculties, but who also have, perhaps due to the manipulations of a Cartesian demon, compelling evidence for believing that their perceptual faculties are unreliable. Call this the *Reverse Evil Demon World* (as opposed to the Standard Evil Demon World). In it, sense experience is reliable but appears unreliable. Is sense experience a source of justification in the Reverse Evil Demon World? There is good reason to think that it is not.

Suppose you hear Glen assert that P, but you have excellent evidence for thinking that Glen is not a trustworthy informant. Glen's asserting that P does not, it would seem, give you a reason for believing that P. Now imagine yourself to be an inhabitant of the Reverse Evil Demon World. You have a sense experience that P. You also have strong evidence for believing that sense experiences are unreliable. It would seem that your experience gives you no more a reason for believing that P than Glen's assertion. This suggests that the reliability of sense experience is not sufficient for making it a source of justification.[9] Minimally, it must be the case that there are no reasons for thinking that sense experience is unreliable. Let us, therefore, modify R-EXREL accordingly, which gives us:

### Moderate Externalist Reliabilism (M-EXREL)
Sense experiences are a source of justification iff (i) they are in fact reliable and (ii) there are no reasons for thinking that they are unreliable.

Though M-EXREL is more plausible than R-EXREL, it is nevertheless problematic. It asserts that sense experience is a source of justification *only* if it is reliable. The *Standard Evil Demon World*—a world in which sense experience is unreliable but appears reliable—suggests otherwise. The inhabitants of this world have mental states that mirror our own, which means that the unreliability of their perceptual faculties is, so to speak, hidden from them. Given the sense of the term 'justification' we have adopted, and assuming that sense experience is a source of justification for us, we get the rather plausible conclusion that in the Standard Evil Demon World sense experience is a source of justification. M-EXREL implies, implausibly, that it is not.

To sum up: In the Reverse Evil Demon World, sense experience is reliable, but appears unreliable and therefore is not a source of justification. This shows that the *de facto* reliability of sense experience is not *sufficient* for making it a source of justification, and motivates the move from R-EXREL to M-EXREL. In the Standard Evil Demon World, sense experience appears reliable and thus *is* a source of justification although it actually is unreliable. This shows that the *de facto* reliability of sense experience is not *necessary* for making it a source of justification. According to M-EXREL, it is. So neither R-EXREL nor M-EXREL is a good answer to the Question.

Next, let us consider an internalist answer to the Question.

## Internalist Reliabilism

Even though the *de facto* reliability of sense experience is neither necessary nor sufficient for its being a source of justification, it would be a mistake to think that reliability is irrelevant. Note the following two points that emerged in our brief discussion of R-EXREL and M-EXREL. Evidence *against* its reliability prevents sense experience from being a source of justification even if it is in fact reliable, as shown by the Reverse Evil Demon World. Evidence *for* its reliability turns sense experience into a source of justification even if it is in fact unreliable. That's what the Standard Evil Demon World shows. So what seems to matter is not reliability itself, but *evidence* regarding reliability. Let's consider, then, the suggestion that evidence of perceptual reliability is both necessary and sufficient for making sense experience a source of justification.[10] Answering the Question accordingly results in a first version of an internalist kind of reliabilism:

> **IR1** A subject's sense experiences are a source of justification for her iff she has undefeated evidence for the reliability of her sense experiences.[11]

Since IR1 employs the term 'undefeated evidence', it is not a good answer to the Question. The analytic goal is to explain in *nonepistemic* terms why sense experience is a source of justification.[12] But this is not an insurmountable hurdle, for we can replace the reference to evidence with a nonepistemic description of that evidence.

Consider my 1988 Honda Accord, still in my possession and put to daily use. It's been a remarkably reliable car. My evidence for attributing reliability to it is this: I remember that is has rarely let me down. Put differently, I remember that it has a good track record. Likewise, I remember that my perceptual faculties have rarely let me down. What I remember is a life-long and wide-ranging track record of perceptual success, a record that involves few perceptual mishaps. My memory of this track record consists of two basic elements. First, I remember that almost invariably my sense experiences support each other. For example, typically I can see what I touch, and touch what I see. Second, I remember a conspicuous absence of experiences indicative of perceptual unreliability. It doesn't happen very often, for example, that I have an auditory experience of a noise, but all things considered it's clear that nothing nearby could make that noise. So let's say I have evidence for the reliability of my perceptual faculties if I remember a track record of perceptual success.

Before we can fix IR1 accordingly, one further problem must be addressed. Since the term 'remember' is a success term, an Evil Demon victim does not, strictly speaking, remember a track record of perceptual success. Yet an Evil Demon victim's sense experiences are a source of justification for him. Consequently, what should count as evidence of reliability will be the mere memory *impression*, *putative* memory, or memorial *seeming*, of a positive track record. In this phenomenal sense, an Evil Demon victim, whose perceptual faculties are in fact unreliable, has a memory impression of a good perceptual track record.

The suggestion, then, is that a subject's evidence for the attribution of reliability to her perceptual faculties consists of memory impressions of a track record of perceptual success. Replacing the *analysans* of IR1 accordingly, we get a second version of internalist reliabilism:

> **IR2**  A subject's sense experiences are a source of justification for her iff she has a memory impression of a track record of perceptual success.

According to IR2, a memory impression of perceptual success is sufficient to make sense experience a source of justification for me. This seems false. Suppose you are interested in what Ben has to say, but you wonder whether he is a trustworthy informant. You have no evidence one way or the other. But there is Fred, and Fred says that Ben is a trustworthy informant. Unfortunately, you have no idea whether or not Fred is a trustworthy informant. Clearly, Fred's testimony fails to turn Ben's testimony into a source of justification for you. Apply this to IR2. Assume your memory tells you that your perceptual faculties are reliable, but you have no reason at all to consider your memory itself reliable. Are your perceptual faculties a source of justification for you under circumstances like that? It would seem not. If a subject's memory is to render her perceptual faculties trustworthy, her memory itself must be trustworthy. Thus we get a third and final version of internalist reliabilism:

> **IR3**  A subject's sense experiences are a source of justification for her iff she has a memory impression of a track record of both perceptual and memorial success.

Henceforth, the label 'Internalist Reliabilism' (INREL) will refer to IR3. It is the view that I wish to defend.

EXREL implies that, for Evil Demon victims, sense experience is not a source of justification. INREL implies that it is. In this regard, INREL and EXREL are fundamentally opposed to each other. There is, however, one thing they are in agreement about: whether sense experience is a source of justification is a *contingent* matter. According to both theories, there are worlds in which sense experience is a source of justification, and worlds in which it is not. They both imply that whether or not sense experience is a source of justification in a given world depends on what that world is like. Next, let us consider a theory that denies such contingency.

### Ipso Factism

Ipso Factism (IPFAC) is the view that a sense experience that P is, *ipso facto*, a source of justification for believing that P. If one has such an experience, then one has a justification for P, and that's it. No further conditions need be met. The point of introducing further conditions would be to rule out counterexamples: possible worlds or situations in which a subject has a sense experience that P but does not have a reason for believing that P. According to IPFAC, such counterexamples do not exist. So IPFAC amounts to the claim that sense experience is a source of justification in all possible worlds (with rational creatures who have perceptual faculties).

IPFAC is an internalist view for the following two reasons. First, sense experiences are prime examples of internal states: states of which we either are aware or can easily become aware. Second, if sense experience is a source of justification in all worlds in which it occurs, then it is a source of justification even in those worlds in which it is not reliable. Even though IPFAC is internalist, it is one of INREL's rivals. INREL asserts that sense experience is a source of justification only if there is evidence of its reliability.[13] IPFAC rejects that, declaring reliability completely irrelevant. For sense experience to be a source of justification, neither must it be reliable, nor must there be evidence of its reliability, nor must evidence of its unreliability be absent.

It might look as though H. H. Price and Roderick Chisholm are representatives of IPFAC.[14] Laurence BonJour describes the view they held as follows:

> The core idea of this view is that the mere occurrence of a physical appearance or state of being appeared to confers *prima facie* justification on the corresponding physical claim.[15]

I take it the significance of the qualifier 'mere' is that, in addition to the occurrence of a sense experience that P, no other conditions must be met if its subject is to have a reason for believing that P. This certainly sounds like IPFAC. BonJour doubts that there really is such a relation between sense experiences and the "corresponding physical claims."[16] William Alston goes even as far as calling what he takes to be the Price/Chisholm view a "cop-out." He says:

> They simply lay it down that perceptual beliefs are to be taken as prima facie credible just by virtue of being formed ... I call this a "cop-out" because it abandons the attempt to find any kind of intelligible connection between the character of the experience and the content of the

perceptual belief formed on its basis, such that this connection would enable us to understand how the experience can provide support for the belief.[17]

It would seem the view that Alston and BonJour attribute to Price and Chisholm is indeed IPFAC. I agree that IPFAC is problematic and should be rejected. BonJour doubts that there really obtains a necessary relation between sense experience and justified belief. We can substantiate his doubt by considering worlds whose inhabitants have memories of significant perceptual failure. In such worlds—call them *Odd Worlds*—sense experience is not a source of justification. According to IPFAC it is. In general terms, IPFAC tells us that whether sense experience is a source of justification is not a *contingent* matter. This seems false. Whether or not it is a source of justification in a given world depends on what's going on in that world. If its inhabitants have memory impressions of a track record of perceptual (and memorial) success, it is; if they have memory impressions of a track record of perceptual failure, it is not. IPFAC is not, therefore, a plausible answer to the Question.

Advocates of IPFAC could reply that in Odd Worlds, sense experience is a source of justification, but one that is always defeated. I don't think this is a good reply. When trying to answer the Question, what we want to know, at least in part, is what the difference is between having a sense experience that P, and, say, wishing that P. Why is the former a source of justification for us, whereas the latter is not? If memories of massive perceptual failure don't bar sense experience from being a source of justification, it's unclear why wishful thinking should not count as a source of justification as well. Thus the reply under consideration would invite the following argument: "Sure, we know that wishful thinking is an unreliable source. But that doesn't mean it's not a source of justification. It just means it is a source of justification that is always defeated." Once we allow for the possibility of permanently defeated sources of justification, it will not be easy to block such obviously preposterous reasoning.

The comparison between sense experience and wishful thinking reinforces Alston's point. What we want is an explanation that helps us understand why a sense experience that P gives us a reason for believing that P, whereas, for example, wishing that P does not. IPFAC does not provide any such explanation, and therefore falls short of meeting our analytic expectations. So I am in agreement with BonJour's and Alston's misgivings about IPFAC. But are Price and Chisholm really advocates of that view? Perhaps they are more charitably interpreted as having advocated a different view, namely conservatism about perceptual faculties. Let us consider that view next.

## Conservatism

Epistemic conservatism, as normally understood, is the view that a belief is innocent (justified) unless proven guilty (defeated by undermining evidence). Let's call that view *Belief Conservatism* (BECON). When applied to sense experience, the innocent-until-proven-guilty approach yields:

### Conservatism About Sense Experience (SECON)
A subject's sense experiences are a source of justification for her iff she does not have memories of perceptual failure.

The basic idea of SECON is that we may trust our sense experiences unless memories of perceptual failure give us a reason for not trusting them. Unlike IPFAC, conservatism implies that whether sense experience is a source of justification is a contingent matter. It depends on whether or not there is evidence against its reliability. Conservatism is therefore an improvement over IPFAC.

To map out the landscape of the five theories we have considered thus far, let us distinguish between *certified* and *undefeated* faculties. A faculty is certified iff it appears reliable. A faculty is undefeated iff it does not appear unreliable. We can now pin down the differences between the five theories as follows.[18] For a subject's sense experiences to be a source of justification for her,

| | |
|---|---|
| R-EXREL says | they must be reliable, but need be neither undefeated nor certified; |
| M-EXREL says | they must be both reliable and undefeated, but need not be certified; |
| INREL says | they need not be reliable but must be certified; |
| SECON says | they need be neither reliable nor certified, but must be undefeated; |
| IPFAC says | they need be neither reliable, nor certified, nor undefeated; they are a source of justification no matter what. |

When it comes to the question of whether a belief source is a source of justification, evidence regarding reliability clearly matters. According to IPFAC and R-EXREL, it doesn't. That's why neither of these views is very plausible. Moreover, evidence regarding reliability seems to be the *only* thing that matters. That's why M-EXREL is not a satisfactory answer to the Question. This leaves us with INREL and SECON. When comparing these two theories, the issue to consider is this: If sense experiences are to be a source of justification for a subject, S, exactly what must S's evidence be regarding the reliability of her perceptual faculties? Is the absence of evidence for unreliability sufficient? Or is it necessary that there be evidence of reliability? According to SECON, the absence of evidence of unreliability is sufficient. According to INREL, it is not. Certification is required as well. Let us see whether we can adjudicate between these views.


## Against Conservatism

According to BECON, for a belief to be justified, it is not necessary that the subject have evidence in its support. It's merely necessary that the subject not be in possession of evidence *against* the belief. This view has a plausibility problem because of two kinds of cases. In the first, a subject, S, believes that P when she has evidence neither for nor against P. In the second, S believes that P when her evidence for and against P is equally good. Let's refer to these two kinds of cases as Evidential Neutrality cases. BECON implies that, in Evidential Neutrality cases, S's belief that P is justified. But it is much more plausible to say that, in cases like that, S should *suspend judgment* about P, and so is *not* justified in believing that P.[19] Consider an example. The number of blades of grass in my front yard is either odd or even. I have no evidence one way or the other. Surely I would not be justified in believing that that number is odd, or, for that matter, that it is even. BECON tells us that, if for whatever reason I were to believe that it is even, my belief would be justified. That doesn't sound very plausible.[20]

It would be surprising if SECON were less implausible than BECON. BECON is undermined by Evidential Neutrality Cases. The problem for SECON arises from similar cases: cases of evidential neutrality with respect to the reliability of sense experience.

Consider, then, a world whose inhabitants have equally good evidence for and against the reliability of their sense experiences. Call this the *Balanced Evil Demon World.* Due to the interference of an Evil Demon, sense experiences in this world are veridical as often as they are not. So when one of these subjects has a sense experience that P, it is just as likely as not that P is true. This is something the inhabitants of this world are aware of. If we assume that evidence of reliability begins at a success rate above 50%, and evidence of unreliability begins at a failure rate above 50%, we may say that the subjects in this world have evidence neither for perceptual reliability nor perceptual unreliability. SECON implies that sense experience is a source of justification in this world. This result would seem no more palatable than the outcome that I would be justified if I were to believe that the number of blades of grass in my front yard is even.

There are several problems with this argument against SECON. To begin with, one may wonder about the details. Can we really coherently describe a world in which sense experience gets things wrong half of the time? Second, an advocate of SECON could challenge the assumption that unreliability begins at a failure rate of 50%. Arguably, perceptual faculties with a much lower failure rate should already be considered unreliable. But this does not seem to be a serious difficulty. Assume unreliability begins when the failure rate reaches 10%. We can simply stipulate that, in the Balanced Evil Demon World, the apparent success-failure ratio lies exactly at this cut-off point, with the result that there is evidence of neither reliability nor unreliability. This suggestion also addresses the first problem. While it may be difficult to imagine a world in which sense experience deceives half of the time, there is no great difficulty involved in conceiving of a world with a, say, 10% frequency of perceptual failure.

A more serious problem is that, as far as reliability is concerned, there might not be a middle ground. Consider your car. Once the frequency of failure reaches a certain threshold, your car stops being reliable and thereby becomes unreliable. The same applies, so it could be argued, to perceptual faculties. If the frequency of failure is high enough to prevent them from being reliable, then they are unreliable. On this conception, evidence of unreliability comes about and increases to the extent evidence of reliability decreases. If this is correct, the Balanced Evil Demon world does not supply us with a very effective objection to SECON.

Let us, therefore, switch to a case in which there is evidence neither for nor against reliability. Suppose an ingenious neurosurgeon invented a procedure to equip humans with the faculty of echolocation, a faculty normally found in bats. Suppose James is the first person to agree to let this surgeon operate on him. The surgeon tells James that there is no guarantee that his new faculty will work reliably. It might, but then it might not. If it does not, it will produce in James hallucinatory experiences of objects that are not really there. To assess the reliability of the new faculty, it will have to be tested. Suppose, then, the operation has been performed, and James begins with a series of tests. He is brought into a pitch-black room. The expectation is that his new sonar faculty will produce a quasi-visual experience of the room's interiors. In due course, although with his eyes he can see nothing, it 'visually' appears to James as though there is a table in the room. The question is: Does James's sense experience give him a reason to believe that there is a table in the room? SECON implies that it does.[21] I seems to me, though, that it does not. Hence I'm inclined to say that this case—call it the *Echolocation Case*—shows that we should reject SECON.

I doubt my verdict about the Echolocation Case will be universally shared. Thus I will raise an additional problem for SECON, a problem that makes it difficult to sustain the judgment that James's sonar experience supplies him with a reason to believe that there is a table in the room. This additional difficulty for SECON arises from the standards we impose on *testimony* if it is to function as a source of justification. Suppose you want to know what the GDP of Poland is. Informant Ben volunteers an answer: $90 billion.[22] Unfortunately, you have no idea whatsoever whether Ben is a reliable source of information with regard to this matter. Does Ben's assertion give you any reason to believe that Poland's GDP is around $90 billion? I think it does not.

Alternatively, consider such things as newspapers and magazines. Suppose while waiting for your dentist appointment, you pick up a journal you are not familiar with. You have no evidence one way or the other regarding its reliability. Reading an article in it, you come across the astonishing claim that eating peanuts protects against tooth decay. Does this give you a reason for accepting that claim? It seems to me it does not.

Examples like that suggest that we consider testimony a source of justification only if we have reason to think it's coming from a reliable source. So when we look at testimony as a source of justification, the internalist reliabilism approach looks more plausible than conservatism. Suppose advocates of SECON were to agree with that. They might say that testimony is one thing, sense experience another. Conservatism is right about sense experience, wrong about testimony. The internalist reliabilism approach is right about testimony, but wrong about sense experience. This move raises what we could call the *Discrepancy Problem*: the problem of having to explain why we should treat testimony and sense experience differently. Why would it be that, if a person is to be a source of justification, there must be evidence of her trustworthiness, whereas if sense experience is to be a source of justification, the absence of evidence of unreliability is enough?

This question ought to be kept in mind when we try to decide whether James' sonar experience gives him a reason for thinking that there is a table in the room. If Ben tells James there is a table in the room, we don't think James has a reason for believing that there is unless he has evidence in support of Ben's trustworthiness. Why should James's echolocation faculty be held to a less stringent standard? James has no evidence whatever for judging whether his new faculty is reliable. Hence, I submit, James has a reason for believing in the presence of a table in neither case. Neither Ben's assertion nor James's experience is such a reason, since neither of them is certified as a trustworthy source of information.

The Discrepancy Problem, then, poses a serious difficulty for SECON. A satisfactory defense of SECON would have to explain why we should treat testimony and perceptual faculties differently, that is, why we should agree that uncertified sense experience, unlike uncertified testimony, qualifies as a source of justification. It is not easy to see how such an explanation might go.

## Huemer

In his book *Skepticism and the Veil of Perception*, Michael Huemer defends a view he calls *Phenomenal Conservatism*.[23] This view asserts the following:

PC  If it seems to S as if P, then S thereby has justification for believing that P.[24]

As it stands, PC does not seem plausible. Asserting that seemings are a source of justification no matter what, PC would appear to be Ipso Factism about seemings. But in worlds whose inhabitants have evidence of perceptual unreliability, perceptual seemings are not a source of justification. Even in our world, seemings are not always a source of justification. Suppose it seems to S as if P because S has an intense desire that P. S does not thereby have justification for believing that P. So not all kinds of seemings are a source of justification. Some are not because we have evidence for thinking they are unreliable. Let's modify PC so as to accommodate this point:

> PC*  If S has a kind K seeming that P, and S does not have evidence for believing that kind K seemings are unreliable, then S has justification for believing that P.

PC* states only a sufficient condition, and is not specifically about sense experience. But if we add an 'only if' and restrict the principle to sense experiential seemings, the result will be SECON. It will be instructive, therefore, to see how Huemer defends PC.

Huemer claims that PC is self-evident, at least once it is seen in its proper light. To put it in its proper light, Huemer appeals to the truth goal: the goal of having true beliefs and avoiding false ones.[25] That strikes me as unobjectionable. After all, the kind of justification we are concerned with is *epistemic*, as opposed to, say, moral or prudential justification. To explain how we are to distinguish between epistemic and nonepistemic justification, typically the truth goal is invoked.[26] Let's see, then, what Huemer has to say about pursuit of the truth goal:

> Now, if my goal is to have true beliefs and avoid having false ones, and if P seems to me to be true, while I have no evidence against P, then from my own point of view, it would make sense to accept P. Obviously, believing P in this situation will appear to satisfy my epistemic goals of believing truths and avoiding error better than either denying P or suspending judgment.[27]

The point Huemer makes in this passage can be summed up as follows:

> (R)  When it seems to me that P and I have no evidence against P, then my pursuit of truth is served better by believing P than denying P or suspending judgment about P.

Suppose (R) is true. It would then be reasonable to conclude that the seeming in question gives me a reason to believe P. That in turn would make it reasonable to conclude that PC (or at least PC*) is correct. But why think that (R) is true? Human psychology is such that sometimes things seem true to people for very strange reasons. Suppose I have a perversely strong preference for even numbers. That's why I believe

(E)  The number of blades of grass in my front lawn is even.

Since (E) seems true to me and I don't have any evidence against (E), (R) tells us that my pursuit of truth is served best by believing (E). That's clearly wrong. My pursuit of truth would be served best by suspending judgment on the matter. It would appear, therefore, that (R) is false.

The problem with (R) is that it does not impose any conditions on seemings as a source of justification. It seem clear, however, that seemings are not always a good guide to truth. Let us therefore consider a version of (R) that imposes the condition that there not be any evidence of unreliability. And since our concern is not so much PC or PC*, but rather SECON, let us modify (R) in this regard as well. Making modifications as indicated yields the following principle:

(R*)  When I have a sense experience that P and I have no evidence for believing that sense experiences of that kind are unreliable, then my pursuit of truth is served better by believing P than denying P or suspending judgment about P.

Following Huemer's example, an advocate of conservatism might defend SECON on the basis of (R*). Now, it seems to me that, unlike (R), (R*) is not obviously false. But when we test (R*) against the Echolocation Case, it tells us that James' pursuit of truth is served best by believing that that there is a table in the room. It would seem, though, that James's pursuit of truth would be better served by suspending judgment. It do not think, therefore, that (R*) supplies us with a compelling reason in support of SECON.

**Pryor**

James Pryor defends a view that he sums up as follows: "When it perceptually seems to you as if P is the case, you have a kind of justification for believing P that does not presuppose or rest on your justification for anything else, which could be cited in an argument (even an ampliative argument) for P."[28] If this view is correct, then INREL is false. According to INREL, a sense experience that P gives you justification for believing that P only if you have evidence for the proposition that sense experience is reliable. So INREL tells us that, when your belief that P is justified because it perceptually seems to you as if P is the case, you have a kind of justification for believing P that *does* rest on your justification for something else, namely the proposition that sense experience is reliable. It would seem, then, that Pryor's view and INREL exclude each other.

In defense of his view, Pryor offers the following consideration:

> For a large class of propositions, like the proposition that there are hands, it's intuitively very natural to think that having an experience as of that proposition justifies one in believing that proposition to be true. What's more, one's justification here doesn't seem to depend on any complicated justifying argument. An experience as of there being hands seems to justify one in believing there are hands in a perfectly straightforward and immediate way. When asked, "What justifies you in believing there are hands?" one is likely to respond, "I can *simply see* that there are hands."[29]

I agree that, for a large class of propositions, it's natural to think that sense experiences give us reasons for believing them. That, by itself, is not at issue when it comes to adjudicating between Pryor's view and INREL. According to INREL, a sense experience with the content that I have hands does give me justification for believing that I have hands. The point at issue is rather whether that experience *by itself* is a source of justification, or whether it is a source of justification *only* if I have reason to think that sense experiences of that kind are reliable.

So why think that evidence of reliability is not needed? Pryor does not address this question explicitly. Nevertheless, we might want to examine whether the reasons he cites in defense of his view are reasons for thinking that evidence of reliability is not needed. In the passage I cited, he makes two main points. First, my perceptual justification for believing that I have hands does not depend on any complicated, justifying argument. This could be understood in either one of two ways:

(i)  there is no dependence on *giving* any justifying argument;
(ii) there is no dependence on *having evidence* for the premises of any justifying argument.

I certainly agree with (i). But why think that (ii) is true? This is where Pryor's second main point becomes relevant. He states that in response to a request for stating a justification for believing "I have hands," a person is likely to respond by saying that she can simply see it. The point, I take it, is that in our ordinary cognitive practice we view this response as entirely satisfactory. This suggests that evidence of reliability, or evidence for the premises of a justificatory argument, are not needed. A suitable sense experience by itself can do the job.

I agree that, in our ordinary cognitive practice, we view the "I-can-see-it" response as perfectly adequate. But this point supports only (i); it does not support (ii). Our perceptual faculties are, in fact, reliable. Moreover, this is perfectly plain and obvious to anybody, and therefore, in ordinary, non-philosophical contexts, hardly worth mentioning. So it might very well be that we view the "I-can-see-it" response as perfectly adequate precisely because we take the reliability of our faculties for granted, feeling no need to dwell on it. It is, however, one thing for a given justification to be appropriate in an ordinary context, and quite another to give a philosophically satisfying account of why a sense experience of one's hands gives a person justification for believing that she has hands. It might very well be the case, therefore, that

    (a) a sense experience of one's hands is a source of justification for believing that one has hands only if one has evidence for a justificatory argument with a premise asserting the reliability of such an experience,

while at the same time it is also true that

    (b) in an ordinary context, people can adequately defend their perceptual beliefs by citing perceptual experiences only, without having to make any appeal to perceptual reliability, because such reliability is in ordinary contexts appropriately taken for granted.

I do not think, therefore, that the rationale Pryor has offered in support of his view supplies us with a reason for rejecting INREL.

## Foundationalism and Coherentism

According to INREL, sense experience is a source of justification. Traditionally, coherentists have denied that it is, holding the view that all justification comes from other beliefs.[30] Thus there is some reason to consider INREL a version of foundationalism. On the other hand, at least on one plausible construal of foundationalism, INREL looks more like a version of coherentism. To explore this point further, let us distinguish between the following two questions:

    (1) Are there beliefs that are justified without receiving any of their justification from other beliefs?

(2) Is it possible for a sense experience that P, *by itself*, to be a justifier for the belief that P, that is, without the subject's having adequate evidence for the reliability of such an experience?

According to INREL, the answer to (1) is yes, the answer to (2) no. Thus INREL allows for basic beliefs of one kind, but not another. Consider the following two conceptions of basic beliefs:

BB1  A justified belief is basic iff it does not receive its justification from any other beliefs.[31]
BB2  A justified belief is basic iff what justifies it is not justification for any further propositions (that could be used as premises in an argument for it).[32]

Suppose I believe that the coffee from which I just took a sip is hot. According to INREL, what justifies my belief is a complex body of evidence, involving evidence for the reliability of both my memory and sense experiences. INREL does not, however, require that I actually *believe* that my memory and sense experiences are reliable. It merely requires that I have evidence in support of believing these propositions. So according to INREL, my belief that the coffee is hot can be justified without receiving its justification from any other *beliefs*. Consequently, it can be basic in the sense captured by BB1. Nevertheless, the evidence that justifies my belief gives me justification for two further propositions: that my sense experiences are reliable, and that my memory is reliable. Consequently, on INREL, my belief that the coffee is hot cannot be basic in the sense specified by BB2. In general terms, INREL implies that, when perceptual beliefs are justified, they are justified in part by evidence for perceptual and memorial reliability. Hence INREL implies that justified perceptual beliefs cannot be basic in the sense of BB2. So if foundationalism is construed as a theory according to which justified nonbasic beliefs ultimately receive their justification from BB2-type beliefs, INREL is not a version of foundationalism.

Yet it isn't a version of coherentism either, at least not according to the standard understanding of coherentism as asserting that nothing can justify a belief except other beliefs. Let us, therefore, distinguish between *holistic* and *monistic* foundationalism. Advocates of monistic foundationalism hold that a perceptual belief that P is basic if, and only if, it is justified by one, and *only* one, justifier: a sense experience that P. Advocates of holistic foundationalism deny the possibility of such basicality, insisting that a perceptual belief's justification always consists of a complex package of multiple justifiers. But they allow for the possibility that perceptual beliefs are justified solely on the basis of experience (conceived broadly as including memory impressions), without receiving *any* of their justification from further beliefs. Holistic foundationalism, then, may be viewed as a kind of compromise between coherentism and monistic foundationalism.[33]

Monistic foundationalism is a version of either IPFAC or SECON. In the former case, its advocates must cope with the problem of Odd Worlds: worlds in which sense experience appears unreliable. In the latter case, a defense of monistic foundationalism calls for a response to the problem of the Balanced Evil Demon World, examples like the Echolocation Case, and the Discrepancy Problem.

### The Problem of Reliability Knowledge

It could be objected that INREL runs afoul of the puzzle arising from the following two propositions:

A1  I can have perceptual knowledge only if I first know that my perceptual faculties are reliable.

B1  I can know that my perceptual faculties are reliable only if I first have perceptual knowledge.

It would seem that, if A1 and B1 are both true, I can have neither perceptual knowledge nor knowledge of the reliability of my perceptual faculties. So to avoid a skeptical outcome, we need to reject one of these propositions. Since B1 enjoys a good deal of plausibility, well-known responses to the puzzle target A1 for rejection.[34] According to the objection I wish to discuss, advocates of INREL must accept A1, or at least some version of it, and thus are prevented from articulating an effective response to the puzzle.

Proponents of INREL need not accept A1. As it stands, A1 is problematic because if it were true, perceptual knowledge could be enjoyed only by subjects with the inclination to consider, and form beliefs about, the reliability of their perceptual faculties. It would seem, however, that there are many subjects who have perceptual knowledge but never bother to do that. A more plausible principle results from replacing 'know' with 'being in a position to know':

A1*  I can have perceptual knowledge only if first I am *in a position to know* that my perceptual faculties are reliable.

It is hard to see on what grounds advocates of INREL could reject A1*. INREL tells us that perceptual justification requires evidence of perceptual reliability. Combine this with a standard account of knowledge, according to which evidence is the sort of thing that puts people in a position to know, and the immediate result is A1*. The modified principle, however, gives rise to a puzzle just as much as A1 does. This puzzle can easily be exhibited by rewording B1 accordingly:

> B1* I can be *in a position to know* that my perceptual faculties are reliable only if I first have perceptual knowledge.

With regard to the puzzle arising from A1* and B1*, advocates of INREL cannot avail themselves of the standard response of rejecting the first of the two problematic propositions. The question arises, therefore, whether INREL offers the resources for defending the alternative response of rejecting the second proposition, B1*. Making, once again, the traditional assumption that what puts a person in the position to know is the possession of evidence or justification, we may restate the two puzzling propositions as follows:

> A2 I can have justification for my perceptual beliefs only if first I am in possession of evidence for believing that my perceptual faculties are reliable.
>
> B2 I can be in possession of evidence for believing that my perceptual faculties are reliable only if I first have justification for my perceptual beliefs.

INREL is a theory about sense experience as a source of justification. Its basic claim is the one expressed by A2. But if A2 and B2 are both true, neither justified perceptual beliefs nor justified belief in the reliability of sense experience would seem possible. So, unless there is a plausible way of rejecting B2, INREL turns out to be a recipe for skepticism.

Why, then, should we think that B2 (or for that matter B1 and B1*) are true? The answer is, it seems to me, that it is ordinarily assumed that reliability knowledge is *inferential*. Let us consider the problem of coming to know that one's color vision is reliable with regard to the color yellow. On the inferential model, I would have to acquire a track record. Suppose at t1, I encounter an object that looks yellow to me. I know it's a banana, so I know that on this occasion my color experience was veridical. At t2, I encounter again an object that looks yellow to me. Turns out it's a lemon. So I can write down another episode of perceptual success. At t3, a copy of the Yellow Pages looks yellow to me, and so forth. Eventually, when I have accumulated a long enough track record, I infer that visual experiences of an object's looking yellow to me are a reliable indication of actual yellowness. But surely this conclusion will be justified only if I am justified in the first place in taking each of the perceptual experiences in my sample to be veridical. And this is the case only if I am justified in believing that the first object I perceived was a banana, the second a lemon, and the third a copy of the Yellow Pages. So clearly, unless I can have, to begin with, perceptual justification for the beliefs needed for verification, I will not be able acquire through inference from these beliefs knowledge of the reliability of my color vision.

If that's the only way in which reliability knowledge—or justification for the attribution of reliability—can be acquired, B2 would have to be true. In that case, INREL would indeed be a recipe for skepticism. There is, however, the alternative possibility that knowledge of sense experiential reliability can be acquired *non-inferentially*. Let us explore this option.

As I already mentioned in the previous section, INREL allows for non-inferentially justified beliefs about physical objects. Consider my belief that the cup of coffee in my hand is hot. According to INREL, this belief receives its justification not from any other beliefs, but from a perceptual experience (having as its content the proposition that the cup is hot) in conjunction with a memory impression of both perceptual and memorial success. The justification of memorial beliefs can be construed analogously. When I am justified in believing that P on the basis of memory, my belief is justified by a memory that has P as its content, in conjunction with a memory impression certifying the reliability of my memory itself.

Let us once again consider my venerable 1988 Honda Accord. What's my justification for taking it to be a reliable car? I do not think my justification is inferential. I do not infer my car's reliability from other things I believe. Rather, it seems to me, my justification is memorial. I *remember* that my Honda has unfailingly served me for fifteen years. This memory gives me noninferential justification for attributing reliability to my car, just as feeling that my cup of coffee is hot gives me noninferential justification for believing that the cup is hot.[35] Let us suppose that my justification for believing my perceptual faculties to be reliable comes about in an analogous way. I remember that my perceptual faculties have served me well in the past. This memory non-inferentially justifies my belief in the reliability of my perceptual faculties.

A satisfactory defense of this suggestion would have to address details that cannot be discussed here. But *if* my supposition is right and my evidence in support of perceptual reliability is memorial, then B2 turns out to be false, for the obvious reason that evidence of that kind does not consist of any *beliefs* that in turn would have to be justified. Rather, it consists of a memory state: a state that is not even capable of being justified or unjustified. INREL, then, does offer us the resources for explaining why B2 is false, and thus affords us a solution to the puzzle of reliability knowledge.[36]

## Notes

1. For an explicit statement of the view that sense experience has propositional content, see Searle 1983, p. 40. Pryor 2000, as well as Huemer 2001, adopt this

view; Brewer 1999 and McDowell 1994 argue that sense experience cannot justify unless it has conceptual content. For opposing views, see Heck 2000 Peacocke 2001.

2. See Conee and Feldman 2001.
3. See Chisholm 1989, p. 76f.
4. For further literature on the internalism debate, see Alston 1989, Feldman forthcoming, Greco forthcoming, Goldman 1997, Kornblith 2001, and Steup 2001a.
5. See Greco, forthcoming.
6. See Engel 1992, Foley forthcoming, and Wolterstorff forthcoming.
7. The 'iff' is to be understood as indicating equivalence, or necessary coextension.
8. As, for example, Goldman's process reliabilism. See his 1979.
9. The Reverse Evil Demon World is a relative of BonJour's Norman case. See BonJour 1985, chapter 3. The latter is meant to show that reliability is not enough for justified belief, the former to show that reliability is not enough to make sense experience a source of justification.
10. In Steup 1996 (pp. 101–105), I called this view *Presumptive Reliabilism*. For objections to Presumptive Reliabilism, see Markie 2004. The view proposed in Steup 1996 is developed further in Steup 2000.
11. A more detailed account would have to state when individual faculties are a source of justification. Obviously, it's possible for one faculty to be a source of justification while others are not. However, the points I am going to make do not require employing a more fine-grained account.
12. For a *locus classicus* regarding the epistemic goal, see Goldman 1979, p. 1f. See also Kim 1988. For dissenting views, see Lehrer 1997, chapter 3, and Wolterstorff forthcoming.
13. When I talk of 'evidence of reliability', what I have in mind is not that there is just *some* evidence, but rather that there is evidence for the attribution of reliability *all things considered.*
14. See Chisholm 1989 and Price 1950.
15. BonJour 1999, p. 137.
16. Ibid, p. 138.
17. Alston 1999, p. 235.
18. A further answer to the Question, which I have not addressed and do not have the space to discuss here, is proposed in Markie 2004. See also Markie's (not yet published) papers "The Mystery of Direct Perceptual Justification," and "Epistemically Appropriate Perceptual Belief."
19. For criticism of conservatism, see Feldman 2003, 143f, and Vahid forthcoming.
20. Admittedly, the example is a bit far-fetched. Few people do in fact believe things like that. For a more realistic example, involving two suspects, see Feldman 2003, p. 144.
21. Actually, to yield this implication, we would need to fine tune SECON as follows: A perceptual faculty of kind K is a source of justification for S iff S has no evidence for believing that kind-K experiences are unreliable.
22. The correct figure for 2002 is $386.1 billion.
23. Huemer 2001.
24. Ibid, p. 99. In Huemer's text, the consequent of PC reads "then S thereby has at least prima facie justification for believing that p."

25. I should mention that Huemer sets forth further arguments in defense of PC that I cannot discuss here. For a critical discussion of these, see Markie 2004.
26. For discussion of truth as the epistemic goal, see David 2001, David forthcoming, and Kvanvig forthcoming.
27. Huemer 2001, p. 104.
28. Pryor 2000, p. 519
29. See Ibid, p. 536.
30. For a list of representative passages, see Van Cleve 1985.
31. For such a conception of basicality, see, for example, Feldman 2003, p. 50.
32. Such a conception of basicality is implied by Pryor's account of immediate justification. See Pryor 2001 and forthcoming.
33. The view defended in Cohen 2002 seems similar to holistic foundationalism, as I construe it here. Pryor 2000 and forthcoming, and Van Cleve forthcoming, defend monistic foundationalism.
34. See Van Cleve 1979 and 2002, and Sosa 1997a and 1997b.
35. I'm using the term 'inferential' in a psychological sense. A belief's justification is, in that sense, *non*inferential if it is not, as a matter of fact, the result of inference. So justification can be noninferential even if it consists of a complex body of evidence that permits various inferences.
36. I would like to thank Michael Bergman, Mylan Engel, Peter Markie, Bruce Russell, and Hamid Vahid for helpful comments and discussion. An earlier version of this paper was read at the 2003 Epistemology and Metaphysics Conference at the Inter-University Center in Dubrovnik, Croatia. I'm indebted to the participants for a helpful discussion.

# References

Alston, William. (1999) "Perceptual Knowledge," in Greco 1999: 223–243.
BonJour, Laurence. (1999) "The Dialectic of Foundationalism and Coherentism," in Greco 1999: 117–142.
Brewer, Bill. (1999) *Perception and Reason*, Oxford: Oxford University Press.
Chisholm, Roderick. (1989) *Theory of Knowledge*, Englewood Cliffs: Prentice Hall.
Cohen, Stewart. (2002). "Basic Knowledge and the Problem of Easy Knowledge," *Philosophy and Phenomenological Research* **65**: 309–329.
Conee, E. and Feldman, R. (2001) "Internalism Defended," in Kornblith 2001: 231–260.
David, Marian. (2001) "Truth as the Epistemic Goal," in Matthias Steup (ed.) *Knowledge, Truth, and Duty. Essays on Epistemic Justification, Responsibility, and Virtue*, Oxford: Oxford University Press.
David, Marian. (Forthcoming) "Is Truth the Primary Epistemic Goal?" in Sosa and Steup (eds.), forthcoming.
Engel, Mylan. (1992). "Personal and Doxastic Justification in Epistemology," *Philosophical Studies* **67**: 133–150.
Feldman, Richard. (2003) *Epistemology*, Upper Saddle River, N.J.: Prentice Hall.
Feldman, Richard. (Forthcoming) "Internalist Epistemic Facts," in Sosa and Steup (eds.), forthcoming.
Foley, Richard. (Forthcoming) "Justified Belief as Responsible Belief," in Sosa and Steup (eds.), forthcoming.

Heck, R. G. Jr. (2000) "Non-Conceptual Content and the 'Space of Reasons'," *Philosophical Review* **109**: 483–523.

Huemer, Michael. (2001) *Skepticism and the Veil of Perception*, Lanham: Rowman and Littlefield.

Goldman, Alvin. (1979) "What Is Justified Belief?" in George S. Pappas (ed.), *Justification and Knowledge: New Studies in Epistemology*, Dordrecht: Reidel.

Goldman, Alvin. (1999) "Internalism Exposed," *The Journal of Philosophy* **96**: 271–293.

Greco, John. (Forthcoming) "Internalism, Externalism, and Epistemic Evaluation," in Sosa and Steup (eds.), forthcoming.

Greco, John and Sosa, Ernest (eds.). (1999) *The Blackwell Guide to Epistemology*, Oxford: Blackwell.

Kim, Jaegwon. (1988) "What is Naturalized Epistemololgy?" *Philosophical Perspectives* **2**: 381–405.

Kornblith, Hilary. (2001) *Epistemology: Internalism and Externalism*, Oxford: Blackwell.

Kvanvig, Jonathan. (Forthcoming) "Truth and the Epistemic Goal," in Sosa and Steup (eds.), forthcoming.

Lehrer, Keith. (1997) *Self-Trust: A Study of Reason, Knowledge, and Autonomy*, Oxford: Oxford University Press.

Markie, Peter. (2004) "Nondoxastic Perceptual Evidence," *Philosophy and Phenomenological Research* **68**: 530–553.

McDowell, John. (1994) *Mind and World*, Cambridge: Harvard University Press.

Peacocke, Christopher. (2001) "Does Perception Have a Nonconceptual Content?" *The Journal of Philosophy* **98**: 239–264.

Price, H. H. (1950) *Perception*, London: Methuen.

Pryor, James. (2000) "The Skeptic and the Dogmatist," *Noûs* **34**: 517–549.

Pryor, James. (Forthcoming) "Is There Noninferential Justification?" in Sosa and Steup (eds.), forthcoming.

Searle, John. (1983) *Intentionality: An Essay in the Philosophy of Mind*, Cambridge: Cambridge University Press.

Sosa, Ernest. (1997a) "How to Resolve the Pyrrhonian Problematic: A Lesson from Descartes," *Philosophical Studies* **84**: 229–249.

Sosa, Ernest. (1997b) "Knowledge in the Best Circles," *The Journal of Philosophy* **94**: 410–430.

Sosa, Ernest and Steup, Matthias (eds.). (Forthcoming) *Contemporary Debates in Epistemology*, Oxford: Blackwell.

Steup, Matthias. (1996) *An Introduction to Contemporary Epistemology*, Upper Saddle River: Prentice Hall.

Steup, Matthias. (2000) "Unrestricted Foundationalism and the Sellarsian Dilemma," *Grazer Philosophische Studien* **60**: 75–98.

Steup, Matthias. (2001a) "Epistemic Duty, Evidence, and Internality," in Steup (ed.) 2001b: 134–148.

Steup, Matthias (ed.). (2001b) *Knowledge, Truth, and Duty: Essays on Epistemic Justification, Responsibility, and Virtue*, Oxford: Oxford University Press.

Vahid, Hamid. (Forthcoming) "Varieties of Epistemic Conservatism," *Synthese*.

Van Cleve, James. (1979) "Foundationalism, Epistemic Principles, and the Cartesian Circle," *Philosophical Review* **88**: 55–91.

Van Cleve, James. (1985) "Epistemic Supervenience and the Circle of Belief," *The Monist* **68**: 90–104.

Van Cleve, James. (2002) "Can Atheists Know Anything?" in James Beilby (ed.), *Naturalism Defeated?* Ithaca: Cornell University Press, 103–125.

Van Cleve, James. (Forthcoming) "In Defense of Moderate Foundationalism," In Sosa and Steup (eds.), forthcoming.

Wolterstorff, Nicholas. (Forthcoming) "Obligation, Entitlement, and Rationality," in Sosa and Steup (eds.), forthcoming.

*Philosophical Issues, 14, Epistemology, 2004*

# SKEPTICAL ARGUMENTS

Jonathan Vogel
Amherst College

## 1. Skepticism as an underdetermination problem

Skepticism about the external world is a philosophical problem, but there are importantly different conceptions of what that problem is. One way of understanding such skepticism, which I find fruitful, is to construe it as an *underdetermination problem*. Let me explain what I have in mind by way of an example. Suppose an art historian is trying to decide whether a certain painting is by Rembrandt or by one of his students. The picture is signed "Rembrandt," but the handwriting is somewhat unusual and was added some time after the work was completed. In general, the execution of the picture is typical of Rembrandt's work, but there are some noteworthy anomalies. These unusual features may be signs of another hand, but they may just as well indicate that Rembrandt didn't completely finish the painting.

The art historian is thus faced with two competing hypotheses about the origin of the work she is examining. Either it was painted (and perhaps left incomplete) by Rembrandt, or it is by one of his followers. The two hypotheses are equally successful in explaining the evidence on hand. For example, they both account for the (imperfect) stylistic affinities between the picture being examined and paintings known to be by Rembrandt. Under these circumstances, it would be arbitrary to favor one hypothesis over the other. Even a correct choice would be, at best, a lucky guess. So, the art historian doesn't know that Rembrandt painted the picture.

What lesson about knowledge should we draw from this example? A straightforward suggestion would be the following:

*Strong Underdetermination Principle*: If q is a competitor to p, and both p and q are logically compatible with all the evidence available to S, then S doesn't know p.[1]

The trouble is that this principle immediately excludes the possibility of any inductive knowledge, as follows. If a hypothesis is supported by inductive evidence, the negation of the hypothesis is logically compatible with the evidence, too. The original conclusion thus has a competitor which, according to the Strong Underdetermination Principle, prevents it from counting as knowledge. But the considerations with which I began hardly seem to count against the possibility of inductive knowledge in general.

At this point a more plausible proposal would be:

> *Underdetermination Principle* (UP): If q is a competitor to p, then one can know p only if one can non-arbitrarily reject q.

Rejection of q would be arbitrary in the relevant sense just in case q is, from an epistemic standpoint, no less worthy of belief than p.[2] So, we have:

> *Underdetermination Principle* (UP, alternate version): If q is a competitor to p, then a subject S can know p only if p has more epistemic merit (for S) than q.[3]

These formulations are meant to be more adequate than the Strong Underdetermination Principle. Accordingly, I take it that the inferiority of q to p on broadly inductive grounds gives p greater epistemic merit than q, and makes the rejection of q in favor of p non-arbitrary. Examples like the one discussed above suggest that the Underdetermination Principle so understood does constrain what we will count as knowledge. In particular, the soundness of this principle would account for the art historian's failure to know that Rembrandt painted the picture she was examining, without eliminating the possibility of inductive knowledge altogether.[4]

Certainly, there is some kind of incompatibility between underdetermination and knowledge. I think that this opposition—which we encounter in everyday life—can give rise to the problem of skepticism about the external world. As we have seen, the fact that her evidence supports two rival hypotheses equally well prevents the art historian from knowing that a particular picture was painted (caused to exist) by Rembrandt. Such situations are utterly familiar. However, it can appear that *none* of our beliefs about the external world counts as knowledge for similar reasons. Suppose you see a tree. You take your sensory experience at that time to be caused by a tree.[5] But if you have just as much reason to think that something *else* is the cause of your experience, your belief that there is a tree in front of you is arrived at arbitrarily and doesn't amount to knowledge. Skeptical arguments, as I understand them, are meant to establish that every one of our perceptual beliefs faces competition from an equally good alternative. It would follow that we are never in a position to know anything about the world around us.[6]

The classic source for such arguments is, of course, Descartes's First Meditation. Descartes considers the skeptical alternative that he is dreaming. He finds that he has no basis for rejecting that alternative, and he concludes that he doesn't know he is sitting by a fire. This point, if sound, generalizes immediately. The unexcluded possibility that your sense experience is merely an extended dream would undercut all, or virtually all, your putative knowledge about the external world. I will call this line of thought the *Dreaming Argument*.

The Dreaming Argument rests on the observation that our sensory experiences might not be caused by anything external to us. Alternatively, our experiences could be caused by an external entity (or entities) thoroughly different from the objects we normally take to exist. Descartes raises the possibility that one's experiences are produced by an evil demon; the more up-to-date version is that one is a brain-in-a-vat whose experiences are caused by a computer. I will call this line of thought the *Deceiver Argument*. Again, the concern is that holding to our everyday beliefs about the world is merely arbitrary, and, hence, that we lack the knowledge we always thought we had.

Let us examine the workings of the Deceiver Argument more closely. It will be helpful to introduce some special terminology and notation. According to the skeptic, we know little or nothing about the external world. I will call those propositions the skeptic says we don't know *mundane* propositions, and beliefs with such propositions as their contents, *mundane* beliefs.[7] One's mundane beliefs are pitted against a hypothesis of massive sensory deception, like the hypothesis that one is a brain-in-a-vat. I will abbreviate the skeptical hypothesis as "SK". The details need not concern us here. What matters now is just that, if SK were true, the world would be thoroughly different from the way we suppose, and virtually all our mundane beliefs would be false.

The Deceiver Argument can be set out as follows:

A1. For any mundane proposition m, if I know m, then my rejection of SK in favor of m is not underdetermined.
A2. My rejection of SK in favor of m is underdetermined.
A3. Therefore, I have no knowledge of any mundane propositions.

This argument is very simple in its structure, and it is obviously valid.[8] The acceptability of the argument therefore turns on the interpretation and correctness of its premises. Premise (A1) invokes a condition on knowledge having to do with underdetermination, and Premise (A2) is the claim that condition isn't met. I propose that we understand (A1) as an application of the Underdetermination Principle set out above. That principle excludes knowledge in cases where a subject has no non-arbitrary way to choose between conflicting hypotheses. The skeptic's thesis in (A2) is that we are in just such a position with respect to the choice between m and SK. To refute the Deceiver Argument as formulated, one has to reject either (A1) or (A2). Since (A1) follows from the Underdetermination Principle, rejecting (A1) requires one to show that the Underdetermination Principle is unsound. I will comment on that way of resisting the argument in the next section.

Now, though, let me make a remark about (A2). What counts as epistemic merit—and therefore what it takes for m and SK to differ in epistemic merit—is a substantive question. There are views according to which m would exceed SK in epistemic merit if: (i) m is appropriately supported by inductive or explanatory considerations; (ii) m is a basic belief, or the rejection of SK is a fundamental epistemic norm; or (iii) m enjoys the benefits of methodological conservatism.[9] And (iv) m would certainly enjoy more epistemic merit than SK, if SK is logically incoherent.

## 2. The Underdetermination Principle, the Closure Principle, and All That

My presentation of the Deceiver Argument as (A1)-(A3) differs from one which many philosophers have taken as canonical. The Deceiver Argument is often analyzed as:

C1. For any mundane proposition m, if I know m, then I know that I'm not the victim of massive sensory deception.
C2. I don't know that I'm not the victim of massive sensory deception.
C3. Therefore, I have no knowledge of any mundane propositions.

(C1) is supposed to follow from the

*Closure Principle for Knowledge* (CK): If S knows p and S knows that p entails q,[10] then S knows q.

There remains the question of how (C2) is supposed to be motivated. One way is by appeal to the Underdetermination Principle itself, and there are others.[11]

The question naturally arises whether the differences between (A1)-(A3) and (C1-C3) make one or the other a more effective argument for skepticism. Consider, in particular, the first premise of each argument. (A1) is supported by the Underdetermination Principle. (C1) is supported by the Closure Principle for Knowledge. The Underdetermination Principle, like the Closure Principle, makes knowledge of mundane propositions depend upon the epistemic status of skeptical hypotheses. The Underdetermination Principle requires, as a condition for knowledge of the world, that our rejection of skeptical hypotheses not be arbitrary, while the Closure Principle requires that we know such hypotheses to be false. The soundness of the Closure Principle has been vigorously disputed.[12] One might think that the skeptic could avoid the difficulties facing the Closure Principle by relying on the Underdetermination Principle instead. But objections to the Closure Principle may count against the Underdetermination Principle as well. For that reason, it becomes important to see how these two principles are related.[13]

In order to do that, I will need to characterize in general terms some epistemic principles and the relations among them. I will begin by introducing some notation. Abbreviate 'S knows that ...' by 'K(...)'. The Closure Principle for Knowledge can then be rendered as:

(CK)  If K(p) and (p entails q), then K(q).

(CK) is the thesis that a certain epistemic operator, namely 'K', is closed under logical implication. Analogous closure principles may be formulated for other operators.[14] For example, 'S is justified in believing that ...', abbreviated as 'J':

(CJ)  If J(p) and (p entails q), then J(q).

Also, 'S's evidence supports ...',[15] abbreviated as 'E':

(CE)  If E(p) and (p entails q), then E(q).[16]

These principles have the general form, where O is an epistemic operator

(CO)  If O(p) and (p entails q), then O(q).

Closure principles of this sort link the epistemic status of one proposition to another proposition's having the same epistemic status, namely that specified by 'O(...)'.

Epistemic operators are also subject to another kind of principle, according to which the application of an operator O*(...) to a proposition is a necessary condition for the application of another operator O(...) to the same proposition. I will call such principles "weakening principles" and where such a principle holds between O* and O, I will say that O* is "weaker" than O. The form of such principles is:

(WOO*)  If O(p), then O*(p).

Of course, specific principles of this form are of keen interest to epistemologists. One is that justification is necessary for knowledge. In the notation adopted here:

(WKJ)  If K(p), then J(p).

Internalists of a certain sort affirm (WKJ), externalists of a certain sort reject it.

Finally, in addition to closure principles and weakening principles, there are what I call *mixed linkage principles*. Such principles make the application of one epistemic operator to a proposition a necessary condition of the application of another operator to a different proposition. The first proposition bears some specified relation to the second; here, that relation will always be entailment. Mixed linkage principles have the form

(MLP) If O(p) and (p entails q), then O*(q).

Two remarks are appropriate at this point. First, a MLP can be generated by combining a closure principle with a weakening principle. If we have

(CO) If O(p) and (p entails q), then O(q)

and

(WOO*) If O(p), then O*(p),

we can apply (WOO*) to the consequent of (CO) to yield

(OO*) If O(p) and (p entails q), then O*(q).

Second, it might appear that if an operator O is closed, and O* is weaker than O, then O* is closed as well. That is,

(CO) If O(p) and (p entails q), then O(q)

and

(WOO*) If O(p), then O*(p)

might seem to imply that

(CO*) If O*(p), and (p entails q), then O*(q).

In many cases, principles related in this way will all be sound. For example, it's widely thought that closure holds for knowledge (CK), that justification is a necessary condition for knowledge (WKJ), and that closure holds for justification as well (CJ). However, it's not true *in general* that an operator which is weaker than a closed operator must itself be closed. Here is an (admittedly artificial) counterexample. I will assume (CK) is sound. Specify an operator Z(...) as follows: 'S doesn't falsely believe that...'. Because truth is a condition of knowledge, Z is weaker than K. Now, say that S doesn't believe the false proposition u = 'Howard drove home during the blizzard', but S *does* believe the false proposition v = 'Howard drove to the doctor during the blizzard or Howard drove home during the blizzard'. U entails v, yet in this case Z(u) is true but Z(v) is false. So, (CZ) doesn't hold. An upshot of this discussion is that showing that closure fails for a weaker operator doesn't conclusively establish that closure fails for a stronger one.

At this point, we can turn to the Underdetermination Principle. The primary formulation of the principle was

> *Underdetermination Principle* (UP): If q is a competitor to p, then one can know p only if one can non-arbitrarily reject q.

I assume that to reject a proposition is to accept its negation. So, if S can non-arbitrarily reject q, then S can non-arbitrarily accept -q. Let me introduce 'N(...)' to stand for 'S can non-arbitrarily accept...'. The Underdetermination Principle can then be written as

> (UP)  If K(p) and (p entails -q), then N(-q).

(UP) has the form of a mixed linkage principle. As I indicated in the previous section, (UP) has considerable intuitive appeal.

(UP) follows from (CK), on the assumption that non-arbitrary acceptance is necessary for knowledge. In the notation I've adopted, that assumption can be put as

> (WKN)  If K(p), then N(p).

I take it that this principle holds because justification is a necessary condition for knowledge

> (WKJ)  If K(p), then J(p)

and non-arbitrary acceptance is a necessary condition for justification

> (WJN)  If J(p), then N(p).

Now, (WKN) can be applied to the consequent of

> (CK)  If K(p) and (p entails q), then K(q)

to yield

(UP) If K(p) and (p entails -q), then N(-q).

That is, assuming (WKN), (CK) entails (UP).

But, for all that has been said, (UP) might hold even though (CK) fails. In fact, (UP) can be derived without assuming (CK). Grant that non-arbitrary acceptance is necessary for knowledge

(WKN) If K(p), then N(p).

Assume as well that closure holds for non-arbitrary acceptance,

(CN) If N(p) and (p entails q), then N(q).[17]

The two principles can be combined to yield

(UP) If K(p) and (p entails q), then N(q).

In short, (UP) can be motivated independently of (CK). So it would seem that the skeptic can deploy a version of the Deceiver Argument which relies on (UP), regardless of how things stand with versions of the Deceiver Argument that proceed from (CK).

Stewart Cohen suggests otherwise.[18] He writes:

> But (CK) cannot really be a weakness of (C1)-(C3) relative to (A1)-(A3)...[T]he premises of (A1)-(A3) entail both premises of (C1)-(C3). But though the premises of (C1)-(C3) entail (A1) they do not entail (A2)...(A1)-(A3) is a sound argument only if (C1)-(C3) is—but not conversely. Thus, (A1)-(A3) can be refuted without refuting (C1)-(C3), but (C1)-(C3) cannot be refuted without refuting (A1)-(A3). In this way, (C1)-(C3) is the stronger argument. (p. 153, with alterations)

I don't see how the logical relations Cohen cites make (C1)-(C3) a "stronger argument" than (A1)-(A3). Compare (C1)-(C3) to the following "set-theoretic argument" for skepticism:

S1. For any mundane proposition m, if I know m, then I have derived -SK from the axioms of set theory.
S2. I have not derived -SK from the axioms of set theory.
S3. Therefore, I have no knowledge of any mundane propositions.

(S1)-(S3) bears the same relation to (C1)-(C3) as (C1)-(C3) bears to (A1)-(A3).[19] First, (C1) and (C2) together imply (S1), and (C2) implies (S2). Second, (S1) and (S2) together imply (C1). Third, (C2) cannot be derived from (S1) and (S2).[20] By Cohen's criteria, (S1)-(S3) is "stronger" than (C1)-(C3), and "stronger" than (A1)-(A3) as well. But, of course, the "set theoretic argument" is worthless. It does less, not more, to serve the skeptic's purposes than the other arguments. We have no reason, at this point, to regard (C1)-(C3) as superior to (A1)-(A3).[21]

Yet it remains to be seen whether (UP) will really be available to the skeptic if (CK) has to be given up. Consider the two most prominent attacks on (CK), those due to Robert Nozick and to Fred Dretske. Nozick introduces the notion of S's tracking the truth of a proposition. We can capture that notion with the operator (If...were false, S would not believe...), which I will abbreviate as 'T(...)'. Nozick argues that tracking is necessary for knowledge. That condition can be represented as

(WKT)  If K(p), then T(p).

Nozick also showed that the tracking condition isn't closed under logical implication. I argued above that it's not generally true that if closure fails for a necessary condition of knowledge, knowledge itself isn't closed. But it does seem that the failure of closure for (T) implies that (CK) fails as well. So if tracking is necessary for knowledge, (CK) is unavailable for use in skeptical arguments. Now, one might think that non-arbitrary acceptance could still be an additional necessary condition for knowledge, over and above the tracking requirement. (UP) would then hold, and the skeptic could proceed despite the failure of (CK). But, as Nozick himself saw things, the tracking condition naturally has its place as a component of a non-justificationist, reliabilist account of knowledge. Such an account rejects (WKJ) and thus leaves no particular motivation to endorse (WKN), nor (UP) itself.

The other principal objection to (CK) is that it seems to be violated in situations like Dretske's Zebra Case. In that example, you are supposed to know Z, that the animal you see at the zoo is a zebra, yet not know -CDM, that the animal at the zoo isn't a cleverly disguised mule made to look like a zebra. Z clearly entails -CDM. So, if you do know Z, but don't know -CDM, (CK) fails. Whether the Zebra Case has any bearing on the status of (UP) depends on why the epistemic status of Z is supposed to diverge from that of -CDM; in and of itself, the example doesn't specify what favorable relation you have to Z that you lack with respect to -CDM. One possibility is that your belief that Z is reliable, in a way required for knowledge, but your belief about the truth of -CDM is unreliable.[22] However, if a reliabilist account of the Zebra Case is adopted, then the status of (WKJ), and also of (UP), is again put into doubt.

Dretske offers a different analysis of why (CK) is violated in the Zebra Case. He assumes that, although you do know Z, you lack evidence against CDM. Because you lack evidence against CDM, you don't know -CDM. Hence, (CK) fails.[23] Now, suppose Dretske is right that you do know Z. CDM is a competitor to Z. If you have no evidence against CDM (and CDM doesn't suffer from some other epistemic defect), then your rejection of CDM would be arbitrary. But (UP) requires that if you know Z, and CDM is a competitor to Z, your rejection of CDM has to be non-arbitrary. So, if this way of understanding the Zebra Case is right, the Underdetermination Principle would fail just like the Closure Principle, and for the same reason.[24]

The analysis of the Zebra Case just given isn't obviously correct; ultimately, I think, it is incorrect. The point I want to make is just that the differences between (CK) and (UP) may not be epistemologically significant. It could be that *both* principles are unsound, and that neither version of the Deceiver Argument goes through. Alternatively, it may be that both principles are sound, so that any difference in efficacy between the different versions of the Deceiver Argument would have to lie elsewhere. To sort this matter out requires a detailed assessment of the considerations Nozick and Dretske have advanced. My own view is that the Closure Principle withstands scrutiny and must be respected. I think that the soundness of the Underdetermination Principle depends on whether non-arbitrary acceptance is necessary for knowledge. I believe that it is, but, as noted above, the issue is very much disputed.

### 3. Epistemic Impairment

On the analysis of the Dreaming Argument provided above, the concern raised by the dreaming hypothesis was that we could be *merely* dreaming that things are a certain way, while in truth they were utterly different. Our inability to exclude the possibility of dreaming would be an inability to rule out the possibility of *error* on our part. To this extent, the Dreaming Argument and the Deceiver Argument do not differ. But, the possibility that one is dreaming, understood in various ways, seems to allow for the construction of skeptical arguments that significantly diverge from the pattern (A1)-(A3) I've been considering so far.[25]

It's natural to suppose that dreaming, by its very nature, is incompatible with knowing. That is, your dreaming that p would prevent you from knowing p *despite the truth of p*, and even despite the fact that the truth of p caused you to believe p in your dream.[26] It's widely thought that the possibility of being in such a state gives rise to a skeptical argument (hereafter, the "Epistemic Impairment Argument"). The point of such an argument is that we can have no knowledge of the world unless we can know that we don't suffer the sort of epistemic deficit dreaming imposes. It need not be assumed that the dreams we undergo are unveridical.

It seems that an argument conducted on these terms has to depart from the pattern (A1)-(A3) and (C1)-(C3), above. In fact, it has been claimed that the failure of (A1)-(A3) and (C1)-(C3) to encompass the Epistemic Impairment Argument shows that they don't capture what is really at stake in the philosophical consideration of skepticism.[27] A regimented version of the Epistemic Impairment Argument would go as follows (as before, "m" stands for any proposition the skeptic says we don't know):

E1. If I'm dreaming m, it's false that I know m.
E2. In order to know m, I must know the falsity of any proposition which is inconsistent with my knowing m.
E3. Therefore, in order to know m, I must know that I'm not dreaming m.
E4. I don't know that I'm not dreaming m.
E5. Therefore, I don't know m.

This argument is defective, however. Consider assumption (E2). Like the Underdetermination and Closure Principles, (E2) is supposed to link knowledge of mundane propositions with knowledge that one isn't dreaming. (E2) is in fact much stronger than the Closure Principle, which it entails.[28] Crucially, (E2) also entails the principle that one knows a proposition only if one knows that one knows it:

(Iterativity Principle) $K(p) \rightarrow K(K(p))$.

The derivation is straightforward. My *not* knowing p is inconsistent with my knowing p. By (E2), if I know p, I must know the falsity of any proposition inconsistent with my knowing p. So, I must know the falsity of the proposition that I don't know p. That is, I know that I know p.[29] The point can be put less formally as follows. A failure to know that one isn't in some knowledge-impairing condition like dreaming would deprive one of second-order knowledge. To argue that this second-order failure results in a lack of first-order knowledge about the world, one must apparently rely on a principle that makes second-order knowledge a condition of knowing *simpliciter*.[30] Hence, the proponent of the Epistemic Impairment Argument seems committed to the Iterativity Principle.

The difficulty here is that the Iterativity Principle is questionable on its face. A further source of trouble is that the Iterativity Principle, when combined with certain plausible assumptions about knowledge, can lead to paradox.[31] Thus, the skeptic seems to take on unwelcome commitments by employing an argument based on the possibility of epistemic impairment. By contrast, the Deceiver Argument in the form (A1)-(A3) yields the conclusion the skeptic desires without reliance on the Iterativity Principle. For this reason, some version of the Deceiver Argument seems to offer better support for skepticism.

Now, the point just made presupposes that the skeptic will have to effect the transition from (E1) to (E3) by way of a fully general principle about knowledge. Perhaps this isn't so. The skeptic might make the more limited claim that *perceptual* knowledge in particular requires knowledge that one is in a perceptual state (rather than a dream state). For example, suppose you see a cat on a bed. The claim now is that you couldn't know that there is a cat on a bed without knowing that you are *perceiving* a cat on a bed. But perceiving is different from dreaming, so it would follow that you couldn't know about the presence of the cat without knowing that you weren't dreaming.

This point would generalize to cover all cases of perceptual knowledge, yielding the premise:

> F1. For any mundane proposition m, if I know m by perceiving m, I know that I'm not dreaming m.

(F1) replaces (E1)-(E3), allowing the Epistemic Impairment Argument to proceed without anything so strong as the Iterativity Principle in the background. The argument continues:

> F2. I don't know that I'm not dreaming m.
> F3. Therefore, I don't know any mundane proposition m by perceiving m.
> F4. Therefore, I have no perceptual knowledge of the external world.

Presumably, if one has no perceptual knowledge of the external world, one would have no knowledge of the external world at all. So, from (F4), we arrive at the full skeptical conclusion:

> F5. I have no knowledge of the external world at all.

What should we make of this line of thought? It's natural to think that one couldn't have knowledge of the external world without knowing that one wasn't dreaming, and I think that this impression should be respected. But, in my view, perceptual knowledge requires one to know that one isn't dreaming because the nature of dream states is that they are unveridical, or at least overwhelmingly likely, to be unveridical. What gives the possibility that I'm dreaming its skeptical force is the connection between dreaming and error. It isn't that dreaming involves any *other* kind of defect or epistemic impairment the skeptic may exploit.[32]

There is a more concessive and less concessive way to support this assessment. First, the more concessive way. Let us grant that it's extremely likely, but not necessary, that dreams are unveridical. And let us grant also that if I weren't justified in believing that I'm not now dreaming, I wouldn't have any perceptual knowledge. But I would still maintain that the incompatibility between dreaming and knowledge is due to the connection between dreaming and error. More specifically, the fact that one is dreaming makes it *unlikely* that the seemingly perceptual beliefs one has are true.[33] Suppose I have experiences I would normally take to be waking experiences of being in Carnegie Hall. Under ordinary circumstances, my having those experiences would make it extremely likely that I was, in fact, in Carnegie Hall. If, however, I'm *not* justified in believing that my circumstances are normal—if I'm not entitled to believe that I'm not dreaming—my having Carnegie Hall-like experiences gives me no good reason to think that I'm really there. Possibly, I've fallen asleep in Carnegie Hall and then dreamt that I'm in Carnegie Hall. But there is, at best, no reason for me to think so. I could just as well be anywhere else.[34] The upshot is that a subject can't properly accept what she ordinarily believes about the world, unless she has some reason to reject the possibility that she's dreaming. If, however, the choice between those alternatives is underdetermined, the subject can accept neither. The skeptical argument can then proceed along the lines we've already seen.

The response just given grants that dreams may be veridical. But I'm not at all sure that such a view is correct. I think that it's plausible that when you dream, you dream that you are awake, that you are seeing things, and so forth.[35] In that case, the truth of what you dream is inconsistent with your dreaming it. To that extent, dreams can't be veridical.[36] Going the other way around, it's part of what you ordinarily believe about the world that you are now awake, that you are now really perceiving things, and that you aren't dreaming. The possibility that you are dreaming *tout court* is, therefore, inconsistent with your body of beliefs about the world taken as a whole.[37]

## 4. The demand for certainty

According to a familiar view, the skeptic holds that knowledge requires certainty. You are certain that p only if you couldn't be wrong about p. The Deceiver Argument serves to make us vividly aware that all our beliefs about the external world are vulnerable to error, hence uncertain, hence not knowledge.[38] To be fully explicit:

G1. In order to know any proposition, one must be certain about that proposition.
G2. Since one can't rule out the possibility of massive sensory deception, it's always possible that one is wrong about any mundane proposition m.
G3. Therefore, one isn't certain that m.
G4. Therefore, one doesn't know m.

The standing response to this line of argument is that the demand for certainty in (G1) raises or distorts the conditions for knowledge. If being certain means being in a position where you can't possibly be wrong, then you can be certain only if your evidence entails the truth of what you believe on the basis of that evidence. Requiring certainty in that sense would immediately exclude the possibility of any inductive knowledge whatsoever. However, we don't ordinarily recognize such a requirement, and instead embrace some kind of fallibilism.[39] The force of the Deceiver Argument, construed as (G1)-(G4), is therefore called into question.[40]

Now, skepticism about the external world may sometimes be motivated by a demand for certainty, but we have seen that the Deceiver Argument can be formulated so that the certainty requirement doesn't enter into it. The skeptic may appeal to the Underdetermination Principle instead. His thesis is that our preference for the commonsense view over the Deceiver Hypothesis is ultimately an arbitrary one. The problem isn't that the reasons we have for that choice fail to give us certainty—it isn't that our reasons for belief are good, but somehow not good enough. The skeptic's claim is rather that we have, at bottom, no reasons for our choice at all.

## 5. Cartesian and Humean skepticism compared[41]

When we affirm, against the skeptic, that we do know things about the external world, we invoke some conception of what knowledge is and what it requires. The skeptic may leave this conception unchallenged. That is, he may attempt to show us that beliefs we hold don't count as knowledge according to norms we ordinarily recognize. I will use the term *domestic* skepticism for a position of the first sort. Alternatively, the skeptic may contest the criteria we use to evaluate knowledge claims, as well as the claims themselves. In the face of *this* kind of skepticism, it would be pointless to show that what we believe satisfies our ordinary criteria for knowing. For, the more radical skeptic doesn't concede that beliefs meeting those criteria ought to be considered knowledge. One way to challenge the standing of our epistemic principles would be to show that they are inconsistent with one another. Such a conflict among our principles, like a discrepancy between our principles and our practice, is an intellectual shortcoming we could hardly ignore. I will call skepticism motivated in this second way *internecine* skepticism. Finally, one might challenge our epistemic principles in some other way, perhaps holding them to other standards according to which ours are defective or wanting. I will call this third variety *exotic* skepticism. The differences among these sorts of skepticism are important, as will emerge below.

I construe the Deceiver Argument as an argument for a form of domestic skepticism. On its face, the argument proceeds entirely within our ordinary conception of knowledge. It seems to rest on epistemic principles which we recognize as correct, notably the Underdetermination Principle. These principles are supposed to have the consequences that:

A1. For any mundane proposition m, if I know m, then my rejection of SK in favor of m isn't underdetermined.
A2. My rejection of SK in favor of m is underdetermined.
A3. Therefore, I have no knowledge of any mundane propositions.

The force of the argument is that we take ourselves to know mundane propositions that, by our own lights, we really don't know. Our usual epistemic assessments conflict with our commitments as to what knowledge requires. The constraints on knowledge applied here are meant to be ones we employ and respect in cases where skepticism is not at issue (especially, the Underdetermination Principle). To that extent, skeptical doubts are no different in kind from doubts that would ordinarily discredit knowledge claims. This line of thought is powerful and philosophically interesting. It would be a *reductio ad absurdum* of our common views as to the nature and scope of what we know. We can't respect the demands of logical consistency and remain indifferent to an argument conducted on these terms. At the same time, though, such an argument can be refuted, and we can see what form the refutation might take. It might be argued that we aren't really committed to the epistemic principles the skeptic appeals to. Alternatively, one might show that those principles don't have the consequences the skeptic supposes, so that either (A1) or (A2) is ultimately unsupported.

My principal concern in this section will be to shed some light on how Cartesian skepticism, so understood, may be related or not related to Humean skepticism (skepticism about inductive justification or inductive knowledge).[42] It would seem that the Cartesian skeptic *need not* be a skeptic about induction. Since a Cartesian skeptic doesn't dispute the legitimacy of our epistemic principles, she would have no reason to deny that true beliefs formed by accepted inductive procedures would count as knowledge. For example, we might know that our sense experience in the future will in relevant ways resemble that of the past. What the Cartesian skeptic denies is just that this experience gives us much knowledge of the external world.

I would expect the account I've just given to be controversial in several respects. One set of issues concerns the nature and role of epistemic principles as I've described them. You might feel that there just aren't any such things—they are at best a bad philosophical fiction. Or you might think that there are epistemic principles, or perhaps epistemic norms, but they can't be captured by propositions about the conditions under which someone has knowledge or justified belief. Or you might think that, if there are such principles, their scope is restricted, and they don't apply—or don't straightforwardly apply—in the cases the Cartesian skeptic brings up.[43] I want to acknowledge these reservations. However, I won't try to address them on this occasion.

Now, I've distinguished Cartesian from Humean skepticism, and I've said that in principle Cartesian skepticism carries with it no logical commitment to Humean skepticism. But it's often thought that the motivations and arguments for the one are pretty much the same as the motivations and arguments for the other. That claim seems right at least so far: If our beliefs about the external world are justified by evidence, and the evidence for those beliefs doesn't entail their truth, then the support for our beliefs about the world is inductive. If a general skepticism about induction holds, then our beliefs about the world don't have the status of knowledge. Cartesian skepticism would follow from Humean skepticism as a special case.

The burden of what I said earlier was that Cartesian skepticism can be understood as a form of what I called domestic skepticism. The question arises whether there is a domestic version of Humean skepticism. If certainty were a requirement for knowledge as we understand it, domestic Humean skepticism would fall out immediately. Let F be some proposition I believe on the basis of inductive evidence. Since my evidence for F is inductive, my evidence doesn't entail F. It follows that my belief that F isn't certain. Then, given the certainty requirement, I don't know F. But if certainty isn't a necessary condition for knowledge, as I've said, then this way of obtaining a domestic version of Humean skepticism stalls at the outset.[44]

In fact, it may be tempting to say something like the following: We use inductive reasoning all the time, and credit ourselves with inductive knowledge as a matter of course. Hence, there is every reason to think that such knowledge is licensed by epistemic principles we accept. In that case, the only way to argue for inductive skepticism would be to challenge our principles. Inductive skepticism, it seems, is bound to be exotic.[45]

But consider a line of thought attributed to Hume himself:

H1. Consider an inductive rule R, which licenses an inference from E to H. You won't be justified in believing H unless you have reason to believe that the application of R will produce a true belief (in this instance).[46]

H2. But to claim that the application of R will produce a true belief (in this instance) is to make an empirical claim about the *world*. (It isn't a claim about what epistemic principles do or don't command your allegiance.)

H3. You have no non-circular justification for that claim about the world; that is, you have no reason to believe that the application of R will produce a true belief (in this instance).

H4. Hence, your belief that H isn't justified.

This line of thought appears to be an argument for domestic Humean skepticism. It aims to show that epistemic principles to which we are committed, including the impermissibility of circular justification, don't allow for inductive justification or inductive knowledge.[47]

Hume's argument so construed is very similar to a skeptical argument based on what Richard Fumerton calls the "Principle of Inferential Justification":

(PIJ) To be justified in believing one proposition H on the basis of another proposition E, one must be (1) justified in believing E, and (2) justified in believing that E makes probable H (Fumerton, 1995, p. 36; notation altered).

There is a lot going on here.[48] As stated, the second clause of the PIJ may seem ambiguous (henceforth, I will ignore the first clause). To get clear about this point, and for purposes of further discussion, let me introduce some more terminology. First, we have an *inductive rule* such that one's evidence, E, justifies H, where E doesn't entail H. Corresponding to that rule is a claim about the world, to the effect that an inference from E to H yields a true belief. The weakest such claim, I think, is a material conditional '(E $\supset$ H)', which I will call the *reduced rule*. Moving in the other direction, there is the proviso that one is justified in believing or accepting that the original rule holds. I will call this the *elevated rule*.

Now, let us return to the PIJ. If we read the phrase 'makes probable' in Clause (2) epistemically, as 'justifies', the PIJ would say that an inductive inference from E to H provides justification for H only if one has reason to believe that E justifies H. That is, the inductive rule holds only if the *elevated* rule does. I will refer to this condition as the requirement that an inductive rule must be *secured from above*.[49]

Suppose that the inductive rule doesn't obtain unless the elevated rule does.[50] Presumably the same will be true with respect to the elevated rule itself. The soundness of the latter will depend upon there being a yet higher-level rule that secures it, and so on. The requirement that an inductive rule needs to be secured from above seems to generate an infinite regress of justification requirements which could never be satisfied. Hence, no inductive rule is sound, and no belief underwritten by such a rule is really justified.

The idea that Humean skepticism is motivated by a certain kind of regress argument is familiar. In fact, Barry Stroud tentatively ascribes such an argument to Hume. Stroud writes:

No one who has observed a constant conjunction between As and Bs and is currently observing an A will reasonably believe on that basis that a B will occur unless he also reasonably believes that what he has experienced is good reason to believe that a B will follow. But, Hume asks, how could one ever come reasonably to believe that? How is one to get a reasonable belief that a past constant conjunction between As and Bs, along with a currently observed A, *is* good reason to believe that a B will occur? (*Hume*, p. 63)

On the face of things, inductive skepticism of this sort counts as exotic. A skeptic who deploys this regress argument attacks the justification of our beliefs by attacking the rules which license those beliefs. That is pretty much the essence of exotic skepticism, as I defined it.

There is more to say, though. The requirement that an inductive rule has to be secured from above is a consequence of the so-called JJ Thesis:

> *JJ Thesis*: If S has a justified belief that X, then S is justified in the belief that her belief that X is justified.

The status of the JJ Thesis is controversial. A prominent view is that it arises from a "level-confusion", and we should not allow ourselves be confused.[51] To be justified in believing a proposition X is one thing, and to be justified in believing that you are justified in believing X is something else again. The former simply doesn't entail the latter.

Nevertheless, the JJ Thesis has appeal to some philosophers, who maintain that it is constitutive for justification as we understand it.[52] In that case, skepticism about induction which invokes the JJ Thesis wouldn't be exotic, in my terminology. Rather, we would have a demonstration that there is a conflict among our epistemic principles, i.e., the principle(s) that license inductive inference, and the JJ Thesis itself. The skepticism that resulted would count as *internecine* rather than exotic. But even if all this were so, it's significant that the argument just considered relies on the JJ Thesis, and that the Deceiver Argument for Cartesian skepticism doesn't. Humean and Cartesian skepticism differ in the kinds of epistemic shortcoming they ascribe to us. Niceties aside, the Cartesian skeptic thinks that we don't have knowledge of mundane propositions because we lack *evidence* for them. By contrast, the Humean skeptic who appeals to the JJ Thesis doesn't claim that our beliefs lack evidential support. The difficulty is rather that, in the absence of any (sound) inductive rules, nothing counts as inductive evidence at all.[53]

We have been considering the skeptical implications of the PIJ, when the phrase 'makes probable' is understood epistemically. The other way to read the phrase is to take 'makes probable' non-epistemically. Then, the upshot of the PIJ is that a necessary condition for S's having a justified belief that H, on the basis of E, is that S have justification for some proposition about the world like $(E \supset \text{Probably } H)$. So far as my concerns go, the probabilistic character of the consequent is a distraction. So I will understand the PIJ to say that the inductive rule doesn't hold unless one has justification for the reduced rule $(E \supset H)$. I will call this condition the requirement that a rule has to be *secured from below*.[54] Skepticism threatens if there is no non-circular justification for the reduced rule.[55] Such skepticism would be domestic Humean skepticism, if we are in fact committed to the PIJ as currently understood and to a principle that forbids circles of justification.

This way of proceeding, like the Humean argument set out earlier in this section, invites the following response. Both suffer from the same defect, viz., that they make non-circular justification for the reduced rule a necessary condition for the soundness of the inductive rule itself. If this requirement were met, you would be independently justified in believing (E ⊃ H). Suppose, in addition, that you are justified in believing E. E and (E ⊃ H) together entail H. In that case you would have *deductive* justification for believing H. Thus, a sound *inductive* rule can be secured from below only if it is superfluous! One might insist that no sound inductive rule needs to satisfy such a condition, or, at least, that we ourselves recognize no such demand on inductive rules. In that event, skepticism about induction motivated by a demand for security from below counts as exotic.[56] And, given the previous discusssion, we might conclude more broadly that no prominent form of skepticism about induction is domestic in character.

However, this judgment may be premature. The point made in the previous paragraph is, of course, related to the objection that the Humean argument for inductive skepticism presupposes that justification has to be deductive. But the twist here is that such a view of justification isn't simply assumed at the outset. Rather, it seems to emerge from the requirement that inductive rules have to be secured from below. The force of this requirement is that, if you are justified in inferring H from E, you are justified in believing (E ⊃ H). (E ⊃ H) is equivalent to -(E & -H), which might be spelled out as "your evidence isn't in this case misleading you about H". Moreover, in line with what I said earlier, -(E & -H) isn't a claim about what justifies what, it rather looks to be a substantive claim about the world. As such, it needs to be justified by evidence—or, at least, so one might think. What would that evidence be? To put the question somewhat provocatively, when you make an inductive inference, what evidence do you have that your evidence isn't misleading you into drawing a false conclusion?

Before pursuing these issues, it might be noted that this kind of worry about inductive knowledge seems closely related to skeptical worries about perceptual knowledge (and, thus, to skepticism about the external world generally).[57] The parallel is this. If you are a brain in a vat, your perceptual evidence P for a mundane proposition M is misleading. That is, SK entails that (P & -M). Since -(P & M) is a claim about the world, you know that claim only if you have evidence for it. What is your evidence in this case, i.e., what is your evidence that you aren't a brain in a vat? Presumably, that evidence is P itself (or P supplemented by other perceptual evidence). How plausible this view might be depends on the nature of your perceptual evidence, and how it is supposed to justify your beliefs about the external world. If P is something like 'It appears to me as though I have a hand' then it's not obvious how P counts as direct evidence against the proposition that I'm a thoroughly deceived brain in a vat.[58] However, that worry might be substantially relieved if P (and other perceptual evidence you have) licenses the acceptance of M, and the rejection of SK, as an inference to the best explanation.[59]

Let us now return to the problem of misleading evidence as it arises in connection with induction. Suppose your evidence is that all observed emeralds are green. You infer, and come to know, that all emeralds are green. You also know that it isn't the case that all observed emeralds are green and yet your evidence has misled you (say because there is a blue emerald buried deep in the earth that no one has seen or will ever see). We may ask, what is your evidence against that possibility? What is your evidence that -(O & -G)? Perhaps your observations of emeralds, O, give you evidence that all emeralds are green, G, and those observations are also evidence for -(O & -G).[60] Nevertheless, one may still harbor the impression that something is amiss with this response. One might think that, in general, E can't be evidence that E itself isn't misleading.[61]

There are many questions at this point which I find perplexing. I'm not sure whether there really is a problem of misleading evidence with respect to induction, and if there is, I'm not sure whether or how that problem might be answered.[62] And, more central to the concerns of this paper, I'm not even sure how this problem should be characterized. Is the threat to inductive knowledge domestic, internecine, or exotic? I feel confident of just this much: We may still ask whether Cartesian skepticism follows from the Underdetermination Principle. A firm answer to that question—even if other questions remain open—would be well worth having.

## 6. Conclusion

My goal in this paper has been to identify and examine a version of Cartesian skepticism, a domestic one motivated by the Underdetermination Principle. Cartesian skepticism so understood can't be ignored or dismissed, but it can be refuted (at least in principle). It seems to me that contemporary discussions of skepticism sometimes go awry because (i) they mistakenly evaluate the relation between the Deceiver Argument and the Epistemic Impairment Argument; or (ii) they overtly or tacitly assume that, for the skeptic, knowledge requires certainty; or (iii) they misjudge the relation between Cartesian skepticism and Humean skepticism. I hope that it's now clearer what Cartesian skepticism is, and isn't.[63]

## Notes

1. This suggestion is very rough, because its scope would need to be restricted to hypotheses that bear some appropriate relation to the data at hand. Otherwise, knowledge is excluded so long as the evidence one has doesn't settle *every* open question where two propositions compete.

2. According to what I've said, you would arbitrarily believe p if p had *less* epistemic merit than some competitor to p. Your so believing would be epistemically defective, but it's odd to characterize the defect as arbitrariness on your part. I think such a point would be well taken, but to set things right would make the exposition much more complicated, without affecting any substantive issues. Consequently, I've left the apparatus as it is.

3. What underdetermination is, and how it bears on the acceptability of beliefs or hypotheses, is a much more complex matter than my very limited remarks indicate. There is a large literature on the topic; two notable treatments are Laudan and Leplin (1991) and Earman (1993). However, I think that for my purposes here, the rough characterization I've given ought to do. That is *not* to say that what follows covers all the important questions about skepticism and underdetermination.

4. I mean to be neutral about whether epistemic principles have truth-values. I will call principles which have positive status for us "sound".

5. This way of describing the problem of skepticism will seem very wrong-headed to someone hostile to foundationalism or friendly to direct realism, and what I've said here is meant to be suggestive rather than definitive. See Michael Williams (1977), Williams (1991), and Alex Byrne (2004) for vigorous objections on this point. I address concerns of this sort in my (1997).

6. I assume that if we had no perceptual knowledge of the external world, we would have no knowledge of the world whatsoever (although see Note 7). That would follow from traditional views about epistemic priority, according to which non-perceptual knowledge about the world is based on perceptual knowledge. It would also follow according to at least some other views; see W. V. Quine (1975).

7. A proponent of the Deceiver Argument may have to concede that we have some minimal knowledge of the world. For example, the belief that my experience is caused by *something* other than myself wouldn't be undercut by the possibility that my experience is caused by some deceptive apparatus. The definition of a mundane proposition given here is meant to accommodate such exceptions.

8. (A2) stands in need of various refinements, especially if epistemic merit is holistic in some important way. An analysis of the Dreaming Argument that parallels (A1)-(A3) can also be given. However, the Dreaming Argument may involve additional complexities of its own, and so I take the Deception Argument as canonical. For a discussion of an important objection to proceeding in this way, see §3.

9. I take epistemic merit to be at least partly constitutive of epistemic justification, and I assume that support by one's evidence contributes towards epistemic merit. See §2. For discussion of (i), (ii) and (iii), see my (1990b), (1992), and (1993).

10. It's hard to give a precise formulation of the Closure Principle. Knowledge isn't closed under logical implication as such; you can know a proposition without knowing all of its logical consequences. The restriction that knowledge is closed under *known* logical implication is more plausible, but still not free of difficulties. Corresponding issues arise in connection with other principles I consider below. However, those issues aren't my concern here, and trying to take them into

account would greatly complicate the discussion. For that reason, in what follows, I treat all principles in unrestricted form.

11. For example, the skeptic might argue that we fail to know -SK, because (i) we aren't certain that -SK; (ii) whatever justification we have for -SK involves an unacceptable circle or regress; or (iii) when we believe -SK, we fail to satisfy a tracking condition for knowledge. See Cohen (1998) and Byrne (2004). I discuss (i), some versions of (ii), and (iii) below.

12. Notably, by Fred Dretske and Robert Nozick. I've defended the principle in my (1987) and (1990a). Current climate is now more favorable towards the Closure Principle than before, but at least some ways of defending the principle seem unsuccessful to me.

13. For recent discussion, see Brueckner (1994) and Cohen (1998). While I disagree with both authors at various points, I think their articles are highly clarifying

14. My approach follows Dretske's as presented in his (1970).

15. "Evidential support" is a term of art, used in various ways. As I think of it, it is a graded notion, so that S's evidence may support a hypothesis more or less strongly.

16. I think that (CK) and (CJ) are right, or close to being right. I have reservations about (CE), though.

17. (CN) follows pretty directly from the way non-arbitrary acceptance was defined. (i) Suppose S non-arbitrarily accepts p. By definition, p is greater in epistemic merit (for S) than any of its competitors, and, therefore, (ii) S can non-arbitrarily reject that competitor. (iii) Suppose further that p entails z. Then -z is a competitor to p. (iv) From (ii), if S can non-arbitrarily accept p, S can non-arbitrarily reject -z. (v) That is, S can non-arbitrarily accept -z, which is to say that S can non-arbitrarily accept z. In short, if (i) N(p) and (iii) (p entails z), then (v) N(z), which is (CN). I'm supposing that the epistemic merit (for S) of p is fixed and doesn't vary as a function of the proposition with which it competes. Dretske, for one, might deny this claim. See below.

18. Cohen (1998) compares (CJ) and (UP) rather than (CK) and (UP) as I have done. But structurally everything is the same. Moreover, if what I say below about (CK) and (UP) is correct, the same goes for (CJ) and (UP). I should note that Cohen later allows that (A1)-(A3) "may provide an independent route to skepticism" (p. 156).

19. (S1)-(S3) also stands in that relation to (A1)-(A3).

20. There is some awkwardness here, because these epistemic principles are presumably necessarily true, if true at all. Consequently, one needs to be careful in talking about entailment relations between such principles, and also in talking about the possibility that a principle "might" be false.

21. What Cohen has shown is that if the Underdetermination Principle can be used to underwrite a *successful* skeptical argument, then the premises (C1) and (C2) will be true, whether the Closure Principle holds or not. That fact licenses no conclusion about the precedence or utility of either principle, so far as the skeptic is concerned.

22. For example, employing Nozick's idea, you do track the truth of Z, but not that of -CDM. In that sense your belief about Z is reliable in a way that your belief about -CDM isn't. Since, in my view, tracking isn't necessary for knowledge, this

particular way of challenging the Underdetermination Principle doesn't work. There is more to the story, however.

23. Using the machinery from above, this position could be characterized as follows. Knowledge and non-arbitary acceptance require support by one's evidence (WKE, WNE). However, (CE) fails, even when the entailing proposition is known or justified. The conclusion is then that closure fails for the other operators as well. Someone concerned to uphold (CK) could do so by defending (CE) or by denying the weakening principles. For example, latter-day relevant alternatives theorists allow that you can know the falsity of the competitor q if, in the appropriate context, the possibility that q is an irrelevant alternative. In that case you know -q without evidence which supports -q, so (WKE) doesn't hold and (CK) can be preserved.

24. I am considering the treatment Dretske gives in (1970). He writes, "The evidence you *had* for thinking them zebras has been effectively neutralized, since it does not count toward their *not* being mules cleverly disguised to look like zebras" (p. 1016). One way of taking this comment is in line with what I say in the text. But, by saying that your evidence is "neutralized", Dretske may have meant that a shift occurs, so that the evidential support, and thus the epistemic merit, of Z isn't comparable with the evidential support, and epistemic merit, of CDM. On such a view, there seems to be no content to a non-relativized notion of non-arbitrary acceptance and rejection, so (UP) is empty or meaningless. It certainly wouldn't be available for use in skeptical arguments. Another remark by Dretske is pertinent. At one point he seems to allow that Z is "more plausible" than CDM, although the implausibility of CDM in these circumstances isn't sufficient for you to know that CDM is false. To that extent, Dretske might deny that Z and CDM have equal epistemic merit, and that a choice between them is forbidden by the Underdetermination Principle.

25. The Underdetermination Principle applies to hypotheses that are competitors, and it underwrites (A1) only if m and SK are logically incompatible. In the versions of the Dreaming Argument I'm about to consider, SK isn't specified to be logically incompatible with m.

26. In an now famous example, G. E. Moore describes how a Duke of Devonshire once gave a speech in the House of Lords, while asleep and dreaming that he was giving a speech in the House of Lords. Moore apparently thinks that the Duke did not know what he was doing. See (1967), p. 47.

27. See Stroud (1984), pp. 14–5; Wright (1985), pp. 431–432, Pryor (2000), pp. 522–523. Pryor considers a version of the skeptical argument that encompasses the possibility of epistemic impairment, but which differs from those I consider here. Pryor takes the skeptic's key premise to be: "If you're to know a proposition *p* on the basis of certain experiences or grounds E, then for every *q* which is 'bad' relative to E and *p*, you have to be in a position to know *q* to be false... *antecedently to* knowing *p* on the basis of E" (p. 528). This proposal raises some difficult issues about epistemic priority. I'm inclined to think that the argument Pryor considers isn't the best the skeptic can deploy, but I won't pursue the point here. However, if what I say below is right, the skeptic can respect the motivations behind the Epistemic Impairment Argument without proceeding in the way Pryor suggests.

28. Let z be a clear logical consequence for me of m; not-z is therefore inconsistent with m and with my knowing m. (E2) provides that I know that not-z is false. That is, I know z. So, it follows from (E2) that I know any clear logical consequence of a proposition I know, which is the Closure Principle.

29. Schematically, (E2) says $[K(p) \& (K(p) => \text{not-}z)] => K(\text{not-}z)$. As an instance of (E2), we have $[K(p) \& K(p) => \text{not-not-}K(p)] => K(\text{not-not-}K(p))$. $K(p) => \text{not-not-}K(p)$ is trivially true, so we can simplify to $K(p) => K(\text{not-not-}K(p))$, or $K(p) => KK(p)$. Strictly speaking, I suppose, the skeptical argument we are now considering doesn't require the Iterativity Principle in full generality. (E2) and the version of the Iterativity Principle that follows from it could be restricted to mundane propositions. But this restriction would lack any real motivation, and wouldn't allow the skeptic to escape all the difficulties (E2) would create.

30. Stroud identifies the skeptic's key principle as $[K(p) \& (K(p) => q)] => K(q)$, which is equivalent to the premise rendered as (E2) (Stroud (1984), p. 28). Wright offers the weaker $[K(p) \& K(K(p) => q)] => K(q)$, which he attributes to Stroud (Wright (1991), pp. 91–92). Wright's formulation yields the Iterativity Principle as long as the knowing subject knows that knowing p entails knowing p—surely, this isn't much of an obstacle. Other authors have claimed that the skeptic's argument explicitly requires a connection between first-order and second-order knowledge. See, *inter alia*, Alston (1989).

31. See E.J. Lemmon (1967) and Thomas Tymoczko (1984) on the status of the Iterativity Principle.

32. I think that what I say here and below would carry over to the skeptical hypothesis that one is suffering from hallucinations.

33. For a related discussion, see David Lewis (1988). Lewis observes that "veridical hallucinations are improbable, and a long run of them is still more improbable" (p. 86). See also Crispin Wright (1991).

34. If you like, you can put the point in explicitly probabilistic terms. The conditional probability I assign to (I'm in Carnegie Hall/I'm dreaming that I'm in Carnegie Hall) is very low. Suppose, then, that I'm having experiences as of being in Carnegie Hall, and that I can assign high probability to my being in Carnegie Hall, given that I'm having such experiences. It must be that I can assign high probability to the proposition that I'm *not* dreaming I'm in Carnegie Hall. Now, John Pollock and others distinguish two ways in which one's reasons to believe a proposition may be undone. On this view, there are *rebutting* defeaters that support the denial of the proposition, as well as *undercutting* defeaters that subvert the evidential connection between one's reasons and the proposition. 'I'm dreaming' would then be seen as undercutting the justification 'I'm having Carnegie Hall-experiences' gives to 'I'm in Carnegie Hall'. I don't accept this dichotomy as drawn, and I'm dubious about the existence of a special category of undercutting defeaters.

35. There is the phenomenon of "lucid dreaming" in which one is aware that one is dreaming. That would be the exception that proves the rule.

36. An objection here is that even if I dream that I perceive that m, and I'm wrong, I may also be dreaming that m *simpliciter*, and I may be right to that extent. This point certainly has some force, but I'm not sure just what. One difficulty is that

it's not true *in general* that if you dream that p, and p entails q, then you dream that q. A more general concern is exactly what it is for dreams to be "veridical" or "non-veridical" in the first place—a good question to which I don't have a good answer. Richard Feldman called these issues to my attention.

37. See my (1990b). There is another twist to the Dreaming Argument I won't take up here. Austin claims that dreams are phenomenologically different from waking states. Dreaming, then, involves a double liability. The dreamer's experience is unveridical *and* the dreamer's ability to recognize that she is dreaming on the basis of phenomenological indications is somehow disabled. The possibility that one is in that kind of state gives rise to complications that a consideration of more straightforward skeptical hypotheses (the brain in the vat) seems to bypass. However, Timothy Williamson maintains that a brain in a vat would be in a situation in some ways quite analogous to the state of the dreamer as just described. See Williamson, *Knowledge and its Limits*, p. 180.

38. What certainty is, or might be, is a complicated matter; so, too, is the relation between certainty and skepticism. For more discussion, one might consult Roderick Firth (1967), Peter Klein (1981), Peter Klein (1986), and, for a nice overview, Richard Feldman (2003). An objection to the construal here is that it conflates certainty with infallibility, and thus belief in any necessarily true proposition would improperly count as certain; a way of responding to this objection is suggested by David Lewis (1996), pp. 551–552.

39. To borrow Austin's remark, "Enough is enough: it is not everything". But one reason to have misgivings about this view is the opposition to it. David Lewis: "It seems as if knowledge must be by definition infallible... To speak of fallible knowledge, of knowledge despite unelimated possibilities of error, just *sounds* contradictory" ((1996), p. 549) and Timothy Williamson: "If one's evidence is insufficient for the truth of one's belief, in the sense that one could falsely believe p with the very same evidence, then one seems to know p in at best a stretched and weakened sense of 'know'" ((2000), p. 174).

40. In the terminology I use later, skepticism which rests on the certainty requirement counts as "exotic". See §5.

41. The characterization I'm about to offer of the dialectic between the skeptic and anti-skeptic has been influenced by Peter Klein (1981), Chapter One. See also Pryor (2000), p. 517.

42. There is a family of positions that can be called "Humean skepticism" or "skepticism about inductive knowledge". Two versions are: (i) knowledge of the observed can't yield knowledge of the unobserved; (ii) knowledge that F requires evidence which entails F. Getting clear about how such views are related to one another is important, but by no means easy, and to do so one would need to reckon with Goodman's New Riddle as well. It might be worth remarking that standard treatments of skepticism about induction frequently describe it as what I would call the unmet demand that inductive rules be secured from below or the unmet demand that inductive rules be secured from above, and these are often conflated. See, e.g., Howson (2000), Chapter One and Swinburne (1974), introduction. Finally, I should note that at least some philosophers with Bayesian sympathies deny that induction poses any problems that require (further) philosophical attention, although they differ among themselves as to

why that might be. See Howson and Franklin (1994) and Howson (2000); for a criticism, see Kaplan (1998).

43. I take Michael Williams to endorse the first or third of these positions, or both. Stanley Cavell may hold the second or the third. And perhaps one or more of these views is attributable to Wittgenstein. However, caution about such an attribution is in order. See Wittgenstein (1969) #634.

44. Similarly, one might take the view that only the possession of evidence which entails P gives one a reason to accept P and to reject its competitors. Then, Humean skepticism like Cartesian skepticism will appear to be motivated by the Underdetermination Principle. To put the same point a little differently, the Strong Underdetermination Principle introduced in §1 yields both Cartesian and Humean skepticism.

45. One might also argue that we credit ourselves with knowledge of the external world as a matter of course, so the epistemic principles we accept must allow for such knowledge (the Deceiver Argument notwithstanding). Hence, Cartesian skepticism must be exotic. For objections to this general line of thought, see Vinci (1983).

46. Hartry Field argues that it's very problematic to ascribe reliability to an inductive method in general, (2000), pp. 125–126, and I'm ready to agree. That said, there is still the question of whether the belief which results from a particular inductive inference is true.

47. I won't enter into the question of what kind of circularity ("rule-circularity", "premise-circularity", or perhaps some other kind), if any, might be involved here, or the question of whether the circularity involved is unacceptable. But one observation may be pertinent. Suppose Humean skepticism is meant to be domestic, i.e., the Humean skeptic concedes the legitimacy of our epistemic principles. If some such principles do accord positive epistemic status to inductive inference, then maybe one could properly appeal to those principles in replying to the Humean skeptic. In other words, an inductive justification of induction *might* have some cogency if deployed against domestic Humean skepticism.

48. In general, it's important to distinguish *impersonal* justification from *personal* justification. The former, as I think of it, has to do with the justification of *propositions*, while the latter has to do with the justification of *beliefs*. How the two types of justification are related to one another, in general, isn't straightforward. The PIJ states a condition on *personal* justification, which is supposed to hold between a justified belief that H and a justified belief that E. The second clause of the PIJ, on one reading, requires *personal* justification for a belief concerning a relation of *impersonal* justification between the propositions E and H.

49. Fumerton rejects this reading of the PIJ, (1995), p. 63.

50. Yet a further complication is whether 'unless' signifies logical implication, or whether it also marks a relation of epistemic priority. My impression is that adopting the latter reading would exacerbate the pressures I identify below, but not otherwise alter them. So, in my presentation, I take the dependence between the various rules to be entailment.

51. See Alston (1989).

52. See Bonjour (1984).
53. The JJ Thesis may count against principles of deductive justification as well as principles of inductive justification. In that event, the JJ Thesis might have the consequence that there is no such thing as evidence of *any* sort.
54. Fumerton himself seems to come down in favor of a non-epistemic reading. But he considers, and rejects, the idea that the force of Clause (2) of the PIJ could be captured in terms of a material conditional like the one in the text. However, Fumerton's reasons for dissatisfaction are different from the ones I express below. In the end, Fumerton's worry about inductive inferential justification seems to have most to do with the unintelligibility to him of a probabilification relation in nature, which, he believes, inductive inferential justification would require. See Fumerton (1995), pp. 85–88. I don't fully agree with Fumerton on this point, and on some others, but to sort out the differences in our views would be a large undertaking. Still, the reader should bear in mind that the interpretation of the PIJ, and the use to which I put it, should not be attributed to Fumerton.
55. If you invoked the original rule in justifying belief in the reduced rule, you would then in some way be relying on the original rule to justify itself. That is supposed to be unacceptably circular.
56. I anticipate the following objection: I have classified inductive skepticism which requires security from below as exotic simply because that demand is inconsistent with the possibility of inductive knowledge. In other words, I deny that this is domestic inductive skepticism just because it is inductive skepticism. My point is rather that, as things stand, the demand that inductive rules be secured from below is no more than an assertion of skepticism about induction. Contrast this demand with an appeal to the Underdetermination Principle. In the latter case, but not the former, the challenge to knowledge has a form that we ordinarily recognize as legitimate and compelling. It may be, though, that demand for support from below does have that form, after all. See the following discussion.
57. On this point, see Byrne (2004) following A. J. Ayer, and Michael Huemer (2001).
58. On the view advanced by James Pryor and others, experience provides you with *prima facie* evidence that m (where m is a mundane proposition, not a proposition about experience or how things appear). Proponents of this view may then want to say that experience also provides you with evidence that -SK. Alternatively, they may say that experience gives you evidence, and justification for the belief that m, from which you infer, with justification, -SK. The prospect of just this kind of resolution of the problem of "misleading evidence" for perception is, perhaps, one of the most attractive aspects of this position. But I have some doubt that this resolution holds up under scrutiny; see "Dismissing Skeptical Possibilities". Timothy Williamson's position, as I understand it, is that a properly endowed subject in a normal environment has knowledge and evidence for mundane propositions like m. Given Williamson's views about evidence, it may be impossible for the subject's evidence for m to be misleading. See Williamson (2000), especially Chapters Eight and Nine.
59. This presentation is very hasty. It should not be assumed that the *explananda*, for which M would be (part of) the *explanans*, are propositions about how things appear to be. On this point, see my (1990b) and (1997).

60. If evidential support obeys something like Hempel's Special Consequence Condition, then, if E is evidence for H, it is likewise evidence for -(E & -H). But the status of this condition is itself open to doubt.

61. What I'm calling the "problem of misleading evidence" is closely related to Goodman's New Riddle of Induction. I should note that the problem of misleading evidence is also related to the status of epistemic "bootstrapping" as discussed in Vogel (2000) and Cohen (2002). I hope to address this connection in future work.

62. Hawthorne (2002) and Bonjour (1998) raise the possibility that one could be justified *a priori* in believing that your evidence isn't misleading; see also Field's view, discussed in Note 46.

63. The ideas in this paper have been on my mind for a long time now, and I'm indebted to many individuals and audiences for their criticisms and suggestions. Most recently, I have benefited from comments kindly provided by Stewart Cohen, Richard Feldman, Richard Fumerton, Thomas Kelly, and Scott Sturgeon. I also want to thank Alex Byrne, Joseph Cruz, Michael Glanzberg, Jeffrey King, Sarah McGrath, Sherrilyn Roush and Susanna Siegel. Some of this material was presented in lectures to the philosophy departments at MIT and Rice University, and to the Rutgers Epistemological Conference 2003. I'm grateful for the helpful discussions on those occasions.

## References

Alston, William. 1989. "Level Confusions in Epistemology", reprinted in *Epistemic Justification: Essays in the Theory of Knowledge* (Ithaca: Cornell University Press, 1989).

Bonjour, Laurence. 1984. "Externalist Theories of Empirical Knowledge" in *Midwest Studies in Philosophy V, Studies in Epistemology*, ed. P. French, T. Uehling, and H. Wettstein (Minneapolis: University of Minnesota Press, 1984).

Bonjour, Laurence. 1998. *In Defense of Pure Reason: A Rationalist Account of A Priori Justification* (Cambridge: Cambridge University Press, 1998).

Brueckner, Anthony. 1994. "The Structure of the Skeptical Argument", *Philosophy and Phenomenological Research*, **54** (1994), pp. 827–835.

Byrne, Alex. 2004. "How Hard Are the Skeptical Paradoxes?", *Noûs*, **38** (2004), pp. 299–325.

Cohen, Stewart. 1998. "Two Kinds of Skeptical Argument", *Philosophy and Phenomenogical Research*, **58** (1998), pp. 143–159.

Cohen, Stewart. 2002. "Basic Knowledge and the Problem of Easy Knowledge", *Philosophy and Phenomenological Research*, **65** (2002), pp. 309–329.

Dretske, Fred. 1970. "Epistemic Operators", *Journal of Philosophy*, **67** (1970), pp. 1007–1023.

Earman, John. 1993. "Underdetermination, Realism, and Reason" in *Midwest Studies in Philosophy, XVIII, Studies in the Philosophy of Science*, ed. P. French, T. Uehling, and H. Wettstein (Minneapolis: University of Minnesota Press, 1993).

Feldman, Richard. 2003. *Epistemology* (Upper Saddle River: Prentice-Hall, 2003).

Field, Hartry. 2000. "Apriority as an Evaluative Notion" in *New Essays on the A Priori*, ed. P. Boghossian and C. Peacocke (New York: Oxford Unversity Press, 2000).

Firth, Roderick. 1967. "The Anatomy of Certainty", *Philosophical Review*, **76** (1967), pp. 3–27.

Fumerton, Richard. 1995. *Metaepistemology and Skepticism* (Lanham: Rowman and Littlefield, 1995).

Hawthorne, John. 2002. "Deeply Contingent A Priori Knowledge", *Philosophy and Phenomenological Research*, **65** (2002), pp. 247–269.

Howson, Colin. 2000. *Hume's Problem* (New York: Oxford University Press, 2000).

Howson, Colin and Franklin, Alan. 1994. "Bayesian Conditionalization and Probability Kinematics", *British Journal for the Philosophy of Science*, **45** (1994), pp. 451–456.

Huemer, Michael. 2001. "The Problem of Defeasible Justification", *Erkenntnis*, **54** (2001), pp. 375–397.

Kaplan, Mark. 1998. *Decision Theory as Philosophy* (Cambridge: Cambridge University Press, 1998).

Klein, Peter. 1981. *Certainty* (Minneapolis: University of Minnesota Press, 1981).

Klein, Peter. 1986. "Immune Belief Systems", *Philosophical Topics*, **14** (1986), pp. 259–280.

Laudan, Larry and Leplin, Jarrett. 1991. "Empirical Equivalence and Underdetermination", *Journal of Philosophy*, **88** (1991), pp. 449–472.

Lemmon, E. J. 1967. "If I Know, Do I Know That I Know?" in *Epistemology: New Essays in the Theory of Knowledge* (New York: Harper and Row, 1967).

Lewis, David. 1988. "Veridical Hallucination and Prosthetic Vision", reprinted in *Perceptual Knowledge*, ed. J. Dancy (New York: Oxford University Press, 1988).

Lewis, David. 1996. "Elusive Knowledge", *Australasian Journal of Philosophy*, **74** (1996), pp. 549–567.

Moore, G. E. 1967. "Certainty", reprinted in *Descartes: A Collection of Critical Essays*, ed. W. Doney (Garden City: Doubleday, 1967).

Nozick, Robert. 1981. *Philosophical Explanations* (Cambridge: Harvard University Press, 1981).

Pryor, James. 2000. "The Skeptic and the Dogmatist", *Noûs*, **34** (2000), pp. 517–549.

Quine, W. V. 1975. "The Nature of Natural Knowledge" in *Mind and Language*, ed. S. Guttenplan (Oxford: Oxford University Press, 1975).

Stroud, Barry. 1984. *The Significance of Philosophical Skepticism* (New York: Oxford University Press, 1984).

Swinburne, Richard, ed. 1974. *The Justification of Induction* (London: Oxford University Press, 1974).

Tymoczko, Thomas. 1984. "An Unsolved Puzzle About Knowledge", *Philosophical Quarterly*, **34** (1984), pp. 437–459.

Vinci, Thomas. 1983. "Skepticism and Doxastic Conservatism", *Pacific Philosophical Quarterly*, **64** (1983), pp. 341–350.

Vogel, Jonathan. 1987. "Tracking, Closure, and Inductive Knowledge", in *The Possibility of Knowledge: Nozick and His Critics*, ed. S. Luper-Foy (Totowa: Rowman and Littlefield, 1987).

Vogel, Jonathan. 1990a. "Are There Counterexamples to the Closure Principle?" in *Doubting: Contemporary Perspectives on Skepticism*, ed. G. Ross and M. Roth (Dordrecht: Reidel, 1990).

Vogel, Jonathan. 1990b. "Cartesian Skepticism and Inference to the Best Explanation", *The Journal of Philosophy*, **87** (November, 1990).

Vogel, Jonathan. 1992. "Sklar On Methodological Conservatism" *Philosophy and Phenomenological Research*, **52** (1992), pp. 125–131.

Vogel, Jonathan. 1993. "Dismissing Skeptical Possibilities", *Philosophical Studies*, **70** (1993).

Vogel, Jonathan. 1997. "Skepticism and Foundationalism: A Reply to Michael Williams", *The Journal of Philosophical Research*, **23** (1997).

Vogel, Jonathan. 1999. "The New Relevant Alternatives Theory", *Philosophical Perspectives*, **13**, ed. J. Tomberlin (Malden: Blackwell Publishers, 1999).

Williams, Michael. 1977. *Groundless Belief: An Essay on the Possibility of Epistemology* (New Haven: Yale University Press, 1977).

Williams, Michael. 1991. *Unnatural Doubts: Epistemological Realism and the Basis of Scepticism* (Cambridge: B. Blackwell, 1991).

Williamson, Timothy. 2000. *Knowledge and its Limits* (New York: Oxford University Press, 2000).

Wittgenstein, Ludwig. 1969. *On Certainty*, ed. G. E. M. Anscombe and G. H. von Wright, trans. D. Paul and G. E. M. Anscombe (Oxford: Blackwell, 1969).

Wright, Crispin. 1985. "Facts and Certainty", Henriette Hertz Philosophical Lecture, *Proceedings of the British Academy*, **71** (1985), pp. 429–472.

Wright, Crispin. 1991. "Dreaming and Scepticism: Imploding the Demon", *Mind*, **100** (1991), pp. 87–116.

*Philosophical Issues, 14, Epistemology, 2004*

# SCEPTICISM AND THE CONTEXT OF PHILOSOPHY

Michael Williams
Johns Hopkins University

## 1. Contextualism: the Basic Diagnosis

Whatever their differences (and they are substantial), philosophers who think of themselves as epistemological contextualists share certain fundamental ideas concerning knowledge and scepticism. I mention three.

1. The standards for correctly attributing knowledge (or justified belief) are in some way sensitive to context, hence variable rather than fixed.
2. While such context-sensitivity is readily seen in ordinary situations of epistemic appraisal, there is an important difference between all ordinary epistemic contexts and the context created by reflecting philosophically about knowledge or "doing epistemology". Whereas everyday epistemic appraisals are always in some way *restricted*, the philosophical examination of human knowledge is *unrestricted*. Since no knowledge-claim can survive unrestricted examination, in the extraordinary context of philosophical reflection—*but only there*—our knowledge of the world seems to evaporate entirely. (Perhaps it does evaporate entirely.)
3. Thus although the sceptic claims to have discovered, while reflecting philosophically, that we lack knowledge of the world, he has discovered (at most) that we lack knowledge of the world while reflecting philosophically.

These ideas constitute what I shall call the Basic Contextualist Diagnosis of Scepticism, or the Basic Diagnosis for short.

There are various ways of fleshing out the Basic Diagnosis, corresponding to different ways of thinking about the nature of knowledge: justificationist, externalist-reliabilist, and so on. However, in my view, the most fundamental division within the contextualist camp cuts across these familiar differences and concerns the question of how we ought to understand the context of philosophy or "doing epistemology". For while all versions of the Basic Diagnosis see the epistemic context created by philosophical questioning as in some way set apart from ordinary justificational or knowledge-attributing contexts, and while all explain the distinctive character of the philosophical context in terms of the unrestricted character of philosophical questioning, a crucial difference emerges when we ask: in what way *exactly* is the philosophical examination of knowledge unrestricted, and how does its unrestricted character lead knowledge to (seem to) evaporate?

There are two approaches to these questions. (Interestingly, both draw on hints from the First Meditation.) The most popular by far focuses on what seems to be the *extreme severity* of the sceptic's (or philosopher's) *standards* for attributing or claiming knowledge. To take this line, I shall say, is thus to adopt the High Standards (HS) version of the Basic Diagnosis, or the High Standards (HS) strategy.[1] The other approach, which I have defended in my own work, directs our attention to the *unusual generality* of the sceptic's (or philosopher's) *questions*. Since I think that the hypergenerality involved in the attempt to understand human knowledge "philosophically" is not just unusual but highly questionable, I shall say that my alternative version of the Basic Diagnosis follows the Spurious Generality (SG) strategy.[2] My purpose in this paper is to explore the similarities and differences between the two strategies and to explain my preference for the second.

## 2. Explanation and Justification

Philosophical scepticism is a problem because, while sceptical conclusions (when clearly understood) are wholly unacceptable, sceptical arguments (at least when we are in a certain frame of mind) can strike us as oddly compelling. As Hume said of Berkeley, we can tell that his arguments are sceptical because, while they admit of no refutation, they produce no conviction.[3] Both aspects of scepticism deserve comment.

Philosophical scepticism is unacceptable because it is extreme both in its *scope* and its *depth*. With respect to scope, the sceptic does not just suggest that we know less than we like to think, which is probably true. He argues that we know *nothing at all*, or (in a more limited but still hyper-general way) that we know nothing at all in certain very broad domains: for example, that we know nothing about the external world. As to its depth, philosophical scepticism is *radical*. The sceptic does not claim merely that we fail to know things by some stricter-than-usual standards. Rather, he argues that we are in no position to draw any invidious epistemic distinctions.[4] For all we can tell, epistemically speaking one belief is as good as another.

Turning to their seductive air of plausibility, sceptical arguments impress because they appear to be highly "intuitive". Not only are they short, to the point and free of obvious logical flaws, they do seem not to depend on any arcane theory. Rather, they seem to invoke only our everyday, average ideas about knowledge and justification, and thus seem to bring to light paradoxes implicit in quite ordinary ways of thinking. Scepticism is *our* problem, not an external threat. Of course, appearances could be deceptive. But if they are, this is something we will need to argue for.

How should we to respond to a problem like this? One way would be to prove, in terms that even a sceptic would have to accept, that we really do know the sorts of things we naturally take ourselves to know. However, the history of attempts to meet scepticism head on is not encouraging. Accordingly, contextualists recommend a more subtle approach. Instead of a proof, they offer something closer to what Robert Nozick called a "philosophical explanation".[5] The need for a philosophical explanation arises from just the sort of paradox that scepticism represents, where philosophical arguments clash with important, perhaps indispensable, pre-philosophical commitments. A philosophical explanation aims to relieve the tension. In the case of the contextualist response to scepticism, the explanatory/diagnostic goal is to sketch an account of the concept of knowledge that (a) is adequate to the basic linguistic data, (b) reveals how the sceptic goes wrong, and (c) shows how nevertheless sceptical arguments can s*eem* so compelling. Such an explanation should offer a complete dissolution of a philosophical paradox.

Such a strategy seems especially well-adapted to dealing with scepticism. A striking feature of the phenomenology of our encounter with scepticism, perhaps first emphasized by Hume, is that sceptical doubts, however compelling in the study, vanish like smoke when we return to everyday pursuits. Contextualism, by linking the sceptical temptation to a particular context of inquiry or appraisal, accounts smoothly for this. This is one of the principle attractions of the contextualist approach.

Accounting for the seductiveness of sceptical arguments is more than a bonus. If we do not identify (and thereby demystify) the source of the attraction that sceptical arguments have for us, we will not be able to rest content with whatever we come up with under (a) and (b). We will seem simply to be *confronting* the sceptic with an anti-sceptical theory of knowledge: Moore's argument on stilts, as it were.[6] If the sceptic's questions still look like good ones, the sense of paradox will not be fully relieved. To put scepticism behind us, we want a response to scepticism that is *diagnostic* rather than (merely) *dialectical*. Lacking a diagnostic component, a response to scepticism will be incomplete.[7]

A philosophical explanation is not a "neutral" proof. But philosophical explanation is not, in a general way, opposed to philosophical justification.

Because of the way it aims to dissolve a paradox apparently implicit in our ordinary epistemic practices, a philosophical explanation, if successful, will amount to a *vindication* of them, thus a kind of justification, though indirect.

How should we judge the worth of a contextualist diagnosis of scepticism? No doubt in all sorts of ways. But I will mention three things that we can reasonably expect from a good diagnosis. First, it should apply to an interesting form of scepticism. Today, this means that it should apply to scepticism that is both general and radical. Second, it should give an illuminating (and of course accurate) account of how such sceptical worries arise. Such an account should indicate how scepticism may be avoided, while allowing for a plausible explanation of its *prima facie* appeal. Such an explanation should not require philosophers who feel the force of scepticism to make egregious mistakes, or be *too* confused. Third, a good diagnosis should not be overly concessive. The history of epistemology is littered with responses to scepticism that, on reflection, turn out to be difficult to distinguish from scepticism itself. Contextualism needs to avoid looking like one of them.

## 3. The HS Approach

The HS strategy is principally designed to dissolve worries created by Cartesian scepticism: paradigmatically, scepticism concerning our knowledge of the external world. Cartesian scepticism is distinguished from Agrippan (regress) scepticism by the use it makes of *sceptical scenarios* (hypotheses, situations). These are apparent "defeaters" to ordinary knowledge-claims (situations such that, if they obtained, our ordinary beliefs would not amount to knowledge) of a special kind. However, they are special in that they involve *systematic* error or deception. Familiar examples are that we are victims of Descartes's Evil Deceiver or brains-in-vats, situations in which our experience is manipulated to mimic the experience we have in (what we take to be) our "normal" world.

The important thing about a sceptical hypothesis is that, however we think of knowledge, it seems at first blush very difficult to explain how we could know that we are *not* in the situation it describes. It seems hard to look for evidence, since anything we appeal to could be part of the deception. But even for externalists, the possibility of such knowledge is less-than-obvious. Suppose, for example, we think that, to count as knowledge, a belief should be sensitive to fact: i.e., if it were false, we should not hold it. Beliefs that sceptical hypotheses are false seem to fail this test. I believe that I am not a brain in a vat. But if I were a brain in a vat, I would still believe that I am not. And there is always the danger of trading scepticism for an equally threatening meta-scepticism. I may have knowledge because my faculties are reliable in a normal world. But can I really be sure what kind of world I am in? Again, merely confronting the sceptic with an anti-sceptical conception of knowledge seems less than satisfactory. (Moore on stilts again.)

Armed with sceptical hypotheses, the sceptic is able to present us with what Keith DeRose calls the Argument form Ignorance (AI).[8] Letting O be some everyday claim—e.g. the Moorean claim that I have two hands—and H be some appropriate sceptical hypothesis, the sceptic argues as follows:

> (AI)   If I know that O, I know that not-H.
>         But I don't (can't) know that not-H.
>         So I don't know that O.

Since we could let just about any claim about the external world stand in for O, it seems that we have no knowledge of external reality.

One reason this argument seems difficult to dismiss is that it conforms to a perfectly familiar pattern. Do I know when the museum opens? Yes, because I looked it up in the guidebook. But now I notice that the book was published some years ago and has not been revised. Perhaps, then, it is out of date and unreliable: I don't know that it isn't. Thinking along these lines, I find myself inclined to judge that I don't know when the museum opens after all. This looks like an everyday variant of AI: a defeater that I have not (and perhaps in present circumstances cannot) know not to obtain under-mines a knowledge-claim. How is the sceptical version of AI different, other than in the outlandish character of the defeater in play? The answer is not obvious. But outlandish does not mean incoherent or impossible. As I said, sceptical arguments seem to be intuitive. It begins to look as though ordinary practical "knowledge" involves turning a blind eye to theoretical problems, which is what Hume thought.[9]

While, by offering a template for a sceptical argument, examples like that of the guidebook may seem to encourage the sceptic, HS theorists see them as offering the key to the sceptic's mistake. Recognising a new error-possibility or "defeater" (the guidebook may be out of date) *raises the standards* for claiming or attributing knowledge. In Robert Fogelin's useful phrase, noti-cing a new error-possibility may serve to raise the "level of scrutiny" to which a knowledge-claim is subject.[10] Bringing into play yet more remote error-possibilities would raise it even higher. But while the level of scrutiny can be raised indefinitely, ordinary contexts of epistemic assessment are always *restricted*. When deciding whether to attribute knowledge, we do not ordi-narily consider any and every way in which the knowledge-claim in question might fail. Rather, we tacitly confine ourselves to a possibly quite extensive but still ultimately limited range of "relevant" or "serious" defeaters.

For everyday purposes, some logically possible ways of going wrong, or otherwise failing to know, are too bizarre to be worth considering. In the case of the museum's opening hours, I may judge that to re-institute my claim to knowledge I need to consult a more recent guidebook. I won't, however, consider the possibility that all guidebooks contain deliberate mistakes, inserted to frustrate the unwary tourist. True, I will not have investigated the possibility of such a conspiracy—such a possibility will not cross my mind—but, ordinarily, failure to exclude such a remote defeater will not undermine my epistemic standing.

Things are different when we reflect philosophically. Philosophical reflection is *unrestricted* in that, when reflecting philosophically, we are open to any coherent error-possibility. The effect of "going philosophical" is thus to raise the standards for attributing knowledge to the maximum. But now disaster threatens, for among defeaters ordinarily treated as too remote to take seriously we find sceptical hypotheses. When we come across them, not merely are we open to considering these bizarre error-possibilities, we have a tendency, as Fogelin insists, to *dwell on* them. And dwelling on them leaves us wondering whether we really know any of the things we ordinarily take ourselves to know.

The HS-strategy tells us not to worry. Standards for claiming or attributing vary with the conversational context, with whatever defeaters or explicit knowledge-claims are in play. In everyday contexts, we are not concerned to claim that we are not brains in vats. The thought that we might be brains in vats never so much as enters our heads, and there is no reason why it should. In such contexts, therefore, sceptical hypotheses *and* their denials are *hors de combat*. Everyday knowledge is thus safe from sceptical undermining. Scepticism works by eliding conversational shifts in epistemic standards. Such a shift can take place *in the course of sceptical argumentation itself*, and indeed does so when explicit mention is first made of a sceptical hypothesis. Making explicit mention of a sceptical hypothesis (whether with sceptical or anti-sceptical intent) takes us out of all everyday contexts of epistemic appraisal and projects us into the philosophical context, with its characteristically extreme standards for attributing knowledge.

Recognizing the contextual variability of epistemic standards, we can see that the sceptic is wrong to suppose that he has undermined everyday knowledge. So why are we tempted to go along with him? In part, because his mistake (or deception) is subtle: it is easy to lose track of standard-shifts, particularly when they occur in the course of what seems to be a single argument. But there is something else. This is that the sceptic *seems* right because he *is* partly right. While he is *wrong* to suppose that our inability to meet the epistemic standards that define the philosophical context casts doubt on everyday knowledge claims, he is *right* about that inability. At a minimum, when doing epistemology we are strongly tempted to impose standards for claiming knowledge that we cannot meet.

What about the standards themselves? As far as I can see, no HS strategist sees anything unintelligible or in principle objectionable about them. They are *different* from ordinary standards, but not for that reason *defective*. Indeed, it is hard to see what theoretical resources the HS strategy commands for arguing that philosophical standards are unreasonable in any sense other than excessively severe (for everyday purposes).

If I am right about this, the HS version of the Basic Diagnosis adopts a rather tolerant attitude towards "doing epistemology". In so doing, it follows what we may call a "pure insulation" strategy. It explains the appeal of scepticism by allowing the sceptic a narrow victory. The sceptic's ruse is just to trick us into thinking that his conclusion, correct in its way, has a wider significance than in fact it has.

Now in explaining why scepticism is a problem, I said that sceptical arguments are seductive because they seem to be highly intuitive. To adopt the HS strategy's tolerant attitude towards doing epistemology is, in effect, to concede that the sceptic's doubts are more than *apparently* intuitive: they are *genuinely* intuitive. They are, so to say, the outcome of an *extreme instance* of an ordinary epistemic procedure. So while, in a way, the context of philosophy stands apart from all ordinary contexts of assertion and appraisal by being unrestricted, philosophical appraisal is not in any deep way discontinuous with ordinary evaluation, but more like a limiting case of it.

I think that this is a concession that we ought not to make. Sceptical doubts are much more peculiar, much less intuitive, than the HS strategy allows for.

## 4. The SG Alternative

With respect to the idea of "doing epistemology" (that is, sceptical or traditional epistemology), the SG strategy is much less tolerant than its HS rival. The main idea of the SG strategy is that sceptical doubts are not really intuitive at all, so that the philosophical examination of human knowledge is radically discontinuous with ordinary epistemic procedures.[11]

The SG strategy takes off from a quite different account of the character of philosophical reflection. Barry Stroud captures it well. "In the traditional question of our knowledge of the material bodies around us," Stroud writes, "we want to know how we know *anything at all* at all about such bodies."[12] We could put it like this: in philosophy, we are not interested in any restricted kind of worldly knowledge—either what such knowledge we have, or how we come by it—but rather in knowledge of the world *as such*. As I sometimes say, the sceptic (or traditional philosopher) imposes a Totality Condition on a properly philosophical understanding of our knowledge of the world.

As Stroud argues, while this traditional philosophical project seems at first blush to present us with "a perfectly intelligible goal", we find that once involved in the pursuit of it we are easily led to a sceptical (or perhaps meta-sceptical) conclusion. Either we conclude that "we do not know the things we thought we knew" or "we cannot see how the state we find ourselves in is a state of knowledge."[13] This happens precisely because of the unusual generality of the philosophical project, for we are easily led to think that, if we are to explain how we know *anything at all* about the external world, we cannot begin by taking it for granted that we have such knowledge: to do so would be to fail to respect the Totality Condition. Thus the pursuit of a properly philosophical understanding of our knowledge of the world leads us naturally to look for a basis or foundation for that knowledge: something that is knowledge, but not knowledge of the world.

Traditionally, this basis has been sought in experience. This is no accident, for it has seemed independently evident to many philosophers that, if we are to have knowledge of the world, experience is ultimately all that we have to go on. But what sort of knowledge does experience provide us with? At this point in the dialectic, sceptical hypotheses make their presence felt. Such hypotheses suggest that our experience could be just what it is, even if the world were very different from the way we normally take it to be. So it seems that experience only tells us how things appear to us, not how they are. But having driven us back to this restricted basis for knowledge of the world, sceptical hypotheses threaten to confine us to it. For precisely because of the way in which they limit what experience tells us, they seem also to show that experience, so conceived, is *neutral* with respect to competing accounts of external reality. For since our experience could be just as it is, even if the world were very different, how can experience be (or how can we see it as) any guide to external reality? The only basis we have for knowledge of the world turns out to be no basis at all.

Ordinarily, we are not troubled by this problem. We take it for granted that experience is an imperfect but still more-or-less reliable guide to how things are in the world around us. But this thought, however natural, is a thought about the external world. So it can easily come to seem to us that, if our goal is to explain how we can know *anything at all* about the world, we cannot take this thought for granted in the way that we do when involved in more restricted inquiries. If we did take it for granted, we would simply be helping ourselves to an instance of the very kind of thing we are trying to explain. We would thus fail to explain how it is that we know *anything at all* of that kind.

Why would we fail? What is wrong with invoking what we know about the world in an explanation of how we come by that knowledge? Perhaps nothing, if all we want is the kind of explanation provided by some empirical discipline, such as cognitive science. But the kind of explanation or understanding that we have traditionally sought in philosophy is not like that. What we want as philosophers is to understand how we can be unproblematically *entitled* to claim knowledge of the world. In that limited sense, what we want from philosophical reflection is a justification of our conception of ourselves as knowers. We want this whether or not we think

that knowledge itself is to be understood always and everywhere in justificational terms. We want it because there are powerful arguments—sceptical
arguments—to the effect that knowledge of the world is impossible, arguments that can be adapted to just about any account of knowledge. We may
cease to hanker after proof, but the need for some kind of vindication
remains strong.

These reflections reinforce a point made earlier: that our need for understanding is thus not fully met by offering a "naturalistic" or purely externalist-
reliabilist account of knowledge. Such an account may indeed show how we
come by our knowledge in a normal world. But the sceptical challenge calls in
question our right to see the world as normal. Notice that to say this is not to
say that such theories are altogether wrong. I would not say this, since I think
that there is an element of truth in externalism. But it is to say that we cannot
fully assuage sceptical worries by simply confronting the sceptic with such a
theory. To do that is just to do in a more elaborate way what Moore did when
he held up his hands. We need to come to terms with scepticism in order to
earn the right to be externalists. Both the HS and SG strategies, because they
are diagnostic rather than dialectical, try to meet this demand. They offer
explanations that are also vindications.

Supposing that philosophical reflection, conceived among the foregoing
lines, pushes towards scepticism. Still, why do discoveries supposedly made
in the context of such reflection threaten everyday knowledge? The answer
is that the sceptic (or traditional philosopher) does not take himself to have
discovered that only knowledge-claims fail to meet some especially rigorous
philosophical standards. Rather, he takes his inquiry into knowledge of the
world as such to have uncovered a disquieting fact about our fundamental
epistemic situation: that experience, the only basis we will ever have for our
beliefs about the world, cannot be seen unproblematically as a source of
worldly *knowledge*. That is to say, he takes himself to have discovered, in the
context of philosophical reflection, an obstacle to knowledge that is present
in all contexts, however mundane.[14]

The fact that, ordinarily, we ignore this problem does not insulate
everyday knowledge from sceptical undermining. Rather, it leads us to see
that everyday "knowledge" is not really knowledge at all, but something
less: knowledge for all practical purposes (or for some practical purpose or
other). The unrestricted examination of knowledge characteristic of philosophy reveals something that we are ordinarily blind to, or choose to ignore.

The line of thought just sketched is of course enormously complex and
can be challenged at many points. But the SG strategy asks what seems to
me an absolutely fundamental question: why do we think that it is so much
as possible to investigate knowledge of the world *as such*. What makes
knowledge of the world so much as a candidate for explanation or understanding? Philosophers do not often press this question. This is understandable. I agree with Stroud that, at first blush, the request for a fully general

understanding of human knowledge seems perfectly intelligible. It looks like lots of other requests for explanation. To that extent, it seems intuitive.

These are the appearances. But is the philosopher's question really so intuitive? This question is worth following up because we can see, on further reflection, that we do not suppose that just any definable category of things is an appropriate object of theoretical inquiry. As Jerry Fodor likes to say, there is no science of things that happen on Tuesdays, though we do not feel that this leaves us with a gap in our understanding. As I have put it, we expect understanding in cases where we already see, however vaguely and inarticulately, some kind of *theoretical integrity* in the things we want to understand. So the question becomes: what kind of integrity does the traditional philosopher attribute to knowledge, or to knowledge of the world, so that we can seek to understand such things *as such*?

To ask this question is to engage in what I call "theoretical diagnosis". As we have noted, the sceptic claims to be a philosophical *naïf*. He raises his questions without having an idea in his head, beyond whatever ideas are implicit in our most commonsensical conceptions of knowledge and justification. As we have noted, this is the principle source of scepticism's problematic character: it appears to be a paradox buried in our most mundane ways of thinking. But the peculiarity of the sceptic's hyper-general questions hints that this may not be so; and if it is not so, then the sceptic's doubts and arguments are not wholly intuitive after all. They may have intuitive elements—if they did not, they could hardly even appear to be intuitive—but they will refract those elements through the lens of unacknowledged theoretical commitments. A good theoretical diagnosis will make explicit how this happens.

We can see right away that, by design, the philosopher neither sees nor wants the kind of integrity that belongs to particular "first-order" subject matters. Precisely not, for he wants to investigate knowledge in a far more general way. So the answer to the question "How can we investigate knowledge in general?" is this: we think that we can do so to the extent that we suppose that knowledge comes from certain *generic sources*—"the senses" or "reason", for example. With that idea on board, we can ask the familiar questions. Are our sources up to the job? Can we defend them in a non-circular way? That is to say, we can ask the sorts of questions that threaten to lead to scepticism.

The idea of generic sources of knowledge is the common property of sceptics ancient and modern. The twist that Descartes gave scepticism was to insist that (what we naturally take to be) the source of our knowledge of the world—sense-experience—is severely restricted as to the kind of information it provides.[15] Experience tells us how things appear to us, where what we want to know is how they are. Thinking of experience as *informationally bounded* in this way, we can ask how we get from experience to knowledge of the world. Giving that question a sceptical inflection, we can ask, is knowledge of the world—any knowledge—so much as possible? Either way, we can investigate knowledge of the world as such.

Actually, things are a bit more complicated even than this. Of course, in a sense, there are generic sources of knowledge: personal observation, testimony, inference from evidence, and so on. But the sceptic, or traditional philosopher, while no doubt borrowing some intuitive plausibility from this mundane fact, understands it in a much more problematic way. Take experience or "the senses": not only is this generic source of knowledge traditionally taken to be informationally bounded, it is also taken to be *autonomous*. That is to say, though it might not tell us everything we want to know, it tells us whatever it can without our needing to be already in possession of collateral knowledge that goes beyond what it can provide. So, for example, we can know all sorts of things about how things appear to us without knowing anything whatsoever about external reality.

There are powerful reasons—familiar from the work of Sellars, Quine, Austin, Wittgenstein, Davidson and others—for doubting whether there are generic sources of knowledge, as the sceptic or traditional philosopher supposes. For example, it is doubtful that observation is informationally bounded, for there seems to be no *a priori* limit on what we can be taught to report on spontaneously and reliably. It is doubtful that knowledge of how things appear constitutes an autonomous stratum of knowledge, autonomous in the sense that we could know any amount about how things appear to us but nothing about how they are. It is doubtful too that we can learn anything by observation without being already in possession of an extensive body of collateral knowledge. More generally, there are reasons to think that, if we did not have many true beliefs, and many reliable methods for acquiring more, we could not be believers at all. That is to say, we could not be believers unless we were knowers.

I am not going to defend these views here: obviously not—we would be here for ever. My point in alluding to them is to throw into sharper relief the central idea of the SG strategy, which is that the intelligibility of the sceptic's demand for a fully general understanding of our knowledge of the world cannot be taken as given. This demand makes sense if we think of knowledge in a certain way. But if we think of it in a different way, the sceptic's question looks like a bad question, as bad as a demand for a science of things that happen on Tuesdays.

If we become suspicious of the generality of "philosophical" questions about knowledge, we are led to a view of knowledge and justification that can reasonably be called "contextualist". It is contextualist in the sense that it holds that all epistemic questions arise in a *definite informational and methodological context*, where *not* everything is up for grabs. This contextualist conception is related to the view of knowledge gestured at by Neurath's well-known metaphor of the boat. Neurath likens our belief system to a boat in which we are always at sea. We can repair or modify any plank, but only by standing on others. There is no philosophical dry dock, where we could take the whole thing to pieces. But it may be that even Neurath's metaphor may be too concessive. It is not clear that, we can always fiddle with just any plank. Wittgenstein argues that, in particular situations, there are beliefs that we cannot even intelligibly call in question. If he is right about this, the contextual limitations on doubting and justifying may be even more severe than Neurath's metaphor suggests.[16]

I said "informational *and* methodological" because one important source of constraint on doubting is the *direction of inquiry*. In a particular context of inquiry or epistemic appraisal, some things are exempted from doubt because calling them into question would change the subject. This does not, of course, make them indubitable. But as long as we are concerned to investigate a particular issue, they remain off the table. In my terminology, they have the status, relative to a particular type of investigation, of *methodological necessities*.

We can use this idea of a body of methodological necessities as constitutive of particular forms of theoretical inquiry to further illuminate the SG strategy's approach to the traditional epistemological project. The key idea is that "doing epistemology" enjoys no exemption from the stricture that theoretical questions always arise in some definite methodological context. *Soi disant* naif, the sceptic thinks that, in the course of philosophical reflection, he has discovered a fundamental fact about—which of course turns out to be a fatal deficiency in—our "epistemic situation". This is that all our knowledge of the world depends ultimately on "experience" (understood as a generic, informationally bounded and autonomous source of knowledge). But all he has really brought to light is how, as a matter of methodological necessity, we must conceive of knowledge if we are to think that he has presented us with a possible form of inquiry. What he thinks of as our epistemic situation is just his own theoretical preconceptions in disguise, preconceptions that are far from obviously correct.

Having explored the two contextualist strategies, I will try to explain why I think that the SG strategy is to be preferred.

## 5. How Interesting?

A good diagnosis of scepticism needs to deal with an interesting form of scepticism: scepticism that is both general and radical. Both strategies acknowledge the generality of the threat of scepticism. But what about scepticism's radical character? The SG approach easily accommodates it: in reflecting on knowledge of the world in general, we are forced to recognize that the ultimate basis for such knowledge is no basis at all. But what about the HS strategy? It seems that, in the nature of the case, the HS strategy only applies to high standards scepticism, which is too weak to be interesting. The radically sceptical worry is not that we lack knowledge by extreme philosophical standards, but that we lack knowledge even by the most relaxed everyday standards. Sceptics take themselves to have put this issue on the table, and since the HS strategy cannot explain how or why, it is diagnostically inadequate.

We might be tempted to make an even stronger claim. In crediting us with everyday knowledge, HS theorists take it for granted that everyday knowledge, even if it doesn't live up to the strictest philosophical standards, is still knowledge. So at a minimum, they take it for granted that our everyday epistemic procedures are not wildly unreliable. What gives them the right to assume this? Isn't our commitment to the reliability of ordinary epistemic procedures exactly what sceptics call in question? Lacking a diagnosis of radical scepticism, the HS approach to everyday knowledge simply confronts the sceptic with our ordinary beliefs.

While, at first, this line of objection may seem powerful—certainly, it used to seem so to me—the question of whether the HS strategy deals with radical scepticism is complex. First of all, we must remember that the HS strategy does not aim to *prove* to the sceptic that, say, he really does have hands, or more generally that the external world really exists. Its goal is to provide a philosophical explanation, combining an account of knowledge with a diagnosis of scepticism's deceptive appeal. To be sure, it is never sufficient simply to confront the sceptic, either with particular common-sense certainties or with a non-sceptical theory of knowledge. On the other hand, the sceptic's attempt to undermine everyday epistemological beliefs should not worry us any more (or less) than his attempt to undermine other everyday knowledge-claims. So let us turn the tables on the sceptic and ask why he thinks that we need to justify the reliability of everyday epistemic procedures. Why, we should ask, does he suspect that they might be wildly *unreliable*? The answer is that he is haunted by sceptical scenarios, and the HS strategy shows that he shouldn't be. The sceptic's more generalized worries thus yield to the same treatment as his attack on everyday knowledge-claims concerning particular matters of fact. So, the reliabilist element in the HS strategy allows for everyday knowledge, while the contextualist element insulates that knowledge from the corrosive effects of sceptical reflections, while explaining their appeal.

In the second place, we must remember that a satisfactory diagnosis need only give a plausible account of how a sceptic might *think* that he has argued for radical scepticism, even if he hasn't. The HS strategy easily meets this requirement. Sceptical arguments work by exploiting unacknowledged shifts in epistemic standards. In this way, they *appear* to falsify everyday knowledge-claims, entered at everyday standards. Of course, they do not really do so; and if we keep track of contextual standard-shifts, we see that everyday knowledge-claims remain true at everyday standards; they *appear* to turn false, but only because sceptical arguments, by making remote defeaters salient, change the context of appraisal. However, if we fail to bear in mind the ways in which epistemic standards shift with context—which is easy to do, when the shift takes place within the course of a single argument—we are liable to fall prey to an *illusion* of having argued for radical scepticism.

We can see, then, that while it might seem obvious that a "high standards" diagnosis can deal only with high standards scepticism, the high standards approach has considerable defensive resources. Nevertheless, I do not find the defence just given fully satisfying. My worry is that the diagnosis of radical scepticism just given makes sceptics (and philosophers who take scepticism seriously) *too* confused. Sceptics are perfectly well aware that everyday knowledge-claims are not held to "philosophical" standards. What they deny is that this insulates them from philosophical criticism What they claim that we discover, in the context of philosophical reflection, is that ordinary knowledge-claims somehow fall short even in everyday contexts. Somehow, their failure to meet the extraordinary standards that we are inclined to impose when doing philosophy reveals some defect that they carry with them even in everyday situations. Sceptics make this claim in full awareness of the fact that there are, or seem at first to be, stark differences between philosophical and everyday evaluation. The conclusion they draw is that what passes for knowledge in everyday situations is really only "knowledge for all (or perhaps some) practical purposes". Philosophical reflection thus reveals that everyday "knowledge" is in some way *deeply* defective, even in its own terms. This sense of a deep and pervasive defect in our epistemic position may be illusory; but it needs explaining and, in my view, the HS strategy doesn't do an adequate job.

## 6. Raising the Standards or Changing the Subject?

Doubts about whether the HS strategy deals convincingly with radical scepticism lead naturally to questions about whether that strategy offers an adequate account of what happens when we "go philosophical". According to the HS strategy, going philosophical raises (to extreme levels) the standards for attributing or claiming knowledge. If all we mean by this claim is that, when doing philosophy, or at least the kind of philosophy that involves dwelling on sceptical hypotheses, we are apt to impose standards for knowing that are difficult—perhaps impossible—to meet, the claim is obviously, even trivially, true. But I have argued that HS theorists mean something more. They are inclined to see sceptical doubts as essentially continuous with ordinary doubts, the only difference being that they encompass error-possibilities that are too remote to be taken seriously in everyday situations. Call this the "Continuity Thesis". It is an aspect of what I earlier referred to as the HS strategy's "tolerant attitude" towards doing (sceptical) epistemology.

The general picture is that the severity of standards for knowing is directly proportional to the remoteness of the defeaters that command our attention. As we come to take seriously ever more remote defeaters, the standards for knowledge go up. We are thus invited to think of defeaters as located on a scale that runs from Pressing to Hyper-remote. In terms of the guidebook case:

> *Pressing*. The guidebook was published several years ago and is likely to contain information that is out of date.
>
> *Remote*. Although the guidebook is up to date, in a fit of pique the museum director has deliberately forwarded false information to the publisher.
>
> *Very Remote*. Companies publishing guidebooks have been infiltrated by members of an underground group bent on undermining the world economy. Part of their plan to disrupt tourism, the world's number one industry, involves corrupting the information in popular guidebooks. As a result, most recently published guidebooks contain substantial inaccuracies.
>
> *Hyper-remote*. There is no guidebook; there is no museum: I'm a brain in a vat.

There are reasons to be suspicious of this picture.

First, if the Continuity Thesis were true, we should expect that, in general, less remote defeaters would be more worrying because easier to take seriously. This doesn't seem to be true. In the right frame of mind, sceptical scenarios seem interesting, important and distinctly disturbing. The story about the global conspiracy to undermine the tourist industry seems merely silly. This is my intuitive reaction anyway. It suggests to me that the epistemic peculiarity of sceptical scenarios—the fact that we are tempted to think that we *cannot* know them not to obtain, because they involve systematic deception—is much more important than, and, in the right context, over-ride, their remoteness ( = commonsense implausibility). This in turn suggests that more is going on than a simple raising of standards.

Second, standards can be raised indefinitely within particular investigative disciplines without our ever getting close to considering sceptical defeaters. Take historical research: a particular documentary source may support a claim I want to make; but I may suspect that source of bias and decide to look for further evidence before committing myself. And even if I find such evidence, I may still not be satisfied. The more distrustful I am of sources, the more I insist on corroboration, the higher my standards. But if I start worrying about Bertrand Russell's sceptical scenario, according to which the world came into being five minutes ago complete with deceptive evidence of great antiquity, am I now being hyper-rigorous about my historical sources?

Again, my intuitive reaction is to say "No". I have stopped doing history and started doing sceptical epistemology. And while both subjects can be done sloppily or rigorously, the epistemologist is not by vocation more scrupulous than the historian. The suggestion is that when we pass from history to epistemology, we do not so much raise the standards as change the subject. And the same holds true when we abandon informal everyday contexts for the context of philosophical reflection.

The SG strategy accommodates these intuitions seamlessly. Reflecting on knowledge in general is a special undertaking, informed by its own theoretical commitments. Those commitments revolve around a particular conception of generic sources of knowledge. Sceptical defeaters are interesting because they are themselves generic: they undermine vast swathes of knowledge, if they undermine anything. To engage in sceptical epistemology is not to raise the standards but to change the subject.

In support of this view, we should recall Fogelin's point that, when doing epistemology, we do not just acknowledge sceptical possibilities: we *dwell on* them. Fogelin's remark, surely correct, suggests that, in the context of philosophical reflection, sceptical possibilities have a special salience. This fits in well with the fact, noted above, that (in the right frame of mind) we take them *more* seriously than the average remote defeater. Prioritizing the generality of the quest for philosophical understanding explains why this is so. The attempt to understand knowledge in general gives the possibility of error in general a special interest.

Noticing that the generic character of sceptical defeaters is more important than their remoteness should lead us to wonder whether talk of remoteness is a good idea at all. After all, they are "remote" in the sense of outlandishly unlikely, given our commonsense and scientific picture of the world. But the radical sceptic doubts our entitlement to that picture. From the sceptic's standpoint, the question of whether sceptical hypotheses are unlikely to be true, given our ultimate epistemic resources, is precisely what is at issue.

Part of what is intended by describing sceptical possibilities as "remote" is that the situations they describe are drastically different from the way we take the world to be. But appeals to similarity (or difference) are always dangerous. To be sure, sceptical hypotheses describe worlds that are factually distant from the world as we ordinarily conceive it. But this does not worry the sceptic. We must remember that the sceptic thinks that, in the course of philosophical reflection, he discovers something about our underlying—by which he means fixed and permanent—epistemic position. This is that, when it comes to knowing about the world around us, in the end experience is all we have to go on. This is so in both "normal" and "sceptical" worlds. So while sceptical worlds may be factually remote, along the dimension that really matters—similarity of epistemic position—they are not remote at all.[17] The SG strategy acknowledges this. It explains the special salience of sceptical hypotheses. But the cost of their special salience is that the sceptic does more than raise the standards: he changes the subject. Philosophical appraisal is radically discontinuous with everyday epistemic assessment.

## 7. Too Concessive

The conclusion reached in the previous section leads to my final reason for thinking that the SG strategy is preferable to the HS alternative. This is that it is much less concessive. Whereas the HS strategist is apt to concede that we do not have knowledge by "philosophical standards", the SG theorist takes a much harder line.

The HS strategy explains why scepticism *seems* right by suggesting that, in the rarefied atmosphere of philosophical reflection, scepticism *is* right. It may seem that the SG strategy makes the same claim. However, we should distinguish two forms that this claim can take. We may agree (weak claim) that the sceptic is *conditionally* correct. That is, with "philosophical" standards in play, we lose all our knowledge of the world. Thus *if* there is nothing objectionable about those standards, the sceptic triumphs, albeit only in the context of philosophical reflection. But if we see nothing wrong with the sceptic's standards, we will conclude that the sceptic is *unconditionally correct*, though again only in the extraordinary context of doing epistemology. To take this line is to offer what I called a "pure insulation" approach to scepticism.

The SG strategy is much less concessive. The whole point of this strategy is to suggest that there is something fishy about the sceptic's standards, so that scepticism is not correct even in the context of philosophical reflection. That is to say, the sort of epistemology that requires us to dwell on sceptical hypotheses is not a well thought-out theoretical enterprise. To give it up would be no loss. It would be like doing without a science of things that happen on Tuesdays. If the aim of philosophical explanation is to get rid of scepticism completely (or as completely as possible), then other things being equal, a less concessive approach is to be preferred.

All the reasons for preferring the SG strategy circle around this one. Explaining how sceptical doubts acquire a radical character, and why becoming prey to such doubts is not best thought of in terms of a simple raising of standards, brought us back repeatedly to the peculiar theoretical underpinning of what Stroud calls the traditional epistemological project. There is a kind of scepticism here. But it is not philosophical scepticism. Rather, it is scepticism about the traditional epistemological project. To explain in a convincing way just how this project is theoretically defective would be a long and complicated affair. Let me just say that to give such an explanation we would have to go beyond epistemological questions narrowly conceived, to engage issues about thought and meaning.[18]

I cannot undertake such an inquiry here. What I do want to claim, however, is this: that in virtue of its tolerant attitude to "doing epistemology", the HS strategy discourages us from going down what strikes me as the most promising avenue of anti-sceptical thinking: theoretical diagnosis, the investigation of the sceptic's rich body of theoretical preconceptions.

Scepticism is a problem because, while wholly unacceptable (and thus a substantive threat), it presents itself as wholly intuitive. The lesson of theoretical diagnosis is that it cannot be both. *Nihil ex nihilo fit.* In philosophy as in life, you need some to get some.

### Notes

1. Here I owe my terminology to Hilary Kornblith. Versions of the HS strategy can be found in the work of Stewart Cohen, Keith DeRose, Robert Fogelin (though he officially repudiates contextualism, being more sympathetic to scepticism), and David Lewis. See Cohen, "Knowledge, Context and Social Standards," *Synthese* (1987), pp. 3–26; DeRose, "Solving the Skeptical Problem," *Philosophical Review* (1995), pp. 1–52; Fogelin, *Pyrrhonian Reflections on Knowledge and Justification* (Oxford: Oxford University Press, 1994); and Lewis, "Elusive Knowledge" in *Papers in Metaphysics and Epistemology* (Cambridge: Cambridge University Press, 1999). Where Cohen and Fogelin connect knowledge with justification, DeRose and Lewis incline towards externalism. Indeed, an important motive in DeRose's treatment, which I do not have space to discuss here, is to save Nozick's subjunctive conditional approach to knowledge from its apparent commitment to the radical falsity of the principle that knowledge is closed under known logical entailment. I discuss Fogelin's views about scepticism in "Fogelin's Neo-Pyrrhonism," *International Journal of Philosophical Studies* (1999), and in "The Agrippan Argument and Two Forms of Scepticism" in *Essays Presented to Robert Fogelin*, ed. Walter Sinnott-Armstrong (Oxford: Oxford University Press, forthcoming). I discuss Lewis's ideas in "Contextualism, Externalism and Epistemic Standards," *Philosophical Studies* (2000); also in German translation in *New Directions in Epistemology*, ed. Thomas Grundmann (Mentis: 2001).
2. I develop this strategy, though not under this name, in *Unnatural Doubts: Epistemological Realism and the Basis of Scepticism* (Blackwell, Oxford: Blackwell, 1992; paperback edition, Princeton N.J.: Princeton University Press, 1996). See especially ch. 3.
3. David Hume, *Enquiry Concerning Human Understanding*, edited by P. H. Nidditch (Oxford: Oxford University Press, 1975), sect. XII, footnote.
4. To be sure, there was a time when less radical forms of scepticism were important: for example, when knowledge properly so-called was thought to demand demonstrative certainty. But since we no longer think of knowledge this way, these forms of scepticism are no longer that interesting.

5. Robert Nozick, *Philosophical Explanations* (Oxford: Oxford University Press, 1981), Introduction. For my take on Nozick and scepticism, see my paper "Nozick on Knowledge and Scepticism" in David Schmidtz, ed., *Reading Nozick* (Cambridge: Cambridge University Press, 2002).

6. For an excellent discussion of this requirement on responses to scepticism, see Marie McGinn, *Sense and Certainty* (Oxford: Blackwell, 1989).

7. This point really needs a lot more argument. When we encounter sceptical arguments for the first time, we may be already dimly familiar with them (particularly these days, when the brain-in-vat scenario has invaded popular culture). More than that, we are introduced to them by instructors who are thoroughly familiar with them and know how to dramatize the problems. So it could be argued that the "intuitiveness" of sceptical arguments and problems is partly an artifact of how we learn about them. But even if this is so, there are limits. Not every problem can be made to look intuitive. There must be something about sceptical arguments that lends itself to this kind of treatment.

8. Keith De Rose, "Solving the Skeptical Problem."

9. Hume thought that, in the end, we are saved from scepticism only by "carelessness and inattention". See *A Treatise of Human Nature*, ed. Selby-Bigge, revised by Nidditch (Oxford: Oxford University Press, 1978), Bk. 1, Conclusion.

10. Fogelin, *Pyrrhonian Reflections*.

11. In making this argument, I mean to correct an impression that *Unnatural Doubts* makes on some readers, namely, that my own anti-sceptical strategy is fundamentally one of insulation. It is true, I think, that there are places in *Unnatural Doubts* where I sound more concessive than I should. I am thinking particularly of the Conclusion, where I discuss the "instability of knowledge": its apparent tendency to evaporate under the philosopher's searching gaze. Robert Brandom takes me to task for being overly concessive in "Fighting Skepticism with Skepticism: Supervaluational Epistemology, Semantic Autonomy, and Natural Kind Skepticism," *Facta Philosophica* (2000), pp. 163–178. Even there, however, my more carefully stated view is the instability of knowledge that the sceptic can derive from his philosophical reflections. But it would be wrong to suppose that I take a tolerant attitude towards the traditional epistemological project. But an appearance of tolerance is created, not just by my willingness to at least contemplate the possibility that knowledge may be unstable, but by my reluctance to declare either sceptical doubts (or traditional epistemology) unintelligible, as opposed to loaded by (dubious) theoretical preconceptions. I retain this reluctance, though I acknowledge that the traditional epistemological project is freighted by theoretical ideas about meaning, which complicates the question of scepticism's ultimate intelligibility.

12. "Understanding Human Knowledge in General," in Barry Stroud, *Understanding Human Knowledge* (Oxford: Oxford University Press, 2000). Quotation p. 101, my emphasis.

13. Ibid., p. 99.

14. This commitment to an unchanging (and unchangeable) epistemic position is an articulation of what I call "epistemological realism".

15. On Descartes's originality, see my "Descartes and the Metaphysics of Doubt" in A.O. Rorty, ed., *Essays on Descartes' "Meditations"* (Berkeley: University of

California Press, 1986). Reprinted in *Oxford Readings in Philosophy: Descartes*, John Cottingham, ed. (Oxford: Oxford University Press, 1998).

16. For more on this, see my *Problems of Knowledge* (Oxford: Oxford University Press, 2001), ch. 14. See also my paper "Wittgenstein's Refutation of Idealism" in Denis McManus, ed., *Wittgenstein and Scepticism* (Oxford: Oxford University Press, forthcoming).

17. In a somewhat indirect way, Keith DeRose notices this problem. It comes up in connection with a counter-example, offered by Nozick himself, to a simple subjunctive conditionals account of knowledge. Nozick notices that a person's belief can fail to be sensitive because, if it were false, the person's way of determining whether it was true would also change. DeRose suggests that, in determining the range of worlds across which S's belief needs to be sensitive, we should place "heavy emphasis... upon similarity with respect to the method of belief-formation utilized by S" ("Solving the Skeptical Problem," p. 21). I think that this concession seriously complicates the HS strategy's response to scepticism. For my own take on Nozick's difficulties, see *Unnatural Doubts*, ch. 8.

18. See my "Mythology of the Given: Sosa, Sellars and the Task of Epistemology," *Proceedings of the Aristotelian Society*, supplementary volume (2003); also in *Sosa and his Critics*, ed. John Greco (Oxford: Blackwell, forthcoming).

*Philosophical Issues, 14, Epistemology, 2004*

# PRÉCIS OF *KNOWLEDGE AND LOTTERIES*[1]

John Hawthorne
Rutgers University

Here is a puzzle: Someone of modest means claims that she knows she will not have enough money to go on an African safari this year. We are inclined to treat the claim as true. But were she to claim that she knows she will not win a major prize in a lottery for which she holds a ticket, we would be far less inclined to accept that judgment as true. But if the person knows that she will not have enough money to go on an African safari, then isn't she in a position to know that she will not win a major prize in a lottery by performing a simple deduction?

As a number of philosophers have noticed, the puzzle generalizes to cases that do not involve lotteries per se. I seem to know that my car is in the driveway right now, but I don't seem to know whether or not it has just been stolen. I seem to know I am meeting someone on Thursday, but I don't seem to know whether I will be one of the unlucky people who suffers a sudden fatal heart attack before then. In each case, the structure of the puzzle is the same. There is what we might call an ordinary proposition of the sort that we customarily take ourselves to know. And there is a lottery proposition of the sort that, while highly likely, is one we would not typically count ourselves as knowing. And in each case the ordinary proposition entails the lottery proposition. We seem to be driven to scepticism, according to which we know little of what we ordinary claim to know. What is the best response?

Chapter one undertakes three tasks. First, an account is provided of when and why we are inclined to think that lottery propositions are unknowable, and thus of the ways that our epistemic space gets organized when we think about lottery-style cases. Particular attention is paid to describing and systematizing the ways that our intuitions are shifty. For example, it is relatively easy to get into a frame of mind where we reckon we know that we will not win the New York State lottery in each of the next thirty rounds. But that attitude gets disrupted when we assimilate that situation to the statistically equivalent situation of an enormous lottery where the chance of winning equals the chance of winning the New York State lottery thirty times in a row.

Second, by way of underscoring the importance of the concept, knowledge is linked to three phenomena: assertion, epistemic modality, and practical reasoning. Simplifying somewhat: assertion is tied to knowledge by way of the rule that one should assert only what one knows; to epistemic modality by way of the rule that, in the epistemic sense, *p* is possible only if it is compatible with what is known; and to practical reasoning by way of the rule that one should use only what one knows as a premise in one's practical deliberations.

Third, single-premise closure is articulated and defended, and multi-premise closure is articulated and motivated. The single-premise closure principle that I favor[2] says that if *S* knows *p* and competently deduces *q* from *p*, thereby coming to believe *q*, while retaining knowledge of *p* throughout, then *S* comes to know *q*. Principles like this have been disputed, notably by Dretske and Nozick. Their objections are answered, some systematic reasons for maintaining single-premise closure are offered, and the gloomy prospects for its detractors are highlighted. I conclude that it seems very unlikely that a denial of single-premise closure is the key to the family of puzzles with which the book is concerned. Multi-premise closure is also highly attractive. However, while its denial is treated as a cost of any view, it is not treated as axiomatic.

Chapter two addresses contextualism in epistemology, giving special attention to contextualist proposals for resolving the puzzle. The contextualist denies that there is any such thing as the semantic value simpliciter of a sentence containing 'know'. Any such sentence will have different semantic values relative to different contexts of utterance, where this is at least in part due to contextual parameters connected to the verb 'know' itself.[3] According to the contextualist, the extension of 'know' can vary from ascriber to ascriber in such a way that 'He knows that *p*', said of a particular person at a particular time, may be false in the mouth of one ascriber, true in the mouth of another.

It is far from clear that contextualist-driven solutions offer proper resources for dealing with epistemic puzzles connected to closure. I detail three such puzzles —ones connected, respectively, to 'junk knowledge', 'easy knowledge', and 'question-sensitivity'—and suggest that in each case it is doubtful that contextualism holds the key to a solution, even supposing that it is correct as a general semantical framework.

In the case of the puzzles at hand, however, the contextualist does seem to have a prima facie attractive solution. In crude outline, the idea is that when the topic of lotteries is raised, the standards for knowing tend to go up, thanks to the salience of certain events. In a high standards context, the sentences 'He knows that he will not be able to afford an African safari' and 'He knows he will not win a major prize in a lottery' are both false. Meanwhile, in those circumstances where we reckon the safari sentence true, our standards are much lower. In such contexts, the safari sentence and the lottery sentence are very often both true, though, in the case of the latter, its truth may well be thanks to its remaining unsaid. For were the lottery sentence to be asserted (or even entertained in thought) this would typically raise to salience certain possibilities of error and thus shift the context to a new, higher standard context.

The resolution of conflicting intuitions is fairly compelling, especially as it offers a solution that appears to be compatible with epistemic closure. The remainder of the second chapter presents a series of problems for the contextualist that fall into four main areas. First, it is very difficult for the contextualist to maintain the intuitive connections between knowledge, assertion and practical reasoning. Second, the contextualist offers no escape route from the sceptical pressures that come via considerations of objective chance. Third, it turns out to be very difficult for the contextualist to save multi-premise closure by appeal to the resources of context-dependent semantics. Fourth, it is hard to reconcile contextualism with the facts of propositional attitude reporting (as well as indirect speech reports). The problems cumulatively provide strong motivation to look elsewhere for a solution to the puzzles.

Chapter three begins with a discussion of sceptical invariantism. The invariantist about 'know' holds that the verb 'know', at least as it appears in 'knows that' constructions (and embedded question constructions) has a single, invariant, semantic value, so that the contribution of 'know' to the truth conditions of an utterance remains constant from utterance token to utterance token. The *moderate invariantist* claims that very many ordinary positive knowledge ascriptions are true. The *sceptical invariantist* holds that all, or nearly all, positive knowledge ascriptions are false. Sceptical invariantism is often dismissed as contrary to common sense. But as the puzzles show, common sense pushes us in competing directions. After all, doesn't common sense tell us that we do not know we will lose the lottery, that we do not know we will not have a sudden heart attack, and so on? A dismissal of sceptical invariantism based on some general appeal to common sense seems too quick.

Various versions of sceptical invariantism are distinguished. According to *error theoretic sceptical invariantism* we ordinarily (and incorrectly) believe the semantic values of positive knowledge ascriptions. According to other versions, we do not believe the propositions that are semantically expressed by ordinary positive knowledge ascriptions; instead, we must find a pragmatic account of why we say things we do not believe in this domain. I argue that an error theory is preferable, suggesting that its competitors put strain on the very notion of semantic value and trade invariably on misleading analogies. I then examine error scepticism in some detail.

The scorecard that emerges for that version of invariantism is not obviously terrible, though its costs are serious. Aside from the obvious cost that it reckons very many of our ordinary and natural beliefs false, it renders problematic the normative connections between knowledge, assertion and practical reasoning. Moreover, it remains unclear whether the sceptic really does have a coherent conception of a relation that some of us hope to (but rarely do) have to propositions (even leaving aside whether the relation deserves the name 'knowledge').

The remainder of chapter three is devoted to discussion of the *simple moderate invariantist*, a moderate invariantist who believes that in nearly all of the puzzle cases described, we do after all know the relevant lottery propositions. The scorecard for that view is not a particularly happy one. The intuitive links between knowledge, assertion and practical reasoning are threatened, multi-premise closure rejected, and various intuitive connections between knowledge and epistemic modality challenged. Chapter three closes with a careful examination of some of Harman's ideas for refining simple moderate invariantism. I argue that they do not, in the end, provide sufficient resources for thwarting the challenges.

The motivating theme for chapter four is straightforward enough. The contextualist adverts to a variety of parameters—attention, interests, stakes, and so on— claiming that insofar as knowledge-ascribers vary along these parameters, the semantic value of 'know' in their mouths will also vary in systematic ways. Suppose instead that (some or all of) these factors had bearing on the truth of knowledge claims only insofar as they were the attention, interests, stakes, and so on of the *subject* of the knowledge ascription. Then, indeed, we would have to depart from a traditional perspective concerning what sorts of considerations are relevant to questions about whether a subject knows. But semantic contextualism would not be forced upon us. I called the family of views that emerges *sensitive moderate invariantism*.

Much of chapter four is devoted to exploring two kinds of parameters that might arguably make a constitutive (as opposed to merely causal) difference to knowledge: facts about what is salient to a subject and facts about the subject's practical environment (what kinds of deliberation the subject is engaging in, and so on). Crudely put, the idea is this. Quite often, one does know the lottery-proposition-entailing ordinary propositions (and even the lottery propositions themselves), but certain sorts of practical environment/salience phenomena have a tendency to destroy such knowledge.

I consider salience first. It is quite easy to provide some prima facie motivation for the idea that certain inferences are 'anxiety-provoking' in such a way that performing them raises certain counterpossibilities of error to salience which in turn destroys knowledge of the premise. But what is it for the possibility that not-$p$ to be salient, in the sense of 'salience' that figures in epistemological discussions? One plausible candidate is an intellectual seeming with the content 'It might be that not-$p$' which, given the standard account of epistemic modals, has a content that is incompatible with one's knowing that $p$. It is hardly surprising that such a seeming induces retraction of the knowledge claim. But why think that salience actually destroys knowledge in those cases in which knowledge was there in the first place? I go on to distinguish three possible models for the knowledge-undermining role of salience. One of them—according to which the relevant kind of anxiety removes the kind of belief necessary for knowledge—is fully in keeping with a highly traditional perspective; the other models I consider are more radical, but also, I contend, less plausible.

Whatever the explanatory power of salience, it cannot do all the work in accounting for our puzzles. (Indeed, I am inclined to think that the work that it can do requires nothing very novel by way of epistemological commitments.) Another place to look—one that strikes me as rather promising—is the parameter of practical environment. The basic idea is that the practical environment of a subject is constitutively relevant to what she knows. The approach has the promise of underwriting the intuitive link between knowledge and practical reasoning. But, of course, it has its costs. Many of our intuitive verdicts about cases are not in keeping with the predictions of this version of sensitive moderate invariantism. (Of course that cannot be taken as a decisive refutation, since no view is innocent in this regard.)

The scorecard that emerges for sensitive moderate invariantism is fairly promising. I also note that even if one is a semantic contextualist, the materials provided in chapter four may nevertheless be employed in resolving the focal puzzles. I end with no firm opinion about which view is correct, though I do admit that: "Put a gun to my head and I will opt for a treatment of the puzzles built around the materials of the 'Practical Environment' section", and I also express a mild preference for invariantism over its contextualist competitor.[4]

## Notes

1. I am very grateful to Tamar Gendler for comments and conversation.
2. Much the same (apart from one refinement) as Williamson (2000).
3. It is also of some importance to see that a contextualist semantics will have to allow that knowledge ascriptions have semantic values even at contexts where they are not uttered. For one thing, this will be important to the evaluation of various sentences that *are* uttered, in particular knowledge claims that quantify into the that-clause. (For example: Everything I know, she knows.)
4. In my recent thinking, I have been exploring two clusters of related topics: the semantics of epistemic modals, and the interaction of chance with both indicative and counterfactual conditionals. I have some hope that these inquiries

(as well as being interesting in their own right) will provide further illumination on the topics of this book.

## Reference

Williamson, Timothy. 2000. *Knowledge and Its Limits*. Oxford University Press.

*Philosophical Issues, 14, Epistemology, 2004*

# KNOWLEDGE, ASSERTION, AND PRACTICAL REASONING

Stewart Cohen
Arizona State University

In his important and illuminating book, *Knowledge and Lotteries*, John Hawthorne considers various solutions to an epistemological paradox regarding lotteries. Hawthorne raises several objections to my own proposal for resolving the paradox, viz., Contextualism. And he proposes an alternative solution he calls "Subject Sensitive Invariantism". In what follows, I will defend Contextualism against Hawthorne's objections and argue that it remains superior to his own proposal for resolving the paradox.[1]

## Contextualism and the Lottery Paradox

Suppose Smith has a low-paying job with no prospect for getting a higher-paying job. He has no investments and no other sources of income. Given his situation, it seems right to say that Smith knows that he'll never be a multi-millionaire. As it turns out, Smith has a ticket in the New York State lottery. Should he win, he would become a multi-millionaire. But it seems wrong to say that Smith knows he will lose the lottery. These intuitions give rise to a paradox given the very plausible premise that entails that Smith knows he will never get rich only if Smith knows he will lose the lottery.

This paradox generalizes in interesting ways. So for example, if Smith recently left his car in lot 2, it seems right to say that he now knows that his car is parked in lot 2. But it seems wrong to say that Smith knows his car has not been stolen.

For virtually any ordinary proposition P (Smith will never get rich, Smith's car is parked in lot 2) we think we know, there is some "lottery proposition" L (e.g., Smith will lose the lottery, Smith's car has not been stolen) such that we think both that we don't know L and that we know

P only if we know L. This can lead us to adopt a skeptical frame of mind and hold that we do not know P after all. A successful anti-skeptical resolution of this paradox must explain how despite our skeptical intuitions, it remains true that we know what we ordinarily claim to know. But this means that a successful resolution of the paradox must explain away our skeptical intuitions. Otherwise the paradox has not been resolved.

Contextualism is the thesis that ascriptions of knowledge are context-sensitive. A common thread in contextualist theories is that the salience of error possibilities raises the standards for how strong one's epistemic position has to be in order for one to know. Contextualism resolves the lottery paradox by construing our apparently inconsistent intuitions as resulting from contextual shifts in these standards. So, for example, our intuition that the sentence, "Smith knows his car is parked in lot 2", is true is explained by the fact that at ordinary contexts, the statement is true. Our apparently conflicting intuition that the sentence "Smith does not know his car has not been stolen" is false, results from our shifting to a stricter context, when we consider the possibility that Smith's car has been stolen. At this new context, the sentence is indeed false. But deductive closure for knowledge is preserved relative to a context. So at everyday contexts, both "Smith knows his car is parked in lot 2" and "Smith knows is car has not been stolen" are true. At stricter contexts, neither sentence is true.

Hawthorne argues that Contextualism is unsatisfactory as a solution to the paradox because it is unable to preserve the constitutive connections that knowledge bears to both assertion and practical reasoning.

### Knowledge and Assertion

Peter Unger has argued that when one asserts P, one represents oneself as knowing P. Given the (defeasible) norm that one should not represent oneself falsely, it follows that one should not assert P when one does not know P.[2] In that same vein, Timothy Williamson has argued that the practice of assertion is constituted by the rule/requirement that one assert something only if one knows it.[3] Following Unger and Williamson, Hawthorne endorses the principle that one may assert P only if one knows P.

Hawthorne argues that Contextualism runs afoul of this connection between knowledge and assertion. Suppose John has recently parked his car in lot 2. Suppose further that John is in a low-standards context (car theft is not being discussed) and someone asks him where his car is. He asserts that it is in lot 2. If I am in a high-standards context where car theft is being discussed, then according to Contextualism, I can truly say, "John does not know that his car is parked in lot 2". This remains true despite the fact that given John's own low-standards context (car theft is not salient), he can truly say, "I know my car is parked in lot 2". Hawthorne suggests that "given a contextualist profile", John has the right to assert that his car is parked in lot 2. Thus we get the odd result that at my high-standards context I can truly say "John may assert that his car is in lot 2 but doesn't know that his car is parked in lot 2".

### Knowledge and Practical Reasoning

Hawthorne also holds that there is a constitutive connection between what one knows and what one can appeal to in practical reasoning. In particular Hawthorne endorses the principle that if $S$ knows $p$, then $S$ can appeal to $p$ as a premise in practical reasoning. Hawthorne argues that this principle makes trouble for Contextualism.

Suppose I am invited to give the keynote address at the APA and I'm at the airport buying my ticket. The ticket agent offers me flight insurance. I reason

I'm giving the keynote address.
So I'll be at the convention.
So I don't need insurance.

This is uncontroversially bad reasoning. Moreover, we can say truly "That reasoning is bad" at *any* context. But notice that if you are in a typical low-standards context, you can truly say, "Cohen knows he's giving the keynote address." But then the following sentence is true at your low-standards context:

"Cohen knows he'll be giving the keynote address, but he should not appeal to that proposition in his practical reasoning".

Thus contextualism violates the practical reasoning principle.

### The Alternative to Contextualism—Subject Sensitive Invariantism

Given these worries about Contextualism, Hawthorne proposes an alternative view he calls "Subject-Sensitive Invariantism". (SSI) Suppose I say, "John knows his car is parked in lot 2". Then I am the speaker/ascriber making the ascription and John is the subject of the ascription.

Contextualism says that the truth-value of a knowledge ascription is sensitive to whether error possibilities are salient *to the ascriber*. So if the possibility that John's car has been stolen is salient to me, then I speak truly when I say, "John does not know his car is in lot 2". This remains true even if this possibility is not salient to John.

SSI denies that there is context-sensitivity in the above sense of ascriber/ speaker sensitivity. Rather, SSI says that the truth-value of a knowledge ascription is sensitive to whether error possibilities are salient *to the subject* of the ascription. On this view, the truth-value of a knowledge ascription is the same regardless of who is doing the ascribing (thus the name, "Subject-Sensitive *Invariantism*"). So if the possibility of error is salient to John, then "John fails to know his car is in lot 2", is true *at every ascriber context*. So if we say "John knows...", because an error possibility is salient to us, we speak falsely if an error possibility is salient to him. Moreover, if the possibility of error is salient to us, we might say "John fails to know...". But if it is not salient to him, again we will be speaking falsely.

Hawthorne's invariantism takes a condition that Contextualism views as a kind of speaker-sensitivity for knowledge ascriptions and construes it instead as a kind of subject-sensitivity—as an element of the subject's circumstances that affects whether the subject knows. Of course, in itself, subject-sensitivity is a mundane phenomenon. The truth-value of a knowledge ascription is sensitive to many features of the subject's circumstances— whether the proposition is true, whether the subject has evidence, etc. What's distinctive about Hawthorne's view is that it includes the salience of error possibilities as an important feature of the subject's circumstances.

According to SSI, the lottery paradox results not from shifting ascriber context, but rather from changes in the subject's circumstances. So S knows that his car is parked in lot 2, provided that the possibility the car has been stolen is not salient to S. Once that possibility becomes salient to S, he stops knowing his car is parked in lot 2.

SSI does not allow either the link between knowledge and assertion or the link between knowledge and practical reasoning to be broken. For the link between knowledge and assertion to be broken, we need a low-standards context at which S may assert P, and a high-standards ascriber context at which "S knows P" is false. But SSI denies that ascriber context can affect the truth-value of a knowledge ascription.

For the link between knowledge and practical reasoning to be broken, we need a low-standards ascriber context at which "S knows P" is true, even though, intuitively, S reasons badly when he appeals to P in his practical reasoning. But again, if S is in the kind of practical situation we envisioned, he will fail to know because error possibilities will be salient to him. The fact that such error possibilities are not salient to some ascriber is irrelevant.

## Contextualist Replies to Hawthorne's Objections

Suppose Hawthorne is right about the connection between knowledge and assertion. (I'm not unsympathetic to the point.) Hawthorne shows that

Contextualism is committed to there being contexts at which the sentence "S may assert P, but S does not know P" is true.

What can the Contextualist say in response? Recall Unger's point that when S asserts P, S represents himself as knowing P. Given this point, the assertion principle turns out to be a special case of the principle that one should not represent oneself falsely. But how should a contextualist view S as representing himself when S asserts P? Surely since S is asserting P within his particular context, insofar as he is representing himself as knowing P, he is representing himself as knowing P by the standards that govern his particular (ascriber) context. This suggests that the contextualist should construe Unger's point metalinguistically:

> When S asserts P in C, S represents himself as being such that "S knows P" is true at C.

But if when S asserts P in C, S is representing himself as being such that "S knows P" is true at C, then given the underlying rationale for the assertion principle, viz., that one should not represent oneself falsely, it follows that

> S may assert P in C only if "S knows P" is true at C.

So the Contextualist should endorse only this metalinguistic version of the assertion principle. But this version of the principle entails that "S may assert P, but S does not know P" is true at the high-standards context. And as Hawthorne points out, this "sounds very odd". But now we can see that the Contextualist can explain away this counterintuitive result. It sounds odd because of a false inference about what is entailed by "S may assert P" when uttered at the high-standards context. Since the speaker is at a high-standards context at which "S knows P" means that "S knows relative to high standards", it would be natural to infer from the truth of his utterance "S may assert P but S does not know P" that S can represent himself as knowing by high standards but S does not know by high standards. And that would be a violation of the principle that one should not represent oneself falsely.

But such an inference is mistaken. Recall the contextualist rendering of Unger's point, viz., when S asserts P in C, S represents himself as being such that "S knows P" is true at C. Given that S himself is in a low-standards context, all that follows from the truth at the high-standards context of "S may assert P but S does not know P" is that "S may represent himself as knowing by low standards but S does not know by high standards". And that surely is unobjectionable.[4]

Now consider Hawthorne's objection that Contextualism allows that "S knows P, but S may not appeal to P in his practical reasoning" can be true at a low-standards context. No metalinguistic maneuver will work against this objection because there is no context at which it would be permissible for S to engage in the kind of practical reasoning Hawthorne describes.

The first thing to note, by way of reply, is that this objection applies to any view that does not require infallibility for knowledge, not just Contextualism. *Any* fallibilist view (besides SSI) will face this problem, i.e., any view that allows that S can know P on evidence E, even though Pr (P/E)<1. For such views, we can always devise a bet where the payoff structure makes it rational for S to bet against what he knows. For example, a fallibilist view will allow that, having just left my car 10 minutes ago, I know my car is parked in lot 2. Suppose you offer me a bet that pays me one billion dollars if my car is not parked in lot 2, but costs me a penny if it is parked in lot 2. Even though the probability my car has been stolen in the last 10 minutes is small, the payoffs are such that it would be irrational for me to decline to take the bet. Despite the fact that I know my car is parked in lot 2, I cannot reason that since my car is parked in lot 2, I will be out a penny if I take the bet. I would be engaging in bad practical reasoning, even though according to Fallibilism, I would be reasoning from a premise I know to be true.

All the same, we have seen that SSI does not allow that S can know P, but be unable to appeal to P in his practical reasoning. This would appear to give it an advantage over competing theories.

So how should a contextualist in particular respond? On my particular version of Contextualism, 'knowledge' talk can be viewed as a heuristic for simplifying reasoning.[5] If we had a considerably greater capacity for storing and computing evidential probabilities, we could do all our reasoning by relying just on the probabilities. But given our actual capacities, we rely on this rough and ready, imprecise notion of knowledge, and allow as a rule of thumb, that when you know P, you can appeal to P in reasoning. So to say that S knows P is to say that the probability of P on his evidence is close enough to 1 for S to appeal to it in reasoning. This works fine most of the time, except for those rare cases where the extent to which probability of P falls short of 1, turns out to matter.

This goes some but not all of the way toward explaining the appeal of the practical reasoning principle. For the question remains: Why does the principle seem more like an axiom than a rule of thumb?

Here the Contextualist can say that the principle appears to be axiomatic because in general, it will be difficult to say things of the form "S knows P, but S cannot appeal to P in his reasoning". When we think about S in those practical situations where intuitively he cannot appeal to P, error possibilities will be salient to us. Thus, "S knows P" will be false at our context of ascription. This could account for the apparent axiomatic status of the principle.[6]

On this way of construing matters, the contextualist will allow that. "Cohen knows P but Cohen can't appeal to P in practical reasoning" remains true at the low-standard context—though as we noted, it will be hard to utter. Is this result unacceptable?

Rather than answer this question directly, I will note that SSI has a similar result. Suppose I know P at t, and at the next instant t′, I will be offered a bet with a payoff structure that makes it rational to bet against P. According to SSI, "Cohen knows P at t, but when he reasons at t′, he will not be appeal to P" will be true at any ascriber context. Now Hawthorne will say that this is because according to SSI, I stop knowing P at t′. But the very fact that I can know P and then stop knowing P, even though I continue believing P, P remains true, I get no new evidence against P, the sensitivity or safety of my believing P has not changed, etc., is itself highly counterintuitive. So I see no clear intuitive gain for Hawthorne's view.[7]

## Objections to SSI

Inevitably the conflict between Contextualism and SSI will come down to which view has the greater intuitive costs. And no doubt Contextualism does have intuitive costs, despite my best attempts to mitigate them. But now I want to look at a serious problem for SSI: It does not meet our constraint on a satisfactory resolution of the lottery paradox. Recall that any non-skeptical response to the paradox must explain the appeal of our skeptical intuitions. But here is a fact about those intuitions. When we are in a skeptical frame of mind, it seems to us that we have made a discovery, viz., there are lots of things we think we know (e.g., where our cars are parked), that in fact we do not know. And not only do we have a strong intuitive inclination to deny that we know, we have the same inclination to deny that others know. Moreover, we are inclined to deny that we ourselves knew previously.

Contextualism can explain why this is so. Our skeptical frame of mind tracks the fact that we are at a high-standards context. And when we are at such a context, those standards will govern not only our self-ascriptions of knowledge, but our ascriptions to others (and to ours earlier selves) as well. So when we judge that others (along with our previous selves) fail to know, we are actually making true judgments.

But SSI is unable to explain why we make these judgements. According to SSI, when we are in a skeptical frame of mind, we fail to know because error possibilities are salient *to us*. But this has no implications for whether others know. That will depend on whether the chance of error is salient *to them*. But we know, even when we are in a skeptical frame of mind, that in many instances, error possibilities are not salient to others or to our previous selves. Yet as we have noted, when we are in a skeptical frame of mind, we have a strong intuitive inclination to deny that others and our previous selves know. But SSI has no explanation for why we are so inclined, given that we know that error possibilities are not necessarily salient to others and to our previous selves.[8] But this is just to say that SSI does not succeed in explaining our skeptical intuitions, and so has not given a satisfactory resolution of the paradox.[9]

Hawthorne is aware of this problem. To handle it, he appeals to the fact that when we reason, we make use of what psychologists call "the availability heuristic".[10] People using this heuristic assess the probability of an event on the basis of how easy it is to recall or imagine tokens of it. Because frequently occurring events are generally more easy to recall or imagine, this heuristic works well most of the time. But the availability heuristic can introduce biases when factors unrelated to the frequency of an event facilitate our recalling or imagining the event. Hawthorne cites studies which show that "...when a certain scenario is made vivid, the perceived risk of that scenario may rise dramatically" (p. 164). Hawthorne then speculates that "when certain non-knowledge-destroying counter possibilities are made salient, we overestimate their real danger; as a result, we may find ourselves inclined to deny knowledge to others in cases where there is in fact no real danger of error".[11] So, for example, when I claim to know that I will be at the conference and the possibility of fatal heart attacks is made salient, I tend to overestimate the probability with which heart attacks occur. This leads me to deny (falsely) that anyone knows he or she will not suffer a fatal heart attack and so to deny (falsely) that anyone knows that he or she will be at the conference.

Does Hawthorne's explanation succeed? First we should note that this explanation, if it succeeds, explains too much. Recall that Hawthorne holds that SSI does explain why we correctly deny knowledge to ourselves when error possibilities are salient to us. So, according to Hawthorne, the task for SSI is to explain why we incorrectly project *our own lack of knowledge* onto others (and onto our previous selves.). But if the availability heuristic leads us to overestimate the probability of error when considering whether others know, then it should lead us to overestimate the probability of error when we consider whether we ourselves know. But if we can explain away our intuitions that others do not know by appealing to our tendency to over-estimate the probability of error possibilities, then why not explain away our intuition that we ourselves fail to know in the same way? Why not say that I do know after all that I will not suffer a fatal heart attack. Moreover, we could then say that I know that I will be at the meeting, even when the possibility that I will suffer a fatal heart attack is salient. But then we lose any motivation for endorsing SSI.[12]

More importantly, it is not at all clear that the data concerning the availability heuristic support Hawthorne's hypothesis. What he needs to explain is why, *in general*, we have skeptical intuitions when error possibilities are salient to us. But it is not always true that when we consider these kinds of possibilities, we tend to overestimate the frequency with which they occur. For example, while people tend to overestimate causes of death that are dramatic and sensational—car accidents, tornados, homicide—they tend to *under*estimate causes of death, which tend to be unspectacular events, which claim one victim at a time, and are common in nonfatal form, e.g., smallpox vaccination, stroke, stomach cancer, and diabetes.[13] People also tend to underestimate risks to themselves. For example, people tend to make countless automobile trips without accidents. Moreover the news media shows them that when accidents do occur, they happen to others. Employing the availability heuristic, they **under**estimate the risk that they themselves will be in an accident. (This leads people to decide they need not bother wearing seatbelts.)

So when error possibilities that are unspectacular, generally non-lethal, or involve ourselves, are made salient, it is not at all clear that we will tend to overestimate their frequency. So I do not see how the availability heuristic can explain, in general, why we have skeptical intuitions when error possibilities become salient to us. But then SSI fails to give a satisfactory account of the lottery paradox.[14]

## Notes

1. Space considerations prevent me from discussing all of the challenging objections that Hawthorne raises to Contextualism. For more, see Cohen (forthcoming).
2. Unger (1975).
3. Williamson (2000).
4. Hawthorne considers a metalinguistic version of the assertion principle (equivalent to mine) and argues that it is not tenable. Unfortunately, space considerations prevent me from discussing his worries. He also argues that Contextualism allows that at low-standard contexts "S knows P, but S may not assert P" can turn out false. Insofar as this is a problem, contextualists can employ the same metalinguistic strategy to account for it.
5. See Cohen (1988), and especially (1999). For other versions of Contextualism, see DeRose (1995) and Lewis (1996).
6. As Hawthorne is aware, matters are more complicated than I have made them out. When error possibilities are salient, there is considerable intuitive pressure to deny knowledge ascriptions. But in some contexts this can be overridden. This phenomenon complicates the accounts that both Contextualism and SSI must give of the relation between knowledge and practical reasoning. Unfortunately, space considerations prevent me from discussing this here.
7. Hawthorne considers one interpretation of how the salience of error possibilities destroys knowledge, whereby such salience destroys knowledge by destroying belief. But Hawthorne rejects this account, correctly I think, because in the event that S persists in believing P even though error possibilities are salient, he may still lose his knowledge. Hawthorne also argues that Contextualism allows that

at high-standard contexts sentences of the form "S does not know P, but he should appeal to P in his practical reasoning" come out as true. These sentences strike me as much less clearly problematic. Insofar as they are a problem, I can handle them in the same way.

8. As Hawthorne notes, since knowledge is factive, our own current lack of knowledge prevents us from ascribing knowledge to others and to our previous selves. But nothing prevents us from suspending judgment about whether others know. Indeed SSI predicts that this is what we would do.

9. For more on this problem for SSI, see Cohen (forthcoming).

10. Slovic, et al. (1982).

11. Vogel (1990).

12. Indeed Vogel (1990) relies on the availability heuristic to provide precisely this kind of general explanation for why we deny knowledge to ourselves as well as others. I should note that Hawthorne's views about how the practical environment, which, regrettably, I do not have space to discuss, are unaffected by this point.

13. Slovic, et al. (1982).

14. I have benefited greatly from discussions with John Hawthorne, Tom Blackson, Earl Conee, John Devlin, Gregory Fitch, Richard Feldman, Jonathan Vogel, Timothy Williamson, and audiences at New York University, University of Rochester, Oxford University, Arizona State University, and University of California, Santa Barbara.

## References

Cohen, Stewart, "How to be a Fallibilist", *Philosophical Perspectives*, 2, 1988 (Tomberlin, ed.).
———"Contextualism, Skepticism, and the Structure of Reasons", *Philosophical Perspectives*, 13, 1999 (Tomberlin, ed.).
———"Knowledge, Speaker, and Subject", *Philosophical Quarterly*, (forthcoming).
DeRose, Keith, "Solving the Skeptical Problem", *Philosophical Review*, 1995, 104: 1.
Lewis, David, "Elusive Knowledge", *Australasian Journal of Philosophy*, 1996, 74: 4.
Slovic Paul, Baruch Fischhoff and Sarah Lichtenstein, "Facts versus fears: Understanding perceived risk" in *Judgment Under Uncertainty: Heuristics and Biases*, Daniel Kahneman, Paul Slovic, and Amos Tversky, eds. (Cambridge University Press, 1982).
Unger, Peter, *Ignorance* (Oxford, 1975).
Vogel, Jonathan, "Cartesian Skepticism and Inference to the Best Explanation", *Journal of Philosophy*, 1990, 87: 11.
Williamson, Timothy, *Knowledge, and its Limits* (Oxford, 2000).

*Philosophical Issues, 14, Epistemology, 2004*

# KNOWLEDGE, ASSUMPTIONS, LOTTERIES

Gilbert Harman and Brett Sherman
Princeton University

John Hawthorne's marvelous book contains a wealth of arguments and insights based on an impressive knowledge and understanding of contemporary discussion. We can address only a small aspect of the topic. In particular, we will offer our own answers to two questions about knowledge that he discusses.

(Q1) Why is it intuitively correct that one can know one will be in San Francisco next year but not intuitively correct that one can know one won't die in the interim?

(Q2) Why is it intuitively correct that one can know using statistical reasoning that a given coin is not heavily biased toward heads by tossing it a few times but not intuitively correct that one can know using statistical reasoning that one's lottery ticket is not the winning ticket?

The paper will appeal to two theses about knowledge that seem to us correct.

(T1) What one knows can and usually does rest on assumptions one justifiably takes for granted without knowing them to be true.

(T2) One knows only if one believes as one does because of something that settles the truth of that belief.

(T1) helps to answer (Q1) and to address issues about strong closure principles for knowledge. (T2) helps to answer (Q2).

## Taking Things for Granted

We begin by observing that one often takes things for granted that one does not fully believe to be the case. For example, consider a perfectly ordinary individual we will call "Sam." In thinking about where he will be next year, Sam takes for granted that he will not before then have suffered a fatal heart attack or have been killed by being hit by a bus. In thinking about what trips he will be able to afford to make, he takes for granted that the lottery ticket he has purchased is not the winning ticket. In thinking about whether he will be able to pick up his daughter at the train station, he takes for granted that his car has not been stolen after he parked it outside the house a couple of hours ago. More generally, he normally takes for granted that he is not dreaming and is not a brain in a vat whose experience of a world of cars and trips and daughters is artificially induced.

It seems to us that Sam does not fully believe any of the things he merely takes for granted: that he will not have a heart attack, that he will not be hit by a bus, that his ticket is not the winning ticket, that his car has not been stolen in the last hour, that he is not dreaming, that he is not a brain in a vat.

But Sam does believe other things that are in some sense supported by things he merely takes for granted. He believes his car is outside in front of his house, for example. Indeed, he *knows* that his car is parked outside in front of his house.

So (T1) seems highly intuitive to us.

(T1) What one knows can and usually does rest on assumptions one justifiably takes for granted without knowing them to be true.

Sam knows he owns a car that is presently outside in front of his house. It seems intuitively correct to us that Sam's knowledge rests on various assumptions that he does not know but justifiably takes for granted: that there is an external world including cars and houses, that he is not a brain in a vat who simply imagines he has a car and a house, and that no one has taken his car away since he parked it in front of his house an hour ago.

Part of the explanation of Sam's knowing that his car is presently parked outside is that he justifiably (and truly) takes it for granted that the car hasn't been stolen. That is not to say that the truth value of the knowledge claim is relative to the things he takes for granted. His claim that he knows his car is parked outside is not elliptical for anything more complex.

Notice that Sam cannot know something just by taking it for granted. He is justified in taking it for granted that he is not dreaming, but that does not mean that, having taken that for granted, he knows that he is not dreaming. Nor, having taken it for granted, is he then justified in believing he is not dreaming.

This also means that knowledge that $P$ which rests on justifiably taking it for granted that $A$ is not just knowledge that, if $A$ then $P$. Sam knows that, if he is not a brain in a vat, he is not a brain in a vat. But he is not justified in coming to believe that he is not a brain in a vat and he cannot come to know that he is not a brain in a vat just because he is taking that assumption for granted.

Similarly, given Sam's present situation, intuitively he knows he will be in San Francisco next year. At the same time, it also seems intuitively correct to us that he does not know he will not die before then. Intuitively, his knowledge that he will be in San Francisco next year rests on the fact that he justifiably takes for granted the assumption that he will not die before then. Alas, the fact that he takes that for granted does not allow him to know he will not die before then.

Hawthorne (2004) notes Williamson's remark, "it is reasonable for me to believe that I shall not be run over by a bus tomorrow, even though I know that I do not know that I shall not be run over by a bus tomorrow" (Williamson 2000: 255). We do not agree with the first part of this. It seems to us that it is not reasonable for Sam fully to *believe* he won't be run over by a bus tomorrow. It is not something he can legitimately *infer* from its small likelihood. Nevertheless, it is reasonable for him to *take it for granted* that he won't be.

Hawthorne also remarks in a footnote, "In a situation where I have no clue what is going on, I may take certain things for granted in order to prevent paralysis, especially when I need to act quickly." He appears to think this is a special case, whereas it seems to us that one normally takes quite a lot of things for granted that one does not know to be the case. Hawthorne does not discuss how knowledge might depend on the fact that one has taken certain things for granted.

## Strong Closure Principles

Intuitively, it is not generally the case that, if one knows that $P$ and one knows that if $P$ then $Q$, one should be able to know that $Q$. $Q$ may be something one takes for granted on which one's knowledge that $P$ depends. Sam knows that his car is parked outside. He has that knowledge in part because he justifiably and truly takes for granted that he is not dreaming. He also knows, that, if his car is parked outside, he is not merely dreaming that his car is parked outside. But, intuitively, he cannot come to know that he is not merely dreaming his car is parked outside by taking it for granted that he is not dreaming.

A number of theorists including Hawthorne defend closure principles for knowledge that conflict with the examples just given. We will refer to such principles as "strong closure principles." By a strong closure principle, we mean one that is incompatible with Sam's knowing that his car is parked outside if he merely assumes and cannot know that the car has not been stolen since he parked it there.

Hawthorne offers a motivation for such principles and then goes on to defend them against attacks. The motivation he offers is perfunctory.

> As Williamson remarks, such principles articulate what is an extremely intuitive idea, namely that "deduction is a way of extending one's knowledge" (2000, p. 117). (Consider, for example, the paradigmatic status of mathematical knowledge that proceeds by way of deductive truth.)

A footnote references a similar claim by Bertrand Russell. A little later, he quotes Feldman (1999, p. 95),

> To my mind, the idea that no version of the closure principle is true—that we can fail to know things that we knowingly deduce from other facts we know— is among the least plausible ideas to gain currency in epistemology in recent years.

Apart from appeals to authority, there are two arguments here.

First, there is Williamson's remark that "deduction is a way of extending one's knowledge." That is (sort of) correct, if it means that deduction is *sometimes* a way of extending one's knowledge. It is incorrect if it means that deduction is *always* a way of extending one's knowledge. But something like the second interpretation is what is needed to defend a strong closure principle. (Furthermore, the presupposition that deduction is something one does represents a serious philosophical error that we will say more about below.)

Second, there is the claim that knowing something is relevantly like having a mathematical proof of something. If you have a mathematical proof that *P* and a mathematical proof that if *P* then *Q*, then you can normally put these proofs together to give a mathematical proof that *Q*. And, given a proof from assumptions *A* to *P* and a proof from assumptions *B* to if *P* then *Q*, you can normally put these together to get a proof from assumptions *A* and *B* to *Q*. But the analogous principle for knowledge conflicts with such intuitions as that Sam knows that his car is parked outside without knowing that he is not merely dreaming that it is.

A more basic worry about the passage from Williamson is its presupposition that deduction is a kind of inference, something one does. Hawthorne apparently presupposes the same thing, since all the strong closure principles he takes seriously assume there is an activity of "competently deducing," a kind of inferring that can provide one with knowledge.

Surely, this confuses questions of implication with questions of inference. A deduction is a structured object, an abstract argument or proof. True, in order to check or exhibit implications, we sometimes construct arguments. And inference can be involved in that construction. But a deduction is the abstract argument that is constructed. Although constructing the argument is something someone does, the deduction itself is not something someone does. The deduction is not the constructing of the deduction. Notice also that a given deduction can be constructed in various ways. One does not normally come up with a deductive argument by first thinking of premises, then thinking of intermediate steps in the relevant order, finally arriving at the conclusion. One often starts with the conclusion and works backwards toward the premises. Or one starts in the middle and works in both directions. Furthermore, although one might construct a deduction as part of a process of coming to accept its conclusion, one might also construct a deduction as part of a process of coming to accept one of its premises via an inference to the best explanation. The conclusion of a deduction is not in general the conclusion of an inference. (The conclusion of an inference might be that a certain construction is indeed a valid deduction. The whole argument is then the conclusion of the inference.)

The same conflation of inference and implication is involved when principles of implication like Conjunction Introduction and Modus Ponens are treated as principles of inference that people might follow. This is generally recognized to be a serious philosophical error. Principles of inference are normative and have a psychological subject matter. Principles of implication are not particularly normative and do not have a particularly psychological subject matter (Goldman 1986, Harman 1999).

Where Williamson says, "deduction is a way of extending knowledge," it is more accurate to say (A) inference is a way of extending knowledge and (B) inference can involve the construction of a deductive argument. But (A) and (B) are insufficient to support a strong closure principle for knowledge.

## Hawthorne's Defense of Strong Closure Principles

In defending strong closure principles against various attacks, Hawthorne argues that denying such principles leads to highly undesirable consequences. Although we lack the space to address all of the arguments he offers, we will briefly indicate why we think his defenses fail to take into account the way knowledge rests on assumptions.

The first consequence that Hawthorne considers depends on the claim that one can appropriately assert something only if one takes oneself to know it. It follows from this that anyone who denies strong closure principles will assert certain things and will refuse to assert their consequences, even when those consequences are pointed out to them. Hawthorne argues that this can lead to an odd conversation: Alice asserts that the animal in the cage is a zebra and agrees that, if the animal is a zebra, then it is not a cleverly disguised mule; however, she is not willing to agree that the animal is not a cleverly disguised mule. But this is a mistake. Alice *accepts* that the animal is not a cleverly disguised mule. In fact, she assumes that. She just doesn't take herself to know it and so does not assert it, although she can assert that it is something she accepts. So, we see no difficulty here.

A further consequence of denying strong closure principles, according to Hawthorne, is that one must give up at least one of three more restricted closure principles that he thinks would be intuitive even to one who denies the more general closure principles. One of these restricted principles is the Equivalence Principle, according to which, if you know a priori that the propositions that $P$ and that $Q$ are equivalent and you know that $P$, then you are in a position to know that $Q$.

However, once it is acknowledged that knowledge can rest on assumptions, the Equivalence Principle has no more intuitive force than more general closure principles. Alice knows this animal is a zebra, on the assumption that it is not a cleverly disguised mule. And the animal's being a zebra is equivalent to its being a zebra and not a cleverly disguised mule. But, just as she cannot know on the basis of her assumption that her assumption is correct, she is not in a position to know on the basis of that assumption that the animal is a zebra and not a cleverly disguised mule.

Hawthorne's final argument in defense of strong closure principles is that the positive accounts of knowledge that have resulted from denying strong closure have significant problems of their own. We leave it to the reader to determine whether that applies to our intuitive claim that knowledge can rest on assumptions one does not know to be the case.

To summarize so far: (T1) is intuitively plausible, it explains (Q1), and it conflicts with strong closure principles. Strong closure principles are not intuitively plausible, they generate problems with respect to (Q1), and they have no good arguments in their defense.


## Variation in Acceptability of Knowledge Claims


Sam says he knows his car is parked out front. April challenges this by asking how he knows it hasn't been stolen since he came inside. Sam says it is very unlikely to have been stolen. April says this is not enough for him to know it hasn't been stolen. Sam agrees. Then what does he say?

He might say it is enough for him to take it for granted that his car hasn't been stolen and, assuming that what he is taking for granted is true, he knows his car is parked out front.

It is more likely that, in the face of April's challenge, Sam takes himself to be no longer justified in taking for granted that his car hasn't been stolen. And Sam recognizes that, if he cannot take that for granted, he cannot know his car is parked out front.

So (T1) might help to explain variations in the acceptability of knowledge claims that some theorists have taken as evidence for a contextual element in knowledge claims.

Here we agree with the account in Hawthorne's final chapter according to which the truth of a knowledge claim about a person can depend on what possibilities the person who is the subject of the knowledge claim ought to take seriously, because the possibilities that one ought to take seriously are those possibilities whose rejection one is not justified in taking for granted.

At this point we would like to say something more substantial about the important question of when one is justified in taking something for granted. But we will have to defer further discussion to another occasion.

### Settling the Truth of a Belief

We now turn to the second of the questions (Q2) we want to address on this occasion.

(Q2) Why is it intuitively correct that one can know using statistical reasoning that a given coin is not heavily biased toward heads by tossing it a few times but not intuitively correct that one can know using statistical reasoning that one's lottery ticket is not the winning ticket?

Anscombe (1957, p. 56) plausibly suggests that the difference between intention and belief has to do with the "direction of fit." We suggest that one such difference between these types of mental state can be expressed in the following two principles.

**Self-referential Guarantee in Belief Content:** The content of a full belief that *P* is: "I am in this mental state because of something that settles it that *P*."
**Self-referential Guarantee in Intention Content:** The content of an intention that *P* is: "My being in this mental state settles it that *P*."

Harman (1976, 1980, 2003) defends these principles and their appeal to self-referential contents of mental states.

The first principle, concerning belief, suggests:

(T2) One knows only if one believes as one does because of something that settles the truth of that belief.

(T2) is a variant of the causal theory of knowledge. In its simplest form that theory says one knows that *P* only if one's belief that *P* is caused by the fact that *P*. This has to be modified to allow, e.g., for knowledge of the future: one knows that *P* only if one's belief that *P* is caused either by the fact that *P* or by something that causes it to be the case that *P* (Goldman, 1967). A further modification is needed to allow for Skyrms' (1967) example in which Alice shoots Bob to death. A short time later Carol cuts off Bob's head. Then Dan comes along and sees that Bob is dead. Dan does not believe that Bob is dead because of something that caused Bob to be dead (since Carol's cutting off Bob's head is not the cause of death) but Dan does believe this because of something that settles it that Bob is dead.

Now, suppose one has two coins, a nickel and a quarter, one biased towards heads to the extent that the probability of its coming up heads when tossed is 0.9, the other unbiased, so that the probability of its coming up heads when tossed is 0.5. After tossing each coin fifty times and noting the outcomes, one comes to believe that the nickel is the unbiased coin, because that explains why about half the tosses of the coin came up heads. Suppose one is right. The nickel is the unbiased coin. One believes that the nickel is unbiased because of the statistical results. And those results are as they are because the nickel is unbiased—that is, because of something that settles the truth of one's belief. So, one believes as one does because of something that settles the truth of one's belief. One can therefore know in this way that the nickel is unbiased, according to (T2).

On the other hand, one cannot in the same way know that one's lottery ticket is not the winner. As in the coin example, one believes as one does for probabilistic reasons. But in this case, the statistical facts are not explained by what settles the truth of one's belief. Suppose that one's ticket is not the winner. The fact that the ticket is not the winner does not explain the fact that it was highly unlikely to be a winner. So, if one were to believe it is not the winner for purely probabilistic reasons, one would not believe as one does because of something that settles the truth of that belief. And so one's belief would not be knowledge according to (T2).

It seems to us that one cannot be justified in fully believing something unless one is justified in taking oneself to know it. So, one would not be justified in believing the ticket is not the winner. Nevertheless, one might be justified in taking that for granted when one considers whether one will be able to afford to go on an African Safari next year. Given the fact that one justifiably and truly takes that assumption for granted, one might know that one will not be able to afford to go. But that does not mean one can know one's ticket will lose.

## Conclusion

In summary, we have put forward two claims, (T1) and (T2), in order to answer two questions, (Q1) and (Q2). (T1) helps to answer (Q1) and explains one thing wrong with strong closure principles for knowledge. (T2) helps to answer (Q2).[1]

## Notes

1. We are indebted to Elizabeth Harman and John Hawthorne for useful comments on earlier drafts.

## References

Anscombe, G. E. M., (1957). *Intention*. Oxford: Blackwell.
Carnap, R., (1950). "Empiricism, semantics, and ontology," *Revue internationale de philosophiie* **4**: 20–40.
Feldman, R., (1999). "Contextualism and skepticism," *Philosophical Perspectives* **13**: 91–114.
Goldman, A., (1967). "A causal theory of knowing," *Journal of Philosophy* **64**: 357–72.
Goldman, A., (1986). *Epistemology and Cognition*. Cambridge, MA: Harvard University Press.
Harman, G., (1976). "Practical reasoning," *Review of Metaphysics* **29**: 431–463.
Harman, G., (1980). "Reasoning and evidence one does not possess," *Midwest Studies in Philosophy* **5**: 163–82.
Harman, G., (1999). "Rationality," in *Reasoning, Meaning, and Mind*. Oxford: Oxford University Press. Esp. pp. 18–23.
Harman, G., (2003). "Adler's evidentialism," unpublished presentation at the Pacific Division Meeting of the American Philosophical Association in San Francisco.
Hawthorne, J., (2004). *Knowledge and Lotteries*. Oxford: Oxford University Press.
Skyrms, B., (1967). "The explication of 'X knows that p,'" *Journal of Philosophy* **64**: 373–89.
Williamson, T., (2000). *Knowledge and Its Limits*. Oxford: Oxford University Press.

*Philosophical Issues, 14, Epistemology, 2004*

# SPEAKING OF KNOWLEDGE

Jonathan Vogel
Amherst College

You've driven your car to the city and parked it on Elm Street. As you return to get it, you remember clearly where you left it. Seemingly, you know (E) that your car is on Elm Street. It would be natural for you to say so, and it would be natural for others to say the same. But suppose that there's an appreciable rate of auto theft in the city, and cars like yours get stolen every day. Do you know (-T) that your car hasn't been stolen and driven away? There is a strong inclination to deny that you do. Once you reflect on the possibility, you may well say that you don't know (-T), and others thinking about your situation may well concur. I'll call this example the *Car Theft Case*.[1]

Three features of the example are noteworthy. First, it might appear to be a counterexample to the Closure Principle for knowledge. The Closure Principle has it that if someone knows a proposition $p$, then she knows, or is in a position to know, any proposition which she recognizes to be a logical consequence of $p$. Here, (-T) is a straightforward logical consequence of (E), yet you seem to know the latter, but not the former. The Car Theft Case thus appears to be a counterexample to the Closure Principle. But it's arguable that this appearance is mistaken, and that the principle holds good in the end. Second, the reason why you fail to know (-T) is distinctive. (-T) is a *lottery proposition*. Under the circumstances described, knowing that your car hasn't been stolen would be like knowing that a particular ticket won't be chosen in a lottery. Such propositions are very likely to be true, yet, even when they are true, we somehow (sometimes) fail to know them. A third feature of the Car Theft Case is that it seems to generalize. A great many of the propositions we ordinarily take ourselves to know entail lottery propositions. If we really don't know those lottery propositions, and the Closure Principle holds, we turn out to lack a great deal of the knowledge we thought we had. We are left with a version of skepticism.[2]

These features of the Car Theft Case pose a problem for epistemologists. If the Closure Principle is non-negotiable, then the straightforward responses to the problem would be either to maintain that we do know lottery propositions after all, or to find a way to live with the skeptical result just mentioned. John Hawthorne explores such "invariantist" views, and finds them quite inadequate. More tempered and complex proposals provide for some kind of shift in the requirements for knowledge or their satisfaction. These views allow that we ordinarily know a good deal about the world. But, when the shift occurs, we do fail to know some lottery proposition and propositions which clearly entail it.

Hawthorne considers two accounts along these lines. One is "contextualism", according to which:

> ... variations in the *ascriber* can affect the truth value of knowledge ascriptions even if we hold fixed the subject of the ascription. Thus, on her account, the relation expressed by the verb 'know' on an occasion of use will depend upon, *inter alia*, what is salient to the ascriber, and perhaps also upon what the interests of the ascriber are, upon whether there is a good deal at stake for the ascriber that turns on the truth value of the proposition that figures in the knowledge ascription; and so on. It is this ascriber dependence that forces the thesis of context dependence. [p. 157]

Hawthorne calls the other position, which he on balance prefers, "sensitive moderate invariatism". On this view, knowledge ascriptions are "*subject*-dependent". That is, whether a subject knows

> ... depends not merely upon the kinds of factors traditionally adverted to in accounts of knowledge—whether the subject believes the proposition, whether that proposition is true, whether the subject has good evidence, whether the subject is using a reliable method and so on—but also upon the kinds of factors that in the contextualist's hands make for ascriber dependence. These factors will thus include (some or all of) the attention, interests, and stakes of that subject at that time. [p. 158]

In what follows, I raise some questions about the workings of Hawthorne's "Sensitive Moderate Invariantist" Lottery-puzzle Explanation (SMILE). I then offer some observations and conjectures about the Car Theft Case, which may contribute to, or constrain, a resolution of the epistemological difficulties it poses.

I

SMILE seems highly counter-intuitive in at least one respect. Think of the Car Theft Case and suppose that someone—call him "Jamie"—parks his car on Elm Street at noon.[3] And let's suppose further that the possibility of car theft isn't salient to Jamie at 1:00, but becomes so at 2:00, with all else equal. Crudely: At 1:00, Jamie doesn't note and take into account the possibility of car theft, while at 2:00, he does note that possibility and does take it into account.[4] Now, assume that in fact (E) Jamie's car is on Elm Street and (-T) Jamie's car hasn't been stolen and driven away. Since, according to SMILE, the requirements for knowledge are *subject*-dependent, facts about Jamie's situation and state of mind at 2:00 don't affect whether Jamie knew at 1:00. But such factors *do* affect what Jamie knows at 2:00. Thus, SMILE provides that at 1:00 Jamie knows both that (E) and that (-T), while at 2:00 Jamie knows neither.

Now, there is no reason why, at 2:00, Jamie can't consider his previous epistemic situation. If he were to report the facts as they are according to SMILE, he would have to say, "At 1:00, I knew that E and -T, but now I don't". There would be something badly amiss with Jamie's saying that, so SMILE faces trouble here. Hawthorne is fully aware of this difficulty, and he offers an ingenious reply:

> If at the later time I don't know the ordinary proposition, then I cannot assert that I used to know it, since knowledge is the norm of assertion. To properly assert that I used to know that p, one needs to know p now. [p. 162]

Let's unpack this point a little. Since knowledge is the norm of assertion, it's proper for Jamie to *assert* at 2:00 that he knew that E and -T at 1:00, only if he *knows* at 2:00 that he knew that E and -T at 1:00. But knowledge is factive: If Jamie knew that E and -T at 1:00, then E and -T. So, if Jamie could properly assert at 2:00 that he knew that E and -T at 1:00, he would have to know at 2:00 that E and -T.[5] However, at 2:00, Jamie *doesn't* know those propositions, because at 2:00 the possibility of car theft is salient to him in some relevant way. It must be, then, that at 2:00 Jamie doesn't know that he *knew* E and -T at 1:00, and that's why Jamie can't properly say that he did. Hawthorne's explanation yields the desired result.

It's worth noting that this analysis can be extended to handle some related problem cases as well. SMILE would presumably allow that, at 1:00, Jamie knew *whether E* and *whether -T*. But at 2:00, Jamie doesn't know whether his car is on Elm Street or whether his car has been stolen and driven away. Under these circumstances, however, it would be unacceptable for Jamie to report at 2:00 that at 1:00 he knew whether E or whether -T, but that at 2:00 he no longer does. Hawthorne's treatment of what's wrong with Jamie's saying "At 1:00, I knew E and -T, but now I don't" doesn't immediately explain why "At 1:00, I knew whether E and whether -T" is true but not assertible by Jamie at 2:00. The disparity exists insofar as "I knew E and -T" entails E and -T, while "I knew whether E and -T" doesn't. But, even so, it seems open to Hawthorne to elaborate a bit. We would assume that Jamie remembers what he thought about E and T previously. He would therefore report, in full, "At 1:00, I knew whether E and -T, and I held that E and -T. But now I don't know whether E or whether -T". Such a discourse would be defective. Given that Jamie remembers at 2:00 that at 1:00 he held E and -T, if he knows *at 2:00* that at 1:00 he knew whether E and whether -T, then Jamie can deduce from those facts that E and -T. That is, Jamie knows, or is in a position to know, at 2:00, that E and -T. But by hypothesis Jamie doesn't know E or -T at 2:00. Consequently, at 2:00, Jamie must not know, and therefore can't properly assert, that at 1:00 he knew *whether* E or -T. Again, Hawthorne's account gives the proper result.[6]

Nevertheless, I fear that Hawthorne's defense of SMILE can't accomplish all that's needed. At least one of the worries I have is very simple-minded. Instead of considering what it's proper for Jamie to assert, let's ask what Jamie ought to believe about his previous epistemic situation. At 2:00, the possibility of Car Theft is salient to Jamie. Jamie reflects back on his conviction at 1:00 that E and -T. Ought Jamie to *believe* at 2:00 that at 1:00 he knew that E and -T, even though at 2:00 he doesn't know, and presumably doesn't believe that he knows, that E (and likewise for -T)? It certainly seems not. But even if knowledge is the norm of assertion, that is of no avail here, since the issue is what Jamie ought to believe, not what Jamie may properly assert. At a minimum, it would be good if more were said about this matter.

My second reservation emerges if we extend the narrative a little bit. Imagine that at 3:00, Jamie returns to Elm Street, and his car is where he parked it. Suppose that Jamie has been worrying about car theft, and he is now relieved that things are all right. But, curiously, it seems that if Jamie *now* reflects back on his situation at 1:00, when the possibility of car theft hadn't yet been salient to him, he has to say that at 1:00 he did know that E and that -T. For, according to Hawthorne, the obstacle to Jamie's asserting that he knew at 1:00 would have to be his *failing* to know at 3:00 that E and that -T. But at 3:00 Jamie *does* know those propositions. SMILE, then, has no explanation of why, at 3:00, Jamie would, or should, withhold the ascription of knowledge to himself, at 1:00, of E and -T.[7]

The difficulty I see here for SMILE seems to be magnified if we consider a third-person analogue of the present example. Here is a case due to Stewart Cohen and discussed by Hawthorne [pp. 159–160]:

> Smith is on an airplane flight with John and Mary. Smith consults a schedule, according to which the flight is supposed to stop in Chicago. Smith believes accordingly, and would claim to know that the flight stops in Chicago. However, it is extremely important to John and Mary whether the plane does or not. They are concerned that the schedule contains a misprint or that the route has recently changed. They have the same information Smith does, but don't regard themselves or him as knowing whether the flight stops in Chicago. They decide to inquire further and are prudent to do so.

The possibility that the schedule is in error and that the flight doesn't stop in Chicago is salient to John and Mary, but not salient to Smith. If SMILE is correct, then Smith knows that the flight stops over, while John and Mary don't know that. What prevents John and Mary from properly asserting what's supposedly true—*viz.*, that Smith knows that the plane lands in Chicago—is that *they* don't know what Smith does. But now suppose that things go as scheduled. When their plane touches down at O'Hare, John and Mary do know that their flight stops in Chicago. At that point, according to SMILE, there is no impediment to their saying that Smith knew that fact all along. But this result seems wrong. It would be natural for John and Mary to say that they have come to know something that neither they *nor Smith* were in a position to know earlier merely by consulting the schedule, and then saying this doesn't stand out as obviously false or defective.[8]

It seems to me that SMILE runs into trouble once again. Moreover, it appears to do so precisely because of the weight it attaches to "subject-dependent" conditions for knowledge. It's true that what is salient to Smith differs from what is salient to John and Mary, just as features of Smith's practical situation may vary from theirs. But variation in these "subject-dependent" factors doesn't have the consequence that it should according to SMILE. For, John, Mary, and Smith all seem to be in the same position epistemically. Whether knowledge can be ascribed to *any* of them appears to turn on the *subject-transcendent* question of whether the evidence equally available to them all (the schedule plus relevant background information) is good enough, under the circumstances, to allow them to know that their flight stops in Chicago.

## II

This last remark may suggest that I am rejecting SMILE in favor of contextualism (see above). For, if there is an epistemically significant shift in Car Theft Cases, and the shift isn't governed by subject-dependent factors, the alternative would appear to be that the shift is governed by ascriber-dependent factors. But here it would be well to distinguish a descriptive question and a normative question. The former is, what explains the variability of knowledge attributions (to oneself and others) in Car Theft Cases? The latter is, which attributions are correct? SMILE and contextualism alike offer answers to both questions. Let me indicate briefly why I'm reluctant to embrace either account, at least at this juncture.[9]

It seems plausible that knowledge ascriptions are governed by the following rule:

*First Conjecture.* The recognition of any substantial probability of error on the subject's part will prompt one to withdraw a knowledge ascription one was otherwise willing to make.[10]

Now, suppose you do try to assign a probability to the event that your car has been stolen in the time since you parked it. You presumably assign such a probability on the basis of relative frequencies you believe to obtain. But frequencies are defined for classes of events. So, to fix a probability for an individual event, one has to select a *reference class* which subsumes that event. A notorious problem arises in this connection. An individual event falls into indefinitely many classes. The choice of one, rather than another, as the reference class affects which relative frequency applies, and thus which probability is assigned to the individual event. In a given case, some choices of reference class seem more appropriate than others, but in general there is no principled way to select a unique reference class which yields a determinate probability for the individual event.

Here is the sort of thing I have in mind. Suppose a gifted, athletic contender for the Olympic gold medal in figure skating named Vladimir has been practicing a special, very difficult maneuver, called the triple Martini. Everyone who has heretofore attempted the triple Martini in competition has fallen. However, Vladimir can carry it off reliably in practice. What are the chances he will succeed when he attempts the triple Martini in the finals? If the reference class we employ is attempts at the triple Martini in competition, we would judge his probability of success to be low. But if the reference class we employ is attempts at the triple Martini by Vladimir, we might well judge his probability of success to be high. Thus, there is some basis for a further suggestion:

*Second Conjecture.* Our assessments of the probabilities of individual events can vary depending upon the reference class we select. Moreover, that selection can be influenced by cues of various sorts.[11]

The selection of a reference class is relevant to our present concerns in light of the First Conjecture. Whether we recognize a substantial probability of error on the subject's part depends on how that probability is determined, which depends in turn on which reference class is selected.[12] Thus:

*Third Conjecture.* At least some of the puzzling phenomena in Car Theft Cases are due to shifts in the selection of a reference class. More specifically, we will characteristically withdraw, or at least hesitate about, attribution to S of knowledge that P, if (i) under some suitable reference class, there wasn't a substantial probability that her belief that P is false; but (ii) under another, comparably suitable reference class, there is a substantial probability that her belief is false.

Much would need to be said by way of exposition and defense of this proposal; I can't undertake that task here. But perhaps the following, foreshortened account may provide some motivation for thinking that the epistemological anomalies that concern Hawthorne have something to do with the selection of a reference class.

Suppose, as before, that initially Jamie is fully confident that (E) his car is now on Elm Street where he parked it. He might extrapolate from a past record of invariably finding *his* car where he parked it, so that the relative frequency, and probability, of his car not being where he parked it is zero. In this setting, he recognizes no substantial probability of error in believing that E, and, other things being equal, he will feel free to claim that he knows E.[13] But Jamie could evaluate the probability that his car isn't where he parked using a different reference class, say that of all cars parked in the city that day. Insofar as Jamie recognizes a non-negligible frequency of car theft in that population, he will assign a non-zero probability to -E. Hence, according to the First Conjecture, Jamie wouldn't be in a position to claim that he knows that E.[14] The pattern overall is that Jamie first finds it acceptable to claim that he knows that E, and then finds it unacceptable to claim that. I'm proposing that this change is due to the shift in the reference class Jamie uses to evaluate the probability of E, along the lines of the Third Conjecture.

I don't claim that this description is definitely the right one, only that it might be. What shifts and why in Car Theft Cases is, at least in part, an empirical question, which I don't see as fully settled. But it strikes me that the answer to this question is important to the fortunes of Hawthorne's position. It may emerge that, in point of fact, knowledge-ascriptions aren't sensitive (solely) to subject-dependent factors, contrary to what SMILE will allow. But there may be a troubling prospect in view for the contextualist, as well. If the variability of knowledge ascriptions does depend upon the selection of a reference class, then it would be a large and problematic step to say that the selection of different classes by different knowledge-ascribers is equally all right, thus licensing different, but equally correct, judgments as to whether the subject knows.[15]

I myself am at a loss to say whether and when we know lottery propositions. But surely we all know a great deal more *about* lottery propositions, thanks to John Hawthorne's fine book.[16]

## Notes

1. I use the Car Theft Case as my primary example, rather than Hawthorne's African Safari Case [p. 1], out of habit and because the explicit inclusion of a lottery in the latter may introduce special considerations that I'd like to avoid.

2. See Vogel, "Are There Counterexamples to the Closure Principle?", in M. Roth and G. Ross, eds., *Doubting: Contemporary Perspectives on Skepticism* (Dordrecht: Kluwer, 1990) and *Knowledge and Lotteries*, Chapter One.

3. Even though Jamie is the same person throughout, he doesn't count as the same subject at different times, insofar as his beliefs, interests, attention, stakes, and the like undergo a change. Note that for the sake of exposition I ignore the possibility that the truth-values of E and -T could change.

4. Hawthorne says that merely thinking of a possibility doesn't give the kind of salience which disrupts knowledge. Assume that whatever further conditions that need to be met, are.

5. Let $A_t$ ( ... ) stand for "S can properly assert ... at t" and let $K_t$ ( ... ) stand for "S knows ... at t". (i) $A_{2:00}$ ($K_{1:00}$ (E & -T)) => $K_{2:00}$ ($K_{1:00}$ (E & -T)) [knowledge is the norm of assertion]; (ii) $K_{1:00}$ (E & -T) => (E & -T) [factivity]; (iii) $K_{2:00}$ ($K_{1:00}$ (E & -T)) => $K_{2:00}$ (E & -T) [from (ii) and the Closure Principle]; (iv) $A_{2:00}$ ($K_{1:00}$ (E & -T)) => $K_{2:00}$ (E & -T) [from, (i), (iii)].

6. I'm indebted here to Stewart Cohen.

7. Compare: Before the lottery drawing, Nate believed that he would lose. The drawing is held, and Nate lost. Should Nate (or I) now say that he knew beforehand that he would lose? [See p. 166, n. 16.] Hawthorne distinguishes one's unwillingness to say, in situations like these, "I used to know that" from one's willingness to say "I never did know that", both of which we have [p. 162–163]. If I read him right, Hawthorne concedes that he has no very happy treatment of the latter, while maintaining that he can account for the former. I am questioning whether he succeeds on that score.

8. Granted, when John and Mary arrive, they could decide that they were mistaken to worry, that consulting the timetable was sufficient after all, and that they had been too nervous or over-cautious earlier. And maybe, in this self-critical frame of mind, John and Mary might legitimately allow that Smith knew what they didn't. However, it's not true in general that John and Mary ought to say or believe that. Hawthorne writes at one point: " ... we do have some tendency to suppose that, as more and more possibilities of error become salient to us, we are reaching an ever more enlightened perspective. Thus when we consider someone who is not alive to these possibilities, we have a tendency to let our (putatively) more enlightened perspective trump his" [p. 164–165].

9. My problem, in a word, is that I'm stuck on the first question.

10. The content of this conjecture is close to that of Hawthorne's "Chance-Knowledge Principle": "If at t, S knows that there is a nonzero objective chance that p at t ... then, at t, S does not know that -p" [p. 93]. One difference in the formulations concerns the chance of p at t versus the chance that S's belief that p is wrong at t. Another is that my version requires "substantial" probability of error, not merely probability that is mathematically greater than zero. It seems to me that my "Hole-in-one Case" counts in favor of the former over the latter [see p. 12], and, although I believe that this point is quite significant, I won't pursue it here. Finally, Hawthorne's principle is restricted to first-person knowledge attributions. My conjecture isn't, although it's less broad in scope than the principle considered by Hawthorne at p. 93, n. 109.

11. The sensitivity of selection of a reference class to cues, and therefore the sensitivity of judgments of probability to such cues, is noted in the psychological literature. See Gerd Gigerenzer, *Adaptive Thinking: Rationality in the Real World* (Oxford: Oxford University Press, 2000), pp. 136–139, 266; see also Kahneman and Tversky, "Intuitive prediction: Biases and corrective procedures", pp. 414–416, in *Judgment Under Uncertainty: Heuristics and Biases*, Daniel Kahneman, Paul Slovic, and Amos Tversky, eds. (Cambridge: Cambridge University Press, 1982).

12. As noted previously, the probability that Vladimir will fall may not be the same as the probability that a belief that Vladimir will fall is correct. On this point, and its broader importance, see Gigerenzer, *op. cit.*, p. 139.

13. Reasoning of this sort (with respect to car accidents rather than car theft) is described by Slovic, Fischhoff, and Lichtenstein, "Facts versus fears: Understanding perceived risk", pp. 468–470, in Kahneman, Slovic, Tversky, *op. cit.*

14. Although I'm convinced that different choices of a reference class play at least *some* role in our shifting judgments about knowledge in Car Theft Cases, there are alternative explanations of what is going on in this particular example. Perhaps Jamie's initial belief that his car is on Elm Street, where he parked it, bypasses any relative frequencies. However, when the possibility that his car has been stolen is broached, an assessment of probability derived from a relative frequency enters the picture. See Gigerenzer on the difference between "local mental models" and "probabilistic mental models", Gigerenzer, *op. cit.*, Chapter Seven. See also Kahneman and Tversky's distinction between "singular" and "distributional" uncertainty ("Varieties of Uncertainty", p. 517, in Kahneman, Slovic, and Tversky, *op. cit.*).

15. The problem worsens if the contextualist is driven to the view that the objective probability of error can have different values, and it's not clear to me how he can avoid that step.

16. I wish to thank Stewart Cohen, John Hawthorne, and Richard Feldman for helpful discussion and comments.

*Philosophical Issues, 14, Epistemology, 2004*

# REPLIES

John Hawthorne
Rutgers University

## Reply to Harman and Sherman

Let me consider in turn (T1) and (T2), which form the basis of Harman and Sherman's reply.

(T1) What one knows can and usually does rest on assumptions one justifiably takes for granted without knowing.

Here is the kind of thing that the authors have in mind: One knows that one is seeing a desk by justifiably taking for granted, but without knowing, that one is not a brain in a vat. One knows that one will be meeting Gilbert Harman for lunch by justifiably taking for granted, but not knowing, that one will not have a sudden fatal heart attack. The authors realize that a consequence of their proposal is that, very often, one knows $p$, does not know $q$, is in a position to competently infer $q$ from $p$ (without thereby losing knowledge that $p$), but is nevertheless in no position to know that $q$. Their package thus requires a rejection of the single premise closure principle that struck me as so compelling.[1]

I do not want to rule out the possibility that, all things considered, the best way to resolve the relevant puzzles is by denying single premise closure. But I do think the costs are more serious than Harman and Sherman let on. Let me briefly go over some of them:

(i) Claims such as 'I do not know whether or not the flight will crash but I do know that I will be at the arrivals gate following my flight' and 'I do not know whether or not I am dreaming right now but I do know that I am in my kitchen' sound extremely odd. Harman and Sherman tell us that they are true, but offer little by way of explanation for their oddity.

(ii) It is hard to fill out the details of their proposal. Harman and Sherman are clear that they do not think that one can know S will lose the lottery simply by justifiably taking for granted that S will lose. On the other hand they think that one's knowledge that S will not be able to afford an African safari this year can rest on justifiably taking for granted that S will lose the lottery. But what about the proposition that S will be showing signs of disappointment on lottery day? Or the proposition that S will never get rich? Or the proposition that S will lose a lottery at some point in the future? Or the proposition that S will be buying a lottery ticket in next month's lottery (something he wouldn't bother to do if he won this month)? Which of these propositions can one know by justifiably taking for granted that S will lose, which not? It does not seem that a satisfying distinction can be made out here.

A related worry: Harman and Sherman are clear enough that I cannot know that I will lose the lottery by justifiably taking it for granted that I will lose the lottery. But what of the suggestion that I can know that I will lose the lottery by justifiably taking it for granted that I will never be extremely rich? Insofar as I have a grip on 'justifiably taking it for granted', it does seem that I can justifiably take it for granted that I will never be extremely rich. But what then prevents one's resting knowledge that one will lose the lottery on that? Again we are given no guidance.

(iii) Harman and Sherman are happy enough to give up an equivalence principle that says that if one knows a priori that $p$ and $q$ are equivalent, and knows that $p$, then one is in a position to know that $q$. They say that 'once it is acknowledged that knowledge can rest on assumptions, the Equivalence Principle has no more intuitive force than more general closure principles' (p. 497)[2] But the authors underestimate just how powerful the principle is. Suppose one knows that S is a zebra and also knows a priori that S is a zebra iff S is a zebra and $\sim$(z is a cleverly disguised non-zebra). As I understand it, Harman and Sherman are happy enough to say that although one knows that S is a zebra, one might nevertheless be in no position to know that S is a zebra and $\sim$(z is a cleverly disguised non-zebra).

Suppose two prizes are offered. I get prize X if and only if the animal in the cage is a zebra. I get prize Y iff the animal is a zebra and (ipso facto) not a cleverly disguised non-zebra. (Suppose the case is set up so that the offering of the prize does not provide special evidence of disguise). Do I really want to say that I know that I will get prize X but do not know whether or not that I will win prize Y, even though I know with a priori certainty that I will get prize X iff I get prize Y? Such thoughts seem altogether bizarre to me.[3]

Note that some of Harman and Sherman's own reasoning tacitly invokes a closure principle. They reason that one cannot know that $\sim$(S is a cleverly disguised mule) on the grounds that in general one cannot know $p$ by justifiably taking it for granted that $p$. They then reason on that basis to the conclusion that one cannot know the conjunction: S is a zebra and ∼(S is a cleverly disguised mule). But why does that follow? Presumably the enthymeme is that if you did know the conjunction, then you would be in a position to know each conjunct. Such an enthymeme is perfectly unproblematic for the proponent of single premise closure. But on what basis do they feel entitled to it?

(iv) Assume that knowledge is the norm of assertion. In the book, I point out that one who tries to conform to this norm but who denies single premise closure will end up behaving like a familiar object of ridicule, Lewis Carroll's (1895) tortoise. Harman and Sherman's Alice will, for certain values of $p$ and $q$, be perfectly willing to say 'Yes' if asked 'Is $p$ the case?' and will assert 'Yes' if asked 'Is it true that if $p$ then $q$', but will be unwilling to assert 'Yes' if asked 'So is it true that $q$?', despite showing no inclination to retract the premises. Despite Harman and Sherman's protestations to the contrary, this still strikes me as an uncomfortable result. Of course it is easy enough to imagine a rational person who retracted an assertion of some premise upon noticing one of its consequences. But that is not Alice.

(v) Harman and Sherman are aware that there are contexts in which one cannot take for granted that one will lose the lottery, and this for practical reasons. If one is offered a cent for one's lottery ticket, then taking for granted that one will lose will lead to undesirable behaviour. But as they are aware, there are other practical environments where all goes well by taking it for granted that one will lose the lottery. What they don't point out is that, in ordinary life, people in those practical environments very often report themselves as knowing they will lose. 'I know full well that I am not going to get that lucky' is a relatively common speech. Why are they so confident that one lacks knowledge in *those* practical environments?

Let me turn to:

(T2) One knows only if one believes as one does because of something that settles the truth of that belief.

The authors use this principle to answer their Q2, viz.: Why is it intuitively correct that one can know using statistical reasoning that a given coin is not heavily biased toward heads by tossing it a few times but not intuitively correct that one can know using statistical reasoning that one's lottery ticket is not the winning ticket? (T2) has some prima facie intuitive appeal. This is due in large part, I think, to the fact that in paradigmatic cases of perceptual knowledge, it is intuitive to think that we are confronted with the very fact that our belief is about. In its general form, however, the principle is less intuitive. Does it extend to knowledge of the future, logic, natural science, and so on? And even in perceptual cases, there are grounds for worry. (It might be suggested that it is the table surface and not the table that causes my belief that there is a table there.) But I do not want to fuss overly about these points here. (The authors are well aware of them.)

Earlier, Harman and Sherman say that one justifiably takes for granted that one's car hasn't been stolen but does not know that one's car hasn't been stolen. Suppose one believes one's car has not been stolen on account of the fact that one has parked it in a fairly safe place. Now supposing it hasn't been stolen, it seems plausible enough to say that its being parked in a fairly safe place is a common cause both of its not having been stolen and of my belief. Is it their view that both in this case and the 'unbiased coin' case (T2) is satisfied but some other factor divides the cases? I am unsure.

It is also worth pointing out in cases like the unbiased coin, our intuitions are much more unstable than Harman and Sherman acknowledge. Suppose that each person on the street sits on his doorstep 90 percent of the mornings when he or she is depressed but only 2 percent of the mornings when he or she is happy. You walk up and down the street and notice which people are away from their doorstep and form the belief of each (say a list of 50 people) that he or she is happy. You realize that it is nevertheless overwhelmingly likely that at least one of the people on one's list is depressed. Granted, it may be that in any particular case a person's happiness may cause her absence from the doorstep which in turn causes the belief. But would one take oneself to know in any particular case that the person is happy? In this context we are not intuitively inclined to self ascribe knowledge in any particular case.

Let me finally connect T2 with epistemic closure. Suppose I form the belief that S will be at lunch on the basis of her intention to be there. I meet S at lunch. We find it very intuitive to say that I knew that I was going to meet S at lunch. Harman and Sherman would applaud the intuition: S's intention is a common cause of my belief and S's being at lunch. T2 is satisfied, and presumably a claim of knowledge is not objectionable on other grounds. But (recalling Harman's *Thought*, p. 161), it may also be true that if S had won the lottery, she would have been at the prizegiving ceremony and not at lunch. This is of course fully compatible with the claim that S's intention causes her to be at lunch. Causes need not necessitate, and need a compliant environment in order to do their work at all. It certainly does not seem that S's intention settles that she will not win the lottery. If I believe that she will not win the lottery, it seems that there is nothing that settles that, and hence I do not know that. This is no problem for Harman and Sherman. But it does suggest that anyone who (like me) endorses single premise closure ought to be suspicious of T2.[4]

## Reply to Vogel

I used 'sensitive moderate invariantism' as a label for a family of views. The rough and ready idea is this: The mechanisms that are appealed to by contextualists to explain the ascriber-sensitivity of knowledge ascriptions can be recast as subject-sensitive conditions. The resulting views, I noted, were worthy of attention and did not require semantic contextualism. I was forthright about the fact that sensitive moderate invariantism has counterintuitive consequences. But one must recognize that other versions of moderate invariantism are no better off in this regard. It is simply a datum that in the sort of setting where we acknowledge to ourselves that, say, we do not know whether or not we will win a lottery, whether we will have a sudden fatal heart attack, whether our car has been stolen in the night, we also become convinced that we do not know whether we will be able to afford an African safari, whether we will be going on vacation next year, whether our car is parked outside. And once we become convinced of such things, we project our epistemological pessimism backwards to our earlier selves and outwards to others. What bears emphasis is that all versions of moderate invariantism will have to concede that while such pessimism is the highly natural outgrowth of very ordinary, mundane, kinds of epistemological reflection, it yields large quantities of mistaken epistemological verdicts. It is clear enough that Vogel wishes for some kind of moderate invariantism, even though he has not yet settled on which version he prefers. But we can see in advance that he, like my sensitive moderate invariantist, will be landed with a host of epistemological claims that are at least somewhat uncomfortable.

Why do I find sensitive moderate invariantism attractive, as opposed to more mundane varieties of moderate invariantism? There is not space here to recap all relevant considerations, but one bears special emphasis. There is an intimate intuitive tie between knowledge and practical reasoning. We operate with a picture of practical reasoning according to which, if the question whether $p$ is practically relevant, it is acceptable to use the premise that $p$ in one's deliberations if one knows it. Suppose we are not sceptics: We allow that in many ordinary situations one knows, say, that one will be vacationing in Scotland in a year's time. Yet it seems clear enough that if offered life insurance, it would be altogether unacceptable to turn down the offer by reasoning that since one will be in Scotland in a year, one will not die beforehand. And note, strikingly, that if someone did try to reason that way, our intuitive reaction would be to let the pessimism override the optimism, and to say that since she might die beforehand, she does not in fact know whether she will be happily vacationing in Scotland. Now one can dismiss that reaction as wrongheaded; whatever view one adopts will require contesting some intuitions. But the overarching importance of the connection between knowledge and practical reasoning seemed—and still seems—like a good reason to uphold those particular intuitions about cases. (Of course one could maintain that connection by declaring that the faulty intuition was the one according to which the practical reasoning is unacceptable. But I took it as blatantly absurd to endorse such practical reasoning.) Meanwhile, if one does not want to be a sceptic, one will also have to allow that in certain practical environments, a person will know that she will be vacationing in Scotland the following year. We are thus led to the kind of sensitivity advocated in chapter four. I am still not confident that such an approach is correct, but it continues to seem well motivated to me.

As Vogel notes, there are some respects in which sensitive moderate invariantism does not have the counterintuitive consequences it may seem to have. If I do not now know that *p* because the stakes have been raised but my earlier self does know that *p*, that does not mean that I am in a position to assert 'I don't know *p* but I used to know *p*' (for the reason I gave in the book and which Vogel explains very clearly). But those considerations don't explain why I am disposed to the negative verdict that I didn't used to know (rather than, for instance, to agnosticism). Nor does it explain why I shouldn't at least give reasonably high credence to the proposition that I don't know but I used to. Nor does it explain why I cannot assert various indicative conditionals such as 'If I don't die soon of a heart attack, I knew in the past that I wasn't going to'. And so on. The point of mine that Vogel outlines was not designed to explain all this away.

So why was my sensitive moderate invariantist not willing to admit defeat? Well, as just noted, my sensitive moderate invariantist realized that similar problems arise for other sorts of moderate invariantisms. And she was also aware of the battery of discomforts awaiting both contextualist and sceptical alternatives to moderate invariantism. Given this, it seemed to her that the jury was still out concerning whether her favored resolution of the puzzles was all things considered the best one. Moreover, chapter four does contain some further suggestions—admittedly rather underdeveloped— about how the faulty intuitions (faulty by the lights of sensitive moderate invariantism) might be explained away.

One helpful resource here is the literature on heuristics and biases, where there is a host of work on the distorting effects of salience when it comes to judgments of epistemic probability. Vogel's own suggestive remarks about the ways that salience affects reference class and in turn probability judgments are rather in the spirit of that literature. (Indeed, some of Vogel's earlier work on this topic—along with much of his other work—was extremely helpful to me in thinking about these topics.).

I am fully in agreement with Vogel that a good entry point to the subject is to ask after the empirical explanations of the various patterns of knowledge judgments that get evoked by differing patterns of questioning, deliberative setting and so on, with a special view to understanding the evolution of an individual's 'epistemic space'. Such an inquiry, as Vogel himself emphasises, will not settle questions about the truth conditions of knowledge ascriptions—since one will still need to decide which reactions are veridical, which distorted. But the inquiry will still form an important part of an adequate perspective upon the puzzles at hand.

I do though wish to raise two queries about Vogel's discussion of probability. First, his discussion draws primarily upon literature on objective probability. But for the most part it does not seem that knowledge verdicts proceed via considerations about objective probability.[5] (Only in certain special circumstances—I here have in mind the literature on the Principal Principle—do we except a match between rational subjective probability and objective probability.) It is not clear to me that, for example, rational subjective probability assignments generally proceed via consideration of relative frequencies.[6] Second, a major decision point concerns whether the notion of epistemic probability that is most relevant to knowledge judgments is one according to which knowing that $p$ entails an epistemic probability of zero that not-$p$. (One place where this choice really matters is in connection with multi-premise closure, the rather attractive idea that competent deductions from sets of known premises invariably yield knowledge. Unless the relevant notion of epistemic probability ties knowledge to probability one, multi-premise closure will have to be discarded. I am unsure as to what extent Vogel would reckon this a cost.) Vogel's 'First Conjecture' is worded in a way that suggests he wishes to allow that knowledge that $p$ be compatible with insubstantial but non-zero probability that not-$p$. But it is then rather striking that his description of the frame of mind in which S claims that she knows where her car is parked is one in which she assigns zero probability to its being elsewhere.

Let me end with a couple of remarks about the following passage in Vogel:

> For John, Mary, and Smith all seem to be in the same position epistemically. Whether knowledge can be ascribed to any of them appears to turn on the subject-transcendent question whether the evidence equally available to them all (the schedule plus relevant background information) is good enough, under the circumstances, to allow them to know that their flight stops in Chicago (p. 505).

First, it is not at all clear to me that the kind of evidentialism about knowledge described here is tenable. It is quite natural to think that a fact is only evidence for me if it is something—epistemically—to me. That there is a leopard in the next room is not part of my evidence if I am unaware of it. And that my phenomenal field has 27 phenomenally red dots is not part of my evidence if I am unaware of it. But now the following thought becomes very natural: Facts become part of my evidence by my coming to know that they obtain. But if this is right, it is of no use to explain knowledge in terms of evidence, or to think that one can identify one's evidence in advance of settling what one does and does not know.[7] Second, it is quite right that having embraced sensitive moderate invariantism, one might still think there is a notion of 'being in the same position epistemically', according to which, for example, one is in the same position epistemically before and after if the only relevant change is from low stakes to high stakes. Even supposing one's knowledge is lost, one might legitimately claim that in some very good sense one is 'in the same position epistemically' throughout. But a more thorough-going version of the position—one that seems more attractive to me—is to insist that just as we were wrong in thinking practical environment makes no difference to knowledge, we were wrong in thinking that it makes no difference to sameness and difference of epistemic position, sameness and difference of evidence and so on. This is in some ways to make sensitive moderate invariantism more radical, but does help to keep knowledge at the center of things.

## Reply to Cohen

I raised a number of concerns about contextualist accounts of the relevant puzzles. Cohen attempts to answer two such concerns. Let me address each in turn.

### (a) Knowledge and Assertion

I pointed out that contextualism delivers results like the following:

   (i) People often assert things that they do not know to be true but are not thereby subject to criticism.
   (ii) There are things people know to be true but ought not to assert because their epistemic position is not strong enough with respect to those things.

Such results are intuitively odd, I thought, and so are a count against the theory.

There are related oddities. If one is a contextualist, it seems that one can allow that someone else can know a sentence of the form '*p* and I do not know that *p*' to be true. (Suppose one has "low standards" and the subject has "high standards". The subject can know-by-my-low-standards that *p* and also know-by-my-low-standards that he does not know-by-his-high-standards that *p*.) But sentences of the form '*p* and I do not know that *p*' are paradigmatically unassertable. So a contextualist will naturally be led to concede that someone may know some sentence of that form to be true yet be in no position whatsoever to assert it.[8]

I also raised a more general theoretical concern. The contextualist typically works within a framework of ascriber independent normative facts—about what one ought to be believing, about which assertions are proper and so on. I then raised the question as to why 'know' should be ascriber sensitive while 'what is assertable', 'what one ought to believe', etc., remain ascriber insensitive. I noted that the contextualist is often willing to discount evidence for ascriber sensitivity for 'assertable'. Suppose, for example, that I have 'high standards' and am sitting on your car, parked in your driveway. Given my high standards I do not reckon you, who have just woken up, know where your car is. You have 'low standards' and flat-out assert that your car is in the driveway. If I am convinced that you don't know where your car is, won't I also think it is a little out of line for you to flat-out assert that your car is in the driveway? Given that intuitions about assertability and knowledge march in step, why regiment things so that assertability ascriptions turn out to be ascriber independent but knowledge ascriptions ascriber dependent?

Let me now turn to Cohen's discussion. He proposes an account of assertion that roughly matches the one I recommended on behalf of the contextualist. The proposed rule is: only assert something if you pass the standards for 'knowledge' in your mouth. But the point remains that Unger's rule, as stated, is extremely intuitive. Cohen's contextualist thinks that it is outright false that, in general, when one asserts something one represents oneself as knowing it. (He explains away the counterintuitive result as stemming from a faulty inference pattern that is, apparently, endemic.) Now of course, having embraced contextualism, one will certainly be inclined to endorse the metalinguistic surrogate rule that Cohen proposes. But it still seems like a cost of the view that the intuitively correct claim—Unger's original one—comes out false. I might also add that it seems to me psycholinguistically implausible that when one learns 'know' one tacitly learns the metalinguistic rule as opposed to the one that Unger and Williamson endorse. Part of the problem is that it does not seem that we have some metric for epistemic standards that would fix a context for 'know' in the way that we do for 'tall'. But even more pertinently, if I think that someone knows what they are asserting to be true, then I will not question the propriety of the utterance. The metalingusitic rule predicts that having settled that someone knows that which they assert, the propriety of the assertion will strike us as an open question. But when evaluating the propriety of an assertion the primary issue is quite obviously what the person knows, not whether the assertion satisfies the assertor's own standards for 'know'. Of course the contextualist can claim that in this respect our practice is founded on a mistake. But I would have thought that such an accusation is best avoided if possible.

Relatedly, it seems to me that part of the function of an assertion that serves its perlocutionary purpose is, as Robert Brandom (1983) noted, to provide a reassertion license. And it is clear enough what the intuitive mechanism is by means of which such a reassertion license is provided: one imparts knowledge that P which in turn provides a license for the impartee to reassert that P. This picture of things does not square with the contextualist perspective. Imparting knowledge that P does not in general provide a license to reassert P because, while knowing that P, the impartee may still not "know by her standards".

None of this leaves me utterly convinced that contextualism is wrong.[9] But these considerations, among others, reinforce my hesitancy towards embracing such a view.

## (b) Knowledge and Practical Reasoning

Sensitive moderate invariantism is, above all, motivated by the intuitive links between knowledge and practical reasoning. Contextualism, I argued, fares less well on that score. In particular, the contextualist will be saddled with claims like the following:

S doesn't know $p$ is false but it is in general perfectly unproblematic for S to appeal to $p$ in her practical reasoning.

S knows $p$ and the question whether $p$ is practically relevant, but it is inappropriate for S to use $p$ as a premise in her practical deliberations.

Cohen focuses on the second of these prima facie embarrassments and offers some thoughtful remarks about how the contextualist might soften its blow. Let me quickly highlight some large issues that cannot be resolved here but which certainly bear on the discussion:

(i) Cohen thinks of knowledge talk as a heuristic for getting at 'evidential probabilities' in a rough and ready way. But how are the companion notions of 'evidence' and 'evidential probability' to be elucidated? Contextualists typically help themselves to a context-independent notion of evidence, against the background of which their favored account of knowledge ascriptions is presented. But if the concept of evidence is intertwined with the concept of knowledge (as I am tempted to think is the case) then this strategy for framing contextualist semantics for 'know' turns out to be deeply problematic, as does the idea that 'know' provides a rough and ready guide to the more fundamental facts about evidence and what is justified by one's evidence. Obviously Cohen is committed to an account of evidence and evidential probability that does not rely in any fundamental way on the concept of knowledge. I merely wish to indicate here that much of what he says stands or falls with the cogency of that commitment.

(ii) Cohen takes it that the sensitive moderate invariantist would at least concede that changes in practical environment do not *ipso facto* change the evidential situation, nor the safety of one's beliefs. As just indicated, a sensitive moderate invariantist who allied knowledge to evidence would not agree with the claim about evidence. What about safety? Cohen is alluding here to the popular idea (which I find appealing) that when one knows $p$ one is in no danger (in the relevant sense) of error. A natural world-theoretic gloss, as various authors have noted, is that if one knows $p$, one doesn't make a mistake about *p* (and perhaps about relevantly similar subject matter) at *close worlds*. Now some may think that one can elucidate the relevant notion of closeness in a way that is not parasitic on questions of knowledge. Most will not. (It is clear enough, for example, that the closeness metric used for evaluating ordinary counterfactuals will not suit the epistemic safety theorist's purposes.) Those who take the latter view, and who are sensitive moderate invariantists, will likely not agree that changes in practical environment make no difference to the safety of one's beliefs. For perhaps such changes make a difference to which worlds count as close. (As a simple model, imagine that as the stakes rise, the sphere of worlds that counts as close increases in diameter.)

This is all to say that there are important general questions about how the concept of knowledge is connected to other concepts of epistemic import whose resolution bears significantly on the prospects for Cohen's own favored approach.

Let me turn finally to Cohen's critique of sensitive moderate invariantism. We do indeed have a strong tendency to suppose that we are reaching an ever more enlightened perspective as more and more possibilities of error become salient to us. This self conception—with its associated sceptical tendencies—will have to be reckoned in some important measure illusory by any moderate invariantist. And, as Cohen emphasizes, it would be nice to have something to say by way of explaining the illusion away. I am less sure than Cohen that contextualism is so well placed to explain away the intuitions of enlightenment that are evoked by the sceptical imagination. For an important part of our phenomenology is that our earlier selves were making myriad errors. His context-shifting semantics does not explain why we should take such a perspective on our earlier selves. (Consider, by contrast, shifting standards of tallness. We do not count our earlier selves as having been mistaken in saying 'He is very tall' when we later say in a basketball context 'He is not very tall'.)

Turn now to the moderate invariantist's efforts to explain away these intuitions of enlightenment. Let me be clear: I do not think that the truth about knowledge, whatever it is, will sit easily with us once we have it before us. We have no clear vision of how the semantic gods would come up with a semantic value for the verb 'know' in the face of its tensions and strains. Nor does our workaday competence with 'know' require that we have any systematic appreciation of how an all-things-considered-best semantic value would be determined. To expect any view to 'explain away' (what by its lights are) errors in such a way that we will be left feeling comfortable is too high a demand. Or so it seems to me. That said, it is still incumbent upon the moderate invariantist to say something about the source of faulty intuitions of enlightenment. As a first pass at part of the story[10] I looked to the work on 'availability' in the literature on heuristics and biases. The findings there were that salience distorts risk judgments, and it seemed to me that this theme might carry over to judgments of knowledge-undermining epistemic danger.

Cohen has two complaints. First he notices that the appeal to availability threatens to explain away too much. If I am willing to use availability to explain away negative knowledge verdicts in the cases that I do, why should I not also be willing to use availability to explain away our belief that, for example, we do not know we will lose a lottery? Why not say that in general we do know that a lottery ticket will lose (unless it is in fact a winner) and that our frequent inclination to think we don't is the outgrowth of a risk distorting imagination that is taken in by the imagined drama of lottery victory?

This misconstrues the proposal somewhat. I never meant to suggest that one could use the availability heuristic as a way of reading off which knowledge judgments were correct, which incorrect. If my all-things-considered favourite theory was one according to which we do invariably know we will lose a lottery (except when we win), then I would indeed 'explain away' the illusion that we do not know that we will lose a lottery by appeal to availability. This is just to say that we stand in need of some independent tests for identifying which knowledge judgments are incorrect in the first place. Once such a tentative identification has been made, one is free to take note of the fact that we have a general tendency to reach negative epistemological verdicts in the face of vivid imaginative confrontation with possible kinds of error, and to explain away our sceptical excesses along those lines. But availability will not tell you which intuitive reactions are sceptical excess, which are right on the money. Insofar as one can make reasonable conjectures there, one has to try to reflect in a general way about what knowledge is important for, what sorts of general structural features knowledge seems to have, and so on. And that was what I tried to do.

Second, Cohen complains that while availability would explain why we are overly sceptical about possibilities of error that involve dramatic and spectacular events, it would naturally predict that we underestimate risks of error when it comes to mundane, undramatic possibilities of error. In reply, it might be helpful to distinguish the following two points, both of which are underwritten by the literature on heuristics and biases:

(a) Discussing or otherwise considering a hazard tends to make it imaginatively salient which in turn tends to make one raise one's estimation of the danger of it occurring.

(b) Dramatic events tend to be imaginatively more salient than mundane ones and hence, other things being equal, one is more likely to distort one's risk judgments in favour of dramatic events than in favour of mundane ones.

Insofar as (a) has application to the knowledge case, it would predict that discussion of possibilities of error would tend to increase one's estimation of the danger of such error being actual, and that it would sometimes do so in a risk-distorting way. This would hold true both of mundane and dramatic kinds of error since (a) predicts that in each case perceived riskiness increases with discussion. Insofar as (b) has application to the knowledge case, it would predict that we are more likely to be sceptical on the basis of possibilities of error that involve dramatic and memorable kinds of events than others. It seems to me that a case can easily be made for both.[11] All I need to point out here is that Cohen's discussion neglects (a) in favour of (b).

I am grateful to my commentators for their stimulating discussions which, like their other work, has been both thought-provoking and instructive in numerous ways. At the time of writing the book I felt highly uncertain as to which of the approaches was correct. In light of my commentators' searching assessments, I am now even more uncertain.

## Notes

1. I had used the verb 'deduce' in stating single premise closure. Harman and Sherman complain that this is to 'confuse questions of implication with questions of inference. A deduction is a structured abstract object' (p. 495). Part of the disagreement is surely terminological. There is a perfectly good use of the English verb 'deduce' where it denotes an activity. There is more to say on this matter, but I shall not try to say it here.
2. Anticipating T2, we should note that if $p$ and $q$ are necessarily equivalent, then it would seem that anything that settles the truth of $p$ settles the truth of $q$. Granted T2 only states a necessary condition on knowledge, but it is worth noticing that it is of no use whatsoever in undermining the equivalence principle.
3. Note that once it is conceded that one knows one will get one prize if and only if one knows one will get the other, then it is very hard to see how matters will be different once it turns out that the prize is truth.
4. A possible reconciliation: Suppose—and admittedly this is not how things normally go—I deduce that $S$ will not win the lottery from the proposition that $S$ will be at lunch: I believe the former on the basis of my knowledge of the latter. Might it not be argued that the fact that I *know* that S will be at lunch itself *settles* the truth of the belief that S will not win the lottery, and that I do believe that S will lose the lottery on *that* basis? This package would suggest that I can know I will lose the lottery, though only if I manage to base that belief on mundane knowledge in a way that is out of the ordinary. (I do not claim that the package is particularly attractive.)
5. That is not to say there are not interesting points of contact between objective probability verdicts and knowledge ascriptions, some of which I discuss in the book.

6. I am not convinced the notion of epistemic probability relevant to knowledge can be assimilated to rational subjective probability either, but I do not wish to fuss about that here.
7. See Williamson (2000) for a powerful statement of this line of thought.
8. This particular oddity was not discussed in the book.
9. It also bears emphasis, as I noted in the book, that one may be convinced of the truth of contextualism but still take much of chapter four on board.
10. I wrote that 'I do not intend that availability take up all the explanatory burden' (p. 179). I also made some further explanatory gestures in connection with the discussion of how practical environment affects knowledge. But I freely admit that all of these suggestions are extremely sketchy and underdeveloped.
11. In connection with (b), think how much more likely it is that a low-risk person will take themselves not to know they will pass a general medical examination on the grounds that they may test HIV positive, as compared to other more mundane sources of failure.

## References

Brandom, Robert. 1983. 'Asserting,' in *Noûs* 17, 637–650.
Harman, Gilbert. 1973. *Thought*. Princeton University Press.
Williamson, Timothy. 2000. *Knowledge and Its Limits*. Oxford University Press.